I0642427

Letters of H. P. Lovecraft

MISCELLANEOUS LETTERS

H. P. LOVECRAFT

MISCELLANEOUS LETTERS

EDITED BY DAVID E. SCHULTZ AND S. T. JOSHI

Hippocampus Press

New York

Copyright © 2022 by Hippocampus Press
Introduction and editorial matter copyright © 2022
by David E. Schultz and S. T. Joshi

The letters of H. P. Lovecraft have been published by permission of
the Estate of H. P. Lovecraft and John Hay Library, Brown University.

Published by Hippocampus Press
P.O. Box 641, New York, NY 10156.
www.hippocampuspress.com

All rights reserved. No part of this work may be reproduced in any form
or by any means without the written permission of the publisher.

Cover design and Hippocampus Press logo by Anastasia Damianakos.
Cover production by Barbara Briggs Silbert.

First Edition
1 3 5 7 9 8 6 4 2

ISBN 978-1-61498-373-6

Contents

Introduction

This volume contains letters to correspondents that survive in relatively small numbers; but one should not assume that this circumstance indicates the insignificance of the correspondent in question. In many instances, the paucity of letters to a given individual is strictly a result of the vagaries of transmission. No doubt many more letters were written to nearly all the individuals included here, but they have not survived. The most poignant example is the correspondence with Lovecraft's wife, Sonia H. Greene. In her memoir she writes that after that initial meeting (at the convention of the National Amateur Press Association in Boston in July 1921), "we kept up quite a steady correspondence." Somewhat later, "After two years of almost daily correspondence—H. P. writing me about everything he did and everywhere he went, introducing names of friends and his evaluation of them, sometimes filling 30, 40 and even 50 pages of finely written script—he decided to break away from Providence" (i.e., to marry Sonia and move to her apartment in Brooklyn). Even after the dissolution of their marriage in 1929, "we still kept up correspondence." But then, just prior to her move to California in 1935, Sonia writes: "I had a trunkful of his letters which he had written me throughout the years but before leaving New York for California I took them to a field and set a match to them."[1] No student of Lovecraft can read that sentence without keen regret. Only a single original document (a one-sentence postcard dating to 1926) survives of this apparently massive correspondence, along with some scraps of letters embedded in two works presented as essays.

Lovecraft's association with amateur journalism, beginning in 1914 with his joining the United Amateur Press Association, resulted in an extensive correspondence relating to amateur matters of all sorts or with transient colleagues in the amateur press; almost none of this correspondence is extant, and we are lucky to have random letters or postcards to such individuals as Henriette Ziegfeld, Jonathan E. Hoag, Victor E. Bacon, and others. At the head of this volume we have included the two earliest instances of round-robin correspondence cycles in which Lovecraft participated—the Kleicomolo (including Rheinhart Kleiner, Ira A. Cole, and Maurice W. Moe) and the Gallomo (including Alfred Galpin and Moe). No doubt even the extensive selections that survive are a fraction of the totality of the cycles.

The extant letters to C. M. and Muriel Eddy, friends in the Providence

---

1. Sonia H. Davis, "The Private Life of H. P. Lovecraft," in S. T. Joshi and David E. Schultz, ed., *Ave atque Vale: Reminiscences of H. P. Lovecraft* (West Warwick, RI: Necronomicon Press, 2018), 132, 136, 141, 145.

area with whom he apparently first came into contact in 1923, are again a small proportion of the total number of letters he must have written to them, especially when he left Providence for a two-year period beginning in 1924. During that time, he became part of a close-knit circle of friends in New York called the Kalem Club. While correspondence with many of its members (Kleiner, James F. Morton, Frank Belknap Long, among others) survives in abundance, the letters to Everett McNeil are nonextant and those to George W. Kirk are few. And yet, Kirk's letters to his future wife[2] indicate that he was one of Lovecraft's closest colleagues during his New York stay. But precisely because Lovecraft met Kirk on an almost daily basis, they exchanged letters only when one or the other of them was out of town or after Lovecraft returned to Providence in 1926.

One of the most interesting correspondents of Lovecraft's final decade of life is Robert Hartley Michael—interesting precisely because so little is known of him. And yet, this person—who presumably came into epistolary contact with Lovecraft through *Weird Tales*, as did many others at the time—elicited some of Lovecraft's most revealing correspondence, both from an autobiographical perspective and from a philosophical and literary angle. As the 1930s progressed, Lovecraft gained numerous correspondents from the world of pulp writing or from the emerging fantasy fandom movement—Henry George Weiss (who published stories under the name "Francis Flagg"),[3] Seabury Quinn, Carl Jacobi, Charles D. Hornig, and many others. "Business" correspondence with Carl Swanson and Allan G. Ullman of Alfred A. Knopf illuminate vital aspects of Lovecraft's literary career, while letters to Edwin Hadley Smith and others provide insight into his late involvement with the National Amateur Press Association. Very late in life he participated in one more round-robin correspondence cycle that came to be called the Coryciani, focused on the study and appreciation of poetry.

To the very end of his life, Lovecraft continued to be a gracious and diligent correspondent, and the legions of fans who were now writing to him—which included such figures as Forrest J Ackerman, James Blish, and Robert A. W. Lowndes, who later attained celebrity in the realms of horror, fantasy, and science fiction—always received replies to their missives. The fact that Blish and his colleague William Miller, Jr. chose to publish extracts of Lovecraft's letters in a fanzine soon after Lovecraft's death bespeaks the importance they set on their fleeting association with the Providence writer.

The letters by Lovecraft that were published during his lifetime are of a

2. For extensive extracts see "The Kalem Letters of George Kirk," in Mara Kirk Hart and S. T. Joshi, ed., *Lovecraft's New York Circle: The Kalem Club, 1924–1927* (New York: Hippocampus Press, 2006), 19–116.
3. Seven letters by Weiss to HPL survive at JHL, one of them 40 pages in length; but it is not practicable to publish these letters here.

variegated nature and provide insights into the issues that animated his mind from an early age. Although, in later years, Lovecraft stated that he was reluctant to bombard local papers with letters to the editor, lest he appear as a crank or an attention-seeker, a number of such letters to the *Providence Journal* and other papers have been found from as early as 1906. Many of these concern scientific controversies in which Lovecraft engaged, as he battled against astrologers and other perceived charlatans whom he believed to be disseminating falsehoods into the community.

Lovecraft's emergence from the hermitry of the period 1908–13—following his dropping out of high school with the onset of what he termed a nervous breakdown—was facilitated by correspondence. Specifically, he was so offended at the romance writing of one Fred Jackson, appearing in a periodical (the *Argosy*) that he read regularly, that he wrote a letter of protest to the editor. The resulting battle of words—in both prose and verse—between Lovecraft and those who defended Jackson extended to *Argosy*'s sister publication, the *All-Story Weekly*, and triggered Lovecraft's entry into amateur journalism. The amateur world itself published random letters of comment by Lovecraft, including extracts of essays that some amateur writers apparently sent in as letters to the editor to various newspapers in Nebraska and elsewhere. Several provocative and lengthy letters also appeared in the *Haldeman-Julius Weekly*, a politically radical paper of the 1920s.

Upon his return to Providence, Lovecraft wrote a paean to the *Providence Journal* about the surviving antiquities in his birthplace. This set the stage for his valiant but ultimately futile attempt to save one such set of old buildings—the Brick Row, dating to the 1810s—that were set for demolition. Lovecraft even enlisted the assistance of his friend James F. Morton, writing a letter to be published under Morton's name. Later, Lovecraft engaged in a lively and at times bantering correspondence with Bertrand K. Hart, the editor of a column in the *Providence Journal* called "The Sideshow," and focusing on Lovecraft's evolving tastes in weird fiction. Other published letters of the 1930s focus on a variety of amateur controversies.

The letters in this volume provide a glimpse of the multitudinous personas that Lovecraft adopted over the course of his life: the devotee of amateur journalism; the writer of pulp fiction; the advocate of science and rationalism; the revealing autobiographer; and, perhaps most vitally, the patient mentor to numerous younger colleagues who sought his assistance and expertise in the craft of writing. It is this last quality that endeared Lovecraft to so many figures in the realm of weird fiction, eliciting a reverence and devotion even among those who never met him in person. Although the correspondence to many of these individuals survives only fragmentarily, what remains testifies to the lasting imprint Lovecraft's kindness and generosity of spirit made upon them.

—S. T. JOSHI AND DAVID E. SCHULTZ

A Note on This Edition

Where possible, the texts of the letters in this volume have been derived from the original manuscripts; in some cases, such manuscripts have been consulted only indirectly (e.g., through access to book dealers' websites where the documents were presented in facsimile). Other letters were derived from the Arkham House transcripts, a series of typescript volumes generated by Arkham House in its preparation of the *Selected Letters* (1965–76), in which August Derleth's secretary, Alice Conger, transcribed extracts of letters that arrived at Arkham House from a wide range of colleagues. The published letters are of course taken from the publications in question, as in nearly every instance no manuscript sources for these letters exist.

We are grateful to Don Albrecht, Mark Alessio, Scott Connors, Kenneth W. Faig, Jr., Christopher Geissler of the John Hay Library, Forrest Jackson, Donovan K. Loucks, Christopher O'Brien, J.-M. Rajala, Peter Ruber, David Tribby, Wisconsin Historical Society, and the archivists at the Library of Amateur Journalism (Special Collections, University of Wisconsin–Madison) for assistance in the preparation of this volume. Special thanks go to Martin Andersson for his care and attention in proofreading the book.

Abbreviations

A.Df.	autograph draft
AHT	Arkham House transcripts
ALS	autograph letter, signed
A.Ms.	autograph manuscript
ANS	autograph note, signed
HPL	H. P. Lovecraft
JHL	John Hay Library, Brown University
NAPA	National Amateur Press Association
TLS	typed letter, signed
T.Ms.	typed manuscript
UAPA	United Amateur Press Association
WHS	Wisconsin Historical Society

AT	*The Ancient Track*
CE	*Collected Essays*
CF	*Collected Fiction: A Variorum Edition*
ES	*Essential Solitude*
FF	*Fantasy Fan*
LFF	*Letters to Family and Family Friends*
LL	Joshi & Schultz, *Lovecraft's Library*
SL	*Selected Letters*
WT	*Weird Tales*

Miscellaneous Letters

To the Kleicomolo

It was at the suggestion of Maurice W. Moe, in the summer of 1916, that he, Lovecraft, Rheinhart Kleiner, and Ira A. Cole began a round-robin correspondence cycle: the Kleicomolo. The members would sequentially write letters discussing one or more controversial topics; as the batches of letters circulated to each member, he would remove his previous contribution and write a fresh letter, commenting on the letters of the others. In an unsigned article (probably by Kleiner), "The Kleicomolo" (*United Amateur*, March 1919), it was noted that "One of the members [Moe] was desirous of keeping a complete copy of the correspondence, and began by copying the letters as they went through his hands. This task soon became so great as to be impracticable, and the rest elected him librarian and promised to send him carbon copies of their instalments." But only the letters by Lovecraft survive.

A few letters to the Kleicomolo and a later correspondence cycle, the Gallomo (Alfred Galpin, Lovecraft, and Moe) survive. Still other cycles referred to in Lovecraft's letters include the Gremolo (Sonia H. Greene, Moe, and Lovecraft)* and the Lokleilo (Samuel Loveman, Kleiner, and Lovecraft).† Presumably some of the round-robin circles, except for the Kleicomolo or the Gallomo, were short-lived or ad hoc affairs, but even the more robust circles dwindled and finally disbanded.

---

*HPL to Alfred Galpin: "By the way—it looks as though the Galpinian cast-asides are going to found a scholastic salon of their own, for this a.m. there blew into the Magnolia P.O. two bulky duplicate letters for Mme. G. [i.e., Sonia H. Greene] & myself, from good ol' Mocrates in Madisonium. He calls the new circle the *Gremolo*, & doubtless intends it as the standard refuge for rejected second-raters" (*Letters to Alfred Galpin and Others* 226).

† HPL to Maurice W. Moe, 18 May 1722 [1922]: "The Lokleilo trio wrote a joint epistle to our kidlet friend in Madison, chinned some more, and then dispersed. Klei hit the trail, and Lolo hit the hay—Samuelus, good ol' scout, insisted that the less hardy and less easily somnolent Theobald take the only available bedchamber whilst he dumped down on the parlour couch—which is convertible into a bed or bedlet of a sort" (*Letters to Maurice W. Moe and Others* 86).

[1]   [AHT]

Vol. I. No. 2.

Providence, R.I.

August 8, 1916.

As London wits at Will's or Button's[1] knew
The letter'd leisure of a favour'd few;
So our small band, more scatter'd and less able,
May meet in mind, if not about the table!

LUDOVICUS THEOBALDUS, JUN.

But after all, what is life and its purpose? What right has man arbitrarily to assume his own importance in creation? Science can trace our world to its source; to the moment of its birth from the great solar nebula in the remote past. More—Science can demonstrate that all the planets of our system had a similar origin. Extending the principle to the sidereal heavens, from whose contemplation, indeed, the nebular hypothesis was originally derived, we find the nebular form is the present condition of all creation—a condition which precludes the existence of life. Therefore we are able to comprehend that the human race is but a thing of the moment; that its existence on this planet is extremely recent, as infinity is reckoned; and that its possible existence in all the expanse of illimitable space is but a matter of yesterday. Space and time have always existed and always will exist. This is the only legitimate axiom in all philosophy. And we are able to see that not only humanity but all other forms of organic life as well are mere innovations; unless, perchance, previous and unknown universes have flourished and perished in the irretrievable recesses of the incomprehensibly remote past. Our human race is only a trivial incident in the history of creation. It is of no more importance in the annals of eternity and infinity than is the child's snow-man in the annals of terrestrial tribes and nations. And more: may not all mankind be a mistake—an abnormal growth—a disease in the system of Nature—an excrescence on the body of infinite progression like a wart on the human hand?[2] Might not the total destruction of humanity, as well as of all animate creation, be a positive *boon* to Nature as a whole? How arrogant of us, creatures of the moment, whose very species is but an experiment of the *Deus Naturae,* to arrogate to ourselves an immortal future and considerable status! How do we know that we have a right to live? Our philosophy is all childishly *subjective*—we imagine that the welfare of our race is the paramount consideration, when as a matter of fact the very existence of the race may be an obstacle to the predestined course of the aggregated universes of infinity! How do we know that that form of atomic and molecular motion called "life" is the highest of all forms? Perhaps the dominant creature—the most rational and God-like of all beings—is an invisible gas![3] Or perhaps it is a flaming and effulgent mass of molten stardust. Who can say that men have souls while rocks have none? Perhaps the best thing a man might do is to annihilate himself! But of this we know nothing. We are here on a grain of dust called the Earth, and endowed with a certain imperfect and unhappy consciousness called "life". It is not for us to destroy what the Gods have given; we might err as sadly in one direction as in the other. It is obviously our right and our duty to heed our own ignorance, and to permit Nature to work out her processes without interference from these puny, shadow-haunted centres of unrest which we call our minds. It is our right and our duty to mould the minor manifestations of human character in such a way that the entire race may derive the least amount of pain and misery from the pitiful satire known as "life". Certain evils are beyond redemption, many are capable of amelioration, whilst a very few might possibly be cured. There is such a thing as pleasure and happiness tho' it is experienced by few, and only to be obtained by a career of such strenuous achievement that the majority are denied more than a sip. False, loose pleasures are not happiness at all, and are invariably compensated for by misery, the certain result of wide deviation from the normal. In short, most of us have no hope of happiness, nor should we waste our energy in striving for it, since it is all but unattainable. As Mr. Campbell[4] well repeats after other moralists, happiness is to be had only incidentally, as a by-product of the pursuit of virtue. But after all, what is the use of happiness? We cannot say we have a right to it, for we do not even know of what it consists. Let us be content with the absence of poignant pain, nor complain should we fail to achieve positive satisfaction. Much has been said of "the sheer joy of living", an ebullient sensation enjoyed by those in close communion with Nature. This feeling undoubtedly exists, but it is in itself a sinister thing, since it is but an atavistic delight in prehistoric things which the intelligent are leaving behind. It is, indeed, a sort of warning against the continued progress of mankind; a finger beckoning us back to the simpler ages we have survived. I have often wondered if mankind would not be happier for a deliberate destruction of learning and civilisation—an absolute and unqualified return to the happy pastoral barbarism of our legendary ancestors! But the magnitude of such a thing is equaled only by its impossibility. We have outlived happiness, and must make the best of our loss. For a few the atoning delights of aesthetic values have arisen; but that mankind as a unit will ever attain to an appreciation of these milder joys is highly improbable. For the majority today, *forgetfulness* is the only road to endurable existence. It is this yearning for relief from the world and its intolerable monotony which undoubtedly gave rise to the spread of drunkenness and its attendant evils. Man has no natural taste for drink, and the solution of the temperance question really lies in providing the race with a substitute means of escaping the realities of existence. In the sodden brawler of the corner saloon we may trace the degraded effigy of the battle-brave Diomedes, who choked the Xanthus with the bodies of his slain.[5]

We have lost all the natural outlets of energy and are blindly groping for new ones. Amidst the bewildering chaos of thwarted instinct and imperfect intellect, the one cry of mankind is "Forget!" Let us then seek to adjust contemporary conditions to man, rather than adapt man to arbitrary conditions. Let us strive for adjustments based on the known nature of the human beast. Let us seek to accomodate his known instincts with harmless activities or painless counter-actives. It is the momentary destiny of that evanescent ephemera called "man" to seek as much surcease as he can from the dulness of life; to do what he can to mould his oft-erring race to the manifest course of Nature, and to await the end prepared for him by the mighty elements which mould not only his own transitory tribe, but all the eternal and unfathomed recesses of existence that yawn about him, even beyond the vision of his excited and disordered fancy. Man knows nothing. Man probably is nothing. But let the poor creatures do what they can to avoid open conflict with destiny. Of all the judgments of man enunciated by the various philosophers and poets of this world, I find most sense and satisfaction in the lines of my own beloved Mr. Pope, who hath writ:

> "Plac'd on this isthmus of a middle state,
> A being darkly wise, and rudely great,
> With too much knowledge for the sceptic's side,
> With too much weakness for the Stoic's pride,
> He hangs between, in doubt to act or rest;
> In doubt to deem himself a God, or beast;
> In doubt his mind or body to prefer;
> Born but to die, and reas'ning but to err;
> Alike in ignorance, his reason such,
> Whether he thinks too little or too much;
> Chaos of thought and passion, all confused;
> Still by himself abus'd, or disabus'd;
> Created half to rise, and half to fall;
> Great lord of all things, yet a prey to all;
> Sole judge of truth, in endless error hurl'd:
> The glory, jest, and riddle of the world!"[6]

Descending from infinity to mine own study, I must needs excuse the delay to which I have subjected the Kleicomolo correspondence. This letter, commenced on August 8th, has been untouched till now, the 22d, on account of my desire to spare my esteemed colleagues the labour of deciphering my uncertain chirography. The vicissitudes of ill health and of critical duties oft-times withhold me from the typewriter during those hours when its clattering is permissible. I am always most in the mood for writing at night, when the machine would disturb the sleeping house, hence make but slight headway in these cases. Unlike Mr. Mo, I have no convenient schoolhouse to serve as a haven of refuge! Also unlike Mr. Mo, I am without pupil-stenographers, hence cannot hope to keep such a complete record of the Kleicomolo correspondence as our pedagogical confrere intends to accumulate.[7] Incidentally, I do not envy the luckless student to whose lot it shall fall to transcribe this tedious and protracted epistle. (Note to stenographer: I hope you have not been typing this in simplified spelling,[8] despite the predilections of your gifted instructor, Mr. Moe; I am an advocate of the most conservative British forms. Also, I hope you have made fewer mistakes than I have!—H.P.L.)

Today, the 22d of August, is one of the hottest days of the season, hence contrary to the general run of humanity, I am unusually in the mood for literary composition. The warmer the weather, the better I like it. But since the hour is late, I find that I cannot include replies to personal communications from Messrs. Klei and Mo. In a measure, this is well, since this rotating letter should in no case interfere with personal correspondence. I will only mention that I have derived a very interesting idea from Mr. Mo's suggestion that I compile a list of Georgian and other pastoral "rubber-stamp" phrases. I intend to spend considerable time at the library searching out the various expressions and conventional proper names used by the classicists, both ancient and English. Most of the classicism of English literature is Graeco-Roman, wherefore the majority of pastoral names used in Milton, Dryden, Pope, Philips, Gay, and others may be found in Theocritus, Bion, Moschus, and Virgil. The subject is no small one and may involve much care and labour. I may publish my results either in the amateur press or the local newspaper, besides communicating the information to Mr. Moe.

But having wearied ye all sufficiently, I will now take my leave, in the hope that this missive may return in the company of three interesting companions.

With heartiest good wishes, I have ye Honour to remain,
    Gentlemen,
        Yr. most Oblig'd and Obedient Servt.:
          LO

Notes

1. Will's was a coffee-house in Covent Garden, London, where Dryden, Congreve, and other 17th-century literary figures congregated. Its standing declined in the 18th century. Button's Coffee House in Russell Street, Covent Garden, London, was established in the early 18th century by Daniel Button. Addison and other literary figures met there after the decline of Will's.

2. In *At the Mountains of Madness,* HPL wrote: "How it [the creature] could have undergone its tremendously complex evolution on a new-born earth in time to leave prints in archaean rocks was so far beyond conception as to make Lake whimsically recall the primal myths about Great Old Ones who filtered down from the stars and concocted

earth-life as a joke or mistake; and the wild tales of cosmic hill things from Outside told by a folklorist colleague in Miskatonic's English department" (*CF* 3.44–45).

3. Cf. *The Dream-Quest of Unknown Kadath:* "The violet gas S'ngac had told him terrible things of the crawling chaos Nyarlathotep, and had warned him never to approach the central void where the daemon-sultan Azathoth gnaws hungrily in the dark" (*CF* 2.156).

4. Paul J. Campbell. HPL alludes to his article "The Pursuit of Happiness," *Invictus* 1, No. 2 (July 1916): 2–5. Campbell also wrote a novel of the same name. It was destroyed in a house fire.

5. See Homer, *Iliad* 5.114–65.

6. Alexander Pope (1688–1744), *An Essay on Man* (1733–34), Epistle II, ll. 3–18.

7. Maurice W. Moe was, at the time, a high school instructor in Appleton, WI. He organized an amateur journalism club with his students, and as HPL suggests, he had them type the Kleicomolo letters for preservation.

8. See HPL's essay "The Simple Spelling Mania."

[2]   [AHT]

Vol. I. No. 6.

Providence, R.I.

October, 1916

Incerta haec si tu postules

Ratione certa facere, nihilo plus agas,

Quam si des operam, ut cum ratione insanias.

TERENCE.[1]

Of the various pretenders to learning that infest this unsettled and degenerate age, no sort is at once so absurd and so disgusting as the tribe of Pindarick[2] little-wits who mask their gross thoughts and want of taste under the veil of pretended genius; and who denominate their irregular productions *vers libre*, after the French fashion. I was not long ago favoured by a correspondent with a copy of THE POETRY REVIEW, a newly founded magazine edited by William Stanley Braithwaite,[3] and so numerous were the specimens of this type of literary monstrosity which I found therein, that I cannot but fear it will work harm with the present generation of readers ere returning sense shall banish it to a deserved ignominy. Not only is such rubbish frequently to be seen in the supposedly poetical column, but 'tis reviewed and commented upon elsewhere to a much greater extent than its insignificance merits.

I think it was Mr. Cowley[4] that first troubled us with Pindaricks in large quantities. After his example, a vast number of bards great and small tried their hand at the pastime, yet in their efforts to be like Pindar, succeeded no further than to grow Boeotian. Of their halting effusions Mr. Addison very justly remark'd, 'that there is in the distortion, grimace, and outward figure, but nothing of that divine impulse which raises the mind above itself, and makes the sounds more than humane'.[5] With the advance and blossoming of our Augustan era, the whole family of metrical contortionists seemed to disappear, notwithstanding some irregular odes by Mr. Gray and others, and not till the nineteenth century did the fever for boorish roughness break out again, this time in the disgraceful Muse of the peasant Whitman. But this second eruption of amorphousness was in many respects vastly unlike the one which Mr. Addison censured. The design of Cowley and his successors was to emulate antiquity and achieve art in Theban fashion, to travel, if I may thus misapply a familiar quotation, *ad astra per aspera*,[6] whilst Whitman, disregardful alike of the precepts of art and decency, used his licence merely to display a swinish and fallacious philosophy of his own making. That Walt Whitman was a degenerate mentally and pathologically, I think no scientist would deny.[7] His fancy was not that of the man, but of the ape, till increasing years and the ascendancy of that touch of real genius which he undoubtedly possessed, combined to elevate his thoughts from the mire to the world above. His coarseness is not the healthy coarseness of Shakespeare, but the fiendishly analytical degradation of an Elagabalus.[8] Only this creature, so vividly portrayed by Mr. Gibbon in his Decline and Fall of the Roman Empire,[9] can be compared to Whitman in utter absence of those instinctive restraints of expression which make even the Earl of Rochester's filth appear decorous in comparison.[10]

Of Whitman's painful egotism and constant posing, Mr. Klei hath sufficiently inform'd us, and with Mr. Mo we may agree that his ravings had no little hint of barbaric chanting or rhythm.[11] We may likewise subscribe to the nobility of some of his real soarings above his native cesspool. But in estimating his worth as an expounder of ideas we must not forget that he based his shriekings wholly upon a fantastic principle of absolute democracy, a condition directly opposed to the plan of Nature, and to the right governance of mankind. Whitman's pseudo-philosophy was something like that of his modern amateur successor, Mr. Isaacson,[12] in its utter disregard of reality and historical perspective. Insensible to the finer sentiments of tradition, and perhaps abetted by the thoughtless fanaticism of the Boston and New York negrophiles and abolitionists of the ante-bellum period, he drew an imaginary line somewhere in the brute creation, betwixt the Guinea black and the gorilla, and pompously vowed that every living thing above that line was equal to every other living thing above that line. Taking seriously the rhetorical flight of the American revolutionists that "all men are created equal", he perpetrated such absurdities as "The Open Road",[13] trusting to the dense sentimentality of his critics to accept and commend its commonplace notions. All men are not equal, nor were they ever intended to be so. In the freest and most primitive states of society the strongest man assumes leadership by physical force, later succeeding to the tripartite functions of King, War-Chieftain, and High-Priest. Those who serve him most valiantly and most faithfully grow into a privileged aristocracy, as do those who by reason of their learning are able to benefit the nascent state. The vast proletariat rightly occupies itself in administering to the needs of those who make possible the defence and advancement of the whole. This system may change, suffer abuse, develop abnormally, and temporarily be overthrown; but will always rise again as soon as demolished. Never so long as the human mind is as it is will there be such a thing as "democracy" save in the speeches of demagogues. As well try to abolish the tides or stop the rotation of the earth, as to essay to overthrow that social order which Nature had enjoined upon her children. Whitman, as an arch-demagogue, has won the rabble to his cause; but to the eye of refinement he will forever stand as a monster. If we must needs call him a giant of American letters, let us concede that he is a Cyclops rather than a Titan. Polyphemus-like, his single vision cannot touch the life or the thought of a cultivated state of society.

I am not inform'd just who was the first pseudo-poet to succumb to Whitman's malign influence; certain it is, that I never heard "free verse" mentioned seriously till an exceedingly recent date.[14] Now, however, it seems the recognised avenue of expression for persons who cannot think clearly, or who are afflicted with concomitant symptoms of radicalism and imbecility in other forms. That the vers librists are preëminently coarse in their ideas, is what one might expect as a result of their radical tendencies. A radical of any sort is by nature an iconoclast, and is never satisfied till he breaks some established canon of reason or propriety. Democracy of thought, with its accompanying rejection of the refined and the beautiful, insidiously leads on to a glorification of the gross and the physical; for the physical body is about all that the boor and the poet have in common. Mr. Mo bids these eccentrics keep off Parnassus and build a mount of their own, but methinks they have their Pierian grove already well established on some farmer's dunghill in Boeotia! From the dissipated "Bohemian" swine of Washington Square in New York, to the more scholarly Amy Lowell, they are all of the same clay. Albert Mordell, a critick in THE POETRY REVIEW, refers to the "poem" of Miss Lowell's wherein grossness hath no small part, saying, 'that if she had written nothing else, this poem would have been sufficient to immortalize her'![15] Wherever radical thought spreads its stench, there may be found the greatest number of vers librists, hovering like maggots about the carcass of decayed reason. I was lately a recipient of a paper or magazine called THE FRA, published by the heirs of the late eccentric, Mr. Elbert Hubbard,[16] which was sent me by my venerable amateur friend Mr. Hoag. In the pages of this publication may be found a vast deal of nonsense and bad English, typical of that flashy, brainless iconoclasm which was characteristic of Mr. Hubbard; but the most significant thing is, that every "poem" in the issue is cast in free verse! Of these one is unfit for perusal, and the residue merely dull.

I am glad that Mr. Co saw fit to celebrate his cliff-shaded bath in pictures rather than in vers libre; in fact, I do not believe such a pleasing spot could possibly excite the cacophonous horrors engendered by the Lowell family tub. And yet, who shall say that a bathtub cannot awake the Muse? Dr. Swift, it will be remembered, found it possible to write a Meditation upon a Broomstick.[17] The following lines, by a little known author, sing the tub with great fervour:[18]

AD BALNEUM
by Lewis Theobald, Jun.

Hail! little sea, in whose bright waters shine
The myriad graces of the boundless brine;
Whose shallow calms and rippling surges bear
Th' eternal sway of Neptune's curule chair:
Thy kindly pow'r a grateful race confess,
And count thy virtues next to godliness;
Blest be thy waves, by no rude breezes blown,
To Britons sacred, and to Jews unknown!
How oft have I, in childhood's blissful day,
Drawn o'er thy face my tiny fleets at play!
See bold Ulysses plough the Grecian main,
And Nelson at Trafalgar die again;
See Pompey's triremes break the corsair's pride,
And Northern Vikings brave the Arctic tide.
Fancy can trace within thy meagre bound
The storied deep, that girds our planet round!
What noble mem'ries thy white banks awake
Of Roman might that made creation quake!
Thy marble ancestors, by Tiber's stream
In tribute to Imperial bounty gleam
Where'er a Caesar's wisdom rul'd the land,
In east or west, the stately thermae stand!
Say, lucid lake, what sylphs and fairies dwell
Beneath the crystal magic of thy spell?
Art as a fount in blest Arcadian mead
Where naiad throngs the sylvan syrinx heed,
Or dost thou bow to Triton's wider rule,
And hold an ocean in thy placid pool?
Do little nereids, suited to thy size,
(Too small to glimpse with our crude mortal eyes)
Sport through thy waves, and ev'ry crest adorn,
Upon the backs of tiny dolphins borne?

Imagination fain would find in thee
The charm, and lure, and glory of the sea!
How swells thy breast when on thy porcelain bed
Descending cloudbursts their mad fury shed!
How whirls thy tide when through thy punctur'd floor
The angry waters in a maelstrom pour!
Then dost thou lie—a dry, deserted thing
For Gods to mourn, and third-rate bards to sing!

If Mr. Theobald hath, in the above, aped somewhat the manner of Mr. Co, he would assure you all, 'tis no conscious plagiarism; but merely the result of a natural taste much akin to that of our Kansan bard.

In commenting upon the poetick productions of the several Kleicomoloes, Mr. Mo hath presented an interesting opportunity for comparison of the manner in which each of us turn'd to numbers. His own case is an example of the virtues of metrical regularity and conventional expression, and should be recommended to the attention of those who argue that form is but a superfluity in poesy. I can well imagine how the artificialities of the French models awak'd in our revered leader that exquisite taste and perfection of harmony which he shows in all his work. For mine own part, I had no use for foreign literature in my youth, being too much of an Anglo-Saxon to care for aught save true-born English verse. Not till later did I realise that my beloved Augustan age derived much of its classick polish from the example of the elegant circle surrounding Le Grand Monarque and centreing in his court. It is my intention, if ever time and health permit, to acquire a greater knowledge of Gallick literature than I now possess. As it is, I have but a slight acquaintance with the tongue of Racine, Corneille, and Monsieur Boileau, for I was ever hostile to a nation which, in the British mind, stood for naught but frivolity and coxcombry. However, now that France hath proven so valiant an ally to Old England, I have conceiv'd rather a fondness for *"les poilus"*,[19] and wish I were more in touch with their refined, even though superficial, civilisation.

Returning to my subject, I would say to Mr. Mo, that I resent not at all his description of me as a "Hand-made product". That I have nothing of actual poesy in my nature, I freely admit; and am convinced that only a childish, semibarbaric fondness for rhythm started me upon my metrical career. Had I not lisp'd in numbers, I should never have troubled the world with my dull "Georgian mosaics"; for poetry, as now taught in schools, would have had no attraction at all for me. All that I have done hath been imitation of older and better bards. To nature I owe naught but a primitive, "tom-tom" sort of liking for regularity; my phrases and images come not from Parnassus but from Pope; I have revell'd not amidst "Leaves of Grass", but amidst leaves of books.

With Mr. Klei, I understand that the opposite condition is true. Whilst I made rhymes first, and later on acquired thoughts to use them with; Mr. Klei was first expert in prose and adequate in culture, later stumbling on poesy as the most natural medium of expression for his native inspiration. That this stumble was a most fortunate accident, a perusal of any of his efforts will shew!

As to Mr. Co, I knew him for a born poet before he ever writ a line of verse. His prose teems with poetick imagery, and his Muse like Minerva, sprang forth from his head full grown and armed. I have flatter'd myself that it was I who first induced Mr. Co to write verse; though my impression may be incorrect. This hath given me much solace when my egotism hath suffered on account of my own verse; which, as an illustrious critick tells me, "ever falls short of true art". An I be no king myself, I can at least be, like Warwick, a King-Maker![20]

The vagaries and eccentricities of Rev. W. Sunday,[21] dwelt upon by Messrs. Co and Mo, are of considerable interest to me, since I know but little of the individual in question. That he is a graduate of college, or of a theological seminary, has been reported in the press more than once, hence Mr. Co's paragraph to that effect is not so erroneous as it might otherwise seem; in fact, Sunday seems already to have become the centre of a vast and variable body of legend. I am uncertain whether or not he is a regularly ordained minister, since the title "Reverend" is very loosely used amongst the lower classes. But his intimate connexion with slum life is perfectly evident from his mode of discourse. I believe that none but a guttersnipe could possibly mouth such vulgarity, save he be a great actor; and if Rev. William were possessed of so great an histrionick gift, he would long ago have graduated from his present vaudeville to the legitimate stage, where he could better serve the interests of art and of his pocket-book. The conservative clergy of this city are much at variance concerning his desirability as an evangelist. The cruder denominations, such as the Methodists, favour his coming next year; but the better elements, represented by Pres. Faunce of Brown University (Baptist)[22] regard his methods with horror and disgust. His next seat of activity will, I believe, be Boston.

I am not able to fathom whether Sunday's performances do more good than harm, or more harm than good, but I am certain that they do both to some extent. His appeal is that of the lowest savage medicine-man, who works in a semi-hypnotic manner upon his auditors and who touches the emotional tendencies below the intellectual exterior. He does not move the mind, but the spinal ganglia; and his effect depends absolutely upon the personal characteristics of his several victims. It is authentically stated, that he has produced violent madness in individuals whose mental afflictions were previously but slight. He belongs in the Congo valley, rather than amongst Anglo-Saxons. Yet I will own, that he may be able to institute temporary reforms among persons of sentimental cast. The very maudlin mind which drink and vice create, responds most readily to neurotic stimuli of this type. One of his thunderous sessions might well cause some modern Silenus or

Clodius[23] to forego at least one of his semi-annual sprees. Though seldom in accord with the dicta of Baptists and Irishmen, I vow, that Mr. Quin of Milwaukee hath best depicted Sunday when he calls him "a strange product of the XX century civilisation."

It was the other night my privilege to hear and see a bit of slum reform of a different sort. A speaker belonging to the Prohibition Party and clad in the vestments of the ecclesiastical rank (Episcopal) had stopped his motor-car in a publick square, and was holding forth to a great assemblage of men made up of every rank and condition of society. Gentlemen waiting for street cars, and riff-raff from the corner saloons, together with every intermediate grade of humanity, were thickly represented. The speaker was a grey bearded man of fifty-one, who described his early and varied career. He had begun as a New England farmer's boy, and had soon commenced to drink in moderation; but after his early youth had become disgusted with liquor and relinquished the vice voluntarily. Later on he had served as a sailor aboard a square-rigger, and still later (as Co will learn with interest) as a cowboy all the way from Montana to Texas. His clerical duties were taken up later on. This man spoke in a voice marked equally with ease, fluency, dignity, and refinement, and expounded the workings of prohibition in the various states which have adopted that it hath indeed no excuse for existence. When a sot near his car declared in uncertain tones that beer was a monstrous valuable food, the speaker quietly contrasted the bloated physique of the heckler with his own spare, wiry strength, remarking without boastfulness that no drinking man had ever excelled him either in the rigging of a brigantine or astride a cowpony. Without the "aid" of rum he had comported himself with distinction in two of the manliest vocations in American life. It was with admiration that I attended his words, and only the lateness of the hour induced me to leave the scene before he had completed his lay sermon.

But scarcely less interesting than the speaker were the dregs of humanity who clustered closest about him. I may say truly, that I have never before seen so many human derelicts all at once, gathered in one spot. I beheld modifications of human physiognomy which would have startled even a Hogarth, and abnormal types of gait and bodily carriage which proclaim with startling vividness man's kinship to the jungle ape. And even in the open air the stench of whiskey was appalling. To this fiendish poison, I am certain, the greater part of the squalor I saw is due. Many of these vermin were obviously not foreigners—I counted at least five American countenances in which a certain vanished decency half showed through the red whiskey bloating. Then I reflected upon the power of wine,[24] and marvelled how self-respecting persons can imbibe such stuff, or permit it be served upon their tables. It is the deadliest enemy with which humanity is faced. Not all the European wars could produce a tenth of the havock occasioned among men by the wretched fluid which responsible governments allow to be sold openly. Looking upon that mob of sodden brutes, my mind's eye pictured a scene of different kind; a table bedecked with spotless linen and glistening silver, surrounded by gentlemen immaculate in evening attire—and in the reddening faces of those gentlemen I could trace the same lines which appeared in full development of the beasts of the crowd. Truly, the effects of liquor are universal, and the shamelessness of man unbounded. How can reform be wrought in the crowd, when supposedly respectable boards groan beneath the goblets of rare old vintages? Is mankind asleep, that its enemy is thus entertained as a bosom friend? But a week or two ago, at a parade held in honour of the returning Rhode Island National Guard, the Chief Executive of this State, Mr. Robert Livingston Beeckman, prominent in New York, Newport, and Providence society,[25] appeared in such an intoxicated condition that he could scarce guide his mount, or retain his seat in the saddle, and he the guardian of the liberties and interests of that Colony carved by the faith, hope, and labour of Roger Williams from the wilderness of savage New-England! I am perhaps an extremist on the subject of prohibition, but I can see no justification whatsoever for the tolerance of such a degrading demon as drink.

Reference to the Governor of Rhode Island reminds me that Hon. Addison Pierce Munroe, father of our fellow-amateur Chester Pierce Munroe, is the candidate of the Democratic party for the leadership of this state in the coming election. Since his opponent is our present wine-bibbing sovereign Mr. Beeckman, I am even more anxious for Mr. Munroe's election than my lifelong personal friendship would in any case make me.[26] I fear he will meet defeat, since the ridiculous folly and atrocious cowardice of Prof. Wilson[27] has made Rhode Island solidly Republican; but I wish, none the less, that I might be able to hail so old and respected an acquaintance as "Gov. Munroe." Then the modest house which I now behold from my east window would be transformed automatically into the Gubernatorial Mansion! Mr. Munroe is generally known as the strongest Democrat in the state, but no Democrat will have much consideration as such this fall. If he wins, it will be a personal rather than a party victory.

Mention of the father leads to mention of the son; and in this connexion I wish to remind Mr. Co that the author of "To Chloris" is not Mrs. Jordan,[28] but Chester Pierce Munroe. How much revision came from the Conservative, Mr. Mo has already seen. Another poem of Munroe's, similarly revised, will appear in the forthcoming October CONSERVATIVE, its title being "Twilight".[29] I have now received proofs of the issue, and the paper may reach even Klei before this epistle—it will certainly reach Co and Mo first. Chester was lately in this city visiting his parents, and seems rather more interested in literary pursuits than he has been for several years.

I received from Mr. Mo the APPLETON CRESCENT describing his address on the use of the phonograph in the teaching of English, and must congratulate him upon the favourable reception with which his idea hath met.[30] That the talking machine will play no small part in the educational activities of the next generation of teachers, I have no doubt. An idea of my own hath been the employment of the cinematograph as an aid to the teaching of history. Films specially prepared to shew the manners of departed ages, to illustrate Greek and Roman antiquities and to aid in interpreting the classicks, would form no feeble addition to the curriculum of and [*sic*] secondary school.

Mr. Mo's description of afflicted Belgium proved of intense interest to me, since it presents at least one advantage resulting from the much vaunted "neutrality" of the United States. This neutrality hath been a source of the keenest distress and humiliation to me ever since the war began, since I believe that the rightful place of America is at the side of her mother nation, defending the Anglo-Saxon civilisation and ideals which both countries hold in common. In fact, I have more than once blushed at the base and selfish attitude of the States at a time when all the forces of humanity should be engaged in warding off the Hun. Never before was I more disposed to make ostentation of the legal provision which makes me still able, as the grandson in direct male line of a true-born Englishman, to call myself a rightful British subject. England is my country as well as America—let those call me "hyphenate" who so desire! (See October CONSERVATIVE)[31]

But in America's ability to assist poor Belgium as a neutral, there is at least some measure of compensation for her evasion of loyalty to the British vigorous American protest at the beginning of the war, as Col. Roosevelt has suggested with no little emphasis. [*Above sentence garbled or mistranscribed.*—ED.] This might not have stopped the war as a whole; in fact it is extremely unlikely that it would have affected the determination of the Hohenzollern to spread his beneficent kultur over France; but I sincerely believe that it would have saved Belgium all its misery. At that time, the shameful weakness of the Wilson administration was not so apparent, and a word of admonition from Washington would have had real weight at Berlin. It was not absolutely necessary for von Kluck[32] to use the more prepared condition of Switzerland made Belgium the easier prey for his damnable vultures. [*Above sentence garbled in AHT.*—ED.] Had America played the nobler part, the objections against Belgium would have been at least equal to those against Switzerland, and some direct route across the actual French border would have been adopted. That the protest of England was without effect, is easily explained by the fact that Germany knew well that England would in any case prove an opponent. But we had poor Wilson—and "he kept us out of war."[33]

A gratifying feature of the American relief work in Belgium is the discovery of one solitary Wilson diplomat who escapes the stupid mediocrity of most of them. Brand Whitlock[34] has certainly shewn himself to be a man of wonderful character and ability, and I shall feel disposed to criticise the incoming Republican administration if they ever think fit to replace such a veritable saviour of mankind with another, for party reasons. Of the Prussian tactics in suppressing art and music amongst the Belgians, no word of contempt is sufficiently strong to speak; in fact, the Huns seem to have lost track of all historical perspective in their disregard for the civilisation of Western Europe. In the formation of modern civilisation it is always the Latin, heir to classical antiquity, who has contributed art and culture; the Teuton's mission is to contribute his own racial stock, which is the highest so far evolved by Nature. From this point contribution of Latin culture and Teutonic blood springs all the glory of modern Europe, culminating in England, whose civilisation contains all the best precepts of the Greeks and the Romans, and whose blood is predominantly Teutonic. It is this transference of older culture to younger and better races which maintains the uninterrupted progress of mankind. The Roman assumed that which was best (and alas—sometimes that which was worst!) in Hellenic culture. The Gaul assumed Roman culture, with its Greek elements, like a mantle. It now remained for the Teuton, highest race of all, to succeed to this mighty heritage. This he did in England, and this he began to do in Germany. Eighteenth century Prussia wisely adopted the polish of the court of Louis XIV, and Frederick the Great became a disciple of Voltaire. But the egotism consequent upon the brilliant success of 1870 and the consequent absorption of the other German states has distorted everything in Prussian eyes, and led Continental Teutons to place full reliance in their racial superiority, regardless of older cultures. France and Italy deserve vast respect, not for the biological grade of their present inhabitants, but for their wonderful traditions of artistic accomplishment. In condemning the Huns, one should not make the common mistake of denying their claim to biological supremacy. They are perfectly correct when they place the Teutonic stock at the head of the human race. Their faulty reasoning is in forgetting that England also is Teutonic, and that their own racial qualities cannot make up for the vastly older culture of the Latins, which they despise, but which England has adopted and adapted. Germany without Latin influences would be like Rome without Greek influences. The race is superior, but the traditions are less refining because they are too recent. Our ancestors were drunken, swinish barbarians at a time when the Graeco-Roman world was ablaze with intellectual and artistic splendour. The Norman Conquest was all that raised us from the level of sots and gluttons. To tell the truth, our forefathers wrested Britain from the Celt by very Hunnish methods—so Hunnish that the Celt well nigh disappeared—but that is far in the past! England now knows how to wage war with equal valour and honour, and it was undoubtedly the chivalrous traditions of France which caused the change. British glory, in its truest sense, dates not from the conquest of the island in 450, but from the fusion with the Normans after the year 1066. So let mankind cease to despise the legacy of the past. It were folly to try and set up new traditions to replace those whose uninterrupted—or only slightly interrupted—flow has gradually but firmly moulded the life, manners, and ethics of Western Europe. Humanity will not permit the coldly scientific and artificial code of the Prussian to displace the dominant ideals of civilisation without the bloodiest struggle in history.

Concerning the work of assimilating foreigners to the American people, a problem in which Mr. Mo hath lately taken an increased interest, I must remark that whilst the eradication of disloyalty is much to be desired, it should nevertheless be provided that certain stocks may never come to taint the original blood of the colonists. The English race, to whom is due the founding and maintenance of the States, and on whose ideals the greatness of the country depends, is a basically Teutonic stock with a slight Celtic admixture. In order to preserve the character of the population, and to avoid that deterioration of manners and morals which is ever consequent upon mongrelism, it is absolutely essential to erect an impassable barrier against the disgusting Italians, Jews, Slavs, Armenians, and other nondescript offscourings of Southern Europe and Asia. In a word, the only immigrants who are real acquisitions, and who can well enter wholly into an American race are those of older type—Germans and Scandinavians as Teutonic elements, and Irish as the Celtic element. It is lamentable that we can secure no more English and Scotch, but the other colonies of the Empire, which are still loyal to the Motherland, seem to gain the best blood which emigrates from the ancestral isle. The assimilation even of the more recent German and Irish elements will take an incalculably long while, since European conditions tend to antagonise them toward the Anglo-Saxon ideal. Singularly—or naturally—enough, the better classes are vastly more difficult to assimilate than the peasantry; since, having been persons of consequence in their own countries, they are less disposed to alter their allegiance. In truth, we should think less of them if they did alter that allegiance. But however much we may admire their ancestral loyalty, they are none the less dangerous to this nation. Prof. Camillo von Klenze,[35] lately a professor at Brown University in this city, is now advocating, in his lectures, a departure from strictly Anglo-Saxon standards in America. Such ideas should be suppressed before they gain ground. If we have created a haven of refuge for those of other lands, it at least behooves the immigrants and refugees to adopt our standards without attempting to infuse their own. It is an ironical truth, that those foreigners who most desire to become thorough Americans, are generally those who are least fitted for amalgamation out of reverence to his vaterland; but the greasy Jew from Russia impudently assumes a pseudo-Americanism to which his race does not entitle him. In considering matters of this sort, the student must free himself from tons of sticky sentimentalism about "broad humanitarian ideals", "America the land of equality", "down with the race prejudice", and other nonsense of like tenor. The question is; do Americans desire to remain a vigorous, clean moraled Teutonic-Celtic people; or do they desire to transform their country to a sordid, amorphous chaos of degradation and hybridism like imperial Rome? Jews, Italians, Slavs and their like must somehow be segregated or gotten rid of before they rise to taint the better classes. Jews have a tendency of keeping to themselves, and of refraining from mixture with the Aryans amongst whom they dwell, provided they exist not in over great numbers. In the mother country they have held and still hold, many important public places. But this condition becomes altered when Semites pour into a nation by the million, as they have into our unfortunate city of New York. I am assured by persons who have seen that city, that the foreign appearance of the populace is at once manifest even to the stranger. Swarthy faces and hook noses affront the aesthetic sense of the passer-by on every street and avenue, save in the better parts of the town. New York is no longer American. It does not belong to the Aryan civilisation of the Western world at all. It has succumbed to the taint of the Orient, and faces the same fate that threatened Europe before the battle of Tours—or earlier in history, before the fall of Carthage. It faces that same Semitic ascendancy which Aryans have been trying to avert since the days of the Phoenicians, or of the Caliphs. That Semites are unfit for Aryan culture is only too manifest. Their own autochthonous civilisation has never risen above the level of the mediaeval Saracen Empire under Haroun al Raschid.

It was not without a smile of sympathetic amusement that I read Mr. Mo's mention of the hapless student who became so lost amidst the tangled verbiage of my previous philosophical and polysyllabic epistle. Yet I regret that I have caused our leader the dull labour of transcribing it himself. It flatters me, to say the least, that so conscientious a critick should find himself able to term my discourse of pantheism "remarkable"; but then, I am aware that the word may have more than one significance! I fully agree with Mr. Mo, that my estimate of human happiness "does leave a great deal to be desired"; but does not the wretched state of mankind also leave much to be desired? Frankly, I cannot conceive how any thoughtful man can really be happy. There is really nothing in the universe to live for, and unless one can dismiss thought and speculation from his mind, he is liable to be engulfed by the very immensity of creation. It is vastly better that he should amuse himself with religion, or any other convenient palliative to reality which comes to hand. In my coming Conservative I shall have a piece called "The Symphonick Idcal", wherein I decry the realists who would discourage the harmless little devices whereby we may trick ourselves into believing we are happy. There is much relief from the burden of life to be derived from many sources. To the man of high animal spirits, there is the mere pleasure of being alive; the *joie de vivre*, as our Gallick friends term it. To the credulous there is religion and its paradisal dreams. To the moralist, there is a certain satisfaction in right conduct. To the scientist there is the joy in pursuing truth which nearly counteracts the depressing revelations of truth. To the person of cultivated taste, there are the fine arts. To the man of humour, there is the sardonic delight of spying out pretensions and incongruities of life. To the poet there is the ability and privilege to fashion a little Arcadia in his fancy, wherein he may withdraw from the sordid reality of mankind at large. In short, the world abounds with simple delusions which we may call "happiness", if we be but able to entertain them. Capacity for happiness, then, is mainly a personal characteristick; varying in individuals, and natural to the species until too much instruction or progress removes it. Mr. Mo slightly misinterprets me when he surmises that I deem happiness beneath the dignity of civilised man. My intention was to state, that it is merely increasingly *difficult of achievement* by civilised man. I am not so ruthless, nay, even criminal, as to wish to strip mankind of what little joy it still possesses. I have sympathy for even the silliest of pleasures, provided it be not too outrageously incompatible with reason, law, and decorum. As to the fundamentals of happiness, I concur not with Sir R. Tagore[36] when he saith that man's existence proves the goodness of life. As I once before inquired, may not man be even a sore, a blemish, or monstrosity in Nature? What is the use of happiness? You say, it keeps us alive. But what is the use of life? This no man can answer! But it is not well, I suppose, so deeply to question Nature. As Mr. Pope hath observ'd:

> Know then thyself, presume not God to scan;
> The proper study of mankind is man![37]

Of the cause of melancholy in individuals, Mr. Mo says that it arises mainly from youthful misfortunes. That my own attitude is tinctured somewhat by early experiences, is not at all impossible or unlikely. My disposition is sensitive, and very keenly dependent upon the atmosphere about me. The death of my grandmother and father[38] gave my first conscious years a cast of gloom which has never been quite dissipated—I have yet a horror of mourning attire, from having seen my mother and aunts continually in it when I was under eight years of age. Then illness played its not inconsiderable part. In a very brilliant family circle I was easily the dullest; my uncle surpassed me in classical scholarship, my mother in elocution, French, and pictorial art, my grandfather in travelled urbanity;[39] in short, I ever felt a sort of constitutional inferiority to those about me, as though I belonged to a lower social class than my parents and relatives. Headaches and deathly fatigue prevented me from achieving distinction in anything that I attempted; while on the other hand, I had learnt too much to be congenial to other children. They deemed my manner of speech odd, as it most undoubtedly was, having been copied either from the discourse of adults, or from the pages of books at least two hundred years old. They had no sympathy with my indifference to their sports, and no toleration for my attempts to introduce classical and dramatic features into their play. I was the most unpopular and disliked child in the neighbourhood; in fact, I do not believe I ever possessed a real friend, save the two brothers mentioned earlier in this epistle. Thus tactilly [tacitly?] ostra-cised both from adult salons and from juvenile merry-makings, I became (as Mr. Mo's friend, Rev. Graeme Davis,[40] quotes from another author) "a veri-table self-conscious Ishmael." Everything I loved had been dead for two cen-turies—or, as in the case of Graeco-Roman classicism, for two milenniums [sic]. I am never a part of anything around me—in everything I am an outsid-er. Should I find it possible to crawl backward through the Halls of Time to that age which is nearest my own fancy, I should doubtless be bawled out of the coffee-houses for heresy in religion, or else lampooned by John Dennis[41] till I found refuge in the deep, silent Thames, that covers many another un-fortunate. Yes, I seem to be a decided pessimist!—But pray do not think, gentlemen, that I am an utterly forlorn and misanthropick creature. I have merely given this cheerful little outline to satisfy Mr. Mo of the correctness of his theory. Despite my solitary life, I have found infinite joy in books and writing, and am by far too interested in the affairs of the world to quit the scene before Nature shall claim me. Though not a participant in the Business of life; I am, like the character of Addison and Steele, an impartial (or more or less impartial) Spectator,[42] who finds not a little recreation in watching the antics of those strange and puny puppets called men. A sense of humour has helped me to endure existence; in fact, when all else fails, I never fail to ex-tract a sarcastic smile from the contemplation of my own empty and egotisti-cal career! In a way, I am supremely ridiculous with my pompous verses, heavy prose, overweighted words, and self-important pseudo-philosophy! What a spectacle! I ought to furnish forth a mighty feast of slander and sneer-ing on the part of Jewsaacson, Edward Cole, and other amiable creatures who, if they ever refer to me at all, wisely do so behind my back! But so much for environment and congenital characteristics. To my mind, a vastly more important influence in shaping the pessimism of Northern philosophers is the hereditary gloom of the Teuton, transmitted, though not in full measure, to all branches of the race today. Our species have not the lightness of the Latin or of the Celt; we are by nature heavy and morose. Our forefathers of the horned helmets, who fought under Ariovistus and Arminius,[43] were all rather frost-bitten in temperament, constantly seeking the surcease of drunk-enness. The Latin and his social glass of wine represent merely the hectic ex-cesses of a buoyant race, but our ancestors in the dark Teutonberg [sic] Forest drank for oblivion's sake—to forget the world and its ill-understood monot-ony between intervals of fighting and hunting. Faugh! what a nasty lot of brutes we all are! The only true happiness lies in the partial ignorance of childhood; either of the individual or of the race. To be happy, we must shed most of our responsibilities, lose our perspective, and place all faith in an un-known future, either this or the other side of the grave. The whole key to happiness is the unknown—those vague anticipations which we all entertain, of "something better coming" (which will probably never come). There is not a man living who would care to continue the farce if he did not think there was something greater in store for him. Even the greatest good fortune we can conceive of, becomes stale, boresome, and common-place as soon as we acquire it. We do not know what we desire—we simply wish for something we lack. If we had what we desire, we should loathe it, and wish for something else.

Concerning the ultimates of time and space, I fear no philosopher would be quite satisfied with Mr. Mo's light rejection of considerations beyond our own terrestrial globe. The whole structure of our chieftain's orthodox Christianity[44] is built upon the relation of Deity with the one crawling atom we call man; and no theologian can sustain his religion unless he can prove that this speck in infinity is the central point of all creation. Mr. Mo leaves us in perplexity whether his God is absolutely omnipotent, or whether he is a local deity, presiding over this particular little world or universe as some minor hamadryad presides over some particular tree or grove. The latter conception, of a God who is confined in action to our visible universe, leaves us to speculate as to what God or forces may preside over the rest of creation—or if we adhere to the commandment of Scripture, and believe only in one God, we must assume that the rest of space is godless; that no personal loving father-deity is there to bless his sons and subjects. But then, if this be so, why did the personal all-wise parent select this one particular little universe wherein to exercise his beneficence? I fear that all theism consists mostly of reasoning in circles, and guessing or inventing what we do not know. If God is omnipotent, then why did he pick out this one little period and world for his experiment with mankind? Or if he is local, then why did he select this locality, when he had an infinity of universes and an infinity of eras to choose from? And why should the fundamental tenets of theology hold him to be all-pervasive? These are monstrous uncomfortable questions for a pious man to answer, and yet the orthodox clergy continue to assert a complete understanding of all these things, brushing inquiry aside either by sophistry and mysticism, or by evasion and sanctified horror. Why must men of sense thus delude themselves with notions of personal and "loving" gods, spirits, and demons? All this sort of thing is good enough for the rabble, but why should rational brains be tormented with such gibberish? It is perfectly true that the conception of a personal force is a vast help in managing the millions, and in giving them much hope and happiness that truth does not convey. Viewing the question in that light, I am a friend of the church, and would never seek to disturb or diminish its influence among those who are able to swallow its doctrines. I even wish I could believe them myself—it would be so comfortable to know that some day I shall sprout wings and go up to Heaven for a talk with Alexander Pope and Sir Isaac Newton! But, provided a man cannot believe in orthodoxy, why grate on his sensibilities by demanding that he believe? We cannot do what we cannot—at least this has been the general idea since the abolishment of the Popish Inquisition. It is only the forcible propagation of conventional Christianity that makes the agnostic so bitter toward the church. He knows that all the doctrines cannot possibly be true, but he would view them with toleration if he were asked merely to let them alone for the benefit of the masses whom they can help and succour. The agnostic becomes bitter only when someone presumes to affront his reason by demanding that he believe the impossible, under penalty of censure and ostracism. The word "Christianity" becomes noble when applied to the veneration of a wonderfully good man and moral teacher, but it grows undignified when applied to a system of white magic based on the supernatural. Christ probably believed himself a true Messiah, since the tendencies of the times might well inculcate such a notion in anyone of his qualities. Whether his mind was strictly normal or not is out of the question. Very few minds are strictly normal, and all religious fanatics are marked with abnormalities of various sorts. It is well known that psychologists group religious phenomena with other and less divine disturbances of the brain and nervous system. Whether, as the novel of Mr. Moore implies,[45] Christ was alive after his nominal execution; or whether the whole Resurrection legend is a myth, is immaterial. Very little reliable testimony could come from so remote a province as Judaea at that time. For the sensitive mind to harass itself over ancient and mediaeval conceptions, to strain over such questions as how many angels can stand on the point of a needle, (this was actually debated in the Middle Ages) or to wear itself to fragments trying to accept that which it can never accept, is as cruel and reprehensible as to deprive the masses of their spiritual and orthodox solace. I think that Mr. Mo really has the same basic conception of creation that I have, save that his long grounded orthodoxy forbids him to express or even to think consciously the stark, bald facts. Mr. Mo's great argument for orthodoxy is that it accomplishes vast good; an argument which neither affirms nor denies its foundation in absolute truth. Many false beliefs have wrought incalculable good—the observed effects are the effects of the belief; not of the possible truth or untruth that may lie behind the belief. Because a certain preacher has helped reform a drunkard, we have no grounds for acclaiming him as vice-regent of some other person or conscious spirit for whose existence we have no other evidence. Mr. Mo's summing up of his own case may be adopted without change as the summing up of my case. "In the face of these phenomena, what does the nature of absolute, ultimate truth matter to you and me? Christianity pure and undefiled is the truth to this world, *for it works!*" That is, Christianity is "truth to this world". All men may perfectly agree when they admit the existence of more than one kind of truth. Christianity is not necessarily logical or actual truth, but it is "terrestrial truth", and that is enough for the majority. Let us be thankful if anything can govern such an unruly race as man. My point of issue with Mr. Mo is, can thinking men ever be satisfied with a truth short of the ultimate and absolute? Dangerous and hurtful as may be this particular brand of truth, mankind has a shockingly perverse way of chasing after it! An arch-pessimist like myself would naturally wish to avoid the true kind of truth, yet it has the same fascination for me that it had for Copernicus and Galileo! But this is the fault of the age. Why are philosophical studies permitted if their result is so disastrous? We may say of true truth what Mr. Pope said of Vice:

> But seen too oft, familiar with its face,
> We first endure, then pity, then embrace![46]

To use Mr. Mo's ant-hill metaphor, my point of issue involves the existence of ants which are "Lovecrafty" or crafty in other ways. Again adopting Mr. M[o]'s own reasoning, the existence of myself, as well as of the hundreds of others who question into the infinities and eternities of things, is enough to prove that "Lovecrafty ants" do exist on this terrestrial anthill, and suffer keenly from the crude enforcement of orthodoxy. When Mr. Mo tells me that Lovecrafty ants cannot exist in an ant-hill, I felt like poor Partridge the astrologer, when Swift endeavoured to prove to him that he was dead and buried![47]

To conclude this weighty discourse, I shall state my attitude toward orthodox theism and Christianity in my own cold-blooded words. I truly believe that Mr. Mo's opinion, if spoken with equal directness, would be precisely the same:

(1) Orthodox Christianity, by playing upon the emotions of man, is able to accomplish wonders toward keeping him in order and relieving his mind. It can frighten or cajole him away from evil more effectively than could reason. Because of its hypnotic and auto-hypnotic power, this faith should be preserved as long as it can be propped up with arguments or diffused through rhetoric. It is a crime publicly to attack the church, since upon that institution rests more than half of the responsibility for maintaining the existing social order. On this account, it is well to refrain from open utterances concerning religion, and at times even to pretend belief. Truth is of no practical value to mankind save as it affects terrestrial phenomena, hence the discoveries of science should be concealed or glossed over wherever they conflict with orthodoxy. It is wisest to invent an artificial sort of "truth" which conforms to the well-being of man. It will never do us any good to know the dimensions of space or the aeons of time, so let us forget all about the universe and the infinity outside the universe. The notion of personal, affectionate Godhead works best with the masses, so let us gently adapt what we know, to what we ought to think. Anything is justifiable in the interests of humanity.

(2) As to naked reality—we only know that we are a speck in the engulfing vortices of infinity and eternity. We know that all creation obeys certain laws or principles whose source we know not, but which apparently result from the interaction of material particles, or modes of motion. It is utter quibbling to differentiate betwixt Nature, and a Deity immanent in nature. The distinction is purely one of words. We know that yesterday in time our

universe and race did not exist. We have no reason for assuming that it will remain in existence save for another moment of eternity. Of our relation to all creation we can never know anything whatsoever. All is immensity and chaos. But, since all this knowledge of our limitations cannot possibly be of any value to us, it is better to ignore it in our daily conduct of life. It is dangerous, and therefore, should not be spread broadcast. But every man has a right to think what he thinks and to believe what he believes.

I have spoken. Is not this, Mr. Mo, the real pith of your theology, and that of every other thinking man save such types as Rev. Graeme Davis? And you, Mr. Co; does not the conception of boundless force, identifiable with Deity, coincide practically with your Pantheism?[48] As for Mr. Klei—he has stated his connexion with the church; but can he not say, at least, that he is not too gravely shocked by so impartial an estimate? I would have him remember, that I censured and satirized Mr. Jas. F. Morton, Jr., as severely as anyone, for his wanton destruction of the public faith and the publick morals.[49]

Trusting, then, to your indulgence in all matters,

I am, Gentlemen,

Yr most Humble and Obedient Servt.

P.S. A courier (the iceman) has just arrived with news from the field of battle. It now seems that Wilson is more likely to prove the victor than Hughes.[50] O Nation of ineffable stupidity!!! GOD SAVE THE KING!!!!

Notes

1. Terence (P. Terentius Afer, 190?–159 B.C.E.), *Eunuchus* 61–63: "If you tried to turn these uncertainties into certainties by a system of reasoning, you'd do no more good than if you set yourself to be mad on a system" (tr. John Sargeaunt). HPL cites Terence as an epigraph to "Metrical Regularity" (1915; *CE* 2.11).
2. HPL alludes to the Greek poet Pindar (518–438 B.C.E.), whose odes are deliberately irregular in meter.
3. William Stanley Braithwaite (1878–1962), book reviewer for the *Boston Transcript* and editor of the *Anthology of Magazine Verse,* was a leading African-American literary figure of his time. He was editor of the short-lived journal *Poetry Review of America* (May 1916–February 1917). HPL corresponded with him briefly in 1930.
4. Abraham Cowley (1618–1667), British poet whose *Pindarique Odes* (1656) popularized the form.
5. *Spectator* No. 160 (3 September 1711).
6. "To the stars through the rough spots," the motto of the state of Kansas, in which Ira Cole lived.
7. See HPL's poem "Fragment on Whitman."
8. Elagabalus (or Heliogabalus), emperor of Rome (218–22 C.E.).

9. See Edward Gibbon (1737–1794), *The History of the Decline and Fall of the Roman Empire* (1776–88), ch. 6.

10. John Wilmot, second Earl of Rochester (1647–1680), British poet and one of the most notorious of the Restoration wits, whose poetry is full of sexual innuendo.

11. Of his poetry, Whitman himself wrote: "I sound my barbaric yawp over the roofs of the world" ("Song of Myself" 52.3).

12. Charles D. Isaacson (1891–1936), amateur journalist and author of *Face to Face with Great Musicians* (1918–21; 2 vols.). In "Concerning the Conservative," *In a Minor Key* No. 2 [1915]: [10–11], Isaacson had strongly criticized HPL's comments on Jews and on Walt Whitman as expressed in HPL's article "In a Major Key." HPL met Isaacson on 1 July 1916 as Kleiner, Isaacson, and others passed through Providence on the way to the NAPA convention in Boston.

13. I.e., "Song of the Open Road."

14. See "The Vers Libre Epidemic."

15. Albert Mordell (1885–1965), "Amy Lowell," *Poetry Review of America* 1, No. 4 (August 1916): 60–61. The poem under discussion is "Patterns."

16. Elbert Hubbard (1856–1915), American printer, editor, and author who, influenced by William Morris, established the Ryecroft Press to publish finely printed and bound books and magazines. He had established *The Fra: A Journal of Affirmation* in 1908; it continued until 1917.

17. Jonathan Swift (1667–1745), *A Meditation on a Broomstick* (1704), a burlesque on Robert Boyle's *Meditations*.

18. The following poem ("To the Bathtub") was not published in HPL's lifetime.

19. Literally, "the hairy ones"; an expression applied to French infantrymen during World War I.

20. Richard Neville, Earl of Warwick (1428–1471) was called the "Kingmaker" because he was largely responsible for establishing Edward IV as king of England in 1461; Warwick actually ruled England for the next three years. In 1470 he helped to place Henry VI on the throne.

21. Billy Sunday (1862–1935), itinerant American evangelical preacher whose histrionic revival meetings gained him notoriety.

22. William Herbert Perry Faunce (1859–1930), president of Brown University (1899–1930). Brown was founded as a Baptist institution.

23. Silenus, in Graeco-Roman mythology, is the tutor and attendant of Bacchus, hence a byword for drunkenness and lasciviousness. P. Clodius Pulcher (92?–52 B.C.E.) was a Roman political figure known for his political opportunism and dissipated lifestyle.

24. See HPL's poem "The Power of Wine: A Satire."

25. Robert Livingston Beeckman (1866–1935), American stockbroker, sportsman, politician, and 52nd governor of Rhode Island.

26. Addison Pierce Munroe (1861–1955), a Democrat and father of HPL's boyhood friends Harold Bateman Munroe (1891–1966) and Chester Pierce Munroe (1889–1943), was defeated by R. Livingston Beeckman (1866–1935), a Republican who became governor of Rhode Island (1916–21). The elder Munroe remarked to Winfield

Townley Scott (an early biographer of HPL) that "in regard to measures that ordinarily would be of no interest to a young fellow of twenty [. . .] he knew more about them than seventy-five per cent of the Senators who would finally vote on them." "His Own Most Fantastic Creation: Howard Phillips Lovecraft" (1944), in Cannon, *Lovecraft Remembered* 13.

27. Before Woodrow Wilson (1856–1924) was twenty-eighth president of the U.S., he was a professor and also president of Princeton University.

28. See Glossary under Winifred Virginia Jackson.

29. "To Chloris" has not been found, but HPL mentions it in "Department of Public Criticism: First Annual Report" (*United Amateur*, August 1916; *CE* 1.123). "Twilight" appeared in the *Conservative* 2, No. 3 (October 1916): [4].

30. "Using Victrola in Teaching of Literature," *Appleton Evening Crescent* 26, No. 303 (13 October 1916): 1, 2. Unsigned, but (except for opening note) by Moe.

31. HPL refers to his essay "Old England and the 'Hyphen,'" arguing that a distinction should be made between Americans of British ancestry and those whose ancestry derives from other nations.

32. Alexander von Kluck (1846–1934), German general who led the German attack through Belgium into France in August 1914.

33. In 1916, the Democratic party campaigned on the slogan, "He Kept Us Out of War," but following Wilson's reelection, the U.S. entered World War I in 1917.

34. Brand Whitlock (1869–1934), journalist and mayor of Toledo, Ohio (1905–13). As President Wilson's minister to Belgium (1913–16), he was of immense help in providing food and other services to the Belgian people during the early years of World War I. See his *Belgium under German Occupation* (1918).

35. Camillo von Klenze (1865–1943), professor of German at the University of Chicago (1893–1906), Brown University (1906–16), and the College of the City of New York (1916–27) and author of *From Goethe to Hauptmann* (1926) and other critical studies. Cf. Lieutenant Klenze in HPL's "The Temple" (1920).

36. Rabindranath Tagore (1861–1941), one of modern India's greatest poets and recipient of the Nobel Prize for literature (1913).

37. *An Essay on Man*, Epistle II, ll. 1–2.

38. HPL's maternal grandmother, Robie Alzada Place Phillips, died on 26 January 1896; his father, Winfield Scott Lovecraft, died on 19 July 1898.

39. HPL refers to his uncle, Franklin Chase Clark (1847–1915); his mother, Sarah Susan Phillips Lovecraft (1857–1921); and his maternal grandfather, Whipple Van Buren Phillips (1833–1904).

40. Graeme Davis (1881–1938), amateur journalist and editor of the *Lingerer*, would become Official Editor of the NAPA in 1917–18 and at that time engage in a controversy with HPL about the respective merits of the UAPA and NAPA; see HPL's "A Reply to *The Lingerer*" (q.v.).

41. John Dennis (1657–1734), British poet and dramatist, but best known for his trenchant and occasionally harsh critical work, notably *The Grounds of Criticism in Poetry* (1704).

42. One of HPL's many pseudonyms was "El Impartial."

43. Ariovistus was king of the Suebi, a German tribe that invaded Gaul around 71 B.C.E. He was defeated by Julius Caesar in 58 B.C.E. Arminius was a chieftain of the Cherusci, a Germanic people living around the Weser river, who dealt a crushing defeat to the Roman legions under P. Quinctilius Varus in 9 C.E.

44. Moe was a Presbyterian.

45. HPL alludes to *The Brook Kerith* (1916) by Anglo-Irish novelist George Moore (1852–1933).

46. *An Essay on Man,* Epistle II, ll. 219–20 ("Yet" for "But" in Pope).

47. In his "Isaac Bickerstaff" articles of 1708–09, Swift had satirized the astrologer John Partridge by first predicting his death and then describing his funeral in very realistic terms, convincing many readers that Partridge was actually dead.

48. HPL published Cole's pantheistic poem "A Dream of the Golden Age" (his second poem) in his *Conservative* (July 1915). Cole also published "The Gods of Our Fathers" in the *United Official Quarterly* (November 1914).

49. HPL refers to the satirical poem "The Isaacson-Mortoniad." Written no later than 14 September 1915 (the date on which HPL copied the poem in a letter to Rheinhart Kleiner), the poem attacks various utterances by Morton and Charles D. Isaacson in Isaacson's amateur journal *In a Minor Key* No. 2 [1915], which themselves were a response to HPL's "In a Major Key." At this time, Morton—whom HPL criticized in his poem for being an evangelical atheist—was not personally acquainted with HPL, but he became one of his closest friends from 1922 onward. HPL did not allow this poem to be published in his lifetime.

50. HPL refers to the Democrat Woodrow Wilson's defeat of the Republican Charles Evans Hughes in the presidential election of 1916. It was initially believed that Hughes had won the election, but returns from the West, reported a day after the election, gave Wilson the victory. HPL's P.S. must have been written c. 8 November.

[3]   [AHT]

Vol. I. No. 10.

Providence, R.I.,
April, 1917

SPRING
By Lewis Theobald, Jun.[1]

Hertha, awake! discard thy snowy sheen,
And greet the dews that drape the sprouting green;
Let sun and show'r revive the sleeping plain,
Whilst April leaflets deck the grove again!
Feel the soft Zephyr, that at glow of dawn
Plays in delight o'er crocus-spangled lawn;
Behold the blossoms that adorn each bow'r,
And breathe the perfume of the op'ning flow'r;

Imbibe the rapture, and with joy attend
The feather'd choir whose notes harmonick blend.
Rejoice, ye Fauns that roam the shaded hill!
Rejoice, ye Nymphs that haunt the sylvan rill!
Eternal Pan a rustick garland weaves,
And leaps, goat-footed, 'neath the tender leaves.
Deep in the hollow, where the willow springs,
The crystal Arethusa softly sings;
Around her banks in modest grace are set
The purple petals of the violet:
'Tis here the gentle Dryads pause to drink,
And pluck their chaplets by the flow'r-fring'd brink;
'Tis here the swain, stretch'd on the bord'ring sod,
Learns to love Nature, and love Nature's God!

Upon the slope that fronts the noontide sun
The sportive flocks and supple eanlings run;
With lissome gambols please the shepherd's eye,
And feel the ardour of the smiling sky:
In golden wealth beneath their prancing feet,
Lie the fair forms of daffodillies sweet;
Whose rising fragrance, delicate and rare,
Gives potent magic to the vernal air.
See the trim orchard, whose all-cov'ring green
Is fleck'd with white, as blossoms burst between;
Before our gaze upon the branches grow
Ethereal drifts of aromatick snow!
As the warm sap the grateful tree ascends,
So to mankind new life its vigour lends:
Our weary race their winter burdens shed,
And young once more, look blithesomely ahead!
Behold the blue, where Sol's Hesperian rays
Dispute the azure with a redd'ning blaze;
Where golden Venus, bright Olympian spark,
Relieves the shadows of the creeping dark.
O'er western slopes with feeble beams expire
The fading embers of Brumalian fire,
Whilst far aloft, in gem-bespangled space,
Majestic Leo glows with warmer grace.
Young, like the year, Diana's silver car
Hangs crescent in pellucid deeps afar;
And hills and woods, responsive to the sight,
Gleam fairy-like in tender, timid light.

Eternal Nature! whose undying pow'r
Wakes to new beauty in the springtime hour;
Whose April skies, enjoin'd by changeless truth,
Arouse the meadows to resurgent youth;
Through frost-curs'd vortices of Scythian strife
Thou bring'st the blessed vernal boon of Life!

'Tis a long-establish'd tradition amongst the small fry and little-wits of Grub-street, that no rhymester may permit the vernal season to pass without scrawling his customary lyrick, ode, or dithyramb to spring. I have therefore perform'd this ancient and honour'd rite before settling down to the more comfortable business of the Kleicomolo Club, here assembled at Will's. Though I am conscious Mr. Mo will object most ardently against the trite subject and heroick cast of my piece, I am consoled by knowing that I am doing at least no worse than a great number of other dunces have done before. Being a great hater of winter, I am more than ordinarily pleas'd at the advent of ethereal mildness, and my spring "poetry" may well be expected to contain a more than common amount of sincerity.

Mr. Co's reference to the crude songs of the primitive cowboy brought to my mind remembrance of my early perusal of Percy's "Reliques",[2] and impelled me to investigate to some extent this second, western growth of English balladry. That certain newspaper criticks should decry the old ditties of the plains, is not to be wonder'd at; for the lays of the British minstrels were likewise in general disrepute, till Mr. Addison pointed out their merits in the Spectator, comparing passages in them with extracts from the Greek and Roman classicks.[3] An excellent collection of cowboy songs hath been made by John A. Lomax, Esq., of the University of Texas,[4] to whom no less a person than Theodore Roosevelt writes as follows of the ancient rhapsodies:

> "There is something very curious in the reproduction here on this new continent of essentially the conditions of ballad-growth which obtained in mediaeval England; including, by the way, sympathy for the outlaw; Jesse James taking the place of Robin Hood. Under modern conditions, however, the native ballad is speedily killed by competition with the music-hall songs; the cowboys becoming ashamed to sing the crude homespun ballads in view of what Owen Wister calls the 'ill-smelling saloon cleverness' of the far less interesting compositions of music-hall singers. It is therefore a work of real importance to preserve permanently this unwritten literature of the back country and the frontier."[5]

Such being the opinion of the greatest living American, I think Mr. Co need waste no thought or resentment upon the cheap slurs and callow cynicism of penny-a-line newspaper hacks! To one unfamiliar with the sources and characteristick qualities of ballad literature, there is doubtless much that is "lugubrious and mirth-provoking" in certain of the old songs. The fact that they were modelled in places from less simple verses which came to the ears of the cowboy minstrels, creates certain incongruities of phraseology which cannot but be unconsciously humorous, as in the following, from "Fuller and Warren":

> "Young man, you have injured me to gratify your cause
> By reporting that I left a prudent wife;
> Acknowledge now that you have wronged me, for although I break the laws,
> Young Warren, I'll deprive you of your life."[6]

This same "Fuller and Warren" ballad commences with the lines:

> "Ye Sons of Columbia, your attention I do crave,
> While a sorrowful story I do tell."

This beginning is undoubtedly derived more or less remotely from the ode of Robert Treat Paine, "Adams and Liberty",[7] which was sung to the historick tune of "To Anacreon in Heav'n":[8]

> "Ye Sons of Columbia, who bravely have fought
> For those rights which unstain'd from your sires had descended."

"Harry Bale" also contains some of the naive qualities which raise a smile amongst the unsympathetick: (It refers to a sawmill accident of fatal end.)

> "On the 29th of April in the year of '79,
> He went to work as usual, no fear did he design;
> In lowering of the feed bar throwing the carriage into gear
> It brought him down upon the saw and cut him quite severe;
> It cut him through the collar bone and half way down the back,
> It threw him down upon the saw, the carriage coming back.
> He started for the shanty, his strength was failing fast;
> He said, 'Oh, boys, I'm wounded; I fear it is my last.'"[9]

But if these passages be ridiculous through associations which tickle the imagination of the sophisticated, they are scarcely more so than some of the most vivid passages in antique balladry, like the following famous extract from "Chevy-Chace":

> "For Witherington needs must I wayle,
> As one in doleful dumpes;
> For when his leggs were smitten off,
> He fought upon his stumps."[10]

To sum up: though there is much in the typical cowboy song to excite the merriment of the casual listener, the serious student of folk-lore may discover a potent sincerity, wild lyricism, and genuine expression in this sort of verse which assures it a place in literature. This body of song was composed by men without books or refining influences; men whose only aids to composition were found in the fertility of their own genius, and in the scraps of song picked up orally from Easterners or from the mothers who rocked their cradles. It undoubtedly required more creative effort and higher mental endowments for these cowboys to compose unaided this array of balladry, than for the mediocre scribbler of the town to compound his flashy criticism—a criticism doubtless made up mostly of meaningless stock phrases filched unintelligently from some last year's magazine or review. It is both unjust and unwise to measure poetick power without a careful analysis of the conditions under which it is manifested and exercised.

I am interested in Mr. Co's researches concerning the occult and the supernatural; particularly so since I have encountered several reviews of poor Oliver Lodge's book "Raymond"[11]—a work which I confess I have not perused at first hand. It may be well to state that Sir Oliver, as well as Sir William Crookes,[12] have received little faith since they turned their attention to [the] fallacy-ridden realm of the supernatural. Their speculations in this direction may well be taken as evidences of freakishness—and in Sir William's case, of senility; since he is now eighty-five years of age. It is Lodge, however, who is under consideration, and he cannot plead old age, since he was born in 1851. Of his reported phenomena, and of other cases of a like nature, it is safest to say that insufficient evidence throws them out of court. Disturbed mentality, auto-suggestion, and deliberate charlatanry will be found at the base of most alleged spiritualistic and telepathic manifestations. They most generally occur amongst the ignorant, or amongst those who ardently *wish* to have them occur. Many of the most plausible cases resolve themselves into the most deliberate imposture upon impartial and authentick investigation. More than one "broad-minded" dupe of spiritualism felt the throes of sheepishness when the exceedingly clever Eusapia Palladino was exposed as a fraud;[13] yet each victim might have known that such magic as she exhibited was impossible according to the recognised principles of Nature. Open-mindedness becomes a fault when it fails to take into account the fundamental probabilities of things. I abhor the sickly attitude of a certain soft-headed class of investigators, who so fear the imputation of bigotry, that they will make fools of themselves by wasting serious thought over obvious cheats and impostors. The very vagueness of human reason, and the very subjectivity of human thought, should warn the student to pay scant attention to the fleeting fancies of the mind. Imagination is a very potent thing, and in the uneducated often usurps the place of genuine experience. I have encountered many instances of children who, without conscious falsification, confuse the real with the unreal, and relate in good faith experiences through which they have not passed. It is reasonable to assume that many apparent instances of supernatural manifestations were devised subconsciously in the brains of the narrators. Atavism hath implanted many dark fancies in man; it needs but a little relaxation of intellectualism to bring up the old ghosts of the past, and revive that intense faith, or tendency to have faith, in the supernatural, which originally grew out of our ancestors' attempts to explain nature. The progress of science will eventually, I believe, enunciate at least two laws, which will forever put an end to spiritualism amongst the educated and even the half-educated. They are:

(1) Life, animal and vegetable, including human life, is a mode of motion which ceases absolutely upon the death of the body containing it.

(2) The future, so far as organic beings are concerned, can never be predicted, since individual and unfathomable caprice has power to direct events into any of the innumerable channels possible under the natural law.

I am very much interested, in Mr. Mo's idea of an oral conversation betwixt the Kleicomoloes, to be conducted by means of a phonograph. I once owned an Edison machine of the primitive type, with recorder and blanks; and I made many vocal records in imitation of the renowned vocalists of the wax cylinder. My colleagues would smile to hear some of the plaintive tenor solos which I perpetrated in the days of my youth!! But sad to say, I gave the old machine away about a year ago to a deserving and not too musical youth who occasionally performs useful labour about the place. I wish now that I had retained it! However, I am sure that I could obtain the use of a commercial dictating machine at some store—to run the records of my associates, if not to make one of my own. I presume that if I were to enter this field, Mr. Mo would expect me to roll my "rrrr....'s" most faithfully. I should indeed be charrrmed to parrrticipate in such a procedurrre! This subject brings up memories of the days of a decade ago, when my phonograph was in constant use. I remember one record—a song called "Starlight", which was truly Western in its cadences: "Good Nity, my Starrrlight, hearrrt of my heartt" . . . etc. etc.[14] Discussing Mr. Mo's arguments, clippings, and cartoons concerning the letter "RRR...",[15] I must give him credit for diligence in research, cleverness in debate and humourr in ridicule. His quotation headed "The Best English" presents one side of the matter with fair force, though I must confess *I* have seldom heard a rolled sound on words like "Emma" and "law". If Mr. Mo would ponder for a moment, he would realise that *this* habit would spoil a *law-war* rhyme as quickly as would the Westerrn roll; for *lawr* and *waw*, rhyme no better than *law* and *warrrh!* I cannot remember hearing such a misplaced roll more than once or twice in my life; the cases in question being only when the word is followed by a vowel. And even then the blunder does not approximate the gargling paroxysm which some New Yorkers fall into when rolling the "RRR:" the intruding "r" sound takes the form of a single "r" attached to the *following* word. For instance, some might speak thus: "I saw (r)Arthur on the street today." And in *this* way the New Englander *does* sometimes sound the "r" in words. It would be quite natural to hear something like this: "The rivah (r)is quite low this morning." Note just *where* the "r" is sounded, and where it is not. This is a phonetic rendering of the manner in which some of the best persons in New England would enunciate the sentence in question. However, there is a growing affectation amongst a certain element to roll the "rrr..." in full glory, so after a generation or so, Mr. Mo may be more right than wrong. But I shall be dead then. I have been informed by one who is in a position to know, that the pronunciation at Oxford University is not representative of cultivated England as a whole. My aunt is well acquainted with Mr. Champlin Burrage, an Oxford man, who is librarian of the John Carter Brown library at Brown.[16] (I hope to meet him very soon.) He gives an entertaining list of what are termed "Oxfordisms," including things as absurd as "la-bór-it-ry" for "lá-bo-ra-to-ry"! Noyes, I presume, endeavours to strike an happy medium between the sundry fads, dialects, provincialisms, and affectations of the several parts of the Anglo-Saxon world. Though as I have said many times in the past, my taste generally rebels at comic-supplement humour; I must confess to many hearty laughs over the particular "Outburst of Everett True"[17] which Mr. Mo cites as a final and crushing blow to the poor Conservative! This forms my first acquaintance with that beefy gentleman of pictorial fiction, since the New-England dailies of the first rank do not use the conventional "comics." Seriously speaking, the humour is not at all inconsiderable, and the point is not difficult to grasp if one can imagine a region wherein everyone uses the Hesperian gargle in enunciation. It is much as though a youthful exquisite, similarly dressed, should mince up to the lift in our 16-story Turk's Head Building in Providence, and lisp out in sweet tones of quaint innocence: "Fourrrrteenth florrr, if you pleathe!" Though I am far from being an habitual gallant, I feel certain that I would uncover my head at such tender naivete! As forr our controverrsy as a whole—'twere best to restore the *status quo ante,* and call it a draw! We have both expended about all the argument and satire we can well spare! However, if Mo be eager for more, I can but speak in the words of Dr. Johnson's obscure correspondent:

"Maxime, si tu vis, cupio contendere tecum!"[18]

Perhaps we will (to use the simple spelling of Artemus Ward)[19] "let it be berried into oblivyun" until our phonographick experiment again exhumes it!

Mr. Mo's recent study of imagism and kindred fallacies, and his wondrously clever specimen of original *vers libre,* excited my most profound interest. The soundness of his conclusions, and the lucidity of his mode of presenting them, admit of no dispute. I was further interested in his assignment of imagistical elements to Mrs. Jordan's singularly graphick verses entitled "Insomnia."[20] This leads me to venture the statement, or surmise, that imagism enters to a greater or less extent into many poems of formal rhyme and metre; and that it forms, indeed, no slight part of the obscurity of certain "deep" poets. My personal opinion of "Insomnia" is much more favourable than Mr. Mo's, since I believe that the confusion of images is an intentional reproduction of the chaotic thoughts of the insomnious brain. It is in this borderland of thought and unreason that Mr. Poe hath placed so many of his themes. I have had moods of this semi-imagism myself, and will herewith submit without comment one of my latest compositions. If the verdict of my colleagues be too unkind, I beg them to pass over the trifle without attaching too much weight to it.

A GARDEN
By Lewis Theobald, Jun.

There's an ancient, ancient garden that I see sometimes in dreams,
Where the very Maytime sunlight plays and glows with spectral gleams;
Where the gaudy-tinted blossoms seem to wither into grey,
And the crumbling walls and pillars waken thoughts of yesterday.
There are vines in nooks and crannies, and there's moss about the pool,
And the tangled weedy thicket chokes the arbour dark and cool:
In the silent sunken pathways springs an herbage sparse and spare,
While the musty scent of dead things dulls the fragrance of the air.
There is not a living creature in the lonely space around,
And the hedge-encompass'd quiet never echoes to a sound.
As I walk, and wait, and listen, I will often seek to find
When it was I knew that garden in an age long left behind;
I will oft conjure a vision of a day that is no more,
As I gaze upon the grey, grey scenes I feel I knew before.
Then a sadness settles o'er me, and a tremor seems to start—
For I know the flow'rs are shrivell'd hopes—the garden is my heart!

But the worst is yet to come! Last winter, whilst reflecting upon my controversy with Mr. Mo concerning absolute and ultimate truth, I was imperceptibly led into a mood of poetick contemplation, and of strangely weird expression in blank verse. I thought of the inconsequentiality—the virtual unreality—of mankind, and of the surging, unfathom'd, half-hideous forces in whose grasp he vainly and impotently writhes. I thought of the ease with which one may become stifled and oppress'd with the infinity of creation; how a mood of morbid gloom or too profound speculation might lead a sensitive mind into painful hallucinations and brain-stultifying imaginings and conceptions of the absolute and immeasurable. With these things in mind, I set to work to record possible impressions in a fashion which Mr. Mo might well call as "imagistic" as the fashion in which "Insomnia" is writ. Whether or not a ray of humour penetrated the gloom, I leave for my three acute readers to conjecture for themselves! At any rate, when my task was over I enjoyed a hearty laugh, and proceeded to place around my horrifick creation a framework of comic verse—this time my adored heroick couplets. I had the Kleicomolo in mind when writing this piece, and will herewith present it for your delectation. Mr. Mo will be able to untangle the Greek mottoes and the Greek name of the blank verse piece at once—if my other colleagues have any difficulty, I will enlighten them. Let me add, that my own acquaintance with Greek is none too familiar!

THE POE-ET'S NIGHTMARE
A Fable

Τρυφή θορυβου ἀεί αἰτία στί.[21]

By Ludovicus Theobaldus, Jun.

Lucullus Languish, student of the skies,
And connoisseur of rarebits and mince pies,
A bard by choice, a grocer's clerk by trade,
(Grown pessimist through honours long delay'd)
A secret yearning bore, that he might shine
In breathing numbers, and in song divine.
Each day his fountain pen was wont to drop
An ode or dirge or two about the shop,
Yet naught could strike the chord within his heart
That throbb'd for poesy, and cry'd for art.
Each eve he sought his bashful Muse to wake
With overdoses of ice cream and cake;
But though th' ambitious youth a dreamer grew,
Th' Aonian Nymph declin'd to come to view.
Sometimes at dusk he scour'd the heav'ns afar,
Searching for raptures in the evening star;
One night he strove to catch a tale untold
In crystal deeps—but only caught a cold.
So pin'd Lucullus with his lofty woe,
Till one drear day he bought a set of Poe;
Charm'd with the cheerful horrors there display'd,
He vow'd with gloom to woo the Heav'nly Maid.
Of Auber's tarn and Yaanek's slope he dreams,
And weaves an hundred Ravens in his schemes.
Not far from our young hero's peaceful home,
Lies the fair grove wherein he loves to roam.
Though but a stunted copse in vacant lot,
He dubs it Tempë, and adores the spot;
When shallow puddles dot the wooded plain,
And brim o'er muddy banks with muddy rain,
He calls them limpid pools or poison pools,
(Depending on which bard his fancy rules.)
'Tis here he comes with Heliconian fire
On Sundays when he smites the Attic lyre;

And here one afternoon he brought his gloom,
Resolv'd to chant a poet's lay of doom.
Roget's Thesaurus, and a book of rhymes,
Provide the rungs whereon his spirit climbs:
With this grave retinue he trod the grove
And pray'd the Fauns he might a Poe-et prove.
But sad to tell, ere Pegasus flew high,
The not unrelished supper hour drew nigh;
Our tuneful swain th' imperious call attends,
And soon above the groaning table bends.
Though it were too prosaic to relate
Th' exact particulars of what he ate,
(Such long-drawn lists the hasty reader skips
Like Homer's well-known catalogue of ships)
This much we swear: that as adjournment near'd,
A monstrous lot of cake had disappear'd!
Soon to his chamber the young bard repairs,
And courts soft Somnus with sweet Lydian airs;
Through open casement scans the star-strown deep,
And 'neath Orion's beams sinks off to sleep.

Now start from the airy dell the elfin train
That dance each midnight o'er the sleeping main,
To bless the just, or cast a warning spell
On those who dine not wisely, but too well.
First Deacon Smith they plague, whose nasal glow
Comes from what Holmes hath call'd "Elixir Pro;"
Group'd round the couch his visage they deride,
Whilst from his dreams unnumber'd serpents glide.
Next troop the little folk into the room
Where snores our young Endymion, swath'd in gloom:
A smile lights up his boyish face, whilst he
Dreams of the moon—or what he ate at tea.
The chieftain elf th' unconscious youth surveys,
And on his form a strange enchantment lays:
Those lips, that lately thrill'd with frosted cake,
Uneasy sounds in slumbrous fashion make;
At length their owner's fancies they rehearse,
And lisp this awesome Poe-em in blank verse:

ALETHEIA PHRIKODES
Πάντα τὰ γέλως, πάντα τὰ κόνις, και πάντα τὸ μηδέν.[22]

Demoniac clouds, up[-]piled in chasmy reach

Of soundless heav'n, smother'd the brooding night;
Nor came the wonted whisp'rings of the swamp,
Nor voice of autumn wind along the moor,
Nor mutter'd noises of th' insomnious grove
Whose black recesses never saw the sun.
Within that grove a hideous hollow lies,
Half bare of trees; a pool in centre lurks
That none dares sound; a tarn of murky face,
(Though naught can prove its hue, since light of day,
Affrighted, shuns the forest-shadow'd banks.)
Hard by, a yawning hillside grotto breathes
From deeps unvisited, a dull, dank air
That sears the leaves on certain stunted trees
Which stand about, clawing the spectral air
With evil boughs. To this accursed dell
Come woodland creatures, seldom to depart:
Once I beheld, upon a crumbling stone
Set altar-like before the cave, a thing
I saw not clearly, yet from glimpsing, fled.
In this half-dusk I meditate alone
At many a weary noontide, when without
A world forgets me in its sun-blest mirth.
Here howl by night the werewolves, and the souls
Of those who knew me well in other days.
Yet on this night the grove spake not to me;
Nor spake the swamp, nor wind along the moor,
Nor moan'd the wind about the lonely eaves
Of the bleak, haunted pile wherein I lay.
I was afraid to sleep, or quench the spark
Of the low-burning taper by my couch.
I was afraid when through the vaulted space
Of the old tow'r, the clock-ticks died away
Into a silence so profound and chill
That my teeth chatter'd—giving yet no sound.
Then flicker'd low the light, and all dissolved,
Leaving me floating in the hellish grasp
Of body'd blackness, from whose beating wings
Came ghoulish blasts of charnel-scented mist.
Things vague, unseen, unfashion'd, and unnam'd
Jostled each other in the seething void
That gap'd, chaotic, downward to a sea
Of speechless horror, foul with writhing thoughts.
All this I felt, and felt the mocking eyes

Of the curs'd universe upon my soul;
Yet naught I saw nor heard, till flash'd a beam
Of lurid lustre through the rotting heav'ns,
Playing on scenes I labour'd not to see.
Methought the nameless tarn, alight at last,
Reflected shapes, and more reveal'd within
Those shocking depths than e'er were seen before;
Methought from out the cave a demon train,
Grinning and smirking, reel'd in fiendish rout;
Bearing within their reeking paws a load
Of carrion viands for an impious feast.
Methought the stunted trees with hungry arms
Grop'd greedily for things I dare not name;
The while a stifling, wraith-like noisomeness
Fill'd all the dale, and spoke a larger life
Of uncorporeal hideousness awake
In the half-sentient wholeness of the spot.
Now glow'd the ground, and tarn, and cave, and trees,
And moving forms, and things not spoken of,
With such a phosphorescence as men glimpse
In the putrescent thickets of the swamp
Where logs decaying lie, and rankness reigns.
Methought a fire-mist drap'd with lucent fold
The well-remember'd features of the grove,
Whilst whirling ether bore in eddying streams
The hot, unfinish'd stuff of nascent worlds
Hither and thither through infinity
Of light and darkness, strangely intermix'd;
Wherein all entity had consciousness,
Without th' accustom'd outward shape of life.
Of these swift circling currents was my soul,
Free from the flesh, a true constituent part;
Nor felt I less myself, for want of form.
Then clear'd the mist, and o'er a star-strown scene
Divine and measureless, I gaz'd in awe.
Alone in space, I view'd a feeble fleck
Of silvern light, marking the narrow ken
Which mortals call the boundless universe.
On ev'ry side, each as a tiny star,
Shone more creations, vaster than our own,
And teeming with unnumber'd forms of life;
Tho' we as life would recognise it not,
Being bound to earthly thoughts of human mould.

As on a moonless night the Milky Way
In solid sheen displays its countless orbs
To weak terrestrial eyes, each orb a sun;
So beam'd the prospect on my wond'ring soul;
A spangled curtain, rich with twinkling gems,
Yet each a mighty universe of suns.
But as I gaz'd, I sens'd a spirit voice
In speech didactic, though no voice it was,
Save as it carried thought. It bade me mark
That all the universes in my view
Form'd but an atom in infinity;
Whose reaches pass the ether-laden realms
Of heat and light, extending to far fields
Where flourish worlds invisible and vague,
Fill'd with strange wisdom and uncanny life,
And yet beyond; to myriad spheres of light,
To spheres of darkness, to abysmal voids
That know the pulses of disorder'd force.
Big with these musings, I survey'd the surge
Of boundless being, yet I us'd not eyes,
For spirit leans not on the props of sense.
The docent presence swell'd my strength of soul;
All things I knew, but knew with mind alone.
Time's endless vista spread before my thought
With its vast pageant of unceasing change
And sempiternal strife of force and will;
I saw the ages flow in stately stream
Past rise and fall of universe and life;
I saw the birth of suns and worlds, their death,
Their transmutation into limpid flame,
Their second birth and second death, their course
Perpetual through the aeons' termless flight,
Never the same, yet born again to serve
The varying purpose of omnipotence.
And whilst I watch'd, I knew each second's space
Was greater than the lifetime of our world.
Then turn'd my musings to that speck of dust
Whereon my form corporeal took its rise;
That speck, born but a second, which must die
In one brief second more; that fragile earth;
That crude experiment; that cosmic sport
Which holds our proud, aspiring race of mites
And mortal vermin; those presuming mites

Whom ignorance with empty pomp adorns,
And misinstructs in specious dignity;
Those mites who, reas'ning outward, vaunt themselves
As the chief work of Nature, and enjoy
In fatuous fancy the particular care
Of all her mystic, super-regnant pow'r.
And as I strove to vision the sad sphere
Which lurk'd, lost in ethereal vortices;
Methought my soul, tun'd to the infinite,
Refus'd to glimpse that poor atomic blight;
That misbegotten accident of space;
That globe of insignificance, whereon
(My guide celestial told me) dwells no part
Of empyrean virtue, but where breed
The coarse corruptions of divine disease;
The fest'ring ailments of infinity;
The morbid matter by itself call'd man;
Such matter (said my guide) as oft breaks forth
On broad Creation's fabric, to annoy
For a brief instant, ere assuaging death
Heal up the malady its birth provok'd.
Sicken'd, I turn'd my heavy thoughts away.
Then spake th' ethereal guide with mocking mien,
Upbraiding me for searching after Truth;
Visiting on my mind the searing scorn
Of mind superior; laughing at the woe
Which rent the vital essence of my soul.
Methought he brought remembrance of the time
When from my fellows to the grove I stray'd,
In solitude and dusk to meditate
On things forbidden, and to pierce the veil
Of seeming good and seeming beauteousness
That covers o'er the tragedy of Truth,
Helping mankind forget his sorry lot,
And raising hope where Truth would crush it down.
He spake, and as he ceas'd, methought the flames
Of fuming Heav'n resolv'd in torments dire;
Whirling in maelstroms of rebellious might,
Yet ever bound by laws I fathom'd not.
Cycles and epicycles of such girth
That each a cosmos seem'd, dazzled my gaze
Till all a wild phantasmal glow became.

Now burst athwart the fulgent formlessness
A rift of purer sheen, a sight supernal,
Broader than all the void conceiv'd by man,
Yet narrow here. A glimpse of heav'ns beyond;
Of weird creations so remote and great
That ev'n my guide assum'd a tone of awe.
Borne on the wings of stark immensity,
A touch of rhythm celestial reach'd my soul;
Thrilling me more with horror than with joy.
Again the spirit mock'd my human pangs,
And deep revil'd me for presumptuous thoughts:
Yet changing now his mien, he bade me scan
The wid'ning rift that clave the walls of space;
He bade me search it for the ultimate;
He bade me find the Truth I sought so long;
He bade me brave th' unutterable Thing,
The final Truth of moving entity.
All this he bade and offer'd—but my soul,
Clinging to life, fled without aim or knowledge,
Shrieking in silence through the gibbering deeps.

Thus shriek'd the young Lucullus, as he fled
Thro' gibbering deeps—and tumbled out of bed;
Within the room the morning sunshine gleams,
Whilst the poor youth recalls his troubled dreams.
He feels his aching limbs, whose woeful pain
Informs his soul his body lives again,
And thanks his stars—or cosmoses—or such
That he survives the noxious nightmare's clutch.
Thrill'd with the music of th' eternal spheres,
(Or is it the alarm-clock that he hears?)
He vows to all the Pantheon, high and low,
No more to feed on cake, or pie, or Poe.
And now his gloomy spirits seem to rise,
As he the world beholds with clearer eyes;
The cup he thought too full of dregs to quaff,
Affords him wine enough to raise a laugh.
(All this is metaphor—you must not think
Our late Endymion prone to stronger drink!)
With brighter visage and with lighter heart,
He turns his fancies to the grocer's mart;
And strange to say, at last he seems to find
His daily duties worthy of his mind.

Since Truth prov'd such a high and dang'rous goal,
Our bard seeks one less trying to his soul;
With deep-drawn breath he flouts his dreary woes,
And a good clerk from a bad poet grows!
Now close attend my lay, ye scribbling crew
That bay the moon in numbers strange and new;
That madly for the spark celestial bawl
In metres short or long—or none at all:
Curb your rash force, in numbers or at tea,
Nor over-zealous for high fancies be;
Reflect, ere ye the draught Pierian take,
What worthy clerks or plumbers ye might make;
Wax not too frenzy'd in the leaping line
That neither sense nor measure can confine,
Lest ye, like young Lucullus Languish, groan
Beneath Poe-etic nightmares of your own!

Fearful and wonderful indeed are the divine arts of the Nine![23] I fear that "Aletheia Phrikodes" requires much—very much—*interpretation!*

Reflection upon the various sorts of unusual verse prevalent in this age, leads me to mention a new bard whose work I have not yet perused, but whose poetry was reviewed by Mr. William Stanley Braithwaite in a recent number of the BOSTON TRANSCRIPT. This bird, Paul Shivell[24] by name, hath lately publish'd a volume entitled "Stillwater Pastorals," which treats of rustick life without the conventional imagery and ornamentation of the polish'd town poet. The orthodoxy of Mr. Shivell should appeal to our arch-pragmatist Mr. Mo, since 'tis said of the former, that "the glowing thing about his faith is that it is direct; direct and open, a thing of wonder and simplicity like a very natural possession, which is more like the note of the Alabasters and Herberts and Trahernes of the seventeenth century. From him all philosophy and criticism have dropped all questioning and doubt, the absolute denial of mystery and secrecy." Like other poets who strive after novelty, Mr. Shivell rejects the elegancies of literary refinement; though refreshingly enough, he hath no use for *vers libre* and kindred fads. His egotism, ever a strong quality amongst would-be philosophick poets, leads him to 'unfold his nature and spiritual ambitions' in a sonnet entitled "My Frank Self-Expression"—which runneth as follows:

"Obscure and down and out as the world goes,
I know I am a seer in plain disguise,
Living above ambition, for a prize
Which angels see, but no man living knows,
And few have ever cared for. I compose
Out of my unapplauded sacrifice

An immortality which proves me wise,
And makes my life acceptable with those
Who shall hereafter understand its aim.
For I who seem to muse of self am singing
The sacred song given me to impart,
The song that was born in me. I disclaim
Fictitious verse, and am through sorrow bringing
Unto my people all I have, my heart."[25]

This thing somewhat fatigues me—the fellow thinks too much on himself. I could easily write a sonnet on myself—in fact, I have done so in imitation of Shivell. It is the first sonnet I have ever written, and is probably the last as well; since I am not fond of the gentle pastime of sonneteering.

LEWIS THEOBALD, JUN., ON HIMSELF:[26]

A transient speck in wide infinity,
A needless incident of endless time,
An empty fool of measure and of rhyme,
One who is not, but only seems to be
Alive to intellect and melody—
Whose struggling thoughts a puny soul confines,
Till their small wit must hide in sounding lines.
Whose only wisdom is to know and see
That he is nothing, and to guard his pen
Against those flights of arrogant conceit
Which soar to mocking Heav'n from bards more bold—
From lords and peasants, great and little men,
Who deem their vain thoughts worthy to repeat,
I tell, for ease; what were as well untold!

Two recent poets, whose work I have perused on account of the singular fame attaching to them, are the military martyrs, Rupert Brooke and Alan Seeger, who laid down their lives in 1915 and 1916, respectively, for the cause of civilisation.[27] Brooke is a lyrist and sonnet-writer whose province is so far from my own, that I can scarce appreciate his undoubted excellence. The one piece of his which does succeed in captivating me, is one that has a noble beginning which will probably rank among the most hallow'd utterances of the Britannick Muse:

"If I should die, think only this of me:
    That there's some corner of a foreign field
That is forever ENGLAND."[28]

The figure of Mr. Brooke is a romantick one; but of scarcely less interest is that of Alan Seeger, the American who fell for France on the fourth of last July whilst charging against the Huns at Belloy-en-Santerre. Seeger lacked some of the poetick talent, and most of the delicacy of Brooke; in fact, his verse is in places marked with the low morality and flagrant pleasure-worship which Parisian dissipation inculcated in him; but his strength as a poet is very considerable, and he exhibits a fidelity to the older models which is truly commendable. Especially is he willing to use that simple, direct, and forcible mode of utterance which his contemporaries seem to have rejected. His masterpiece is an ode intended to be read at the celebration of Decoration Day in Paris before the statue of Washington and Lafayette, and in this he shews his shame at the protracted neutrality of the United States, saying of the deeds of the American serving France:

> "Something that we can look upon with pride
> Has been achieved, nor wholly unreply'd
> Can sneerers triumph in the charge they make
> That from a war where Freedom was at stake
> America withheld, and daunted, stood aside."[29]

Seeger's "Message to America" is potent and virile in its tribute to the one great man of our generation:

> "You have a leader who knows—the man
> Most fit to be call'd American,
> A prophet that once in generations
> Is given to point to erring nations
> Brighter ideals toward which to press
> And lead them out of the wilderness.
>
> I have been too long from my country's shores
> To reckon what state of mind is yours,
> But as for myself I know right well
> I would go through fire and shot and shell
> And face new perils and make my bed
> In new privations, if ROOSEVELT led!"[30]

Seeger's lines on pacifists, in the same poem, are worthy of immortality:

> "Oh, bury them deeper than the sea
> In universal obloquy;
> Forget the ground where they lie, or write
> For epitaph, 'Too proud to fight!'"[31]

The less martial poetry of Seeger is positively exquisite in its classick taste, suggesting Mr. Swinburne, though inexact rhymes and false syllabick values are not wholly absent. I recommend the following to the admiration of Mr. Klei, begging him to forgive the "grandeur–amber" rhyme out of deference to the beauty of the whole:

> "Have ye gaz'd on the grandeur
> Or stood where it stands
> With opal and amber
> Adorning the lands,
> And orcharded domes
> Of the hue of all flow'rs?
> Sweet melody roams
> Through its blossoming bow'rs,
> Sweet bells usher in from its belfries the train of the honey-sweet hours.
>
> A city resplendent,
> Fulfilled of good things,
> On its ramparts are pendent
> The bucklers of kings.
> Broad banners unfurl'd
> Are afloat in the air.
> The lords of the world
> Look for harbourage there.
> None finds save he comes as a bridegroom, having roses and vines in his hair."[32]

The preceding is part of a choral song in a long and heterogeneous poem entitled "Paris." I see that I have rambled on about Seeger at great length, thus proving how marked an admiration I bear for his style. The secret is to be found in his archaism of thought and conservatism of expression; things hinted at in his first sonnet, address'd to Sir Philip Sidney:

> "I give myself some credit for the way
> I have kept clean of what enslaves and lowers,
> Shunn'd the ideals of our present day
> And study'd those that were esteem'd in yours."[33]

It is to a poem quoted by Mr. P. J. Campbell that I owe my introduction to Seeger and his verse, an introduction for which I cannot sufficiently thank our esteemed President.

As the Mo–Lo theological controversy narrows down to fewer points of difference, it may be correspondingly given a smaller and smaller space in each successive epistle. I perceive that my erudite opponent challenges my assumption that scientific progress must be "concealed or glossed over" in order to ensure the preservation of religious belief. He declares that the church is willing to admit all the discoveries of science, reconciling them to some increasingly vague theistical plan—that is, to use plainer language, altering religion to suit science, and making of God a plastic character to be remodelled whenever obvious truth disproves one of His original legendary attributes. This I am willing to admit; but I am not equally willing to abandon the basic idea of my statement, that it will be found necessary in the end to minimise science in order to preserve faith. Not every man is as happily incurious as Mr. Mo; and for many persons, a mere knowledge of the approximate dimensions of the visible universe is enough to destroy forever the notion of a personal godhead whose whole care is expended upon puny mankind, and whose only genuine and original Messiah was dispatched to save the insignificant vermin, or men, who inhabit this one relatively microscopic globe. Not that science positively refutes religion—it merely makes religion seem [so] monstrously improbable that a large majority of men can no longer believe in it. And to go a step further—sooner or later the relation betwixt organic and inorganic life will be discovered. It will be clearly demonstrated how carbon, hydrogen, oxygen, nitrogen, and other elements combine to form substances possessing vital energy. Probably the chemist or biologist will be able to create in his laboratory some very primitive sort of animal or vegetable organism. This will be the death knell of superstition and theology alike; and unless it be sacredly concealed, the church will cease to exist save amongst the very ignorant. But of course, since this has not yet come to pass, I am aware that it forms no truly legitimate part of my case against orthodoxy. However—the probability is strong!

When Mr. Mo charges me with inconsistency in asking whether thinking men can ever be satisfied with make-shift terrestrial truth as opposed to stark absolute fact, I fear he misapprehends my meaning. I did not ask, can *a thinking man* be so satisfied; my question relating to thinking men as a class—to the majority of the scientists and philosophers of today and tomorrow. Surely Mr. Mo does not deem me so ignorant as not to know that many men of vast culture and attainments are devoutly orthodox. Indeed, there is much in pure humanitarian culture, as opposed to rigid scientific training, which encourages absorption in the affairs of mankind, and more or less indifference to the unfathomed abysses of star-strown space that yawn interminably about this terrestrial grain of dust. Perhaps I am a barbarian at heart—sometimes I believe I am—to be so anxious to know what *is,* and not what *ought to be.* I cannot attach so much importance to mere mankind as I should—the *"Homo sum"* sort of enthusiasm never appealed greatly to me.[34] I am not very proud of being an human being; in fact, I distinctly dislike the species in many ways. I can readily conceive of beings vastly superior in every respect. But to be orthodox, one should have less imagination!

Mr. Mo's frank admission that he is satisfied with the empirical "truth" which results from an evasion of astronomical facts, is in a way surprising to me; yet after reflection I can understand the mental attitude, the direct opposite of my own, which enables him to make such a statement. He is to some extent, consciously or unconsciously, a disciple of that not unknown Oxford don, Prof. Schiller, concerning whom an article lately appeared in THE IN-DEPENDENT.[35] This philosopher, like our Appletonian comrade, has a rather elastic notion of Truth, giving that supposedly inflexible abstraction a curiously adaptable nature. In a word, he is a pragmatist of extreme type. Until I read of Prof. Schiller, I was unable to understand how such theories could be held; but I now perceive that there is a not inconsiderable school of pragmatists, who hold to similar ideas. This controversy has taught me many things, foremost among them being my own comparative ignorance of formal philosophy and its subdivisions. I intend to give some attention to this subject in future, in an endeavour to comprehend views which seem to me now too absurd for credence on the part of thinkers. I have a notion that I shall become ardently interested in this subject, for I am a born speculator. (In the academic, not the financial sense!) Mr. Mo's final statement: "All your argument has not shown me why it (absolute truth) interests you," brings to my mind an interesting train of thought. Is there, then, no genuineness in that instinct of truth-seeking which we commonly suppose to reside in the human mind? Does nothing matter which has no direct bearing on our daily life? Were the Papists right in torturing men who believed in the Copernican system? Verily, it matters little to man whether the earth revolve around the sun, or the sun around the earth! No one has really shewn why this matter should interest us! It is sufficient if we eat, sleep, and worship! But with all due respect to Mr. Mo, I must reiterate my belief in the necessity of truth to the human mind. All in my argument does not need to show why truth interests me—all my argument cannot show why, for I do not know! The fact remains that it *does* interest me, as it has interested thousands of other men. The pages of history are red with the blood of those who have died for their intellectual convictions. Truth-hunger is a hunger just as real as food-hunger—it is equally strong if less explicable; indeed, who can assign a direct reason for any of the obscurer desires and aspirations of man? It is all according to the plan of Nature. In flouting the absolute truth because of its lack of application of the affairs of mankind, Mr. Mo reminds me of the Florentine astronomer Sizzi, who thus argued against the existence of Jupiter's satellites: "Moreover", quoth this sage in the course of his argument, "the satellites are invisible to the naked eye, and therefore can exert no influence on the earth, and therefore would be useless, *and therefore do not exist!*"[36] 'Twas vastly inconsiderate of Galileo to see these troublesome orbs, after they had been conclusively demonstrated not to exist at all! How complex is the mortal brain!

Though this ends for the present my contribution to the debate proper, I cannot refrain from remarking upon the agnosticism of the poet Swinburne, as revealed in his works. Though not a deep student of the modern poets, I was lately forced to give this bard considerable attention in order to pass intelligently upon the merits of a manuscript submitted to me for criticism. Swinburne deified man and Mother Earth as one and the same, his belief standing out vividly in such poems as "Hertha" and the "Hymn to Man." God, in the personal sense, he quite scientifically judges to be a creation of the human imagination. A remarkable thing in Swinburne's "Hertha" is his contempt for [the] act of *worship* in the formal sense. We see about us the invincible and omnipotent presence of Mother Earth (Hertha) or Nature. We know that this assemblage of forces has absolute power over us to make or unmake, sustain or destroy us. We are its helpless children. And yet—why should we make ourselves ridiculous with genuflections and prayers which do no one any good? Why indulge in anything so empty and whimsical as ritual worship? We know that Nature is great. We appreciate its boons, and fear its rigours; we admire its beauties, and abhor its defects. But why should we feel anything so unmeaning as personal reverence? Nature is in existence. We know that it is in existence. Why pray to it merely because it exists and is powerful? We are not children, and therefore know that it cannot hear and answer our prayers. I am not now speaking of what the masses should feel—I am speaking in terms of the absolute, leaving the proletariat at their candle-lit niches wherein repose idols of the Christ and the Virgin. All this I say—but see how much more briefly and graphically Swinburne says it in verse: (Mother Earth is speaking)

> "I bid you but be;
>   I have need not of pray'r;
>   I have need of you free
>   As your mouths of mine air;
>   That my heart may be greater within me, beholding the fruits of me fair."[37]

Of course, Swinburne's deification of Man merely amuses me; but it is a refreshing departure from the Oriental self-abasement of orthodoxy, and would delight the invincible spirit of Paul J. Campbell. Observe the following climax of the "Hymn of Man":

> "They cry out, thine elect, thine aspirants to heavenward, whose faith is as flame;
>   O thou the Lord God of our tyrants, they call thee, their God, by thy name,
>   By thy name that in hell-fire was written, and burn'd at the point of thy sword,
>   Thou art smitten, thou God, thou art smitten; thy death is upon thee, O lord.
>   And the love-song of earth as thou diest resounds through the wind of her
>   wings—
> Glory to Man in the highest! for Man is the master of things."[38]

But having already rambled on too long, I must needs bring the present Kleicomolo to a close. If I have seemed negligent in chronicling mine own activities as others of the circle have done, 'tis because the uneventfulness of my life gives me little or nothing to chronicle. As I close, I would fain suggest to Mr. Klei that he include in his section a prospectus of the proposed poetick society which he lately mentioned to me in an epistle.

I regret very much my inability to make my sections of the Kleicomolo more interesting, and am sensible that they lack much of the charm possessed by those of my associates. I have not the sober tone of a Kleiner, nor the delicious imaginative charm of a Cole, nor yet the erudition and colloquial crispness of a Moe. I am a clumsy thinker and a heavy writer, and should feel flattered that a trio as brilliant as Kleicomo are willing to endure the ponderous flights of fancy I inflict upon them.

Conscious, therefore, of your manifold indulgences, I am, Gentlemen,:

Yr. most oblig'd & obt. Servt.:

Lo.

Notes

1. *AT* 277–78 (entitled "April" in published versions).

2. Thomas Percy (1729–1811), British clergyman who compiled *Reliques of Ancient English Poetry* (1765; *LL* 752), a landmark volume collecting early ballads.

3. See Addison, *Spectator* No. 70 (21 May 1711).

4. John A. Lomax (1867–1948) compiled *Cowboy Songs and Other Frontier Ballads* (1910), *American Ballads and Folk Songs* (1934) and *Our Singing Country* (1941). With his son Alan (1915–2002), he made numerous field recordings of folk music on plantations and in prisons.

5. The letter (dated 28 August 1910) appears in Lomax's *Cowboy Songs and Other Frontier Ballads* (New York: Sturgis & Walton Co., 1910), [ix–x].

6. "Fuller and Warren," ll. 21–24; in *Cowboy Songs and Other Ballads* (1910), 126–27.

7. Robert Treat Paine (1773–1811), "Adams and Liberty" (1798).

8. The melody "To Anacreon in Heaven," a drinking song, was first published in England c. 1780, the melody probably written by John Stafford Smith, the words written by Ralph Tomlinson, both members of the Anacreontic Club of London. "To Anacreon in Heaven" was their theme song. The melody was popular in America during the War of 1812, and several Americans (the most famous of them Francis Scott Key) wrote patriotic songs to it.

9. "Harry Bale," ll. 9–16; in *Cowboy Songs and Other Ballads* (1910), 172–73.

10. From "The Hunting of the Cheviot" (Chevy Chase), a hunting ballad dating to the 15th century.

11. Lodge's book claims that he had established contact with his son Raymond's spirit after the latter's death in World War I. Lodge had previously been a respected physicist, but destroyed much of his reputation with this book and others expressing credulous belief in spiritualism.

12. Sir William Crookes (1832–1919), British chemist and physicist. His most important work was in the investigation of the conduction of electricity in gases. He developed the Crookes tube (mentioned in "The Shunned House") and in it produced

cathode rays for the first time. He also wrote *Researches into the Phenomena of Modern Spiritualism* (Rochester, NY: Austin Publishing Co., [1904]).

13. Eusapia Palladino (1854–1918) was a peasant woman from Naples who claimed extraordinary powers such as the ability to levitate tables, communicate with the dead through her spirit guide John King, and to produce other supernatural phenomena. Most investigators who examined her work dismissed her as a charlatan, but Lodge and others maintained belief in the reality of the spiritual manifestations.

14. "Starlight," music by Theodore F. Morse (1873–1924) and lyrics by Edward Madden (1878–1952). HPL probably writes of the performance in 1905 by Byron G. Harlan (1831–1936).

15. See HPL's poem "Epitaph on ye Letter Rrr.......", included in a letter to Maurice W. Moe (29 August 1916) and written as part of a dispute with Moe regarding the propriety of dropping the letter "r" in such words as "far" and "father" (Moe had objected to HPL's rhyming "born" and "dawn" in a poem).

16. Burrage (1874–1951) had been a librarian at Manchester College, Oxford, becoming Librarian at the John Carter Brown Library in 1915. It does not appear that HPL met him.

17. "The Outbursts of Everett True" was a short-lived two-panel comic strip written by J. W. Raper and drawn by A. D. Condo. True was noteworthy for losing his temper.

18. "I very much wish, if you are willing, to compete with you." Quoted by Thomas Babington Macaulay in his article, "Samuel Johnson" (*Encyclopaedia Britannica*, 1856), from a Scotsman who wished to challenge Johnson to a battle of wits. HPL quotes the line at the end of "The Case for Classicism" (1919; *CE* 2.38).

19. Artemus Ward (pseud. of Charles Farrar Browne [1834–1867]) was an American humorist much given to the use of slang and dialect.

20. Winifred Virginia Jordan, "Insomnia," *Conservative* 2, No. 3 (October 1916): [2–3].

21. A Greek version of the Latin motto *Luxus tumultus semper causa est* (Disturbance is always caused by excess), coined by HPL. The Latin version appears in the published version of the poem.

22. A Greek version of the Latin motto *Omnia risus et omnia pulvis et omnia nil sunt* (All is laughter, all is dust, all is nothing). Both versions appear to date from the Renaissance; it is unclear where HPL found them. The title of this section is Greek for "the frightful truth." HPL uses the Greek motto again at the head of "Waste Paper" (1923?; *AT* 252).

23. I.e., the Muses.

24. As a first-year student at Phillips Andover Academy, Paul Shivell (1874–1968) won the Means Prize for original poetic declamation, but he was unable to sustain his early successes as a poet.

25. Poem VII under "Sonnets to H. L. H.," *Stillwater Pastorals* 67–68.

26. Published as "Sonnet on Myself."

27. Rupert Brooke (1887–1915) was a British poet who died of blood-poisoning while the British Army was proceeding to the Dardanelles. Alan Seeger (1888–1916) was a minor American poet who joined the Foreign Legion and gained brief celebrity fol-

lowing his death in World War I. In his honor, HPL composed the poem "To Alan Seeger."

28. From "The Soldier" (1915), ll. 1–3. Quoted by HPL at the end of his introduction to *White Fire* by John Ravenor Bullen (1927; *CE* 2.139).

29. "Ode in Memory of the American Volunteers Fallen for France" (1916), ll. 11–15; in *Poems* (New York: Charles Scribner's Sons, 1916), 170.

30. "A Message to America" (1916), ll. 53–58, 79–85; in *Poems*, 164–65.

31. "A Message to America," ll. 75–78; *Poems*, 164.

32. "Paris" (1914), ll. 123–40; *Poems*, 55.

33. "Sonnet I" (1916), ll. 5–8; *Poems*, 145.

34. HPL refers to the celebrated saying by Terence, *Homo sum: humani nil a me alienum puto* (I am a human being: nothing human is alien to me) (*Heauton Timoroumenos* 77).

35. Ferdinand Canning Scott Schiller (1864–1937), German-born British pragmatist philosopher and author of *Studies in Humanism* (1907). See Edwin E. Slosson, "A British Pragmatist: The Philosophy and Personality of F. C. S. Schiller," *Independent* 89 (12 February 1917): 265–68.

36. The passage is quoted in Thomas Dick (1774–1857), *The Practical Astronomer* (New York: Harper & Brothers, 1846; *LL* 255). Francesco Sizzi was an Italian astronomer of the 17th century, credited with being the first to notice the annual movement of sunspots.

37. Algernon Charles Swinburne (1837–1909), "Hertha" (1871), ll. 156–60.

38. Swinburne, "Hymn of Man" (1871), ll. 195–200.

To the Gallomo

The Gallomo was another round-robin correspondence group, like the Kleicomolo. The members were Lovecraft, Maurice W. Moe, and Moe's former pupil Alfred Galpin, Jr. (1901–1983). Galpin had entered high school in 1915 and quickly became a fixture in the Appleton (Wisconsin) High School Press Club, headed by Lovecraft's colleague Maurice W. Moe. Galpin was brought to Lovecraft's attention by Joseph Harriman, a recent graduate of Appleton High School. Lovecraft states that Galpin had been added to the Kleicomolo circle in 1918 (without a change of the name), but that around that time Ira A. Cole dropped out, leading to the formation of the Gallomo (*SL* 1.171). The group disbanded when Moe felt unfairly set upon by the others in religious arguments.

[4]   [AHT]

Providence, R.I.,
Tuesday, September 30, 1919

Concerning l'art cinematographique and the sundry idols of Galmo therein, I may say that I find nothing outrageous in their taste; though I can't say that I see anything particularly brilliant in the eternal Mary of the Movies.[1] In my judgment her art consists mainly of a certain gelatinous saccharinity which is not at all hard to achieve—chance and press-agenting doing the rest. She has not even the originality of Chaplin[2]—who is at least master of a number of effective ideas and essentials of comicality which would not have been despised by the mimes and buffoons of Graeco-Roman days. Klei, though, thinks otherwise, and says he hath her framed picture in his room! I formerly attended the cinema quite frequently, but it is beginning to bore me. My interest lay more in the plays than the players, and I have no special enthusiasm for any of the artists of the shadow. If I have ever singled out any stars above the rest, it has been a pair about one whom relatively little—Henry B. Walthall[3] and the Japanese Sessue Hayakawa.[4] The latter was my late young cousin's favourite.[5] Walthall possess tragic potentialities all too seldom utilised on the screen. His part in the "Birth of a Nation", though a leading one, failed to do him justice. He could create a sensation if some of Poe's tales were dramatised—I can imagine him as Roderick Usher or the central character in "Berenice". No one else in filmland can duplicate his delineation of stark, hideous terror or fiendish malignancy. Hayakawa excels in tragical pathos, and would soar high if he were a white man. I would not be surprised if he had a dash of white blood somewhere. Both Walthall and Hayakawa are too good for films—they ought to be known more widely.

As to Rabelais—he is to me unexplored territory, and is likely to remain so till the day of my demise. I cannot seem to acquire any enthusiasm for French things, and the quality of coarseness would be enough to deter me anyway. I suffered all the horrors of P. Ovidius Naso[6] because he was a classick author and could not be skipped, but I'll be gracioused if I'll repeat the experience for any gracioused Frenchman! Cook and McDonald[7] are trying to get me to read de Maupassant and Flaubert, who are by me untouched, but I'll tell them to go to O. Dear! If I ever become more Gallick than Victor Hugo and Jules Verne makes me, it will be through M. Anatole France, who seems to be such a Galpinian favourite. The only furriner I've read lately is Vicente Blasco Ibanez, whose "Four Horsemen of the Apocalypse" was sent me by a correspondent who evidently wanted to take no chances about my absorbing it.[8] It was disappointing—all the characters but one were damned scoundrels. The one worthy thing about the book was its absolutely faithful picture of the Hun beast in all its native ugliness.

This neighbourhood is quite honoured today, His Eminence Cardinal Mercier of Belgium[9] being entertained in the McElroy mansion only four houses west of Castle Theobald on Angell St. My aunt is now there at the reception being given in his honour. The extensive grounds are all fenced off to deter curious crowds, and awnings cover the long drives whereby the mansion is reached from the street. His Immanence will sleep there tonight, then depart for the lawless town of Bosting. I should like to see the Cardinal, but feel too confoundedly miserable today to breast any bustle, formality, or excitement. I am saving my strength for H. R. H., the Prince of Wales,[10] whom I intend to see or die in the attempt. The McElroy home is the only local stronghold of Hibernianism. It was built by the late Joseph Banigan, sometimes called "The Rubber King", who was Mrs. McElroy's father.[11] He was a poor Irish peasant who succeeded in business and lived to found a family whose innate good qualities gave them a definite social standing hereabouts. He married an American lady, and gave his children the best education obtainable, so that they are rather influential in the community. One of our principal skyscrapers—where my grandfather had his office the last two years of his life—was named the "Banigan Building"—though Providence pride has led to its recent renaming as the "Grosvenor Building"[12] (some change from peasantry to aristocracy, eh, what?). My mother and aunts knew the daughters of Joseph Banigan from childhood, and found them really worthy in every respect. The grandchildren were my earliest playmates, though it made me shudder in my British soul to know "Dicky Banigan", "Robert McElroy", "Edmund Sullivan", etc!! However, there is some consolation in the fact that Dick, Joe, and John Banigan, who lived nearest me (next house to #454 Angell) were only a quarter Irish.[13] Their father had followed the example of his own father and married into an old American family. Still, I wished they could have been solidly Saxon! The Banigan heirs are the recognised leaders of Catholic circles here, and have entertained all the visiting Popish dignitaries such as Cardinal Sartori of Italy, Gibbons of Baltimore,[14] and now Mercier. Mercier, by the way, is rather Galpinesque in altitude. My aunt went to the college exercises this morning to see him obtain his LL. D., and says that the tallest professor was selected to confer upon him his academic cap. The registrar (whose wife told my aunt) is supposed to perform this ceremony, but is such a pygmy that he felt he could not do it gracefully, so called in more suitable assistance! The Banigan or McElroy Mansion, where Mercier is now receiving the homage of local society, is one of the "show places" of the neighbourhood, and excited Klei's vast admiration when he was here. It is a Gothic manor-house of brick and stone, such as its peasant builder may have seen and admired at a distance in his boyhood in Ould Oireland. The grounds are extensive and beautifully kept, with hedges, trees, and stables of pleasing architecture. It lies almost exactly half way betwixt the house where I was born, and that which I inhabit. Altogether, I fancy the Irish have helped rather than harmed the locality!

Concerning the posthumous publication of epistles, I sincerely hope that no one may ever be fatuous enough to embalm my folly thusly! Never have I entertain'd the Galpinian hope of such a thing—and I trust that I may never have to acquire a Lollian dread of it. For heaven's sake, Galba,[15] permit posterity to observe me in relaxed moments such as the present one! You must realise that the Gallomonistic Tibaldus is not the stern ascetick whom the rest of the world knows. Shew one of these Gallomoes to anyone save five or six intimate correspondents, and they wou'd vow I never writ it! For one thing— no one but Galmo ever beheld a word of profanity from my pen. The Kleicomolo is frankly written with a view to semi-publicity, but not this closer document—Gawd, no! I can't kick if Galba wants to keep these outbursts of microcephaly, but I can at least adjure him to keep 'em private. I've had one experience with Galloian publicity! (Vide chronicles of A. H. S.)

I am sorry the respected P. G. W. K.[16] falls for the "league" bunk.[17] The matter of the six British votes is simple—if voting in the league means anything, which it doesn't. It provides that Britain shall have a better chance to control decisions than otherwise—which is well and good. The veto power of the U.S. is a Wilsonian jester, a Congolese Bantu in the stack of fuel—for no country votes where its own affairs are concerned! Having no vote on its own affairs, the U.S. could do nothing to stay decisions affecting it. What Johnson, Borah,[18] and those other objectors want, is an equalisation of votes so that on general questions the U.S. can have an equal chance with the Motherland to sway decisions. As one of the articles—the 15th, I think, shews, disputes referred to the assembly are decided by majority voting. As you must know, there will be sharp competition amongst the larger powers to control the votes of the lesser powers. England will control Persia, Hedjaz, etc., whilst America will control Hayti, San Domingo, Cuba, etc. Johnson and his ilk want to be sure that England controls no more than America. Now this merely makes me tired. The fortunes of both Anglo-Saxon nations run side by side, and it matters not which one has the votes—but if it will help defeat the whole chimerical league plan, let Johnson talk! The voting would only affect minor matters. When a nation is in earnest, it will break through all the flimsy league paraphernalia. It would take force to break out of the league if that body were a reality and most of the members opposed withdrawal. Keller says that any nation could withdraw on two years' notice. That is plain error. All such questions would have to be submitted to the council for arbitration and decision. The covenant is full of little jokers that riddle the Wilson claims. Heaven knows, I haven't time to look them all up, for the scheme amounts to nothing anyway! By the way—I shall not try to answer Galba's sophistical defence of that fellow Wilson in a previous GALLOMO, but will enclose a bit of verse copied from a Western paper. Read it and pass on to Mocrates, little one. (N.B. Lapsus calami[19]—I meant KLEICOMOLO when I said GALLOMO, but I will send the verse just the same.) The most infernally silly thing that league advocates say, is that the opponents of their plan are pro-German. That is not so. The only shady characters on our side are the Sinn Feiners, and Gawd knows we're ashamed enough of them. Germany knows that the league amounts to nothing, and is placidly indifferent as to what becomes of it. But allee samee if Allied folks no lookee out, German get much dangerous again! It behoves the publick to regard the future attitude and opportunities of this unrepentant and far from weak enemy. Despite the taking of territory from Prussia, the Balkans again lie open for Hun exploitation. Sooner or later Austria will either join Germany or reëstablish the dual monarchy with Hungary, in any case being on the German side. The best thing would have been to let Roumania take Hungary, as suggested a few weeks ago. Bulgaria—but we all know Bulgaria. And if we continue to mistreat Italy, she will be against us in the next war. The Dago loves not the gentle Boche, but he will hate us a great deal worse than he will hate Germany if we permit the Fiume blunder of the Paris council to be perpetuated.[20] As to Russia—if it stays Bolshevik, Germany will exploit it and wax corpulent upon it. If it regains sanity, it will hate us with a cold, steely hate for our neglect in its hour of need. At this moment French, English, and American troops ought to be helping Kolchak and Denikine, for Russia was our ally whilst it lasted. When these elements triumph, if they do, they will have small reason to forgive us, and will in all reasonable probability align with Germany. I am no diplomat, but I am quite sure from what I read that a little common sense could turn the future course of two great nations—Italy and Russia. These hang in the balance—will they go with us or with the Hun? Our best possible ally in the event of Russo-German hostilities with us is Poland. This new nation has an undying hatred both of Russia and of Germany. If helped by us to the limit of our ability—given every stimulus for development into a great nation, and bolstered up commercially and financially—it will be no mean influence in our favour in the years to come. Of Japan I have not so far spoken, because I think it a certain enemy of the future, which no plan can permanently make a friend. It demands free access to Anglo-Saxon soil for its citizens, and this can never be given. Orientals must be kept in their native East till the fall of the white race. Sooner or later a great Japanese war will take place, during which I think the virtual destruction of Japan will have to be effected in the interests of European safety. The more numerous Chinese are a menace of the still more distant future. They will probably be the exterminators of Caucasian civilisation, for their numbers are amazing. But that it all too far ahead for consideration today. The next war, I think, will see England, America, France, Spain,? Greece, Scandinavia,? Holland, Switzerland, and the South American countries, against Germany, Russia, Austria, Italy, Japan, Mexico, and Bulgaria. I forgot to add Poland to our side—also Belgium, of course. Italy and Russia might be doubtful—might even be friends if treated properly in time. Also, future German colonisation might make enemies instead of Allies in South America. But at any rate, it is a duty to maintain the solidity of the Anglo-Franco-American *bloc*, and to win to it as many friends as possible; all bound by ties of substantial self-interest. This Anglo-Franco-America is the only real league of nations. These three nations have no diverse aims, and can bear triple harness infinitely. I once thought Italy could make a fourth, but see that the other three are not sufficiently considerate of its interests. Anyone fostering disunion amongst these three countries ought to be shot—which means the many Irish curs who go about the United States preaching Anglophobia. It will be best to keep up Saxon dominance until the final crash—and it is not extravagant to hope that the English ideal can be kept through the new Dark Ages to blossom forth again after the next Renaissance—just as the Roman influence reappeared in European culture. But it is too late to talk of any separate destinies for America and England. They must stick together for the advancement of their common culture.

Concerning a reading course 1600–1800, stressing minor poets—let me lean back in my chair for a moment and think! I should hardly advise stressing minor poets, but if thou'rt determined, here goes: Of course, 1600 finds us in the heyday of the Elizabethan aera. I don't have to tell you to read the w. k. author of *Hamlet, Macbeth,* and other popular melodramas and comedies, but I will drop a word in behalf of my fat old friend Ben Jonson, whose *Catiline, Sejanus, Volpone, Alchemist, Silent Woman,* and *Cynthia's Revels*—plus of course *Every Man in his Humour,* ought to receive the o. o. from your penetrating O. K. Glimmes. Nor should Messrs. Beaumont and Fletcher be scorn'd. Doubt has been expressed as to their authorship of *Alfredo,* a Tragedy,[21] but you may accept as their genuine and meritorious work such things as

The Maid's Tragedy, Faithful Shepherdess, Knight of the Burning Pestle, etc. Read 'em. And now for your poets, minor and otherwise. We come at this point upon a group called by Dr. Johnson the "Metaphysical Poets", of whom I shall first mention a favourite of Klei's—George Wither. George hath a sort of pastoral cast, hence he appealeth to me also. Read "The Shepherd's Hunting", one passage in which would be appreciated by the new romantick poet whom Mistress Hoyt[22] likes so well:

> So, my WILLY, shall it be
> With Detraction's breath and thee,
> It shall never rise so high,
> As to stain thy poesy.[23]

Well, who's this? That celebrated old fellow Dr. Donne, about whom our former Chairman of Private Criticism, W. F. Melton, Ph.D.,[24] hath writ a book! Read as much as you can stand of old John—it won't hurt you. And at this point note how the old Elizabethan luxuriance of fancy is petering out in the artificial *conceit*. 'Tis an aera of transition, plain to see. Minor bards come thick and fast—Dick Corbet, Dr. Henry King, Sir J. Beaumont, Tho. Carew, a gallant like Waller and Klei, Phineas and Giles Fletcher, Francis Quarles— pious old duffer—George Herbert, another pious gink some of whose verse my aunt had to learn when she was even more of an infant than thou, O Galba. Sir J. Suckling, the arch-gallant, Robert Herrick, a really meritorious lyrist, Richard Lovelace—the "stone walls do not a prison make" fellow,[25] Bill Davenant, the playwright, who was so unscrupulous for fame that he used to hint at being a left-handed son of Shakespeare, Dick Crashaw—pious guy— Edmund Waller, the Kleiner of his age, first of the neatly correct writers—

> "He caught at love, and fill'd his arms with bays"[26]

Abraham Cowley, quite some poet—writ all sorts of junk including an epick, the "Davideis", which though writ in the Heroic Couplet hath met with unaccountable oblivion—Sir John Denham, author of "Cooper's Hill", wherein occurs the famous comparison of an author's work to the Thames:

> "Oh, cou'd I flow like thee, and make thy Stream
> My great Example, as it is my Theme!
> Tho' deep, yet clear; tho' gentle, yet not dull;
> Strong without Rage; without o'er flowing, full."

But I mustn't forget the prose artists in spite of your preference. Could you stand Burton's *Anatomy of Melancholy?* If not, try Sir Tho. Overbury or Sir Tho. Browne. I suppose you already know Walton's *Compleat Angler* by heart, to say naught of the diaries of Sir J. Evelyn and Saml Pepys. Therefore I turn to verse again, and hail the mighty name of MILTON. Read him through. Skip not Andrew Marvell, nor for thy life overlook the hilarious Samuel Butler, whose Hudibras is a text-book of wit and enchiridion of humour. John Philips' *Splendid Shilling* is a rather good light diversion—a parody upon Miltonick style. We are now arriv'd at the Restoration aera, and faced with the illustrious name of DRYDEN. His contemporaries who deserve a reading are John Oldham the satirist,[27] Sedley, the gallant poet, Wentworth Dillon, Earl of Roscommon, rhetorician and didactick poet, and the brilliant dramatists. Of the latter you must not miss Otway, author of Venice Preserv'd, Nat Lee, Dryden's enemy Shadwell the Laureate, Nicholas Rowe, and (since you are a devotee of Rabelais) the comical authors Wycherly, Vanbrugh, Farquhar, Etherege, and Congreve. Congreve brings us down to the age of Pope, but belongs to the Restoration school so far as technique is concern'd. He writ not only comedies but tragedies, of which the most famous is *The Mourning Bride,* containing the celebrated couplet:

> "Heav'n has no rage like love to hatred turn'd,
> Nor hell a fury like a woman scorn'd."

By the way, it is this same play which contains "Musick hath charms to soothe the savage breast". Coming back to prose, miss not the philosophical Hobbes, Locke, and perhaps Boyle, nor the essayist Sir W. Temple.

Now hail to the dawn—Aetas Augustana! Poets in profusion await thine eye—John Sheffield, Duke of Buckinghamshire, the immortal Prior, Thos. Parnell, ADDISON, Tickell, Gay, Somerville, POPE, SWIFT, THOMSON, Ikey Watts, Ambrose Philips, Collins, Dyer, Garth, Shenstone, Young, Akenside, Allan Ramsay the Scotchman,—but stay—we are quitting the Augustan age for that later period of romantick beginnings. GRAY, the Churchyard Man, Falconer, author of the *Shipwreck,* Beattie, Blair, Percy's Reliques, COWPER, Dr. Darwin of Botanick Garden fame (grandfather of the immortal Charles), Wolcot—Peter Pindar, the biting satirist, Churchill, Anstey of the New Path Guide, poor Chris. Smart, Elizabeth Carter, the learned old maid, Macpherson, the Ossian faker, Goldsmith, the brothers Warton, Matt. Green, Sheridan, Rogers, Crabbe, Burns,—but we are getting rather near the present! To go back—I forgot to mention the Restoration burlesque on Dryden—*The Rehearsal,* by George Villiers, Second Duke of Buckingham, which perhaps furnished Mr. Sheridan with a model for *The Critick.* Prose writers from this age downward are Sir R. Steele, Addison, Swift, Budgell, Hughes, Arbuthnot (read his *History of John Bull*), Ld Bolingbroke (*Letters, Patriot King*) Lady Mary Wortley Montagu, (*Letters*) Mandeville, utilitarian moralist, Smollet[t], Sterne,—the philosopher and historian Hume, who exploded a great deal of theistic nonsense—EDWARD GIBBON, SAMUEL JOHNSON, Mr. Burke, Jimmy Boswell, "Junius", P. D. S. (Philip Dormer Stanhope, Earl of Chesterfield), Beckford, author of *Vathek* in French and English, Miss Burney, afterward Mme. D'Arblay, Gilbert White, author of the *Nat. Hist. of Selborne,* Horace Walpole,—but we are getting close to the end. The nineteenth century is near, and we now see new and strange authors publishing their first works, who will be better known a quarter of a century later. Campbell, Southey, Wordsworth, Coleridge—all are above the horizon, but still partly obscured by the thick vapours of that region. A great age is closed—an age in which men saw that reason is the paramount quality, and that emotion and passion are mere secondary things unworthy of serious treatment. Verse was then what it should be—a light tinkling amusement of the idle—for men's minds were on greater things. Hume was brushing away the clouds of miraculous superstition; Gibbon was re-creating the declining Roman world; Johnson was refining the publick morals as Addison did before him. Prose and verse had attained their utmost elegance of form, and were tottering on the brink of decline. Science was arising—that young giant later to carry everything before it. Probably my survey has been but imperfect. I have doubtless omitted in this hasty catalogue many writers who ought to be read, and included many who are scarce worth perusal—but tired as I am today it is the best I can do. Let me express the hope, O Galba, that thou mayest extract at least a grain of help or amusement from what I have writ.

Great was my delight to behold the Mocratic domicile in pictured majesty. Verily, Sir, thou art well off both materially and aesthetically. The place is exceedingly attractive both inside and out, and the views are thoroughly delightful. The sweep of lake horizon would delight my astronomical soul. The roof of 598 Engelstrasse is approximately flat, and in the days of my youth I had a set of meteorological instruments there. Hither I would sometimes hoist my telescope, and observe the sky from that point of relative proximity to it. The horizon is fair, but not ideal. One can see the glint of the Seekonk through the foliage of Blackstone Park, and the opposite bank is quite clearly defined. With a terrestrial eyepiece of fifty diameters on my telescope, I can see some of the farms in the heart of East Providence, and even Seekonk, Mass., across the river. One in particular delights me—a typical bit of ancient agrestick New England with eighteenth century farmhouse, old-fashion'd garden, and even archaic well and well-sweep—all this bit of primitive antiquity visible from a roof in the prosaic modern town!! One of the houses within range is a seventeenth century structure—1650 or thereabouts—but this is not nearly so picturesque as the more recent one above mentioned. A good telescope, or even a binocular glass, is a great pleasure when one has a wide vista. I am fortunate in having an almost ideal battery of optical aids, including a Warner and Swasey—hell, no, I mean Bausch and Lomb—prism binocular which cost me $55.00 about twelve years ago. Ah, them golden days when I didn't have to worry about what I spent! I'd like to see meself buying a $55.00 plaything today!!! Well, if Mocrates can make a lit'ry success of me, maybe prosperity will bless me humble hearth once more! The Gay Bldg. is attractive, as is the view therefrom and I congratulate Mocrates upon his good fortune in having so thoroughly pleasant an atmosphere to work in.

Providence has some excellent skyscrapers, the newest and tallest of which is the Turk's Head Building—sixteen stories.[28] The dominant view from Providence tall buildings includes the state capitol on the north, and the attractive bay on the south. Into this bay used to come the shipping of all the world, and about a century ago it was a veritable forest of masts. The great storm of 1815 caused the bay to overflow and inundate the whole waterfront. Full-rigged ships were cast up on Market Square, and one schooner was driven some distance up Westminster Street—past the corner known as Turk's Head, above hinted at. Never hath so great a storm lash'd the shore since. The shipping has sadly fallen off during the last fifty or sixty years, but the bay is still beautiful—as it will always be in spite of decadence and Bolshevism. The eternal sea is the one thing which the degenerate creature man can never mar! But Oh, the deuce, what sort of senile rambling is this!

I am, Gents, yr obt &c

M. LOLLIVS

Notes

1. I.e., Mary Pickford (1893–1979), who, with Charlie Chaplin, was the first "star" of the film industry.

2. Charlie Chaplin (1889–1977), British-born actor. HPL countered Rheinhart Kleiner's poem "To Mary of the Movies" (*Piper*, September 1915) with "To Charlie of the Comics."

3. Henry Brazeale Walthall (1878–1936), silent film star in D. W. Griffith's Biograph stock company, whose work includes *Judith of Bethulia, Avenging Conscience,* and *Birth of a Nation.*

4. Sessue Hayakawa (1889–1973), Japanese stage and film actor who was featured in many Hollywood films from 1914 to 1962.

5. Phillips Gamwell (1898–1916), son of HPL's aunt Annie E. P. Gamwell.

6. HPL alludes to Ovid's *Ars Amatoria, Remedia Amoris,* and other works notable for their sexual explicitness.

7. Philip B. McDonald (1888–1959), a professor of Engineering English at the University of Colorado, amateur journalist (and husband of Edna Hyde Macdonald), and contributor to HPL's *Conservative.*

8. A popular but lurid novel about a Frenchman who returns from overseas to fight in World War I. It reveals a violent hatred of the Germans.

9. Désiré Joseph Mercier (1851–1926), Belgian theologian and philosopher. He became Archbishop of Mechelen in 1906 and thus leader of the Catholic church in Belgium.

10. Later Edward VIII (1894–1972); still later (following his abdication), Edward, Duke of Windsor.

11. Mary Ann Banigan (1861–1923) married William B. McElroy. She was the daughter of [Michael] Joseph Banigan (1839–1898), an Irish-born entrepreneur who made millions with the Woonsocket Rubber Company and other firms in Rhode Island.

12. The 10½-story Banigan Building (later Grosvenor building; now AMICA Building), constructed at 10 Weybosset Street in 1896, was the first tall, fireproof, steel-frame building erected in Providence.

13. Richard Davis Banigan (1890–1973), Robert McElroy (Robert Bernard McElroy (1886–1953), and John J. Banigan Jr. (1894–1967).

14. James Gibbons (1834–1921), Bishop of Richmond (1872–1877) and ninth Archbishop of Baltimore (1877–1921).

15. It is not clear why HPL referred to Galpin as Galba (presumably alluding to the Roman general who was emperor for less than a year in 68–69 C.E.), aside from the approximate similarity of their names.

16. Evidently a reference to someone named Keller, perhaps a friend of Galpin's or Moe's. See further letter 7 (p. 93).

17. The reference is to the League of Nations, the brainchild of Pres. Woodrow Wilson. The U.S. Senate rejected U.S. participation in it in March 1920.

18. Hiram Johnson (1866–1945), U.S. senator from California (1917–45), and William Edgar Borah (1865–1940), U.S. senator from Idaho (1907–40), two Republicans who led the fight against U.S. entry into the League of Nations.

19. *Lapsus calami:* Latin for "slip of the pen."

20. HPL refers to Fiume, a city now in Croatia. On 12 September 1919, while the Peace Conference at Paris was in session, the city (then part of the Austro-Hungarian Empire) was taken over by a band of Italian soldiers led by the writer Gabriele d'Annunzio, who established it and the surrounding area as an independent state.

21. The play (1918) is by HPL, and is signed "By Beaumont and Fletcher." It involves Galpin, Moe, HPL, and Rheinhart Kleiner as characters. HPL once signed a sonnet "Jonson Flomont-Betcher."

22. Unidentified, although a youthful Helen Hoyt lived in Appleton, WI, and attended Lawrence University there; so may once have been one of Moe's pupils.

23. George Wither (1588 –1667), prolific English poet, pamphleteer, satirist, and writer of hymns. The quotation is from "The Companionship of the Muse," ll. 9–12.

24. Wightman Fletcher Melton (1867–1944), *The Rhetoric of John Donne's Verse* (Baltimore: J. H. Furst Company, 1906).

25 "To Althea, from Prison" (1642), l. 25.

26. "The Story of Phœbus and Apollo Applied," l. 20.

27. See HPL's "John Oldham: A Defence." The poem was written in response to Rheinhart Kleiner's "John Oldham: 1653–1683," published on the same page as HPL's poem.

28. The 17-story V-shaped Turks Head Building (1913, 1978) at 7–17 Weybosset Street, dominating the intersection of Weybosset and Westminster streets, has a high-relief sculpture of a Turk's head in the frieze above the third story.

[5] [AHT]

Providence, R.I.,
December 11, 1919

BELLS

I hear the bells from yon imposing tower;
    The bells of Yuletide o'er a troubled night;
Pealing with mock'ry in a dismal hour
    Upon a world upheav'd with greed and fright.

Their mellow tones on myriad roofs resound;
    A million restless souls attend the chime;
Yet falls their message on a stony ground—
    Their spirit slaughter'd with the sword of Time.

Why ring in counterfeit of happy years
    When calm and quiet rul'd the placid plain?
Why with familiar strains arouse the tears
    Of those who ne'er may know content again?

How well I knew ye once—so long ago—
    When slept the ancient village on the slope;
Then rang your accents o'er the starlit snow
    In gladness, peace, and sempiternal hope.

In fancy yet I view the modest spire;
    The peaked roof, cast dark against the moon;
The Gothic windows, glowing with a fire
    That lent enchantment to the brazen tune.

Lovely each snow-drap'd hedge beneath the beams
    That added silver to the silver there;
Graceful each col, each lane, and all the streams,
    And glad the spirit of the pine-ting'd air.

A simple creed the rural swains profess'd;
    In simple bliss among the hills they dwelt;
Their hearts were light, their honest souls at rest,
    Cheer'd with the joys by reas'ning mortals felt.

But on the scene a hideous blight intrudes;
    A lurid nimbus hovers o'er the land;
Demoniac shapes low'r black above the woods,
    And by each door malignant shadows stand.

The jester Time stalks darkly thro' the mead;
    Beneath his tread contentment dies away.
Hearts that were light with causeless anguish bleed,
    And restless souls proclaim his evil sway.

Conflict and change beset the tott'ring world;
    Wild thoughts and fancies fill the common mind;
Confusion on a senile race is hurl'd,
    And crime and folly wander unconfin'd.

I HEAR THE BELLS—THE MOCKING, CURSED BELLS
    THAT WAKE DIM MEMORIES TO HAUNT AND CHILL;
RINGING AND RINGING O'ER A THOUSAND HELLS—
    FIENDS OF THE NIGHT—WHY CAN YE NOT BE STILL?

—H. PAGET LOWE

Before quitting the subject of Loveman and horror stories, I must relate the frightful dream I had the night after I received S.L.'s latest letter. We have lately been discussing weird tales at length, and he has recommended several hair-raising books to me; so that I was in the mood to connect him with any thought of hideousness or supernatural terror. I do not recall how this dream began, or what it was really all about. There remains in my mind only one damnably blood-curdling fragment whose ending haunts me yet.

We were, for some terrible yet unknown reason, in a very strange and very ancient cemetery—which I could not identify. I suppose no Wisconsinite can picture such a thing—but we have them in New-England; horrible old places where the slate stones are graven with odd letters and grotesque designs such as a skull and crossbones. In some of these places one can walk a long way without coming upon any grave less than an hundred and fifty years old. Some day, when Cook issues that promised *MONADNOCK,* you will see my tale "The Tomb",[1] which was inspired by one of these places. Such was the scene of my dream—a hideous hollow whose surface was covered with a coarse, repulsive sort of long grass, above which peeped the shocking stones and markers of decaying slate. In a hillside were several tombs whose facades were in the last stages of decrepitude. I had an odd idea that no living thing had trodden that ground for many centuries till Loveman and I arrived. It was very late in the night—probably in the small hours, since a waning crescent moon had attained considerable height in the east. Loveman carried, slung over his shoulder, a portable telephone outfit; whilst I bore two spades. We proceeded directly to a flat sepulchre near the centre of the horrible place, and began to clear away the moss-grown earth which had been washed down upon it by the rains of innumerable years. Loveman, in the dream, looked exactly like the snap-shots of himself which he has sent me—a large, robust young man, not the least Semitic in features (albeit dark), and very handsome save for a pair of protruding ears. We did not speak as he laid down his telephone outfit, took a shovel, and helped me clear away the earth and weeds. We both seemed very much impressed with something—almost awestruck. At last we completed these preliminaries, and Loveman stepped back to survey the sepulchre. He seemed to know exactly what he was about to do, and I also had an idea—though I cannot now remember what it was! All I recall is that we were following up some idea which Loveman had gained as the result of extensive reading in some old rare books, of which he possessed the only existing copies. (Loveman, you may know, has a vast library of rare first editions and other treasures precious to the bibliophile's heart.) After some mental estimates, Loveman took up his shovel again, and using it as a lever, sought to pry up a certain slab which formed the top of the sepulchre. He did not succeed, so I approached and helped him with my own shovel. Finally we loosened the stone, lifted it with our combined strength, and heaved it away. Beneath was a black passageway with a flight of stone steps; but so horrible were the miasmic vapours which poured up from the pit, that we stepped back for a while without making further observations. Then Loveman picked up the telephone output and began to uncoil the wire—speaking for the first time as he did so.

"I'm really sorry", he said in a mellow, pleasant voice; cultivated, and not very deep, "to have to ask you to stay above ground, but I couldn't answer for the consequences if you were to go down with me. Honestly, I doubt if anyone with a nervous system like yours could see it through. You can't imagine what I shall have to see and do—not even from what the book said and from what I have told you—and I don't think anyone without ironclad nerves could ever go down and come out of that place alive and sane. At any rate, this is no place for anybody who can't pass an army physical examination.[2] I discovered this thing, and I am responsible in a way for anyone who goes with me—so I would not for a thousand dollars let you take the risk. But I'll keep you informed of every move I make by the telephone—you see I've enough wire to reach to the centre of the earth and back!"

I argued with him, but he replied that if I did not agree, he would call the thing off and get another fellow-explorer—he mentioned a "Dr. Burke," a name altogether unfamiliar to me. He added, that it would be of no use for me to descend alone, since he was sole possessor of the real key to the affair. Finally I assented, and seated myself upon a marble bench close by the open grave, telephone in hand. He produced an electric lantern, prepared the telephone wire for unreeling, and disappeared down the damp stone steps, the insulated wire rustling as it uncoiled. For a moment I kept track of the glow of his lantern, but suddenly it faded out, as if there were a turn in the stone staircase. Then all was still. After this came a period of dull fear and anxious waiting. The crescent moon climbed higher, and the mist or fog about the hollow seemed to thicken. Everything was horribly damp and bedewed, and I thought I saw an owl flitting somewhere in the shadows. Then a clicking sounded in the telephone receiver.

"Lovecraft—I think I'm finding it"—the words came in a tense, excited tone. Then a brief pause, followed by more words in a tone of ineffable awe and horror.

"God, Lovecraft! *If you could see what I am seeing!*" I now asked in great excitement what had happened. Loveman answered in a trembling voice:

"I can't tell you—I don't dare—I never dreamed of *this*—I can't tell—It's enough to unseat any mind————wait————what's this?" Then a pause, a clicking in the receiver, and a sort of despairing groan. Speech again—

"Lovecraft—for God's sake—it's all up—Beat it! *Beat it!* Don't lose a second!" I was now thoroughly alarmed, and frantically asked Loveman to tell what the matter was. He replied only "Never mind! Hurry!" Then I felt a sort of offence through my fear—it irked me that anyone should assume that I would be willing to desert a companion in peril. I disregarded his advice and told him I was coming down to his aid. But he cried:

"Don't be a fool—it's too late—there's no use—nothing you or anyone can do now." He seemed calmer—with a terrible, resigned calm, as if he had met and recognised an inevitable, inescapable doom. Yet he was obviously anxious that I should escape some unknown peril.

"For God's sake get out of this, if you can find the way! I'm not joking—So long, Lovecraft, won't see you again—God! Beat it! *Beat it!*" As he shrieked out the last words, his tone was a frenzied crescendo. I have tried to recall the wording as nearly as possible, but I cannot reproduce the tone. There followed a long—hideously long—period of silence. I tried to move to assist Loveman, but was absolutely paralysed. The slightest motion was an impossibility. I could speak, however, and kept calling excitedly into the telephone—"Loveman! Loveman! What is it? What's the trouble?" But he did not reply. And then came the unbelievably frightful thing—the awful, unexplainable, almost unmentionable thing. I have said that Loveman was now silent, but after a vast interval of terrified waiting another clicking came into the receiver. I called "Loveman—are you there?" And in reply came a *voice*—a thing which I cannot describe by any words I know. Shall I say that it was hollow—very deep—fluid—gelatinous—indefinitely distant—unearthly—guttural—thick? What shall I say? In that telephone I heard it; heard it as I sat on a marble bench in that very ancient unknown cemetery with the crumbling stones and tombs and long grass and dampness and the owl and the waning crescent moon. Up from the sepulchre it came, and this is what it said:

"YOU FOOL, LOVEMAN IS DEAD!"

Well, that's the whole damn thing! I fainted in the dream, and the next I knew I was awake—and with a prize headache! I don't know yet what it was all about—what on (or under) earth we were looking for, or what that hideous voice at the last was supposed to be. I have read of ghouls—mould shades—but hell—the headache I had was worse than the dream! Loveman will laugh when I tell him about that dream! In due time, I intend to weave this picture into a story, as I wove another dream-picture into "The Doom that Came to Sarnath". I wonder, though, if I have a right to claim authorship of things I dream? I hate to take credit, when I did not really think out the picture with my own conscious wits. Yet if I do not take credit, who'n Heaven *will* I give credit tuh? Coleridge claimed "Kubla Khan", so I guess I'll claim the thing an' let it go at that. But believe muh, that was *some* dream!![3]

Well, God rest you, Merry Gentlemen, may nothing you dismay.

Your affectionate Grandfather,

M. LOLLIVS. TIBALDVS

Notes

1. "The Tomb" did not appear in Cook's *Monadnock Monthly*, but in Cook's *Vagrant* (March 1922).

2. The reference is to HPL's being declared "totally and permanently unfit" to serve in the U.S. Army in December 1917. Ironically, Loveman probably was more neurotic than HPL.

3. HPL soon afterward wrote the dream into the story "The Statement of Randolph Carter" (*Vagrant*, May 1920). HPL was fictionalized as Randolph Carter, Samuel Loveman as Harley Warren. The story contains no character named Burke.

[6]   [AHT]

[April 1920]

It is seldom, O Gentlemen, that I have anything new to write ye of. So uneventful is my career that a trip to Boston is the occasion for four or five closely typed pages. But I now have another slightly out of the ordinary incident to relate—albeit one which hath not taken me out of my secluded study. To come to the point—I have been spending all my time since Monday correcting arithmetic papers for pupils in the two upper grades of the Hughesdale, R.I.[1] Grammar School, and in concocting examples and problems and laying out work for them to do! Behold Theobaldus the long-distance pedagogue! The explanation? Simple and lucid! One of the still semi-rural branches of my maternal family inhabit the township of Johnston, wherein lies the village of Hughesdale. They are by nature scholastically inclined, and are largely represented on the school board. Last week there was dire need of a substitute teacher to take the place of the grammar-school principal, whose vacation is due; and in view of the amazing energy and versatility of my aunt they decided to keep the job in the family, so to speak. They are aware of the rather tenuous state of local finances, and rightly guessed that the unexpected emolument might not prove unacceptable. Now be it known that my aunt has never before taught school a day in her life. Though fond of children, and very capable and tactful in managing them, she has known schools solely from the pupil's point of view; and has been a stranger to all the educational novelties which have sprung up since her graduation from Miss Abbott's fashionable seminary for refined young females.[2] Can you imagine such an one guiding the destinies of a village grammar-school? No? But then—you don't know my aunt! As a person of ample culture and general education, there was of course no difficulty for her in directing the classes in the non-mathematical subjects. With amazing skill she seized on the complicated routine, and kept her classes busy at reading, reciting, writing exercises, and the like. But then arose the grim spectre—the hated, damned thing—ARITHMETIC! Fancy for a moment a person out of schoolbooks since the early 'nineties, endeavouring to grapple with the fad-ridden arithmetic of the day—the absurdly pedantic science wherein such terms as "common denominator", "plus", "minus", etc. are, or seem to be, abolished, and wherein it is deemed treason to tell a child to divide fractions by inverting the divisor and proceeding as in multiplication! Such was the thing faced by my aunt, who candidly confessed her inability to attend to all the insistent needs of those two restless upper classes, and to explain to them each step of every example as scrawled on their daily exercise papers. They worked much of the time according to methods new to her, and to follow and correct their attempts in itemised fashion was practically impossible. All her evenings, anyway, were obviously to be taken up with the correction of other papers. But here behold the mighty redactor of amateurdom! All is well, for is not Tibaldus the Great at hand? Ecce homo! It is not alone bad verse with which my mighty talents can grapple! Which means that I offered my assistance, and have undertaken to be the Power Behind the Throne in the mathematical department of the Hughesdale Grammar School! Now I suppose Gahal-Bah, the Wonder, and Mocrates, the Superman, will marvel that the mere correction of 7th and 8th arithmetic should be any sort of task. But suppose, O Great Ones, ye were like unto me, who do abhor 'rithmetic with all the loathing of an ethereal nature? Most of the methods are as new to me as to my aunt, and the text-book is a crime—the work of a local dignitary who has a pull with the school board. But natheless the principles of mathematicks are through all the ages unvarying, and brains were made to use; so I mastered the damned thing Sunday night and have now set up as a pedagogue of the new school; albeit I will on my knees praise the Creator Friday, when I can dismiss it as a bad dream and go back to my old ways whenever ill fortune compels me to make mathematical computations! My aunt says she *could* not today do some of the complicated problems in the back of the book. I wishtagawd I could say the same; that my conscience might enable me to slide over them lightly—but unfortunately I still remember enough to do them, detest them as I do! Therefore picture me last night, waist deep in papers covered with everything from vulgar fractions to cube root, and tinkering at stupid mistakes as if I were patching up D. V. Bush's latest metrical misdemeanour. Oh, Boy! Yuh'd orter see Grandpa marking up examples with a real red pencil, austerely, just as reg'lar teachers do! In the old days I used to long for the authority represented by one of those forbidding red pencils—but now I perceive that the authority is dearly purchased in the coin of fatigue and headache! And Holy Pegāna! The mistakes those kids make! Much as I loathe arithmetical pursuits, I'd have been ashamed in my grammar school days to turn in such work! Some of them do fairly well on the plain sailing—but the problems knock 'em all down! Yuh hafta go after 'em wit' a diagram! Sometimes I find certain blunders strangely duplicated—and I smile to think of the slips of paper exchanged in classroom behind my aunt's back. I know, because I have myself been a scholar—in my day I used to revise my class's work about as I do the United Amateur today—though of course without pedagogical sanction. I hope that the stuff I furnished my youthful clients in those days was not as bad as some of the suggestions passed around by these Hughesdale hopefuls—if so, my aid was not of much value! What would you think of a seventh-grade class in which not a single member can tell how to find the depth of [a] box when the length, breadth, and cubical contents are given? They have had all this, but the least jar in the routine throws their little brains all helter-skelter. Just now the trouble is coming from a mistake which the regular teacher made in her haste to escape vacationwards. At the last moment she put a problem on the board in which she must have written cu. in. when she meant cu. ft. Not one in the school could see any light, and the theory above outlined is due solely to Theobaldian deduction. But there is another good one on my aunt! In devising problems yesterday for today's papers, and putting them on the board, she was distracted by the incessant chatter of an amiable and friendly-intentioned fellow-teacher; and made a question asking how much profit a farmer would make if he bought 3¾ bu. apples at $3.00 per bu., and sold them at 5¢ per quart. D'ya get it? *Profit?* The poor kids were all at sea—they knew something was the matter, but not just what! I am taking pity on them, and explaining very kindly that the apples got rotten or worm-eaten or something, so the unfortunate swain hadda sell 'em at a bargain! Yuh'd laff tuh see the bluff some of the kids made—and yet not one seemed to remember the second term of the common expression "profit and ———". It taketh not much to puzzle the faculties of infancy, and there are no Galpinii in Hughesdale! The racial composition of the school is appalling. Dagoes exist in amazing numbers—children of the thrifty peasants who settle on little farms and shun the congested urban Italian colony. My aunt says that they are much superior in conduct and appearance to city Italians, and I can testify that the brightest kid in the institution is named Joe Merluzzo! By the way—devising problems ain't the easiest work this side of Cleveland! If yuh'd don't watch out yuh'll make some absurd condition which the eye of youth will demur at. I hope I have escaped all pitfalls, making examples that come out well and fairly evenly. It is hard to tell just how hard or how easy the work should be made, and how to differentiate betwixt the 7th and 8th grade intelligences; but anyhow—'tis but for a week! To my mind, a teacher's job is no job for one person. Team-work is needed—one to hold down the youngsters through the day, and another to wrestle with the papers at night. My aunt says she positively could not manage the thing without aid, and I am sure I don't see how anyone else can! She wants to give me a share of the financial spoils, but I scorn remuneration for labour performed in the cause of upholding the family's scholastic honour! The house is now a veritable branch office of the school. Arithmetical paraphernalia abound in my room, whilst my aunt has set up another table in the library to hold her linguistic, orthographical, geographical, historical, etc. matter. At this point I am going in there to get one or two of the freak exercises handed in, which I shall copy in these columns! Ah! Here's a good grammar one:

JOHN HUNSPERGER 6B

Parse "I thought the school bell was broken".
I, pronoun; *thought*, verb; *the*, l. adj.; *bell*, noun; *was*, adverb; *broken*, noun.

"Boys should be very brave."
Boys, noun; *should*, adj.; *be*, prep.; *very*, adj.; *brave*, noun.

What a fine crop of Millars etc. is growing up to replace those who pass from our midst! Ah, well! Probably inefficient tuition is to blame for some of the dulness in rural schools. I'll wager the regular teacher of the higher grades has been monstrous remiss in explaining arithmetical matters to her young charges. I am having to make copious marginal notes on their papers, explaining principles they should have known ages ago. In short, gents, Grandpa Tibaldus is getting to be quite some schoolmaster! If only I could keep up and about longer at a time, I should take my rattan in hand and seek an appointment in some institution of l'arnin—after I had tried everything else and failed! Congrats, O Sage, on getting out of it! I should "need more beefsteak" too, if I were to do a millionth part of what thou didst. If nocturnal home correction is to me such a burthen, you can fancy what sort of a classroom despot I would make. I'd last just about ten to fifteen minutes!

But my new and evanescent professional pedagogy is not my only contemporary care—would that it were! The United is bound for trouble again, this time because of the idiotic way some members have been nagging Cook about the lateness of the official organ. They ought to know that he is practically giving them this de luxe thing as an act of charity—but they don't; and instead of being grateful they ask for more! Such is mankind. These naggings, coupled with his scant sympathy (which I share) for the professionalism of the present editorship, have caused the worm to turn at last—and Cook has just sent me the rough draft of his resignation, as he means to forward it to Miss D. and Mrs. R. DAMNATION! Kin ya imagine the result? The year's programme ruined, and that nasty wretch Dowdell gloating and triumphant![3] I have written Culinarius a note of ultimate appeal, imploring him for the sake of old and hallowed memories not to desert the flag in time of need. Will he heed? I hope so! If not, back to Ericson—higher rates, less intelligent work, and just as much delay after all. It is that filthy Cleveland sewer-rat and that disgusting Columbus hippopotamus-jellyfish[4] who have done all the malevolent work by their raucous howls, and I fervently wish them both a swift and rough passage to the abode of Beëlzebub.

B/t/w—I s'pose youse geezers have saw the new BEARCAT.[5] What an odd contrast—essay by Martin and poem by Loveman—and that damned fool editor's own mouthings! Dowdell amuses me when he does not anger me. So he thinks his poor old Grandpa Lollius is boss of the United does he? Well, well, ain't it a shame! If I really were, you can wager that Dowdell would have been kicked out long ago—as he may be yet! "What will hold the recruit?" sneeringly quotes young William. "A rope!" he cynically replies. Well, Willie, I notice they ain't throwin' many ropes out in your direction! The only way the United will ever use a rope on that little thief is to give him a necktie party beneath the spreading sycamore or the genial telegraph pole! Oh, hell! But I must not sour my angelic nature by thinking of that unwashed brat. It'll make me cross with my pupils when I correct their mistakes! Let's turn to poetry—no, I mean my verse. I have really sworn off, but t'other day I received a touching request from young Nicol, out in dreary Saskatchewan (that's almost as dreary as Alberta, where Al Fred Willie lives!), who wants a few lines for his crude SARDONYX. I am a kind-hearted soul when I ain't mad, so within ten minutes I had scrawled off the following:[6]

ON READING LORD DUNSANY'S BOOK OF WONDER

> The hours of night unheeded fly,
> And in the grate the embers fade;
> Vast shadows one by one pass by
> In silent daemon cavalcade.

> But still the magick volume holds
> The raptur'd eye in realms apart,
> And fulgent sorcery enfolds
> The willing mind and eager heart.

The lonely room no more is there—
For to the sight in pomp appear
Temples and cities pois'd in air,
And blazing glories—sphere on sphere!

H. PLANTAGENET LYTTLEWYT

This reminds me of Gahal-Bah's postcard request for information on the 'tendencies of modern verse'.[7] Gracious! What do I know about modern verse? I should say, at a guess, that poetasters are striving after formlessness, obscure rhythm which is not rhythm at all, commonplaceness and colloquialism in language and imagery (naturalness, they call it!), introspectiveness, subjectivity, and merciless realism. Half with and half against the current is imagism—which is a species of idiocy wherein sensation replaces reason. I am mightily glad I have ceased to cultivate poesy. It's going to the dogs, and it would pain me to see it go if I were a poet. Let me see thy collegiate theme on the subject, O Parvule! And b.t.w.—congratulations on appointment to the debating team! Now Lawrence will win every contest of wits in sight! Happy will be the U. of Wis. next year!

Speaking of the "Carter" story, I have lately had another odd dream—especially singular because in it I possessed another personality—a personality just as definite and vivid as the Lovecraft personality which characterises my waking hours.

My name was Dr. Eben Spencer, and I was dressing before a mirror in my own room, in the house where I was born in a small village (name missing) of northern New York State. It was the first time I had donned civilian clothes in three years, for I was an army surgeon with the rank of 1st Lieut. I seemed to be home on a furlough—slightly wounded. On the wall was a calendar reading "FRIDAY, JULY 8, 1864". I was very glad to be in regular attire again, though my suit was not a new one, but one left over from 1861. After carefully tying my stock, I donned my coat and hat, took a cane from a rack downstairs, and sallied forth upon the village street. Soon a very young man of my acquaintance came up to me with an air of anxiety and began to speak in guarded accents. He wished me to go with him to his brother—my professional colleague Dr. Chester—whose actions were greatly alarming him. I, having been his best friend, might have some influence in getting him to speak freely—for surely he had much to tell. The doctor had for the past two years been conducting secret experiments in a laboratory in the attic of his home, and beyond that locked door he would admit no one but himself. Sickening odours were often detected near that door . . . and odd sounds were at times not absent. The doctor was aging rapidly; lines of care—and of something else—were creeping into his dark, thin face, and his hair was rapidly going grey. He would remain in that locked room for dangerously long intervals without food, and seemed uncannily saturnine. All questioning from the younger brother was met with scorn or rage—with perhaps a little uneasiness; so the brother was much worried, and stopped me on the street for advice and aid. I went with him to the Chester house—a white structure of two stories and attic in a pretty yard with a picket fence. It was in a quiet side street, where peace seemed to abide despite the trying nature of the times. In the darkened parlour, where I waited for some time, was a marble topped table, much haircloth furniture, and several pleasing whatnots covered with pebbles, curios, and bric-a-brac. Soon Dr. Chester came down—and *he had aged*. He greeted me with a saturnine smile, and I began to question him, as tactfully as I could, about his strange actions. At first he was rather defiant and insulting—he said with a sort of leer, "Better not ask, Spencer! Better not ask!" Then when I grew persistent (for by this time I was interested on my own account) he changed abruptly and snapped out, "Well, if you must know, come up!" Up two flights of stairs we plodded, and stood before the locked door. Dr. Chester opened it, *and there was an odour*. I entered after him, young Chester bringing up the rear. The room was low but spacious in area, and had been divided into two parts by an oddly incongruous red plush portiere. In the half next the door was a dissecting table, many bookcases, and several imposing cabinets of chemical and surgical instruments. Young Chester and I remained here, whilst the doctor went behind the curtain. Soon he emerged, bearing on a large glass slab what appeared to be a human arm, neatly severed just below the elbow. It was damp, gelatinous, and bluish-white, and the fingers were without nails. "Well, Spencer", said Dr. Chester sneeringly, "I suppose you've had a good deal of amputation practice in the army. What do you think, professionally, of this job?" I had seen clearly that this was not a human arm, and said sarcastically, "You are a better sculptor than doctor, Chester. This is not the arm of any living thing." And Chester replied in a tone that made my blood congeal, *"Not yet, Spencer, not yet!"* Then he disappeared again behind the portiere and emerged once more, bringing another and slightly larger arm. Both were left arms. I felt sure that I was on the brink of a great revelation, and awaited with impatience the tantalisingly deliberate motions of my sinister colleague. "This is only the beginning, Spencer," he said as he went behind the curtain for the third time. *"Watch the curtain!"* And now ends the fictionally available part of my dream, for the residue is grotesque anticlimax. I have said that I was in civilian clothes for the first time since '61—and naturally I was rather self-conscious. As I waited for the final revelation I caught sight of my reflection in the glass door of an instrument case, and discovered that my very carefully tied stock was awry. Moving to a long mirror, I sought to adjust it, but the black bow proved hard to fashion artistically, and then the whole scene began to fade—and damn the luck! I awaked in the distressful year of 1920, with the personality of H. P. Lovecraft restored! I have never seen Dr. Chester, or his young brother, or that village, since. I do not know what village it was. I never heard the name of Eben Spencer before or since. Some dream! If that happened to Co,[8] he would be surely seeking a supernatural explanation;

but I prefer actual analysis. The cause of the whole is clear—I had a few days before laid out Mrs. Shelley's "Frankenstein" for re-reading. As to details—Ambrose Bierce supplied the Civil War atmosphere, no doubt; whilst it is easy to trace in Dr. *Chester* and his brother—facially, I mean—the likenesses of my boyhood friends *Chester* and Harold Munroe; those brothers of whom I spoke in one of my ancient KLEICOMOLOES. I am not sleeping much this week, but last night I had a promising fragment of a dream that was cut short by premature awakening. I was alone in a black space, when suddenly, ahead of me, there arose out of some hidden pit a huge, white-robed man with a bald head and long snowy beard. Across his shoulders was slung the corpse of a younger man—cleanshaven, and grizzled of hair, and clad in a similar robe. A sound as of rushing wind or a roaring furnace accompanied this spectacular ascent—an ascent which seemed accompanied by some occult species of levitation. When I awaked, I had an idea for a story—but queerly enough, the idea had nothing to do with the dream![9]

At the recommendation of James F. Morton, Jr., I am perusing the works of a modern imaginative author named Algernon Blackwood—but Hell! I mentioned that before, didn't I! I can't say that I am very much enraptured, for somehow Blackwood lacks the power to create a really haunting atmosphere. He is too diffuse, for one thing; and for another thing, his horrors and weirdness are too obviously symbolical—symbolical rather than convincingly outré. And his symbolism is not of that luxuriant kind which makes Dunsany so phenomenal a fabulist. Just to see what he's like, youse fellers might read "Incredible Adventures", a collective of five very long "short" stories.[10] It ain't half bad, and if the first one tires you out, you are not compelled to swallow the remainder.

As to my friend Ed Plunkett—I am sorry to hear of the way the Middle West has treated him—not that the effete east was any too courteous.[11] Rascoe[12] of the CHITRIB sums the case up well when he speaks of the discrepancy betwixt the writings and personality of an author. But really, the publick should shew more tact. The only reason why an author leaves his privacy is because the morbid curiosity of the rabble about his face, figure, and favourite breakfast food drags him out. He does not wish to parade on a platform for two bucks a look! If the crowd like him not, the crowd alone is to blame for its disappointment. If left alone, he would never have come before it. Critics, expecting so much, sadly exaggerate the awkwardness of Dunsany. In absolute fact, he is a very tall, thin man with just a touch of awkwardness—and it is an engaging, boyish sort of awkwardness which does not offend the eye at all. His voice is *not* of the "mush-in-the-mouth" sort, but is merely a bit mellow and throaty after the British pattern, rather than thin and nasal after the Yankee style. Perhaps there is a slight lisp, but it appears only at rare intervals. Obviously he has been at pains to correct it. The only trouble with Dunsany as a public speaker is that he makes no pretence of *stage presence*. As a successful dramatist, one expects him to have a bit of the actor about him, but he is essentially of a non-dramatic type. His striving for dramatic effect is an intellectual one—exercised when he *writes*, not when he *reads* his plays. He addresses his audience not as a performer declaiming to a crowded pit, but as a gentleman entertaining friends in his own drawing-room. He is at home with his audience—he mingles with them in spirit, as it were, and is not conscious of the platform and the gulf it is supposed to create between reader and auditor. He makes no effort at bodily pose—he is merely himself. Accordingly he seats himself and crosses his long legs when he chooses, and occasionally resorts to the water-pitcher. But he does not do this in an absurd or ungraceful way. There is not a trace of the clown in his acts. As to that "dumping a pitcher of ice water over his head"—I rebel at the callous remark of a half-baked reporter who probably knows nothing of headaches. When he lectured at Boston I heard him remark after the address, in speaking to a friend, "I have a fearful headache". Now I know *all* about headaches. All there is to be known. Some of mine seem impossible to live through. And I know that if Edward J. M. D. Plunkett's are anything like mine, he *must* put water to his head when they are near their climax. He did not do so the night I saw him—in fact, he did not even rub his brow until after he had descended from the platform. But it takes no great amount of deduction to infer that in Chicago he was more sharply afflicted whilst on the platform. Instead of descending, he stuck it out like a stoic to please his audience—and in return a writer jests about his antics with the water-pitcher! I am eloquent about headaches tonight, because I have just emerged from a veritable "killer", contracted by working half the forenoon and all the afternoon on Bush junk. *I* have been using water on my forehead, and I give not a river-regula[to]r[13] on what any critick or reporter says of me!

I wonder that some of these journalists do not speak of Dunsany's face and expression—but they are obviously concerned only with things about which they can find fault. Dunsany is really handsome, and has one of the most kindly, winning, wholesome expressions I have ever beheld. Whether serious or whimsically humorous, his blue eyes are alight with an indefinable quality which makes one sure that he is a very good and very generous man. Dunsany left in my mind an exceedingly favourable impression—an impression which made me wish that he were a personal friend of mine. He is, I think, a trifle *unworldly*—if such may be said of a man who has travelled all over the globe and served through two wars.

Next on the programme is the Einstein theory, which I must confess at the outset that I cannot discuss authoritatively. I have as yet seen no really coherent account, and many of the articles by professors in local papers admit freely imperfect comprehension on the part of the respective writers. Einstein himself says that only twelve living men can fully comprehend his theory. I am intensely interested, and at the very beginning of the present publicity wrote McDonald for a key to the mystery. As you may or may not know, he teaches the history of science and mathematics as well as "Engineering English". His answer was—zero! Evidently he is not sure himself, and did not wish to let Grandpa see his deficiency. In such matters he is my very opposite—when I don't know a thing, I never try to cover up my lack. But now for my puerile observations. Einstein has two distinct theories—one relating to the nature of light, gravitation, and ether; the other relating to time and space. One of the two may be correct whilst the other is erroneous; and personally I think he is partly right on light and gravity but at sea on infinity and eternity. Coming down to the simple things I can comprehend—Einstein believes, and has apparently proved fairly well, that the direction of light can be changed by gravity. Not that light tends to follow anything but a straight line, but that gravity can act as a deflecting agent like refracting and reflecting media. Now the significance is this: if gravity can affect the course of a luminous ray, *then light does not consist of ether waves!* Think of the significance of this fact, if fact it be: All our basic theories of optics must be revised, and perhaps all our conceptions of radiant energy revolutionised. We are thrown back to my own beloved periwig days, when my old friend Ikey Newton held out for the old emission theory in spite of the undulatory doctrines of Huyghens and Euler! Back to the Queen Anne period! And woe unto Ambrose Bierce—his "Damned Thing" is altogether out of the running! Einstein is cautious—he confesses himself unable to explain the nature of light. He shows merely that the commonly accepted wave theory is improbable if not impossible, and shows this on a solid experimental basis—but further than that he is unable to go. It is worth noting that Einstein denies altogether the existence of the ether. For him there is no substance whatsoever in interplanetary and interstellar space; radiant energy being something substantial projected through utter nothingness. So far I have been speaking of Einstein's first and simpler theories. I cannot state my own position yet, for I am bewildered by the conflict of evidence. Eclipse observations certainly have shown a strange deflection of light rays by solar gravity; yet on the other hand, the mass of accumulated evidence in favour of ether-wave light is certainly immense. The conflict is baffling—no foot hath trod the new trail opened up. For mine own part, I am wondering whether or not some compromise theory cannot hit the truth. Perhaps there is an universal ethereal medium susceptible of waves, but perhaps wave-effect is only *for the conveyance of material particles susceptible of gravitational deflection.* I am slow—extremely slow—in relinquishing a theory which fulfils so many varied conditions as well as the wave theory fulfils them. Whatever of Einstein's may be true, it does not seem possible that the older doctrines can be utterly void of foundation. As with the periodic system in chemistry, we seem to be almost on the verge of some universal truth which eludes us! Lest I seem too reactionary in clinging somewhat to the older theories of light, let me say that the Einstein theory is not without its contradictions. In one point it fails to agree with observed phenomena, this being the displacement of the lines in the solar spectrum. So far the rapid displacement required by the theory has not been detected. This point, however, would positively disprove the larger and more complex relativity theory, but would not disprove the possibility of a material light affected by gravitation. The presence of one flaw makes it still possible to accept all of Einstein's work on a purely probational basis. Einstein has certain original ideas on the nature of gravitation itself; ideas partly conflicting with the law of Newton. These, however, have never been clearly explained in any article which I have yet seen. They seem to be involved inextricably in the theory of light, but to be independent of the general relativity theory—which scientists are slow in endorsing.

As to relativity on the whole, the commentator must proceed with extreme caution. As I said, I do not fully grasp the key to Herr Einstein's mode of thought; but so far as I can piece out his meaning from the unsatisfactory and fragmentary articles I have seen, I am inclined to think that he is falling into that most reprehensible habit of theorists—running ahead of experimental and practical science with speculations *for which observed phenomena and accepted hypotheses make no demand.* In other words, I think he is dipping into metaphysics and constructing some ingenious notions which *might* account for observed phenomena, but which are not *required* by the known conditions. This I deem a practice not to be encouraged. Such things as "dimensions" are merely terms invented to describe and define observed things. When we let the nomenclature run away with us and try to imagine conditions with one, two, three, four, five, or six "dimensions", we approach the borderland of sophism and fallacy. Now, O Galba, be not as glib as usual in calling Grandpa "dogmatic". (How youse two guys do overwork that woid in speaking of Theobaldian ideas—as if there *were* such a thing as "dogmatism" in science!) What I am trying to convey is this: that so far I have not seen any account of any natural phenomena which call for explanation by an hypothesis as extravagant as Einstein's. Is it not just possible that the personal equation and the desire of the individual enter in, as in religion? That is, is it not possible that Einstein has been influenced by a certain instinctive reaction against the starkly realistic conception of infinity and eternity? He may be right—I am not fighting yet—but how doth it look to thee, O Gahal-Bah? Remember, I judge from imperfect data. I may change my mind after reading some really authoritative article on the question. W. r. m.—for Pete's sake, Kid, send me anything you find about it. If it's something you don't wish to spare permanently, remember that Grandpa treats books and papers very carefully, and will pay the postage with pleasure for the sake of enlightenment.

If Einstein minimises the importance of present systems on the ground (O what familiar ground!) that human perception and conceptions are imperfect, he must be prepared to have the same objections levelled against his own doctrines. He contends, I seem to gather, that Time is a sort of motion in a hitherto unknown time-dimension. According to him, a clock runs slower when in motion, because it is bucking up against the current of Time itself. Now with all due respect to metaphysics and to Herr Einstein, and with due knowledge that the super-mind of Gahal-Bah will accuse me of "dogmaticism" (where t'ell didya get that spellin', kid?), I will venture the calm opinion—(mindya I said only *opinion*) that all this talk about Time and Space is damned nonsense. Whatever evidence there is for the relativity of Time and Space, I feel sure that the evidence for their absoluteness is vastly greater. Take Time, for example. Time is a definite thing. A planet revolves around the sun once—twice—thrice—and so on. There is a difference between one, two, and three. If its rate be uniform, something different has happened between the first, second, and third revolutions. What is the difference? It is Time—which is not an entity but a condition. At an uniform rate, two separate bodies always cover the same distance if they move in one direction simultaneously from a given point. Why does not one move farther than the other? Or in other words, there is a certain relation in Nature which causes certain things to occur concurrently, and which establishes a definite quality in certain processes whereby they occur in a fixed manner presenting them to our perception at a time when we are not perceiving corresponding stages of parallel processes. All this is the detached and abstract way of saying that there is such a thing as absolute *Time*—that some things are more swift than other things, and that the quality of swiftness is a definite one. Certain phenomena are evolutional, being characterised by continuous change. Such is the growth and development of an organic being or race of organic beings. We know that there is an absolute relation between this organic change and such changes as that of our planet's position in space, or of the place of some known star. We know that this organic change can be ranged by the side of other phenomena and found to conform to certain laws of uniformity. When the birth of two children reaches our perception simultaneously, we know that no matter what the subsequent conditions attending each, the future steps of their development will exhibit a correspondence. We know that there are no conditions whereby one will present himself to our perceptions as a child side by side with the presentation of the other as an adult. In other words, the development of organic beings is measured by a certain inexorable law of duration which we must call something—and might as well call *Time*. If our senses are not reliable in informing us of the various time-relations; if there is no such thing as order and precedence as we know it, then our perceptive apparatus is strangely out of harmony with that regularity which seems omnipresent in the cosmos. Einstein tears down more than he realises! For my part, I cannot say that my conception of Time is at all shaken. The contrary evidence cannot outweigh the vast bulk of perfectly consistent and intimately correlated evidence in support of the generally accepted notions.

Much the same thing applies to space. We know that there is such a thing as distance. No matter how unreal the evidence of our senses may be, it is positive that the relation of Providence and Pawtucket is different from the relation of Providence and Appleton. No geometrical scheme can make it possible for a man to journey from Providence to Appleton with the same amount of energy which takes him from Providence to Pawtucket, or to reach Appleton with a perception of as little change in the position of the sun and stars as that experienced in reaching Pawtucket. In other words, it takes more time and energy to get to Appleton than to get to Pawtucket; shewing that Providence and Appleton have a fixed relation which is different from the fixed relation of Providence and Pawtucket. Nothing can controvert this—the evidence of the human senses cannot be made to vary, so that even if they are delusive, a true difference exists in the same ratio as that which appears to exist. Now what applies to this small globe applies as well to outer space. By methods as definite and conclusive as those which demonstrate terrestrial relations, we have established a knowledge of certain celestial relations. We know, for example, that we are nearer the sun than Saturn is; and we know that this relation is of exactly the same sort as that involved in terrestrial distances. The solar system is positively no illusion—its dimensions exist in *exactly* the same absolute manner as those of a small orrery standing on the neighbouring table. As the ball of the orrery representing Jupiter is to the ball of the orrery representing Mercury, so *in every respect* is the actual planet Jupiter to the actual planet Mercury. There is positively not the least ground for denying this exceedingly obvious and overwhelmingly supported truth. So far, so good. Of course, the facilities for measuring siderial space—[*sic*] parallax and spectrum displacement, are less direct than those available for measuring the solar system. In the latter case, there are means of confirming the parallax results, and the conditions for noting parallax are much more favourable. But the perfect consistency of the results which have been attained, and the prodigiously great probability—practical certainty—that all known laws are not arbitrarily and abruptly broken off at some definite point at the artificial "boundary of the solar system", make it impossible for us to doubt seriously the reality of space and magnitude as universal, cosmical things. That a definite order which holds good so far as we can see should break off just beyond our perception, is inconceivable. How odd that the limit of familiar nature should coincide so exactly with the limit of our perception! Altogether, no really open mind can conceive of any boundary to space. Space and distance are proven to be real things, and this having been proved, it is impossible to limit them. The relation of Providence to Appleton has a positive analogue in the relation of the earth to the sun, and to deny that the analogy cannot extend to the relation of the solar system to Canopus would be puerile. So while freely conceding Einstein a place among real scientists, and eagerly looking for truth in his observations upon light, I must respectfully decline to take seriously his attack upon the fundamental structure of all things. He has not shewn us, or at least the prevalent articles on his system have not shewn us, any definite thing about our sense which justifies our substituting for recognised perception some equally uncertain and much less probable alternative series of perceptions. I await further light.

As a closing word on Einstein, I will add that many scientists reject his speculations *in toto,* believing that even the observed deflection of starlight during solar eclipses is due to refraction by some hitherto unsuspected outer atmosphere of the sun. This may prove the end of all the perplexity—an end reached by the complete rejection of Einsteinism.

I cannot resist taking a fling, at this point, at Galba's too hasty mode of jumping at conclusions. (Pardon the awkwardly repeated *at's!*) He confidently states that Grandpa cares no more for astronomy because no mention has been made in these epistles of the silly maunderings of "Prof." Porta.[14] Really, Child, I thought better of yuh! It never occurred to me to mention something which by its extravagance and baselessness is altogether excluded from serious thought, and I am honestly surprised that one with Galba's vast store of information should accept anything like the Porta farce as being in any way connected with sober astronomical matters. To be blunt, there was nothing in Porta's outburst to capture the attention of a real astronomical student for so much as a second. It was pure amateur charlatanry, since anyone having a primer knowledge of planetary motions realises that combinations almost as "ominous" as that of Dec. 17 are of constant and un-disastrous occurrence. Searching history for precedents; one can easily see that no conspicuous weather perturbations have attended these groupings of the planets. Moreover, the large planets move so slowly, that the practical effects of the "pull" would have been manifest long before December in this particular case. Hadst thou been exercising thy usual alertness, O Babe, thou couldst have detected the earmarks of charlatanry in the extravagant *language* of the "Professor". (Who is an unknown amateur with a little home-made tin telescope and a few old almanacks, out somewhere on the Pacific Coast.) Pipe this "give-away" flourish—cheap stuff:

> "Owing to a strange grouping of six mighty planets, such as has not been seen in a score of centuries, the United States (why only the U.S.?) next December will be swept by the most terrific weather cataclysm experienced since human history began.
>
> It will be caused by the hugest sun-spot on record—a sun-spot that will be visible to the naked eye. (How wonderful!)
>
> Since men first began to make a record of events, no sun-spot has been large enough to be seen without the aid of instruments. (Haw! Ya damn liar, there have been dozens! I've seen one myself, and such things have been announced in the papers scores of times within the past decade.) This one will be.
>
> The sun-spot that will appear December 17, 1919, will be a vast wound in the side of the sun. (Ya fathead, sun-spots never appear suddenly, in one day—they form gradually, developing in intensity like cyclonic storms.)

It will be a gigantic explosion (sic) of flaming gases, leaping hundreds of thousands of miles out into space. It will have a crater large enough to engulf the earth, much as Vesuvius might engulf a football. (Ya poor boob, any ordinary sun-spot is like that! I knew as much when I was eleven years old—wonder how *old* you are, Porta old sport?)

Such a sun-spot will be rich enough in electro-magnetic energy to fling the atmosphere of our planet into a disturbance without precedence (spose ya mean *precedent,* ol'scout!) or parallel." (O mother, shoot me while I'm happy! If every spot that size could do all that harm, we'd be havin' cataclysms 'bout every year!)

Well, Kid, is this enough nonsense to quote? An' tuh think you expected Grandpa to discuss this seriously in the GALLOMO! Only one person ever mentioned this thing to me—a mediocre correspondent who sent me the clipping of the prophecy wherefrom I quote. I replied in explanatory vein, but never thought of mentioning it to a guy of Mogal's mental calibre! Later I saw some clever spoofin' about the thing in the papers, but no one took the affair to heart. The best comment I saw was in the CLARION—young Keller gave the event a witty write-up. It seems that some sensationalist must have magnified the Porta prophecy to a prediction of the end of the world—though I never heard that till I saw the CLARION. One word more, O Boylet. Not long ago I saw an item about Porta's claim that present weather conditions had verified his raving. Haw! We've had some weather, all right, but Porta said it was coming from a sun-spot—and *there ain't been no big sunspot!* Porta's claim of "verification" is about as sound as the claim of the average charlatan! I can imagine that B. L. T.[15] and his contribs may have had a good time about the joke, and wish I had seen some of the colyum matter published during the crucial period.

Speaking of astronomical things—is either of youse guys interested in (a) the supposed new trans-Neptunian planet, (b) the talk of telegraphic communication with Venus or Mars, and (c) the Goddard plan for sending a rocket to the moon? If so, just speak up! Grandpa has heaps to say about all these things!

T'anks fer de remarks on "Dagon", kid! I rather liked that thing myself. It was written in 1917, and is the second tale I wrote after resuming my fictional pen after a nine years' lapse. I think I told youse ginks that I quit writing fiction in 1908, despairing of my ability to shape anything with the grace of a Poe. I went over all my old MSS., bade most of them a last farewell, and saved out only two—"The Beast in the Cave", written in April, 1905, when I was 14 years and 7 months old, and "The Alchemist", which I had just finished. Thereafter I sent in "The Alchemist" for a credential; thinking that in an immature organisation stories might be better appreciated than verse or essay matter. I never expected to see that published, but later the chance came, and I tinkered with it a while, preparing the slightly revised version which appeared in 1916. So far I had never thought of resuming my old pastime. But then I chanced to send Culinarius "The Alchemist", and he immediately told me that fiction is my one and only province! Mildly amused, I sent him the "Beast", which he snapped up as though it were worth printing. My stock of tales was now quite exhausted, but Cook kept urging me to improve my supposed gift for weird tales, so I decided to revive the old atmosphere. For a long time I was too indolent to do anything, but one June day in 1917 I was walking through Swan Point Cemetery with my aunt and saw a crumbling tombstone with a skull and crossbones dimly traced upon its slaty surface; the date, 1711, still plainly visible. It set me thinking. Here was a link with my favourite aera of periwigs—the body of a man who had worn a full-bottom'd wig and had perhaps read the original sheets of *The Spectator*. Here lay a man who had lived in Mr. Addison's day, and who might easily have seen Mr. Dryden had he been in the right part of London at the right time! Why could I not talk with him, and enter more intimately into the life of my chosen age? What had left his body, that it could no longer converse with me? I looked long at that grave, and the night after I returned home I began my first story of the new series—"The Tomb". My narrative pen was very rusty—believe me, boys, very rusty indeed! To drop back into the forms of fiction was exceeding hard after nine quiescent years, and I feared that the result would be the limit of absurdity. But the spell of the gruesome was upon me, and I finally hammered out the hideous tale of Jervas Dudley. At last—a Poe again! Honestly, I was afraid to send the deuced thing to Cook—especially afraid because he had himself just begun to write stories again after an eleven year lapse, and said he had lost all his talent. I really felt that the new attempt was inferior both to the "Beast" and "Alchemist". Meanwhile I had been reading Poe again—for about the ten millionth time. The new or rather revived mood was hard to dismiss, and after limbering up my style a bit with practice work I perpetrated "Dagon" in August. To me it seemed better than "The Tomb"— smoother, less halting and angular. I felt that my practice had done me a bit of good. Meanwhile Cook paid me a personal call—in September. We talked about everything under the sun, and in observing some little rusticities and plebeianisms in his dress and demeanour, I lost some of my awe for his fictional greatness. Before he bade me a reluctant farewell, I had placed the manuscript of "The Tomb" in his hands—not being quite ready to part with "Dagon", which I was still polishing in places. With eagerness I awaited Cook's verdict on my revived art—and fancy my delight when he wrote enthusiastically, saying my new tale immeasurably surpassed all my juvenile attempts, and declaring he would print it in his de luxe MONADNOCK at some indefinite future date! Tickled, I at once began work on "Psychopompos"—as yet unable to cast off my beloved heroicks altogether, even in fiction. Duties pressed, and I worked slowly. "Psychopompos" was abandoned midway, and not resumed till the summer of 1918, when I sent it to Cook and received a glowing acknowledgment. My egotism was now becoming almost Galpinian again, and I hustled with a new yarn—"Polaris"—which you fellers saw before anyone else. That really was an important milestone in muh brilliant career—for its unconscious resemblance to the work of Dunsany is all that finally led to my acquaintance with that then unknown source of inspiration. My next job was more mechanical.[16] A singular dream had led me to start a nameless story about a terrible forest, a sinister beach, and a blue, ominous sea. After writing one paragraph I was stalled, but happened to send it to Mrs. Jordan. Fancy my surprise when the poetess replied that she had had a precisely similar dream, which, however, went further. In her dream a piece of the shore had broken off, carrying her out into the sea. A green meadow had loomed up on the left hand side, and horrible entities seemed to be hiding among the trees of the awful forest behind her. The piece of earth on which she was drifting was slowly crumbling away, yet this form of death seemed preferable to that which the forest things would have inflicted. And then she heard the sound of a distant waterfall and noted a kind of singing in the green meadow—at which she awaked. It must have been quite some dream, for she drew a map of it and suggested that I write a story around it. After a little consideration I decided that this dream made my own proposed story a back number, so I abandoned my plan and used my original opening paragraph in the new story. Just as I was speculating how I should infuse a little life and drama into the rather vague fragment, my mother broke down, and I partially broke down as a result of the shock. For two months I did nothing—in fact, I can hardly remember what I even thought during those two months—I know I managed to perform some imperative amateur work mechanically and half-consciously, including a critical report or two. When I emerged, I decided to add piquancy to the tale by having it descend from the sky in an aerolite—as Galba knows, for I sent the thing to him. I accordingly prepared an introduction in very prosaic newspaper style, adding the tale itself in a hectic Poe-like vein—having it supposed to be the narrative of an ancient Greek philosopher who had escaped from the earth and landed on some other planet—but who found reason to regret his rashness. As it turned out, it is practically my own work all through, but on account of the Jordanian dream-skeleton I felt obliged to concede collaboration, so labelled it "By Elizabeth Neville Berkeley and Lewis Theobald, Jun." I sent it to Cook, who will soon print it. Then came "Beyond the Wall of Sleep"—written spontaneously after reading an account of some Catskill Mountain degenerates in a N. Y. TRIBUNE article on the New York State Constabulary.[17] By this time I was beginning to hear Dunsanian urgings, but I paid them scant attention. My next—"Juan Romero"—was written merely as a reaction from copying a dull yarn by Phil Mac.[18] He had made such a commonplace adventure yarn from such a richly significant setting, that I yearned to shew what ought to be done with such a setting. Youze gazinks have seen both Mac's and my yarns. And then, having been told so often that my "Polaris" was exactly like Dunsany, I idly began to read "A Dreamer's Tales"! The rest is history—or would be if I amounted to anything. I had a new interest in life—EDWARD JOHN MORETON DRAX PLUNKETT. A week before I had wished to die—now I had something to live for! In succession have appeared "The White Ship", "The Street", "The Doom that Came to Sarnath", "The Statement of Randolph Carter", "The Terrible Old Man", and "The Tree"—this last being the living tree yarn which I choked off when I thought The Boy was going to publish his Bog-Batty without spoiling it with a realistic ending.[19] In a word, Dunsany has restored my lost childhood, and I am again spinning stories for the pure fun of it—just as I used to do from 1897 to 1908. Viva Plunkett!

Well My Gawd—wot a lotta space I ben wastin' on muhself!! Galba, your introspection and autobiographical fluency is ketchin'! By the way—my Dunsanian library is getting enlarged. My mother has just given me "The Gods of Pegana", and as a token of gratitude for lending her the "Dreamers' [*sic*] Tales", Miss McGeoch[20] has just ordered Little Brown & Co. to send me the Bierstadt biography—"Dunsany the Dramatist"! That's wot I calls high int'rust for merely lendin' a small book, believe muh! Now I'm gonna lend the Tales to Cook—wonder if he'll print me a CONSERVATIVE for the favour? As to professional publication of the fabulae Theobaldianae as a book—ferget it, kid! Upstarts and nobodies have to finance their own books—I know, because Sherman, French & Co. made me what they called an "offer" after reading my ode for Jul. 4, 1917, in the NATIONAL MAGAZINE.[21] And I hain't so anxious to squirm into the publick eye that I'd risk six hundred iron men on a damn fool scheme that would never pay. No, gents, I ain't got no ambition whatsoever! The older I grow, the more futile life seems to me. What does fame mean? What would I do with it? Would it make any difference to me if my work were mentioned in the ATLANTICK and the leading reviews? It would be fun at first, but I'll wager I'd be tired of it all in two weeks. Life is an empty thing, and if one can keep reasonably contented, and dismiss thoughts of suicide, he ought to be satisfied. I write what I feel like writing because I feel like it. The writing is all the fun—I am even getting less eager for amateur publication. To think out a plot and raise in fitting language some image of horror or fantasy—that is now my favourite indoor sport. To prove that my words are true—I have not even tried to place "Sarnath" anywhere! If I can extract a good word from a few gazinks—Mogal, Loveman, Cook, or Morton, my egotism is entirely satisfied. For the publick I have only profound contempt—dear, dear, how theatrical that sounds! Oh, b.t.w.—at the repeated nagging of my aunt I sent "The Tomb" to THE BLACK CAT, and received it back in a month with nothing but an insulting printed rejection slip. I am not sorry for the incident, for after this I can with clear conscience turn a deaf ear to all who urge me on toward publicity!

Concerning radicalism—I see no excuse for tolerating it in any form. The more radicals are allowed to utter both orally and in print, the quicker their nasty doctrines will spread. Cut off their advertising, and a good work is done. I wished to suppress the Wahlstrom article in THE CREDENTIAL, but Mrs. R. insisted on its retention with a footnote—and that footnote has aroused Campbell.[22] Another time I would withdraw all support from THE CREDENTIAL unless the offending article were removed. As it is, I am going to have a word to say about Campbell's position—am going to tell him he ought to be ashamed of himself. This reminds me—I have recently joined the Loyal Coalition of Boston, which is fighting the Sinn Fein movement in America, and wish youse guys would join also.[23] Any contribution of a dollar or more makes you a member. The object of the Coalition is to combat with propaganda the deadly and insidious campaign of Irish hyphenates to intimidate our venal and vote-craving politicians into recognising the mythical "Irish Republic" and thereby committing an international crime against that friendly power and motherland whose continued friendship means more to civilisation than anything else. Few realise the perilous nature of the agitation which criminals like that mongrel wretch De Valera[24] are conducting against Anglo-American harmony. The passage of such a thing as that infamous Mason bill providing for diplomatic recognition of a seceded Ireland would be an indescribable calamity—it has been said that it would cause the British ambassador to withdraw. These Irish malcontents, with their vast power to "swing the Oirish vote", must be killed off or throttled somehow, and to do this the Loyal Coalition is leaving no stone unturned. Its battles with Hearst's slimy BOSTON AMERICAN are refreshing to read of. I have promised the Coalition to circulate their printed matter widely through the United, and intend to mail a judicious selection with every issue of the UNITED CO-OPERATIVE,[25] besides having an anti-Irish editorial in that paper. I enclose one of the booklets—Gal to Mo, Mo to Lo. I am asking for its return because I have relatively few of these, and cannot get them at less than a nickel apiece. I wish the contents to reach as many amateur eyes as possible. Later I shall send both of you more matter—to keep. I suppose Galba will have a sneer ready—but these Micks have got to be crushed despite the sneers of all the 18-year-olds in or out of the nursery! If either or both of you can find time to help in distributing Coalition matter and fighting the Sinn Fein, let me know; and I will see that you receive a goodly supply of printed matter, including the booklet I am now asking you to return. I first heard of the organisation from Mrs. Jordan, who is so devoted to the cause that she does secretarial work at the offices two or three days every week without remuneration. I later heard of it from Miss Hamlet, whose aunt is equally active in its behalf. It certainly deserves all the support anyone can give it, for the Sinn Feiners in this country are a devilish force; with dangerous opportunities to influence politicians. A word of advice to those who take Sinn Fein propaganda lightly: remember the German propaganda, and how some adjective-adorned fools laughed at it at first, and then kicked themselves when they found out how real a menace it was! As to prohibition—I doubt if any gradual process could have equalled the eighteenth amendment in real efficacy. If anything is too drastic it is not the amendment, but the Volstead law. Undoubtedly some of the provisions for drastic enforcement are excessive and troublesome to the medical profession; but when one reflects on the abuse of privilege sometimes practiced by that same profession, one is less sympathetic. I doubt if any reaction of dangerous strength could ever develop against the amendment, because the whole question is so infinitely less grave than other matters confronting the country—matters involving the existence of all civilisation. There will never be harmony during the present generation, but when a new generation, largely unused to drink, grows up, I fancy that pro-liquor sentiment will sink to a minimum. Galba's rage and disgust at the prohibition of bibulous idiocy in the individual seem to me ill-founded. The number of drunken men must be reduced, irrespective of principle. O Principle, how many sins are committed in thy name! A man who gets drunk is not merely an idiot but a potential menace to society. Drink has turned law-abiding men to murderers many times before, and will many times again. Let there be as few as possible of these cases. Of course, the manufacture and traffic is the great thing to strike at, but if you allow home brewing and distilling, and free possession of liquor, you will have a good-sized share of drunkenness left. For that matter—we still have. But the more firm the law the less we shall have. Remember that all the object of this prohibition reform, however the movement may assume various aspects in its various phases of operation, is this: *to keep men from becoming intoxicated.* Anything tending toward this is proper. Anything tending in an opposite direction is mere sophistry.

I was afraid those disjointed things bored you, but since they seem not to have done so, I will give you a few more, as I have recorded them for future fictional development in my commonplace-book. Remember, gents, that these crude sketches are the mere dreams themselves, not the stories. I relate only exactly what I dreamed, not what I am going to build up around the dreams.

I

I was walking or rather wading through a seemingly interminable and treeless marsh, under a leaden sky. My companion was an old man—a man so old that he frightened me, although I felt that I knew, or had once known him. His white hair streamed about his shoulders, and his beard nearly trailed the ground. Despite his age, he was stronger than I, for he set a pace that fatigued me. Then suddenly I saw a lonely house upon the horizon ahead. It was a very ancient house—a New-England farmhouse of the type built from 1640 to 1680, with a peaked and exceedingly steep roof, and shingled over all its surface. It appeared to be rotten—in the last stages of decay. As we approached the house, the old man said to me, "It has not changed". I did not reply. Then he said, "For two hundred years it has not changed". I remained silent. Then he said, "You were foolish to wait and be re-born; I am wiser, and have lived all along." As he said this, I fancied I remembered him. He was now clad in a garment so discoloured and nondescript that I could not analyse it—it may have been a mere robe made of old burlap sacks sewed together—but as I have remembered him he was young, clad in high boots and red coat, and having a black full-bottomed wig and three-cornered hat. His face in this vague memory was smooth, although bluish from the shaven roots of a prodigious growth of beard. Then I said "It has not changed". We approached and entered the house, finding the interior a mass of fallen plaster and general ruin. Up a rotting staircase we began to climb, and the old man said, "We shall find it just as before". And I said, "The thing is still the same after two centuries, we shall find it above". Still we climbed. The house had but two stories, but the top of the ancient staircase seemed no nearer. Up, up, up—until the walls about us melted into mist and swirling cloud—yet ever on and up—on and up—"We shall find it as of yore—it has not changed".—on and up—on and up—and there ended the dream!

II

I was in an ancient castle at the foot of a damp stone staircase. All about me were men-at-arms—every churl of them fast asleep! I seemed enraged, and shook several of them, yet could not rouse them. The castle seemed to be my own. I then clanked interminably up the staircase—for I had on armour and a heavy sword—until sounds from the plain below arrested my attention. Peering down through a narrow window I beheld our men of England, mounted, and with red tabards bearing the golden lions of Britain over their armour, in mortal combat with an unknown foe. The foe was also mounted and armoured, and wore tabards of yellow with red dragons depicted thereon. The fight grew demoniacally furious, and I experienced a wild desire to get into it. Then the leader of our men rode out before the army and challenged the leader of the foe to single combat. The challenge was accepted and the two armies drew back, leaving an open space between. The leader of the foe was a mighty figure in his heavy armour, and the fight was fierce. Finally the foeman was unhelmeted by our leader—*but beneath that helm there was no head*. At this moment the whole force of the enemy seemed to melt from sight, and I also felt a change. No longer was I at the window, but on an horse before the ranks of our men, a gigantic sword unsheathed in my hand. At this point I remembered the window on the staircase, and recalled with a start that the face of our leader had been the exact replica of my own. I glanced about, and on my left saw the form of a vast and interminable castle whose turrets reached up into the clouds beyond visibility. Then the dream abruptly changed, and though I did not awake, was conscious of drifting down some hideous stagnant river in a rotting boat, between terrible overhanging cliffs of basalt. There was no wind, and I wondered why I moved down so still a stream. The insects were of strange form, and made me shudder as their numbers increased and they began to light all over me—I had been sleeping at my table, my head resting on my arm.[26]

III

I was in a museum of antiquities somewhere in Providence, talking with the curator, a very old and very learned man. I was trying to sell him an odd bas-relief which I had just modelled myself from clay. The old man laughed at me, and asked me what I meant by trying to sell a new thing of my own workmanship to a museum of ancient things. I answered him in words which I remember exactly—a rare thing for me. Usually I recall no exact words beyond isolated sentences from my dreams. I said:

"Why do you say that this thing is new? The dreams of men are older than brooding Egypt or the contemplative Sphinx, or garden-girdled Babylon, and this thing was fashioned in my dreams."

Then the curator bade me shew him my product, which I did. It was of old Egyptian design, apparently portraying priests of Ra in procession. The man seemed horror stricken, and asked in a terrible whisper—"WHO ARE YOU?" I told him that my name was H. P. Lovecraft—adding that I was the grandson of Whipple V. Phillips, who I thought would probably be better known to a man so old. He replied "No, no,—*before that!*" I said that I had no memories before that save in dreams. Then the curator offered a high price, which I refused; because I saw from his face that he meant to destroy my sculpture as soon as it was his—whereas I wished it hung in the museum. My refusal clearly perturbed the man, who asked me to name my own price. Humorously, I cried "One million pounds sterling!" (currency mixed up!), when to my amazement the old man did not laugh, but looked only more deeply worried. He had taken me seriously! Then he said in a perplexed, baffled, frightened tone, "I will consult with the directors of the institution—please call a week from today." I do not think the dream ended there, but I recall nothing beyond. My remembrance of dreams is often affected by a sort of sense of unity—I can recall only things which have a connected sequence, hence my narratives stop as soon as the main subject is exhausted. Dream II in this letter is exceptional in this regard.[27]

But enough of dreams. When the weather is hottest, and I am therefore at my best, I shall weave many of these nocturnal phantasies into short stories, though I am aware that the amateur press can never accomodate them all, especially now that Culinarius hath failed us. And speaking of stories—Mocrates, never mind about Mocraftising that "Beyond the Wall of Sleep" of mine. The comparative comment of Loveman, Morton, and other authorities places it so much below "Dagon" that I am sure you could not possibly have any success with it. Try "Dagon", if you want a story to experiment on. My British recruit, James Hull Goss—who is a teacher—says that he has taken the liberty to try to place "Beyond the Wall of Sleep" in some British professional magazine without securing my permission. Nice fellow, Goss, but he doesn't know what a hopeless task he hath undertaken!

Some diary! Well, I got news this trip, fellers! EDWARD JOHN MORETON DRAX PLUNKETT, 18th BARON DUNSANY, is the 1920 Laureate Judge of Poetry for the United Amateur Press Association! Yep—'s true! I thought of the thing a month or two ago, but did not dare write Ed. Then I decided that he might prove kind if the letter came from one with whom he had previously corresponded, so I asked Miss Hamlet to write him, which she did % the J. B. Pond Lyceum Bureau. For a long time no answer came, and we gave him up for lost. Miss Durr[28] asked me to find another judge, and I wrote a Capt. Fielding-Reid of Baltimore, one of the Bookfellows.[29] But Friday Miss Hamlet received a telegram from Ed accepting the post!! The letter had chased him all around the British Isles, finally reaching him at his mother's place, Dunstall Priory, Shoreham, Sevenoaks, Kent. So the 18th Baron is ours!! Think what it will mean to have Lord Dunsany's name at the head of our Honorary Membership list all next year!! And that gives us an excuse to send him papers and the like!! I vow, I shall get out a CONSERVATIVE some time soon if I have to blow a safe to cop the coin—just for the sake of having something to send Dunsany.[30] I will take care that one of my Dunsanian tales, plus some critical puff of Dunsany himself, shall appear therein. At least, that is my momentary dream—probably I shall do nothing of the sort in reality! I hope the Convention will frame a nice resolution of thanks to send him. But amidst this burst of felicity I am not unmindful of the lowlier writers. A week ago I asked Fielding-Reid to serve, so the question naturally arose: what the hell shall I do if he accepts? I hate to offend any person who has graciously consented to perform a favour, and to shelve Fielding-Reid after asking him seemed rather awkward. To relieve this embarrassing situation I devised the following simple plan: to resurrect the obsolescent short verse class, enter the requisite number of "pomes" without the respective authors' consent, and send it to Fielding-Reid as if nothing had happened—he'd never know the difference, and would fancy he was doing just what we asked in the first place. I had said "short poems" anyway, so that he would not be discouraged from the task—providential adjective! So I have notified Miss Durr, and sent the list of entries to Mrs. Campbell,[31] requesting both to deal with Fielding-Reid as they would have originally. Thus if he accepts, we shall have an extra Laureate Class this year; though if he does not accept, the thing can be dropped. But believe muh, boys, I sure am tickled at Dunsany's acceptance. A damn good fellow, if ya ask me! Vivat Dunsanius!

Anent the Rt. Hon. Samuel Langhorn[e] Clemens, I read the Bradford critique in the ATLANTICK,[32] and now have from the library both "What is Man?" and "The Mysterious Stranger".[33] I never read any of his work before, on account of a sort of instinctive doubt of the solid worth of native American authors aside from those of the Atlantick Coast, but from considering the depth of philosophical reasoning in "What is Man?" I am coming to believe that Clemens was a genuine genius. Really, the old fellow agrees with me to a surprising extent regarding the human ape, which at once proves his greatness! I think I shall like Marcus—I may even read his humorous works.

As to any especial "creed of speculative scepticism", as Gahal-Bah describes his present need, I would advise Epicureanism as a base. That old geezer had the right idea, and drew from the right sources, largely my old friend Democritus. Read Lucretius' "De Rerum Natura" for the best possible exposition of this unsurpassed philosophy. There are many reasons why moderns can never surpass Epicurus, among them racial inferiority. We are certainly as far below the Greeks as, for example, the Mongolians are below us. That Pelasgian stock which gave rise to the dominant qualities of the Greeks and Romans alike has no parallel today. As to a creed of pure and absolute selfishness, O Child, I should have to ascertain exactly what you mean before criticising it. Certainly, selfishness is the only strong motive force in human life, but it must be restrained and guided. It is on this point that poor Nietzsche loses track of reason. The general tranquillity of that part of mankind which is most highly organised and sensitive is the logical aim of life. This really means the general tranquillity of the whole, for to concede unusual privileges to lower and coarser elements would not give them enough happiness to make up for that taken from elements which are more capable of feeling pleasure and pain. In order to establish this general tranquillity, everyone must sacrifice a little for the general good. If no one made sacrifices, no harmonious existence would be possible; if only a few made sacrifices, to benefit the majority, they would soon tire of it and revert to primal selfishness. And if the majority made all the sacrifices to benefit the few, the equilibrium would be equally unstable. A civilised order can be maintained only by the sacrifice of power by the ignorant and coarse, and the sacrifice of superfluous emotion by the educated and refined. The animal-like labourer must refrain (if he can be made to do so) from using his physical strength to overturn his superiors and rise to the leadership of a savage state, whilst the man of position must sacrifice the natural impulsiveness which if unchecked would cause conflict and wreck the cultural fabric which his mind has evolved. Neither, for purely selfish reasons, can afford to be selfish! It actually pays, in the end, to make the necessary small sacrifices. The Old Man in "What Is Man?" speaks the purest wisdom when he tells the Young Man: "Diligently train your ideals upward and still upward toward a summit where you will find your chiefest pleasure in conduct, which, while contenting you, will be sure to confer benefits upon your neighbour and the community." Yes, Sir— Clemens was a deep, realistic, and accurate thinker—I have done him injustice in neglecting him heretofore. These are the hard, cold, practical facts which the Christians twist to suit themselves, enshroud with a cloak of idealistic nonsense, and metamorphose into a code of abasement and self-inflicted misery. They scorn pleasure and speak of the "sanctity" of sacrifice. We exalt pleasure, but know that the greater pleasures are obtainable only by the sacrifice of the lesser; so that we recognise sacrifices as plain common sense rather than sanctity. And we know—or ought to know—that the greater pleasures are not hectic or animalistic things, but delicate aesthetic perceptions and unemotional tranquillity. Those are the only pleasures that last, and that are not conducive to subsequent pains which more than neutralise them. The hedonist, following Aristippus and Gidlow–Mills,[34] believes in seeking the wildest delights of sense, and in accepting all the consequences both to the individual and to society. That is what he calls "living"—the poor fish! He thinks the calm and unemotional Epicurean is only half alive; that he actually misses something in avoiding the violent alternation of emotional exaltation and depression. But it would not take long to demonstrate that the Epicurean loses less pleasure and escapes more pain in the long run, thus ending up with a better balance than the hedonist. And if the hedonist shall say to him that he has missed "life" by his even course, he can fling back the unanswerable reply—"Well, what the hell of it?" Pleasure is purely relative and measured by the attitude and emotional and intellectual organisation of the individual. Probably the sensual hedonist secures very little more pleasure at any time than the delicate and finely organised Epicurean who lives his calmer, more ethereal life; whilst of course he is continually subject to agonising emotional reactions and depressions which the colder man escapes altogether. As a matter of fact, the hedonist does not "live" any more than the Epicurean. He merely lives differently and on a less highly evolved plane. The hedonist has much more in common with the religious man than with the rational Epicurean. The crude emotional attitude of the Christian toward what he calls deity, and the spasms of sloppiness into which he goes about what he calls "universal love" are mere perverted manifestations of the same physical and psychic forces that drive the hedonist to his riot of apparently opposed but actually analogous sense-gratification. Above all this mess of emotional overdevelopment stands the Epicurean rationalist; his emotions educated down to insignificance, and his higher qualities cultivated for the benefit of himself and of society. I am aware that these candid opinions of mine are not very well calculated to pleasure either of my readers, but must enunciate them in the interest of truth and unprejudiced investigation. Galba will see that I am not likely to favour his plan of 'developing his emotional senses more strongly'. Believe me, kid, emotion is a false will o' the wisp. There is only one quality in man or for that matter in all the cosmos that calls for anything like worship. Only one quality which represents really exalted evolution and finely organised complexity of structure—and that quality is REASON. If thou wouldst know what is God, I answer thee, REASON!

Notes

1. Hughesdale is a neighborhood in Johnston, RI, about 6.5 miles due west of Providence.

2. Josephine L. Abbott (1840–1928) was principal of the young ladies' school at 280 Benefit Street in Providence from 1873 until 1892, when she married Francis A. Gaskill. HPL's aunt Annie Gamwell was a member of the class of 1885 of Miss Abbott's school.

3. HPL had opposed Dowdell for official editor of the UAPA in the election of July 1919 (see "For Official Editor—Anne Tillery Renshaw").

4. I.e., Dowdell and Ida C. Haughton, a member of the Woodbees (an amateur group in Columbus) and a vehement opponent of HPL.

5. I.e., *Dowdell's Bearcat*, Dowdell's amateur journal. The issue in question is that of December 1919, containing Harry Martin's "James Russell Lowell as a Poet and Critic" (1–4) and Samuel Loveman's translation "A Song of Chamisso's" (5).

6. John R. Nicol. It is not known if HPL's poem appeared in the journal. The poem did appear in the *Silver Clarion* (March 1920).

7. See Galpin's "Some Tendencies of Modern Poetry" (*Philosopher*, December 1920; in *Letters to Alfred Galpin and Others*, 408–11).

8. I.e., Ira A. Cole (of the Kleicomolo).

9. HPL's later tale "Herbert West—Reanimator" may incorporate some features of this dream.

10. In later years HPL revised his opinion of the volume, regarding it very highly.

11, HPL refers to the American tour that Lord Dunsany conducted from the fall of 1919 to the summer of 1920. HPL saw him lecture in Boston on 20 October 1919.

12. Burton Rascoe (1892–1957), journalist, critic, and editor who was literary and drama editor of the *Chicago Tribune* (1912–20) before going to New York to work on several newspapers there.

13. Mistranscribed in AHT. HPL clearly was using "river-regulator" as a euphemistic substitution for "dam[n]."

14. Albert Porta, a meteorologist, announced that the conjunction of six planets on 17 December 1919 would "cause a magnetic current that would pierce the sun, cause great explosions of flaming gas, and eventually engulf the Earth." His announcement resulted in worldwide panic, isolated outbreaks of mob violence, and several suicides.

15. "B.L.T." refers to Bert Leston Taylor (1866–1921), American journalist and author of the "A Line o' Type or Two" column in the *Chicago Tribune* (1909–21).

16. HPL refers to the collaborative story "The Green Meadow."

17. The article HPL refers to is F. F. Van de Water, "How Our State Police Have Spurred Their Way to Fame," *New York Tribune* (27 April 1919): Sec. VII, pp. 2–3.

18. I.e., Philip B. McDonald (see letter 4n7).

19. "Marsh-Mad: A Nightmare," *Philosopher* 1, No. 1 (December 1920): 7–8 (as by "Consul Hasting").

20. Verna McGeoch (Murch after marriage, 1885–1949), Official Editor of the UAPA (1917–19) and hence editor of the *United Amateur.*

21. HPL's poem "Ode for July Fourth, 1917" had been reprinted in the *National Magazine* (July 1917).

22. The *Credential* (April 1920) was an amateur journal of which Anne Tillery Renshaw was editor and HPL assistant editor. It featured the "credentials" (proofs of literary ability) of new members. HPL refers to an article by Emil C. Wahlstrom of Dillon, CO.

23. On this subject see further HPL's "Lucubrations Lovecraftian."

24. Éamon de Valera (1882–1975), a vigorous proponent of Irish independence. He became president of the Irish Republic in 1921–22.

25. An amateur journal, jointly published by HPL and Winifred V. Jackson, for December 1918, June 1919, and April 1921. *United* in the sense of the UAPA.

26. See "Commonplace Book" (entry 26).

27. See "Commonplace Book" (entry 25).

28. Mary Faye Durr, who would be elected President of the UAPA for 1919–20.

29. Francis Fielding-Reid (1892–1960) served during World War I and later as a physician in Baltimore. He does not seem to have published anything.

30. HPL did not in fact issue a *Conservative* between July 1919 and March 1923.

31. Eleanor Barnhart Campbell of Ridgefarm, IL (wife of Paul J. Campbell), who was Laureate Recorder for the UAPA in 1919–20.

32. Gamaliel Bradford, "Mark Twain," *Atlantic Monthly* 125, No. 4 (April 1920): 462–73.

33, *What Is Man?* (1906) is a philosophical dialogue in which Twain asserts a rigid determinism and denies the existence of altruism. It is now available in Twain's *What Is Man? and Other Irreverent Essays*, ed. S. T. Joshi (Amherst, NY: Prometheus Books, 2009). *The Mysterious Stranger* (1916) is a work of black humor in which Satan presents a bleak view of human life.

34. HPL refers to the amateur writers Elsa A. Gidlow (1898–1986) and Roswell George Mills (1896–1966), later editors of *Les Mouches Fantastiques.* Gidlow had written an article, "Life for Life's Sake" (*Wolverine,* October 1919), advocating a hedonistic attitude to life. HPL responded with "Life for Humanity's Sake."

[7]   [AHT]

Friday, Sept. 3, 1920

ON A GRECIAN COLONNADE IN A PARK

From the green shore the gleaming marble towers
    Against the dusk and verdure of the trees;
Beyond, there rise the odours of rare flow'rs
    To swell the fragrance of the Eastern breeze.

That breeze, which o'er Hymettus' slopes hath play'd,
    Finds beauty here, like that it fondled there;

And to these scenes, in classic semblance made,
　　Adds the old magic of the Grecian air.

In the calm twilight, as the hush'd wood
　　Darkens the mystery, obscure and deep,
Forgotten shadows come to dream and brood,
　　Wak'd for a moment from Elysian sleep.

The dim past beckons thro' the marble gate,
　　Stately and silent, distant and divine,
While the still pool reflects a duplicate
　　Within its depths—a shadowy ocean shrine.

Once in the gloom beyond that porch of white
　　I heard a murmur of ethereal sound,
And seem'd to see, as by some eery light,
　　A shimm'ring band, with woodland myrtles crown'd.

The waters, too, a strange enchantment breath'd,
　　And old, old thoughts rose spectral from the grave;
I saw Leucothea, in damp blossoms wreath'd,
　　And young Palaemon from his coral cave.

That shrine of white, deep in the glassy mere,
　　Upon my soul a charm resistless cast;
The dark gate lur'd, as to my straining ear
　　Came voices, calling from the cherish'd past.

And now at eve there lingers in my soul
　　The haunting mem'ry of that placid scene;
While in my dreams I strain to reach a goal
　　Where Glaucus waits me, clad in kelpy green.

The portal calls; beyond that wat'ry door
　　Lies all the bliss my heart hath ever known;
The past is there—yet I stand on the shore
　　In the cold present, alien and alone.

So as pale forms by sunken altars praise
　　Deserted gods of years remote and blest,
I, too, shall tread again those ancient ways,
　　And in the templed deeps sink down to rest.

HENRY PAGET-LOWE

I am interested to hear of the Mocratic experiments in road construction, an art dear to the Romans, and invaluable in the extension of empire through easy communication. I am myself no viafactor, though I have in winter made efforts to qualify as a nivicide; and next to making a road, I fancy it is a good distinction to be an effective clearer of roads. My days of manual exertion were in my youth—what pride I took in my little world in the vacant lot next the house! When I was very small, my kingdom was the lot next my birthplace, 454 Angell St. Here were trees, shrubs, and grasses, and here when I was between four and five the coachman built me an immense summerhouse all mine own—a somewhat crude yet vastly pleasing affair, with a staircase leading to a flat roof from which in later years I surveyed the skies with my telescope. The floor was Mother Earth herself, for at the time the edifice was constructed I had a definite purpose for it. I was then a railway man, with a vast system of express-carts, wheelbarrows, and the like; plus some immensely ingenious cars made out of packing-cases. I had also a splendid engine made by mounting a sort of queer boiler on a tiny express-waggon. The new building, therefore, must needs be my grand terminal and roundhouse combined; a mighty shed under which my puffing trains could run, even as the big trains of the outside world ran under the sheds at the old depots in Providence and Boston—depots long since razed to the ground to make way for the Union, Back Bay, and South Stations of today! So the building became in familiar household parlance "The Engine House"—and how I loved it! From the gate of our yard to the Engine House I had a nice track—or path—made and levelled for me; a continuation of the great railway system formed by the concrete walks in the yard. And here, in supreme bliss, were idled away the days of my youth. As I grew older, I took the road and its buildings more and more under my personal management. I began to make repairs myself, and when I was six I constructed many branch lines. Once I carefully laid track with wooden rails and sleepers—forgetting the trivial detail that I had nothing to run on it! But it looked nice, anyway! Then came changes—one day there was not any coachman to help me, whereat I mourned; but later on I had compensation—the horses and carriages were sold too, so that I had a gorgeous, glorious, titanic, and unbelievable new playhouse—the whole great stable with its immense carriage room, its neat-looking "office", and its vast upstairs, with the colossal (almost scareful) expanse of the grain loft, and the little three-room apartment where the coachman and his wife had lived. All this magnificence was my very own, to do with as I liked! Many were the uses to which I put that stable. The carriage room was now the main terminal of my railway, whilst in other parts were my office, theatre, and other institutions. But the call of the pastoral could not be resisted! Despite my new possession, my interest in the vacant lot and the Engine House was unflagging. One day I decided to alter my scheme, and instead of a railway system my domain became a pastoral countryside. I invited all the boys of the neighbourhood to co-operate in building a little village under the lee of the high board fence, which was in due time accomplished. Many new roads and garden spots were made, and the whole was protected from the Indians (who dwelt somewhere to the north) by a large and impregnable fort with massive earthworks. The boy who suggested that fort and supervised its construction was deeply interested in military things and followed up his hobby. Today he is a Lieutenant-Colonel in the U.S. Army, having attended West Point and served brilliantly as Captain and Major through the World War, being twice wounded. My new village was called "New Anvik", after the Alaskan village of "Anvik", which about that time became known to me through the boys' book "Snow-Shoes and Sledges", by Kirk Munroe. As you see, I then read juvenile matter as well as the classics, and liked it! As the years stole on, my play became more and more dignified; but I could not give up New Anvik. When the grand disaster came, and we moved to this inferior abode, I made a second and more ambitious New Anvik in the vacant lot there. This was my aesthetic masterpiece, for besides a little village of painted huts erected by myself and Chester and Harold Munroe, there was a landscape garden, all of mine own handiwork. I chopped down certain trees and preserved others, laid out paths and gardens, and set at the proper points shrubbery and ornamental urns taken from the old home. My paths were of gravel, bordered with stones, and here and there a bit of stone wall or an impressive cairn of my own making added to the picture. Between two trees I made a rustic bench, later duplicating it betwixt two other trees. A large grassy space I levelled and transformed into a Georgian lawn, with a sundial in the centre. Other parts were uneven, and I sought to catch certain sylvan or bower-like effects. The whole was drained by a system of channels terminating in a cesspool of my own excavation. Such was the paradise of my adolescent years, and amidst such scenes were many of my early works written. Though by nature indolent, I was never too tired to labour about my estate, attending to the vegetation in summer, and shovelling neat paths in niveous winter. Then I perceived with horror that I was growing too old for pleasure. Ruthless Time had set its fell claw upon me, and I was seventeen. Big boys do not play in toy houses and mock gardens, so I was obliged to turn over my world in sorrow to another and younger boy who dwelt across the lot from me. And since that time I have not delved in the earth or laid out paths and roads. There is too much wistful memory in such procedure, for the fleeting joy of childhood may never be recaptured. Adulthood is hell.

Valete—

LO.

[8]   [AHT]
Wednesday, August 31, 1921

Well, Gents, I can't tell youse how it delights yore Grandpa's heart to get back to the old GALLOMO mode of expression! Nevermore let the thought of dissolution cross the threshold of our minds, but let us remain for ever the Three Musketeers of amateur philosophy—one for all, and all for one!

Where shall I begin? I left Mocrates in the grey of the morning before I departed on that trip to Boston to meet Mrs. Renshaw, and Galba a few days later, just as I had received an urgent invitation to repeat my Hampstead-Haverhill visit. Verily, my mail records more of social activity than in the old days; though I shall soon plunge once more into the unbroken solitude of former years. It is strange to move among mankind—I smile sardonically as I mingle with the race of which I am only nominally and physically a part; for is not my spirit of the cold aether and the far spaces beyond the Milky Way? And yet I shall open my missive with more social chronicles—beginning with a simple event which pleased me more than any elaborate convention, yet which took me no more than twenty miles from home.

I have frequently lamented in my accounts of travel, the absence of that carefree kind of activity to which I was accustomed in youth. Amidst the formal and heterogeneous gatherings of amateurdom, I have longed for a return to boyish life; and for a mingling with crowds of youths only, bent on crude song and innocent merriment. You will recall that in describing my Allston–Boston walk of July 2, with Morton, Kleiner, and Dench,[1] I compared its songful stagness with the atmosphere of those older, happier walks with "the fellers" back in 1906, '07, '08, or '09, when I was young and all the world was gay. And now I am able to record a brief return to just that youth, with promise of occasional repetitions in the future! Truly, the hand of time is not proof against all the artifices of mankind!

On Monday, August 8, as I was splashing in the bathtub about 9 a.m., I was summoned on the telephone by my best of all boyhood friends—Harold Bateman Munroe, with whom I played joyously through long years of primary, grammar, and high school experiences or their chronological equivalents. Not for any mortal other than Harold, youse guys, and perhaps Klei, would I have stirred out of that refreshing thermal tide; but H. B. M. is H. B. M., so I made shift to conquer the difficulties of the situation as best I might. Attaining the instrument at last, I was rewarded for my fraternal devotion; for what should Harold propose but a trip through our boyhood play-scenes—East Providence, Seekonk, and Rehoboth—in his camouflaged Ford! Was I on? I'll enlighten the universe! In less than an hour we were spinning over the old Taunton Pike, drinking in the sights on which we had once gazed with the eyes of youth. Much was changed—green fields had here and there become tainted with the sties of foreign canaille, white houses had turned red and red houses white, and one old mill through whose rotting timbers we had played had collapsed from sheer old age,—but the spirit of rock-ribbed and immutable New-England was unconquered, and among remembered vistas we were boys once more. I had not been there for eight or nine years, and the happy sequence of old panoramas was paradise to me. There lay antique Rehoboth Village beneath its centuried canopy of giant oak branches, dreaming stilly in the green twilight it has known since Queen Anne sate on the throne; its simple houses ever the same, and its soul lingering in the past. There too lay the hills and the woods where Indians and Englishmen once fought, and where in our time we too fought showy frays; happy legions with the bloodthirstiness of boy-barbarians. Our ride took us to sleepy Taunton, a city unchanged since the forties, where a boy who had run away to Civil War might return and find nothing strange save the trolleys on the old horse cars. And as we returned, we resolved to visit the most sacred shrine of all, that spot on Great Meadow Hill where we had made a clubhouse by enlarging an old wood-cutter's shanty, and where we had for years assembled for rites of juvenile fellowship. At Wheeler's Corner we turned from the level pike to enter the familiar rutted road and feel the familiar bumps—almost as bad in the Ford as on our boyhood wheels. Not a thing was changed—one might dream that scarce a leaf had fallen, and that the whole country had lain quiet under a spell until the coming of the old crowd to waken it. Up the long slope we jolted, past the last farmhouse—the mournful old Moore place where even the young children seemed old and wan with strange solitude—and finally attained the entrance to the forest that marks the neighbourhood of the summit. Leaving the Ford, we plodded along the stony path between the oaks and maples, marvelling at the new growth of trees which had been cut down in our time. The clubhouse, we soon realised, would no longer stand bleakly under the sun commanding a vast horizon; but would hide its old age in a leavy covert of young saplings. We speculated on how much of the edifice we should still find—Harold believed that only the fireplace—built with the aid of old James Kay the Civil War veteran—would be left standing. That was of great stones, and James Kay was a splendid mason who had worked on Carolina fortifications during the war. He died long ago, God rest him, but we felt that his work would survive his body. I, on the other hand, maintained that we might find some of the newer walls; not indeed the original woodman's hut, but the portion of new pine boards that we had added. And so, still speculating, we rounded the bend in the path and prepared to see what the monster Time might have left for us—when behold! Our youth came again upon us a flame. For there amidst the growing trees in awkward grace stood the symbol of our old days in wonted wholeness—*the boyhood clubhouse, erect in its tar-papered grotesqueness, and intact in every part through all the years!!* There was neither vandalism nor decay—the lock was gone, but that was all. Even the old pictures hung on the walls of this haunted place; this little world of the past, where even Time had eased his scourging in the absence of any human audience. What shadowy companies, moreover, could we picture about the grey cement heart where the pebbled initials G. M. C. C. still lay fixed as we had stamped them when it was new and wet! We seemed to see the old gang as it was—Ron, and Ken, and Stuart,[2] with the fresh faces and clear eyes of youth. They are not dead, but the boy in them is dead, so that their ghosts appear only in this silent and forgotten place. And as we gazed about, Harold conceived the idea of regaining for brief snatches the youth that we have lost. If all goes well, we shall refit this house of miraculous preservation, and bring back to it the men who were once the old gang; and perhaps on some nights in the golden autumn when the logs burn red in the stone fireplace the ghosts may pass back into the aging bodies to which they belonged of old, and the gang will live once again. And perhaps we shall sing in the olden way, and teach the birds of autumn the songs known to the birds of other autumns, and awake the old trees to memories of strains that stirred leaves now fallen. Then as we drive home in the late night the long road will echo as of old, and the voices of men shall sing the songs of boys—the songs of fifteen years ago—"In the Golden Autumn Time, My Sweet Elaine",[3] "When the Mocking Bird is Singing in the Wildwood",[4] and all the others that we learned with such care, and taught with such care to J———— S————, who was a trifle dull and who was our mascot. And perhaps we may some day have J———— with us at a session, and chide him as we go back for his slovenly dress, and straighten his tie and re-crease his felt hat as we approach East Providence Six Corners, where we are ashamed to be seen with him under the strong electric lights. Who the deuce says we are over thirty? He's a liar! But we shall be careful to include only such boys as have not imbibed too strongly the persistent delusion of having grown up. Only these shall gather as of old around the hearth and plan for the still distant years of adulthood. To others we shall seem odd—but what the hell do we care? Who would not be odd, if he might thereby re-enter the sealed door of his youth? But I'd better turn off the wosh.

My next trip, that of Wednesday, August 17, was of prosaic modernness. On account of the innumerable feuds amongst the Boston amateurs, Miss Hamlet insisted that I make a call at Dorchester separately from the main event of meeting Mrs. Renshaw. I missed two trains through the delay of a beastly headache, arrived just as Miss H. had departed on a trip to see poor old Mrs. Bell,[5] and though I gave not a damn about it, was forced by an over-hospitable family to promise to make a special trip another day, lest the disappointment quite break their hearts! Gawd, what a lot of fuss over a poor old nobody—flattery is the universal order of things around Boston. What moved me to promise was the sight of my own work saved and pasted in a scrap book. It is not everywhere that Grandpa can pose as a great man! After I broke away from the cordiality of Elsinore, I made for the Curry School of Expression,[6] where Mrs. Renshaw was holding forth, and there found the great leader, attended by her inseparable satellite Miss Crist.[7] Mrs. R. was about as her pictures shew—stout and homely, but highly cultivated and as urbane an arguer as James F. Morton Jr. We departed immediately for Newton Centre, where Mrs. R. is visiting a sister of Miss Crist, arguing violently on the way about Haeckel, Hegel, Kant, Schopenhauer, Nietzsche, cosmogony, and other pleasant things. Mrs. R. is still an idealist, but I think she is waking up gradually. Geology has radically modified her formerly bland theism, and within a decade she ought to be a thorough materialist. She is not one to stand still—the only trouble is that she may move in a circle like Morton. The argument was civil throughout, and interrupted only during the wait at Trinity Place Station, where occasional passing trains would cut one or the other off just as the fate of the universe was being decided. At Newton Centre the first stop was made at the Wurtz household where Mrs. R. is visiting. Here Miss Crist was temporarily dropped, whilst the Renshaw–Theobald arguing team forged onward to Mortonstrasse 53, where Mrs. McMullen[8] had invited us to dinner. Here came quite a surprise for me, for despite the new feuds I found Mrs. Miniter there! She was very cordial, and just as flattering as ever. At dinner were Mesdames Renshaw, Miniter, & McMullen, to say nothing of Grandpa. I had the honour of telling Mrs. McMullen of her new laureateship, and she was vastly pleased. Later there arrived the Crist–Wurtzes and the Aonian W. V. J., the latter having an interesting tilt with Mrs. Miniter in cattishly civil dialogue whose iciness was delectably veiled with politeness. Afterward, I am told, Mrs. Miniter decided to introduce fiction into her account of the meeting; and has been telling the world that "W. V. J. did not speak to her for over an hour after she arrived". Hell, how the cats fight! But I am outside it all—a cosmic being apart, as 'twere. Although I am of course on the United or Jackson–McMullen side in any real warfare, I shall be civil to Mrs. Miniter as long as she is civil to me, despite the view of W. V. J. that I ought to observe a more marked coolness as a mark of United loyalty. No mere poet can tell me anything about United loyalty! Hell—who is the United anyway? (toot-toot!) But speaking of cats—the best one present was the real thing, a tiny grey kitten, part Angora, that a neighbour brought in at Mrs. McM's suggestion—Mrs. McM being aware of my predilection for the (genuine) feline species. He was a good double handful, with an inexpressibly pretty face and eyes, and a collar with tiny bells that tinkled as he cavorted with the innocent sprightliness of youth. Most of the time he sat in his Grandpa Theobald's lap, chewing either my waistcoat buttons or my fingers according to his juvenile taste. This neighbour also brought in twin collie dogs—an interesting pair, which completed rather a quaint menagerie. Conversation ranged from the grave and scholastic to the gay and humorous, and was diversified by songs by the two musical members—Mesdames McMullen and Renshaw. I was asked to sing, but knew enough to refuse. Among the subjects broached was a commercial arrangement whereby I might revise English themes for Mrs. R.'s classes at Research University—by mail, of course. That would not, perhaps, be as bad as Bush work if the pay were adequate. A wilder suggestion of Mrs. R.'s was that I write a text-book of rhetoric![9]

The riot broke up at 11:10, and I departed for my usual night train. The next evening Mrs. R. was to meet the Hub Club[10] (whom W. V. J. and Lilian Middleton will no longer meet), and Mrs. Miniter invited me to stay over at 20 Webster, but I was wretchedly tired and decided to omit the sequel. I reached home at 1:20, drenched by a sudden shower which caught me just before I attained the portal. Mrs. R. later said she was surprised at my aspect. She had expected something conspicuously awkward, eccentric, and hermitish.

On the following Friday I received still another invitation, as Galba already knows. This time Hampstead and Haverhill again, by request of the super-hospitable Littles, who so delightfully approximate the state of England's rural gentry. It was for a longer time than the other visit, but I compromised on two nights, and arranged to use the final evening on my homeward trip to discharge the debt of courtesy by calling at the Hamlet Castle. Leaving Providence Thursday morning at 11:00, I arrived in Haverhill at 2:15, and was met with a horseless carriage containing Miss Little, her mother, and a bearded and pleasant uncle whom I had not seen previously but whom I liked at once. In describing these rural magnates I am happily able to discard that tone of sarcasm with which I describe certain more urban amateurs; for verily, they are of the wholesome Saxon gentry that needs no apology or allowances. In a word, they are all right; of one's own sort, as it were. We first proceeded to 408 Groveland, where we found no visible Smithy. We thought he was out, but later learned he was merely asleep. After that we visited picturesque Winnikenni Castle, a mock-chateau of ivied stone that crowns a noble steep. Here, in certain angles of the hoary wall, one's mind is wafted magically back to the tenth or eleventh century; and it should not surprise one to behold the wraith of some armoured knight or retainer pacing silently up and down the platform. Haverhill is some town, we'll tell the world! After a long drive over gentle hill from parts of which spread wondrous panoramas of steeple-studded valley, we attained Little Manor once more, and I made at once for the crowded library. Later I saw strawberries growing for the first time in my life, and even condescended to soil my hands by picking some. In the evening I produced the binoculars, planisphere, and astronomical handbook I had brought with me, and sought by a flashlight's aid to ascend the neighbouring "Pinnacle" for purposes of celestial observation. It was a wild climb through the spectral wood in the dusk, the light gleaming fitfully, and the sentient boughs reaching out to claw at the faces of the travellers. And finally when the summit was attained, fancy my curses at discovering that the god damn sky had clouded up too much to permit of observation! The descent was accomplished by another route, including strange shadows where goblins danced in the shadow. Though the expedition was a failure, the climb itself may perhaps furnish an idea or two for a story. Next day I read some of my new hideous yarns aloud at the hillside camp, and received one good suggestion from the audience regarding the improvement of "The Outsider". Not that I hadn't thought of the point before, but I was not sure. In the afternoon an Haverhill trip was planned. First came Smiffkins, who had received the note I had put in his mail slot the day before, and who was ready and waiting under a gnarled tree. How I like that queer old cuss! He is in truth a wild woodland thing—a real faun if there ever was one—and if I were an artist I would draw him with goat's feet, or half merged into the trunk of some gigantic and shadowy tree. Among other things, he told me of a coming split in the National, engineered by the vindictive Hyde–Outwater gang[11] who were so beautifully licked at the Boston convention. Not that I relish seeing the enemy suffer—but this thing will not hurt the United any! Now who will call us the "Divided Amateur Press Association"![12] After Smithy came the big event—a trip through the museum of the Haverhill Historical Society. This is not supposed to be open Fridays, but the influence of the Littles is far from Little, and it was opened for the special benefit of the present expedition! Of all fascinating places, this comes near the top of the list. In its nucleus it is still a private Colonial mansion of brick, inhabited by the original family, whose head is the director of the museum. This family dates from the early eighteenth century, and its natural accumulation of rare furniture is more vital and time-annihilating than any formal collection in a more formal museum. Not least pleasing of the items is the lord of the manor himself, Leonard Smith, Gent., in whose blood is combined all the best strains of the land. In him we behold the true British Colonial—the purest of the ancient stock—and I found his conversation a delight; later telling the Littles that I like all Haverhill Smiths, both patrician and plebeian. I took a picture of Mr. Smith in his entrancing old-fashioned garden, and will shew you a copy if it turns out well. He is venerable, white-headed, and white-bearded, and a true artist in soul. His landscape gardens are a joy, and his interior decorations something to admire. Annexed to the old mansion is the new museum building, where repose a multiplicity of Merrimack Valley antiquities. One could stay in this paradise indefinitely, but other attractions called. On the premises, not far from the main buildings, stands a small white house of one story and loft. This is the ancient Ward house, built in 1640, and the oldest edifice of any kind I have ever beheld. The musty odour of the place is appalling, but deters no one from entering—for who would not like to stand within walls that were reared but a decade after the Massachusetts-Bay Colony was founded, and but a score of years after the first white pilgrim landed at Plymouth? On the wall was a framed copy of the MERRIMACK ADVERTISER for some date in 1815. There is nothing new under the sun—I noted a poet's corner with verse almost as bad as some of the stuff I revise! But who could tell in one letter—even a GALLOMO—of all that such a museum contains? It amused me to note that despite their influence none of the Littles had ever visited the place before. Only Miss M. A. Little made this trip, but now they are all going! It was now evening, and after a detour to the business section to pick up the younger Little sister the party returned to Little Towers. After dinner the family again demanded that Grandpa amuse them with some of his theatrical impersonations—and believe us, you'd never know the old man in some of the things they made him put on! In my acting days I went in for the heavy villainous stuff; but the Hampsteaders seem partial to the Julian Entinge[13] stuff, and could not be satisfied till they had Grandpa laced into a hoop-skirt outfit with bonnet and parasol to match! Though it was hard to think of dialogue for such a makeup, they seemed satisfied with my improvisations; and compensated by prolonged applause for the injury inflicted upon my patriarchal dignity. The evening concluded with an attempt to solve a new checkerboard puzzle of Mr. Little's; and here I must confess that I failed as miserably as all the rest. I have asked them to let me know if they ever solve it. On the next and final day there was a morning session at the camp, during which I used my binoculars to sweep the valley below—to sweep yet not clean it, for what could need cleaning in a region like Hampstead? Believe Grandpa, but that panorama of spires and roofs amidst foliage is something which would make anyone but a hardened modern write heroick couplets indefinitely! I was surprised to note that the Littles had no telescope or binoculars, and that the younger sister had never used any before—strange are the lacunae of rural life. The noontide period was occupied in the construction of a cake by Miss Little for our friend Tryout—a masterpiece designed to outdo the one sent him some time ago by honest old Mrs. K. Leyson Brown. There was a large cake for Smiffkins himself and several little cakes for his grandchildren; and I am sure that poor Mrs. Brown's eclipse was complete! We took it to him on the trip which carried me to my train, and I had the honour of carrying the main cake and handing it to Tryout, thus obtaining an infinitesimal spark of reflected glory at the achievement. He seemed transported, and has evidently decided to immortalise the whole Little gens in his next TRYOUT, for he has just written me asking the name of the father—which is Albert, as I shall presently tell him. After the presentation I was whirled to the station and duly dumped, later puffing southward on the uncertain Boston & Maine amidst many courteous invitations to come again and often. Some hospitality! I am convinced that I am by nature a simple rustic, whose genuine aesthetic sympathies are excited only by rural virtues and scenery, and to whom the pastoral is therefore the only authentic medium of expression. My urbanism and sophistication are but an intellectual cloak assumed academically through philosophical conviction, and touching no spring of real creative art. I shall never really care for modernistic expression, no matter how long I try, for I am of the old order, with every perceptive faculty attuned to the old and simple images. After the country, the city seems cheap and tawdry to me—I can sneer loftily and intellectually at the ecstasy of a Nature-poet over a sweep of hill, but damn it all, that same view will move me to admiration when the alleged emotional stimuli of the modern and disillusioned poet leave me cold! I must stay in my room and keep my eyes from Nature if I expect to become truly sophisticated. Otherwise, I shall be strongly moved by things which are too simple to move a true poet of today. But stay! I must not display prejudice—and after all, the rural landscape would probably bore me to death after a week or two. Everything is a bore in the end.

And speaking of bores—as I puffed out of Haverhill the Hamlet call still lay ahead of me. I had given a forewarning that I might be "unavoidably" delayed till evening, and hoped my prospective hosts would not do anything elaborate—but Gawd 'elp us! When I finally reached there via B. & M., elevated, and surface car, I found that they had a near-convention staged for me! There was an ambitious dinner of lamb and sundry fixings, and many reproaches at my "unavoidable" tardiness. As a local delegate Miss Hamlet had unearthed a literary protege of hers—the Mildred LaVoie whose name has lingered inactively on our lists since 1916, and who is a young person of undistinguished aspect and ancestry; not uncomely, but more suggestive of the artless nymph than of the fictional titan. This quiet and unassuming individual writes stories, but is afraid to send them anywhere—even to TRYOUT—for publication; hence has remained an amateur nonentity for five years despite the efforts of Miss Hamlet to bring her genius to the world's notice. I was not very enthusiastic about the process of LaVoian assimilation till after the maid in question had departed, and Miss H. produced a story of hers which she had secured surreptitiously. Then I perceived that the work was not half bad in its way—shewing at least clear observation, command of detail, and a keener picture of the subject matter than mere words. It is surely worth printing, and I shall accomodate Miss Hamlet by placing it somewhere where its appearance will duly surprise its over-modest creator—Lawson's WOLVERINE ought to stand for it.[14] But after all, I was paid for my politeness in making the Dorcastrian detour. Just before I beat it for the 11:45 I was given the loan of a new book which I am told is the most horrible collection of short stories recently issued! It is called "The Song of the Sirens", and is by one Edward Lucas White, who claims he dreamed all the ghoulish things described. I have not yet had a chance to peruse it, but am expecting a fine time when I get around to it. Returning to the trip—I returned to the South Station via Andrews Sq. subway, and was home at the usual 1:20. I slept till the next evening, and am still drowsy from the three days unwonted exertion.

This ought to be enough of a social programme to hold me for a while—but Gawd 'elp us! when one gets to be a social butterfly the thing gets beyond one's control! Am now notified that I must act as an host next Saturday and Sunday or Sunday and Monday, when there will descend upon Providence no less a whirlwind than Galba's new friend and admirer, Mrs. Sonia H. Greene, the Champion Long-Distance talker of Muscovy and Lands Adjacent! What can one do to entertain such a human dynamo and phonograph combined is beyond me, but I must think of something lest a $50.00 Fund contributor be offended into financial sterility. Galba, yuh'd orta hear what she says about you in her latest 12-pager! If your ma don't watch out, she'll kidnap yuh! Galpinitis? We'll spill it to the solar system! I never before saw a nut quite like Mme. Greenevsky—it must be Slavonic blood! For pure hot air she may have rivals, but the joke is that there is sound sense and profound literary erudition beneath all the nonsense. So she thinks Grandpa is egotistical? Hell! That's what she told me at the convention—and then added that she never would have wasted her valuable time in trying to convert me if I were not an unusual specimen, or something like that. Her worst trouble is an absent sense of humour—the poor fish thought it was serious egotism when I told her that I despise all mankind and consider myself a cosmic intelligence aloof from the race. In letters Mme. G. is not at all egotistical—I was surprised at the Uriah-Heepness[15] of her written as distinguished from oral arguments. But Holy Yahveh, what floral rhetoric! However, let me not libel an honest and learned thinker, who is really the most remarkable accession which amateurdom has had for some time. Klei likes her, and calls on her often, though that may be partly due to her possession of a beauteous daughter who scorns the sedateness of our bookish Brooklyn bard, and who must therefore be a tantalising object to a professional heart-breaker like the rhythmic Rheinhart. Mme. Greenevitch is nothing if not generous—Monday I received from her a present of a new book, Shaw's latest emanation, yclept "Back to Methuselah". Surely gratitude will impel me to forget the charge of egotism and be as courteous an host as possible—besides, philosophy and its great Appleton exponent will furnish an unlimited variety of topics for rational discussion. And despite the surface, there is no denying that Mme. G. *is* rational and highly cultivated to boot. I have just read proofs of my RAINBOW article, which consists of some cynical aphorisms culled from two letters of mine.[16] I fear this stuff will shock friend Mocrates—but it may help prepare him for the fuller shock of my "Confession of Unfaith" in Campbell's next LIBERAL.

Friday, Sept. 12, 1921

Oh, Boy! Gents, yuh'd orta see Grandpa today! Am I a beauty? I'll tell the woild! From underneath my hair to a point perilously close to my left eye there stretches a beautiful and gory welt acrost me marrble brow, adding to muh classic features the one charrm they lacked beforre—the devilish scarriness of the pirate or Heidelberg duellist. What's the trouble? Some experience, boys! I'll hev ta write it up into a story—earthquakes, avalanches, and all that sort of thing. At about 6 a.m. yesterday morning, as I was concluding an all-night literary session at my desk, I stopped in the kitchen to secure my solitary second meal. Perhaps you know that I am a singularly light eater, taking but one full meal and one self-prepared cracker-and-milk lunch each day. Well, as I was a-sayin', this was the light second meal. I had sot muhself down at the table and was daintily toying with my epicurean repast, when I seemed to hear a sort of crackling sound, and saw a fine grey dust gathering on the board before muh. Before I could rouse my sleepy head to connected thought, something else happened to the aforementioned cranium—for suddenly and without further warning the roof of the cosmos busted up and fell on poor Grandpa!! Gawd, wot a cataclysm to spring outa nothin! Some last days of Pompeii! It knocked me flat down against the table, burying me and the latter in one indistinguishable heap of lava and scoriac chaos. Were I not possessed of a record-breaking shock of hair, which just now needs cutting at that, the moon would be laying pale lilies of light on dead Grandpa!!! As it was, I sure was sanctified with dust, albeit not star-dust. To lay all mystery and symbolism aside, what really happened was this: the plastering of the ceiling had perversely loosened and fallen from a point directly above the grey head of the lone diner! It was some wreck, take it from me! The room looked like devastated Belgium as I surveyed it through the curtain of blood trickling from my injured dome. But I managed to dig out, shake off the worst of the dust and debris, and finally free myself from the fine grains of plaster which had sifted all over me. Today I am very comfortable, relatively speaking. The wound is healing, but it sure is a thing of beauty! And soon a gang of plasterers will be at work—not on me, but on the room.

The Hampstead–Haverhill pictures are now done, and I will enclose some for Gallomonistick inspection—Lo to Mo, Mo to Gal, Gal to Lo. They will, I think, bear out my narrative in convincing you of the scenick beauty of southern New-Hampshire. The upper story windows of the "ell" of the house, as shewn in the picture, are those of the antique room I occupied—a room with not a fitting changed for 150 years. The vertical scenic view is that of the willow lane forming the subject of Miss Little's poem in a recent TRYOUT. In the next GALLOMO I shall probably enclose another set of pictures taken during the coming Greenevsky visit; pictures of more interest to Galba because of his acquaintance with their subject. I shall dodge the camera this time unless my gashed forehead returns to something more like normalcy. It would take a pirate's costume to give that scar an appropriate setting!

But enough of Grandpa's social whirl! As to the Galpinian satire about the fanciful kingdom—go to it, kid! You can make something of it if anyone could! I am getting too damned cynical to appreciate satire lately—I am so disillusioned about the institutions of mankind that the ridicule loses its point— why the hell should anyone *expect* the shams of statecraft and society to be true? Is it not a trifle naive to *ridicule* pomposity and pretence when there is nothing else in the world? It becomes, methinks, only the outer gods to judge man—and then may not the outer gods as well be hypocrites and fools? I dismiss life with one contemptuous "bah" and shrug of the shoulders—let the fools stew in their own lies and puerilities! "It is good to be a cynic. It is better to be a contented cat. It is best not to exist at all."[17] Boy, the cyanide! This leads me—the subject, not the cyanide—to consideration of our little friend's code of philosophy as outlined on the 8½ × 13 GALLOMO sheet. I am asked to criticise it—but I can't, for it expresses mine own present views so closely that the difference is negligible. I can only endorse, and express my pleasure that once more the Galban and Lollian orbits should intersect. One cannot get beyond these simple assumptions and preferences without leaving behind the solid data of fact and experience. More elaborate and dogmatic systems may be beautiful, but they rest on thin aether. Like Galba, I have sympathy for reformers—and indeed, in my youthful simplicity I once had reforming tendencies myself. But lately I see the huge futility of it all, and must needs mix pity with my admiration. The world is a beastly mess, and will never be anything else. All that one may do is to train down the worst crudities for the same of smoother existence. As to the relative value of love and contempt, I am undogmatic. In me liking springs from two distinct sources—admiration for intellect, which is personal admiration, and admiration for picturesqueness, which is akin to aesthetic admiration. I like only great minds, or minds which are beautiful, picturesque, or individual in any way—even a comic way. The two kinds of liking are very distinct—the first is intense and fixed, and regards the object as a human being with dignity. I save this for a very few persons, most of them dead and famous, but a few living and acquainted with me, as Galba and Mocrates. The second kind is whimsical and impersonal—I do not instinctively recognise these non-great but picturesque minds as wholly human, and do not take them seriously; but am fond of them in a pictorial way—as I am of a landscape or a cat. My liking of this kind is variable, and more or less mingled with tolerance and even kindly contempt. I think of such minds as toys to amuse my fancy. Still, such likings are sometimes strong—it is thus, for instance, that I cherish my old pal Smiffkins of the TRYOUT, and poor Jawn Samples[18] of the austral backwoods. They are pleasingly quaint, and I like them because they please me and add to my sense of importance. They are like the grotesque vignettes in certain old books, or the gargoyles upon some antique cathedral. But the real article in liking is that which I possess toward Galmo, in whom I perceive the evolved minds that spell superiority, which is the only absolute value in the cosmos.

I perused with much interest the Galbanian "In Memoriam" and allied phenomena. Surely it is some hoax, and I am strongly tempted to use it despite an undeniable lack of enthusiasm concerning "The Decline and Fall of the College Library". Not that I fail to appreciate the excellence of that masterpiece—but the author is so great that it is overshadowed by his other and more titanic performances. Gimme more time to appreciate it, boy. My taste may clarify, and my point of view alter. I like the distinctly memorial part vastly—and the pome as well. I'll hold on to it a while and do some deciding—

perhaps Gahal-Bah will find some Hastingian[19] specimen even more clever than the "Decline". I have no cut appropriate for the thing, but if in his h. s. and college experience Galba has acquired any freakish looking halftone from CLARION, LAWRENTIAN, or some such publication, I would be glad to use it. B. t. w.—"The Gods in the Gutter" is rather good—I never read much of Service,[20] but deem him very capable in his chosen field of ostentatious virility.

About the U. of Wis. course—Gawd, kid! D'ya wanta lap up the whole damn college? I tykes off me 'at to a bloke as can tackle a course like that! As to advice—who the deuce am I—a non-collegian—to pass judgment upon the studies of my betters? However, I should choose (in the order of the table) Jastrow's Psychology[21] to French Poetry, Divine Comedy and Contemporary Philosophy to Genl. Survey French Lit., English Philology to Cont. Drama and Rise of Russia, Human Traits to Abnormal Psych.—and I guess this is all, the two other points being the same in both second year semesters. My main method of advising is to promote diversity and to minimise studies of a general literary nature which a mind like Galba's would hardly need in addition to his exhaustless general reading. But since all this pertains to an intellectual world far in advance of my meagre attainments, I would advise Gahal-Bah to go ahead and do as he damn pleases without listening to Grandpa's senile twaddle.

And now, Mawruss, mein knabe,[22] I'm gonna get after you for an hasty judgment! Hee-haw! So Mocrates thought his Grandpa wrote "The Eye Above the Mantel"!!![23] Sage, the only thing I did to that thing was to straighten out one split infinitive and improve one fanciful name. Otherwise the thing stands verbatim as written by its real author—a genuine human being without a pseudonym; a real, live boy of nineteen, about to enter his sophomore year at New York University—Frank Belknap Long, Junior, son of Frank Belknap Long, Esq., a prosperous dentist of 823 West End Ave., New York City. Young Frank is the latest of my adopted grandchildren, and is some kid, albeit hardly in the exalted Galpinian sense—or even the Spoerrian[24] sense. He is a true artist, and a devotee of Poe and America's older literature, and I think he is about to become a leading amateur. He is, moreover, our new First Vice-President. Yes, my son, Frank is no empty cloak for his Grandpa Theobald, but is a highly independent youth, wholly responsible for his own stories. I like "The Eye Above the Mantel" very much—so much so that I snapped it up for the Official Organ the moment Long sent it to me; but pray do not fancy I wrote it. There may be crudities—even Mocrates' objection may be partly valid, though that kind of "sensibility" belongs more to the languid effeminacy of Cowper than to the vigour of a Nietzschean,—but the whole is certainly a good job. Yes, a damn good job for a kid of nineteen!

And whilst I am in the mood for literary disavowals, let me chide Father Mocrates for a second hasty guess—that concerning "The Crawling Chaos".[25] Brudder, although I had a hand in that job, I swarta Gawd I didn't do more than half or three quarters of it. I thought I told you all about that composite piece work, but I must have been thinking of the earlier "Green Meadow". It is true that I once used the pseudonym of "Elizabeth Berkeley" in conjunction with its more rightful owner W. V. J.—in 1916 the name covered certain verses by both authors, in an effort to mystify the public by having widely dissimilar work from the same nominal hand.[26] But that is past history, and today Elizabeth ain't me at all, but exclusively my eldest daughter Winifred. Since Loveman rates "The Crawling Chaos" ahead of all my strictly original stories, and since Mo's friend thinks the author must be a real snowbird or hop-hound, it may be worth while to clear up the constituent elements once for all—so here goes, with documentary evidence 'n' everthin! The enclosed fragment of a Jacksonian letter, written late in 1918 or early in 1919, is the nucleus of the story. As you will perceive, the whole bizarre setting comes from an actual dream of the poetess whilst in the clutches of influenza. This element of illness may account for much of the fantastic colouring, though in actual truth no drug was administered. I have, I think, mentioned before, that the genius of W. V. J. can produce hideous conceptions far outdoing any of mine, and remaining ineffective solely because of their creator's singular helplessness in prose. This is one of them—others you will see in the remarkable CONSERVATIVE I am trying to get out. I kept this dream outline a long time without utilising it—for being basically egotistical, I put mine own work first. Finally, last December, the authoress became impatient about it, so I threw the story together in a hurry. The colouring impressed me as opiate, so I supplies the dopy prologue. Then in analysing the nature of the dream, I found that the dominant points were a hellish pounding and an encroachment of the sea upon the land. Using these two latter "starters", the denouement was fairly inevitable to me; so that although everything after the ninth line of page five in the printed version is my own, it is only broadly so; the impulse having been supplied by the original data. When I sent the finished story to W. V. J. I was amused by her idea that I must have actually seen the same supernal sights that she saw in the dream. Her overpowering imagination, conjoined to very scanty scientific attainments, makes her vaguely credulous of the supernatural; and she cannot get rid of the notion that there may be an actual region of dream and vision which can be independently and objectively seen by different individuals. In this case she declared that I had described details of the strange interior, and of the architecture of the dream-house, which she had plainly noticed but had not described to me; which to her is proof that a common dream experience must underlie the work of both collaborators. She does not realise that imagination can seize on new things and subconsciously project them backward into association with past things—just as all prophecies are written after the occurrence of the things prophesied. In the case of "The Green Meadow" I related to her a dream of mine, and she claimed to have had exactly the same dream, with a subsequent development which mine lacked. This was certainly her honest belief, yet I could swear that she had no such dream till she had seen my account. Then, doubtless, she did have the dream in its amplified form; automatically putting it backward in time when later thinking of it and repeating it. I will send the epistolary extract to Mocrates, who seems most interested in the tale. He can return it either directly to me, or to me via Appleton. And by the way—don't mention to W. V. J. that I sent the thing. She has a fad for destruction, and wishes all her epistles burnt without exhibition, though they are in truth far less slanderous than the presumably preserved GALLOMO. I usually comply with the wish, though in this case had to save this one sheet for the sake of the story. One more point—about that woshy paragraph which Mocrates cites. Here I plead guilty and have not the least excuse to offer. It is all in my own part of the story, and was slung in purely for verbal effect. Tinsel ornament pure and simple. I wanted something poetic and bizarre, and since the story wasn't mine, neglected to be particular. I am a damnably selfish cuss—don't ever expect me to be conscientious in a collaborated work! I'll write any old rot if I can escape responsibility for it, and frankly, I didn't think the "Crawling Chaos" was going to make such a hit that anyone would notice it. When I did that job my egotism was at its height over Loveman's praise of my "Nyarlathotep", and I failed to see the real superiority in W. V. J.'s richly and exotically ornate dream nucleus. I looked down upon something to which I should have looked up! But Loveman took down my pride in short order!

I perused with much interest the account of Mocratic vacation activities, and congratulate our Sage upon his natatory exploits. Mocrates could be me awright—d—n me if I can swim a stroke! I always hated sea bathing, and have not voluntarily indulged in it since the age of nine. The only time I have been in bathing since is once when I was about 16 or 17—when I had to merge with the waters of a crystal lake in order to prove to the gang I was with that I was not afraid of the cold ripples. I leaves the beach to them as likes it—mine be the warmer billows of the bathtub! I am, very literally, a *poor fish!*

About them new United rates—forget the four bucks, Mocrates! If you are two years overdue, merely renew for one—it is just as well to have been technically a non-member for one year—what the devil do you care so long as you are paid up a year ahead? Call it a reinstatement and let Grandpa be your sponsor—I'll send ya a blank an' get the credit for a splendid new recruit!

But Oh, Boy! Mebbe I ain't got a fight on my hands in the United! Ida[27] has just written me that she and her Columbus henchman expect next year's UNITED AMATEUR to be conducted in a more commonplace and democratic manner; with less of the purely artistic and more of the chatty and plebeian. Only on such conditions, she implies, will the Columbus purse strings be liberally open. I have been dreadfully polite in replying, and have courteously ladled out wosh to the effect that I'll see her in hell first. As long as I'm editor, the organ will be exactly as it is now—exactly as good a thing as I can produce. If they don't like Grandpa they can get another boy—and that will be some job just now.[28] They can keep their money if they wish—I had rather edit a good four-page leaflet than a 20-page mess of Columbus junk. But anyhow, I think hell's gonna break loose somehow. Either they will try to starve me out and leave me to struggle on in my own way without support, or they will fire me and set up some Woodbee bonehead for editor. If the latter, I shall get out a UNITED CO-OPERATIVE as a rival official organ if I can scrape up the cash—ridiculing the administration's bourgeois foibles, and making 'em sorry they ever tried to monkey with the boss. If they expect to depend on me, they've gotta take things as I hand 'em out! I have long been patient with Columbus, but now that I've made up with Cleveland I simply must fight somebody or something else. A pug gets stale if he doesn't get into a mill once in a while—me an' Dempsey is lookin' for a brisk match!

I look forward with eagerness to future APPRENTICES[29]—especially illustrated ones. Them's the stuff amachoordom needs! The present one will certainly win vast favour—I have already heard it complimented in no uncertain terms. Let's have a contrib, O Sage, as soon as ya get something nontheological. What we're lookin' for is less the didactic than the essay of belles-lettres type. I noted with interest the Palaestina essay and the sundry jests and howlers. How Mocrates can remember speeches verbatim is beyond me! If I can carry all the ideas I feel proud enough—the words are too much for Grandpa in his old age! I will forward the items to Galba.

Well, I gotta quit. If you could see the hopeless mess of unanswered mail before me, you would realise what Gallomonistic devotion prompts these eleven pages just now. My Bush work is going to the devil, and I am ashamed to write Mr. Hoag till I can shew him something in the way of accomplished work.[30] My nerves are in a chaos this year—I seem better and more active outwardly, but I am getting to be an old man, fonder of dozing by the fire than of exerting myself. Life is such a beastly bore—I shall have to get hold of that laudanum some day soon. But until then, I shall remain, as ever, Gentlemen,

Yr most obliged and obedient Servant,
HENRY PAGET-LOWE

Notes

1. Ernest A. Dench (1895–?), British born Brooklyn amateur, living in Sheepshead Bay, NY, author of *Making the Movies* (1915) and other books about the cinema. HPL saw him frequently during his residence in Brooklyn (1924–26).

2. The references are to HPL's boyhood friends Ronald Kingsley Upham (1892–1968), Kenneth [James] Tanner (1890–1979), and Stuart Tiepke Coleman (1892–1969).

3. 1905; lyrics by Richard H. Gerard, music by S. R. Henry.

4. 1906; lyrics by Arthur J. Lamb, music by H. B. Blanke.

5. Unidentified, save that HPL once referred to her as an "impoverished invalid."

6. Samuel Silas Curry (1847–1921) founded the School of Elocution and Expression (now Curry College) in Milton, MA, in 1879.

7. Unidentified. Of her, HPL wrote: "—a colourless young woman who acts as her [Renshaw's] secretary, typist, & general caretaker; reminding her when she leaves her handbag behind or fails to put on her hat."

8. Susan Lilian McMullen ("Lilian Middleton"), an amateur poet. See HPL's essay, "The Poetry of Lilian Middleton" (1922; *CF* 2).

9. Late in life HPL revised just such a treatise for Renshaw, *Well Bred Speech* (1937).

10. The Hub Amateur Journalism Club in Boston ("The Hub"), of which HPL was a member (1920–24). He wrote "The Moon-Bog" for presentation at one of its meetings.

11. I.e., the amateur journalists Edna Hyde and Marjorie H. Outwater of the NAPA. Nothing is known of this "split." Outwater was an Official Editor of the NAPA (1920–21).

12. Members of the NAPA were fond of referring to the UAPA in this manner because in 1912 it had split into two factions because of a disputed election.

13. Julian Entinge (born William Julian Dalton, 1881–1947), American actor who, after working on Broadway and in vaudeville, began making films in 1917, becoming one of the highest-paid actors in Hollywood. He appeared mostly in musical comedies, and also was a female impersonator (hence HPL's remark about being dressed up in "a hoop-skirt outfit").

14. Horace L. Lawson was editor of the *Wolverine*, an amateur paper for which HPL was conducting the "Zoilus" column.

15. Uriah Heep is a (falsely) humble clerk in Charles Dickens's *David Copperfield* (1849–50).

16. "Nietscheism [*sic*] and Realism."

17. The quotation is from "Nietzscheism and Realism."

18. John Milton Samples (see Glossary of Names).

19. Referring to "Consul Hasting," i.e., Alfred Galpin.

20. Robert W. Service (1874–1958), "Gods in the Gutter," in *Ballads of a Bohemian* (1921), a poem attacking Baudelaire, Wilde, and Verlaine.

21. Presumably a class on the psychological theories of Joseph Jastrow (1863–1944), Polish-born American psychologist and author of such works as *Character and Temperament* (1915) and *The Psychology of Conviction* (1918).

22. "Maurice, my boy."

23. Frank Belknap Long, "The Eye Above the Mantel" (*United Amateur*, March 1921).

24. J. Fuller Spoerri (1899–1969), an amateur living in Washington, D.C.

25. A collaborative story with Winifred V. Jackson.

26. HPL's poems "The Unknown" and "The Peace Advocate" were published as by "Elizabeth Berkeley."

27. Ida C. Haughton (1860–1934), president of the UAPA (1921–22). The feud between her and HPL became so bitter that HPL wrote the vicious satire "Medusa: A Portrait," directed at her. See letter 10. Her "henchman" was Leo Fritter (1878–1948),

lawyer, amateur journalist. HPL supported Fritter's campaign to be president of the UAPA (1915), which Fritter won. (HPL was first vice-president.) Both Haughton and Fritter were members of the Woodbees.

28. In fact, HPL was ousted as Official Editor of the UAPA in the election of July 1922, Leo Fritter taking his place; but the official board for 1922–23 proved ineffective, and HPL and his associates were returned to office in 1923.

29. A journal issued by Moe.

30. HPL's comment suggests that he was doing revision work for Hoag.

[9]   [AHT]

Providence, R.I.,

October 6, 1921.

Concerning Ireland, I would ask Gahal-Bah what he means by "rights". What "right" exists on earth, save that of strength? If the Irish had the "right" to independence they would possess it. If they ever gain it, they will possess it—until they lose it again. England has the right to rule because she does. When she ceases to rule it will be time to talk of "rights" of others. It is not chance, but racial superiority, which has made the Briton supreme. Why have not the Irish conquered and colonised the earth if they are so deserving of regard? They are brainless canaille. Galba asks why he should worry about how hard a time the powers of Europe have. I will answer, because their overthrow would mean the overthrow of art, science, literature, and civilisation. If Galba respects the one, he must respect the other. Personally I agree that neither nations nor civilisations matter ultimately, but I do think it contributes to our immediate comfort to maintain the status quo. If Galba were truly cynical he would leave college, spend what money he has in drink and pleasure, and then commit suicide. The fact that he continues to live and waste time in reading and study proves that he cares for civilisation, and he who cares for civilisation had best be on the side of the Empire which alone sustains it. What if we are hypocritical? Is there either good or bad in the cosmos? What works, is best. Shew me another modern nation capable of keeping as much order as the British Empire keeps, and I will listen to drivel about our decadence. The decadence is not in Britannia but in all mankind—of course we know that man is now on the down-grade. As to the coming supremacy of the Prussian and Slavonic world, I should not be surprised at another challenge from Germany, but do not think any Slav nation will rise even to semi-civilisation. Whatever the Slav conquers will be lost to civilisation, for the race-stock is deficient. Slavs are emotional and irrational—the leaders of their nations are mostly non-Slavs with a veneer of Slavic culture. The ruling classes of the Slav nations are mainly Teutonic—clearly dolichocephalic Xanthochroi.[1] The brachycephalic masses are incurable peasants incapable of governing themselves or anyone else—they constitute part of the dull peasantry of many nations outside their nominal linguistic boundaries, including the characteristic South-German with his stupid face, broad head, and wholly non-Teutonic qualities. Germany may have a chance for leadership toward the end of the civilised period, but I hope that the Anglo-Saxons can prevent it. It is a free fight, with the strongest entitled to victory. Cosmically it does not matter, but I am an Englishman and have the healthy instinct of the animal to see its own pack win. I am not in the least uncynical about it, but certainly do not see what use there is in doing anything save stand by the old order. We are in the saddle now, and will prevent the maximum of chaos most easily by keeping there. If we cannot, all very well—it does not matter much—but so long as we have such vile things as lives the best we can do with them is to dedicate them to the service of Old England, whose influences gave us all we have. GOD SAVE THE KING!

I would like to disillusion Galba regarding his "brilliant and downtrodden" Ireland. So far as any evidence goes, the majority of men who have brought eminence to Ireland are nearly or wholly Anglo-Saxon by blood. Lord Dunsany is frankly an Englishman, with not one drop of the Celt—a Cheam School, Eton, and Sandhurst man whose voice and accent are as Londonese as any I have ever heard, and whose sympathies are ardently with the Empire. Even the self-conscious "Irish" intelligentsia are nine-tenths Anglo-Saxon, including Yeats, Synge, and everyone of any reputation. The ancient Irish civilisation is an ephemeral vision of the past, dead long before Britannia brought to the accursed island the only enduring culture it has ever possessed. That English culture in Ireland has certain local modifications no one wishes to deny. They are pleasing and appropriate, like the local variations of other cultures. We have Scottish, North-of-England, South-of-England, Welsh, Irish, American, and perhaps Australian variants of our English root-culture; but it is all English at the fountain-head, for none of it would have existed if our ancestors had not invaded the abandoned Roman province, driven out the Celts and Gallo-Romans, and founded the most solid and powerful civilisation since the Roman age. I will stand or fall with "fat John Bull", for he is mine own.

"England, with all thy faults I love thee still".[2]

In the NEW YORK TRIBUNE for last Sunday is a review which should interest our youthful sceptic; an account by Burton Rascoe, Esq. of the CHITRIB, of a striking fictional portrait of the modern bloodless intellectual: "Erik Dorn", by Ben Hecht, G. P. Putnam's Sons $2.00.[3] I believe that if I have a little more energy I shall try to obtain this work for perusal, for it seems to describe the modern with almost scientific comprehensiveness. I advise Gahal-Bah to peruse it at any cost. In commenting upon it Mr. Rascoe observes:

"Modern artists and aestheticians are rapidly eliminating from art all emotions which are not concerned with abstract form, and are thus helping to minimise sentiment in the life of the sentient being. The tendency is toward a biological atavism, highly intellectualised. A philosopher has said that we have lived emotionally beyond our means, and that we are reaping a harvest of complexes and neuroses which cripple the nervous system and weaken the body. Perhaps Erik Dorn is a prototype of the not unusual man of tomorrow."

The discussion on modernism hath served to confirm me in my belief that, so far as I touch art at all, I am not only a non-modern but a violent anti-modern. Intellectually I believe in nothing; aesthetically I believe only in the irradiate dreams of childhood. Sophistication I loathe and abhor with all the venom inherited from aeons of reptile and saurian ancestors in palaeolithic abysms of terrestrial history, and I even despise intellect when not directly concerned in the process of philosophical and scientific intellection. By this latter paradox I mean that I see nothing of beauty or pleasure in intellect, but only the hideous fascination of the forbidden Golden Door for the miserable Agib who stands before it.[4] All reality is a putrid mess, and whilst an intellectual negation of it is a stigma of inferiority or senility; I deem an aesthetic negation of it not only justified, but perhaps the only true art as well. It is not, however, romanticism which I deem art. In the negation of the obvious, whether intellectual or aesthetic, there is only puerility and absurdity. It is in a more subtle, conscious, and phantastick way, that the mind must seek its momentary surcease from the hell with which it is normally environed. The evolution of art during the coming half-century will be worthy the study of philosopher, scientist, and aesthetician alike. Decadence or reaction are the two obvious alternatives; with a parallel development of both as a not impossible third course. Progress I deem impossible—reason has dealt healthy emotion its death blow.

Concerning the question of Hibernia, and of the Britannick race, I need say no more than that Galba is misled by a false species of analysis whereby the observer cannot behold the wood for the trees. The fact remains that our race alone hath founded the circle of culture embracing all the elements which Galba is sophistical enough to class as non-English. But for England, there would be no Irish or American civilisation, and if at the present moment the Mother Isle chances to be below its normal degree of intellectual fertility, the circumstance is of no ultimate significance in the appraisal of the entire civilisation. If the Empire be decadent, it but shares the general decadence of this age; a decadence inevitable to all civilisations in the end, and detracting nothing from the historical merit of the nation itself. We do not respect Rome the less because she fell; indeed, any man had rather be an antique Roman, though the republick be dead, than a modern Italian, though the kingdom be shakily living. Of modern races the Britannick is so indisputably the greatest that argument is futile. I am not even disturb'd by the cries of those who challenge it. That the Gauls are the most uniformly artistick and cultivated of peoples, I do not dispute; but as I grow older I respect art the less, and power the more. It is not improbable that all art is merely an unsatisfactory substitute for physical supremacy; the imaginative gratification of that will to power which is frustrated in the objective attainment of its objects. It may be that the finest work of the aesthetick fancy is but a poor makeshift for the victory of one vigorous tribe or individual over another. Were I stronger, I might have gone to West Point, adopted a martial career, and found in war a supreme delight which scribbling can but faintly adumbrate. At heart I believe I despise the aesthete and prefer the warrior—I am essentially a Teuton and barbarian; a Xanthochroic Nordic from the damp forests of Germany or Scandinavia, and kin to the giant chalk-white conquerors of the cursed, effeminate Celts. I am a son of Odin and brother to Hengist and Horsa . . . . Grrr . . . Give me a drink of hot blood with a Celtic foe's skull as a beaker! Rule, Britannia . . . GOD SAVE THE KING!

Concerning my pessimism, it is well to differentiate betwixt the general and the personal. The general is of course theoretical, and subject to change as evidence warrants; being merely a present conviction that the pains of life overbalance the joys. The personal, to which I fancy Galba alludes, is based on my own mind and condition; and is a sentiment of inferiority rather than superiority. I have not the energy to study with that vigour and pleasure which mark the researches of Galba, and while freely granting that better men have put on paper a pleasure which hath cheered multitudes, must simply affirm with regret that I am unable to extract sufficient pleasure to make consciousness preferable to oblivion. From study I derive pleasure, but not so much as I could derive from non-existence. As to the despising of mankind, surely Galba realises that all despising is necessarily relative and empirical. In the cosmos there are no values whatsoever, so that the vilest insect is ultimately equal to the most magnificent spiral nebula. When I say I despise man, I do not mean to single him out as the one most loathsome object in creation, or on the other hand to differentiate him from myself in a spirit of assumed superiority. Indeed, I despise myself fully as much as the average fellow-louse; having what amounts to a positive personal dislike for the fellow called H. P. L. I despise man as compared with his own prevailing opinion of himself, that is all. There is no such thing as absolute beauty; what is called beauty is purely subjective and variable. Galba argues well that the quest for beauty forms as profitable a pastime as any, but he does not explain how one can avoid being bored by it ultimately, when he realises that it is all no more than a matter of fortuitous molecular, atomic, and electronic arrangement. The cosmos is a mindless vortex; a seething ocean of blind forces, in which the greatest joy is unconsciousness and the greatest pain is realisation. It is useless to point to the trivial pleasures of existence as justification for the numberless pains thereof—that they are truly pleasures, none disputes; yet how fleeting and how satiating! It is my present conviction that one must be either a downright pessimist or a complete dupe of mythology and religious delusion. Real extasies exist only in the fancies of the poets and priests. But after all, how absurdly trivial is the whole controversy on pleasure and pain—for what does it matter whether we suffer or not? Our feelings are the most trivial of incidents in the unending cycle of existence.

Concerning materialism, I believe that all ultra-modern objections to it arise from mere reaction and confusion in nomenclature. The resolving of the atom is interesting, and to chemical and physical science quite revolutionary, but that it constitutes any affirmation for the silly idea of permanent cosmic evolution in one direction, or for the notion of human personality as something apart from physical organisation, is quite unthinkable and certainly unwarranted by the least particle of genuine evidence. It is not for the philosopher to quibble over the exact definitions of matter and energy, or their possible identification. The minutiae of the operation of the blind infinite vortex are quite immaterial. Vitalism is a pleasing fad, but it cannot overcome the evidence for determinism or establish so absurd a doctrine as one-direction progress in an eternal universe. If Galba hath more evidence to present in these matters, I shall be pleased to hear it; though perchance he will not care to discuss the question till I have perused Santayana. I have now finished "Back to Methuselah", and deem it vastly clever. I knew about the struldbrugs[5] before Galba was born, and can see the resemblance, though it is not great. The struldbrugs were examples of the futility and misery of old age, whilst the ancients of Shaw are examples of the virtues of that condition. What Shaw does suggest, is the glowing oration upon struldbrugs which Gulliver deliver'd to the Luggnaggians before he had seen those pitiable creatures. Shaw, I think, is by no means so great a man as Swift; he is too much preoccupy'd with trivial questions of society, and doth not perceive to the full the tragedy of existence. He is too humorous—the truly great pass beyond humour, and retain only a terrible admixture of infinite disgust and soul-rending pity.

Well s'long,

H. PAGET-LOWE.

Notes

1. The racial terms are derived from various essays in Thomas Henry Huxley's *Man's Place in Nature* (1894), referring to "long-headed blond-haired" peoples (i.e., descendants of the "Nordic" barbarians in Europe) as opposed to broad, short skulls.

2. William Cowper, *The Task* 2.206.

3. A novel concerning a jaded intellectual. HPL apparently later read the work, for in later years he continually regarded it (along with T. S. Eliot's *The Waste Land*) as a landmark in modernist literature. The review by Burton Rascoe was "Striking Portrait of Modern Skeptic Drawn in 'Erik Dorn,'" *New York Tribune* (2 October 1921): Part V, p. 9.

4. Referring to the "Story of the Third Calendar, Son of a King," *The Arabian Nights' Entertainments*, ed. Andrew Lang.

5. In *Gulliver's Travels*, humans in the nation of Luggnagg who are seemingly normal, but are in fact immortal.

[10]   [TMs., JHL]

THE GALLOMO

PROVIDENCE, R.I., TUESDAY, NOVEMBER 29, 1921

MEDUSA: A PORTRAIT
By Theobaldus Senectissimus, Gent.

TO THE HON. IDA COCHRAN HAUGHTON, VISCOUNTESS WOODBY————

MY LADY:—

I shou'd be but a Cheater, and unworthy of the poetick Art, were I not to acknowledge to you by this Dedication the Indebtedness I bear you. For 'tis plain that I may my self claim but partial Credit for a Picture which, without so illustrious a Model, wou'd never have been drawn with any Sort of Fidelity. Truly, the Satirist desiring to shew certain Traits of Mind, wou'd be hard put to it, had he not before him some sort of living Example; and I am in Candour forc'd to concede, that of the Qualities I here seek to pourtray, no human Being cou'd display so great and flourishing an Abundance as your self. I shall ever count it a Piece of the greatest good Fortune, if my Satire succeed, that your Hatred of me mov'd you to slander and vilify me behind my Back; for lacking that Provocation I shou'd have neither had the Temerity to expose your Failings, nor possest so compleat a Fund of Lies and Calumnies from which to draw a Picture of such Venom as I never thought before to exist upon Earth.

Conscious, therefore, of my Debt, I will commend this unpretentious Effort to your well-known Graciousness, and beg leave to subscribe my self,
MY LADY,
Your Ladyship's most obedient,
most devoted, humble servant,
THEOBALDUS SENECTISSIMUS, ARMIGER.

Soak'd in her noxious venom, puff'd with gall,
Like some fat toad see dull MEDUSA sprawl;
Foul with her spleen, repugnant to the sight,
She crudely whines amidst eternal night.
From wit and sense by slothful brain debarr'd,
And with the chains of age and sourness scarr'd,
Her half-liv'd life one hateful wish reveals:
To give to others all the pain she feels!
Unschool'd in youth, unchasten'd by the years,
Grotesque with ignorance, absurd with fears;
Shunn'd for her ugly face and fretful mind,

She crawls alone, at war with all mankind.
In her black heart no love or kindness dwells,
But hate that shocks, and malice that repels;
Her narrow thoughts an equal vileness shew,
For there but envy and suspicion grow.
Blind to the truth, by jealous passion fann'd,
She slanders all she cannot understand,
And with loose tongue the sinner and the saint
Alike befouls in one inclusive taint.
Slow to see goodness, quick to smell a fault,
She scours the earth for victims to assault;
With what strain'd words she doles her lagging praise!
With what glad force her instant hatreds blaze!
Sluggish of wit, her loathsome bulk attests
One spark alone—a rage that never rests!
But not content to be an open fool,
Or candid knave, she seeks to cheat by rule;
Her want of sense in quoted saws she cloaks,
And with trite pelf a double laugh provokes,
Whilst all her cruelty must candour seem,
Tho' doubly evil for the stratagem.
So lurks MEDUSA, scourge of all around,
With hate, spleen, vanity, and dulness bound.
Anxious the wretch that courts her tardy smile,
And hapless he that knows her sneers and guile;
For since her envy flays all greater minds,
In ev'ry one alive a foe she finds—
Save for a little band of kindred sort,
In torpor mighty, but in wisdom short.
Void of all humour but the sly grimace,
She sees a challenge in each smiling face,
And spreads with twofold zeal her net malign,
Since she as injur'd innocence may shine.
From such a pest what rescue may we gain?
What spell may crush her hypocritic strain?
Her human form (perchance 'twas human once)
Forbids us smother the offending dunce;
Besides, we hesitate to smother such
A reptile thing, repellent to the touch.
A musket-ball but little harm could do
Where there's no brain or heart to hurtle through,
So still the monster heaves and puffs and rolls,

The toothless tearer of a thousand souls!
So must she fume, insatiate, sour, and wild;
Deaf, stupid, blear'd; by ev'ry tongue revil'd:
So must we wait, till Heav'n the curse revokes,
And the swoln snake in her own poison chokes!

To Jonathan E. Hoag

Jonathan E[lihu] Hoag (1831–1927) lived in and around Troy, N.Y., and entered amateur journalism late in life. Lovecraft compiled and wrote an introduction to Hoag's *Poetical Works* (1923). Lovecraft, Samuel Loveman, and James F. Morton revised some of Hoag's poetry for the volume. The book constituted the first appearance of a work by Lovecraft in hard covers. Lovecraft wrote birthday poems to Hoag from 1918 to 1927, and the elegy "Ave atque Vale" (*Tryout*, December 1927), upon Hoag's death. Hoag's descriptions of the Catskill Mountains may have contributed to the topographical atmosphere of "Beyond the Wall of Sleep" and "The Lurking Fear," which are set there. Hoag may have been a partial inspiration for the character Zadok Allen in "The Shadow over Innsmouth," whose life-dates exactly match Hoag's.

[11]   [ANS][1]

[No stamp; not addressed; not posted]

H. P. Lovecraft [*written by Hoag*]

Notes

1 *Front:* County Farm Dam / Cocheco River / Dover N.H.

[12]   [ANS][1]

[Postmarked Providence, R.I.,
3 July 1920]

Today I have another welcome visitor—R. Kleiner, Esq. We shall go to Boston together Monday.

Ward Phillips

Best wishes
and sincere respects.

Rheinhart Kleiner

Notes

1. *Front:* State Armory, Providence, R. I.

[13]   [ANS][1]

[Postmarked Brooklyn, N.Y.,
[?] September 1922]

Your interesting letter, with its delightful enclosures, received. Will answer soon. Am in Brooklyn, on my way back from Cleveland. ¶ Loveman recd. your letter, but was not able to attend to anything at the time—physically well, but very nervous. I shall try to transfer our work to more effective hands—don't lose hope! More anon.

H. P. L.

Notes

1. *Front:* Reviewing Stand, Entrance to Flower Garden, Prospect Park, Brooklyn, N. Y.

[14]   [ANS][1]

[Postmarked Brooklyn, N.Y.,
22 September 1922]

Visited this historic spot recently—wish you could see it. N.Y. is full of interesting sights & antiquities, including the old tavern—Fraunce's [*sic*]—where Gen. Washington bade farewell to his army.[2] ¶ Will write soon. Loveman has been unusually silent, but I'll wake him up if it kills me! H. P. L.

Notes

1. *Front:* Washington's Headquarters 1776, 160th Street and Edgecombe Avenue, New York

2. Fraunces Tavern, a tavern in lower Manhattan purchased in 1762 by Samuel Fraunces (1722?–1795), an African American restaurateur. George Washington bade farewell to his troops there on 4 December 1783.

[15]   [ANS][1]

[Postmarked Marblehead, Mass.,
6 July 1923]

How do you like the book? Am exploring old Marblehead & Salem—have been to Hub Club convention in Boston.

Best wishes,
H P L.

[*Note by Hoag:*] Rec'd July 9' / 23.

Notes

1. *Front:* A Quaint Old Street in Marblehead, Mass.

[16]   [ANS][1]

[Postmarked Providence, R.I.,
19 September 1923]

Well, here are both of your friends & literary collaborators, together in solemn conclave! Your letter just came, & I believe one of mine has gone astray, for I was the last to write . . . . It was a thick letter, with many enclosures—too bad it's lost!

Yr moſt obt   H P Lovecraft

It gives me pleasure to join in sending cordial greetings. We have been viewing many interesting scenes together.

James F. Morton, Jr.

Notes

1. *Front:* Manning Hall Brown University.

[17]   [ANS][1]

[No stamp, no postmark]
259 Parkside Ave.,
Brooklyn, N.Y.
May 14, 1924

My very dear friend Scriba:—

This is just to herald the letter I have owed you so long, & which I shall certainly write in a few days! Pressure of work has been enormous, as I shall duly relate. ¶ and here are your two splendid poems, duly sandpapered. Pray send me copies when they are printed. ¶ United trying to get ahead under difficulties—of this more anon.

H. P. L

[P.S.] The new household sends unanimous regards!

Notes

1 *Front:* Poe's Cottage, Bronx, N. Y.

[18] [ANS][1]

[Postmarked Staten Island, N.Y.,
10 March 1925]

Exploring quaint Staten Island with my friend George Kirk. Delightful antiquities! Am writing this on flat-topped grave in a half-deserted village churchyard![2]

Yr obt Servt H P Lovecraft

Being a friend of HPL's I consider you a friend of mine. Best wishes

George Kirk

Notes

1. *Front:* Old Billopp House, Tottenville, S. I. (Erected 1668)
2. Reformed Church on Staten Island; an historic Dutch Reformed Church and cemetery at 54 Port Richmond Avenue in Port Richmond.

[19] [ANS][1]

[Postmarked Alexandria, Va.,
12 April 1925]

Still on my wanderings! Absorbing the National Capital & its antiquities, & incidentally meeting the local amateur leaders—

H P Lovecraft

Notes

1. *Front:* The National Cathedral, Washington, D. C.

[20] [ANS][1]

[Postmarked Newport, R.I.,
5 August 1926]

Your letter recd.—Will answer soon. The two of us are revelling in Colonial sights!

——H P Lovecraft

It is long since I have heard from you. I hope you are enjoying excellent health.

James F. Morton, Jr.

Notes

1. *Front:* The Old Mill and Channing Monument, Touro Park, Newport, R. I.

[21] [ANS][1]

[Postmarked Newport, R.I.,
14 July 1927]

Am shewing a young friend of mine the antiquities of colonial Newport—
now seated on a high cliff overlooking the sea.
Yr obt Servt. HPL

If I approach closely enough, I shall stop at Greenwich. But nothing is certain
in my eccentric peregrinations. I have met the enemy, and I am theirs!
Very sincerely yours
Donald Wandrei

Notes

1. *Front:* Interior Trinity Church Built 1726, Newport R. I.

[22] [ANS][1]

[Postmarked Providence, R.I.,
21 July 1927]

Assembled in conclave in Providence:
[signed]
Frank B. Long, Jr.
Donald Wandrei
James F. Morton (late "Jr."), who sends cordial greetings and wishings for an-
other visit with you.
C. M. Eddy, Jr.

We are holding quite a convention of kindred souls, & wish you could be
here to take part in the deliberations. Tomorrow the party goes to Newport.
—Theobald

Notes

1. *Front:* The Carrie Tower Brown University.

[23]   [ANS][1]

[Postmarked Portland, Me.,
26 August 1927]

Still on the road! Portland is a fascinating place, & full of recollections of Longfellow. Now for Portsmouth, Newburyport, & Haverhill—at which latter place I shall see the genial Tryout editor. Stopping at YMCA & seeing the town thoroughly. It is quite a city, but full of old time seafaring colour.
    Best wishes—Theobald

Notes

1. *Front:* Longfellow's Home, Portland, Me.

[24]   [ANS][1]

[Postmarked Bretton Woods, N.H.,
27 August 1927]

Was so near the White Mts. in Portland that I decided to take advantage of a cheap excursion. Ascended Mt. Washington & had some fine views en route, though rain spoiled view at summit.
            Sincerely—
            H P Lovecraft

Notes

1. *Front:* Crawford Notch from Mt. Willard, White Mountains, N. H.

[25]   [AN][1]

    This place has the best existing collection of Colonial household objects—I wish you could see it. This winter I am making a particularly thorough study of the Colonial atmosphere, & am visiting as many of these houses & museums as possible.

Notes

1. *Front:* Rhode Island School of Design /Southeast Bedroom / Pendleton Collection / Colonial House

[26]   [AN][1]

    Here is a feature of Old Providence which I don't think I've shewn you before.

Built in 1816.
It was designed by John Holden Greene, a Providence architect, & is one of the finest Georgian churches in New England; though its steeple is not as perfect as that of the old First Baptist (1775).

Notes

1. *Front:* First Congregational (Unitarian) Church / "An Old New England Meeting House"

[27]   [AN][1]

This likeness is only an hypothetical one made in the 18th Century. Actually, Roger Williams had no pictures painted; so that we do not know how he really looked. The costume shewn in the picture is 100 years too recent for Williams's time.

Notes

1. *Front:* Roger Williams—Copies of Engraving. Engraved by F. Halpin from an Original Painting for "Benedict's History of the Baptists".

[28]   [AN; Hoag to Lovecraft][1]

[no stamp; not posted]

To H. P. Lovecraft: 598 Angell St., Providence, R.I.

From Prospect St.
Greenwich, N.Y.

Now Philip, when on Fashion St. you go.
You meet a freckl'd face you too well know,
Foxy hair bobb'd short and her dress the same,
A number 6 on rubber heels; and lame,
You'd feel a thrill of joy you ne'er felt before!
Pray don't tarry long to search the whole world o'er,
But dye that scanty crop on top your grizzl'd head
Like hers you met on Fashion St., a foxy red.—

A New year's Greeting.   The advice of Scriba.

Notes

1. *Front:* Elmira State Reformatory, Elmira, N. Y.

To Henriette Ziegfeld

Henriette Ziegfeld (1894–1976) was a member of the Woodbees, an amateur journalism club in Columbus, Ohio, along
with her brother Arthur F. Ziegfeld, editor of the amateur journal *Ziegfeld's Follies*. She was a schoolteacher and businesswom-
an. In 1921 she went to India as an educational worker and met
Bernhard Strasen, a missionary worker; they married in 1923
and had six children. The family returned to the U.S. in 1951,
eventually settling in Fort Wayne, Ind.

[29]   [TLS]

598 Angell St., Providence, R.I.

November 6, 1920.

Dear Miss Ziegfeld:—

I must lose no time in thanking the Woodbee Club for
its splendid generosity in this season of peril for *The United Amateur*. The gift
of $25.00 to the fund, just received, is a surprise of the most welcome sort,
and will make certain the issuance of an adequate November number. The
action of the Woodbees is a splendid example of United loyalty, and places
the Association heavily in the club's debt. It has been noted in the September
issue just going to press, and will certainly earn for the Columbus members
the unstinted thanks of all on our rolls. In addition, I must express my personal thanks as Official Editor, for my position as the first to depart from the
high standard made possible by W. Paul Cook's generosity is rather trying; and
overwhelmingly so when the very existence of the organ becomes imperilled.

The splendid gift of the Woodbees—the largest single gift so far received
in the Fund—brings the Fund up to $82.25.[1] Of this amount about $50.00
will go toward the 16-page September organ today mailed to Ericson for
printing, leaving a residue which with later scattered contributions will make
possible a November number of equal size. The September number will contain all Convention matter, one poem, one sketch or story, and a large number of reports, from which the President's will unfortunately be missing. I
tried my best to obtain it in time, but the young man is very busy and evidently placed other matters first.[2] When I had word that Ericson was ready for his
copy, I did not feel justified in delaying any further. In the November issue I
hope to have a poem or two, a story, official reports, and a membership list,
which will not occur in September. News notes will if possible be included in
both—which reminds me that Woodbee items are always welcome.

Again thanking the club for its extreme generosity, I am
Very sincerely yours,
H P Lovecraft

Notes

1. HPL refers to the Official Organ Fund, a fund whose proceeds were used to publish the *United Amateur*, the official organ of the UAPA. A year or so after this letter was written, Ida C. Haughton of the Woodbees accused HPL of mismanaging the Official Organ Fund.
2. The president of the UAPA for the 1920–21 term was Alfred Galpin.

To John Ravenor Bullen

John Ravenor Bullen (1886–1927) was a Canadian poet and amateur journalist. He possibly introduced Lovecraft to the Transatlantic Circulator (an Anglo-American correspondence group) in early 1921. Some of his poetry later appeared in Lovecraft's *Conservative*. When Bullen died, his mother asked Lovecraft to prepare an edition of Bullen's poetry, and Lovecraft did so. The Recluse Press of W. Paul Cook published *White Fire* in 1927 (a second edition was printed in 1929 but never bound). Lovecraft said that the printing of *White Fire* almost ruined Cook (it "proved rather a costly venture, since the expenses exceeded all calculations"). Lovecraft's preface is a revised version of his essay "The Poetry of John Ravenor Bullen" (*United Amateur*, September 1925). "That Bullen article is a bit flattering—he isn't as important as I imply—but he is so amiable & eager that I thought it wouldn't do any harm to let him have his glory before a none too discriminating audience" (*LFF* 569).

[30] [AL][1]

598 Angell St.,

Providence, R.I.,

Decr 27, 1920

Dear Bullen:—

       Your kind holiday wishes are keenly appreciated & heartily reciprocated; none the less so because the winter festival is for me not literally a *Christmas*, but the old solstitial celebration of our pagan Saxon progenitors, wherein the cause of rejoicing is the northward turning of the sun with its concomitant prophecy of spring.

       Your interesting letter & attractive card duly arrived, & I was very glad to see the arguments which you advance on your side of the philosophical & metaphysical controversy. It gratifies me to know that I have been instrumental in helping you form a definite philosophical attitude, even though that attitude is the reverse of my own; & I trust you will be charitable enough to forgive me if I cannot share it.

       The argument you employ—that of transcendental idealism—is a familiar one to me; but I must warn you that it is today practically abandoned. The supposition that all objects form only a subjectively created series of illusions, with existence in the mind alone, is indeed a possible & legitimate one; but having less probability than realism, & surely no more justification, it is hard to view as anything more than an ingenious fancy. Certainly we *know* nothing—even our own existence is in doubt—but in the absence of proof it is safer to accept provisionally that theory which is best correlated with observed phenomena. *Probability* is not to be slighted. When we see a railway train we assume that it came from its starting point on the track

[31]   [AL]

598 Angell St.,
Providence, R.I.,
Jany. 7, 1921.

Dear Bullen:—

I was exceedingly glad to receive your interesting letter & card of holiday greeting last month, & would have replied earlier but for execrable health & accumulated duties. The Circulator, despatched by Mr Munday^2 Dec. 20, reached me Dec. 29; but I was unable this time to get it off within the prescribed week. It is now ready for transmission to Rock Island, & will go this afternoon if I am able to get down town to the express office. I observe that my imaginative work is not greatly favoured by the majority of members, & fear I shall be regarded as rather a bore if I cannot find something else to insert. Possibly I will next time send something by some other member of the U.A.P.A. For your own very kindly criticisms I am immeasurably grateful—although you really give me vastly more credit than I shall ever deserve! Your new novel^3 opens most promisingly, arresting the reader's attention at once & arousing a keen expectancy for future instalments.

Jany 9.

Was not well Friday, but sent off the Circulator yesterday.^{4} I regret very much having delayed it, & hope you can excuse the lapse. ~~Your card of Dec. 10 & interes~~ Let me reciprocate the kind seasonal wishes contained in your letter, & the benevolent [. . .]

[32]   [AL]^5

III.

[. . .] Old Dickon resolved to concoct something likely to make the kid sit up & take notice. He is still awaiting word from Appleton.

I note your remarks anent N.A.P.A. politics, & assure you that if I vote at all in the National it will be pro-Houtain.^{6} I am his recruit, & will support any candidate of his so long as he does not pick one from the non-Lovemanic part of Cleveland. For the National & its government I give not a solitary "dab"—(remember my cold!) but am agin' Cleveland on principle, as it were! So the slang-employing Marjoria Exaquaria is a Cleveland spy, eh? Down with her![7] I have an extra grudge anyway, for she does not mail me the *National Amateur*. I only extracted the September number after an oral request at the Newton Hub meeting, & have not seen the November one yet. (Have just asked M^rs. Miniter to get me a copy if possible.) I wonder if the Dowdell gang have instructed her to keep as much National matter as possible away from me, lest I become an interested Nationalite & transfer the fight from the United? If so, Willie doesn't know his Grandpa Theobald yet. I am not interested in the National, & shall never be an active factor in its campaigns. Except for a general dislike of Cleveland & a mild wish to please the Hub–B.P.C. party,[8] which seems to me the best element to say naught of being the only element whose members I know

Notes

1. Both items are fragments found on the versos of the A.Df. of "The Horror at Red Hook."

2. John Munday, one of the participants (along with HPL and Bullen) in the Transatlantic Circulator, an Anglo-American group of amateurs who exchanged stories, essays, poetry, and other works in manuscript and commented on them.

3. In the preface to *White Fire* HPL states that Bullen was the author of "at least one unpublished novel, a refreshing romance of old seaways and pirate treasure entitled 'From the Mouth of the Golden Toad'" (*CE* 2.139).

4. The material included HPL's essay "The Defence Reopens!" (January 1921; *CE* 5).

5. Either a part of the above letter or a separate letter.

6. E. Dorothy Houtain (wife of George Julian Houtain) was elected president of the NAPA in the election of July 1921.

7. HPL refers punningly to Marjorie Outwater, Official Editor of the NAPA (1920–21). In Latin, *ex* = out; *aquaria* is a derivative of *aqua* (water).

8. The Hub Club and the Blue Pencil Club, amateur groups in Boston and Brooklyn, respectively.

To Myrta Alice Little

Myrta Alice (Little) Davies (1888–1967) was a graduate of Colby College (B.A.) and Radcliffe (M.A.). After several teaching jobs, she settled in Hampstead, N.H., writing for the McClure Newspaper Syndicate. She also published in the *Tryout* and other amateur journals and was acquainted with the *Tryout*'s editor C. W. Smith, who lived in nearby Haverhill, Mass. Lovecraft's first visit to Little in New Hampshire occurred on 8–9 June 1921. See Goudsward for further information on Little and Lovecraft's ties to New Hampshire.

[33]   [ALS, JHL]

598 Angell St.,

Providence, R.I.,

May 17, 1921

My dear Mifs Little:—

Pray accept my sympathy regarding the process of domestic upheaval, & the hope that your chain of symbolic icons may by this time boast complete colouration! That there exists in the task some redeeming spark of pleasure for you, is indeed fortunate. I abhor all manual labour, & am unutterably bored by the necessity of taking care of my own quarters. Many a night have I slept in a dressing-gown on the top of my bed to avoid making it the next day—in fact, I believe I am the most basically & constitutionally indolent person on this terraqueous globe. Last week occurred a tragedy—I was forced to clear my table & files of a year's accumulation of papers, since I could no longer find anything I wished amidst the general chaos! I am now resting after this unwonted exertion, & enjoying the singular spectacle of the whole surface of my table, exposed to view after several months of burial beneath sundry strata of literary debris. I pine for Oriental magnificence & luxury—to rest at ease amidst silken pillows in a vast tapestried chamber, cheered by the scent of incense & attended by a horde of submissive slaves responding to my commands. Thus might one be free to observe without the pettiness of action; to reflect without the annoyance of practicality; to write without the fetters of the commonplace—but up to now I have found no slaves on the market, whom I could trust to keep my papers & books in order; hence my condescension to the disagreeable routine of helping myself. Life in these parvenu communities of the Western hemisphere is a beastly bore!

Your critic, if she has been moving, deserves sympathy. I moved once—in June 1904—& have not yet recovered from the nervous shock.[1] The next time will probably be the end of me—at least I hope it will. Any acerbity & cavilling you may receive from her within the next few weeks may be safely discounted as pathological. When I moved I could not bear to go "home" to the new quarters at #598, but would remain away as much as possible, mostly on long cycling trips. I hardly recall what happened during that summer, but the horror is still vivid after seventeen years. Still—moving from one's *birthplace* is an extreme case.

You would not find a Remington very satisfactory for migratory purposes. Mine[2] resembles a grand piano in dimensions & weight, & I detest the exertion of moving it from its stand by the window to the table under the gaslight. I should like to have a Corona also, & almost obtained one a few years ago; but the dual arrangement would really be unwise for one with my financial limitations.

I note your correction regarding your literary encampment, which I shall view with interest & pleasure if the Parcae permit my Arctic expedition next month. And regarding said expedition—surely Junius is better than Maius, & I am not sure but that Quintilis would be better still. Heat is my breath of life—I never really live till the mercury reaches 90°. As to duration; the fatigue I felt on the second day both times I stayed overnight in Boston, warns me that it were well not to extend my absences too abruptly. Wherefore I fancy I had better plan for the single night only, at the same time extending sincerest thanks for the ampler invitation. When you have observed the almost unbelievable tedium & dulness of my conversation, & the grotesque & melancholy awkwardness of my demeanour, you will be grateful for the weak nerves which prevent me from imposing more considerably upon your hospitality! Indeed—I am growing monstrous sensitive about my want of social amiability, & last week declined another Boston invitation because of the settled melancholy I was in.

Concerning the *date*—I have decided to disregard the Wednesday matinee for reasons to be stated forthwith. When I came to consider the matter, I found that the performance seemed more or less immaterial—I think I am beginning to be bored by all ordinary events, so that a dramatic spectacle no longer possesses any glamour for me, unless it be of singular merit or magnitude. My change of plan is for this reason: to my regret I am informed that my simple Damoetas[3] of Haverhill is suffering from a nervous breakdown, so that it would probably be really unkind of me to vex him with a call. Accordingly, the Groveland St. event is abandoned. Eodem tempore, I am invited to the Hub Club meeting of Thursday, June 9—just the date of the projected journey; so that a plan to include that enters my dense cranium. Behold, then, the revised programme—which is, however, to be adopted only if perfectly convenient to all in your household. (a) Matinee abandoned. (b) Advance to Westville Wednesday, June 8, 1921; to arrive about the time Robert Gray, Jr. is grinding out the overture at the Albee Theatre.[4] (c) Bivouac for night among the ghosts of abandoned wing at Little Towers. (d) Early part of June 9 at the Towers & the literary lodge adjacent thereto, with afternoon departure in time to reach (e) Boston at 7:30 p.m. for Hub Club meeting, after which will come (f) the 11:45 night express, & (g) home, James, at 1:30 a.m. June 10. This, you see, merely retrogrades the schedule XXIV hrs., & substitutes the Hub for the Merrimack metropolis. I am, though, vastly sorry to hear that Tom's[5] genial master is indisposed—I have just written him a note of sympathy, telling him that I can understand any malady springing from neural fatigue or maladjustment. Poor *Tryout!*

Considerations of weather & time-tables arise. Probably it would not do to be too particular about the skies, since a postponement would no doubt play havock with your crowded calendar of activities. As to the B. & M. rail facilities—I shall seek enlightenment tomorrow if the local headquarters of the N.Y.N.H. & H. can supply such information regarding their northerly contemporary. Does one go to Westville or Hampstead? Possibly you might supplement the lore obtainable from the humble leaflet. And more—does daylight saving prevail in the Granite State? I am in sooth an alien to those climes—I have *seen* but never *set foot in* New-Hampshire. How exciting an adventure to enlarge my list of visited states from three to four! My record will be—R.I. 1890, Mass. 1890, Conn. 1903, N.H. 1921. Will the list ever be further augmented? Last year Houtain & Kleiner almost persuaded me to add N.Y., but this spring I feel more weariness & less ambition; so that I half fancy I shall return to oblivion without ever having seen any part of this wretched planet outside New-England. If I had a yacht with perfect luxury, I might be a traveller in my old age; for I should like to see the Motherland with its green fields, ancient oaks, & ivied manor-houses; Rome with its crumbling memorials of unexampled supremacy; Hellas with its fallen columns & olive-groves telling of more beauty than earth ever knew elsewhere; & Ægyptus with its awesome stones & tenebrous crypts that carry the fancy back to vague ages. All these should I like to behold, yet lacking wealth & ease of transportation I shall see them only in dreams. And who shall say that dreams are less than reality? Have I not beheld the willowed streams of England, the majesty of Greece & Rome in all their youth of 2000 years ago, & the living swarthy throngs that hailed the greatness of Se[s]ostris in Thebes & Memphis?

Since art, save Graeco-Roman art, is not a specialty of mine; I perceive that my ignorance of the Worcester gallery has not been such a deprivation as I imagined. In matters of pictorial art I have not enough taste to warrant the airs of a connoisseur—& I never assume enthusiasms which I do not possess, in the manner of conventional persons. Probably I am fond of Graeco-Roman art mostly because it is *old*—in modern art I have no appreciation of portraits, & can be enthusiastic only over landscapes or certain scenes involving quaint edifices. My standard is partly pastoral, & partly bizarre. I like the horrible in art—Doré is my favourite, & Dunsany's elderly illustrator S. H.

Sime appeals to me. Impressionism as far as Degas is not wholly outside the range of my sympathy, but the post-impressionism of such persons as Cezanne & Matisse is as bad as *vers libre* in my estimation. Such puerile blots & twists as one sees in *The Dial* are beneath my contempt.[6]

My eyes are practically free from the inflammation which lately beset them, but I have been depressed with the twin afflictions of an unparallelled cold & a paralysing pressure of professional verse revision. The latter, I think, is the worse evil—how cheerfully could I strangle the dunce who expects me to make something of doggerel equally devoid of form & ideas!! Labour is an unmitigated evil except for peasants—one should be free to search for beauty & horror without obligations of any kind, & to create art with no thought of commercial considerations. In either labour or leisure, however, there is little reward. Both wear on one atrociously. Life is too long by far—one should not outlive the naturally ecstatic & optimistic days of early youth. Keats & Shelley were luckier than they knew.

I learn with interest the nature & identity of your especial Cook—he of the sabbatico-scholastic narrative. Something bears in upon me the conviction that he & I would not agree anent thrills. This is probably the sort of thing he would like:

George's Sacrifice
By Percy Vacuum, age 8.

George was a good boy who went to Sabbath-school every week and never forgot his golden text. Each Sunday the kind teacher gave a pretty picture to every little boy who was not late, and at the end of the year promised a nice red-covered testament to every little boy who had not been late at all.

It was the very last Sunday of the year, & George had never been late. See him as he trips along to sabbath-school, his face glowing with the light of his soul, & his eyes looking only ahead, never at the gaudy flowers that sacrilegiously bloom beside the road! The sun is so bright, & George will get his red-bound testament if he is not late!!

But what is this we see? A tiny waif crying at the cross-roads! Poor little thing, it is indeed tiny Joe, the blacksmith's boy, who lives a mile hence & has strayed away & become lost!!!!!

Heavens! what is our good George to do? Shall he leave little Joe crying and lost, or shall he take him home and be late to sabbath-school? He does not know what to do, for although he reads his quarterly and learns his golden text faithfully, he is not a good cas'-u-ist. How his golden head swims with the great problem before him! Really, it is quite too much!!

Then he thinks of the glory of sacrifice and resolves to help little Joe even if he is late to sabbath-school! So he takes the tiny fellow's hand and leads him to the modest smithy of his loving parents; though crying softly over the red testament he fears he will not get.

Now he draws near the abode of the good smith—and what is this he sees? Oh, Wonders!!!!!!! *It is his dear sabbath-school teacher's buggy standing outside the door of the forge!!* Inside he hears the clink of the anvil. His teacher's horse has lost a shoe, so his teacher has had to stop at the blacksmith's! He will not be late! Delirious with joy, he enters the forge.

In one second little Joe is ecstatically smothered in his father's brawny arms, whilst George's teacher listens to the thrilling tale. "My boy", says the teacher, "you did right! Now let us drive gaily to sabbath-school, where you will get your red testament!" Thus is Christian sacrifice ever rewarded. Boys, always follow George's example!!

Coming out of the ether—certainly a tale should be plausible—even a bizarre tale *except for the single element where supernaturalism is involved*. It is thus with Wilde's "Dorian Gray", & with all imaginative masterpieces.

I am glad to know that you have heard from my Alfredus child, & hope he will write frequently. To know him is worth all the dues, fees, & responsibilities of membership in amateur journalism! You will find him the clearest, keenest, & most ruthlessly honest & thorough thinker you ever encountered. His only god is truth—& having shed all illusions he grimly attacks the stronghold of knowledge with the engines of sincerity. I have never beheld his equal, & never expect to do so. Future years will justify the seeming fulsomeness with which I describe him.

I think I read something about the adaptation of Briggs' drawings for the cinema—but it was two or three years ago, & I never beheld any of the pictures on the screen. I saw "Kismet" in cinema form a few weeks ago, & thought it unusually good.[7] There was much scenic lavishness impossible in a stage production, & to my mind the arrangement was highly artistic—not excepting the opening & closing struggle of the worthy plebeian with the rather Woodrow-Wilsonian donkey. I could find no fault with any part, & I liked the well-managed drowning of the Vizier—or Wazir, as the more accurate Orientalists say—in the pool. In the stage version one merely sees the gentleman go over the side, but in the cinema we behold the sinister surface, the bubbles, & all that sort of thing. I am certainly fond of artistic murder—it is a delicate accomplishment & a balm to jaded nerves.

Which leads me to the Grand Guignol & Maurice Level. Nay, I have never read a tale of M. Maurice's, but have yearned to do so ever since beholding the announcement of his book of tales in the reviews a year or so ago.[8] Our library has none of his work—Providence is really rather provincial. *Hearst's* is a publication unknown to me[9]—I shun all the publications of that pro-German traitorous scoundrel, from his low *Boston American* to his flashy *Cosmopolitan*.[10] It is my desire to see the fellow hanged—or held beneath the surface of a pool till the bubbles grow faint! But for M. Level I have only the respect most profound—I would that I could create plots as delicious as his! How relieving it is to fly from the pitiful commonplaces of futile, trivial, superficial, ethics-mad, mock-important, sentimental, romantic, false-idea'd, American namby-pamby Sunday-school tales, to something that actually digs under the illusory surface of conventional values & feigned motives, & shakes the real fibres of the human animal! Actually—the motive forces of the average American story are so pitifully false that one must needs weep for the travesty on art. Things which do not matter, but which loom large in the primers of Victorianism, form the bases of the most pretentious tales—with bathos & elephantine tinsel as a result. What a horde of heavy, thick-witted, hyper-moral dunces are about to be swept into eternal oblivion from the petty fame they now enjoy amongst ribbon-clerks, sunday-school teachers, & elderly ladies—dunces with their harping on progress, "spiritual" struggles, nobility of "soul", unselfishness, & such infernal nonsense! What a force American idealism is—from the oracular Emerson down to the oozy Harold Bell Wright![11] It has had its day, but must pay the penalty of all emotional extravagances that distort facts, exalt mere expedients to cosmic principles, & interpret life in terms of artificial, wholly fictitious, & often diametrically wrong motives. It cannot remain a force in literature because its appeal was based only on a passing mental fashion; the cords it thrilled—or tried to thrill—were not the real cords of intense human feeling, but the transient gossamer threads of an abnormal sentimentality. When the fad of ethics is gone, the literature of ethics will be an absurd curiosity. "No artist", says Oscar Wilde, "has ethical sympathies. An ethical sympathy in an artist is an unpardonable mannerism of style . . . . . . No artist desires to prove anything."[12] America has had just one great literary artist—Edgar Allan Poe. Ambrose Bierce was a true artist, but with greater limitations. But art is foreign to the snivelling Puritan temperament of most Americans—they are mad about *wholesomeness, rightness,* & kindred non-essentials. It never occurs to them that the only real art is the creation of pictures of intense phases of actual life—real life, & not life as misrepresented in Presbyterian prayer-meetings. To seize an idea or image bearing on some really tense apex of human experience—some genuine emotional or imaginative exaltation—that is art. But the herd of "right-thinking"[13] scribblers are forever debarred by their false conceptions of life, from recognising the real apexes & exaltations. For one thing, they must learn that the one great emotion is *despair*—the one logical & inevitable result of the conflict of man's will with his iron-hooped limitations. Then they must learn that nothing ever "comes out right"—that Nature abhors neat compartments & obvious results, but delights in complexities, contradictions, & paradoxes—that good men are generally simple & unsuccessful persons, & that evil is what usually wins rewards—if there be such things as good & evil in a blind cosmos. They must learn that man as a whole can be regarded in only two possible moods—pity & ironic humour—that all struggles are trivial except the ghastly eternal struggle of the will against Fate—in which the will is always foredoomed to defeat. All these things they must learn—but they will not, since such ideas are not nice & pretty & "inspiring". And so America will never produce great literary artists except for rebels like Poe, strong enough to defy tradition & overcome heritage. Real vividness will continue to be left to the European Continentals. Vive Level!

To return from my senile maunderings & Menckenoid invective—I always knew "Nemesis" was a mere tinkle of sound, but you are the first reader to expose its hollowness! That thing has been so often referred to as my best piece of verse, that I almost came to believe it a solitary treasure among the trash of my near-literary emanations! I suppose its main trouble is too much imagery & too little idea—a leading defect of ulalumish rhapsodies. Speaking of the diversity of taste—young Horace L. Lawson[14] tells me that "The House" in *The Philosopher* is the best verse I ever wrote! In truth, no verses of mine are of much merit. If I ever wrote anything worth reading, it is to be found amongst my prose nightmares. Which reminds me—did not the explanation of "The Tree"[15] appear hidden under the externals? I meant to *suggest* it without *stating* it. Musides slowly poisoned Kalos because the latter's statue was turning out the better; but Kalos, with the aid of the tree-spirits by whom he was beloved, effected a revenge. Out of his grave Kalos sent a living tree—an emissary which in time killed Musides & destroyed his work so that he could not enjoy the fruits of his crime, but the dull public never knew. The public never knows what lies behind the exterior of so-called "noble" men & "noble" acts.* So they built a temple to the brotherly piety of Musides. But the olive trees know, & to this day whisper significantly to one another, & sigh in the night wind, οἶδα! οἶδα! In this tale the idea of *justice* forms an artistic error from the absolute point of view; but the idea is Hellenic, & is permissible in fantasies assuming the supernatural. The fantastic tale, indeed, may legitimately admit the deeply-seated illusions of man; since it is primarily a study of the human imagination, of which illusions form a prominent part. Illusion may always be treated, *as illusions.*

But I must have pity upon the ennuied reader & cease, lest the visit of so monumental a bore be either hailed with dread, or revoked altogether!

Most cordially & sincerely yrs—

H P Lovecraft

P.S.—Pray pardon *envelope!* Am all out of the "real thing"—must get some tomorrow.

Notes

1. HPL and his mother had to move from 454 Angell Street to more modest quarters

---

*Loveman once wrote an impressive prose-poem—"The Departed"—on this theme.

at 598 Angell on the occasion of the death of his grandfather, Whipple V. Phillips. He even contemplated suicide at the time.

2. I.e., HPL's 1906 Remington typewriter.

3. A figure who appears in Greek and Latin poetry as a prototypical shepherd. Here it refers to Tryout Smith, whom HPL described thus: "I find Smith a very interesting person, since his character renders him almost a living incarnation of the conventional types of pastoral poetry. As he roams the fields & woods with his diminutive mascot, I fancy he is much like the old poets' conception of some Sicilian or Arcadian Damoetas, who spent the day in innocent sport, & danced to the homely melody of the oaten reed" (*Letters to Rheinhart Kleiner and Others* 86).

4. Robert Gray, Jr. was the longtime director of the Albee Theatre (320 Westminster St., Providence), which opened in 1919.

5. Tryout Smith's cat, about whom HPL wrote "Sir Thomas Tryout: Died November 15, 1921."

6. The *Dial* (1880–1929) was a journal of literary and political commentary. Around this time it became a vigorous proponent of cultural modernism.

7. *Kismet* (Waldorf Film Corporation, 1920), American silent film version of the play *Kismet* (1911) by Edward Knoblock, directed by Louis J. Gasnier; starring Otis Skinner and Elinor Fair.

8. Maurice Level, *Tales of Mystery and Horror*.

9. *Hearst's Magazine* (1912–14), later titled *Hearst's International Combined with Cosmopolitan* (1914–21) and *Hearst's International* (1921–25), a popular magazine. Some of Level's stories (in English translation) appeared there.

10. William Randolph Hearst established the *Boston American* (1904–61) as a tabloid newspaper. He acquired the magazine *Cosmopolitan* in 1905.

11. Harold Bell Wright (1872–1944), bestselling American novelist whose work was held in low esteem by critics.

12. From the preface to *The Picture of Dorian Gray*. Also quoted in HPL's essay "Final Words" (September 1921; *CE* 5.62).

13. HPL has derived this derisive phrase from the journalism of H. L. Mencken.

14. Amateur journalist in Utica, Mich., and editor of the *Wolverine* (1919f.), to which HPL contributed stories and his "Vivisector" column.

15. It is unclear how Little came to read "The Tree," since it was not published until it appeared in the *Tryout* (October 1921). Perhaps she saw proofs of the story at Tryout Smith's house.

To Victor E. Bacon

Victor E[dward] Bacon (1905–1997) was born in Somerset, England. He was an amateur journalist—one of Lovecraft's recruits—and editor of *Bacon's Essays,* which published work by Lovecraft and Clark Ashton Smith. Edgar J. Davis, President of the United Amateur Press Association, appointed him its Official Editor (1925–26).

[34] [ALS]

Same old dump—
3/11/22

Dear B:—

Had I not been knocked flat by a combination of D V Bush & George Julian Houtain, I should have sooner expressed my sincere regret at hearing of your recent indisposition. Permit me to do so now, & to add the assurance that I will not diffuse the tidings. I hope very much that your recovery will complete itself with thoroughness & celerity, so that your customary programme may be resumed under favourable conditions. With illness of any kind I can sympathise most understandingly—the difficult thing for me is to imagine anyone without it. My younger aunt says she has never had a headache—only a confidence in the probity & veracity of the Phillips blood makes me accept this statement literally . . . . especially at the present moment, when my own cranium is agitated with some sort of earthquake, civil war, or political election in the anterior part of its interior.

There need be no overwhelming regret about missing the Hub orgy—their regular meetings on the second Thursday of each month are almost as amusing, though not so many of the animals turn out on such occasions. At any one of these solemn conclaves your welcome would be profound & unaffected, & the members who might be absent would probably be the least important. And as I said before, any trip including a glimpse of the divine Castor & Pollux—I mean Kenneth & Robin[1]—would have to be separate unless you had a second day to spare—or unless the multiform local feud should undergo another realignment. These feuds are picturesque things—in far away Brooklyn the local club is planning a constitutional amendment providing for the expulsion of any member publishing abuse or slander. Pax omnibus!

I am not attending the Maldenese *coena Trimalchioni*[2] this evening—I am too bored with mankind to waste the fee, car-fare, & energy. What a futile thing the bally race is, anyway—humanity—a snake writhing in the dirt after its head is cut off! . . . . . . verily, a pleasing image! I must remember that to put in some cleverly cynical essay or story. . . . . . . if I ever write anything deserving the adverb.

No hurry about the enclosures—& don't read the story till you are fully recovered. The punch at the end is no food for an enfeebled system! Herewith I enclose the next of the series—that bird Houtain hustles the poor old gentleman unmercifully. The title of the fifth will be "The Horror from the Shadows."[3] My lawd! I wonder if I can keep up the crescendo of ghoulishness? It will take something positively fiendish to outdo this last sunshiny phrase when titling the sixth & last (thank 'eaven!!) of the series. This series business is a beastly bore—all technique & mechanics without a loophole for real creative art. I have fallen into a formula, & grind 'em out with all the delicate individuality of a sausage-factory. I make myself think of that Poe spoof—"How to Write a Blackwood Article." To use a Wisconsinism—Bah!

Enclosed is a letter from one of the tender Galpinii of your own locality—a 13-year-old poet & student of Norse mythology who was 'written up' in the Haverhill paper. Smithy sent me the cutting, & I am Unitedising the kid before Groveland St.[4] can Nationalise him. He is some boy—he shall be the latest & smallest of my grandsons! You might write him when you have more health & leisure. The Merrimack Valley shall yet be a great amateur centre!

Hoping to hear of your full restoration to health & vigour ere long, I remain yr sympathetic & obt Servt

L

P.S. I've written a new horror—"Hypnos"—but am not sure it's worth typing. It is one of those would-be artistic ambiguities—dreamy stuff.

Notes

1. The sons of S. Lilian McMullen, Kenneth (b. 1911?) and Robin (b. 1914?). Middleton (1877–1946) was a poet who wrote under the pseudonym "Lilian Middleton." See HPL's essay "The Poetry of Lillian Middleton" (*CE* 2).

2. I.e., dinner at the home of Edith Miniter and Charles A. A. Parker at 30 Waite Street in Malden, Mass. HPL alludes to Trimalchio's lavish banquet in Petronius' *Satyricon* (the proper Latin would be *cena Trimalchionis*).

3. An installment in his serial "Herbert West—Reanimator."

4. Tryout Smith was a member of NAPA, but not of UAPA. The youth is unidentified.

To C. M. and Muriel Eddy

C[lifford] M[artin] Eddy, Jr. (1896–1967) of Providence was a writ-er of horror fiction and later a theatrical booking agent for 25 years. His wife was Muriel Elizabeth (Gammons) Eddy (1896–1978). According to the Eddys, they were in touch with Lovecraft and his family as early as 1918; Muriel maintained that their mothers knew each other through the woman suffrage movement. But it seems unlikely that the Eddys knew Lovecraft that early. There are no mentions of C. M. Eddy in Lovecraft's correspondence prior to 1923; Lovecraft never mentions Muriel in his surviving letters. He revised four stories for Eddy in 1923–24 and visited their home in East Providence before he left for New York in March 1924. The Eddys had three children: Clifford Myron Eddy (1918–2003), Fay A. Eddy Dyer (1920–2016), and Ruth Muriel Eddy Bell (1921–2009). Lovecraft's letters to Zealia Bishop tell of the great impoverishment of the Eddy family in the late 1920s, and although Lovecraft himself was not financially well off, he did what he could to provide or direct funds to the Eddys.

[35]   [ALS]

[Hotel Statler / Detroit]
598 Angell St.,
Providence, R. I.
Sept. 5, 1923

My dear Mrs. Eddy:—
                    I am glad to learn that you & Mr. E. liked "The Music of Erich Zann"—& to such an extent that you would like to see more of my effusions. Enclosed are several tales—which are my own favourites among the 30 odd things I have written, & which you can peruse at leisure. I hope that at least one or two of them will be of some interest—"Dagon" is the one which *Weird Tales* accepted, so may be regarded as theoretically "professional" even though it was written in the amateur spirit & may, in the course of events, never get into actual print.

Yes—I read "The Floor Above", & thought it one of the best things yet to appear in W.T. The atmosphere was handled with admirable power & re-straint—a rare thing in fiction of the novel W.T. grade. Another good thing in that magazine was "Beyond the Door"—in an earlier issue, I think. The latest issue strikes me as rather poor; & curiously enough, one of the most poorly & carelessly written of all the stories is perhaps the very best in atmosphere &

background. I refer to "The Weaving Shadows",[1] which although clearly the work of a novice—& probably a none too highly educated person—really has a finer command of phantasmal horror than most of the other & technically superior tales. I never saw *The Thrill Book*, & was distinctly tantalised by what you say of "The Sargasso Sea".[2] This theme has been used before in fiction & fantasy—Dunsany has a sketch touching the general idea in his "Last Book of Wonder"[3]—but is always legitimate material for original treatment. There is really a "Sargasso Sea" in the Atlantic at a confluence of ocean currents, but the presence of hordes of lost ships is of course mythical. The actual place is merely a more or less tranquil expanse covered with floating weed & a certain amount of scattered driftwood & minor wreckage. However—the prosaic facts didn't prevent Dunsany from drawing the picture of _ __, ruined temple of the [sea], & _ _ _ the dead ships of all the ages come to do __ ___ [. . .]

[*pages 2–4 not available*][4]

Very sincerely yours,
H. P. Lovecraft

P.S. Batch of new *Tryouts* just came—I'll enclose a copy.

Notes

1. M. L. Humphreys, "The Floor Above" (*WT,* May 1923); Paul Suter, "Beyond the Door" (*WT,* April 1923); W. H. Holmes, "The Weaving Shadows" (*WT,* March 1923).
2. Chester L[eigh] Saxby (1891–1969), "The Sargasso Sea" (*Thrill Book,* 15 June 1919).
3. "The Secret of the Sea" in *The Last Book of Wonder.*
4. The dealer who sold this letter included several other lines from the letter in his description of it: "It was the old style which I venerated in youth, & with which I became so saturated that it grew to be my instinctive utterance." And "I should be floundering about as clumsily & artificially as if I were using a half-foreign dialect." And "And the ironic part of it is, that I have a very keen intellectual appreciation of what the moderns are doing, so that (as in the Conservative I sent you) I am often forced to defend them against the reactionaries whom I myself resemble in my actual use of language. Truly, a grotesque cleavage between theory & practice!"

[36]   [TLS;[1] Place of Hawks (transcript)]

598 Angell St., Providence, R.I.,
October 20, 1923

My dear Mrs. Eddy:—

Here, at last, is the amended "Ghost-Eater", whose appearance I trust Mr. Eddy will find satisfactory. I made two or three minor revisions in my own revised version, so that as it stands, it ought to be fairly acceptable to an editor. I certainly hope Baird will take it—in fact, I would be willing to wager heavily that he will.

Speaking of Baird, he has just written me a letter which sends my egotism up to quite unbearable heights. He has been getting such favourable comments on "Dagon" that he says my work 'makes a peculiar appeal to his readers', and wants to use all my stuff—one after another. He accepts "The Hound" for the December issue, and hopes I'll keep him constantly supplied, sending my mail to his personal address in Evanston instead of to the Chicago office. Pretty good, all told—though he apologises for slow pay these days, and sends a promise instead of a cheque. Incidentally, he says I haven't offended Vincent Starrett,[2] whom he knows well, and denominates a thorough good fellow.

I am indeed glad that the Hoag book found such an appreciative audience, and would suggest that you write the venerable poet how much you enjoyed his work. He is keenly delighted by the numerous acknowledgments he receives, and at his age one cannot have too many delights. His address is: J. E. Hoag, 17 Prospect Street, Greenwich, N.Y. Considering the number of copies I had, it was no favour at all to supply your sister,[3] which I did yesterday. I am only too glad to know that my good old friend's efforts are so enthusiastically appreciated in my native part of the world! In accordance with your request I wrote on the fly-leaf, though as I assured your sister in an accompanying note, there is no value whatever in the scrawlings of an unknown and insignificant nobody. If signatures are any good, I shall be perfectly willing to write all over the fly-leaf of the Eddy copy when next I am in East Providence! I hope your sister will enjoy the verses as much as you have—I suggested that if she does, she might write Mr. Hoag about it.

I shall shortly make my report on the MSS. I took home—and I know that I shall find them delightful. What changes I make, I'll make lightly and as non-defacingly as possible.

With all good wishes to you and Mr. E., and trusting that the enclosed will be satisfactory, I remain,

Most sincerely yours,

HP Lovecraft

Notes

1. First and part of second paragraph quoted in *The Dark Brotherhood* 98–99.

2. In a letter to Edwin Baird, editor of *WT*, HPL had written: "'Penelope' [*WT*, May 1923] is clever—but Holy Pete! If the illustrious Starrett's ignorance of astronomy is an artfully conceived attribute of his character's whimsical narrative, I'll say he's right there with the verisimilitude! I wrote monthly astronomical articles for the daily press between 1906 and 1918, and have a vast affection for the celestial spheres." To HPL's chagrin, Baird published the letter in *WT* 2, No. 3 (October 1923): 82.

3. Muriel Eddy had two half-sisters, Gertrude and Ethel.

[37]   [ALS]

[Pantlind Hotel / Grand Rapids, Mich.]
259 Parkside Ave.,
Brooklyn, N.Y.,
July 21, 1924

Dear C M E Jr:—

Once more a prodigal adopted grandfather sues for pardon anent epistolary delinquencies! Only asterisks & exclamation points could adequately express the rush I have been in—a rush, by the way, of the most wearisome & least encouraging sort; since it mainly involves revision of the most arduous & least remunerative variety—for that eternal pest David V. Bush. The extent of this rush may be gauged by the fact that I haven't been able to keep track of Henneberger, Baird, & Wright at all—although of course my young friend Long generally gives me the latest. Long is in Maine for the summer now, but writes his old grandpa frequently . . . . . & so far without eliciting any reply from that delinquent & reprehensible old gentleman. Henneberger, apparently, is a bad egg altogether so far as stability is concerned. He never sent me the cash due me, & I have not bothered to write him at all—although I fancy I will drop him a line soon if I get time, asking if he really does wish to do anything about that *School for Scandal* thing. The present aspect of things at Chicago appear to be this: Henneberger is out of *Detective Tales*, & Baird is publishing uncomplimentary things about him in the various writers' magazines. Wright is out of *Weird Tales*,[1] but intends to found an entirely new magazine of the same sort though somewhat higher quality, to be called *The Weird Story Magazine*. Henneberger is now the nominal editor of *Weird Tales;* but he owes the printer $43,000·00, & the latter may take over the magazine & publish it himself in Indianapolis. That would be a rare thing for weird writers—two magazines where one grew before—provided, of course, that both or either will pay the hapless authors whom they waft onward to immortality—or the poorhouse.

It certainly is a beastly shame that things went up in chaos just as your work was so firmly intrenched—but at least you have the psychological satisfaction of knowing that so much of your work was editorially acceptable. Besides—if Wright starts his new magazine & W.T. really does "carry on" under the regime of the present printer, you will have an excellent chance of placing all that is now on hand & all that you may write in the future. Long is left in the lurch in much the same way. He doesn't know if his stuff will ever be used—or if that splendid September cover design drawn for his story will ever appear. Wright says he is sorry that *Weird Tales* has a claim on this story & design, for he would like to use them in his new magazine. As for me—I've simply been too damned busy to afford the luxury of worry or disgust! Somebody—Wright, Baird, Henneberger or the (printer's) devil—has "The Unnamable" & "The Festival"; but I haven't had a second's leisure to inquire.

Now that I'm reminded of it, though, I may write today if the day doesn't end too quickly. By the way—have you any shadow of satisfaction regarding "The Loved Dead"? Wright tells Long that you succeeded in properly shocking his gentle readers with that wholesome little tale![2]

Oh yes—thanks for that *All-Story* tip! This time I *did* get the issue in time, & I have now accumulated all four numbers, though I've had no chance to read "The Radio Man" so far.[3] The title is deucedly insipid, but possibly the carefully concealed & sagely discussed author has surpassed it in the text . . . . or perhaps it isn't his title at all, but merely the mild-mannered choice of Sister Bob Davis, that delicate soul for whose fastidious readers our rough frightful tales seem to be altogether too horrid & shocking & unpleasant.[4] By the way—I read "12:30 in Eternity",[5] & found it mildly clever although not especially original or in any way atmospherically striking. If this is what dear Bobbie calls "weird" stuff, then I can see where my assorted terrors draw a fine collection of pale pink rejection ships from the Munsey offices! Leeds—who, by the way, is in a fearful financial fix as the result of unsold stories & the failure of the *Writer's Monthly* to pay him for his "Thinks & Things" column— says that Davis has a hard time using any weird material, since his nominal superior, Matthew White, Jr., is dead set against the acceptance of anything of the sort. It's a fight against White every time Davis uses a weird story.

Don't hurry about sending that Moon Pool sequel, but on the other hand, don't fail to send it some time.[6] I think I'll prepare for it by reading the good old pool itself again. Long went wild over it, & this week I'm going to lend it to old McNeil. I shall also sub-lend them the sequel when you send it—& I think you'll hear from them about it . . . which will give you a good entree into a corresponding membership in our circle of The Boys. Speaking of the li'l' ol' circle, Kleiner has just proposed a new member—a rather likeable chap named Dwight Anderson[7]—whom we expect to see at the next meeting, but whose final admission depends on the will of our fastidious social censor Morton! Morton is very anxious to limit our gatherings to fellows who are proved to be congenial down to the last shadow & detail, so that the gang will be really more of a family than a club. Our last meeting was here, & our next will be at McNeil's[.] Better move here—I can guarantee you instant membership! We miss young Long now that he is away. Oh, say! Shoot us "The Better Choice",[8] & we'll give it a critical discussion at an early meeting! Quick action there, even if I turn out a bit tardy in the revision. The same goes for that corpse story of Mrs. E's. Speaking of mutual help & all that sort of thing—accept my most verbose & expansive gratitude for typing that endless "Nameless City" MS.! Count me for reciprocation at the first opportunity. Can I do anything in sandpapering off "The Doll"? Your mention of it as possibly weird in spots excites my interest.

Yep—the stories came safely, & Morton read aloud "The Better Choice" at our meeting last night. It was voted a good story, except for the frequent *stock phrases;* (a defect against which, as you'll recall, I've issued many a warning) & the only reconstructive change suggested was a condensation of the possibly sentimental prison reflections of the hero (p. 10 of MS.) The sort of phrases that need deletion are such things as:

> countless centuries
> hollow of her hand
> sweet, innocent, dreamless sleep of childhood
> invisible hand
> myriad twinkling stars
> rubbed elbows
> loved & cherished
> according to my own dictates
> resign himself to the inevitable
> Cimmerian darkness
> wild-eyed, staring
> brains of the combination
> modern Midas
> cold, grey walls
> untold agony
> ——&c &c.

The idea is to get away from formulae & state things in some new & arresting form. Of course it's darned difficult—but it's worth it!

Too damn bad that the S N E[9] has struck snags—but here's hoping that the publication of "Mammy's Bill o' Fare" will net enough jack to float it again. That song is certainly a winner; & if intrinsic merit means anything nowadays, it will find recognition in spite of all the music trusts & kindred conspiracies which hell can breed! I'd like to see a copy of it—shoot us one, & expect proper cash by return mail. The presence of your own cover design adds double zest to my anticipation.

Those clipped illustrations for D D & B[10] are very apt—at least the Dr. Morehouse one is. The only objection to the other one is that it refers to a chance metaphor in the text, & not to any actual incident in the plot of the tale. I return them in case you find them of value in giving hints to other publications handling the story. Speaking of cuttings & the like—I enclose herewith some things which Leeds gave me, & which you may retain permanently if you like. Leeds himself is writing a novelette on the traffic in heads—as practiced by certain tribes in the northern extremity of New Zealand, where the art flourishes to a limited extent despite the assertions in the accompanying article. This reminds me that I ought to be fixing up a criticism of Leeds' story, as I promised. It's a bit heavy, I fear, & damnably overweighed with rambling dialogue.

I hope you received "La Bas" safely. It's contraband goods now, as it were, so be damned careful of it. When you are through with it, you might send it on to

W. Paul Cook,
    Box 215, Athol, Mass.
As you see, I'm conducting something like a circulating library—Cook in his turn will send it on to Paul J. Campbell in Illinois! The Pompeii volume[11] will go forward to you in a day or two. No hurry at all about this.

Hope to have more interesting news next time, but for the past month Bush has tied me down to a devilish monotonous grind—and a devastating stone-brokeness has cut off all interesting travel save around N.Y. City. I ought to be satisfied, though, since N.Y. is crammed full of ancient & incredibly colourful byways if one knows where to look for 'em. I've spent some time among Colonial warehouses & alleys & curving hilly streets which evoke the old seaport of the 1770's with surprising vividness I'd like to take you around as I did last November! ¶ Hoping for a line when you can drop it, & sending the very best regards of both my wife & myself to all the members of the Eddy corporation,

    I am ever
        Yr faithful grandfather   H P L

Notes

1. Actually, Wright stayed on at *WT* until 1940.
2. *WT* (May–June–July 1924). HPL revised the story.
3. A serial by Ralph Milne Farley in *Argosy All-Story Weekly* (28 June–19 July 1924).
4. Robert H. Davis (1869–1942), American journalist, editor, dramatist, and photographer; editor of *Munsey's Magazine* from 1904 to 1925 and also editor of the *Argosy*, to which HPL submitted "The Rats in the Walls." See HPL to Frank Belknap Long (8 November 1923): "Davis, tho' admitting it hath some merit, holds it too horrible for the tender sensibilities of a delicately nurtured publick" (*SL* 1.259). Davis's superior, Matthew White, Jr. (1847–1940), editor of *Argosy* (1886–1928), was even more dead set against it.
5. Robert W. Sneddon, "Half Past Twelve in Eternity," *Argosy All-Story Weekly* (28 June 1924).
6. "The Conquest of the Moon Pool" by A. Merritt.
7. Dwight Anderson of Cleveland, Ohio, secured that laureate award for poetry at the 1899 UAPA convention.
8. *WT* (March 1925).
9. Unidentified. Possibly something relating to Eddy's song-writing.
10. Eddy's story "Deaf, Dumb and Blind," revised by HPL.
11. HPL owned several books on Pompeii. The one in question might be Marc Monnier (1827–1885), *The Wonders of Pompeii*, translated from the Original French (1870; New York: Scribner, Armstrong & Co., 1872).

[38]   [ALS]

259—
Sept. 5[, 1924]

Dear C M E Jr:—

Since this is the first non-business letter I have written in gawd knows when, except to my aunts, I will let the situation speak for itself, & omit apologies. However, you can imagine the apologetic spent which, for lack of space, denies itself expression! Financial exigencies have kept me from taking time even to think, & heaven only knows what the end will be! I am now looking for a regular job—advertising or trade paper work if possible—which will give me some decently dependable stipend with at least a shadow of ability to know what my working hours will be. Free-lancing is hell when so much time & effort are needed to bring in such beggarly returns. Just now I have two jobs vaguely in sight, though probably I shall get neither. One—the best one, I think—is on the well-known trade organ *The Haberdasher*.[1] Lack of commercial experience is a beastly obstacle—everybody is polite and complimentary enough, but it's tough work leading 'em up to the hiring-point! You are to be congratulated on the regular berth you have landed. Stick to it, kid! I'll do the same if I ever land one of my own provided the other guy is willing. Heigho! It's a great life.

I'm glad to hear that you have made an advantageous residential move. It must be delightful to have the park only a stone's throw away—which reminds me that this joint is very close to Prospect Park, Bklyn., where I do considerable work & reading on sunny summer days.

Your "block" design for your business stationery is delightful. I envy you your pictorial ability, & am anxious to see the music cover which exemplifies it. I'm glad that your new affiliation will benefit your independent business, & really believe it will be a vast help, since all your work needs is marketing opportunity in order to "go over big", as colloquialists phrase it. An' doan yo' fergit, boy, to sen' yo' gran'paw dat "Mammy's Bill o' Fare" w'en dey gits it out in Philadelphy!

Let me thank you for the *All-Stories,* which safely arrived, have been perused, & are now loaned to our portly & erudite friend James Ferdinand Morton, Jun. The Moon-Pool sequel was very good, though its diffuseness, romanticising & explanatory quality made it a bit less powerful than the "Moon-Pool" itself. There is some more good material in this file, especially a novelette by Max Brand called "That Receding Forehead". I noted "The Girl in the Golden Atom", which is the forerunner of the more recent "Man Who Mastered Time"—& have since read the intermediate matter* in book form.[2] Quite a clever series, I'll say! Other recent weird reading of mine has included a not very interesting volume of classic devil tales, & a really splendid collec-

---

*by the way—what about "The Fire-People"? Does that come in the series, too?

tion of short stories (entitled "The Listener") by Algernon Blackwood, whose perusal I most heartily recommend to you if the Prov. Pub. Libe will yield 'em up. Glad you got Pompeii. Cook recd. "La Bas" OK, & is now forwarding to Campbell. And La Touche Hancock promises to send you Machen's "Three Impostors" as soon as his boss (Leslie Stratton, ed. of Coney Island Times) is through reading it.

That misdirected letter did arrive safely enough, & here's the much appreciated picture to prove it. I receive so much mail that the postman knows me backward & forward! Me & the frau were exceedingly glad to see the view, & only regret that we can't retain it. The upper half, by the way, still bids me bid you to bid your upper half to trust patiently in the coming epistle. The hectic rush of events goes for both sides of the household, & opportunities for writing are devastatingly few!

Concerning pictures–I haven't had anything but snap shots in nine years, but here's the best I can find. Thanks for the honour of the request! Both of these are to keep. One dates to 1920, the other is strictly contemporary— although I don't note any marked physiognomical differences. I'm a very conservative person—it just occurred to me that as I sit writing today, I have on the same blue suit which I had on when the 1920 picture was taken! And it was two years & four months old even then! Yes—& more yet besides! The suit I have on in the 1924 picture was purchased in 1915! . . . . the same one I used to wear down to 61 Furnace in order that my late grandchild might have an appropriate fabric to claw & shed fur on. Eheu! Poor Felis! To lay flowers on her bier just as I was ready to send rattles & teething-rings for her prospective brood! How does her small mistress bear up under the blow?

Speaking of an Eddilet—I am glad to hear that they all sparkle & ripple with accustomed felicity. Regards to their mater, whose epistle I faithfully delivered to the ruler of this establishment, & who will before long receive an appreciative reply thereto.

I'll do what I can toward making time to polish up the tale—perhaps if I land a regular position I'll have some evenings free from mental strain. Next Thursday the gang will consider Mrs. E's "Grey of the Dusk"[3]—which has, as I said when first I heard it, a strikingly excellent plot. "The Doll"[4] is excellent—adroit plot cleverly handled, & certainly weird enough in colouring for Editor Wright. I've sent it to him with the expressed hope that he'll accept it . . . . . & pay for it!

I've bought the A-S. with "The Nameless Doom",[5] & am awaiting a chance to read it. Sounds good! In the next W.T. I have a short weird poem, "To A Dreamer", but nothing else so far as I know. I think Wright has lost "Festival" & "Unnamable". I've now sent him the Eddy-typed "Nameless City", & some single-spaced things which I promise to re-type on acceptance.

Thanks prodigiously for the envelope pertaining to Providence views. Yes—please send me the full address if you can get it. Nothing interests me so much as Old Providence. I can't purchase at once—dead broke—but want to be ready to order as soon as I can remit. Meanwhile I've been doing some tall colonial exploring around N.Y. & the adjacent regions. Some fine colonial churches in Newark, & Perth Amboy has one of the most fascinating colonial waterfronts (of the dingy, sinister type) I have ever seen.

Our gang is prospering—two new members now, Edward Lazarre[6] [*sic*] & George Kirk, both from Cleveland. They're close friends of Samuel Loveman, whom we expect to have with us next week.

But I must quite in a hurry—hellish rush! Pardon the bum penmanship & all that, & let me hear how everything goes. Your card came, & here's the Houdini letter, such as it is. I haven't seen H. since last spring, but possibly he may recall who I am. Anyway, try your luck, for I fancy you'll find an interview enjoyable. Yes—I heard of that Baird serial. Thanks.

With best regards of wife & self to you & all the accompanying & subsidiary Eddies, I remain

      Ever

        Yr most obt Grandpa

          H P L

Notes

1. The *Haberdasher* (1887–1926), a trade magazine published by the Haberdasher Company (New Brunswick, NJ).

2. HPL refers to several stories in the *All-Story Weekly:* Max Brand, "That Receding Brow" (15 February 1919); Ray Cummings, "The Girl in the Golden Atom" (15 March 1919), later expanded into a novel (1920); Ray Cummings, *The Man Who Mastered Time* (12 July–9 August 1924); Ray Cummings, *The Fire People* (21 October–18 November 1922).

3. In her posthumous book *Erased from Exile*.

4. Apparently unpublished and nonextant.

5. By Charles A. King, Jr. (*Argosy All-Story Weekly*, 16 August 1924).

6. Edward Lazare (1904–1991), a member of Hart Crane's literary circle whom HPL met in Cleveland and New York in the 1920s. He was later a longtime editor of *American Book-Prices Current*.

[39]   [ALS; Grill #500]

             [Hotel Vendig / Pennsylvania]

                           Novr. 20 [1924]

Dear C M E Jr:—

          Telegram just arrived. Sorry to have delayed so, but have recently been in a turmoil of engrossing misfortunes, financial & otherwise, amidst which not a moment of unworried leisure has existed.

For one thing, my wife has suffered a nervous breakdown—in hospital 10 days, later on farm in Somerville N. J. for rest, & now back again pending breaking up of housekeeping, which her health necessitates. Just where I shall board depends on what comes of my latest effort at a commercial affiliation—am hanging on here for present, & will tell you my new address when I have one.

Not a moment to touch D D & B, but here it is.[1] And you can tell that ass Wright for me that the story is much better with its present cumulative beginning than it would be with any popular-magazine abrupt opening. Tell him to study the work of Arthur Machen & note how "The Great God Pan" starts.

Hope all goes well with you. Did Hancock[2] ever send you "The Three Impostors"? If not, I must get after him.

More later—& meanwhile pray accept my apology for delay of your tale. Hope it gets a good art heading. I've seen the Brosnatch[3] drawings for my "Festival" & "Randolph Carter", & although they're good, they don't fit the narratives any too well.

Well—that's that. Hope you place D D & B to advantage, & that the readers take to it. Meanwhile best wishes for your musical ventures & general financial state.

Till breathing time—
as usual
Yr most obt Servt
H P L

[P.S.] Regards to all the household

[P.]P.S. Song came—thanks & congratulations!

Notes

1. "Deaf, Dumb, and Blind," the final story HPL revised for C. M. Eddy.

2. Ernest La Touche Hancock (1857–1926), a minor poet, journalist, and short story writer, and author of *Desultory Verse* (1912). *The Three Impostors* is an episodic novel by Arthur Machen. HPL must have lent Hancock his copy.

3. Andrew Brosnatch (1896–1965), *WT* illustrator.

[40]   [ALS; Place of Hawks (transcript)]

169 Clinton St.,
Brooklyn, N.Y.,
June 2, 1925.

Dear Fellow-Strainer-After-Effect:—

I am glad to hear that the Ishtar business reached you safely. This tale, I think, is hardly equal to Merritt's earlier work—certainly not to "The Moon Pool".[1] Popular magazine traditions &

attitudes are "getting" him—which may be good for his pocketbook, but certainly not for his art. It's hard to say exactly what stamps a piece of writing as popularly commonplace—all one can do is to complain that there seems to be no reflection of convincing scenes & events, or of any perspective save the conventional outlook of the hack-writer. But this tale certainly had possibilities, & shows any amount of superficial ingenuity.

I thought you'd hear from Black,[2] who seems to be a novice anxious to correspond with those a trifle less novicer than he. He wants advice about writers' correspondence schools, & I told him that you would be much more likely than I to know about such institutions. Here's hoping he doesn't prove a nuisance—& that he gives you some good revisory jobs, since he said he would shortly have some stories to be looked over. I've also put him in touch with amateur journalism, which I hope to see revived this year through the combined efforts of a younger generation led by Davis & by Victor E. Bacon of St. Louis, formerly of Boston.

Glad you liked "The Unnamable" in print. I've been too busy to read *Weird Tales* since December, so don't know whether it's going to the devil or picking up. Some time I must try to snatch the leisure to skim through the whole batch of piled-up copies. I bore up well under the condensed D D & B— the one item I did glance at. Good luck with your next shiver-generator, whenever it may appear! Incidentally, I'd give a lot to see a new book just published by Lippincott, of which McNeill has given me circular—"Haunted Houses", by Charles G. Harper. It must contain a wealth of sinister material, & if I had $4.50 to spare I'd annex it on the spot!

I'm delighted to hear how much you have been benefited [by?] Houdini, & am sure you must have vastly enjoyed that three weeks in Boston. Let us hope you may shortly use the hard-earned "atmosphere" in a highly remunerative novel!

As for "Mickey", I am utterly consumed with envy! What would I not give to be cleaved & bitten by so sprightly a sprig of feline juvenility? Your four-birthday'd heiress is to be congratulated most profoundly—& may the good Saint Patrick preserve the kitten from such mishaps & untimely extinction as overtook his predecessor! The cat poem is indeed excellent—I return it in case you keep a scrap-book of such material. Incidentally, I'll throw in a couple of other cat items for good measure, neither of which need be returned.

My own household now is of a much more lugubrious character, chronicling what is little short of a cataclysm to one in my constant state of beatific brokenness. It is, to come to the point, nothing less than the robbery of my dressing alcove a week ago Sunday whilst the household slept, & the loss of virtually all the wearable clothing I possessed—three suits & an overcoat— besides a blanket, a wicker suit-case of my wife's, & a $108.00 radio set I was storing for a friend. This calamity leaves me in the most embarrassing imaginable state as regards wardrobe, for although the thieves left three overcoats, their depredations removed every blessed suit I possess except the one I had been wearing & had left carelessly on a chair in the room proper—which they did not enter. This one remaining suit is a thin & ancient blue serge in very dubious condition, & must soon be supplemented by something a little more dependable—which amidst my appalling fiscal vacuity is a problem indeed! And to think I had *just* had most of the others all fixed up at the tailor's to fit my now thinner figure—for I have been *reducing* during the past few months, & have succeeded to a degree which I would not have believed possible a year ago . . . . weight *155* lbs, waist 31', collar 14¾. The robbers were a pair of youths who had hired the adjoining room two weeks before; & who, by the way, departed without paying their second week's rent after securing their plunder. Entrance to my alcove was affected by forcing the lock of the always-closed door leading to their room. They worked by stealth, & made not a wakening sound at any time, though only a portiere separated my room from the alcove which they visited. I have, of course, sent the most careful descriptions of all my missing goods to the police; but one cannot often expect the return of property in a city with so intricate an underworld as this. One must instead be a philosopher, & save the energy of grief for the more profitable task of devising a way to get new clothes!

But I must desist & get to work! About a month ago I discovered that I was wasting half my time in profitless idling with various members of our local group, who would call around now and then till the whole crowd got to meeting almost daily. My work suffered seriously, till at last I turned over a new leaf & adopted a policy of rational seclusion, to which I am adhering with Spartan determination. Except on special occasions, I now confine meetings to the regular Wednesdays; & the results have appeared already in an amplified output. Others, too, are buckling down to business. George Kirk, in partnership with a chap from Cleveland,[3] has opened a fine new bookshop at #97 Fourth Avenue—in the final arrangement of whose stock & dressing of whose window I assisted during the crowded small hours of the morning preceding the debut. It is called "Martin's Book Shop", & I heartily recommend it to the patronage of all booklovers who may chance to be in or pass through New York. Loveman is back in Cleveland for a while—though intending to return in the autumn with more of his goods, prepared for greater domestication here. Leeds is connected with a new (or newly reorganised) financial & commercial magazine, in connexion with which Long & I are trying to pick up a little hack work to eke out our disastrously lean inbound purse tricklings. And I think I told you that good old Morton, most fortunate of us all, has been solidly fixed for the rest of his life by an appointment as curator & absolute head of the new municipal museum at Paterson, N.J. Kirk's new shop gives the gang a brand new meeting-place—& we are to assemble in its cosily furnished back room tomorrow evening. Oh, yes—one more domestic detail. I buy food now, & keep it in a bread-box & crudely carpentered cupboard in my wash alcove; thus avoiding the expense of diurnal restaurant patronage. Once a week, though, I blow myself to a full spaghetti dinner at John's—an excellent Italian place I've discovered a few blocks from here. It's surprising how much I save by getting my own meals— I run largely to bread, canned stuff, cheese, & cookies in bulk—besides a sort of health food, "whole grain wheat" which my aunts continually send me.

But I must really quit this time! Best regards all around,

Most cordially yours,

HPL

Notes

1. A. Merritt, *The Ship of Ishtar.*
2. Possibly B[iddle] Coursin Black (1900–1984), who published a weird prose sketch, "The Ultimate," in the *United Amateur* (May 1926).
3. For Kirk, see headnote to letters to him. His partner was Martin P. Kamin (1897/1899–1976), with whom Kirk lived in Manhattan before establishing his own bookshop.

[41]　[ANS; on telegram to HPL]

[c. 30 October 1926]

[DETROIT MICH　409P
H P LOVECRAFT
10 BARNES ST PROVIDENCE RI

HOUDINI SERIOUSLY ILL STOP PLEASE HOLD MANUSCRIPT UNTIL FURTHER NOTICE
STOP ADVISE EDDY STOP

MRS HARRY HOUDINI.]

This came tonight—use your own judgment about what to do & what not to do.[1]
Hastily—

H P L

Notes

1. HPL and Eddy had been ghostwriting a book for Houdini, to be called *The Cancer of Superstition.* They had worked up an outline for the book and Eddy had started writing it, but they ceased when news of Houdini's illness arrived. HPL owned his exposé *A Magician among the Spirits* (1924; LL 470). Houdini died on 31 October. His wife, Wilhelmina Beatrice Rahner (1876–1943), better known as Bess Houdini, was his stage assistant. She elected not to pursue the project.

[42]   [ALS]

10 Barnes St.
Providence, R.I.
April 25, 1927

Dear CME Jr.:

Contrary to superficial evidence, I am not yet a subterraneous inhabitant of Swan Point[1]—but superabundant tasks plus limited energy have conspired to make my late-winter hibernation a very complete one. I am only just beginning to crawl out of my burrow & take a preliminary vernal survey of the visible world—one long-distance exploring trip forming so far the entire extent of my open-air activities. Doubtless I need all the spring inspiration I can accumulate—for I have a tedious siege of dentistry to face . . . . on whose details I will not dwell with ghoulish insistence!

Meanwhile I trust you have been reasonably well, & that your wife has by this time fully recovered from her recent indisposition. I shall be over to see you next Friday evening—the 29th—if that time is convenient as any other, the hour being about 8 p.m., more or less . . . to be interpreted as custom may lead you to interpret it. In case of any doubt, I guess I'll enclose that postal which I had so neatly addressed to myself on that evening when your telephone call saved the need of sending it. Upon its smooth surface you can indite whatever message may be in order—saying whether next Friday will be convenient or suggesting an alternative date if it is not. I'm glad the card won't have to be wasted, after all!

Speaking of enclosures—in making further demolitions of my duplicate *Weird Tales* I came across this story of yours, the added copy of which may perhaps be welcome. As I told you, wherever I come across a tale by a friend, in such dismantlings, I always send [its contents?] to him. I've done a deal of writing since seeing you last. The [short?] tale I was then planning turned out to be a 150-page novelette—which, in addition to the 110-page one finished in January, makes a batch of typing which I have not yet had the courage to approach.[2] I was, however, forced to type my weird tale history, (& without the added research from the library list) owing to a hurry call from Cook, who is to publish it.[3] It came to 75 pages—gawd what a job! I am now reading proof on it. Cook means later to issue my "Shunned House" as a thin cloth-bound book with a preface by Frank B. Long. And I have written still another tale—a long short story with a rural setting called "The Colour Out of Space," which I may bring along for you to see. Not long ago the well-known critic Vincent Starrett of Chicago asked to see some of my stuff—which flattered me greatly, though I don't know how well he'll like the assorted batch I sent him.[4]

With every good wish, & trusting too see you soon—most cordially yrs,—
HPL

[P.S. What] do you think of the questionnaire craze? It seems to me more sensible than crosswords, since its scope is more general. I follow the *Bulletin* specimens regularly—they are very easy, but I almost always "fall down" on the *sport* question, since I am not well-informed in that field.

Notes

1. HPL was interred at Swan Point Cemetery in the family plot when he died in 1937.
2. The 150-page ms. was *The Case of Charles Dexter Ward;* the 110-page ms. was *The Dream-Quest of Unknown Kadath*. Neither was published in HPL's lifetime.
3. HPL refers to "Supernatural Horror in Literature." He had intended to look up additional weird works in the Providence Public Library, but never got the chance.
4. The stories HPL sent to Starrett are unknown.

[43]   [ALS;[1] Place of Hawks (transcript)]

Sunday
[26 January 1930]

Dear C M E Jr:—

I am happy to notify you that I have not only succeeded in switching that typing job your way, but have put you in touch with a client who may have considerable work for you to do in the future—the woman in Kansas City whose crude stuff I recall showing you back in 1927. Long & I have been dividing most of her recent jobs, but she has a whole lot of old material on hand which we have given up as hopeless for any market we can cater to. You might be able to fix this material up for magazines of the "confession" or Macfadden type. In some cases she might pay in advance, while at other times the cheque might come later. She is strictly reliable,[2] & will never attempt the evasions you have encountered from some clients. Belknap & I can attest this after many years' dealings. Besides the revision she will probably want some attempted placing done—giving you (besides the revision fee) a fixed percentage of the proceeds on all work accepted & paid for by editors. But you can discuss that with her directly. She will probably drop you a line—but in case she doesn't, I'll give you the name & address to place on file beside John Milton Samples'—which I trust was the one you had in mind last week. It is: Mrs. Zealia B. Reed, 4125 Walnut St., Kansas City, Mo.

Now about the present typing job. It is a long weird novelette of which I am really the author[3]—my job being to write some sort of a story around the idea of a mound haunted by two ghosts near Binger, Okla.—an actual legend. How well or ill I have succeeded, I'll leave for you to judge. Belknap—to whom I showed it before sending to Mrs. R.—thinks I did rather well. The thing—which has been returned to me—runs to 61 standard size pages in my usual hieroglyphics; which I calculate (using the analogy of my recent de Castro job)[4] will make about 78 double-spaced typewritten pages . . . . . Gawd help you! I have told Mrs. R. that you will do this at the standard rate (for Belknap & me) of 25¢ per page, with carbon copy—which, assuming that my 78-page figuring is nearly right, would make your bill $19.50. She agrees to this rate, & has sent me a blank cheque, signed, in case incidentals alter the figure. I calculate that registered first class postage will be around half a dollar, so guess I'll fill the cheque out for twenty bucks. For your convenience, I'll try to cash it directly & bring you the proceeds in advance. The job is not especially a rush one, although reasonable promptness would probably be appreciated. When done, I will take care of the MSS.—giving them a final ink correction if necessary & sending the original off to *Weird Tales*. You may have difficulty with some of the interlineations, corrections, artificial names & words, & Spanish passages, but I'll fix up any slips or gaps you may leave. Also, I'll forewarn you about the worst places when I bring the MS. over. When I come along I'll bring all the necessary paper, (of this sort—Woolworth—2 70-sheet pkgs.) carbon paper, & second sheets—& also a typewriter ribbon if you will tell me the kind to get. I think you said your machine is an L. C. Smith[5]—but perhaps there are different kinds. If you drop me a line the day you receive this—Monday—I can get your reply the next day & purchase the stuff on my regular Tuesday expedition down town. If it is warm enough, & if that night is convenient for you, I will come over with the MS. that same evening—Tuesday—& give you all the tips you may need in order to get effectively to work. Enclosed is a card on which you can reply whether or not this date suits you. If it is not warm enough, I will either come some later night or mail you the cash & MS. with such instructions, accessories, suggestions, &c. &. as may be available. Let me know, then, if you'd like the stuff delivered at 8 p.m. (or thereafter!) on the evening of Tuesday, Jany. 28, 1930.

I trust that luck has given you at least a few good turns since the other night, & that the cash for this order will be able to do some good service in keeping the Mart establishment going & furnishing Tom & Jack with a good egg-sandwich & dark coffee patron![6] It occurred to me the other day to ask you whether or not you could find a helpful use for various items of apparel which might or might not be a good fit, as they stand, for you & for your son & heir. Of course it would take cash, in all probability, to get them in really fitting shape; but it might be worth your while to have them in reserve—awaiting such seasons of windfall as might enable you to patronise some skull-capped knight of the shears & needle. Not that they'd be any of *my* junk—heaven knows, I wear my veteran garments myself! Once an old Jew came to the door & asked me 'if I had any old clothes'—& I replied "Yes—look at them!"—pointing to what I had on! But I know more than one guy who sheds stuff from boredom & not from real worn-ness—& especially, one kid of 14 whose outgrown things (in perfectly good shape) might come in marvellously handily for your Crown Prince. Of course I don't know how much I could assemble right now—but if you give the word I'll keep my eyes open. You might let me have a chart of your correct sizes some time so that I could know what bimboes to watch most closely!—always provided, of course, that you really want such material. I don't intend to emulate your late tenant in filling your attic with undesired heaps of cloth! But we can discuss that when I see you—next Tuesday or later.

Let me know on the card, then, whether the $19.50 price is all right for a typing job (with carbon) liable to reach above 78 pages, & whether Tuesday night is the best time for you to discuss the details of the ordeal—temperature permitting. Best wishes to you & all the household—including the furry incarnation of my old Nigger-Man[7] of thirty years ago! ¶ Yr obt Servt H P L

Notes

1. A brief extract is quoted in *The Dark Brotherhood*, pp. 99–100
2. However, late in life, in his "Instructions in Case of Decease," HPL noted: "Mrs. D. W. Bishop, 5001 Sunset Drive, Kansas City, Mo. owed H. P. Lovecraft $26 for revision work" (*CE* 5.239).
3. I.e., "The Mound." *WT* rejected the story. It appeared (under Zealia Bishop's name) after HPL's death.
4. "The Electric Executioner."
5. The L. C. Smith Typewriter Company was founded in 1903 by Lyman C. Smith (1850–1910), although Smith had established his first typewriter company in 1886. It specialized in portable typewriters. In 1926 the company merged with the Corona Typewriter Company to become Smith Corona.
6. Tom and Jack's Restaurant at 283 Broad Street.
7. HPL's black cat in youth. It ran away when HPL's family moved from 454 to 598 Angell Street in 1904.

[44]   [ALS, JHL]

Tuesday, Feby. 18[, 1930]

Dear C M E Jr:—

The "Mound" MS. is long ago safely corrected & off to Wright. Mistakes were surprisingly few—far less than I would have made—the principal pair of them being in places where I had indicated large-scale transpositions by means of signs which were probably inadequate. Congratulations on a fine job—& best wishes for future work!

But my purpose in dropping this line is to mention that my sartorial canvass has brought in some more returns—some of them of juvenile nature—comprised in a bundle too large to carry comfortably . . . . or at least, for an old man like me to carry comfortably. It occurs to me that you might drop over some evening at an hour convenient to yourself, & that on the return trip I might (the weather being decent) go along with you to hold up one end of the bundle. Then, when the thing is safely within your portal, we can take a more leisurely round ending up at the refectory of Thomas & John. This will reach you on Wednesday, & you can get the enclosed card back to me by Thursday. Almost any night would do for me, but for definiteness's sake I'll nominate Saturday, Feby. 22, as a tentative date . . . . making a double holiday of it! Let me know if this is all right; & if it isn't, nominate another date on the card. If the night is cold, we can attempt a division of the bundle's contents—you taking along as much as you care to carry, & I bringing along the residue on my next call. Besides the habiliments, there is a lot of malted-milk chocolate which might come in handily when other nourishment runs low. It is in chunks which can be either eaten as they are or dissolved in hot water to form a drinking cocoa.

By the way—tell Mrs. Eddy that I received her postal the other day, & that I am sending a copy of the Bullen book to her sister in Attleboro as she suggested. It'll be slow work disposing of all the copies I have around here, but I may do it in the end!

Glad to hear that Mrs. Reed is agreeing to your proposition, & hope you'll hear from Samples also. I've just written Belknap about the Associated Secretaries business—advertising, letter-heads, &c.—but haven't had time for a reply from him. Sundry tasks have inundated me, but I am still hoping to snatch time for some original story-writing soon.

I'm *still* wavering about exchanging the fountain pen—perhaps it's too late to do it now, even if I decide to try. The specimen works admirably—this note is written with it—but undeniably flows too freely when I first begin to use it after a rest, & when it verges toward emptiness. But even as it stands, it's the best-working cheap pen I've yet seen.

Just had five sonnets accepted for use on the Journal's Wednesday page. You'll no doubt see them as they appear one by one.[1]

Well—let me know on the card about your coming over—whether Saturday will be all right, & if so what hour I may expect you. Or, if Saturday isn't so convenient, what other day & hour will best suit your programme.

Best wishes—& hoping you've had some luck in one or another of your various lines of endeavour.

Yr most obt

H P L

Notes

1. HPL refers to five sonnets from *Fungi from Yuggoth* (see Bibliography).

[45] [ANS]

[postmarked _?_ February 1930]

Just a line to say that I think it will be all right to go ahead on some of the Reed revision; for in a letter today recd. from Mrs R. she asks whether you have made any progress—evidently believing that she had authorised you to start in, & had accepted your 50% offer. Possibly you heard from her after our colloquy of last Saturday–Sunday.

¶ However—use your judgment about beginning. Maybe you ought to see the original MS. ("The Unchaining") before trying to tackle the story now entitled "On the High Places".[1]

¶ And don't tackle "Lesson 8". From what Mrs. R. writes, I judge that this was sent to you *by mistake,* & that it is merely the opening of the novel which Belknap revised for her last summer.

¶ In a day or two you ought to receive one of those patent hair-cutters—a tribute from the Associated Secys. Carp'er, which thus equips all its members.

¶ Incidentally, though, Belknap can't join in just at present—he is up to his neck in a new novel.

——Yr obt servt—H P L

[*On front:*] _____ I am _____ unexpected & _____ batch of rush work—which _____ from two directions! ¶ Wright rejected "The Mound" because of its length. The idiot!

Notes

1. HPL, Frank Belknap Long, and Thomas Uzzell all had a hand in revising "The Unchaining" in mid-1927. Mrs. Reed submitted the story to *WT* but it was rejected.

[46] [ALS]

Monday [10 March 1930]

Dear C M E, Jr—

Out of the depths comes Grandpa's tomb-like voice! Still buried beneath the unforeseen avalanche—& the worst of the thing is, that it's stuff I can't sidetrack! Student themes from a school in Washington (the Renshaw School of Expression, conducted by the ex-amateur Mrs. Anne T. Renshaw) to be criticised & graded in a certain way—a way purely literary & aesthetic, & having no reference to popular commercial standards. I've handled this stuff before, & know what kind of a job it is. It's really a job for an English teacher, but I generally get by. But it means *work,* damn it . . . . an institution for which I have a lifelong & unconquerable aversion! Added to this job is a series of philosophic articles from a guy in Vermont[1]—stuff that needs strengthening in the light of historic background. Another thing which it would be difficult to pass on! But every tunnel has an exit somewhere, so I live in hope of seeing the light of day again sometime! I'll drop you the usual postal-enclosing message when I have an evening to call my own! One or two decently warm afternoons I've taken advantage of the weather to the extent of toting my work along in a bag to Blackstone Park or the Swan Point river road.

I have *not* yet heard from Mrs. Reed on the subject of having her Belknap-revised novel done over—although a couple of months ago, before getting in touch with you, she said she might have me read it & give a sort of general opinion on it. Most assuredly I shall advise her to let you tackle the job—if she doesn't bring up the point herself I'll find a way of introducing it the next time I have occasion to write her. I don't think the "Mound" rejection will deter her greatly from attempted authorship. The hopefulness of some beginners dies hard! Trust you'll have good luck with the "High Places", & hope Mrs. R. will send you the original version—"The Unchaining"—without that clumsily engrafted pseudo-weird ending.

Hope you can work the "Trimette" adequately after a little practice. The other day I gave my greying & thinning locks another once-over, since I was too broke to get the real haircut I needed; & my aunt really thought I had been to the barber's until I told her! The more you practice with the thing, the better work you'll do. And of course you'll have to use the scissors in grading the hairline at the back of the neck. I've learned to do this fairly decently with a hand-mirror in my spare hand—you saw the degree of success I attained a month ago.

That cat item is certainly interesting! It would be odd if a new race of wildcats or panthers were to be evolved in New England from the abandoned & atavistical house cats of Cape Cod!

My story of the Vermont horror made quite a little progress before the avalanche hit me, but now it's stalled at page 26. I'm afraid it'll be a novelette before I'm through with it—& chances are that Wright will reject it on the ground of length as he did "The Mound".

Heard Joseph Wood Krutch deliver his lecture on Poe Wednesday night at Sayles Hall, but he didn't say anything more than is in his book on Poe published in 1926. He is a slim chap of 36 who looks younger than his age, but who has a nervous mannerism which makes one think he is about to vault over the desk in front of him!

Got the new *Weird Tales* last week, but don't think much of it. Unusually poor even for W.T. ¶ Well—more when I see more daylight!

Regards—yr most obt H P L

[Envelope postmarked Providence, R.I., 10 March 1930.]

Notes

1. Woodburn Harris.

To Sonia H. Greene

Sonia H[aft] Greene (1883–1972) was married to Lovecraft from 1924 (3 March) to 1929 (although Lovecraft did not sign the divorce papers). She was born Sonia Haft Shafirkin in Ichnya (near Kyev), in Ukraine. Settling in the United States, she eventually joined the amateur journalism movement, publishing two lavish issues of the *Rainbow* and becoming president of the UAPA (1924–25). After her "divorce" from Lovecraft, she moved to California and married Dr. Nathaniel Davis.

[47]   [TLS, JHL]

259 Parkside Avenue,
Brooklyn, N. Y.
August 1, 1921.

My dear Mr. Lovecraft:

Besides the unique conception which I find in your idea, and which should at all times be the only justification for the expression of any Art, I am pleased to find that yours embodies both this, and the other great Art, a wonderful command of language.

Your well written story of "The Temple," gave me a source of pleasure not often found in works produced for monetary compensation.

Your conception of the superman as characterized in 'Carl Heinrich' seems to be consistent with monarchic and oligarchic theories and principles. While I may agree with the ruling of the "select few" over the weak and ignorant masses, I have no wish or hope ever to see or know of a superlatively strong and intellectual machine-rule which is not generously tempered with the wisdom of unblind justice or the "milk of human kindness." And the arrogance of absolute power knows no limit!

To be strong in time of great stress is not a virtue that can be acquired. It is a quality that no amount of "Deut[s]che Kultur" or *any* culture can ever produce.

The quality is only inherent in the unique individual (Der Einzige) which, through centuries of his forebears may, sometimes, inherit along with a specific trait of his race. But this is not infallible. The swing of the pendulum may alter the case.

Gorky, the Russian tramp author, risen through strife, amid poverty and ignorance, under the oppression and suppression of recent Czaristic Russia, created a character in his admirable short stories, one "Chelkash".[1] In this unique individual he incarnates the scums and the dregs, the flotsam and jetsam, of the lowest "basyak" translated, would be the equivalent of the most sordid tramp-hobo-bandit. A pirate whose composition embraces a quality of strength, a mental and psychological power and vigor, at once of a deity and satan combined.

A motley potpourri of Dyonisian [*sic*] activity and Apollonian passivity embracing the entire gamut of the human emotions, from a violent and deadly temper when justly roused to the most docile self-control when life, power or scheme are at stake; not only tempered with but dominated by a superior power to will.

By far this is not the type to select as the model for the superman. Reverse the circumstances of your "Carl Heinrich" and "Chelkash" and you will find in each the revserion [*sic*] to type. The only difference is that one is reared in the lap of wealth and luxury, with the advantages of education, culture and position, and whose fervid religion is "Gott und der Kaiser", instead of the "Individual versus State," and his education is made up mostly of militarism; while the other imbibes his kind of supremacy from the actual facts of his sordid life.

In each case, the stress of the moment, the necessity for quick thought and action, or calmly calculated plans for a definite and necessary purpose, may prove to be lodged in a Chelkash more definitely and permanently than in a Carl Heinrich.

One evening a few years ago, I went to Carnegie Hall to hear the son of the great Tolstoi.[2] I was eager to hear of him from one who was at once his son, friend and exponent. You may imagine my disappointment when I found him to be a mediocre individual with nothing more striking and original to offer than the proper usage of words and phrases, with quotations interspersed; without casting one ray of light upon Tolstoi other than had already been gleaned from his books and biographies.

I aspire to the artistic and constructive originality of the human great mind regardless of outer polish. I will accept the mistakes of its expression, the faults of its construction, but it must be primarily original, independent and sincere in its conviction; whether it agrees with my point of view or not does not matter. There must be the spark of genius that can light the candle of other, dormant minds, which, [*sic*] also may possess a slumbering tardy genius that gently needs to be awakened.

I have no wish or desire to see the mil[l]ennium brought about; I seek no reforms. It is through the channels of bungled reform that civilization advances one step and falls back two. Our modern reforms are like the opiate,—it eases the pain but kills the patient. Nor do I wish to see the world ruled by absolute monarchy.

Only when the intellectually and physically strong will learn how to rule wisely and humanely, and the weak will recognize their limitations and will be willing to serve and follow the strong to the limits of their natural ability; being humanely and properly compensated for their efforts; given their chance to develop according to their lights; when property and the accummulation [*sic*] of wealth and dominant power will not be placed above human life and comfort; then, and then only, I believe, might civilization rise to heights not yet achieved in the history of Time! There must be neither master nor slave! Then [*sic*]

Then and then only might there be a justifiable hope for the advent of the Super-man.

As an exponent of Nietz[s]che's superman, G. Bernard Shaw illustrates this fully, both in practice and in theory, in his superb play of the same name. Though employer and employe are depicted, there exists neither the master in the one, nor the slave in the other.

Being aristocratically inclined you may not agree with this point of view, but it doesn't matter, for when one is sincere in his conviction, others may also see the light.

. . . .

All the little fantasies you sent me I have read with keen pleasure. They are gems of literature, beautifully woven. By the description you give of submarine steeps and subterannean [*sic*] depths one would really believe that the creator of these had actually been at sea and had delved down into the very bowels of the earth.

Knowing that the unfortunate condition of your health does not permit of such physical luzuries, [*sic*] you deserve indeed to be congratulated; my young 'Robert Louis Stevenson.'

Assuring you again of my gratitude to you for my membership, I am,

Sincerely yours,

S. H. G.

Notes

1. Maxim Gorky (1868–1936), Russian writer and political activist. His story "Chelkash" (1895) is about a clever thief. It was translated into English in the volume *Chelkash and Other Stories* (1916).

2. Leo Tolstoy (1828–1910) had ten children who survived to maturity, including six sons. Sonia probably refers to Count Ilya Tolstoy (1866–1933), who lectured across the US in 1916–17 about his father's work. He lectured at Carnegie Hall on 19 January 1917.

[48]

[Nietzscheism and Realism][1]

Concerning the quality of mastery, and of poise in trying situations, I believe that it arises more from hereditary than environmental considerations. Its possession cannot be acquired through the culture of the individual, although the systematic culture of a certain class during many generations undoubtedly tends to bring out such strength to a degree which will cause that class to produce a higher average of dominant individuals than an uncultivated class of equal numerical magnitude.

I doubt whether it would be possible to create any class strong enough to sway permanently a vast body of inferiors, hence I perceive the impracticability of Nietzscheism and the essential instability of even the strongest governments.[2] There is no such thing—there never will be such a thing—as good and permanent government among the crawling, miserable vermin called human beings. Aristocracy and monarchy are the most efficient in developing the best qualities of mankind as expressed in achievements of taste and intellect; but they lead to an unlimited arrogance. That arrogance in turn leads inevitably to their decline and overthrow. On the other hand, democracy and ochlocracy lead just as certainly to decline and collapse through their lack of any stimulus to individual achievement. They may perhaps last longer, but that is because they are closer to the primal animal or savage state from which civilised man is supposed to have partly evolved.

Communism is a characteristic of many savage tribes; whilst absolute anarchy is the rule amongst the majority of wild animals.

The brain of the white human animal has advanced to such a stage that the colourless equality of the lower animals is painful and unendurable to it; it demands an individual struggle for complex conditions and sensations which can only be achieved by a few at the expense of the many. This demand will always exist, and it will never be satisfied because it divides mankind into hostile groups constantly struggling for supremacy, and successively gaining and losing it.

When there is an autocracy, we may be sure that the masses will some day overthrow it; and when there is a democracy or ochlocracy, we may be sure that some group of mentally and physically superior individuals will some day overthrow it by establishing a more or less enduring (but never wholly permanent) supremacy, either through judgment in playing men against each other, or through patience and ability in concentrating power by taking advantage of the indolence of the majority. In a word, the social organisation of humanity is in a state of perpetually and incurably unstable equilibrium. The very notion of such things as perfection, justice, and improvement is an illusion based on vain hopes and overdrawn analogies.

It must be remembered that there is no real reason to expect anything in particular from mankind; good and evil are local expedients—or their lack—and not in any sense cosmic truths or laws. We call a thing "good" because it promotes certain petty human conditions that we happen to like—whereas it is just as sensible to assume that all humanity is a noxious pest which should be eradicated like rats or gnats for the good of the planet or of the universe. There are no absolute values in the whole blind tragedy of mechanistic nature—nothing is either good or bad except as judged from an absurdly limited point of view.

The only cosmic reality is mindless, undeviating fate—automatic, unmoral, uncalculating inevitability.

As human beings, our only sensible scale of values is one based on the lessening of the agony of existence. That plan is most deserving of praise which most ably fosters the creation of the objects and conditions best adapted to diminish the pain of living for those most sensitive to its depressing ravages.

To expect perfect adjustment and happiness is absurdly unscientific and unphilosophical. We can seek only a more or less trivial mitigation of suffering.

I believe in an aristocracy, because I deem it the only agency for the creation of those refinements which make life endurable for the human animal of high organisation.

Since the only human motive is a craving for supremacy, we can expect nothing in the way of achievement unless achievement be rewarded by supremacy.

We cannot expect justice—justice is a mocking phantom—and we know that aristocracy has many undesirable features. But we also know—sadly enough—that we can never abolish the evils without abolishing everything of value to civilised man.

In an aristocracy some persons have a great deal to live for. In a democracy most persons have a little to live for. In an ochlocracy nobody has anything to live for.

Aristocracy alone is capable of creating thoughts and objects of value. Everyone, I fancy, will admit that such a state must precede democracy or ochlocracy in order to build the original culture. Fewer are willing to admit the cognate truth that democracies and ochlocracies merely subsist parasitically on the aristocracies they overthrow, gradually using up the aesthetic and intellectual resources which autocracy bequeathed them and which they never could have created for themselves. The rate of squandering depends upon the completeness of the departure from aristocracy. Where the old spirit lingers, the process of deterioration may be very slow indeed—certain belated additions compensating for the decline. But where the rabble gain full sway taste is certain to vanish, and dulness reigns darkly triumphant over the ruins of culture.

Wealth and luxury are essential alike to the creation and the full appreciation of beauty and truth. Indeed, it is the existence of wealth and luxury, and of the standards which they establish, that gives most of the pleasure felt by the non-wealthy and non-luxurious. The masses would rob themselves by cutting off the real source of that slight enjoyment which they secure, as it were, by reflection.

When, however, I praise autocracy, I do not by any means refer to such absolute monarchies as czaristic Russia or kaiseristic Germany. Moderation is essential in all things, and overstressed political autocracy produces an infinity of stupid checks on art and intellect. A tolerable amount of political liberty is absolutely essential to the free development of the mind; so that, in speaking of the virtues of an aristocratic system, the philosopher has in view less a governmental despotism than an arrangement of well-defined traditional social classes, like those of England and France.

Governmental aristocracy need go no further than to safeguard an aristocratic class in its opulence and dignity so that it may be left free to create the ornaments of life and to attract the ambition of others who seek to rise to it.

The healthiest aristocracy is the most elastic—willing to beckon and receive as accessions all men of whatever antecedents who prove themselves aesthetically and intellectually fitted for membership. It gains, moreover, if its members can possess that natural nobility which is content with a recognition of its own worth, and which demonstrates its superiority in superior works and behaviour, rather than in snobbish and arrogant speech and attitude.

The real aristocrat is ever reasonable, kindly, and affable toward the masses—it is the incompletely cultured *novus homo*[3] who makes ostentation of his power and position. Yet in the last analysis it is futile to pass judgment upon any type of social order, since all are but the blind result of uncontrollable fate and utterly beyond the power of any statesman or reformer to alter or amend.

All human life is weary, incomplete, unsatisfying, and sardonically purposeless. It always has been and always will be; so that he who looks for a paradise is merely a dupe of myths or of his own imagination.

The will and emotion of man crave conditions that do not and never will exist, so that the wise man is he who kills will and emotion to a degree enabling him to despise life and sneer at its puerile illusions and unsubstantial goals. The wise man is a laughing cynic; he takes nothing seriously, ridicules earnestness and zeal, and wants nothing because he knows that the cosmos holds nothing worth wanting. And yet, being wise, he is not a tenth as happy as the dog or peasant that knows no life or aspiration above the simplest animal plane.

It is good to be a cynic—it is better to be a contented cat—and it is best not to exist at all.

Universal suicide is the most logical thing in the world—we reject it only because of our primitive cowardice and childish fear of the dark. If we were sensible we would seek death—the same blissful blank which we enjoyed before we existed.

It does not matter what happens to the race—in the cosmos the existence or non-existence of the earth and its miserable inhabitants is a thing of the most complete indifference. Arcturus would glow just as cheerfully if the whole solar system were wiped out.

The undesirability of any system of rule not tempered with the quality of kindness is obvious; for "kindness" is a complex collection of various impulses, reactions, and realisations highly necessary to the smooth adjustment of botched and freakish creatures like most human beings. It is a weakness basically—or, in some cases, and ostentation of secure superiority—but its net effect is desirable; hence it is, on the whole, praiseworthy.

Since all motives at bottom are selfish and ignoble, we may judge acts and qualities only by their effects.

Pessimism produces kindness. The disillusioned philosopher is even more tolerant than the priggish bourgeois idealist with his sentimental and extravagant notions of human dignity and destiny.

"The conviction that the world and man is something which had better not have been," says Schopenhauer, "is of a kind to fill us with indulgence toward one another. It reminds us of that which is after all the most necessary thing in life—the tolerance, patience, and regard and love of neighbour, of which everyone stands in need, and which, therefore, every man owes to his fellow."[4]

Notes

1. A series of cynical reflections on ethics and politics, chiefly derived (despite the title) from Schopenhauer, specifically *Studies in Pessimism* (1890), a posthumous compilation of his essays. HPL noted that the "essay" was a selection by Sonia H. Greene from two letters he had sent her (HPL to the Gallomo, 31 August 1921). A note prefacing the item reads: "This article is taken from correspondence not originally meant for publication."
2. HPL refers to Nietzsche's concept of the superman, one of a group of intellectually and culturally superior individuals who would lead society altruistically for its own good.
3. "New man," a term used scornfully by the Romans to indicate the first man of a family or clan to achieve entry into the aristocracy.
4. *Studies in Pessimism* 29–30. HPL's quotation is somewhat truncated.

[49]

[Lovecraft on Love][1]

[c. 1922]

The mutual love of man and woman for one another is an imaginative experience that consists of having its object bear a certain special relation to the aesthetic-emotional life of its possessor, and depends upon the fulfilment of certain aesthetic conditions by the object.

Love is generally linked with subsidiary conditions such as pride, admiration, eroticism, intellectual congeniality, etc., and in practice it may be taken for granted that all other things being equal, the possessor generally prefers to have the object close at hand, although a purely ethereal and imaginative force such as real love is sometimes independent of time, space, or corporeal existence. True love thrives equally well in presence or in absence, proving that the force is an exalted and imaginative one, and directed toward the most permanent spiritual and aesthetically responsive part of the personality. It need not disavow a parallel erotic appreciation but it inwardly eclipses and transcends it.

Such love primarily presupposes a profound and sincere mutual attachment, possibly born of close propinquity, or sometimes taking fire instantaneously at the first meeting. When born and nurtured of slower time, its development embraces a sense of peace, tranquillity, repose, confidence, security, protection, permanence, spiritual solace as well as physical proximity, assurance of permanent welcome home, mutual understanding, physical, mental, cultural, and traditional harmony and a tacit assurance of effort exerted toward and for the well-being of the beloved.

Time, moreover, brings with it a powerful array of glamorous memories and tender associations. During a normal lifetime there are several stages of love: there is the love of springtime youth, of mature middle age, and that ripe, mellow love of the elder years. Each stage in progress has its specific kind and quality of love, some element of which may be found in all three stages and other stages developing or becoming modified with time.

With long years of slowly nurtured love comes adaptation and perfect adjustment; memories, dream-pictures, delicate, aesthetic stimuli, and usual impressions of dream-beauty become permanent modifications through the influence of which each tacitly exercises upon the other. A familiar melody, a scene, an impression reaching down into the consciousness and memory of one or both when both live in the same mental and spiritual world; both harbouring conceptions of life sufficiently similar to enable the two to share an existence in common, seeing the same thing when looking at the same object; each considering the life of the other as a natural and inevitable kind of life to live, so that it is not too abstract and visionary to have any significance for the tastes and temperaments and aspirations of the other.

It is important that each knows *what* the other is. Is life to one a series of delicate, illusive, and fantastic adventure-visions beckoning the spirit to untrodden paradises and unattainable feats of creative arts, while to the other, life is something quite material, to be tolerated, somehow, while immersed in the plodding effort of commonplace living, thinking, feeling, and doing? Thus, brutelike debasing life, thought, sensibility and action instead of exalting and being exalted by them?

Does the quality of affection as manifested by the one, bear sufficient kinship to the quality of affection envisaged by the other, to form an adequate basis for mutual sentimental life?

One may think and love in dream-pictures of beauty and mystery; how nearly does such thinking and loving coincide with the normal thinking and loving as the other reckons such things? These, I believe, to be real points of love, and not such absurdly imaginative attraction as makes of love merely lust, and of the loved one an object of its expression and gratification.

There are so many separate branches of thought, mood and feeling in which each must be able to summon up a very strong and genuine quota of affection. There is the purely aesthetic, the domestic, the whimsical, and humorous, the childish and diminutive, and even the historic and geographic. Each must try to understand the sphere of the other, and these spheres themselves must not be too antipodal in their values, motive-forces, perspectives, and modes of expression and fulfilment to evoke an adequate appreciation of their purport. Yet each must frankly recognise the essential fixed limitations of the other and serenely abide by them. Nor must there be extravagant theoretical ideals of perfection which are impossible in view of probable basic differences which cannot be eradicated.

Very often ostentatious passion belonging to the exquisiteness of a few early years is erroneously regarded as love and is essentially incompatible with maturity.

There is a universal difference between the romances of youth and of maturity. By forty or perhaps fifty a wholesome replacement process begins to operate, and love attains calm, cool depths based on tender association beside which the erotic infatuation of youth takes on a certain shade of cheapness and degradation. Mature tranquillised love produces an idyllic fidelity which is a testimonial to its sincerity, purity and intensity.

At forty or fifty the more mental and deeply seated affection is a far more appropriate subject for sentimental interest and rhetorical celebration than is the undisguised animalism of youth.

Eros calls up visions of springtime bowers and virginal delicacy. Hymen, of cheerful hearths, long shared dreams and little, familiar ways that time has made sweet and sacred; delicate ways and images of beauty and tenderness are built up through the many years of joint living and close companionship, creating an ineffable kindness and unflagging devotion such as hot and impetuous youth can never achieve.

Youth brings with it certain erogenous and imaginative stimuli bound up in the tactile phenomena of slender, virginally-postured bodies and visual imagery of classical aesthetic contours symbolising a kind of freshness and springtime immaturity which is very beautiful but which has nothing to do with domestic love.

No conservative man or woman expects such extraordinary physical exaltation except for a brief period in extreme youth; and any high grade person can soon transfer his or her psychic needs to other fields when middle age approaches; other forms of stimulation mean much more than sex-expression to such persons, so that they hardly give it more than a cursory thought.

Mature men and women might regard youthful beauty as an exquisite statue or carving to be admired but not necessarily desired, while more mature or elderly persons would be regarded simply like themselves, interesting or otherwise, to be liked and admired or conversely—according to their personalities and sociability.

Love in extreme youth is more a matter of physiology than psychology and wholly independent of the genuine love of mature middle age.

Since in most cases of youth, love has been imperfect or unsatisfactory, in later life there comes a wholesome craving for another chance to find true love which maturity alone seems capable of fashioning and keeping unimpaired without expecting to thrill with the physical exaltation which is the rightful heritage of springtime youth only.

Notes

1. The text is derived from an essay Sonia wrote after the dissolution of her marriage with HPL, "The Psychic Phenominon [*sic*] of Love" (T.Ms., JHL), where Sonia claims to have included this extensive passage from a letter HPL wrote to her. In a note on the ms. she has written: "It was Lovecraft's part of this letter that I believe made me fall in love with him; but he did not carry out his own dictum; time and place, and reversion of some of his thoughts and expressions did not bode for happiness." The text has been amended to reflect HPL's customary orthographical usage.

[50]   [ANS][1]

[Postmarked New London, Conn.,
25 September 1926]

Glorious trip home through Sunny New England paradise![2]
—H P

Notes

1. *Front:* Old Huguenot House, New London, Conn. At the time, Mrs. Greene was in Chicago.
2. HPL had just concluded a visit with Sonia (at her request) in Brooklyn (c. 13–19 September), after which HPL went to Philadelphia, back to New York, then home on 25 September. This postcard must have been written as the train made a stop in New London.

To Harry Houdini

Harry Houdini (pseudonym of Ehrich Weiss, 1874–1926) was a magician, escape artist, and debunker of spiritualism. In early 1924 J. C. Henneberger, owner of *WT*, in an attempt to salvage the magazine, hired Houdini as a regular columnist. Henneberger then commissioned Lovecraft to write an account of an adventure that Houdini purportedly had in Egypt; the result was "Under the Pyramids" (published in the May–June–July issue as "Imprisoned with the Pharaohs"). In the fall of 1926 Houdini came in touch with Lovecraft again. He first asked Lovecraft to write an article attacking astrology, for which he paid $75. (A partial manuscript of this article has recently surfaced.) Then he commissioned Lovecraft and C. M. Eddy jointly to ghostwrite a full-scale book, *The Cancer of Superstition,* but his sudden death on 31 October put an end to the plans, as Houdini's widow did not wish to pursue the project. The only surviving correspondence of Lovecraft to Houdini is a brief postscript on an envelope.

[51]   [ANS, envelope only]

[Postmarked Brooklyn, N.Y.,
25 March 1924]

[. . .]

P.S. Your recent note just came. Congratulations on the Poe desk! I hope to see & ponder over it!!

Thanks exceedingly for forming another link in the chain of forwarding by which the Turner letter reached me. That letter is indeed a nobly heartening influence!

Pardon informal postscript.

H P L

To the Homeland Company

The Lovecrafts had been married only since 3 March 1924, taking up residence at Sonia's apartment at 259 Parkside Avenue, Brooklyn. In May, they purchased two home lots in Bryn Mawr Park, a development in Yonkers. They soon found they would be unable to develop the property. Sonia managed to retain control of at least one of these lots for a few more years.

[52] [T.Df., JHL]

259 Parkside Ave., Brooklyn, N.Y.,
July 29, 1924

The Homeland Co.,
    28 N. Broadway,
        Yonkers, N.Y.,

Gentlemen:—
        Owing to financial difficulties of the most acute and unforeseen sort, I find myself unable at present to make the remittances now due on the property which I purchased last May at Bryn Mawr Park—Lots No. 3 and 7 of the Parkway Section.
        Since I expect to be less hard pressed in early autumn, I should greatly regret having to give up the lots at this stage; and am therefore venturing to inquire whether you could—as I am told is occasionally [. . .]

[Letter Seeking Employment]

Included with the draft letter is a leaf with a copy of Lovecraft's advertisement in the *New York Times* for Sunday 10 August 1924. A single response to the advertisement (though there may have been others) was from M. A. Katherman, "Merchandising Counselor" (11 August 1924). On the page, Lovecraft also wrote the following possible recipients for the letter. The significance of his symbols is not clear: they may indicate publishers to whom he actually submitted his letter, or they may indicate publishers who had replied.

Newspapers

N.Y.	Boston
>Herald-Tribune	Transcript
>Times	Herald
Evening Post	Post
Sun	Christian Science Monitor
World	
Brooklyn Eagle	

Magazines

>Century	Atlantic
~~Harpers~~	
Munsey	

Publishers
>Harpers
>Scribners
Dutton
>Putnam
>Doubleday, Page
Doran
Boni Bros
Boni & Liv.
Knopf

[53]   [A.Df., JHL]

[29 July 1924?]

Dear Sir:—
   If an unprovoked application for employment seems somewhat unusual in these days of system, agencies, & advertising, I trust that the circumstances surrounding this one may help to mitigate what would otherwise be obtrusive forwardness. The case is one wherein certain definitely marketable aptitudes must be put forward in an unconventional manner if they are to override the current fetish which demands commercial experience & causes prospective employers to dismiss unheard the application of any situation-seeker unable to boast of specific professional service in a given line.
   The notion that not even a man of cultivation & good intelligence can possibly acquire rapid effectiveness in a field ever so slightly outside his own routine, would seem to be a naive one; yet recent events have shewn me most emphatically what a widespread superstition it is. Since commencing, two months ago, a quest for work for which I am naturally & scholastically well fitted, I have answered nearly a hundred advertisements without gaining so much as one chance for a satisfactory hearing—& all, apparently, because I cannot point to previous employment in the precise industrial subdivision represented by the various firms. Faring thus with the usual channels, I am at last experimentally taking the aggressive.
   The situation of which I am in search, & which I believe your establishment might afford, is one where the services of an author, reviser, re-writer, critic, reviewer, correspondent, proofreader, typist, or anything else even remotely of the sort, are required. In these lines I am prepared to display a mature & effective proficiency despite the fact that I have never been systematically employed by another; yet am willing, in deference to custom & necessity, to begin most modestly, & with the small remuneration which novices usually receive. What I wish is an initial foothold; after that I am confident that my work will speak for me.
   I am by vocation a writer & reviser—composing original fiction, criticism, & verse, & with exceptionally thorough experience in preparing correct & fluent text on subjects assigned, or meeting the most difficult & intricate problems of re-writing & constructive revision, prose & verse. For over seven years I have handled nearly all the writings of a very prominent American author, editor, & lecturer; including several books & many poems which have subsequently achieved no little popularity in traversing the rounds of the press.[1] I have also edited & revised books for others, & can if desired submit samples of this as well as of less extensive work—published stories, reviews, association organs which I have edited, & the like.

This free-lance industry, however, is obviously uneven & uncertain; & I am now—being married & settled in New York—extremely desirous of exchanging it for a regular & permanent salaried connection with any responsible enterprise of not too dissimilar nature. That I can adequately fill any ordinary position involving English composition & rhetoric, literary creativeness, & familiarity with typographical forms & practices, seems very clear to me. Experience in the details of any one commercial enterprise I may lack, but I nevertheless believe that I have assets of at least equal value in an ability to compose rapidly, vividly, fluently, & correctly from outlines, notes, or suggestions, & in such qualities as quick & discriminating perception, orthographical accuracy, stylistic fastidiousness, & a keenly developed sense of the niceties of English usage. As regards these qualities, I am willing to take any sort of practical examination such as composing continuous text from hints or synopses submitted, or reading proof under your supervision, with reference to speed & freedom from error.

I am thirty-four years of age, & of pure English-American-Protestant ancestry. My education, while not including the university or a professional translator's knowledge of modern languages, is that of a gentleman, & embodies all the essentials of liberal culture, literary technique, disciplined observation, & balanced conservatism. With this equipment—ordinary as it is—I cannot doubt but that I am capable of filling some position offered by such organisations as yours, even though lack of earlier employment form a factitious barrier. Round pegs find round holes, square pegs find square holes. And by the same token, albeit with rather greater difficulty, I am sure that there must somewhere be a corresponding hole for such a peg as proverbial metaphor may dub trapezohedral!

Hoping—rashly or not—to hear from you & to receive a fuller opportunity for displaying my industrial qualifications, I am

Very truly yours,

H P L

Notes

1. HPL refers to David Van Bush.

To Edgar J. Davis

Edgar J[acobs] Davis (1908–1949) was a young amateur journalist of Merrimac, MA, with whom Lovecraft explored Newburyport and other locales in New England. Davis began corresponding with Lovecraft soon after his recruitment into the UAPA in March 1922. He was so young (13 when they first connected) that Lovecraft referred to him as his "small greatgrandson," whereas he typically called his other protégés grandsons. He was elected president of the UAPA (1925–26), but by then the organization was largely moribund.

In regard to their correspondence, Lovecraft relates the following: "And now young Davis—our little Merrimac pal—hath just written the Old Gentleman an epistle ninety pages long—forty-five reg'lar Dodge Report sheets! Watch that li'l rascal—if he isn't a second Galpinius, I'm a bum judge of babes!" (*Letters to James F. Morton* 45). But despite the enthusiasm they shared initially, their correspondence and friendship soon diminished.

[54]   [AHT]

169 Clinton St.,
Brooklyn, N Y
May 12, 1925

My Child:—

Your experience must indeed have been a trying one, with pain and peril in the past, and if not ennui, at least the possibility of ennui, at present. However, you are a philosopher, and can no doubt extract vast compensation from the languid luxury which your situation entails. You can learn to appreciate the wish of Baudelaire for vast basalt grottoes under the seas, where he might have perpetually fanning him a host of slaves whose only care would be to invent methods for driving away his boredom.[1] Up to last October, your description of hospital life would have excited no visual mnemonic imagery in my consciousness, for I had never seen the interior of such an institution at any great length. In that month, however, my wife was ill for some time at the Brooklyn Hospital, and from visiting her each day I acquired no little familiarity with the sights, sounds, and atmospheric touches peculiar to the temples of Hygeia.[2] I trust that your emergence from pamper'd solitude to the relative publicity of a limited ward is not attended by any serious regrets. Your soul and personality are still your own, and if the burthen of the herd mind presses too seriously upon you, you can always retire haughtily within their impregnable recesses. Then, too, it may at times be amusing to compare pulses, temperatures, and the like with your fellows in affliction. Certain types of persons, indeed, are said to derive their prime intellectual and emotional sustenance from discussions and comparisons of maladies, treatments, operations, and similar physiological curiosities.

Your most obt great-grandfather and h^ble Servnt
H. P. Lovecraft.

Notes

1. HPL refers to the poem "XII. La Vie antérieure" in *Les Fleurs du mal* by Charles Pierre Baudelaire (1821–1867).
2. Hygieia was the Greek and Roman goddess of health, cleanliness, and hygiene.

To George W. Kirk

George Willard Kirk (1898–1962) was a bookseller, publisher, and friend of Lovecraft. Born in Akron, Ohio, he entered the book trade at an early age. He spent the years 1920–22 in California, where he became acquainted with Clark Ashton Smith. In early 1922 he published Samuel Loveman's edition of *Twenty-one Letters of Ambrose Bierce*. He met Lovecraft when the latter came to Cleveland in August 1922; at that time Kirk gave Lovecraft a copy of Smith's *Odes and Sonnets* (1918), thereby encouraging Lovecraft to get in touch with Smith. In August 1924 Kirk came to New York to establish a bookshop. By this time he was engaged to Lucile Dvorak but did not have enough money to support her. His numerous letters to her provide vivid descriptions of Lovecraft and his friends in New York, mostly members of the Kalem Club. (Extensive extracts of the letters were published in *Lovecraft's New York Circle: The Kalem Club, 1924–1927*, ed. Mara Kirk Hart and S. T. Joshi [New York: Hippocampus Press, 2006].) He participated in numerous all-night walks around New York with Lovecraft and other Kalems. In early 1925 Kirk moved into the same apartment house at 169 Clinton Street, Brooklyn, where Lovecraft was residing, but stayed only a few months. From August to October 1925 Kirk resided at 317 West 14th Street in Manhattan. Lovecraft later used the building as the setting for "Cool Air" (1926). Kirk married Lucile Dvorak on 5 March 1927, setting up the Chelsea Bookshop at 58 West 8th Street (which is not in fact in Chelsea), remaining there for more than a decade. He and his wife visited Lovecraft in Providence in early September 1929. Lovecraft continued to meet Kirk on his visits to New York in the 1930s, but otherwise their contact appears to have been slight.

[55] [ANS][1]

[Postmarked Providence, R.I.,
2 August 1926]

IN MEMORIAM
OSCAR INCOUL VERELST[2]
OF MANHATTAN
1920–1926

Damn'd be this harsh mechanick Age
That whirls us fast and faster,
And swallows with Sabazian Rage
Nine Lives in one Disaster.

I take my Quill with sadden'd Thought,
Tho' falt'ringly I do it;
And, having curst the Juggernaut,
Inscribe: OSCARVS FVIT!

—L. Theobald, Jun.

Pray send me the elegies by S L & R K![3]

Notes

1. *Front:* Memorial Arch and Brown University, Providence, R. I.
2. Oscar was a cat owned by a neighbor of Kirk's that was killed by an automobile. HPL was by this time returned to Providence, so he only heard of the incident from Kalem Club members. "Oscarus fuit" is Latin for "Oscar was" (i.e., is no more).
3. Loveman's poem was "For a Cat"; Kleiner's was "On a Favorite Cat: Killed by an Automobile."

[56] [ANS][1]

[Postmarked New London, Conn.,
25 September 1926]

On my way—Glorious time![2]

——H P

Notes

1. *Front:* Ye Old Town Mill, Erected 1650. Still in Operation. New London, Conn.
2. See letter 50n2.

To Leonard E. Tilden

Leonard E. Tilden (1861–1937) was a veteran amateur journalist of New Hampshire and later Washington, D.C. Of him Lovecraft once wrote: "Leonard Tilden proved very interesting. He opined that the salvation of amateurdom lie in pound postage for amateur papers, & pleased me by saying that he likes my weird tales" (*Letters to Rheinhart Kleiner and Others* 172).

[57] [ANS]

[Postmarked Brattleboro, Vt.,
23 August 1927]

Memorable amateur outing! This is the Vermont Laureate's[1] first sight of an amateur in person since Cook blazed the trail. Also my first sight of Vermont—exquisite country!
Am stopping with Cook in [Athol.]
    Regards—H P Lovecraft
Arthur H. Goodenough
W. P. Cook

Notes

1. I.e., Arthur Goodenough.

To William Bryant

William L. Bryant (1871–1947) was the curator of the Roger Williams Park Museum of Natural History and Planetarium within Roger Williams Park in Providence. He was also president of the Audubon Society of Rhode Island and a member of the Providence Art Club.

[58]   [ALS]

> 10 Barnes St.,
> Providence, R.I.,
> April 25, 1927

William Bryant, Esq.,
    Curator, Park Museum,
        Providence, R.I.,

My dear Sir:—

You will probably recall my visit of last August to the Museum in company with Mr. James F. Morton, Curator of the new Museum at Paterson, New Jersey. Mr. Morton was highly grateful for the many courtesies extended him, & intends at no distant date to forward you the assortment of New Jersey minerals which he promised.

I am once more imposing on your consideration in his behalf in an effort to learn the exact location & conditions surrounding several local mineral beds which he is anxious to visit on his coming trip here. His time will be exceedingly limited, & he has left to me the task of ascertaining the details about certain quarries mentioned in a recent article in *The American Mineralogist.*[1] Knowing that deposits are sometimes exhausted, & that rich localities are often privately owned & closed to the public, he is especially anxious not to follow any false leads during his crowded sojourn; hence asks me to discover particulars in these directions in order that he may attempt only feasible trips. He also wishes to be very sure in the matter of reaching the respective deposits, since there is no time to lose in mistakes.

Now my own knowledge of mineral conditions is absolutely *nil,* & even my geography is by no means equal to the task of identifying the various regions & quarries named in the quoted article. Clearly, I must have expert & specialised advice—& I know of no source more likely to yield definite results than yourself. I am aware how great an imposition it seems to burden you with such a long & detailed set of questions, & can only plead in palliation that it is all in the cause of science—Mr. Morton being assuredly a highly worthy upholder of that honourable cause! I am endeavouring to make the answering as easy as possible by drawing a sort of crude questionnaire, which you will find enclosed, together with a self-addressed stamped envelope. Let me add that if this forms too great a demand on your time, I shall be equally grateful for merely the name & address of someone else likely to furnish the needed data. I believe that the Brown professor of Geology lives only a block or two from my own door,[2] but not knowing him personally, I hesitate to bombard him with inquiries. Your own former favours to Mr. Morton have singled you out as a first victim!

With sincere thanks in advance for anything you can do to set me on the track of the data which Mr. Morton needs, & with renewed apologies for troubling you, I am

Very truly yours,
H. P. Lovecraft

P.S. I am not certain of the exact date of Mr. Morton's visit, but when he is in the city he will in all probability call upon you.

Notes

1. Lloyd W. Fisher and Edwin K. Gedney, "Notes on Mineral Localities of Rhode Island: 1. Providence County," *American Mineralogist* 11, No. 12 (December 1926): 334–40. Fisher (1897–1951) was an instructor of geology at Brown University and later taught at Bates College (Lewiston, ME).
2. Bryant himself lived at 19 Barnes St. The 1927 Providence city directory gives Fisher's address as 13 Brown St.—but this is more than a half-mile south of HPL's residence.

[59]   [TLS]

April 27, 1927

Mr. H. P. Lovecraft
10 Barn [*sic*] Street
Providence, Rhode Island

My Dear Mr. Lovecraft:
I have inclosed your questionnaire with the letter to Dr. Fisher of Brown University with a request that he fill it out and return it to me. As soon as I get it, I will send it on to you.

Dr. Fisher no doubt has all the information you wish as he told me he has been visiting most of the localities and knows far more about them than I do as yet. I have only lived here two years and have not had a chance to see many of the outcrops.

With kind regards,

Yours very truly,
William L. Bryant
Director of the Museum.

[60] [ALS]

10 Barnes St.,
Providence, R.I.,
May 18, 1927

Dear Mr. Bryant:—

When I communicated the very kind favours of yourself & Mr. Fisher to Mr. Morton, his gratitude was extreme; & he has now written particulars concerning the first of his spring-&-summer visits to these parts.

If all goes well, he will reach here late in the afternoon of June 6th, staying over night & devoting the following day—*Tuesday, June 7th*—to the mineralogical excursion. On that occasion he will probably have to be at the New York Boat by 6:30 p.m. or thereabouts; but even so, there will be a reasonably decent period of time for rock-gathering on a modest scale. Mr. Morton's preference—as determined wholly by what he has read & heard—is for *Cumberland* as a field of action; but he holds himself very ready to defer to the judgment of yourself & Mr. Fisher in mapping out his itinerary.

If you & Mr. Fisher have the leisure to guide & accompany the Morton expedition on this particular date, it is needless to say how gladly & gratefully your participation will be hailed. In such a fortunate eventuality you might let me know, as far as possible in advance, of the exact conditions involved—time & place of meeting, & so on. The almost three weeks intervening will no doubt give you & Mr. Fisher time to decide or arrange details without inconvenience. If the trip will be unfeasible for you, I would also appreciate hearing—& am enclosing a self-addressed envelope for reply in any case. This will probably form the first of three New England visits made by Mr. Morton during the coming season, hence there need not be too great disappointment if good arrangements cannot be hit upon for June 7th.

Thanking you again for your courtesies, & hoping that conditions may turn out auspiciously for the full-strength expedition,

I remain
Most sincerely & cordially yours,
H. P. Lovecraft

To Robert Hartley Michael

Michael (1912–1973) lived in Pittsburgh and was the proprietor of the Werewolf Bookshop there. Portions of letters 61 and 62 were published as "The Incantation from Red Hook" (in *The Occult Lovecraft*). Other portions of letter 62 were published as *E'ch-Pi-El Speaks*. Portions of letter 64 were published as "The Cosmos and Religion" (in *The Occult Lovecraft*) and "Some Self-Criticisms" (in *The Fantastic Worlds of H. P. Lovecraft*).

[61]   [ALS]

10 Barnes St.,

Providence, R.I.,

June 28, 1929

Dear Mr. Michael:—

Your letter about my stories in *Weird Tales* gives me a very flattered & important feeling, & I am truly glad to hear that you have found the stuff of so much interest. It may interest you to know that the ancient alleys in "Pickman's Model" were drawn quite faithfully from the topography of Boston's crowded North End & that old brick tunnels (used by smugglers in the 18th century) have actually been found there. Unfortunately this region is rapidly changing; so that in 1927, when I tried to shew a friend[1] the scene, we found nothing left of the tangled courts save a cluster of old cellars laid ruthlessly open to the prosaic sun! But in other days it did not require much imagination to conjure up sinister notions from the teetering lanes where old gables almost met overhead!

About that incantation from "Red Hook"—it is actually a relic of ancient rituals, & is mentioned in more than one history of magic, so that I can hardly sign it in such a way as to indicate authorship. However, I will enclose a copy with signature properly qualified, trusting that this will be acceptable to you. Would that my humble signature were a more valuable commodity!

As for good stories of the sort I write—it gives me extreme pleasure to mention a few which wholly eclipse mine in merit. You may have read some or most of these—if so, let me know & I'll recommend some more. Some time ago I prepared a sort of historical sketch of weird literature,[2] a copy of which I will cheerfully lend you if you care to do any really intensive reading in the weird fictional field. My recommendations deal only with more or less standard material, for I haven't time to keep track of popular magazine fiction. For "tips" anent the latter you might write my young friend & fellow-Weird-Taler H. Warner Munn, 451 Main St., Athol, Mass., who is quite a specialist in that line! But here are some recommendations: [*note to side:*] (These are all easily available published books)

Arthur Machen	⎰ The House of Souls
	⎱ The Three Impostors
	The Terror
	John Silence—Physician Extraordinary
Algernon Blackwood	The Listener & Other Stories
	The Lost Valley ' ' '
Montague Rhodes James	⎰ Ghost Stories of an Antiquary
	⎱ More ' ' ' ' '
	A Thin Ghost & Others
	A Warning to the Curious
E. F. Benson —	Visible & Invisible
H. R. Wakefield —	They Return at Evening
Leonard Cline —	The Dark Chamber
Herbert S. Gorman —	The Place Called Dagon
Ambrose Bierce	⎰ Can Such Things Be?
	⎱ In the Midst of Life

I assume you are familiar with Poe. If not, don't fail to familiarise yourself with all of his short tales. And, as I have said, I can recommend others later on when you have looked up these titles.

As for my own stuff—I haven't had much published outside W.T., although you will find one of my best things—"The Colour Out of Space" (which received a three-star mention in O'Brien's 1928 yearbook)—in *Amazing Stories* for September 1927. There are also some things in Ms. which W.T. has rejected—I could lend you some of these if you would care to see them. I don't know where you could get W.T. prior to July '25 if the publishers can't supply it—but I could lend you the Mss. or tear-sheets of a number of my tales which appeared before that.

Thanking you for your interest & hoping that you may find much pleasure in the books recommended,

   I am

      Yrs. most cordially,

            H. P. Lovecraft

[*Enclosure:* Signed copy of the incantation from "The Horror at Red Hook."]

Notes

1. Donald Wandrei.
2. "Supernatural Horror in Literature."

[62]   [ALS]

10 Barnes St.,
Providence, R.I.,
July 8, 1929

My dear Mr. Michael:—

 I am glad you found something of interest in the reading recommendations, & that you have access to some Machen material in your camp. Yes—"The White People" is a great piece of work—perhaps the subtlest & finest of all Machen's weird products. It has a potent, brooding atmosphere & deep reservoirs of malign suggestion. Superficial critics prefer the spectacular "Great God Pan", but to me the latter is mechanical, artificial, & hopelessly coincidence-ridden as compared with "The White People." I know only one weird story equal to this brief masterpiece, & that is Algernon Blackwood's "The Willows"—which occurs in the volume called "The Listener & Other Stories."

 I am sending a few things of mine—to be returned eventually, though not necessarily in a hurry—in the hope that you haven't seen them before. I couldn't tell, without dragging out all my files, just what items appeared before July 1925 & what came later; but I am herewith enclosing a list of all the tales which I consider good enough for preservation, & you can check those which you would like to see. In general, I think my later tales are better—at least technically— than the earlier ones, for with the years I have learned to use a certain moderation of tone & simplicity of style which I rather badly lacked a decade ago.

 I don't wonder that your Latin teacher was stumped by that Hebraic-Hellenic incantation in "Red Hook", for it is a piece of late-ancient or mediaeval illiteracy which probably has no straightforward syntactical sense anyway! E. B. Tylor, the well-known anthropologist, calls it "an illustration of magical scholarship in the [*sic*] lowest stage."[1] When I wrote "Red Hook" in 1925 I thought this formula was of Alexandrian origin, but later reading makes me inclined to place it in the Middle Ages. It was first used, no doubt, by Jewish Cabalists, & later adopted by European magicians generally. I am no scholar— knowing sadly little Greek & no Hebrew at all—hence can't pretend to give a real translation. I merely took it as I found it in a history of magic (where there was no attempt to translate either this or any other formula) & tried to get as good a notion as I could of the principal words—recalling my meagre & long-ago Greek course & relying on Dr. William Smith's Bible dictionary for Hebraic lore. The result was something like this:

> "O Lord God Deliverer; Lord-Messenger of Hosts; Thou-art-a-mighty-god-forever; Magically fourfold assemblage; And anointed one, together & in succession!"

But I don't fancy this is accurate; for as I have said, I am no savant & the incantation is a decadent ungrammatical & misspelled piece of crudeness which would baffle even the wisest. The magazine version, I believe, is misprinted slightly, but here is the correct reading:

HEL · HELOYM · SOTHER · EMMANUEL · SABAOTH · AGLA · TETRAGRAMMATON · AGYROS ·

OTHEOS · ISCHYROS · ATHANATOS · JEHOVA · VA · ADDONAI · SADAY · HOMOVSION · MESSIAS · ESCHEREHEYE ·

Taking the words one by one:

Hel is clearly the Hebrew *el*, meaning Lord or Deity. Illiterate translations always take liberties with aspirates.

Heloym, by the same token, is *Elohim*, the Hebrew word for deity in its less tribal & more generalised sense.

Sother is simply bad Greek for *Soter*, meaning *Deliverer*.

Emmanuel is Hebrew for *God-with-us*, usually applied to the prophesied future incarnation of deity in the Old Testament, whose fulfilment Christ is assumed to be.

Sabaoth is an Hellenised form of the Hebrew *Tsebaoth*, meaning hosts found in the scriptures in the *Lord God of Hosts*. It was a favourite word with mediaeval occultists & with them probably came to signify *hosts* or *armies* of elemental spirits. I have often wondered if this, rather than *sabbath* (day of rest) is not really the parent-word for the term *sabbat* (*Witches' Sabbath*) applied to the hideous secret orgies of the witch-cult followers. Surely a word signifying *throngs* is much more appropriate for the obscene convocations of May-Eve & Hallowe'en than is a word signifying a weekly *rest* period.

Agla is a frequent word among occultists, being often engraved on the wands & knives of magicians. It is formed of the first letters of the Hebrew words composing the sentence "Thou art a mighty god forever."

Tetragrammaton is a Greek term of magical conjuration identified with a certain cabalistic diagram. It represents a mystical symbolisation of the four elements—air, water, earth, & fire, & is used for evoking their elemental spirits—respectively the sylphs, undines, gnomes, & salamanders. There are four generally recognised magical diagrams which recur repeatedly in occult rites. The other three are the triangle (equilateral), sign of the Trinity or mystical threefoldness of things; the double triangle or Sign of Solomon, representing the Macrocosm or Entire Universe; & the all-potent pentagram, or five-pointed star, which represents the star of Bethlehem & is the greatest of all conjuring forces. With one point up, the Pentagram is the sign of Christ & an aid to White Magic. With two points up it is the Sign of Satan & the Black Magicians' ally. But this is a digression.[2]

Agyros is probably a misspelling of the Greek *agris*—an *assembly*.[3]

Otheos is probably an even worse misspelling of the Greek *Othneios*, meaning *strange*.

Ischyros is good Greek meaning *mighty*.

Athanatos is also good Greek & means *immortal*.

Jehova is the common modern pronunciation of the Hebrew *Yahweh* meaning the supreme & awe-inspiring tribal god whose name was too terrible to be pronounced save by a high priest once a year.

Va? I give up. Can't make head nor tail of it!

Adonai is the Hebrew alternative word for *Yahweh*—used commonly because the familiar use of the real god-name was forbidden.

Saday is another term beyond me, although I have seen it repeatedly in the many ancient formulae which I have copied from different sources as colour-touches for future tales.

Homousion is probably a decadent variant or compound involving the Greek *Homou—together*.[4]

Messias is the Hebrew *anointed*, & under the more common form *Messiah* is a frequent term for Christ.

Eschereheye stumps me again—it being only a guess of mine that the barbaric word involves the Greek meaning *in a line* or *in a row*.[5]

And that is all I can make of the thing! However, it looks just as impressive in a story as if it meant something in particular—which no doubt it did to the naive wizards & Cabalists of the Dark Ages.

As for Black Magic—I fear I'm not any such expert as you suppose! In fiction I prefer original horrors to flat transcripts of folklore, & my knowledge of actual mediaeval formulae & practices is really abominably fragmentary. I've read some of A. E. Waite's & Eliphas Levi's[6] rather dry & pompous treatises, but hardly know just how one would start an informal discussion of the subject—it has so many facets! Some day, though, I'll try to sketch out a few high spots in the history of sorcerous practices—though you could probably pick up more from one of Waite's books, or from a more popular treatise by the well-known Sax Rohmer ("The Romance of Sorcery"—1914).

[. . .]

As for myself & the conditions under which I write—I'm afraid that's a rather unimportant subject, since in plain fact I am a very mediocre & uninteresting individual despite my queer tastes, & have hardly produced anything worth calling real literature. However—here are a few data.

I am a prosaic middle-aged creature about to turn 39 on the 20th of next month—a native of Providence, of old Rhode Island stock on my mother's side & more closely English on my father's side. I was born on what was then the Eastern Edge of the settled district, so that I could look westward to paved streets & eastward to green fields & woods & valleys. Having a country-squire heredity, I looked east oftener than west; so that to this day I am three-quarters a rustic. At the present moment I am seated on a wooded bluff above the shining river which my earliest gaze knew & loved. This part of my boyhood world is unchanged because it is a part of the local park system—may the gods be thanked for keeping inviolate the scenes of which my infant imagination peopled with fauns & satyrs & dryads!

My taste for weird things began very early, for I have always had a riotously uncontrolled imagination. I was afraid of the dark until my grandfather cured me by making me walk through vacant rooms & corridors at night, & I had a tendency to weave fancies around everything I saw. Very early, too, began my taste for *old* things which is so strong a part of my present personality. Providence is an ancient & picturesque town, built originally upon a precipitously steep hillside up which still wind the narrow lanes of colonial times with their carved, fanlighted doorways, iron-railed double flights of steps, & tapering Georgian steeples. This dizzy, ancient precipice lies on the route between residence & business sections, & from infantile glimpses of it I acquired a fascinated reverence for the past—the age of periwigs & three-cornered hats & leather-bound books with long ſ's. My taste for the latter was augmented by the fact that there were many in the family library—most of them in a black windowless attic room to which I was half-afraid to go alone, yet whose terror-breeding potentialities really increased for me the charm of the archaic volumes I found & read there.

Weird stuff always captivated me more than anything else—from the very first. Of all the tales told to us in infancy the fairy lore & witch & ghost legends make the deepest impressions. I began to read fairly young—at four—& Grimm's Fairy Tales formed my first continuous reading. At five I read the Arabian Nights, & was utterly enthralled. I made my mother fix up an Arabian corner in my room—with appropriate hangings, lamps, & objets d'art purchased at our local "Damascus Bazaar"—& I assumed the fictitious appellation of *Abdul Alhazred;* a name I have ever since whimsically cherished, & which I have latterly used to designate the author of the mythical *Al Azif* or *Necronomicon.*

At about six I turned to Graeco-Roman mythology, lead gradually by Hawthorne's "Wonder Book" & "Tanglewood Tales", & by a stray copy of "The Odyssey" legend in Harper's Half-Hour Series. At once I dismantled my Baghdad corner & became a Roman—turning to Bulfinch's "Age of Fable" & haunting the museums of classical art here & in Boston. It was around this time that I first began my crude attempts at literature. I was literate on paper—with printed characters—as soon as I could read; but did not attempt any original composition till around my sixth birthday, when I painfully acquired the art of writing in script. Curiously, the first stuff I wrote was verse; since I had always had an ear for rhythm, & had very early got hold of an old book on "Composition, Rhetorick, & Poetic Numbers" printed in 1797 & used by my great-great grandfather at the East Greenwich Academy about 1805.[7] The first of these infantile verses I can remember is "The Adventures[8] of Ulysses"; or, "The New Odyssey", written when I was seven. This began: "The night was dark, O reader hark! & see Ulysses' fleet all homeward bound, with vict'ry crown'd, he hopes his spouse to greet. Long he hath fought, put Troy to naught, & levell'd down its walls. But Neptune's wrath obstructs his path, & into snares he falls."

Mythology was my life-blood then, & I really almost believed in the Greek & Roman deities—fancying I could glimpse fauns & satyrs & dryads at twilight in those oaken groves where I am sitting now. When I was about 7 years old, my mythological fancy made me wish to be—not merely to *see*—a faun or a satyr. I used to try to imagine that the tops of my ears were beginning to get pointed, & that a trace of incipient horns was beginning to appear on my forehead—& bitterly lamented the fact that my feet were rather slow in turning into hooves! Of all young heathen, I was the most unregenerate. Sunday school—to which I was sent when five—made no impression on me; (though I loved the old Georgian grace of my mother's hereditary church, the stately First Baptist, built in 1775) & I shocked everybody with my pagan utterances—at first calling myself a Mohammedan & then a Roman pagan. I actually built woodland altars to Pan, Jove, Minerva, & Apollo, & sacrificed small objects amidst the odour of incense. When, a little later, I was forced by scientific reasoning to discard my childish paganism, I was to become an absolute atheist & materialist. I have since given much attention to philosophy, & find no valid reason for any belief in any form of the so-called spiritual or supernatural. The cosmos is, in all probability, an eternal mass of shifting & mutually interacting force-patterns which our present visible universe, our tiny earth, & our puny race of organic beings, form merely a momentary & negligible incident. Thus my serious conception of reality is dynamically opposite to the fantastic position I take as an aesthete. In aesthetics, nothing interests me so much as the idea of strange suspensions of natural law—weird glimpses of terrifyingly elder worlds & abnormal dimensions, & faint scratchings from unknown outside abysses on the rim of the unknown cosmos. I think this kind of thing fascinates me all the more because I don't believe a word of it!

Well—I began to write weird tales at the age of 7½ or 8, when I had my first glimpse of my idol Poe. The stuff was very bad, & most of it is destroyed; but I still have two laughable specimens done when I was 8—"The Secret of the Grave" & "The Mysterious Ship". I didn't write any really passable tales till I was 14. When between 8 & 9, my whole tastes took an abrupt turn, & I became wild over the sciences—especially chemistry. I had a laboratory fitted up in the cellar, & spent all my allowance for instruments & textbooks. In these whims I was much indulged by my mother & grandfather (my father having died), since I was very sickly—almost a nervous invalid.

When 7 I took up the violin, but abandoned it in boredom 2 years later & have never since had a good musical taste. I could not attend school much, but was taught at home by my mother & aunts & grandfather, & later by a tutor. I had brief snatches of school now & then, & managed to attend high school for four years—though the application gave me such a nervous breakdown that I could not attend the university.[9] As a matter of fact, I never had any decent heath until eight or nine years ago—though now, oddly enough, I seem to be developing into quite a lean, tough old bird!

My youthful science period proved of long duration; though I carried on literary attempts at the same time, also played much like any youngster. I was not interested in games & sports, & am not now—but liked forms of play which included the element of dramatic impersonation; war, police, outlaw, railway, &. From chemistry I gradually shifted to geography & finally to *astronomy*, which was destined to enthrall me & influence my thought more than anything else I ever encountered. I obtained a small telescope, —which I have still—& began writing voluminously on the heavens. I still have some of my old mss., & a hectographed copy of my juvenile periodical "The Rhode Island Journal of Astronomy". At the same time my curious antiquarianism began to get more & more emphatic. Living in an ancient town amidst ancient books, I followed Addison, Pope, & Dr. Johnson as my models in prose & verse; & literally lived in their periwigged world, ignoring the world of the present. When I was 14 my grandfather died; & in the financial chaos ensuing, my birthplace had to be sold. This dual deprivation gave me a tinge of melancholy which had hard work wearing off; for I have very strong geographical attachments, & worshipped every inch of the rambling house & park-like grounds & quaint foundations & shadowy stable where my youth had been spent. It was long my hope to buy back the home "when I became rich"—but before many years I saw that I utterly lack the acquisitive instincts & ability needful for monetary success. Commercialism & I can't get on speaking terms, & since that gloomy year of 1904 my history has been one of increasing constriction & retrenchment.

Till the death of my mother we had a flat near the old home.[10] Then came ill-starred excursions into the world, including two years in New York, which I learned to hate like poison. Now I have a room in a quiet Victorian backwater on the crest of Providence's ancient hill,—in a sedate old neighbourhood that looks precisely like the residence section of a sleepy village. My elder aunt[11]—in frail health & unable to keep house—has a room in the same dwelling; & since both she & I retain as much as possible of the old family furniture, pictures, & books (the rooms are very large) there is still much of the old home atmosphere hereabouts. Knowing I shall never be rich, I shall be very contented if I can hang on here the rest of my days—in a quiet place much like my early scenes, & within walking distance of the woods, fields, & river-banks where I roamed in childhood. My principle remunerative occupation is the professional revision of prose & verse for other writers—a hateful task; but more dependable than the hazards of original writing when one does not produce popular & easily saleable work.

I do my own tales whenever I get the chance, which isn't as often as I'd like. Whenever possible, I take my writing out in the open in a black leatherette case—sometimes to my beloved wooded river-bank, & sometimes to the wilder countryside north of Providence. My one purely recreational hobby is antiquarian travel—visiting other ancient towns & studying examples of Colonial architecture. My lean purse makes my excursions sadly limited, but even so I have arranged to cover quite a little historic ground from Vermont to Virginia during the last few years.

The first stuff I ever had printed was a regular monthly series of astronomical articles in a local daily.[12] I was sixteen when these began, & I surely felt important. Meanwhile I was beginning to doubt my fictional ability, & was turning to verse. At 18 I decided I couldn't write stories, & burned all my tales save a few grotesque infant experiments & two of my later things—"The Beast in the Cave" & "The Alchemist". I am not sorry for this, for the stuff really was detestably immature. What does make me feel ridiculous is the serious way I took my verse-writing at this period—for in cold truth I never was or will be a real poet! My illusions persisted because at that time I was a semi-invalid & much of a recluse, so that I did not receive a wide array of salutary criticism. Then—at age 24—I joined an amateur literary society whose activities were conducted by correspondence; & thereby secured some highly valuable encouragement & critical suggestions. I wish that organisation were as vigorous today as then—but unfortunately it has become moribund beyond all ordinary powers of resuscitation. My ambitions, which had dropped from science to literature when it became clear that my health would not permit of the arduous application of astronomical or chemical research, now became further clarified; & I was made to see little by little that prose & not verse was my rightful medium. At the same time the most conspicuous 18th century eccentricities began to drop away from my style.

In 1916 I let one of the amateur editors in my literary group print one of the two tales[13] which I had saved from the holocaust of 1908; & was immediately thereafter told by a friend that weird fiction was my one & only real forte—the one & only point at which I had any chance of making an actual contact with genuine artistic achievement. I was half incredulous at first, for I had distrusted the worth of my tales; but upon persuasion decided to try again after my 9-year fictional silence. The results were "The Tomb" & "Dagon", written respectively in June & July of 1917. I half-feared that my rustiness in story-telling would make these new attempts worthless, but was soon assured that they greatly surpassed the 2 surviving tales of my youth. Then I started in earnest, producing a vast number of new stories of which I have saved about ⅞ I had no idea of a steady professional market till "Weird Tales" was founded—& I still doubt if any other periodical would stand regularly for my stuff. It doesn't look so bad beside the unutterable junk forming the bulk of "W.T.'s" contents, but I fear it wouldn't stand very high considered as literature—beside such real literature as the work of Poe, Machen, Blackwood, James, Bierce, Dunsany, de la Mare, & so on. The highest honour I've so far received is a three-star mention & bibliographical note in O'Brien's "Best Short Stories of 1928" —based on my "Colour Out of Space".

Well—that's about all there is to me! Not much, but you see how garrulous a vain old man becomes when someone gives him provocation for talking about himself! That's the kind of guy I am—a cynic & materialist with classical & traditional tastes; fond of the past & its relics & ways, & convinced that the only pursuit worthy of a man of sense in a purposeless cosmos is the pursuit of tasteful & intelligent pleasure as promoted by a vivid mental & imaginative life. Because I believe in no absolute values, I accept the aesthetic values of the past as the only available points of reference—the only workable relative values— in a universe otherwise bewildering & unsatisfying. Thus I am an ultra-conservative socially, artistically, & politically, though an extreme modernist despite my 39 years in all matters of pure science & philosophy. Loving the illusory freedom of myth & dream, I am devoted to the literature of my escape; but likewise loving the tangible anchorage of the past, I tincture all my thought with overtones of antiquarianism. My favourite modern period is the 18th century; my favourite ancient period, the virile world of unspoiled republican Rome. I can't get interested in the Middle Ages—even the magic & legendry of that dreary era seems to me too naive to be really convincing.

Turning to my love of getting out of the real world into an imaginary world, I tend to prefer night to day when not in the open country. Accordingly my hours are fearful & wonderful at home—usually up at sunset & to bed in the morning. I am seldom out late—but seldom up early! In winter I virtually hibernate, for I am abnormally sensitive to the cold. Even a little coolness knocks me silly! On the contrary, I don't know what it is to be hot. I begin to tighten [*sic*] up at 95 in the shade!

All told I am pretty much of a hermit, as I was in youth. Most of my literary associates—a congenial "gang" some of whose names you'll recognize from W.T. tables of contents (Frank Belknap Long Jr., Donald Wandrei, Clark Ashton Smith, H. Warner Munn, Wilfred B. Talman, August W. Derleth, &c., &c.,)—live in other localities, & I'm getting too old to enjoy conversation on other than my favourite topics.

Old age claimed me early. Temperamentally I am about the same as I was 20 years ago, as I'll be 20 years hence if I'm alive then. As for writing—I usually know what I want to say before I start a tale, but often change the plot midway if the actual penning suggests some new idea. I do all work in long hand—I can't even think with a cursed machine in front of me—& correct very minutely. The extreme rapidity with which I write matter not destined for publication gives place to a very slow-moving caution when I tackle a piece of seriously intended prose. I apply great attention to details, including rhythm & tone-colour; though my aim is for the greatest possible simplicity—the art which conceals art. I usually spend about three days on a tale of medium length—in sessions of varying duration. I don't like to break the train of thought, so don't let any other task interrupt.

I never write except when the inward demand for expression becomes insistent. Nothing excites my contempt so much as forced or mechanical or commercial writing. Unless one has something to say, he had better keep quiet! I have a commonplace-book in which I jot down weird notions & plot germs for later use, & also have a file of weird newspaper cuttings as a possible source of ideas & colour-touches. A few tales I have founded on actual dreams—my own being very weird & fantastic. In youth I had more nightmares than I do now—when at six I used to encounter quite regularly a frightful species of dream-demons which I named "night-gaunts". I've used them in one of my tales.[14] I do my best writing between 2 A.M. & dawn. What I dread most is typing my Mss., for I abhor the sight & sound of a machine. I can't get anyone else to do it for me, since nobody can read my Mss. in their scrawled, interlined, & repeatedly corrected state. Sometimes I can't decipher them myself! Now I guess there isn't much more to be said about either the would-be author or his effusions!

Finally, I must apologise for this present flood of senile garrulity! This is the way old age gets when given occasion to recall bygone days—especially when the environment is unchangedly suggestive of the past as is this wooded river-bluff. But the west is blazing red with a departed sun, & above the ancient treetops the thin silver sickle of a young moon is trembling. I must get home. . . .

Yrs. most cordially—

H. P. Lovecraft

[*Enclosure:* List of stories by HPL.]

Notes

1. For "the" read "its." *Encyclopaedia Britannica,* s.v. "Magic," by Sir Edward Burnett Tylor (1832–1917), British anthropologist, p. [15.203 in 1901 ed.]
2. Originally, "Tetragrammaton" referred to the four Hebrew letters usually transliterated as YHWH or JHVH (Yahweh or Jehovah) to represent the name of God, for the reasons HPL gives below (see *Adonai*).
3. Actually, the word is derived from *aguris* (itself an Aeolian form of *agora*), meaning "a gathering, crowd."
4. HPL is considerably in error. The term means "of the same substance," and is generally taken to refer to the orthodox Christian belief that Jesus Christ is of the same substance as God.
5. HPL appears to be referring to the word *scheros* (found only in the dative case, *scheroi:* "in a line, one after another, uninterruptedly, successively"), but it is unlikely that this is a proper definition of the word in the incantation.
6. Arthur Edward Waite (1857–1942), American-born British mystic and poet who wrote extensively on magic and occultism. Eliphas Lévi (pseud. of Alphonse Louis Constant, 1810–1875), French poet and occultist. HPL did not own any books by either author, but appears to have been familiar with *The Mysteries of Magic* (1886; rev.

ed. 1897), a compendium of Lévi's writings selected and translated by Waite. HPL derived the incantation in *The Case of Charles Dexter Ward* (1927) from this book.

7. HPL refers to Abner Alden's *The Reader* (1802), a volume HPL consistently misdated to 1797. He has given an erroneous subtitle.

8. Should read "Poem."

9. Actually, he did not complete high school.

10. HPL and Sarah Susan Lovecraft (1857–1921) lived at 598 Angell Street from 1904 to 1924.

11. HPL and Lillian D. Clark (1856–1932) lived at 10 Barnes Street from 1926 to 1933.

12. HPL contributed at least 17 astronomical articles to the *Pawtuxet Valley Gleaner* in 1906 (and perhaps more in 1907–08).

13. "The Alchemist." The other tale, "The Beast in the Cave," later appeared in W. Paul Cook's *Vagrant*. Cook is the friend HPL cites later in the sentence.

14. *The Dream-Quest of Unknown Kadath,* but also in the sonnet "Night-Gaunts."

[63]   [ALS]

10 Barnes St.,

Providence, R.I.,

July 20, 1929.

Dear Mr. Michael:—

I am glad to know that the arrival of my tales proved such a pleasantly exciting event, & assure you there is no hurry about their return. Take your time & read them as gradually as you wish. I can appreciate your reluctance to spoil the fresh effect of certain kinds of reading matter by taking it in too large doses—that is why some people say they had rather read a weird story in a general magazine than read a magazine containing nothing but weird stories. Let me know when to send the next batch—& I will include the privately printed magazine with my history of supernatural horror in literature. Meanwhile Wright tells me that he is reprinting my old story "The Hound" in the next issue of W.T.

I am glad, too, that the rather copious autobiographical notes interested you; & surprised to learn that they describe a personality so similar to your own. "Ivan Tchor"[1] seems to be the spiritual brother to "Abdul Alhazred", & I wouldn't be surprised if he had read the "Necronomicon" at some forgotten period of his youth. I can picture the bearded Ivan in the turret room of the castle above the Volga, reading The Necronomicon in Theodorus Philetas' Byzantine Greek translation & now & then glancing sardonically at that part of the inner wall where there is a patch of masonry more recent than the ancient stonework of the haunted pile! Your cemetery incident sounds entertaining—I wish you had had as sinister & picturesque a setting for it as some of our old Eastern cities affords. In Providence, for example, there is a very ancient churchyard back of St. John's Cathedral[2] on the precipitous hill—

completely concealed from all public highways, & shadowed by mossy back-walls & lush greenery. The earliest interments go back to 1723, when the first church was built, (the present stone church dates from 1810) & there are many old slate slabs, crumbling marble urns & grotesque table-slabs & altar-tombs which give the whole picture an inimitably elder-world effect. By day it recalls Stoke-Poges* & Gray's Elegy, & by night it suggests almost anything connected with evil, horror & the outer-abyss. Adding to its spectral charm is the fact that in the '40's it used to form a favourite promenade of no less a person than Edgar Allan Poe himself, during his not infrequent visits to Providence! Last January I took a guest there at midnight—for it is only about five squares from my home, down the steep hill & a bit south along Benefit St.— & flashed my electric pocket light among the tombs as if it were a ghoulishly dancing corpse-light. My guest, though a middle-aged poet[3] of much sense & ordinary daylight courage, refused to descend to the lowest parts of the churchyard where the oldest slabs brood beneath overarching willows in the lee of the ivied cathedral wall—not because he was really afraid, of course, but because the scene reacted on his imagination too powerfully for comfort.

Your room, with its Altar of the Goat, inverted crucifixes, & other appurtenances of the Black Altars, must be a highly impressive place—& you may be reminded of it when you read "The Hound" next month. When I was very small—about 7 years old—my mythological fancy made me wish to *be*— not merely to *see*—a faun or satyr. I used to try to imagine that the tops of my ears were beginning to get pointed, & that a trace of incipient horns was beginning to appear on my forehead—& bitterly lamented the fact that my feet were rather slow in turning into hooves!

I'm glad you've read "The Willows", & believe you'd find it worth another perusal. I haven't read "The Old Dark House",[4] although I saw it advertised a couple of years ago. I was told that it was of the "popular novel" type rather than a piece of genuine weird literature, However, if you think it's worth a glance I may try to get hold of it.

With all good wishes—
  Most sincerely yrs,
    H. P. Lovecraft

Notes

1. In June 1930 the émigré translator and conservative thinker Ivan Tchorevskij (1876–1951) issued an anthology of "new" French verse in his Russian translations.

---

*I.e., the village of Stoke Poges (Buckinghamshire, England) in which Thomas Gray completed "Elegy Written in a Country Churchyard."

2. St. John's Episcopal Church (1810), 275 North Main Street. The churchyard is mentioned in "The Shunned House" (1924) and "The Messenger" (1929). It was there that HPL wrote his Poe acrostic, "In a Sequester'd Providence Churchyard Where Once Poe Walk'd" (1936).

3. Samuel Loveman.

4. By J. B. Priestley.

[64]   [ALS]

> 10 Barnes St.
> Providence, R.I.
> Sept. 20, 1929

My dear Mr. Michael:—

[. . .] There lay a pall of darkness and secrecy upon that house—it subtly discouraged from the first one's inclination to speak aloud, & at times one felt a faint miasmal tangibility in the circumambient air. The great high rooms had something of the mausoleum in their crumbling stateliness, & in the halls at night one always had to be sure that the great white flamboyant Corinthian pilasters never moved just the least bit. Something unwholesome—something furtive—something vast lying subterranely in obnoxious slumber—that was the soul of 169 Clinton Street at the edge of Red Hook, & in my great north-west corner room "The Horror at Red Hook" was written.

"In the Vault" was written to order, as it were—to please an old gentle-man who asked me to write a tale about an undertaker locked in a vault & es-caping on piled-up coffins—& I never do well with other people's suggestions. However, I fancy I've written just as poor things independently. "From Beyond the Wall of Sleep" [*sic*] is detestably mediocre, & "Cool Air" doesn't wear very well on rereading.

What is more, I myself greatly dislike "The Hound". I find it, nowadays, melodramatic & overstrained. The real fact is I find a curious rawness & im-maturity in all the stuff I have written up in the last two or three years. This ought not to be, considering my age (40), but it is so none the less. The rea-son probably is that I was too glibly self-confident about my work in earliest youth. I had sort of superficial fluency, & mistook that for maturity—so kept right on using the same kind of tone & imagery from year to year, & not mel-lowing with age as I ought to have done.

Stuff that I have written in my thirties has in many ways retained the rawness & naiveté that ought to have been shed before twenty-five. You will see it in the affected atmosphere of "The Tree", & the mawkish overtones of "The Quest of Iranon". The thing that has helped me shake off this incubus is, without doubt, my critical & revisory work—which compels me to analyse a vast array of diverse & immature writing very closely, & to pick out flaws & weaknesses for correction. Bitterly as I hate this work, it has done me good by compelling me to pay more attention to the fundamentals of the writing process—so that I ought to bless it instead of cursing it. Gradually I have come to recognise, in the Mss. of others, certain characteristic faults & extravagances of my own—trite phrases & images, overstrained situations & denouements, mawkish & artificial tone, &c.—& to correct these tendencies in such little as I am still able to do amidst the pressure of work.

"The Colour Out of Space", written only 2½ years ago, is the earliest thing of mine which I can regard as in any way a finished specimen—and I should certainly give the older stuff a very extensive revision & toning down if it were ever to be collected in book form.

Hope you can make out "Sarnath"—of which I haven't any types copy. I really ought to change that name to "Zarnath" or something else, because after writing the story I actually came across the name "Sarnath" in Dunsany—whose system of imaginary nomenclature is surprisingly like my own, although I devised mine before ever hearing of him.[1]

I was rather gratified this fall to find that I have been included for a second year in the three-star Roll of Honour in Edward J. O'Brien's short story year-book. Last year it was for "The Colour Out of Space"; this year for "The Dunwich Horror". O'Brien also gave a lesser ovation to my "Silver Key"—which was also mentioned in the O. Henry Memorial Prize volume for 1929.

I have [not] written a story since "The Dunwich Horror", being utterly driven to the wall by revisionary work. I am, however, trying to get my revision programme cleaned up this winter so that I can get some more material of my own.

[. . .]

[. . .] high-sounding officers,* but not much behind 'em nowadays—like a Guatemalan or Costa-Rican army! [. . .]

[. . .]

[. . .] [You have a] keen appreciation of the substratum of barbaric feeling in contemporary 'jazz'—for in all truth it is not a very far cry from the bleat of a saxophone to the howling of a frenzied ring of sweat-drenched cannibals around the monolithic altar of a Congolese crocodile-god. [. . .]

Although the churchly tradition is an important part of our folklore, which must be respected because of its influence on history, it becomes hypocritical for an adult or nearly adult mind to continue in the empty forms after all illusion of their substance has worn off. There is no need for ostentatious irreverence or bitter scoffing—such things, indeed, belong only to the first period of nascent revolt against a still arrogant dogmatism. Nowadays we can afford to recognise religion as an anthropological phenomenon quite natural and inevitable in its day, and even yet possessed of the residual beauty and dignity which it gained from its former position as focus of the

---

*Of NAPA.

highest human feelings and ceremonial symbolisation of the principal phenomena of life.

But it is, after disillusionment, almost as much a matter of doubtful taste
to practice the meaningless rites as to scoff at them; so that it seems to me a
non-churchgoing policy is the only honest and artistic course for a rational
materialist. I don't attend church myself, though I have a keen eye for the ecclesiastical architecture and many parts of the ceremonial ritual—especially in
the Episcopal and Catholic sects.

I love, too, the pastoral calm suggested by a distant church-tower or
steeple in a spreading landscape, and I have often celebrated such things in
prose and verse. It is all a graceful mythology like that of Greece and Rome,
or of the Odin-worshipping north, and as such deserves our aesthetic reverence and affectionate recollection.

Today, however, we have learned too much about the structure of the
universe and the origin of our own feelings (including the religious feelings)
to fancy that these pleasant legends have any real relation to things as they
are. So far as can be seen, the immediate cosmos within the curved space-
time continuum envisaged by Einstein (which is all the cosmos we can ever
plumb or even form guesses about) is a perpetual and impersonal affair consisting solely of streams of force circulating in regular patterns and involving
the alternate building-up and breaking down of that temporary form called
matter. It has always been so and always will be so.

The very conceptions of "beginning" and "ending" have no meaning in
such an eternal flux, being derived wholly from our limited experience with
temporary forces. A cosmos like this can hardly be said to have *consciousness,
direction,* or *purpose;* since the whole regular pattern (like that of a crystal) is
merely the automatic result of balanced streams of force, while every muta-
tion of its contents is the product of inevitable reactions preceding and surrounding the given one.

There is a progressive change away from any one state toward any other
state—for what is built up is soon broken down again, leaving the net aggre-
gate always the same. When a universe condenses out of the ether in one part
of space, another is evaporating into the ether elsewhere. The sum total is
fixed—there never has been and never will be anything in the cosmos save
automatic rearrangement; rearrangement of the parts of a larger whole which
is eternally the same. Amidst all this unending pattern-motion, the history of
our present galaxy and solar system and earth and organic life and human
species is the merest temporary flash and incidental by-product—something
not dreamed of a cosmic second ago, and to be utterly obliterated and forgotten a cosmic second hence. Life is, indeed, a rather rare occurrence (i.e., the
juxtaposition of two stellar spheres in such a way as to raise, upon one of
them, huge gaseous tides which break off and form a planet system without
wholly wrecking the parent mass) which probably don't occur more than

once or twice in incalculable aeons, and therefore seldom existing in more than one or two places in the cosmos at any given time.

It is the most complex form of cosmic organisation yet known, and forces act through its units in such an elaborate way that we get the illusion of "free will" amongst its topmost subdivisions; but actually it is no more than a variant of these same forces which elsewhere manifest themselves as rocks or oceans or suns or planets. Prof. Harlow Shapley[2] well describes life as "a minor crustal phenomenon in the history of a planet." It arises spontaneously from the elements of the crust under certain conditions of light, heat, pressure, and chemical reaction, and eventually returns to inanimate dust after a long course of natural development during which it sometimes attains vast complexity and occasionally achieves that peculiar quality of environment-registration and reduplication which we term "consciousness".

All this is a plain matter of physics and chemistry and it is simply idiocy for us—in this age—to repeat the very natural mistakes of our forefathers and invent a mythical "spiritual" world which half pervades our real substance and furnishes a basis for "immortality". Our modern knowledge of force and substance, and our realisation that personality in organic beings is a result of the complex arrangement of their material parts—glands, brain-cells, etc.—leave no room or need for the naive and ancient idea of a "soul" or "ka" or any other sort of double for the body which we recognise as the substance of a human creature. That body is shaped by natural patterns of force; and when it dies, there is no possibility of a continuance of the thought or personality-phenomena which resulted solely from the functioning of its material particles. When the fuel is gone, there can be no flame.

Of course, all this seems shocking and bewildering to a generation naively brought up with the notion that insignificant Man is the chief concern of the cosmos, and that his acts and fate are deeply related to the governing powers of all entity. It is a frightful jolt for them to realise that mankind and the world on which he dwells are only a momentary and negligible incident in the history of vast and eternal processes which have no consciousness and no concern as to whether the human world does or doesn't exist. Heredity, egotism, pomposity, and fear get a knockout blow from the real facts, and one can't really expect an elderly person of the present—whose dominant emotions were hopelessly fixed in childhood—to accept anything so shattering to his conventionally acquired basis of thought of life. To the universe it makes no difference whether or not organic life appears to exist on any of its planets. The individual is too trivial to be of importance—and indeed, life cannot exist for more than the merest fraction of a planet's total existence. It is a mistake to regard the cosmos as either favourable or unfavourable to it. It is simply indifferent and unconscious. All we can do is to let the old folks alone, for emotions of great depth absolutely bind them to their ancestral folk-myths.

Even my own middle-aged generation is touched by the early inhibiting influence; so that it tends to produce desperate *compromisers* between myth and fact, such as to the eloquent Dr. Harry Emerson Fosdick[3] and his ilk. But to the mind which takes a *fresh start*, there is nothing very terrible about the facts of the cosmos as they really are. Even mankind's self-esteem needn't suffer; for although we know he isn't the principal pet of an omnipotent "old man upstairs", we also know that he probably forms the most distinctive and completely organised form of matter now in existence; a form of very rare occurrence and strikingly unique properties.

As to the ethical side—it doesn't require a system of mythology with high-blown conceptions of cosmic "good" and "evil" to demonstrate that people get along more comfortably under certain systems of regulation than under a wild regime of unrestrained individual caprice! The only thing we can sensibly call an "object" in life is to derive a maximum number of satisfactions from the process; and when we investigate the sources, the relative intensity, and the relative permanence of the various kinds of satisfactions at our disposal—physical, emotional, imaginative, and intellectual—we find as a matter of scientific truth that we have to limit the lesser in order to enjoy the greater, in a manner very closely corresponding to the major principles of theologic ethics. That is, indeed, the real origin of ethics; for after all religion did no more than give an easily understandable raison d'etre & authority to laws of conduct which actually arose from utilitarian experience and the play of the aesthetic emotions. Certain things have a tested value in promoting the strength, survival, and emotional contentment of the group—and these are what come to be endorsed by theology and called "good". Of course they vary as environmental conditions vary, and are therefore different for different races and periods; but in the main, their limits of variation are not so wide as to destroy all suggestions of a coherent code. This code, in its various forms, does not need to perish when its supporting theology perishes—hence it is asinine to claim that society will break down as soon as faith vanishes.

On the contrary, it is probable that the code can be far more rationally and flexibly formulated, once its natural and variable background is recognised. Of course, elders will protest whenever it departs from its religion-backed form—but men of sense will recognise that changes may be for the better rather than for worse. The changes, though, are not likely to be as great as many young radicals imagine; since, after all, a great deal of our contentment depends on our retaining some linkage with an historically familiar pattern. When we depart from familiar ways we have vast difficulty in retaining the illusion of *significance* in anything—we begin to lose interest and test every idea and feeling by the yardstick of "what of it?" in a manner rather impoverishing to our mental lives. All this is a problem in itself—the only proximate answer to which is a cautious conservatism.

So far as I can see, all non-materialistic interpretations of the cosmos are pure mythology—though the very natural and age-long holding of supernatural beliefs by the majority gives them an emotional and aesthetic value independent of their actual baselessness. Supernatural assumptions in art—though known to be false—afford a convenient mode of emotional escape for those who feel oppressed by the rigid limitations of time, space, and natural law. Actually, if Western Civilisation must have some form of supernatural superstition, I really think the old gods are much more appropriate than the pretense of Christianity which we have been externally flaunting since historic and political accident fastened it on us. Christianity has never really fitted us—our whole record is one of actual conduct belying the protestations we make on Sunday. On the other hand the old gods are *really* ours—they were the imaginative product of the same culture-stream which produced our genuine subconscious instincts and folkways. If we openly worshipped them, our habitually ruthless and predatory conduct would not be hypocritical. I'm sure that Thor and Odin seem much closer and more vital than the anaemic, crucified saviour. However, as a practical issue, it's simply asinine and sentimental to fancy that we can ever set the Valkyries to riding again. Long centuries have taught the herd to embody their ignorance and superstition in the Christ-image and there'd be no advantage in a shift which for most would be meaningless. The trend of reason and enlightenment is toward no gods at all—and it doesn't matter much which of the old delusions the unthinking cling to.

It has always seemed doubtful to me whether any one person answering to the traditional Jesus ever existed in fact. In many respects the forms of Christianity closely follow those of the popular mystery-cults of the period—Dionysiac, Apollonian, Pythagorean, etc.—which joined Oriental and Hellenic concepts in a variety of ways. With this cult-background (wherein the idea of sacrifice and atonement was so marked) to start with, and with the age-old Jewish idea of a messiah superadded, it would be easy to build up a religious and heroic myth around any one of the sporadic evangelists of the East—or around several of them, fusing their various personalities into one idealiased hero or demigod. This, it seems to me, is what must have happened. The tissue of miracles and too-neatly-dramatic episodes undoubtedly represents the purely mythic element; but certain touches of verisimilitude now and then suggest a substratum of fact. Incidents in the lives of several rustic preachers may be involved—though possibly one figures more extensively than others. Just who this one was, and to what extent the padded and myth-decked gospel narrative relates his actual history, it seems to me can never quite be settled except through the discovery of hitherto unknown source-material. Parts of the popular tale—sacrifice, resurrection, etc.—are obviously derived from the nature-myth of Linus, Dionysus or Zagreus. Other parts—trial, etc.—might be tested by certain comparisons with contemporary accounts. But the lack of really reliable sources is almost fatal. That is, so far as general scholarship knows.

[. . .]

Yrs. for bigger & better daemons—

H. P. Lovecraft

Notes

1. HPL is in error: the name Sarnath does not appear in the work of Lord Dunsany. It is an actual place-name in India, although HPL probably did not know that.

2. Harlow Shapley (1885–1972), American astronomer and director of the Harvard College Observatory (1921–52).

3. Harry Emerson Fosdick (1878–1969), pastor of the Park Avenue Baptist Church (1925–30) and the Riverside Church (1930–46) in New York City, and a central figure in the Fundamentalist-Modernist controversy within American Protestantism in the 1920s and 1930s.

[65] [ALS]

10 Barnes St.,

Providence, R.I.,

[Dec. 18, 1929.]

My dear Mr. Michael:—

[. . .]

[. . .] I place it[1] among the best things I have written [. . .]

[. . .]

[. . .] [The review contains][2] the first mention my work has ever received in the press of my own town! [. . .]

[. . .]

[. . .] Your generous enclosure[3] quite overwhelms me [. . .]

[. . .]

[. . .] If you take that aestival pilgrimage, depend on a warm welcome in Providence! [. . .] Surely you must see Salem & Marblehead—Arkham & Kingsport! [. . .]

[. . .]

H. P. Lovecraft

[*Enclosure:* Copy of the *Recluse*.]

Notes

1. "The Nameless City."

2. A review of *Beware After Dark* in the *Providence Journal* (in B. K. Hart's "The Sideshow" column).

3. Of money.

[66]   [ALS]

10 Barnes St.,

Providence, R.I.,

Feby. 4, 1930.

Dear Mr. Michael:—

I was very glad to hear from you, & to learn that you found my sketch of weird literature interesting. It is rather incomplete & careless, I fear; & I would make many changes if I were to prepare a second edition in book form. I wish somebody would write a really scholarly & inclusive thing of the sort—I'd be the first to buy it! Glad to hear also that the large *National Amateur*[1] reached you safely.

It surely argues brilliancy if, at your age, you have a prospect of entering college next year! Amherst is about 70 miles from Providence in a straight line, & would probably be reached through Worcester or Springfield. If you go there you must certainly get down to this city now & then. Amherst is a very pretty place—shady & reposeful & traditional—as I can attest from having passed through it once or twice.

Too bad the "Beware after Dark" review got lost—but it doesn't really matter. The book, I recently learned, proved a commercial failure—which really surprises me in view of the generous amount of first-rate standard material it contains. But perhaps your own case is typical—everybody likely to appreciate it would probably have read most of the items before!

I've had that Drake book—"The Shadow[y] Thing"—on my want list for some time, having read favourable reviews of it. Your added recommendation increases my wish to see it, & I shall make it my first library item when I get a chance to do any leisurely reading at all. This has been an atrociously crowded winter for me—with little time for either reading [or writing] of original tales.

About that subtlety in Machen's "White People"—I don't wonder you have to inquire, for I find that 'four out of five' have the same difficulty! The point is—as I recall from memory, for my copy of the book is lost—that *suggestion* often has the power to produce physical results in its own image, so that the *symbolic enactment* of a thing (as in mimetic magic & various forms of religious sacrament) may cause the equivalent reality to occur without any direct physical cause. In the prologue incident, a mother's finger is injured in this sacramental-mystical or suggestional way, because she is in a certain emotional rapport with the child who physically receives the injury. In the story itself, the adolescent heroine probably becomes sacramental[ly] pregnant with a brat of some evil elder god, through having *seen*, with appropriately mystical emotions, some obscene Roman statue-group depicting the physical conception of such a brat. The nature of the early witch-cult, the account of the hateful sculpture, & the description of the girl as menaced by an awful yet innocent shame from which she delivers herself only by suicide, would appear to make Machen's intent unmistakable. But for this suicide, the heroine would have been the accursed Madonna of a Virgin Birth as hideous as that of the creature Helen Vaughan in Machen's Great God Pan.

You have the advantage of me in having seen the new W.T., for I haven't yet procured a copy. It amuses me to hear that good old Abdul is being inquired after! Perhaps I'll furnish some of the hoax-data which I've concocted about the dippy old Damascene![2] I've just received $11.00 for "The Ancient Track." I write loads of verse, but never set up any pretensions to being a poet. Some day I'll shew you my hellish sonnet sequence "Fungi from Yuggoth", which I wrote last month.

I surely hope that aestival migration plan of yours will materialise—whether through hitch-hiking or through motorcycling. I'm not saying that New England's old churchyards would necessarily *scare* you, but I'll wager they couldn't help *interesting* you. You'll be near some great old places at Amherst. Don't miss *Deerfield*, which is probably within the scope of an afternoon's trip.

With best wishes,

Most cordially & sincerely yrs—

H. P. Lovecraft

Notes

1. Presumably the "July 1919" issue of the *National Amateur* (actually issued in 1921), containing HPL's "Idealism and Materialism—A Reflection" and "The Picture in the House."

2. HPL refers to the March 1930 issue of *WT,* where a reader, N. J. O'Neail, wished further information on "Abdul Alhazred the mad Arab, and his *Necronomicon.*" HPL supplied the "hoax-data" in "History of the 'Necronomicon'" (1927).

To W. Chesley Worthington

W[illiam] Chesley "Chet" Worthington (1903–2002) served as an editor of the *Providence Journal,* then as editor of the *Brown Alumni Monthly* (1931–68). It was to Worthington that Lovecraft sent poetry for publication in his column, "These Plantations," which appeared Wednesdays in the *Journal.* Worthington published "The East India Brick Row" and five sonnets from *Fungi from Yuggoth.*

[67]   [ALS, Providence Athenaeum]

> [H. P. LOVECRAFT
> 10 BARNES STREET
> PROVIDENCE, R. I.]

Decr. 7, 1929

W. Chesley Worthington, Esq.,
    Providence, R.I.,

Dear Sir:—
         Though the enclosed may be absurdly long for use in "These Plantations", I cannot resist submitting it on the slender chance that you can tuck it in somewhere. It fills me with rage to think that the city is permitting a group of Babbitesque Goths & Vandals to destroy wantonly one of the finest & most distinctive things we have, without more than the palest & feeblest of regretful remonstrances. Last spring I suggested in a letter to the Editor of the Sunday Journal that the old South Water St. warehouses be carefully restored instead of destroyed, & provided with new fireproof interiors suitable for use as a Hall of Records. I well knew that it was of no use to suggest—but the process formed at least an emotional catharsis. These lines do likewise— & I hope that by some miracle you may find them worth printing. I'd like some of those town-wreckers to read them—if indeed such persons ever turn to a page as civilised as "These Plantations."
         Hoping against hope—
                 Yr most obt Servt
                 H P Lovecraft.

[68]   [ALS, Providence Athenaeum]

[H. P. LOVECRAFT
10 BARNES STREET
PROVIDENCE, R. I.]

Jany 10, 1930

Dear Mr. Worthington:—

Let me thank you for the copy of the Wednesday page with my stanzas—elegiac indeed, alas, as a glance at the subject-locale now shows—on the ancient Brick Row. No doubt you share my oaths regarding the depeditation of *Comes* to *Come* in Stan. 7, l. 1, & the curious metamorphosis of *steepled* to *stepped* in Stan. 9, line 2—though according to standards of modern newspaper linotypography that is indubitably getting off easily. Such light regrets are drowned in the major regret that the Brick Row itself is now beyond the help of the most perfervid rhetoric. But at least I did all the feeble remonstrating I could—winding up the losing fight by inducing a New Jersey friend to present the visitor's point of view in a letter to the Sunday Journal.[1] And now the end is nigh. The towers by the gate of St. Romanus have toppled, & The Sultan's destroying hordes have entered a breach in the walls. Nothing remains for me to do—artistically speaking—but perish on the spot like Constantinus Palaeol[o]gus before me!

I am very grateful for the space spared for my effusion, & hope that it did not cause you any really nerve-racking problem of format. The neat, symmetrical location of the piece is highly pleasing.

Again expressing my appreciation, believe me,
         Yr most h^ble o^bt Servt
              H P Lovecraft

Notes

1. See letter 213.

To William Stanley Braithwaite

William Stanley Braithwaite (1878–1962) was literary editor for the *Boston Transcript* and compiler of the *Anthology of Magazine Verse . . . and Year Book of American Poetry*. He received the Spingarn award from the NAACP. Lovecraft was outraged when he learned that the *Transcript*'s literary editor was not Caucasian (Braithwaite was one-eighth Black—or, in the pejorative formulation of the time, an "octoroon"). Braithwaite was the alleged lover of Lovecraft's erstwhile collaborator Winifred Virginia Jackson. The two founded the B. J. Brimmer Publishing Company, which for many years published Braithwaite's annual anthology of the year's best magazine verse. Lovecraft was amused to find that in the 1921 edition, Braithwaite printed seven poems by Jackson, noting that they had been published in Lovecraft's *Conservative*. They were not. Presumably Jackson had informed him they would be. Braithwaite wrote the introduction to Jackson's *Backroads: Maine Narratives, with Lyrics* (Boston: B. J. Brimmer, 1944). Lovecraft's suggestion to Jackson that he might name a black kitten "William Stanley Braithwaite" may have caused the cessation of communication between the two.

[69] [ALS, JHL]

Feb. 7, 1930

Dear Mr. Braithwaite:—

I am glad to hear that you found merit in Mr. Long's poem,[1] & wish his work could be better known—for the encouragement of recognition would undoubtedly have the effect of stimulating him to more & more poignant utterance. There are provokingly few poets—just as there are provokingly few prose writers—who fully express that sense of the cosmic & the marvellous which is so potent a reality to many kinds of sensitive people. You would not find *Weird Tales* a very rich harvesting-ground for poetic material; although it does frequently contain excellent verses by Clark Ashton Smith, whom you have occasionally mentioned in the anthology.[2] If Mr. Smith could only curb a frequent tendency toward extravagance, I think his work would be of even greater importance than it is. He is now entering the prose field to some extent—with exotic phantasies & tales.

It pleases me highly to learn of the continued progress of Miss Jackson, whose work gave me such an instant impression of authentic genius a decade ago. I have seen & appreciated later verses of hers here & there, & am interested by the prospect of a novel from her pen. I shall be on the lookout both for this & for the short stories. It seemed certain to me from the first that her work had that sureness of insight & expression which marks genuine art, & the more authoritative confirmation of that judgment is very gratifying.

Another early judgment of mine, which I hope later developments may confirm, relates not to an actual poet, but to a hierophant of poets—in other words, to a manual or text-book on the subject of poetic appreciation, which I think will be more effective than anything hitherto published in arousing ordinary minds to the beauty of poetry, explaining as much as can be explained of the poet's appeal, & inculcating standards by which the genuine can be distinguished from the spurious. This book—"Doorways to Poetry"—is by Maurice Winter Moe, a teacher of English in the West Division High School, Milwaukee, Wisconsin; & a reading of it in manuscript has aroused my enthusiasm to almost inordinate bounds.[3] It is so perfectly & incisively analytical, yet so appreciatively sympathetic & so free from pedagogical sterility. There is a chance of its acceptance by the Macmillan Co., & in the event of its publication I confidently expect qualified critics to sustain my own instant & unofficial verdict. There is no doubt but that you will receive a copy upon its issuance.

Again expressing my appreciation—
    Yr oblig'd ob[t] Servt
    H P Lovecraft

Notes

1. Apparently "On Icy Kinarth" by Frank Belknap Long, *WT* 15, No. 4 (April 1930): 444.

2. Braithwaite's *Anthology of Magazine Verse for 1926* listed but did not reprint Smith's "To Omar Khayyam" (*Lyric West*, May–June 1926).

3. The book was never published.

To Lee Alexander Stone

Lee Alexander Stone (1879–1955), who had served in the Spanish-American War, was so disgusted with the U.S. Army health standards that he undertook a public health career of national importance and international reputation. He wrote numerous articles on public health for scientific and medical journals, including books dealing primarily with sex hygiene and marriage. He also wrote four books concerning Chicago. In 1929, he published a 16-page item reprinted from the *Chronicle of Chicago* that appeared as a pamphlet titled *Chicago: Greatest Advertised City in the World, Not the Wickedest* (1929). Presumably this is the item Lovecraft refers to in his letter to James F. Morton, in which he transcribes his letter to Stone: ". . . take a look at this sample of polite insult, which I have just handed to a goddam dead beat in Chicago, who has owed me a revision bill dating partly from Feb. 1929 & partly from Sept. 1929. He has paid no attention whatever to courteous statements, & in the following words I wash my hands of him & his'n. 'Is Chicago a Crime-Ridden City' is the title of an absurd defence of Chi which I knocked in shape for him a year & a half ago" (*Letters to James F. Morton* 233; N.B. the footnotes were glosses intended for Morton's benefit).

Lovecraft later regretted sending this tart letter, when he learned from Farnsworth Wright (who had recommended Lovecraft to Stone) that Stone had taken ill around the time he was dunning him for payment.

[70]   [transcription in letter to James F. Morton]

10 Barnes St.,
Providence, R. I.,
Septr. 18, 1930.

Lee Alexander Stone, M. D.,
    Chicago, Illinois

Sir:
    In the matter of your persistently unpaid revision bill—concerning which you so persistently withhold all explanations despite repeated inquiries—I have decided, at the risk of encouraging sharp practices, to forego the use of a collecting agency & make you a present of the amount involved.

This is my first encounter with such a hopelessly bad bill, & I believe I may consider the sum ($7.50) as not ill spent in acquiring practical experience. I needed to be taught caution in accepting unknown* clients without ample† references—especially clients from a strident region which cultivates ostentatious commercial expansion rather than the honour customary among gentlemen.

Meanwhile I am grateful for so concrete an answer to the popular question, "Is Chicago a Crime-Ridden City?"

With such consideration as is appropriate to the situation, & trusting that my small gift may prove of financial aid to you, Believe me, Sir,

Yr most obedient h^{ble} Servt.

H. P. Lovecraft

---

*He was Supt. of a branch of Chi. Pub. Health Service during the war!
†Farnsworth Wright was the guy who wished him onto me.

To H. Warner Munn

H[arold] Warner Munn (1903–1981) was an American writer of fantasy and horror tales, and a friend of Lovecraft. His first story, "The Werewolf of Ponkert" (*WT*, July 1925), was based on a remark in Lovecraft's letter to *WT* (March 1924): "Take a werewolf story, for instance—who ever wrote a story from the point of view of the wolf, and sympathising strongly with the devil to whom he has sold himself?" It appears that Munn misunderstood the import of Lovecraft's remark, for he has the werewolf regret his condition. Munn wrote several more werewolf stories under the generic title "Tales of the Werewolf Clan"; some were gathered as *The Werewolf of Ponkert* (1958). He was introduced to Lovecraft by W. Paul Cook in the summer of 1927; Lovecraft visited him in Athol, Mass., in the summer of 1928, at which time (on June 28) Munn took Lovecraft to Bear's Den, a remarkable forest gorge later cited in "The Dunwich Horror" (1928). Cook and Munn visited Lovecraft in Providence in June 1929, and Lovecraft visited them in Athol the next June. Lovecraft and Munn communicated only sporadically in the 1930s; Lovecraft suggested that Munn's increasing religiosity caused him to keep his distance from Lovecraft. Munn went on to write many stories for the pulps as well as fantasy and historical novels.

[71]   [ALS]

10 Barnes St.

Providence, R.I.

September 19, 1930

My Dear Wladislaw:—

Well, I'll be damn'd! Nearly everybody I know seems to have something to do with Vermont sooner or later! I recall driving through Putney with Cook three years ago—it seemed a very attractive place, like all the idyllic villages along the route. Trust you're enjoying your sojourn—though I hope your cessation of regular Athol duties is only temporary. What you say about the deserted village is surely provocative to the imagination, & I hope you can manage to get out to see it. The circumstances of its wiping-out ought to inspire more than one incident in the "master" cycle. *Black Sickness* . . . . . ugh! . . . . . perhaps some one amongst the inhabitants had made the Black Pilgrimage to Chorazin, & returned with more influences than he had expected! And so the houses stand today, vacant & sinister, with gaping black windows that peer like daemon eyes into the haunted night, whilst honest folk go miles out of their way to avoid that which broods & stalks in darkness . . . . Yes, Sir, you must tell me about that place when you see it—if you return.

I am glad to hear that Cook is safely resting. Is his emancipation from the transcript routine a permanent one? Many have been frightfully worried about his epistolary silence—especially the survivors of the late John Ravenor Bullen, who are wondering what he means to do about that [?typically] needless second edition of "White Fire"—which I believe is sidetracked at some binder's in Boston. I surely hope that W P C's recuperation will be thorough enough to let him wind up these loose ends to everybody's satisfaction!

No doubt you received my card from Quebec, hence are aware of the ecstasy I experienced upon my first visit to that ancient & lovely town. I haven't been able to think about much of anything else since—for truly, it is the most utterly exquisite & picturesque thing that has ever met my aged eyes. I'd move up there in a second for good if it weren't for the unendurable winter temperatures. All my former standards of urban beauty are suspended & obsolete. A mighty headland missing from a mile-broad river & crowned with a medieval fortress—*city walls* climbing precipitous cliffs or towering above green table-lands—tangles of pointed red-tiled roofs & silver belfries & steeples glistening in the sun—great arching *city gates*, & labyrinths of ancient streets & alleys climbing vertical heights or burrowing in the dark shadow of beetling precipices—houses of primordial ambiguity & of a quaintness unknown elsewhere on this continent—horse-drawn vehicles in abundance, & all the evidences of a mellow, mature & leisurely elder civilization—all these are only a fraction of the marvellous totality that is Quebec. My whole sojourn there seems like a fantastic dream extending over vast periods of time—I can hardly believe that any such place really exists! Have you seen it? If not, do so the first chance you get! It truly does not belong to this age & scene at all, but to an old bourbon France contemporaneous with witches' Sabbaths & the subtlest antics of the Master's brood.

On my way home I stopped off a day in Boston for the boat trip to Provincetown. This was notable to me as my first experience on the open sea—all my previous navigation having been on harbours, rivers, & bays. To be out of sight of land gives on[e] the acutest sensations of mystery & expectancy . . . . What, one wonders, will loom suddenly ahead on that vacant & alluring horizon? One shares to some extent the adventurous sensations of Ulysses, Madoc, Columbus & all the great sea-rovers of songs & story. Another stupendously fascinating thing is entering Boston Harbour amidst the glamour of a misty sunset. Out of vaporous vacancy rise the mysterious grey headlands, monolith-like lighthouses, & low-lying, cryptical islets—till one wonders whether one is really approaching a part of Earth, or some Ethereal Dunsanian shore beyond the East or over the Edge of the world.

Meanwhile our friend Orton[1] sends word that he is doing some traveling, too—from Montreal down the St. Lawrence on a yacht to Quebec, & there to Burlington & back to Rutland. I hope he enjoyed Quebec as much as I did—though I'd wager a good sum he couldn't!

As for further gang news—Morton is back from his long trip, & repeats that he appreciated Charleston to the full, although ancient St. Augustine fascinated him more than anything else. Loveman has left the Argosy Book Shop & gone back to Dauber & Pine's—a damn wise move on his part. He ought never to have left there in 1927. Belknap flourishes as usual—I was glad to see him last month & spend a few days with him & his parents around Cape Cod. No doubt you got our joint card from Hyannis.

Best wishes—& don't forget to let me know about the accursed village where the Black Man breathed on the people—that is, provided you get out alive.

Yr obt Servt,
Grandpa Cthulhu

P. S. Shall be glad to see "The Cat Organ" in print next month.[2] P. P. S. Saw Montmorency Falls near Quebec—which beat Doane's Falls in magnitude, though not by a long shot in picturesqueness of setting.

Notes

1. Vrest Orton (1897–1986), member of the Kalem Club, was working at the time for The Tuttle Company, a publisher in Rutland, Vt. He was for a time an editor at the *Saturday Review* and later the founder of the Vermont Country Store.
2. "The Cat Organ" is a section of "The Master Strikes" (*WT*, November 1930), part of the "Tales of the Werewolf Clan."

[72] [ALS, JHL]

66 COLLEGE ST.,
Providence, R.I.,
Dec. 29, 1935.

Mighty Werewolf:—

Welcome back from the tomb! Young Petaja has spoken of hearing from you, so that I was aware of your presence atop the ground in at least a vampiric or zombeian capacity. Shall be on the lookout for your new story—tell me when it gets accepted.

I was certainly glad to get the "Mts. of Madness" accepted. It was placed through the agent Julius Schwartz (255 E. 188th St., N.Y. City)—the guy who wants to publish your survey of bizarre fiction[1] in his *Fantasy Magazine*. *Astounding* has also taken a new novelette of mine—"The Shadow Out of Time".[2] This dual acceptance is certainly gratifying, though I am no such fatuous optimist as to expect the winning streak to continue. Last month I wrote a short story called "The Haunter of the Dark"—not yet professionally submitted—based in a way on the view from my west window.

Hope all has lately been well around ancient Pequoig. Cook is anxious to hear from you. Last September he pulled up stakes & went out to the St. Louis region to help the old-time amateur journalist Paul J. Campbell in a neighbourhood newspaper project.[3] The venture seems to have encountered difficulties, & W P C may find himself in rather a tight position—stranded far from home. His present address is *5720 Westmoreland Place, East St. Louis, Illinois.*

I spent last summer in De Land, Florida, with young Barlow—thus repeating the programme of 1934. Previously Barlow & I had simultaneously visited New York—around New Year's—& mingled in many meetings of the group there—Long, Wandrei, Wandrei's brother, Loveman, Talman, Leeds, Kleiner, &c. &c. Perhaps you know that both the Wandrei boys have made a tremendous commercial success of hack fiction-writing, as has Belknap on a slightly smaller scale. On my return from Florida I made the usual antiquarian stops—St. Augustine, Charleston, Richmond, Washington, Philadelphia,—& spent 2 weeks in N.Y. as Wandrei's guest.

Later trips included one to the Wilbraham ("Dunwich") country with the old-time amateur E. H. Cole, one to Marblehead, one around Cape Cod, & one to New Haven. In mid-October Loveman visited New England, & I shewed him a bit around Boston & Cambridge.

Had a good Yule—with lighted tree, various presents, &c. Now I am about to hop off on a week's visit to Long, during which I expect to see most of the gang. Hope the weather will be decent. We had a rather late autumn, & there is now snow on the ground even yet, but the past few days have been disconcertingly cold.

Weird magazines seem to be languishing of late—at least, W T has had discouragingly few stories of any value. Clark Ashton Smith, C. L. Moore, & Robert E. Howard are the great standbys nowadays. The little "fan magazines" struggle along bravely—though *The Fantasy Fan* has succumbed. *Fantasy Magazine* will in future be printed by William Crawford, publisher of *Marvel Tales* & *Unusual Stories,* & a newcomer—*The Phantagraph*—is laying plans for permanence.

Hope the Werewolf Clan had a pleasant Yule, & that 1936 will prove one of its most prosperous years. Every good wish—

Yrs most cordially,
H P L

Notes

1. See HPL to Lillian D. Clark, 11 June 1930: "Munn brought out several samples of his recent work for criticism, & I shall read them at leisure—some here & some after

I get home—giving him an opinion on them at a later date. One of them is an article on popular weird fiction for *The Recluse*" (*LFF* 859). The work was never published.

2. The story was sold by Donald Wandrei, acting without HPL's knowledge and refusing a fee or commission for his work as informal agent.

3. Campbell and Cook worked briefly for the *Canteen*.

To Earl C. Kelley

Earl C. Kelley, Jr. (1905–1932) of Burlington-on-Lake-Champlain, Vermont, was an amateur journalist and editor of *Ripples from Lake Champlain,* which published "The Pigeon-Flyers" from Lovecraft's *Fungi from Yuggoth.* Kelley apparently had accepted "A Memory," but died by his own hand before the poem could be published. At the time, he was president of the NAPA.

[73] [ANS]

[Postmarked Providence, R.I.,
7 November 1930]

Thanks exceedingly for the new issue of your delightful magazine. Such an ample & regular treat as this reminds me of the palmier days of amateur journalism, & raises the hope that a renaissance may really be under way. Truly, your *Ripples* form a marvellously stimulating breath of the old times! Vermont is getting to be the chief of all amateur states, & I am glad to see leading laurels come back to old New England. It is very likely that the splendid old-timer W. Paul Cook (a native of Vt.), will soon be added once more to your list of actual residents, so that your supremacy will be placed absolutely beyond all hope of challenge.

Best wishes—& good luck & long life to *Ripples.*
Sincerely yrs—
H P Lovecraft

To Henry George Weiss

Henry George Weiss (1898–1946) was an American poet, writer, and novelist. His science fiction stories and poetry appeared under the pseudonym "Francis Flagg" in *Amazing Stories, Astounding Stories, Tales of Wonder, WT,* and elsewhere. Of him Lovecraft wrote: "He is [. . .] a victim of communistic illusions; and fears that his real-name authorship of much radical verse would make him unfavourably known in his own person to conservative business interests" (*ES* 330). He is the author of *The Shame of California and Other Poems* (1925) and *Lenin Lives* (1935).

[74]   [AHT]

Dunedin (Florida)

June 5, 1931

Dear H G:

[. . .] I am, most certainly, having the veritable time of my life;[1] for Whitehead is one of the most fascinating personalities I have ever encountered. He is generosity & good-fellowship personified, & has a searching erudition that makes his conversation an endless pleasure. Though rector of the local Church of the Good Shepherd, he has nothing of the musty cleric about him; but dresses in sport clothes, swears like a he-man on occasion, & is an utter stranger to bigotry or priggishness of any sort.

The scenery here is hauntingly appealing, & I am at this moment on the sun-baked gulf shore under a palm-tree. The *climate* beats even St. Augustine, & I feel active & braced up beyond all comparison with my usual state in the north. At the same time, I think I'd rather live in St. Augustine than here;[2] since the *newness* of everything in this region would get on my nerves eventually. I need a touch of historic tradition & antiquarian architecture in order to achieve imaginative satisfaction.

I expect to move along next week—going back to St. Augustine for a week, though trying to work in a cheap excursion to the South of Florida—Miami & possibly (dare I dream it?) Key West. A couple of belated revision cheques arouse a hope in this direction which I lacked before. After quitting Florida, I want a shot at Savannah—& then a week in Charleston. Whether, after that, I can manage to stop off at Richmond, remains to be seen. Despite the superiority of the Florida climate I shall be glad to get into the real *old South,* where an unbroken 18th century tradition survives. Charleston is the place for me—& I may have to live there, or at St. Augustine, yet. More & more people are impressing upon me the folly of trying to eke along in the north with a heat-craving physique like mine. All this blazing Florida weather is a sheer tonic to me—I'm wearing some of Whitehead's West Indian white drill clothing, his physique being almost identical with my own. I appreciate your verses on the tropic scene—indeed, I was inveigled into concocting a couple of quatrains of my own the other day; for the autograph album of a young fellow from New York (Allan Grayson—cousin of Wilson's physician Admiral Cary T. Grayson)[3] who has been visiting down here. This kid is only 17, & displays his sensitive reactions to the mystery of sunset & moonlight in prose-poems worthy of a much older person. It turns out—by amazing coincidence—that he is a dental patient of Frank Belknap Long's father; & I am telling him to look up Belknap & the rest of the gang when he gets home. Well, anyway—when he asked me to write in his album I let loose the following:

To A Young Poet In Dunedin

You haunt the lonely sand where herons hide,
 And palm-framed sunsets open gates of flame;
Where marble moonbeams bridge the lapping tide
 To westward shores of dream without a name.

Here in a haze of half-remembering,
 You catch faint sounds from that far, fabled beach.
The world is changed—your task henceforth to sing
 Dim, beckoning wonders you could never reach.

Now as to the argument—I really don't see that we've made much progress in trying to find a non-religious basis for *the sense of obligation.* You have done some noble & subtle reasoning—all valid & clarifying in many directions—but the gist of the basic question still remains untouched. Why "should" anybody do anything which nature doesn't *force* him to do, & which would not advance his own individual satisfaction?

Your first argument is that non-cruelty is natural within certain limits, & that with growing civilisation those limits tend to expand. This is, to a moderate extent, quite true—as I have myself previously pointed out—*aesthetics* being the basis of the change. But to fancy that this essentially passive softening & refinement of taste could account for the fanatical & assertive emotions of radicals & equalitarians is beyond the utmost boundary of probability. No ordinary emotion of this sort could conceivably take on such grotesque extremes. To account for hysterical devotion & martyrdom, some potent conception of *imperative obligation*—such as the material world does not provide for—is absolutely necessary. Incidentally, your mention of an "economic interpretation" of enemy-eating implies a definite & demonstrable error. It is a matter of common anthropological knowledge that such practices are mystico-religious or magical in background & motivation; often involving the conception of absorbing the victim's strength & prowess with his substance.

To sum up my position—the *whole concept* of a rigid *right* or *justice* or *obligational element* (as distinguished from the mild & passive mercy-feeling resulting from aesthetics) has *no conceivable basis* outside mystical religion. I have tried in vain to find anything in your arguments which would challenge that position. Your Marxian quotations from Cole are all tremendously apt, & I agree with them.[4] But this sort of interpretation of materialism does not account for the obligation concept. Your Marx quotations regarding intangible values—sugar-weighing—& your comparison with ants & bees regarding an obligational "labour bond"—are likewise what I would call interesting but irrelevant. True—but what has it to do with the validity of any obligational element apart from necessity? Ants & bees react as they do *because they have to*— because they are made that way. So do human beings & all other natural objects. Whatever the way they *do* react, is the natural & inevitable way, & that's all there is to it. Ideas of *preference* in the matter—i.e., *any choice of courses within the limit of material possibility*—are manifestly artificial & without natural basis. Only aesthetic feelings (to a mild degree) or religious feelings (often to a fanatical degree) could account for the origin & persistence of such preferential notions. This, of course, applies to *all* obligational & preferential feelings— not merely those connected with social adjustment.

As for *mind*—we may most briefly define its essence as a mode of motion in the material cells of the body—primarily the brain. In its essence it is most distinctly *not a social product* but a pure biological product—the typical natural response of nerve tissue (both general & cerebrally localised) to external environment. Far from being social in basis, it may be said to represent the lone wolf—the individual—learning how to protect itself against its surroundings. Various arbitrary forms of mental expression, however, (such as speech) are indeed social products. You err in thinking that man has been gregarious from the start—though of course this whole matter has nothing to do with the question of an obligation-sense. Gregariousness preceded speech, of course, but it was in turn (so far as comparative evidence indicates) preceded by a solitary phase of life—such as is still found in connexion with the gorilla.

All your Marx–Engels observations form good & subtle reasoning so far as they go, but they wholly dodge the primary question *of the nature of the quality of obligation*. You give no sound reason *why* any individual "should" (and what is the *real* meaning of "should", or "ought", anyhow?) follow any other course than that prompted or made imperative by nature & demonstrated by cool reason to be most satisfying to his peculiar individual instincts.

When you turn to consider various possible outcomes of the present awkward social & political situation, I can agree with you to a surprising extent. Any of the courses you enumerate is distinctly possible—but so, I must insist, is likewise a gradual palliation & capitalistic letdown without social & aesthetic overturns. You are too cocksure when you insist that the present leaders will not make any tangible concessions till after the mob becomes dangerously conscious of its power. Note that I am by no means so cocksure in the opposite direction. I don't say that any such compromise is *bound to succeed.* Only a damn fool pretends to be a prophet where vast unknown, unstable, & complex forces are concerned. I merely say that the compromise *may* succeed; & that I hope very much, personally, that it will. But I am free to admit that any sort of catastrophe—from tyrannous communism to complete savagery—may come instead. It is a sheer gamble whether or not the existing leaders will see the need of a letdown before the mob grows universally conscious of its destructive physical power.

As for my own attitude on the subject—of course environment has given me certain natural *inclinations* in the matter of opinion, just as it plays a vast part in the formation of all human opinion; but so abstract & impersonal are my general mental processes that I don't think this element can be held as paramount. If you ever saw me arguing with the blind upholders of an aristocratic tradition for its own sake, you would realise how far from stereotyped & derivative my own ideas & sentiments are. Such reactionaries regard me as a hopelessly non-human semi-bolshevik myself! My frank position is, that I think no conceivable system of communism could bring civilised people any possible recompense for the damage its establishment would inevitably involve. Otherwise, I'm impersonally neutral. I don't give a damn whether my grandfather's ex-coachman knows more or less Latin, or appreciates literature more or less, than I do. It's all one to me. I wouldn't give a nickel either to teach him or to keep him from learning. But I'm god damned if I'll stand for being held back myself, merely waiting for him to catch up! As for communism—I don't give a damn whether it exists or not so long as it lets gentlemen alone, & does not alter the relationship betwixt the individual & the best opportunities for free intellectual & aesthetic expression. I oppose it because I believe the odds are against its adoption in a civilised way. Russia is certainly the last model for an Anglo-Saxon to follow. In my honest opinion, your belief that a mass standard could equal an individualistic standard is an error based on an only partial subjective appreciation of the intangibles involved. You do not realise the drag imposed by the whole equalitarian & equalisation concept on the bold & non-social outreaching of the ego which creates beauty, & on the type of pleasure-education necessary to the cultivation of artistic sensitivities of the first order. But on the other hand, I am willing to admit that many forms of modified communism might not be so totally destructive of all real art & cultivation as most thinkers today assume.

As for the essentially artistic motive at the base of high-grade communists' & reformers' fanaticism—I have never disputed this. I have merely sought to inquire why the artistry of these persons seeks so indirect & concretely unfruitful a channel of expression. The rewards of the more typical artist, though sometimes ethereal & intangible, are at least *direct;* & closely connected with the normal functioning of basic instincts & emotions. They form a clear-cut case of sublimated ego-expansion. In the case of the social artist—the Lenin or Carrie Nation or Mussolini or King Carol[5]—we are, when the elements of sheer eccentricity & unsublimated egotism are disposed of, forced to account of the *direction* of his artistic energy. Social service may easily form the same basic kind of ego-expansion as pure art, but no ordinary or materialistic motivation could make one choose this highly indirect & arduous form in preference to easier, more direct, & more profitable (in terms of actual pleasure derived) forms. Some other kind of choice-motivation must be sought for—& in seeking we encounter that *sense of obligation imposed upon the individual from outside, as distinguished from the natural & ineluctable imperatives of a deterministic cosmos.* This, of course, can be nothing other than mysticism or religion, no matter how well & speciously masked.

Thanks for the bolshevik paper—interesting as a social curio, if not exactly convincing. And later on, when I get a chance, I'll look at your friend Bakunin[6]—though social matters could never form a major interest of mine. The tariff cartoon is pretty good—quite typical of a certain school of thought. As for books outlining my own position—I'm hanged if I can pick any one particular volume, unless Krutch's "Modern Temper" covers the ground. I'm not an exact or interested student in this field—I read carelessly & fragmentarily, & depend as much upon original reflection, or magazine articles whose titles & authors I forget unless I get a chance to clip & file them, as I do on formally published volumes. But Krutch, or Santayana's "Life of Reason" & "Scepticism & Animal Faith", ought to give you a fair notice of my position. [. . .]

I gave your regards to Whitehead, & he sends you his own in the most cordial fashion. I think I'll let him read your letter, since it would be likely to interest him as much as it did me. In the new W.T. you'll find one of his tales—"Hill Dreams"—as well as a poem by Long, a fine yarn by Clark Ashton Smith, & a reprint of my old "Outsider".[7] My "Whisperer in Darkness" is due for next month—the August issue, out July 1st.

By the way—there's a highly interesting article on the "scientifiction" story by Capt. S. P. Meek[8] in a recent number of *The Writers' Digest*—an article enumerating the few stereotype plots favoured by popular commercial editors. Whitehead is thinking of composing an extension of it—possibly with my collaboration—dealing with available ways of getting out of the rut & finding new angles for "scientifictional" expression. [. . .]

Yrs. most sincerely,
H P L

Notes

1. As part of an extensive tour of the South, HPL spent the period 21 May to 10 June in Dunedin, FL, with the weird writer Henry S. Whitehead.

2. HPL visited St. Augustine for the first time on 7 May, spending the next two weeks there.

3. Rear Admiral Cary Travers Grayson (1878–1938), surgeon in the U.S. Navy, personal aide to President Woodrow Wilson and chairman of the American Red Cross. The youth was Allan Brownell Grayson (1913–1967), who later became a pastor in the Episcopal church.

4. G. D. H. Cole (1889–1959), English political and economic theorist who was inclined toward Fabian Socialism.

5. Carol I (1839–1914), King of Romania (1866–1914).

6. Mikhail Bakunin (1814–1876), Russian anarchist and socialist.

7. *WT* (June–July 1931) contained, in addition to the works mentioned, Long's "The Abominable Snow Men" and Smith's "The Venus of Azombeii."

8. Sterner St. Paul Meek (1894–1972), American military chemist, early science fiction author, and children's author. The article in question is "The Pseudo-Scientific Story," *Writer's Digest* 11, No. 6 (May 1931): 37–39, 69 (as by "Captain S. P. Meek").

[75]   [AHT]

> 66 College St.,
> Providence, R.I.
> Aug. 30, 1933

Dear H G:—

[. . .] I am at last doing what I have wanted to do all my life— *living in a genuine Georgian house 130 years old!* [. . .]

Our house—yellow & wooden—is on the crest of the great hill in a quaint grassy court just off College St.—behind & next door to the marble John Hay Library of the university. It is about half a mile south of 10 Barnes St. The fine colonial doorway is like my bookplate (which I think I've shewn you) come to life, though of a slightly later period (circa 1800), with sidelights & fan carving instead of a fanlight. In the rear & on the western side are picturesque, village-like gardens—those behind being at a higher level than the front of the house. In front there are some flower beds, a hedge, & a row of old-fashioned posts to keep off vehicles. The upper flat we have taken contains 5 rooms besides bath & kitchenette nook on the main (2nd) floor, plus two attic storerooms—one of which is so attractive that I wish I could have it for an extra den! My quarters—a large study & a small adjoining bedroom—are on the south side, with my working table under a west window affording a splendid view of the lower town's outspread roofs & of the mystical sunsets that flame behind them. In general, the interior is fully as fascinating as the exterior—with colonial fireplaces, mantels, & chimney cupboards, curving Georgian staircases, wide floor-boards, old fashioned latches, small-paned windows (which fasten up in an antique way without cords or weights), six-panel doors, rear wing with floor at a different level (3 steps down), quaint attic stairs, &c.—just like the old houses open as museums. After admiring such all my life, I find something magical & dreamlike in the experience of actually *living in one* for the first time. Our furniture, paintings, & accessories blend with the Georgian architecture very well—& the generous space has enabled us to get out of storage many things (such as a huge oil painting by my elder aunt) which have not seen the light since the dissolution of the old home years ago. [. . .]

In July—while my aunt was at the hospital—I had a most delightful visit from E. Hoffmann Price, who had come north for the summer in a newly-acquired Ford of ancient vintage. He brought his car into the service of antiquarian exploration, taking me to many historic spots in Rhode Island (such as the old Snuff Mill where Gilbert Stuart was born in 1755) which I had never seen before because of the absence of public transportation lines. During this exploration—which centered in the old "South County", where before the Revolution there were great plantations like those of the South—I saw one of the most exquisite landscape vistas that imagination can depict—a vast expanse of green valley with the bends of a sky-blue river far below; dim lines of shadowy forest; a distant white-steepled church on a headland; & the remote edge of the mystical, limitless sea. I also saw two splendid old villages virtually unchanged since colonial days, together with endless acres of quaint, stone-walled countryside, & occasional ancient houses in varying degrees of repair, desertion, or decay. [. . .]

I myself have written very little of late—revisory work taking the bulk of my time. Just now, however, I am trying to clear my programme for some original writing—& have completed a new tale called "The Thing on the Doorstep". [. . .]

Regards & best wishes,
  H P L

[76] [AHT]

Providence, R.I.
Feb. 4, 1936

Dear H G:—

[. . .] Yes—since about 1931 my political & economic views have moved quite considerably toward the left as a result of wider observation & closer consideration of the problems involved. I don't subscribe to any patent ready-made theories, but believe that a governmental oversight (or ownership, if private large-scale industry can't or won't function under state oversight) of manufacturing & commerce has now become essential, & that opportunities for employment must somehow be artificially allocated. While I am against all violent social & cultural upheavals, I believe that there is no sense in making all the processes of industry dependent upon profits which really benefit no one in particular. Equalitarianism is all bunk, for of course service should be rewarded in proportion to its value; but profits apart from service are a sort of luxury which a complex mechanical civilisation can hardly afford. If the state owned industry, high-grade executive services would continue to command ample salaries, while less skilled labour would receive a lower though adequate & dependable wage. Nothing of importance in existing society would need to be uprooted. But the absence of a profit-motive, & the recognition of universal employment (or remuneration in lieu thereof) as a civic necessity, would give to the population a comfort, security, & general stability beyond any hitherto experienced. Such, I hope, is the goal which will be attained by degrees. A start has certainly been made—or at least, the psychological preparation for a start. Transient periods of reaction may intervene, but I think the major direction is quite well marked out. I only hope that no injudicious moves or irrational impatience may precipitate a catastrophe before the time is really ripe for important changes—i.e., before the people are truly convinced of the need for readjustment, & are as ready to support a bold step toward profitless state ownership as they were to support the milder steps of the present administration. [. . .]

[. . .] Ackerman's egotistical eagerness to plaster his name over everything he can makes me smile. I, on the contrary, greatly dislike to sign any tale which is not wholly my own. I've had a hand in over half a dozen recently published or accepted yarns of others, but wouldn't under any circumstances let my name be used in connexion with them.

I haven't written a thing in verse since 1930, but have perpetrated one or two tales. The only recently *published* thing of mine is "At the Mountains of Madness", a long antarctic story once rejected by Wright, which appears as a 3-part serial in *Astounding*. The opening instalment (Feby.) is now on the stands. *Astounding* has also accepted another long thing of mine—"The Shadow out of Time"—which will appear later on.

Probably postcards have kept you apprised of my major motions. I had a long visit with Barlow last summer, during which we printed a book of verse—"The Goblin Tower"—for Long. On the way home I stopped at my favourite antiquarian shrines—Charleston & St. Augustine—& visited Wandrei a fortnight in New York. Later in the year I took some minor trips around New England—Marblehead, Wilbraham, Cape Cod, New Haven—& around New Year's I visited Long a week in N.Y.—seeing all the gang & visiting the new Hayden Planetarium (a tremendously interesting device) for the first time. Reaching home Jany. 7, I found myself engulfed by an utterly prostrating flood of insistent work—& then came this damned grippe & general exhaustion. Beastly cold weather—I shall certainly welcome the spring!

All good wishes, & hope to hear from you.

Yrs. most cordially,

H P L

[77]   [AHT]

66 College St.
Providence, R.I.
Feby. 3, 1937

Dear H G:—

[. . .] Yes, my opinions on political & economic matters have been undergoing quite a gradual shift toward the left during the past few years, until I believe I may now be classified as definitely a socialist in ultimate principles. Not that I accept any of the extravagant theories & flimsily synthetic "ideologies" (with mythical linkages among all sorts of separate fields, & a savagely uncivilised depreciation of intellectual & aesthetic activity for its own sake) of the extreme radicals, but that I believe more & more that only a public control & non-profit operation of the larger industries can ensure for the bulk of the population a dependable & adequate return for services rendered. As you know, I have for some years conceded that only through governmental *regulation* can industry be made to afford every citizen a decently compensated situation. I have been a "New Dealer" from the start. But now I am convinced from sundry arguments in & out of books that private industry cannot stand the regulation necessary to produce tolerable conditions. That is, that the widespread basic industries can never count on enough profit to keep them going without imposing on the nation hardships too severe to be permitted. Therefore the government, *beginning* logically with simple regulation, must be prepared gradually to take over the basic industries one by one as they cease to yield private profit under the conditions necessarily imposed. This can be done without violence, & may well be inaugurated by the mere process of encouraging non-profit competition—through governmental enterprises or consumer coöperatives. The constitutional framework can be altered step by step to accomodate the change, & experience will show how far it will be necessary to go in absorbing the smaller commercial enterprises. And needless to say, no dislocation of the national life & tradition, nor any interference with free intellectual & artistic activity for their own sakes—in the old way, & without the taint of propaganda—need be attempted.

Your comments on the present situation & possible developments are extremely interesting, & I find it possible to agree in many ways. The recent election gratified me extremely, since it seemed to show a certain degree of awareness & cohesiveness among the bulk of the population—which if maintained will be sufficient to keep reaction in check & eventually wear down the obstacles in the way of public ownership, non-profit industry, governmentally regulated salaries, guaranteed positions, & the other social measures needed to give our civilisation a fresh equilibrium in the light of modern machinery, modern knowledge, & the revised values & objectives which spring from these things. Of course, the collective mind must be moulded very gradually. Just now it is willing to demand much more than it ever demanded before, but balks at the *word* "socialism" & the outright idea of public ownership. That is natural—& the thing to do is to consolidate present gains & prepare the public mind—slowly but pervasively—for the next logical step. The average citizen is ready to try something new when he has seen its apparently only alternative proved a definite failure. That has already occurred with Hoover's laissez-faire capitalism—which the majority now realise will never be anything but an oppressive influence. Now the mass of citizenry must have an opportunity to test the present half-way measures of government regulation. Let them see how these measures work, as they saw before 1933 how Hooverism worked. If in a few years they find that controlled capitalism cannot give them the steady decent remuneration & security which they very properly demand, they will be ready to forget their fear of the word "socialism" & to back up a gradual governmental absorption of the great industries one by one, as each finds itself unable to fulfil the demands of modern social organisation. That is the rational, normally evolutionary way of the Northwestern European peoples as distinguished from the emotionalism & violent extremes of Central, Eastern, & Southern Europe. It is the way we have always traversed in the past, & which I hope will continue to hold good for an indefinite future. If anyone fancies such evolution has *not* always been at work among us, let him survey our condition in the Middle Ages, or even in the 18th century when tendencies toward economic concentration dispossessed thousands & swelled the masses of the urban indigent in England. The great evils bring their own public will for correction; & when an evil recurs a second time, popular psychology supports a deeper-reaching & more drastic remedy than before.

The next few years in America will be intensely interesting to watch. I agree with you in attaching vast importance to the influence of organised labour in its more modern forms—as typically represented by John L. Lewis.[1] A compact & effective alliance of wage-earners, capable of unified action when advisable, will be even more potent than an awakened general electorate in forcing the concessions necessary for better distribution & control of resources. Both through strikes & through political blocs vast pressure can be exerted in a perfectly legal way—& with wider & more intelligent organisation there will be fewer chances for the unjust or injudicious application of pressure (i.e., to secure in certain cases industrial rewards which may at the time be actually excessive, or out of just proportion with the rewards obtainable in other equally exacting but less shrewdly organised branches of industry). Organised labour, acting within the law & according to the spirit of a free nation, really has far vaster possibilities than most have hitherto supposed. In the past it has been frustrated through poor leadership & confused organisation; because the best minds of the nation have sincerely believed that its demands & methods were unjustifiably drastic, hence have tended to side with capital against it. The present generation is witnessing a change. To-day the disinterested thinkers & noncommercial trained leaders have reached new conclusions because of fresh evidence & more thorough study of the past, hence are gradually changing sides. This will make all the difference in the world. No longer will the unscrupulous pressure-mechanism & legislation-bending agencies of organised capital find a clear track ahead, with only naive blunderers to interfere. At last, the invisible government of money will be checked by an opposition led by brains of equal power, training, & competence. And with this effective opposition, reactionary venom & stubbornness will be likely to do much less harm than they otherwise would. I doubt whether the growing Catholic-fascist movement will make much headway in America. Like communism, it is too dogmatic & patently international to be swallowed by a strong, free people. It may cause a soft-pedalling of the *word* "socialism", but it can do precious little against a practical, concrete demand for guaranteed work, decent remuneration, & whatever is needed to ensure these things. You can see what became of Fr. Coughlin.[2] In all the United States I don't believe a Gen. Franco could find enough sympathisers to raise an effective fascist army. 16 million people voted Republican—but would they dare to launch an armed revolt against those determined to move ahead?

As for the position of Pres. Roosevelt—I hardly fancy he means to play the reactionary. He knows that change must come gradually, & that immediate objectives must have safe-sounding names. For the present it is advisable to antagonise capital as little as possible, since capital is to be asked to function under government regulation—the utmost curb which the people as a whole are *yet* willing to impose. Compromise is the order of the day. The government & labour must perform a little quiet teamwork, each seeming to be independent of the other. Let labour demand much, & then let a technically impartial government help effect a settlement. The whole people could not support labour directly—but they will support a government which remains apparently neutral yet which in the end will gradually see that labour gets its share. Later on, labour will become able to command more direct support from the people—& then we may see many open moves in its direction on the part of the liberal Democrats. I fancy there will be great caution in offering a pure-and-simple labour man—even one as forceful & competent as Lewis—as a presidential candidate, since such a figure might scare off millions of timid voters & sweep them into the camp of some reactionary candidate. However, there will perhaps be more than one avowed labour president during the lifetime of today's younger generation.

As for things abroad—they certainly are in a hell of a mess, & I only hope there won't be a wholesale explosion dragging the Anglo-Saxon world in. Poor Spain seems to be an arena in which Germans, Russians, Italians, & everybody else—including even some Spaniards!—are fighting out their social & political ideas! I sympathise definitely with the leftist government, notwithstanding the extent to which extreme elements have gained ascendancy within it—& this for three reasons: first, because the barbaric & church-ridden tyranny of the other side would probably be as bad as even the worst excesses of a communist or anarchist regime; second, because the government is the one legally elected by the Spanish people; & third, because the general trend of all evolution is leftward, so that a fascist Spain would have another period of bad equilibrium ahead, whereas a leftist Spain, however chaotic, would represent one with its worst struggles probably over. I feared last summer that the government hadn't a chance, but the ensuing deadlock & defence of Madrid told another story. The outcome seems to be something of a toss-up—depending, of course, on the amount of foreign aid each side gets. Nazi Germany, with her interferences in the affairs of outside nations, is rapidly getting to be the same sort of international nuisance that bolshevik Russia was before the present Stalin period. I saw a review of that book you mention, & fancy it must be rather illuminating. Whether the fascist nations & Japan will ever get together for a war on Russia is perhaps dependent on a dozen unpredictable elements—especially the attitude of other strong nations. China meanwhile is a baffling puzzle. I doubt very much whether the Chinese people can ever properly organise their sprawling congeries of provinces, since their culture-tradition (admirable though it is) is woefully deficient in those qualities of accuracy & steadiness which make for successful large-scale administration. They are like the Celts in this respect. Eventually, it will take an outside nation of high administrative capacity to organise the life & resources of China—& the choice is probably between Japan & Russia. Of the two, Japan is probably the better-fitted, since her culture is itself largely permeated with Chinese influences. Unfortunately, however, the Japan of today would probably exploit a vassal China in such a way as to make its strength a potential world menace. Still, one cannot tell. If given a free hand in China, Japan might be willing to abandon all designs of expansion elsewhere. However, the vast extent, antiquity, & ingrainedness of the Chinese culture would prevent China from ever being completely subordinated to an outside master. I doubt whether either Japan or Russia could successfully unseat its language & other basic traditions. Either conqueror would probably emulate Rome's policy in the Hellenistic world, where the preëxisting & tenacious Greek culture was always let alone even after complete military & political subjugation. Another question is that of how long a suzerain nation could hold China after the latter's teeming millions—a quarter of the human race— had become inculcated with the methods of orderly life, self-sustaining industry, & effective administration. Centuries hence, despite the almost inevitable period of foreign tutelage ahead, China may yet form a titanic world force to be reckoned with. It would be curious if the oldest of all the civilisations of today were to survive its younger rivals in the end. [. . .]

   All good wishes,
     Yours most cordially,
      H P L

Notes

1. John L. Lewis (1880–1969), president of the United Mine Workers (1920–60) and a founder of the Congress of Industrial Organizations (CIO).

2. Charles E. Coughlin (1891–1979), Canadian-American Roman Catholic priest who in 1934 founded a purportedly leftist organization, the National Union for Social Justice, but who later revealed himself as an anti-Semite and supporter of Hitler and Mussolini. In 1936 he supported William Lemke, a third-party candidate, to express his opposition to Franklin D. Roosevelt; but Roosevelt won re-election in a landslide.

To Seabury Quinn

Seabury [Grandin] Quinn (1889–1969) was an American writer
and editor, and a prolific author of tales about the psychic detective Jules de Grandin, mostly published in *WT*. After serving
in World War I, he began writing, editing, and teaching in the
field of medical jurisprudence, specializing in mortuary law.
Among the publications he edited was the trade magazine *Cas-
ket and Sunnyside*. His reference book *A Syllabus of Mortuary Jurisprudence* was published in 1933. Lovecraft enjoyed his early tale
"The Phantom Farmhouse" (*WT*, October 1923) but felt other
tales to be formula-ridden hackwork. Lovecraft first met Quinn
at Wilfred B. Talman's apartment in New York City on 6 July
1931; they met again in early January 1936, during Lovecraft's
last New York visit.

[78]   [*SL*]

Sept. 11, 1931

My dear Quinn:—

Mixed congratulations & commiserations on your rise in
the editorial world! I can understand how it feels to be kept from developing
clamorous plots—for that is just the state into which an excess of revisory
drudgery has lately plagued me. Added to this oppression in my case, is the
turmoil of steam-heat installation in the Victorian backwater which harbours
me & my overcrowded belongings. Everything is reduced to the primal *'rudis
indigestaque moles',*[1] & I am fleeing to the woods & fields for quiet. Fortunately,
the absence of a neighbouring aunt in Maine leaves me a vacant flat to serve as
a shelter when the weather makes outdoors inhospitable. Just now, though, the
weather is treating me very well—blazing summer sunshine, & a thermometer
which was 87° yesterday & probably more today! I think I mentioned that I am
a tropical bird—knocked out by the cold, & in my element from 80° upward.
  [. . .]
  Glad you liked "The Strange High House"—which was written in 1926,
once rejected by Wright, & later recalled for reconsideration. It is one of the
last of the things I wrote in the semi-poetic Dunsany manner—a manner to
which I may or may not revert in future. The trouble with that style & mood
is that if one doesn't catch exactly the right keynote, the result is very pathetic
indeed. Nothing is more utterly mawkish & namby-pamby than a flat, misfire
tale of that type—like my "White Ship"—which makes me sick whenever I
think of it! I was immeasurably pleased with the Doolin illustration, which

showed an actual comprehension of the text & mood of the story. Doolin[2] is the best artist they've had since Rankin's[3] heyday, & I surely hope he won't go down hill like the others. Your recent pointed words to Wright may cause him to keep a sharper eye on the "art" department than he has heretofore. [. . .]

        Yr most obt hble Servt

         H P L

Notes

1. "A crude and unfinished mass"—Ovid's description of the chaos at the beginning of creation in *Metamorphoses* 1.7.

2. Joseph Patrick Doolin (1896–1967) was an artist for *WT* and other pulp magazines.

3. Hugh Doak Rankin (1878–1956), early illustrator for *WT* (1927–36).

To Carl Swanson

Carl Swanson (1902–1974) was a fan and book dealer from Washburn, N.D., who wrote to authors of weird and science fiction asking for contributions to a magazine he hoped to publish, to be called *Galaxy*. His plan initially was to issue short stories as separate booklets. Financial difficulties, as well as opposition by Farnsworth Wright (who pressured his authors not to grant Swanson permission to reprint their stories), prevented the publication of *Galaxy*, though he considered issuing a mimeographed magazine or series of booklets. He did issue the mimeographed *The Metal Giants* (1933) by Edmond Hamilton through his Swanson Book Company. A few years later, when Swanson lived in Coleharbor, N.D., he sold magazines to collectors.

[79]   [ALS, JHL]

10 Barnes St.,

Providence, R.I.,

Jany. 12, 1932

Carl Swanson, Esq.,
   Washburn, N.D.,

Dear Mr. Swanson:—

I am indeed greatly interested & pleased to hear of your magazine, & hope that it may become a successful fixture in the periodical world. It would delight me to be able to contribute to it, & I enclose herewith two stories[1]—one of them the one mentioned by Mr. Flagg—in the hope that either or both may be of use. These have never been published. If you would care to use any reprints of my published tales, I would surely be glad to have them appear again.

The list of authors you mention sounds very encouraging. May I suggest that you try to secure material from one or two others of proved excellence? I might mention Frank B. Long, Jr., 230 West 97th Str., New York City, (The Black Druid, The Man with a Thousand Legs, The Space-Eaters) & Dr. Henry S. Whitehead, Box 414, Dunedin Isles, Dunedin, Fla. (The Black Beast, Passing of a God, The Tree Man)[2] You are undoubtedly familiar with the work of both. Also Robert E. Howard, Lock Box 313, Cross Plains, Texas.

Financial circumstances have forced me to abandon bookbuying for a long time, but whenever I do feel able to re-indulge I shall certainly provide you with a want list. I might say in passing that some of the first things I shall try to get when I can get anything at all are M. P. Shiel's "Pale Ape & Other Stories" (containing the magnificent "House of Sounds" which I wish you could reprint—pub. by T. Werner Laurie, London, 1908), Maturin's huge "Melmoth the Wanderer", & some of the less technical works of Arthur Edward Waite touching on magic in its various traditional phases. All of these, however, would probably command prices far beyond my present reach.

With best wishes for the new magazine, & hoping that something of mine may be found suited to its pages, I am

Yrs most cordially & sincerely,

H. P. Lovecraft

Notes

1. "The Nameless City" and "Beyond the Wall of Sleep." Swanson accepted both.
2. Frank Belknap Long, "The Black Druid" (*WT*, July 1930), "The Man with a Thousand Legs" (*WT*, August 1927), "The Space-Eaters" (*WT*, July 1928); Henry S. Whitehead, "The Black Beast" (*Adventure*, 15 July 1931), "Passing of a God" (*WT*, January 1931), "The Tree-Man" (*WT*, February/March 1931).

[80]   [ALS, JHL]

10 Barnes St.,

Providence, R.I.,

March 30, 1932

Dear Mr. Swanson:—

Precise mimeographing is undoubtedly an art which improves with practice. In the amateur press association one youth published a duplicator paper with perfectly even right-hand margin, but I imagine it cost him a good deal of time & troublesome calculation. Approximate evenness is about all one could expect in rapid & extensive work.

Let me know if you decide to issue a booklet with my stuff. In that case, would the existing two tales be just right, or could you use more in case I have any you'd like? There are 3 or 4 of my favourites which no magazine has yet taken, & I'd rather welcome the chance to get some good lending duplicates. I'll send the $2.00 when the time comes. How does one go about getting a copyright—that is, where does one apply for blanks & all that? I've never copyrighted anything myself as yet.

I hope you can later on make printing arrangements—but printers are lamentably high-priced nowadays. One good firm—which prints a trade magazine for a man I know—is the Meador Publishing Co., 470 Atlantic Ave., Boston, Mass.[1] Good inexpensive printing—of a semi-amateur kind—is done by a friend of mine in Vermont who publishes a poetry magazine of his own—Walter J. Coates, North Montpelier, Vermont.

With best wishes for all your various enterprises—
Yrs most sincerely,
H P Lovecraft

Notes

1. HPL elsewhere described the company as a vanity press. It printed *Props* for J. Bernard Lynch.

[81]　[ALS]

Memphis, Tenn.

Home Address—
10 Barnes St.,
Providence, R.I.,
May 30, 1932

Dear Mr. Swanson:—

Yours of the 17th has just reached me after several forwardings, for I am taking a scenic & antiquarian vacation—a trip to New Orleans, with various stops at points of interest en route. Was in Chattanooga yesterday—& was fascinated by the views from Lookout Mountain & by the caverns (including a 145-foot subterranean waterfall) inside the mountain. Tomorrow Vicksburg & Natchez—New Orleans Wednesday.

By this time I presume my magazines & MSS. have arrived at my Providence address. Glad you found the magazines of interest. *Home Brew* was really an abominably wretched mess—& my story in it was none too good.[1] As you say, if revised for second publication it ought to be made one solid story, with all the duplicate descriptions cut out. Personally I detest this *series* idea, for the repetitions at the start of each new story are frightfully boresome to those who have read the earlier tales. I wouldn't undertake to prepare a mess of hash like that today.

I have noticed the retrenchment in the Clayton magazines, & am sorry to see the weird field narrowing so. It is to be hoped that *Strange* & *Astounding* can weather the depression—but of course no one can tell. Things seem to get worse instead of better.

With best wishes—
Yrs most sincerely,
H. P. Lovecraft

Notes

1. *Home Brew* published two stories by HPL in serial form. He refers to "Herbert West—Reanimator," in which HPL felt the need to write synopses of previous episodes at the beginning of each new episode.

To Carl Jacobi

Carl Jacobi (1908–1997) of St. Paul, Minn., wrote more than 100 stories in pulp magazines including *WT, Terror Tales, Amazing Stories, Short Stories, Galaxy, Fantastic Universe, Mike Shayne Mystery Magazine, Thrilling Adventures,* and *Thrilling Mystery.* Lovecraft enjoyed Jacobi's "Mive" (a prize-winning story in the Fall 1928 issue of *Minnesota Quarterly,* the student magazine of the University of Minnesota) in *WT* (January 1932) and wrote to Jacobi about it. His stories "The Tomb from Beyond" (*Wonder Stories,* November 1933) and "The Aquarium" (in August Derleth's *Dark Mind, Dark Heart* [1962]) show Lovecraftian influence. Jacobi published three collections with Arkham House: *Revelations in Black* (1947), *Portraits in Moonlight* (1964), and *Disclosures in Scarlet* (1972); a final collection of tales, *Smoke of the Snake,* appeared in 1994.

[82] [*SL*]

10 Barnes St.,

Providence, R.I.,

Feby. 27, 1932

Dear Mr. Jacobi:—

[. . .]

"Mive" pleased me immensely, & I told Wright that I was glad to see at least one story whose weirdness of incident was made convincing by adequate emotional preparation & suitably developed atmosphere. Most of the stuff in the cheap weird magazines is utterly & irredeemably flat because of the lack of any substance to lend a semblance of actuality to the extravagant & overcrowded incidents. I also read "The Coach on the Ring", & wish the editor had had the discernment to let the original title stand.[1] Many things in this tale captivated me exceedingly, though as you realise it was a little nearer the popular magazine formula than "Mive". I hope to see the other items of yours which you mention—& congratulate you sincerely on your success in making varied placements. Your versatility is decidedly greater than my own for I can never hit the popular formula well enough to land anywhere but in *Weird Tales*—or in the forthcoming & as yet standardless *Galaxy* to be issued by Swanson of Washburn, N. D.[2] Moreover, I think my days of contribution to *W.T.* are decidedly numbered; for Wright rejected my best story last year,[3] & is likely to do the same with my later work on account of its greater length & slower motion as compared with my earlier stuff. I can no longer be satisfied with the glib, machine-clipped type of tale which editors demand—& unfortunately there is no likelihood of editors ever being satisfied with the kind of story I now write. Repeated rejections began to get on my nerves so badly last autumn that I was almost unable to write anything at all—so now I have resolved to let professional magazines alone for a while & write to please myself only; letting the results pile up for whatever ultimate disposition the Fates may provide. Of course, though, I would probably try my professional luck with any especially short or obvious story which might happen to drop from my pen in the course of varied composition.

Derleth spoke very highly of your work & future promise, & admiringly heralded "Mive" long before it appeared. He himself strikes me as one of the most remarkable youths I have ever encountered—gifted alike in serious & popular writing, & with an inexhaustible driving energy which most others must envy in vain. No doubt you have seen the MSS. of his serious work— "Evening in Spring", "A Town Is Built", &c.[4] Possibly you also know my brilliant young friend Donald Wandrei, of your own Twin Cities.

The address of Robert E. Howard is Lock Box 313, Cross Plains, Texas. Just now he is travelling in the southern part of his state, hence may be tardier in receiving & replying to correspondence than at other times. He is an old-time Texan steeped in the virile & sanguinary lore of his native region, & writes of his local traditions with a force, sincerity, & genuinely poetic power which would surprise those who know only his more or less conventional contributions to the magazines. His letters form a veritable epic of primitive emotions & deeds in a grim & rugged setting—the last free play of the old Aryan tribal & combative instincts of which Homer & the Eddas & Sagas sing.

Hope you won't be disappointed with "In the Vault", which is an old piece of mine once rejected by Wright but accepted on a second submission (instigated by Derleth) five years later. It is not very typical—at least in style—of what I am writing now.

With best wishes, congratulations on your work, & appreciation of the kind opinion you express concerning mine, I am,

Yours most cordially & sincerely,

H. P. Lovecraft

Notes

1. "The Haunted Ring" (*Ghost Stories*, December 1931–January 1932); title restored in *Revelations in Black*.

2. For Carl Swanson and *Galaxy*, see below.

3. *At the Mountains of Madness*.

4. "A Town Is Built" (ms., WHS) is unpublished.

To Kirk Mashburn

Wallace Kirkpatrick Mashburn (1900–1968) did not make the trip to New Orleans (he was not an admirer of Lovecraft's work).

[83]   [ANS by HPL and E. Hoffmann Price, privately held][1]

[postmarked New Orleans, La.
15 June 1932]

Come over Sunday.

The Throne Room has been the scene of a noteworthy enclave, which will be attested by the hand & seal of the undersigned.

نظام الملك الرئيس

Regards—I've read your work with great admiration!

—H. P. Lovecraft

Notes

1. *Front:* Lacework in Iron, Royal Street, New Orleans, LA.

With Harold S. Farnese

Harold S[ulzire] Farnese (1890–1945) was assistant director of the Institute of Musical Art in Los Angeles and a composer. Lovecraft told a correspondent: "He is a native of Monaco, educated in Paris, & winner of the 1911 Prize at the Paris Conservatory" [*Letters with Donald Wandrei* 387]. He was a reader of *WT* since its earliest days and had seven letters published in "The Eyrie."* In July 1932, Farnese asked Lovecraft's permission to set to music two sonnets from *Fungi from Yuggoth.* Lovecraft granted permission, and by September Farnese had written and performed music for "Mirage" and "The Elder Pharos." Lovecraft never heard or saw the pieces (which were for solo voice and piano), and it was not until after Lovecraft died that Farnese had the sheet music circulated. The pieces were not published; Farnese simply had a few photostats made after he learned Lovecraft had died.† Farnese tried to enlist Lovecraft's help in writing a libretto for a planned opera entitled *Yurregarth and Yannimaid* (later *Fen River*), but he declined, suggesting Clark Ashton Smith as librettist. Two versions (by Farnese) of the synopsis of *Fen River* are provided. One lists Lovecraft as a co-author, but Lovecraft did not work on the libretto. It does not appear that Farnese approached Smith. After Lovecraft moved in 1933, the two fell out of touch.

When Lovecraft died, Farnese composed his "Elegy" (see Appendix), a musical response ("just finished" 27 April 1937) to the poetic elegy August Derleth had written. This piece was published by the G. Schirmer Co. Farnese became the unwitting source of the spurious "Black Magic" quotation attributed by August Derleth to Lovecraft, and thus generating a gross mischaracterization of the nature of Lovecraft's work. His letters to Lovecraft are included herein for the reader to compare what Lovecraft wrote and how Farnese interpreted those remarks. See Schultz regarding other errors of memory and interpretation Farnese made in his letters to August Derleth.

---

*April 1925, September 1925, February 1926, May 1926, June 1926, May 1927, August 1931, and July 1937.
†See Kenneth W. Faig, Jr., "A Note Regarding the Harold Farnese Musical Pieces," *Dark Brotherhood Journal* 1, No. 1 (June 1971): 12–14.

[84]   [HSF to HPL]   [TLS, JHL]
[Institute of Musical Art
4001 South Harvard Boulevard
Los Angeles, Calif.]

7/11/1932

Mr. H. P. Lovecraft,
℅. Weird Tales Magazine,
450 East Ohio Street,
Chicago, Ill.

Dear Sir:

I would like to ask your permission to set music to your poems "The El-der Pharos" and "Mirage" from your collection "Fungi from Yuggoth" which appeared in the "Weird Tales" Magazine some years ago.

As a composer of instrumental and piano works I might say that I have never been much interested in the composition of songs until I read your po-ems some years ago; your highly picturesque atmosphere and setting stimulat-ed my creative ability into wanting to compose these poems.

There is something about your work (poetry as well as prose) that no-body else seems to have: an originality of a marked degree which rests on the fact that you have built a world of your own imagination which your pen knows how to people. No matter how imaginative, your work breathes life and proves a great stimulant to the creative artist of another art.

Needless to say, my musical setting will try to prove an apt background to the eeriness of these poems, modern and impressionistic.

Hoping to receive a favorable answer,

Yours very truly,

Harold Farnese

(Graduate of Paris Conservatory, Paris, France.
Winner of the 1911 prize for composition.)

[85]   [HPL to HSF]   [nonextant]

30 August 1932

[86] [HSF to HPL] [TLS, JHL]

[Institute of Musical Education, Ltd.
715 South Park View Street
Los Angeles, Calif.]

Sep. 3rd 1932.

Mr. H. P. Lovecraft,
10, Barnes Str.
Providence, R.I.

Dear Mr. Lovecraft:

I was very pleased with your exceedingly kind letter of the 30th ult. which I received yesterday upon my return from the North-West where I went on a tour, visiting Northern California, Oregon and Washington.

I have finished the music to both the "Mirage" and "The Elder Pharos" and played them in Seattle and Chehalis, Wash.[1] before a select group of musicians who were very enchanted with them and the critics (private, of course, as I had not yet received your kind permission for their performance) said that the atmosphere created by you was admirably maintained by your composer. Of course, a composer can always do his best when he actually falls in love with a subject, instead of being asked by any poet to compose this or that.

Regardless of the attitude taken by Putnam's[2] or others on stories or poems of a weird character, I cannot understand how these publishers can be blind to the genius displayed in your work which is not only serious, dignified and classic in its form and content, but highly original as well. The outstanding feature of your work seems to me to lie in the fact that in the realm of your imagination you have built up not only a unique atmosphere, but a dreamland of moving characters and motives, at no time forced upon the reader's imagination, but very subtly suggested or insinuated. If I comprehend your work correctly, I take from it the suggestion of an outer sphere of (may I call it) Black Magic, at one time ruling this planet but now dispossessed, awaiting "on the outside" a chance for a possible return. On this vast canvass [*sic*] of your creative ability, such pictures as depicted in "The Festival" (Weird Tales, Dec. 1924), "The Elder Pharos", the two stories about Randolph Carter, a flash or two of the dream-city of Yaddith,[3] the water-dripping grottos of the sunless realm of Yuggoth etc. appear to me as dashes of rich and exquisite colour and appealing strongly to my creative suggestion to express in tones what you have wrought in words. To you, therefore, belongs the distinction of having created a marvelous world of the mind, and as to myself, I am very grateful to you to be accorded the privilege of entering with you in to this outer world of dreams and brooding mystery.

While meandering in spirit through the land of Yuggoth, I am impressed with an idea of whether at some future time, when you should feel at leisure we might not cooperate on a stage-work, say a music-drama on this very subject, and in accordance with your ideas I had somehow conceived two figures (male and female) in the foreground, which I have tentatively called: "Yurregarth and Yannimaid" which might form a good title for such a play. While in the North West I found my trip across the swampy rivers of Oregon, with their high reed grass, their black and silent forests, their moist and ice-cold grottos of stone a great stimulation to a scenic setting for such a play.

I would naturally like to hear from you on this idea and whether you would be willing to collaborate in writing the libretto. In the meantime, I am sending you a catalogue of the school of which I am the Dean, giving the pictures of our faculty, and also a letter to a publisher in Boston, who is well known for his partiality to original works, which you might make use of for the collection of stories which Putnams rejected.

Thanking you repeatedly for your kind letter and promising you to send you "Mirage" and "The Elder Pharos" as soon as I can make copies of them,

I am,

Very sincerely yours,
Harold Farnese

My private address is still:
4001 So. Harvard Blvd.
Los Angeles, Calif.

Notes

1. The complete sheet music for the two "atmospheric tone poems" may be found in *Fungi from Yuggoth: An Annotated Edition.* The music was recorded, both with and without the "lyrics," as was Farnese's "Elegy," on the CD *Fungi from Yuggoth: A Sonnet Cycle* (Nampa, ID: Fedogan & Bremer, 2015).
2. In the summer of 1931, G. P. Putnam's Sons had rejected a proposed collection of HPL's stories.
3. Yaddith appears to be a planet; see "Alienation," "Through the Gates of the Silver Key," "The Haunter of the Dark," and "Out of the Aeons" (for Mount Yaddith-Gho). HPL often used "Yaddith" as part of his own fictitious address.

[87]   [HPL to HSF]   [AHT]

10 Barnes St.,
Providence, R. I.,
Sept. 22, 1932.

Dear Mr. Farnese:—

Your much appreciated letter, & the catalogue with its interesting portrait & sketch of yourself, awaited me upon my return from an antiquarian trip to Montreal & Quebec. I was delighted to learn that the melodising of my "Fungi" had been accomplished in a way satisfactory to yourself & others, & am eager for an opportunity to hear the scores—which I feel sure must not only reproduce the spirit of the lines, but possess an artistic merit far beyond that of my halting attempts.

Furthermore, let me thank you for the all-too-complimentary introduction to the Gorham Press,[1] which I have sent on with an account of what I have to offer. I rather fear that this firm is one which requires a cash advance from its authors—a thing I am unable to furnish—but if management is ever disposed to make an exception in this matter, it surely ought to do so in the present case, under the influence of your thrice-generous statements! I will let you know the outcome of my inquiry.

I can understand the reason for Putnams' rejection of my work, & have been led to institute a sort of stock-taking since thoroughly digesting the final letter from the firm's reader. The fact undoubtedly is, that despite my *conscious* resolutions to steer clear of the cheap claptrap & oversimplicity of the popular commercial tale, I have been more or less *unconsciously* influenced by the demands of editors—so that my attempts have come to possess a crude *obviousness*, lack of subtlety, & heavy laying-on of pigments, which really have no place in fiction of the first quality. This fact was lately confirmed by the wholly disinterested verdict of a new acquaintance—a man of very wide literary experience & undoubted critical acumen. Whether I shall ever be able to produce work of the desiderate grade remains to be seen. Meanwhile I regard my past performance with an increasingly critical eye, finding only a few of them even approximately satisfactory to my present taste . . . . . & naturally, one effect of my attempted reform is to make my newer stuff more & more unacceptable to the cheap editors.

Of course, I have always realised that my especial province is fundamentally a very minor one; & that even if I achieved the level of literature, it would be merely a trivial phase of the 'literature of escape'. What I *do* insist upon is that this field, however minor, is a genuine & serious one; & not a mere aspect of naive crudity to be brushed aside by an enlightened age. To my mind, the *sense of the unknown* is an authentic & virtually permanent—even though seldom dominant—part of human personality; an element too basic to be destroyed by the modern world's knowledge that the supernatural does not exist. It is true that we no longer credit the existence of discarnate intelligences & superphysical forces around us, & that consequently the traditional "gothick tale" of spectres & vampires has lost a large part of its power to move our emotions. But in spite of this disillusion there remain two factors largely unaffected—& in one case actually *increased*—by the change: first, a sense of impatient rebellion against the rigid & ineluctable tyranny of time, space, & natural law—a sense which drives our imaginations to devise all sorts of plausible hypothetical defeats of that tyranny—& second, a burning curiosity concerning the vast reaches of unplumbed & unplumbable cosmic space which press down tantalisingly on all sides of our pitifully tiny sphere of the known. Between these two surviving factors I believe that the field of the weird must necessarily continue to have a reason for existence, & that the nature of man must necessarily still seek occasional expression (even though in limited degree) in symbols & phantasies involving the hypothetical frustration of physical law, & the imaginative extrusion of knowledge & adventure beyond the bounds imposed by reality. That this must be done more subtly than in the past, goes without saying; but I insist that it still must be done now & then. The emotional need for escape from terrestrial certainties is still, with a definite & permanent minority, a genuine & sometimes acute one.

In my own efforts to crystallise this spaceward outreaching, I try to utilise as many as possible of the elements which have, under earlier mental and emotional conditions, given man a symbolic feeling of the unreal, the ethereal, & the mystical—choosing those least attacked by the realistic mental & emotional conditions of the present. Darkness—sunset—dreams—mists—fever—madness—the tomb—the hills—the sea—the sky—the wind—all these, & many other things have seemed to me to retain a certain imaginative potency despite our actual scientific analyses of them. Accordingly I have tried to weave them into a kind of shadowy phantasmagoria which may have the same sort of vague coherence as a cycle of traditional myth or legend—with nebulous backgrounds of Elder Forces & trans-galactic entities which lurk about this infinitesimal planet, (& of course about others as well), establishing outposts thereon, & occasionally brushing aside other accidental forms of life (like human beings) in order to take up full habitation. This is essentially the sort of notion prevalent in most racial mythologies—but an artificial mythology can become subtler & more plausible than a natural one, because it can recognise & adapt itself to the information & moods of the present. The best artificial mythology, of course, is Lord Dunsany's elaborate & consistently developed pantheon of Pegāna's gods. Having formed a cosmic pantheon, it remains for the fantaisiste to link this "outside" element to the earth in a suitably dramatic & convincing fashion. This, I have thought, is best done through glancing allusions to immemorially ancient cults & idols & documents attesting the recognition of the "outside" forces by men—or by those terrestrial entities which preceded man. The actual climaxes of tales based on such elements naturally have to do with sudden latter-day intrusions of forgotten elder forces on the placid surface of the known—either active intrusions, or revelations caused by the feverish & presumptuous probing of men into the unknown. Often the merest *hint* that such a forgotten elder force *may* exist is the most effective sort of a climax—indeed, I am not sure but that this may be the *only* sort of climax possible in a truly mature fantasy. I have had many severe criticisms because of the *concrete & tangible* nature of some of my "cosmic horrors". Variants of the general theme include defeats of the visible laws of time—strange juxtapositions of widely separated aeons—& transcensions of the boundary-lines of Euclidean space; these, & the always-fruitful device of a human voyage into forbidden celestial deeps. In every one of these seemingly extravagant conceptions there is a certain amount of imaginative satisfaction for a very genuine emotional need of mankind—if only the subject be handled with adequate subtlety & convincingness.

In the matter of this handling, though, most fantaisistes (including, alas, myself) generally fail miserably. We are all tempted to 'lay it on too thick'—with results varying in disastrousness from mere flatness to hilarious absurdity. Critical theories differ regarding the extent to which one may, without producing weakness or suggesting the puerile, overtly employ the paraphernalia of supernaturalism. A large body of taste opposes absolutely the use of *coined names* as applied to strange things & places—thus outlawing my "Yuggoth", "Thok", "Nithon", &c., along with Machen's "Voorish domes" & "Aklo letters", & Poe's "Yaanek", "Nis", "Auber", &c. It is really a perplexing question to determine just what will strike the sensible reader right, & what will impress him as childish & meaningless stage-paraphernalia. No two readers, of course, are alike, so one must use his own judgment about how wide a circle to aim at. I doubt if it is necessary or advisable to cater to the most pervasively sophisticated wing of the reading public—the wing which pursues sophistication for its own sake & cherishes Aldous Huxley & T. S. Eliot as twin Bibles—since that wing finds even serious realism ridiculous, & is, moreover, wholly a stranger to the emotions which call fantasy forth. On the other hand, one must beware of introducing anything so naive, traditionally hackneyed, or obviously contradictory of nature as to excite the reasonable ridicule or boredom of the average intelligent reader. An absence of Gothic melodrama, cheap ghostliness, & extravagance of incident, is imperative. The supernatural ought properly to be *suggested* rather than openly presented, & the impossible marvels ought as far as feasible to consist of *hypothetical extensions of reality* rather than direct & obvious *contradictions of reality*.

But pray pardon this overdose of rambling theory & abstraction! Regarding your suggestion that I coöperate in a musical drama with the score by yourself—I really feel quite overwhelmed by the force of the implied compliment! If I were able to do justice to such an enterprise, there is certainly nothing I would rather attempt—for despite a profound ignorance of music, I am acutely sensible of its marvellous power, & keenly appreciative of its ability to enhance the effect of allied forms of expression. But over against this looms the fact that I have *no experience whatever in dramatic composition*—& how is a frank novice to evolve anything capable of correlation with the score of an accomplished composer? I am only too well aware that the construction of an effective drama demands a vastly greater fund of technique than one can pick up haphazard from the plays & operas one has casually & uncritically read or witnessed.

Despite my tremendous admiration for things like Dunsany's "Gods of the Mountain" or O'Neill's "Emperor Jones", I have never as yet employed drama as a medium of expression. Probably the reason is that in the sort of work I am trying to do human characters matter very little. They are only incidental details, & can well be left in the puppet stage—since the real protagonists of my tales are not organic beings at all, but simply *phenomena*. I doubt if I have the ability to handle human characters in a lifelike way, for they impress my imagination so much less than do the more impersonal forces of nature. This being so, it is clear that dialogue has never been of much use to me. If I had characters talk, it would be merely to register through them the abnormal mutations of their environment. To create the living figures necessary to vitalise a music-drama of any ordinary sort, therefore, would seem to be a task definitely beyond me. I judge that you do not wish to depart too far from the conventional, since you mention having in mind two figures, male & female, to occupy the foreground. That, I suppose, implies romance of a more or less orthodox sort—in the delineation of which I would be as helpless as an infant trying to write Sanskrit. I tend to deal not with couples but with lone figures confronting the unknown—projection, no doubt, of the idea of the individual dreamer caught in the toils of nightmare. In the intense development & climax, few if any human emotions save awe or fear play a part. I do not like to lose the effect of unity—of the single impression.

That, then, is the way I stand. I would like enormously to coöperate if I thought I could—for the picture of those swampy rivers choked with noxious reeds & trickling sluggishly through sunless tangles of grotesque & gigantic trees, or lapping at cave-riddled cliffs of basalt carven with non-human hieroglyphs, is one which surely catches poignantly at my imagination! But you see the limitations under which I labour. If you still think that I could be of any aid despite these limitations, I would be glad indeed to hear more of your design—indeed, I would in any case, even though I might not be able to participate in the work. Incidentally—one who might do much better than I in this line—who has, in fact, written a poetic drama with an Atlantean theme—is Clark Ashton Smith, Box 385, Auburn, California. I really believe it would pay you to get in touch with this fellow-Californian.

Apologising for my verboseness, & full of appreciation of your kind opinion of my work, I remain,

Yrs. most cordially & sincerely,
H. P. Lovecraft

Notes

1. Richard G[orham] Badger (1877–1937), a publisher in Boston, known for publishing the work of poetical novices. That firm was widely regarded as a vanity press. Gorham Press was the printer for Richard G. Badger.

[88]   [HSF to HPL]   [TLS, JHL]

[Institute of Musical Education, Ltd.
715 South Park View Street
Los Angeles, Calif.]

September 24, 1932.

Mr. H. P. Lovecraft,
10 Barnes Str.
Providence, R.I.

Dear Sir:

I beg to confirm my letter to you dated Sep. 3rd or 4th, which I wrote in reply to your kind epistle of August. The delay, as I took pains to explain, was caused by my trip to Washington and Oregon during the month of August.

You will pardon my impatience in writing again, but I thought that maybe my letter did not reach you or else your reply might have gone astray. I am rather interested in your reaction to the matters put in my letter, so I thought I type these lines at the same time pointing out that either at 715 So. Parkview, %. above school or at 4001 So. Harvard Blvd. both addresses at Los Angeles, Cal. will find me home.

Will you have the kindness to let me know whether you received my (second) letter in reply to yours?

Thanking you,

Very sincerely yours,
Harold Farnese

[89]   [HSF to HPL]   [TLS, JHL]

Los Angeles, Cal. Sep. 28th 1932.
4001 So. Harvard Blvd.

Dear Mr. Lovecraft:

Many thanks for your highly interesting letter, which I enjoyed immensely. Not being a "literateur" nor having many connections among writers your letter gave me the first sight "from behind the wings" into the machinery of story writing. I have always been attracted by the weird and eldritch which bears the stamp of serious and dignified recital and which is neither puerile nor ridiculous. Perhaps, because (as you say) it offers an escape from the humdrum existence that a goodly number of us try to elude or at least to interrupt for a few hours in our time of leisure. Somehow, I have received most of my inspiration for my compositions from odd and outoftheway paintings rather than stories or poems, because, no doubt, the latter lacked something. When I selected No. 8 and No. 9[1] from your "Fungi" I did so because they offered more of a picture (perfectly rounded out) than the other poems in that same collection. To explain in detail is indeed difficult to do. The creative musician usually receives a general idea of conception of a suggestion which we call roughly "atmosphere", and which within him opens the door of his creative self to give birth to a background suitable to such subject. This reaction luckily differs in all artists and runs the gamut from the most ordinary to the most grotesque. Charpentier (a French composer famous thru his opera "Louise")² wrote the most beautiful music inspired by an everyday bourgeois story. Rich. Wagner needed the inspiration of Norse mythology, Edward Grieg was inspired by populating woody glades with dwarfs, elves and other creatures of folk-lore and the great Debussy turned inevitably toward Greek mythology in order to give to the world such as his "Afternoon of a Faun".

Your own creation of an "artificial" mythology somehow attracted me at once to your work as something out of the ordinary, and though I also admire the writings of Lord Dunsany, I find your work more unaffected than his. In other words there is greater scope in your work for the added embellishment of music, a combination that no doubt impresses more and is less apt to proclaim: "Of course, Dear listener, all this does not exist, but is merely fantasy."

I understand fully what you say as to your difficulties with regard to dialogue and reversing the importance of persons over conditions, and if you wish we might keep the idea of a libretto in abeyance, but I would like to tell you what made me write to you the suggestion. Somehow, the paraphernalia of your work gave me the idea, that here was an author who with the creation of his own pantheon might write such a thing as a "Modern Faust" or a "Modern Parsifal". After all, from Mythology to Legend is merely one step, since most of the old European legends are extensions of folk-mythology. Goethe and Wagner have made use of "Faust" and "Parsifal", quite a few authors have made use of "King Arthur", etc. etc. there are many but not very good treatments of that great Romanesque Legend of "Don Juan", and none at all of the more modern legend of the French Duke of Luxembourg.

There is the legend of "Klingsor, the necromamcer" [*sic*] (partly used in Wagner's "Parsifal") and even that adventurous tale of "Cagliostro" and many more. There is no need to treat these in the orthodox manner, most of these legends are vague to begin with and quite flexible under a writer's pen. Mozart's "Don Juan" of course is childish, but not so the original legend, or the more modern drama by Hans Bethge.³

Anyway, I may clarify my thoughts a little after a while and give you a resumé of what might lend itself to musical treatment. If the idea should support itself upon the fascinating array of your paraphernalia, it goes without saying that I would wish to give you credit for it, assuming your gracious permission to build a story on an atmosphere originally created by yourself.

Thanking you repeatedly for your kindness in explaining to me in detail the devious factors entering into your work and for writing to me the most interesting letter I have received in a long time and promising to keep you "au courant" with regard to the "Fungi",

I am, Very sincerely and cordially yours,
Harold Farnese

Thanks for the name and address of A. C. [*sic*] Smith of Auburn Cal.

P.S. The only story by another writer who seems to exude a similar atmosphere as your work is "The Willows" by Algernon Blackwood! I wonder whether you ever read it, as no doubt you would enjoy it. It is in a book with other short stories of the weird.

H. F.

Notes

1. So numbered by *WT,* because it used only a selection of ten from HPL's ms. of 35 sonnets. Both poems appeared in the same issue.
2. Gustave Charpentier (1860–1956), French composer best known for his opera *Louise* (1900).
3. Hans Bethge (1876–1946), German poet and author of the drama *Don Juan: Tragikomödie in drei Akten* (1910).

[90]   [HPL to HSF]   [AHT 2.2]

From Providence
Oct. 12, 1932

Dear Mr. Farnese:—

I appreciated exceedingly your very kind & interesting communication of 28th ult., & would have acknowledged it sooner but for the devastating pressure of accumulated work around me. Only recently have I even begun to get my programme under control—an event which I celebrated last Sunday by taking an antiquarian trip to Salem (the "Arkham" of my tales) & Marblehead (my "Kingsport"). I never tire of picturesque & ancient places, & can revisit them endlessly without loss of the original glamour.

Your remarks on the sources of musical inspiration interested me vastly. In general, I imagine that all arts involving a free play of fancy have much the same sort of stimuli. Stories often result from the oddest & most seemingly irrelevant ideas & glimpses. I am most often moved to composition by vague landscape, atmospheric, & architectural effects—either first-hand or in pictures—though stories, newspaper cuttings, dreams, & all sorts of other things have lain behind many of my efforts. Some writers have built stories & poems on things no more tangible than stray lines or even titles of other works of literature, while vast numbers have received an impulse from music, painting, & sculpture. I think my own imagination is predominantly *geographical,* for to me there is nothing so fascinating as antiquity & unreality as manifested in the aspect of some strange *region.* I love to dwell almost disproportionately on topographical & architectural details, & have a great predilection for describing ancient towns whose crumbling roofs & tangled, shadowy alleys suggest brooding, unimaginable secrets bequeathed from limitless gulfs of time & space.

My one objection to Dunsany is his anxiety to "rub in" the purely fictitious & non-serious nature of his conceptions—an anxiety which grows upon him with the years. I like best his earlier things—"The Gods of Pegāna", "Time & the Gods", "A Dreamer's Tales", & "The Sword of Welleran"—in which he kept this tendency more or less under control. Unfortunately the ironist in him has tended to triumph over the fantaisiste, so that his recent work lacks very largely the qualities which enchant me. The change seems to have begun about 20 years ago with "The Book of Wonder".

I agree with you that my synthetic pantheon is capable of being used as the basis of a cycle of terrestrial legend. That, indeed, is exactly what Dunsany has done in "The Sword of Welleran" & "A Dreamer's Tales". But it is not every theogonist who could summon up the dual skill to invent a convincing fantastic framework on the one hand, & people it with vital & plausible characters on the other hand. Different types of imagination, not always conjoined in the same person, would seem to be called upon. In my case, the linkages of the pantheon to the earth are always perceived through a confusing haze & at a baffling distance—the indistinctness & remoteness being part of the mood I am endeavouring to capture. Accounts of the "Elder Ones" come down through slender, unreliable, & often conflicting channels, & it would of course be possible for a writer with a certain type of imagination to reduce all these dark hints to a coherent & self-consistent system, & to treat vividly of a primal age when Yog-Sothoth & Cthulhu were open & dominant factors in the life of our immediate planet. Of course, the heyday of these entities was long before the existence of organic life as we know it; but we may assume that the earliest men found enough vestiges of their dying power to form the foundation of an adequate legend-cycle. In certain tales still unpublished,[1] I have treated of my artificial mythological background rather more specifically than in any which have seen print—& have brought it into relationship with the artificial mythology of Clark Ashton Smith (with its Tsathoggua & its Hyperborean legends)—but on the whole it is a sadly uncodified & uncorrelated mess of casual allusions & possibly conflicting attributes. It wouldn't be a bad idea for me to read over all my stuff & try to straighten out the overshadowing daemonology.

I shall, as I said before, be exceedingly glad to hear more of your ideas for a fantastic libretto—& it may well be that I could collaborate on such a thing to much better advantage than I could create it outright. No doubt you would wish to lay the scene on some sunken or forgotten continent such as Atlantis, Mu, or Lemuria—or in the (then tropical) Arctic or Antarctic. The *Antarctic* has always exerted a peculiar fascination over me, & my most ambitious story (rejected by *Weird Tales*) has its scene laid there. However—the figures in that story (except for the expedition which crosses the mountains & finds the city) are not human beings or anything approaching the human type. As I have said, I believe that Clark Ashton Smith (Box 385, Auburn, California) might help you greatly in preparing a fantastic libretto. He once wrote a sort of drama or opera called "The Fugitives", with an Atlantean theme.[2]

Blackwood's "Willows" is, in my opinion, the greatest weird story ever written—as I have repeatedly said both in print & out. No one has even approached Blackwood in the minute & serious treatment of man's sense of the unreal—although, oddly enough, he has also written some of the most infantile drivel on record. His style, too, has suffered as a result of his early journalistic work. Blackwood's greatest material, besides "The Willows", is perhaps "Incredible Adventures", "John Silence", (except the opening & closing tales) "The Centaur", & such short stories as "The Wendigo" & "The Listener". Some time, if I can find a copy, I'll send you the article on weird literature which I wrote six years ago for a privately printed magazine.

With every good wish, hoping to hear more of your libretto design, & trusting to see the melodised "Fungi" in due course of time, I remain,

Yrs most cordially & sincerely,

H. P. Lovecraft

Notes

1. Notably "The Mound" (where he borrows Smith's Tsathoggua), *At the Mountains of Madness,* and "The Shadow over Innsmouth."
2. Actually, only a few "songs" (poems) from the opera were ever completed.

[91]   [HSF to HPL]   [TLS, JHL]

Los Angeles, Calif. Oct. 25th 1932.

751 So. Parkview

Dear Mr. Lovecraft:

I want to thank you for your interesting letter of the 12th which I read with great pleasure. I feel somewhat remiss in not having sent to you as yet copies of "Mirage" and "The Elder Pharos" but am negotiating at present with a Blueprint house to have photostat copies made. Photostat is quite expensive, but it is (thus far) the only efficient way to have music multiplied. Mimeograph is out of the question (when it comes to staves and notes), the so-called Ditto process is too smeary and the Blueprint process not very feasible as it necessitates using MS paper with staves on one side only (which is more or less legendary). As soon as I have copies made I will send them to you.

I agree with your criticism of A. Blackwood. Among some very fine weird stories one finds utter drivel at times and very astonishingly so. A new revised Engl. edition which contains "The Listener" and "The Willows" offers also a string of very mediocre stories, very wearisome and not at all keeping the reader up to attention. I thoroughly enjoyed the Cat story "Ancient Worship" in "John Silence" also "The Haunted Island" from another collection.[1] Among other authors, I rather enjoyed the "Ghost stories" and "More Ghost stories" of James, which are no doubt known to you.

The story for my libretto is still quite vague within my cerebellum and what there is of it is not quite what you thought. I do not choose a very legendary background, but a more feasible location, which in my opinion will throw a fantastic story into much stronger relief. For instance: a miracle in "Miracle-Land" will not astound us as much as a miracle in one of the backwaters of America or England, or still better a country not named at all. The synopsis is briefly this:

The title is to be: "FEN-RIVER", as the river with its marshes is the main background of the tale. Fen River, through centuries has encroached upon dry and cultivated land and by slowly but surely inundating the surrounding land has swallowed up villages and hamlets in its ever increasing swamps. One of these villages, however, has somewhat survived, though entirely surrounded by swamps and cut off from the rest of [the] world. The once healthy race of people have deteriorated into a pale-skinned lazy tribe who in spite of all exhortations of their parish priest have gradually succumbed to the lore of the Elders and the worship of Yog-Sothoth. There is a particularly mysterious personality, "Nickelmann" (the name derived from the Norse "Noeck", a legendary god or spirit of rivers or waterfalls), who appears in human guise, but whom the audience is to suspect as the bad spirit of the swamps, the "River-god", (without being told so much.) Into this milieu is projected a young man, a traveler from the outside who falls in love with a girl of the people of the marshes. Thus far the extraordinary atmosphere of the libretto. The story itself, I suppose will have to develop along the approved lines with a love-episode, a jealousy play, a violent death and possibly the sinking of the doomed village into the swamp.

[In margin:] Perhaps this may inspire you to a new weird story in which you are welcome to use this "locale"!

Unfortunately, as you pointed out yourself in one of your letters, an operatic libretto is rather limited as to story, though sufficiently elastic as to background or atmosphere. The audience quite naturally demands a coherent story of human passions, a so-called foothold with things real, as we know them to be. The great English actor Ben Jonson said that "unfortunately, people are more interested in domestic than in imperial tragedies", [2] and the playwright cannot leave this out of consideration. Thus Wagner may introduce Lohengrin in a skiff drawn by a swan, he may present the giant Fafner in the guise of a dragon, he may entertain us with the magic of Klingsor in "Parsifal", but he is nevertheless required to give us a story of human interest, of human passion, love and death, into which the other more fantastic features fit like pieces of a puzzle.

I shall be very interested to hear what you have to say about this vague outline and likewise in the article written by yourself 6 years ago with regard to weird literature, if you should come across a copy of it.

I am keeping the name and address of Clark Ashton Smith on file, as his advice or help might come in handy later on and wish to thank you for your kind interest in my work. I value this interchange of thought very highly indeed, as I have few acquaintances or friends with whom I might discuss these matters, as in creative art tastes differ widely and there is little encouragement in talking to people who cannot be sympathetic to one's line of inspiration.

With best wishes for yourself and the projected publication of your book,
Very cordially and sincerely yours,
Harold Farnese

Notes

1. *The Empty House and Other Ghost Stories.*
2. HSF mentions Benjamin Jonson (1572–1637), the English actor, playwright, and poet, but the quotation seems to be from Samuel Johnson: "The passions rise higher at domestic than at imperial tragedies" (*Johnsoniana*, London: John Murray, 1836, p. 100).

[92]   [HPL to HSF]

10 Barnes Str.
Providence, R.I.
Nov. 7th 1932.

Dear Mr. Farnese:—

I have read your letter of the 25th ult. with the keenest interest and pleasure and am exceedingly glad to hear of your plans for a libretto. Incidentally—let me urge you not to exercise the least haste about supplying copies of the melodised "Mirage" and "Elder Pharos". It may—for such is my state of hermitage—be some time before I can find any musician capable of playing the compositions as they deserve to be played; and in view of the expense of photostatic copies, I would feel guilty in imposing any sort of additional burthen. However, it will of course gratify me immensely to have them in the end.

I am sorry that new editions of Blackwood mix the potent with the inane. Someone ought to prepare a choice anthology with things like "The Willows", "The Listener", "The Wendigo", "Episode in a Lodging House",[1] and other things including some of the "Incredible Adventures" and all the "John Silence" tales except the first and the last. But one thing in his unevenness consoles me. If he is able to write both good and bad stuff, then some of my own recent disappointing things do not necessarily argue that I can never attain a more poignant level!

You are right in saying that a weird plot gains force by taking place amidst familiar scenes. I have written very few things in which the entire setting is exotic—indeed, I incline more and more toward absolute realism except in the one direction chosen for departure from the limitations of the objective world. What you outline of FEN RIVER fascinates me extremely, and I can almost see the dark spectral land of which only one lonely swampgirt isle drags out a decadent and retrogressive survival. Have you, by the way, read Herbert S. Gorman's "The Place called Dagon", where a sinister communal retrogression (without, however, the distinctive features of your setting) is rather well suggested? The idea of a malignant "Nickelman" makes me think vaguely of the aqueous spirit Kuehleborn in La Motte Fouque's UNDINE—who haunts the spectral wood and assumes various forms. This character could be developed into a figure of perpetual veiled menace—representing an undercurrent of terror and always suggesting unknown and evil forces behind his doubtful and mocking anthropomorphism. The human characters, too, could be greatly removed from conventional puppetdom despite an approximate adherence to the standard operatic formula. In short, the entire outline, arouses in me the most hopeful and fascinated anticipations, and I shall watch its development with the utmost interest. I hope to see the script upon its completion, and later trust, that some good fortune will enable me to hear a rendering of the drama with its proper music. Incidentally—I may indeed accept your offer of the FEN RIVER locale as a story setting. If I were to do so, it would be after seeing your full text—in order not to conflict with any attributes with which you may endow the dark and fabulous region and its people. Many thanks for the suggestion! An ultimate sinking, by the way, would make a magnificently catastrophic denouement.

I hope that you and Clark Ashton Smith can collaborate to advantage some day. He is, of course, much more of a poet than you could possibly suspect from the salable material with which he floods the pulp magazines. He has four small books of published verse to his credit, and his unpublished translation of Baudelaire is the best I have ever seen.[2] Besides all this, he is a fantastic pictorial artist of no mean power, whose paintings of Saturnian landscapes and trans-galactic nightmares have had at least one exhibition in San Francisco.

By separate mail you will receive a copy of the magazine containing my "Supernatural Horror in Literature", which is in sad need of revision since it was written six years ago, but which I hope you will enjoy nevertheless.

With congratulations on your coming libretto and promising you my help at least as a critic, and also with every good wish for every other enterprise of yours, I remain,

Yours most cordially and sincerely,

H. P. Lovecraft

Notes

1. Actually "Smith: An Episode in a Lodging House" (1906).
2. Mostly unpublished in Smith's lifetime; now gathered in volume 3 of Smith's *Complete Poetry and Translations*.

[93]   [HSF to HPL]   [TLS, JHL]

Los Angeles, Cal.

715, So. Parkview, Dec. 7th 1932.

Dear Mr. Lovecraft:

I am a little late in answering your interesting letter of Nov. 7th, as I wanted to read your article first before replying. I enjoyed it immensely and it also drew my attention to the reading of a few books which I had not previously perused.

First of all, I read Gorman's "The Place called Dagon" which I thought was interesting. The only technical criticism that I might make (which might interest you as a writer) is that the impression of horror would have been much stronger, if the author had given the idea that this Devil Worship had been carried on interruptedly in this out-of-the-world-corner since the days of Salem's witch trials, and not only been revived by an eccentric. I cannot state why, but the former way of writing the story would have been much more eldritch than the latter.

Walter De La Mare's "The Riddle" in which most of the stories mentioned in your article appear did not impress me as much as his book "The Midnight King" (Lewis II of Bavaria) which I had read some years ago.[1] I take exception to his style, which I find abstruse and unnecessarily obscure in many spots. His style reminds me of the more absolute kind of music such as a symphony by Bruckner or some works by Brahms. (Can only be digested in small doses.)

I enjoyed some of the stories in Miss Asquith's collection of mystery stories "The Black Cap", particularly the "Footsteps in the Jungle" by Somerset Maughan. [*sic*] This book I followed up with (Provost) Montague James' "Ghost Stories" (a new edition containing all of them) which I can always reread without ever getting tired of them. I just borrowed E. F. Benson's "Invisible and Visible", [*sic*] which seems very good, if I may judge from the first story. Strange, that this man has not written more books on weird subjects!

Here is a bit of news which might interest you. One of the local Book Stores (Dawson's) which goes in for collection[s] of rare and out-of-print works, has a book on sale, which I saw once before in my life, in the library of a wealthy collector, the author's name of which I had forgotten. It is the BOOK OF BLACK MAGIC AND PACTS incl. Rites and Mysteries of Goetic Theurgy, Sorcery and Infernal Necromancy by ARTHUR EDWARD

WAITE. (London 1898). This work is priced as $30.- but can now be had for $10.- [In margin: Dawson's only have *one* copy of it!] As far as I can remember it contains many invocations, incantations, spells etc. of infernal spirits and how to protect one's self when calling upon such spirits etc. Rather interesting and perhaps just the proper background for some of your stories. It has a frontispiece showing the demonologist Edw. Kelly[2] causing a departed spirit to appear. The sacrifices ordained are very weird and could be drawn upon by you in more than one story. If you would like to buy it through me, let me know.

I have not started "Fen River" as yet, because I want to finish some other works first. I dislike starting too many things at the same time.

However, I will keep you "au courant" with regard to the libretto.

Which book by A. Machen do you consider his best? I mean a book which is forcible, interesting and weird.

Hoping that you are well and enjoying your work,
Yours very cordially and sincerely,
Harold Farnese

Notes

1. A novel (1927) by George Delamare (b. 1886).
2. Edward Kelley (1555–1597/8), occultist and colleague of John Dee.

[94]   [HPL to HSF]   [nonextant]
22 December 1932

[95]   [HSF to HPL]   [TLS, JHL]
[Institute of Musical Education, Ltd.
715 South Park View Street
Los Angeles, Calif.]
Jan. 9th 1933.

Dear Mr. Lovecraft:

Many thanks for your letter of the 22nd ult. I wish to thank you for your magnificent offer to draw books from your private library and I shall with pleasure avail myself of the opportunity if the occasion should arise. That is to say: I have made a copy of your list of books (which I herewith return to you) and shall first try the L.A. Public Library for the books that sound interesting. Those not on the shelves of the P.L. I shall make a note of and later on ask you for the loan of them. I am also very grateful for the compilation of the list, as it gives me an idea just what to look for. Thank you so much.

Since writing to you last I have tried to read Buchan's "Witchwood", [*sic*] but it is so filled with Scotch dialect which is not easy to understand, and (for shame) I returned the book to the library only half-read. It is certainly reminiscent of "The Place Called Dagon" in many spots. Don't you think so?

Incidentally, have you ever read Hubert Wales' "Brocklebank Riddle"? A marvelous weird and interesting book, which is, unfortunately, out of print.

I just borrowed Buchan's "Runagates' Club" from the P.L. and will let you know later how I liked it.

I will draw this to a close as the mail is going out and I would like to send it along at once. So, please excuse the brevity of my letter.

With best wishes for the New Year,
Sincerely and cordially yours,
Harold Farnese

[P.S.] I was sorry to hear of Mr. Whitehead's demise. Remember one effective story of his particularly well: "The Fireplace".

[P.P.S.] Wasn't he a clergyman and lived at one time in the West Indies?[1]

Notes

1. Henry S. Whitehead died on 23 November 1932. "The Fireplace" appeared in *WT*, January 1925. Whitehead was an Episcopal minister who served as Archdeacon of the Virgin Islands (1921–29).

[96]   [HPL to HSF]   [notes on photograph of Providence County Court House, 1933]

Building with white belfry is original College Edifice (1770)

66 College St.
Note Brown Univ. Clock tower above, & adjacent John Hay Library

[97]   [HPL to HSF (spurious)][1]   [AHT 2.3]

[. . .] Dialogue of any form seems to tear the veil that I like to throw over my stories. Somehow, it seems impossible to cling to my technique of the weird, when I must indulge exclusively in dialogue. [. . .] I am fascinated by your project of creating an opera, & wish with all my heart that I could help you. For you, a musician, & I, a writer, seem to see things in the same light. The story & plot of "The Swamp" please me mightily. I wish with all my heart that I could breathe life into the forms of Yurregarth & Yannimaid. And as to the sinister figure of Nickelman, a modernised version of "Undine" should be a novelty to American audiences.

[. . .] You will, of course, realise that all my stories, unconnected as they may be, are based on the fundamental lore or legend that this world was inhabited at one time by another race who, in practicing black magic, lost their foothold & were expelled, yet live on outside, ever ready to take possession of this earth again. . . .

[He was] the merest tyro [when it came to music. [. . .] I am no student of music, but it warms my soul. [. . .]

Notes

1. The text is from a letter by Farnese to August Derleth (11 April 1937), which accompanied his letters from HPL for transcription by Arkham House. These extracts were transcribed and are part of AHT, along with text from actual letters by HPL. In other letters to Derleth, Farnese wrote: "I am afraid that during the years I have lost one of HPL's letters, for I remember him discussing Blackwood's 'Dr. John Silence' and waxing into a regular tirade about the cheap love interest woven into the last story 'Howling Dog', which does not seem to occur in the letters I sent you" (17 April 1937); "I regret to have lost one of HPL's letters in the interval of the years. Yet I am glad to have been able to have given you all the salient points which I noted down in my book of reference" (21 April 1937). It would seem that the text of this letter is the "lost" letter, as rendered in Farnese's notebook. His letters to Derleth are held at WHS.

[T.Ms., labeled "Copy," Place of Hawks]

"FEN RIVER".

A Fantasy in one act by

H. P. Lovecraft and Harold Farnese.
Music by Harold Farnese.
(Projected in 1932.)

Yurregarth	Tenor
Yannimaid	Soprano
Chlorander	Tenor
Nickelman	Bariton or Bass (?)
Aril	Mezzo Soprano
Sarac, the priest	Bariton
Terrete, the ferryman	Bass

People of the Swamp Village.

Place: The "lost" town in the fens of Yuggoth.

Time: Imaginary.

PRIVATE NOTES.

Scene of inspiration: Northern California, somewhere between Crescent City and Eureka. (Duck Inn.)

Yurregarth, Yannimaid, Chlorander and Aril are young, Nickelman and Terrete middle-aged, Sarac of an undefined age.

The main quality of "FEN RIVER" must be its intangible weirdness and eeriness. It must follow the lines of H. P. Lovecraft's poems "FUNGI FROM YUGGOTH". It must exude the fragrance of his "MIRAGE[']" and "ELDER PHAROS". "Fen River", of course, is an entirely different story, original in itself, against a Lovecraft background and surrounded by a Lovecraft atmosphere. Fog and haziness of outline are essential, nor should the plot be quite rounded out. We must leave the "lost city" as we round it; the whole must remain something akin to a nightmare in our memory.

"Fen River" is an attempt to present a music-drama in which the action is subordinated to the atmosphere of the play. The latter governs everything; the logical development of the plot depends upon it. The Attempt is not entirely novel. Debussy played with the idea and Lapparra made use of it in his "La Habanera". Likewise in Kienzl's opera "The Evangeliman[n]" we find the domination of atmosphere, though here perhaps it crept in unintentionally.

DIALOGUE. The dialogue must be written in words that are not commonplace, on the other hand, must not be stilted. (That indeed is true with all libretti written in English.) The effect must be weird and dreamlike. At all times "The Swamp" must be in our mind as governing the actions of the DRAMATIS PERSONAE. If there is no precedent for it, a style must be invented!

[T.Ms., WHS; enclosure with letter to August Derleth, 30 December 1938]

FEN*RIVER.

(A Fantasy in one act)

Chlorander, a denizen of the outside world, has lost his way in the swamps and reed-choked rivers of Yuggoth, but is finally rescued by the ferryman Terrete and brought to the "lost" town on the banks and islets of Fen River.—Here he meets a pale-faced, sullen and solitary race of people, partly dehumanized by the miasmic vapors of the poisonous swamp-land and forgotten by the outside world.—

Here he watches the priest Serac celebrating mass before empty pews of a half-ruined chapel, going thru the holy ceremony with a meaningless babble.—Here he meets Nickelman, the swarthy and diabolic character, who believes in black magic and the infernal powers and who has even among the townfolk an unsavory reputation.—Here he falls in love with the lily-white Yannimaid who loves and is beloved by Yurregarth, the uncrowned prince of the town.—Here he finds Aril, a strange and passionate Maenad who loves him at sight but whom he fears and detests.—

Nickelman, always bent on mischief, bewitches Yannimaid to lure Chlorander to her place in the stillness of the night.—But while be goes to inform Yurregarth of their tryst, his infernal spell is broken thru his absence and Yannimaid has dismissed her unwelcome suitor.—The astonished Yurregarth finds Yannimaid alone and accepts her protestations of innocence.—Meanwhile, Chlorander is waylaid by the shrewish Aril who desires his love or else will ruin him.— Her cries bring the townsfolk to the scene and even the priest who goes thru his ritual undisturbed.—Chlorander is told to leave the place and embarks with the ferryman Terrete, but Aril jumps into the boat at the last moment resolved to leave also.—They are seen struggling in the rocking barge while Yannimaid clings to Yurregarth and Nickelman bursts into diabolical peals of laughter.—

SCENE.

(Left and Right from the Audience.)

In the background the sluggish and reed-choked Fen-River.—
At the left a small chapel in disrepair. (toward background)
At the right, Yannimaid's house built of wood. (toward foreground)
The road toward the town is assumed to wend toward the right.
The chapel is lit dimly and at night the glow of torches is seen from the right.—The scene is at all times plunged in fog that never lifts entirely.—

PRIVATE NOTE.
Submitted to H. P. Lovecraft in Sept. 1932. Because of a vacation trip of his to Massachusetts I did not hear from him until late in Oct.—HPL is delighted with the idea, but makes several suggestions:
"Muffled sounds; hazy lights; uncanny whisperings; etc.—"
"By all means leave it to audience whether Nickelman is a demon of the swamps or only a malicious character.—Modern stage-craft does not fancy ghosts "per se".—The more question-marks, the better.—Do not commit yourself. Then your work will be original.—I'll do what I can."—

HAROLD FARNESE.

To Edwin Hadley Smith

Edwin Hadley Smith (1869–1944) was a leading amateur journalist of the period, chiefly associated with the NAPA. The Library of Amateur Journalism (also known as The Edwin Hadley Smith Collection and The Fossil Collection), initially housed at the Fossil's headquarters in New York City and moved to the Franklin Institute in Philadelphia 1934, is now at the University of Wisconsin–Madison. Lovecraft directed that, upon his death, his amateur journals be turned over to Smith. R. H. Barlow informed August Derleth that Smith never kept letters, and so this published letter is all that has survived.

Smith had commented on Lovecraft's "Verse Criticism," the first of eight such articles that appeared in the official organ of the NAPA.

[98]

March 10, 1933.

Regarding my latter-day leniency in the critical notes in the *National Amateur* toward poor verse technique, pointed out in Mrs. Smith's[1] postscript to your note, this is perhaps an unconscious reaction against my martinet-like pedantry in the United days of 1914–1922.

In that period I paid supreme attention to form and tore nearly everything to pieces in a technical way, on the theory that good writing ought to come first in any effort to master the poetic art.

Nowadays I am not so sure about the proper order of development. It sometimes seems that the logical first step is the acquisition of a general poetic taste and feeling quite apart from prosody—the cultivation of perspective, mood, type of imaginative utterance, and degree of discrimination, without which the creation of real poetry is impossible. Good technique can come later, but this matter of the true poetic conception is a crucial and all-important thing. If the beginner cannot master this, it is really useless for him to acquire a smooth technique, since the result would be no more than a glib rhymed prose.

In Amateurdom, real poetic vision is even rarer than smooth writing, and it ought to be encouraged accordingly. Whenever it occurs, it deserves to be pointed out, be its continuing medium good or bad. Whenever it just fails of occurrence, the path toward correction may well be indicated.

Of two would-be poems, one with hints of genuine poetic feeling but with poor versification, and the other with a commonplace prosaic attitude concealed by clever technique, the former is the potentially superior product. I neglected to emphasise this valuation in my early amateur days, hence am now trying to atone for the delinquency.

However, I freely and sadly admit that the bulk of amateur versification is woefully bad, and may later on prepare a more or less generalised article on the simpler poetic metres, and the necessity of sticking to them if the result is to be anything but slovenly.

Incidentally, it is amusing that Official Editor Spink saddled the job of verse criticism on me, since I have not seriously attempted poetry in years. Virtually all my contemporary efforts are in prose.

Notes

1. Nita Gerner Smith (1881–1969).

[99]   [In *Boys' Herald*]

[c. February 1936]

[. . .]

Omitting important figures in mailing papers should be attacked in print. Such omissions are especially reprehensible when a paper contains matter adverse to the person omitted.[1] I believe an amendment providing a penalty would be very much in order. A law requiring that a member must be supplied with a copy of an attack by registered mail (to avoid false claims of having sent a copy) not later than the mailing of any other copy. The penalty could be suspension of mailing-bureau privileges or suspension of membership for a stated period. Attacking a member behind his back, circulating hostile material before he has a chance to formulate a timely reply, is the flagrant thing that needs the sternest rebuke. The matter might well be brought up as an editorial theme. It would focus the members on an evil becoming increasingly prevalent, and in need of correction through drastic speech or legal enactment.

[. . .]

Notes

1. HPL refers to Ralph W. Babcock's printing of a story by Hyman Bradofsky in his *Enterprise* (Fall 1935) peppered with Babcock's sarcastic comments on Bradosfky's prose without Bradofsky knowing about it until the story appeared in print.

To Allan G. Ullman

On 1 August 1933, at the suggestion of Samuel Loveman, Allan G. Ullman of Alfred A. Knopf wrote Lovecraft requesting manuscripts of his work to evaluate for publication. Ullman (1908–1982) was a bookseller (not an editor) at Knopf from 1931 to 1934. The proposed volume was ultimately declined, chiefly because Knopf could not secure a commitment from Farnsworth Wright to sell 1000 copies of the book through *WT*. For the readers' reports on the stories Lovecraft submitted, see David E. Schultz, "'Whaddya Make Them Eyes at Me For?': Lovecraft and Book Publishers," *Lovecraft Annual* No. 12 (2018): 51–65.

[100] [ALS]

66 College St.,
Providence, R.I.,
Aug. 3, 1933

Allan G. Ullman, Esq.,
℅ Knopf Co.,
New York, N.Y.,

Dear Mr. Ullman:—

    In reply to yours of the 1st. I am sending (enclosed & under separate cover) a few tales for examination at your leisure. Since most of these are my only copies, I must ask that they be treated with some care—& returned if unacceptable. These represent about the best I have done in the domain of fiction—& no doubt a reading of even part of them would be enough to let you decide whether you would care to undertake the issuance of a collection. Very recent items are not included because of length—these being really outside the limits of the short story proper.

    The present bunch consists of seven items, as follows. Dates are of writing—not publication:

The Picture in the House (1920) Pub. in *Weird Tales*. Mentioned by E. J. O'Brien
    in 1924—1 or 2 stars (I forget which)
The Music of Erich Zann (1921) *Pub. in Weird Tales*. Reprinted in anthology
     "Creeps by Night" (+ British Edition) & *London Evening
     Standard*. Probably to appear in future anthology issued by
     Denis Archer.[1]

The Rats in the Walls (1923) Pub. in *Weird Tales* 1923. Reprinted in Selwyn &
Blount Anthology, London. Also reprinted in W.T. 1930.
The Strange High House in the Mist (1926) Pub. W.T. 1st class mention O. Henry
Mem. annual 1932
Pickman's Model (1926) pub. W.T., minor mention O. Henry Mem. annual.
Reprinted S & B Anthology, London
The Colour Out of Space (1927) pub. *Amazing Stories*. 3-star O'Brien 1928. In my
own opinion, my best story.
The Dunwich Horror (1928) pub. W.T. 3-star O'Brien.

I am glad that "The Dreams in the Witch House"[2] has impressed you favourably, & hope that the additional tales may not prove disappointing. It
would of course gratify me exceedingly if the publication of a collection could
be arranged.

It was very kind of Mr. Loveman to mention my attempts to you. He has
always encouraged my fictional experiments most generously—so that in a
sense he is responsible for the existence of most of them. I presume you
know how poignant & graceful a poet he is—I wish your firm could some
day issue a volume of his selected lyrics.

Appreciating your inquiry very much, & hoping that I have not imposed
too many of these tales upon you, I am
Very sincerely yours,
H. P. Lovecraft

Notes

1. This anthology never appeared.
2. Possibly Loveman lent Ullman the magazine appearance of the story.

[101] [ALS]
66 College St.,
Providence, R.I.,
Aug. 16, 1933
Dear Mr. Ullman:—
Our friend Mr. Loveman has just informed me that you
would like to see more specimens of my fiction, & suggests that I send you
'everything which I or others have thought good in the past'. A more or less
literal adoption of that suggestion (except that I mercifully refrain from in-
flicting two long MSS.—115 & 72 pp—written in 1931) is responsible for the
accompanying avalanche.

I am (God help you!) including 18 stories, as follows:
(my own favourites asterisked) (especial favourites of others—†)[1]

The Tomb (1917) Stiff in diction, but liked by many. (Pub. Weird Tales)

*Dagon (1917) A favourite of mine, though some of the melodramatic diction ought to go.

*The Statement of Randolph Carter (1919) Almost literal transcript of an actual dream—in which I am "Carter" while Loveman is "Warren". (Pub. W T)

The Temple (1920) Nothing remarkable, but my most extended embodiment of my favourite undersea theme. (Pub. W T)

*Facts Concerning the Late Arthur Jermyn & His Family (1920) I rather like this. (Pub. W T)

*The Cats of Ulthar (1920) Brief phantasy. I like this—& cats! (Pub W T)

√†*The Outsider* (1921) A great favourite with readers, but rather bombastic in style & mechanical in climax. (Pub W T & later reprinted there)

The Moon-Bog (1921) Liked by many, but not a favourite of mine. (Pub. W T)

†*The Lurking Fear* (1922) Written to order for a cheap magazine called *Home Brew*, hence the gory, mechanical sub-climaxes. Reprinted W T. A favourite of readers—but not of mine.

†*The Festival* (1923) A readers' favourite. Pub. W T & soon to be reprinted there.

†*The Unnamable* (1923) Another readers' favourite (Pub W T)

†√ *The Shunned House* (1924) Loveman's favourite. Rejected by W T. About to be issued as a brochure by the Driftwind Press, North Montpelier, Vt.

√*In the Vault* (1925) Pub. W.T. Second-class mention O. Henry Mem. 1932.

†√ *The Horror at Red Hook* (1925) Not a favourite of mine, but reprinted in the Selwyn & Blount anthology & included in the American pirated edition—"Not at Night", ed. by Herbert Asbury, Macy-Masius. (Pub W T)

*The Call of Cthulhu (1926) Pub. W.T. Reprinted in "Beware After Dark", ed. by T. Everett Harré. (Macaulay). Not so bad.

†*Cool Air* (1926) Liked by some. Pub. *Tales of Magic & Mystery*. Phila. 1927.

†*The Silver Key* (1926) Pub. W.T. 1-star O'Brien 1929.

*The Whisperer in Darkness (1930) Pub. W T. I like the Vermont atmosphere, which attempts to be authentic.

I don't envy you the task of wading through all these MSS., but perhaps the perusal of a few of the starred or daggered specimens will give you all the idea of my stuff that you need. Loveman wants you to be sure to read "The Shunned House."

Regarding a special story 'more gruesome than anything I have ever done'—I dare say I could evolve one if the venture advanced far enough to demand it!

Appreciating your patience in reading these tales, & hoping that by some miracle a published collection may be found practicable,

I remain

Yrs very cordially,

H. P. Lovecraft

Notes

1. The significance of the four pencil checkmarks is not known. They may have been made by Ullman, since Loveman had recommended that he read "The Shunned House," one of the checked items.

To Charles D. Hornig

Charles D[erwin] Hornig (1916–1999) was the youthful editor of *FF* (September 1933–February 1935), the first important fanzine in weird fiction. Hornig, residing in Elizabeth, N.J., accepted Lovecraft's offer to serialize a revised version of "Supernatural Horror in Literature" there, but the serialization had progressed only to the middle of Chapter 8 by the time of the magazine's folding. He also published four stories and four poems from *Fungi from Yuggoth*. The October 1934 issue was dedicated to Lovecraft. While Hornig was still in high school and still editing *FF*, Hornig became editor of *Wonder Stories* (November 1933–April 1936). On 25 May 1935 (his nineteenth birthday), he met Lovecraft in Providence. He edited *Science Fiction* (1939–41), *Future Fiction* (1939–40), and *Science Fiction Quarterly* (1940–41) but abandoned them all by 1941. Isaac Asimov said of Hornig: "Charles D. Hornig is the only science fiction notable who has absolutely no talent" (*Before the Golden Age: A Science Fiction Anthology of the 1930s* [Garden City, NY: Doubleday, 1974], 728).

Hornig himself in an advertisement in 1947 said he had "58 letters and cards" from Lovecraft. Only 22 are represented here, and most are truncated. (Eric Kramer has once offered for sale "a file of 27 post-cards and one letter from H. P. L. to Hornig. These are informative and lengthy cards in the usual diminuative [*sic*] script of H. P. L. and cover a vast and important literary area. All were written during the early through mid nineteen thirties.")

[102] [ALS]

> 66 College St.,
> Providence, R.I.
> July 27, 1933

Dear Mr. Hornig:—

        I read yours of the 24th with great interest—Smith[1] having previously mentioned your coming venture. Most sincerely do I hope you will succeed; for fantasy has been a lifelong interest of mine, & I welcome every new influence which can give it scope. Your policy seems to me to be very well chosen, & the 'scientifictional' opening will doubtless aid in establishing popularity. The advertisements seem to be in the right media—& I will certainly do all I can to call the favourable attention of friends & correspondents to the newcomer. Of course—as you state—the difficulties are many & vast; but if extensive profit be not the motive, there certainly ought to be an excellent chance of success.

Enclosed is a dollar bill, for which please enter me for the 18 months' subscription mentioned. I certainly hope that the magazine may weather these months & establish itself as a permanent enterprise.

Smith speaks very warmly of your experiment, & I am glad you are using some of his work. To my mind he is the best & most dependable weird writer in America today, & I regret that there is not a larger market for products such as his.

As for my tales—I'll be glad to contribute any of those which I now have on hand, & am sending herewith five specimens which I hope you will like— at least, to some extent. Use one, or all, or none, or any number you wish. "The Nameless City" is my own favourite, although Smith is partial to "Beyond the Wall of Sleep".[2] Return what you don't like, & I'll refund the postage.

With every good wish for your venture, I am

Yrs most cordially & sincerely—

H P Lovecraft

P.S. I've sent all the miniature circulars to correspondents, & could probably distribute about 50 more if you care to send a supply.

Notes

1. Clark Ashton Smith. See HPL to Smith ([29 June 1933]): "The circular you sent is the first I've heard of *The Fantasy Fan*" (*Dawnward Spire* 423).
2. Besides these, HPL also submitted "From Beyond," "The Other Gods," "Polaris," and the poems "The Book," "Pursuit," "The Key," and "Homecoming" (all from *Fungi from Yuggoth*).

[103] [ANS]

August 7
[Postmarked Providence, R.I.,
7 August 1933]

Dear Mr. Hornig:—

Congratulations on your appointment with *Wonder Stories!* You surely did walk into a surprising piece of good fortune. Wish I could call on Farnsworth Wright & come away with a regular job—which heaven knows, I need badly enough! I'm sure you'll find your new work eminently congenial.

Glad to hear of the coming change of the *Fantasy Fan* to the weird field. I may send some articles on weird fiction for your approval. Back in 1926 I wrote a short history of weird fiction which appeared in a privately printed magazine. Would you care to serialise such a thing if I could dig up a copy to lend? (I couldn't spare one permanently.) I would in such a case bring the text up to date by mentioning things published since it was written. ¶ I suggest that you have reviews of important weird books as they appear. ¶ By the way—Knopf lately asked to see some of my stuff with a view to book publication, though I don't believe anything will come of it. Similar requests by Putnam's & the Viking[1] came to nothing in the past.

Best wishes & renewed congratulations
            —Yrs most sincerely,
                 H P Lovecraft.

Notes

1. HPL means Vanguard Press, which had approached him for a possible book project in 1932. The Viking Press is not known to have queried HPL during his lifetime.

[104] [ANS][1]

[Postmarked Providence, R.I.,
11 August 1933]

The weird-fiction article is technically copyrighted in the name of W. Paul Cook, who issued the amateur magazine containing it, but he will offer no objection to the reprinting of the thing. If you need to get in touch with him when you begin publication, you can do so. His address is 7 Hancock St., Boston, Mass. I haven't time just now to prepare the article for publication— that is, to revise & insert matter as I would like—but I could surely do this before you would want to use it. Or if you'd like to give the thing a preliminary survey just as it is, I can send it along temporarily. It is quite long—would make a swell book. ¶ Glad you liked the Witch House. ¶ Renewed congratulations on your congenial job. Hope it lasts. Writers complain of Gernsback's slow paying, but I presume he is more regular with his actual staff.
Best wishes—HPL

Notes

1. *Front:* Cape Cod Auto Map.

[105] [ANS][1]

[Postmarked Providence, R.I.,
15 August 1933]

I'll send the weird fiction history later—remind me if I forget it. Glad young Derleth is contributing. Why not ask for a story from Bernard Dwyer, Box 43, West Shokan, N.Y.? He has some very good stories which Wright has turned down for some reason or other. ¶ I see that 3 new weird magazines are due to appear—one of them *Astounding* as revived by Street & Smith. The field is certainly getting populated again! Glad the *Wonder* staff get their due stipend.

Best wishes
—HPL

Notes

1. *Front:* Hospital Section, West Balcony, Crane National Exhibit, Boardwalk, Atlantic City, N. J.

[106] [ANS][1]

[Postmarked Providence, R.I.,
22 August 1933]

I'll let you have the history by Oct. 10. It probably comes to 25,000 words, but is divided into chapters. If I can't get around to correcting I'll send it along just as it is—for of course the items since 1926 are relatively few. The changes would consist of added passages—each lettered, with a corresponding letter on the printed text to indicate place of insertion. Deletions & minor corrections would be made in ink on the printed text.[2] ¶ Hope your W.T. advertisement will bring results. Shall be eager to see #2. ¶ Glad Barlow sent material. You'll also like Dwyer's stuff. ¶ No doubt about revival of *Astounding*. First issue went to press Aug. 15. They have just bought a story of Wandrei's for $95.00. The editor is Orlin Tremaine, but most of the active work is done by the Associate Editor, Desmond Hall.[3] ¶ It is wise, I fancy, to cut down the purely weird element in *Wonder;* though of course there is a middle ground where weird & science elements are hard to separate—especially in the realm of interplanetary fiction.
Best wishes—
H P L

Notes

1. *Front:* Steam Exhibit, West Side of Foyer, Crane National Exhibit, Boardwalk, Atlantic City, N. J.
2. This comment, along with one in letter 104, indicates that HPL sent Hornig a marked-up copy of the *Recluse* appearance of the essay, rather than a revised T.Ms.
3. F[rederick] Orlin Tremaine (1899–1956), editor of *Astounding* (1933–37) whom HPL blamed for butchering *At the Mountains of Madness* when it was serialized there in 1936. Tremaine later published two volumes of HPL's stories as editor of Bartholomew House: *The Weird Shadow over Innsmouth and Other Stories of the Supernatural* (1944) and *The Dunwich Horror* (1945). Australian-born Desmond Hall (1911–1992) was assistant editor of *Astounding* under Harry Bates (1930–33) and briefly under Tremaine (1933–35) before becoming editor of *Mademoiselle.*

[107] [ANS]¹

[Postmarked Providence, R.I.,
29 August 1933]

I'll surely let you have the history by Oct. 10—revised or not. It's really not so obsolete just as it stands. Glad Derleth is going to supply something. Another young chap who might have a weird story thesis to contribute is J. VERNON SHEA, JR., 5705 JACKSON ST., PITTSBURGH, PA.² I shall certainly wait eagerly for *Astounding*—hope it lives up to its promises. Glad the new *Wonder* will have good stuff. Carl Jacobi is a young author worth watching—he has a command of genuine weirdness not often found, & his recent "Revelations in Black" was a high spot of W.T.³ ¶ I may take a trip to Quebec later this week—my first real vacation of the summer. Old towns like that fascinate me—which reminds me that your own city has a good many interesting old houses. I used to explore ancient Elizabethtown frequently in 1924 & 1925, when I was in Brooklyn.
Best wishes—
HPL

[P.S. on front] This scene is less than 100 yds. from my east windows.

Notes

1. *Front:* The Carrie Tower, Hope, Manning and University Halls at left. / Brown University, Providence, R. I.
2. J[oseph] Vernon Shea (1912–1981), correspondent of HPL (1931–37) and longtime devotee of weird and science fiction.
3. It was published in the issue of April 1933.

[108] [ALS? "Our Readers Say"]

[c. September 1933]

Vol. 1, No. 1, looks to me very much what the younger science fiction devotees want. Later on it might be a good idea to use matter of interest to weird tale enthusiasts—articles on the classics of weird literature, and information concerning weird magazines. As for Ackerman's ebullition, I fear he can hardly be taken seriously in matters involving the criticism of imaginative fiction. Smith's story was really splendid, except for the cheap ending on which the Editor [of] Wonder Stories insisted. Ackerman once wrote me a letter with a very childish attack on my work—he evidently enjoys verbal pyrotechnics for their own sake and seems so callous to imaginative impressions. [. . .]¹

Notes

1. The debate about Clark Ashton Smith's story "Dweller in Martian Depths" and Forrest J Ackerman's denunciation of it was carried in *FF* in a column called "The Boiling Point" from September 1933 through February 1934. The inaugural column consisted only of a lengthy complaint by Ackerman that the publication of a horror story in a science fiction magazine was unacceptable. The following five issues of *FF* consisted primarily of brief paragraphs in favor of Smith. The entire contents of the column are now reprinted in *Dawnward Spire* 689–98.

[109] [ANS][1]

[Postmarked Providence, R.I.,
24 September 1933]

Well—at last I'm sending you the history of weird fiction under separate cover. Don't hesitate to reject it if it is not what you want. As you'll see, it deals only with literature of standard grade—not cheap popular stuff. Of the modern magazine writers, Smith is the only one who really makes the grade. An article on the cheap writers would be a wholly different proposition—you might get one from *H. Warner Munn, Route 1, Athol, Mass.,* if you asked him. ¶ This is my only copy of the enlarged article. Hope you can read the parts added on the margin. Please return if not used—& also, I'd be glad to have the copy back in the end even if you do use it. It is my only duplicate. By the way—you'll find other features of interest in the magazine containing this article. ¶ Best wishes for the F F. One or two people tell me they are subscribing. Hope it gets a firm foothold. Regards—

HPL

Notes

1. *Front:* Hospital Section, West Balcony, Crane National Exhibit, Boardwalk, Atlantic City, N. J.

[110] [ANS][1]

[Postmarked Providence, R.I.,
26 September 1933]

Trust the article will reach you safely, & that you'll find it interesting. Let me know if any of the interpolated paragraphs on the margin are hard to decipher. I'd be glad to give the proofs a reading when the time comes, if that would be convenient to you. ¶ Shall be very glad to see second issue. ¶ Just read the first issue of the new *Astounding*. Not so bad for pulp stuff, but essentially mediocre from a literary point of view. ¶ Best wishes—

HPL

Notes

1. *Front:* Faneuil Hall, known as the 'Cradle of Liberty,' was the focus of Revolutionary movement in Boston and the colonies. In the background is the tower of the Customs House, the tallest building in Boston.

[111] [ANS][1]

[Postmarked Providence, R.I.,
23 October 1933]

Thanks exceedingly for the liberal supply of Oct. Fantasy Fans. It looks to me even more interesting than the first. Smith's tale[2] was splendid—the remunerative editors were certainly fools to turn it down. Glad to see that a large number of readers are shewing up Ackerman's nonsense. People like Ackerman are peculiarly ridiculous—one can plainly see that their bombinating is merely an egotistical gesture to call attention to themselves. However, most people outgrow this stage. Glad you were able to use something from young Barlow[3]—he's distinctly worth encouraging. Hope you won't find my article too long & ponderous. I fear your younger readers will think it's a long time getting really started.

All best wishes—H P L

Notes

1. *Front:* Betsy Williams Cottage, Roger Williams Park, Providence, R. I. The text was partially published in *FF* (November 1933).
2. "The Kingdom of the Worm"; rpt. in *Other Dimensions* (1970) as "A Tale of Sir John Mandeville."
3. "Annals of the Jinns: I. The Black Tower."

[112] [ANS; "Our Readers Say"]

[c. November 1933]

Delighted to see the November issue. All the items and departments seem well calculated to interest the weird fiction devotee; and since there is no other magazine in this field, TFF ought certainly to be able to build up a solid clientele in the course of time. [. . .]

[113] [ANS; "The Boiling Point"]

[c. December 1933]

Glad you are giving the vociferous Master Ackerman a hearing—it's always well to let both sides of a debate have an equal chance. But I fear that Effjay the Terrible and his allies don't make out a very strong case. The tirade to which exception was taken was not merely an assertion that Smith's "Dweller in Martian Depths" is unsuited for a science fiction magazine. It is a wholly gratuitous and intemperate attack on the story itself, written with a slap-dash extravagance and obviously sadistic gusto which plainly shewed either a complete lack of analytical understanding and imaginative sensitiveness, or (as was probable) a mere boyish desire to shew off and attract notice. However, Ackerman is young, as proved by his tendency to regard ordinary civilised language as alien and incomprehensible. Now that he's had a good barrage from the general public, it would be just as well to leave him in peace. Five years from now he'll go beyond any of us in laughing at his explosions of today. [. . .]

[114] [ANS]¹

[Postmarked Providence, R.I.,
20 January 1934]

Glad your subscription plan is working, & hope you can arrange the monthly programme after all. Sorry I couldn't get in touch with you while in N Y—I did say on a card that I was coming, & I had some idea of paying you a call; but I was so utterly swamped by engagements (it happens that a large majority of my friends live in the N.Y. area) that I hadn't a second extra. As it was, I couldn't get around to half the things I wanted to do. ¶ Hope you can get to Providence this summer—let me know when you're coming, & I'll tell you how to get up to the house. I live almost on the crest of the precipitous hill which separates the residence from the business district—in the university section next [to] the college library (see over). Providence is a quaint old town like Elizabethtown, & I think you're feel quite at home here! ¶ Have you any extras of your very first issue—Sept.—to spare? I gave away all my duplicates by mistake, & would like to get 2 or 3 for the sake of the first [instalment] of my article. ¶ Best wishes
—HP

[P.S.] [left margin] entrance to the quaint court where I live [right margin] I live next door to this building

Notes

1. *Front:* John Hay Memorial Library, Brown University, Providence, R. I.

[115]　[ANS][1]

[Postmarked Providence, R.I.,
26 January 1934]

So you've lived in the red Barnet–Mayo–Scott house? I envy you! My present abode—the oldest I have ever inhabited—is only 130 years old, but it has a fan-carved doorway, small-paned windows, six-panel doors, wide floor-boards, old-fashioned latches, &c. It grieves me beyond measure to learn that the ancient Scott house is gone—& in such an ignominious way.[2] Such wanton vandalism is all too common nowadays. Providence needlessly sacrificed a fine old row of brick waterfront warehouses in 1929—I protested loudly but it didn't do any good. The Scott house—built in 1763—once had finely landscaped grounds going all the way to Jefferson Ave. There was a stream which ran around an artificial island shaped like Great Britain, with trees marking the location of the principal cities. Of course—all this vanished generations before I saw the place. The house is described in the "Historic Houses of N. J.".[3] Have you the book-let "Historic Elizabeth" by Kelley & Dix which the Eliz. Journal published for the 250th Anniversary in 1914?[4] If not, I can lend you a copy. It is highly inter-esting. I could get it in 1924, but don't believe it is available today. Yes—I know how long the Staten Island route is, but that 25¢ fare appealed to me!
Best wishes—
HP

Notes

1. *Front:* John Hay Memorial Library, Brown University, Providence, R. I.
2. HPL refers to the house at 1105 East Jersey Street, Elizabeth, NJ, built for Dr. Wil-liam Barnet in 1763. It was later owned by Col. John Mayo, whose daughter Maria married General Winfield Scott, who then took up residence there. The house was de-stroyed in 1928 to make way for a gas station. HPL saw the house in 1924 (*LFF* 189).
3. See Mills pp. 127–31.
4. Frank Bergen Kelley and Warren R. Dix, *Historic Elizabeth, 1664–1914* ([Elizabeth, NJ]: Elizabeth Daily Journal, [1914]).

[116]　[ANS][1]

[Postmarked Providence, R.I.,
31 January 1934]

Sorry your present quarters are so uncongenial, & hope you'll be able to find a quieter & larger place in spring. Late in 1924 I tried to find a room in Eliza-bethtown—as a relief from Brooklyn & Manhattan—and almost took a large one in E. Jersey St. not so very far from the old Boudinet house[2] (now the Ladies' Home); but the rent was high & the room was dark & inconvenient, so I finally kept on in Bklyn. till I could get back to Providence. E. Jersey is a great

old street. The Bonnel House—out beyond the Boudinet—was built in 1682, & is one of the very few gabled, pre-colonial houses surviving outside New England. It is second only to the Hatfield house in age. Too bad so many of these fine old places have been half spoiled by modernisation. The ugly French roof added to the Boudinet house is very annoying, & even the Belcher house has some unfortunate modern changes. But of course that's not as bad as if they were torn down. I can't get over the pity of the loss of the Scott house! Glad you've read the Kelley & Dix brochure. It is really a splendid guide—better than anything we have in Providence. It tells just what the antiquarian & historical student wants to see, & shows clearly how to get everywhere. There ought to be a new edition. ¶ All good wishes—
H P L

Notes

1. *Front:* John Hay Memorial Library, Brown University, Providence, R. I.
2. Now the Boxwood Hall State Historic Site, 1073 East Jersey Street, Elizabeth, NJ, built about 1750. Also a National Historic Landmark for its association with Elias Boudinot (1740–1821), who lived there from 1772 to 1795. Boudinot was president of the Continental Congress (1782–83).

[117] [ANS; "Our Readers Say" and "Your Views"]

[c. February 1934]

Very glad to see the new issue. Smith's article is extremely apt and timely. I find that James tends to be popularly under-appreciated. Barlow's tale is the best yet—he seems to improve constantly. The verses of Messrs. Lumley and Searight are haunting and excellent. It's a good idea to substitute a department of general discussion for "The Boiling Point".[1] [. . .] It can be said that anything which vividly embodies a basic human emotion or captures a definite and typical human mood is genuine art. It requires an [*sic*] especial morbidity to enjoy any authentic word-depiction, whether it is conventionally "pleasant" or not. Indeed, it argues a somewhat immature and narrow prospection [*sic*] when our jud[g]ment is by the mere conventional appeal of its subject-matter or its supposed social effects. The question to ask is not whether it is "healthy" or "pleasant", but whether it is *genuine* and *powerful.*

Notes

1. *FF* (February 1934): Smith, "The Weird Work of M. R. James"; Barlow, "The Time Machine: A Biographical Note"; William Lumley, "The Dweller"; and "Winds," Richard F. Searight. The column of general discussion was "Your Views" (beginning with the March 1934 issue).

[118] ["Our Readers Say"]

[c. March 1934]

The March *Fantasy Fan* looks like an excellent issue—typographical impression improved. But may I ask that some extremely misleading misprints in my letter be corrected? One is especially bad, giving a direct contradiction of what I really wrote—this being the substitution of AN for NO in the phrase meant to read "*no* especial morbidity" (Your Views department). Other errors are "prospection" for "perspective" and the omission of "g" from the word judgment. ¶ Glad to see the interesting tale by Robert E. Howard and the powerful poem by Clark Ashton Smith.[1] [. . .]

Notes

1. "Gods of the North" and "Revenant" (*FF*, March 1934).

[119] [ANS][1]

[Postmarked Providence, R.I.,
27 March 1934]

Congratulations on the sale of your article! Hope you can manage to insert a note correcting the worst errors in the letter, for that AN for NO really puts me in a very bad position—directly contradicting my meaning & destroying the sense of the argument. Ordinary readers are completely misled by this kind of thing—they don't stop to study the context & ____. With the letter as it is, one couldn't blame anyone for inferring that I am 'crazy, or have a deceased mind'! Glad, though, to see the general improvement in typographical correctness. ¶ I may possibly get to Florida next month to see Barlow. If so, there's a chance of my meeting Edmond Hamilton & Jack Williamson, __ in Key West.[2] ¶ All good wishes—

HPL

[P.S.] Just read Machen's new book—The Green Round.

Notes

1. *Front:* Industrial Trust Co. Bldg. and Depot Park, Providence, R. I.
2. HPL did not in fact end up seeing the science fiction writers Hamilton and Williamson on his extended stay with R. H. Barlow in De Land, FL (2 May–21 June).

[120] [ANS "Our Readers Say"]

[c. April 1934]

"The Ancient Voice"¹ is a splendid tale, with overtones of subtle terror and macabre suggestion that linger disquietingly in one's memory. It is certainly refreshing to see the shades of opinion represented in the "Your Views" department, and I feel sure that this discussion will be much more intellectually fruitful than the earlier type with its occasionally sharp personal digs. Smith's "Chinoiserie" is exquisite. [. . .]

H. P. Lovecraft

Notes

1. By Eando Binder (*FF,* April 1934).

[121] [ANS]¹

[Postmarked Cassia, Fla., 11? June 1934]

Greetings! Travelling in the south & paying our friend a long visit in De Land. Enjoyed the latest Fantasy Fan—an excellent issue. The cover of different colour² adds to the effect. But how comes it that Barlow's article appears under the name of "Daniel McPhail"?³ ¶ Had hoped to get to Havana, but this hope is almost gone now. Shall spend a week in St. Augustine & return north by [?easy] stages. De Land is very pleasant, & the subtropical climate has quite set me on my feet. The Barlow place is in the open country, 14 miles west of the village, in a very pleasant region. Behind the house is a lake on which we go rowing. My host is an extraordinary brilliant young fellow, though handicapped by poor eyesight. He is a writer, painter, sculptor, pianist, landscape gardener, book collector, & then some! ¶ Regards—Hope I can see you when I re-pass through the NY zone.

HPL

Notes

1. *Front:* A cocoanut tree, Florida.
2. I.e., pink.
3. "About H. G. Wells," *FF* 1, No. 9 (May 1934): 143–44.

[122] [ANS][1]

[Postmarked Saint Augustine, Fla.,
23 June 1934]

Greetings! Saw the new F F at Barlow's & must congratulate you on an excellent issue. After a 7-week visit in De Land, I am amongst my favourite antiquities again. Staying in St. Augustine a week, & absorbing ancient atmosphere by the carload. North again by the middle of July.

Regards & best wishes—

H P L

Notes

1. *Front:* Old City Gates, St. Augustine, Fla.

[123] [ANS][1]

[Postmarked Providence, R.I.,
13? July 1934]

Glad to see the new F F which arrived today. An unusually good issue: Smith's story has a deep, macabre power, & Keller's—though conventional in theme—is extremely clever & attractive.[2] Let me thank you also for the generous supply of the June issue with "From Beyond." ¶ Had a fine week in St. Augustine, & reluctantly started north June 28. 2 days in Charleston, 1 in Richmond, 2 in Washington, 1 in Philadelphia. In NY found the Longs about to go to Asbury Park for the week end & went along with them. Too broke to stop in N.Y. any length of time; & couldn't look anybody up. It was, altogether, a great trip, but I'm glad to be home among [familiar scenes].

Best regards—

HPL

Notes

1. *Front:* Van Wickle Gates, Brown University, Providence, R. I.
2. *FF* (July 1934): Clark Ashton Smith, "The Epiphany of Death"; David H. Keller, "Rider by Night."

[124] [ANS][1]

[Postmarked Providence, R.I.,
26 July 1934]

The trip certainly was enjoyable, & I hope you can arrange to take a similar jaunt later on. Glad to hear that Wright is going to give the F F a good notice in the Eyrie.[2] That amply makes up for his refusal to accept the advertisement

a second time last year. Probably he thought at first that the F F was a *competing* venture, but now he doubtless realises that it is *supplementary*—that it promotes interest in W T & perhaps actually increases his sales. Interested to hear of future cover stocks—& hope the anniversary issue will command an especially good range of contributions. I'll be sending in my second year's subscription during August. Did Bloch tell you that he's at last crashed W T?[3] I'm always glad to see the younger generation coming along. Still rushed to death with piled-up work, & today still another job arrived—which will certainly have to be postponed. Got the new *Marvel Tales* the other day—a great improvement over the first number, but something ought to be done about the misprints or bad spelling—whichever it is. Long & Howard easily lead the issue. Again, thanks for the generous F F supply.
Best wishes—
H P L

Notes

1. *Front:* Campus, Brown University, Providence, R. I.
2. "The Eyrie" (*WT,* September 1934): "From time to time we are importuned by our readers to devote several pages of WEIRD TALES each month to a forum in which the lovers of fantastic fiction can exchange views. We are asked to have articles on weird fiction generally, information about our authors, debates between the fans. It has been suggested that we expand the Eyrie for this purpose, and make it a battleground for the conflicts of the weird fiction fans. This we have stedfastly refused to do, for WEIRD TALES, after all, is a magazine of fiction, and undue expansion of the Eyrie, or the opening of a new department to satisfy the fans, would take just that much space away from weird stories, which are our primary interest. So, instead of reducing our story space to make room for such a department, we suggest to those of you who are interested that you write to Charles D. Hornig, editor of The Fantasy Fan, whose home address is 137 West Grand Street, Elizabeth, New Jersey. We have been receiving The Fantasy Fan for several months, and we think it is just the forum you want—that is, those of you who make weird fiction your hobby. The Fantasy Fan does not appear on the news stands, but Mr. Hornig can supply you with detailed information about it." (394)
3. Bloch's story "The Secret in the Tomb" (*WT,* May 1935) had been accepted in mid-July 1934, but "The Feast in the Abbey" (*WT,* January 1935), accepted later, turned out to be his first published *WT* story.

[125] [ANS; "Our Readers Say"]

[c. August 1934]

Read the new TFF yesterday with great interest and pleasure. The sketches by Barlow and Morse are very notable.[1] Let us hope that the success of volume one will be brilliantly duplicated in 1934–5.

Notes

1. *FF* (August 1934): Richard Ely Morse, "Ebony and Ash: A Tale of Three Wishes"; R. H. Barlow, "The Fall of Three Cities."

[126] ["Our Readers Say"]

[December 1934]

I am extremely glad to see the new TFF, which manages to hold much of interest despite the space I use up. As I said before, I surely appreciate the courtesy of the dedication.[1] I shall be anxious to see the coming Smith and Poe numbers.

Notes

1. The issue for October 1934 was dedicated to HPL. Besides another installment of "Supernatural Horror in Literature," it published "The Book," "Pursuit," "The Key," "Homecoming," "Beyond the Wall of Sleep," and a brief letter. The issues for November and December were dedicated each to Smith and Poe.

[127] [ANS]

[Postmarked Providence, R.I.,
13 December 1934]

Just recd the December issue. This [is] very welcome indeed & seems to have an especially interesting variety of contents. The stories by Bloch & Rimel are both extremely good, & Nelson's "Feast of the Centaurs" has a curious nightmare charm. Smith's "Passing of Aphrodite" is sheer music & poetry. A notably important contribution is Koenig's article on Hodgson[1]—which reminds me . . . will you return to me that addition to my article which contains mention of Hodgson? I have recently read "The Night Land" & may want to mention it.[2] I'll have it back in your hands very quickly. Glad to see the article on Price.[3] After all, the contents frame the important thing. Hope you won't have to depart from your monthly schedule. Best wishes—yours sincerely, HPL

Notes

1. *FF* (December 1934): Robert Bloch, "The Laughter of a Ghoul"; Duane W. Rimel, "The Sorcery of Aphlar"; Robert Nelson, "The Feast of the Centaurs"; Clark Ashton Smith, "The Passing of Aphrodite"; H. C. Koenig, "William Hope Hodgson."
2. *FF* ceased publication before "Supernatural Horror in Literature" with the note on

Hodgson could appear. A separate article, "The Weird Work of William Hope Hodgson," was published in *Phantagraph*.

3. Fred Anger and Louis C. Smith, "An Interview with E. Hoffman [*sic*] Price."

[128] [ALS]

[Postmarked Providence, R.I.,
18 December 1934]
Dec. 18

Dear C H:—

    Thanks for sending back the Hodgson note—it now covers the ground fairly well. Wish I could get hold of more of H's stuff—I haven't seen the short story—"Voice in the Night"[1] which Koenig mentions, & no doubt there are stray items which even K. hasn't seen. I can't conceive how H. managed to be so totally forgotten among weird fans. Koenig deserves the highest credit for rediscovering him, & I hope you'll add the little note to that effect which I've appended to my insert. It could go anywhere in the issue containing that passage. The late Henry S. Whitehead discovered "Carnacki"—but of course that is the very least of Hodgson's achievements. It is "The House on the Borderland" which gives the best impression. All the others have vitiating qualities which detract from the net impression. "The Night Land" contains some of the most powerful weird images & suggestions in all literature—yet is so insufferably drawn out, & has such an atrocious mock-archaic style (unlike any English ever used), that Derleth didn't even have the patience to finish it.

    I hope very much that the plan for making the F F self-supporting will work out successfully. I constantly urge all my correspondents to stand by the magazine—for, as I tell them, they'd miss it keenly enough if it were forced to suspend publication or adopt a curtailed schedule! It really fills a tremendous need as a general exchange bureau for ideas & information, & a medium of encouragement for the beginner. Though it has been going only a year & a quarter, I can scarcely imagine how we ever did without it! It certainly gratifies me to hear that my own enthusiasm has played a part in keeping it going.

    I can cordially endorse your sentiments regarding winter weather—for cold is the one enemy I simply cannot fight. When the mercury is under +20° the only thing I can do is stay in the house—all sorts of trouble & symptoms having resulted from my occasional exposure to lower temperatures. If I had the cash, I'd never be north of Latitude 30° from August to June—for actually, late June, July, & early August are the only time I'm ever thoroughly comfortable up here.

    Your vacation plans sound delightful indeed—although I couldn't bear to come back to these hellish temperatures after a brief, tantalising taste of decent weather. For me, that would be worse than sticking it out here. In

1930 I went to Charleston & came back in mid-May—& nearly froze to death when I struck Philadelphia. Since then I've vowed never to go south unless I can arrange to return not earlier than the middle of June.

However—every one to his tastes. And I share your enthusiasm for Greyhound travel. We seem to be in a small minority there, for most hate 'bus riding—but I find it fascinating, & very reminiscent of the old-time stage-coach. There is a sense of adventure & expectancy in riding over historic highways, & passing through the streets of unknown & picturesque towns, which one could not possibly get from train travel. Too bad you can't stop anywhere—you ought to see Chattanooga, Tenn., & ascend Lookout Mountain . . . & Richmond, Charleston, Savannah, & St. Augustine are ineffably fascinating. If I were you I'd cut out Palm Beach & Jacksonville in favour of *St. Augustine.* I don't give a hang for Miami, either—except the climate. If I got that far, I'd try to make the rest of the distance to Key West—which I visited in '31. On that occasion I desperately wanted to cover the remaining 90 miles by water to Havana, but was too broke. Hope you can weather the 6 nights on the coast! If you can really sleep to any extent, you'll probably be all right. I don't sleep very well on wheels, but have always stood the 2 nights between Providence & Charleston finely. That's the most I've ever done at a stretch.

Hope I shall see you in Providence next spring or summer—plenty of sights in these parts to keep you busy! Long has invited me to N.Y. for the post-Christmas period, & I may accept—since the subway system helps one to get about without exposure to the cold. In any case, I shall be envying you the Florida sun! ¶ Best wishes—H P L

Notes

1. "The Voice in the Night" (first published in *Blue Book Magazine,* November 1907) was reprinted in Hodgson's story collection *Men of the Deep Waters* (1914) and in Colin de la Mare's anthology *They Walk Again* (1931); but HPL apparently did not have access to these volumes.

[129] [ANS, JHL][1]

> [Postmarked Providence, R.I.,
> 26 January 1935]

Glad to see the new F F with its wealth of good verse.[2] I think the substitution of a straight editorial department for a column of readers' letters is a good idea—provided, of course, a chance remains for readers to express themselves on really important topics in the body of the magazine. ¶ Hope you had a pleasant trip to Florida—Koenig is there now, lucky devil! ¶ My visit to Long was very pleasant. Barlow was in town, & both Wandreis simultaneously blew in . . . Donald by boat from San Francisco, & Howard directly

from St. Paul. At a general meeting at Long's 15 were present—Barlow, the Wandreis, Leeds, Talman, Koenig, &c. On another occasion Samuel Loveman showed me his collection of about 400 Clark Ashton Smith drawings. The Wandreis have taken a flat in Greenwich Village—155 W. 10th St.—& we held several sessions there. On one occasion Koenig shewed Long, Barlow, & me over his Electrical Testing Laboratories—a fascinating place, full of strange-looking devices to measure the safety & durability of household electrical appliances. We did some book hunting, & both Barlow & I landed several bargains. Home Jany. 8, & busy dealing with accumulated work ever since. ¶ *Miss Elizabeth Toldridge,* whose *new* address is *The La Salle, Washington. D.C.,* says she has not recently recd. the F F. Didn't she have an 18-months' subscription? I've sent her Oct. & Dec. issues—the only ones I could spare. Better see how she stands on your books.
All good wishes—
HPL

Notes

1. *Front:* Brown University, Van Wickle Gates and University Hall, Providence. R.I.
2. *FF* (January 1935) was a "special weird poetry number." It contained R. O. P., "Dream"; HPL, "Homecoming"; HPL, "The Key"; Duane W. Rimel, "Late Revenge"; Robert E. Howard, "Babel"; Natalie H. Wooley, "The Alien"; Robert Nelson, "Fragment"; William Lumley, "The Elder Thing"; Lionel Dilbeck, "The Ghoul's Parade"; Richard F. Searight, "The Dead World"; Robert Nelson, "Trilogy of Death."

[130] [ANS][1]

[Postmarked Providence, R.I.,
14 March 1935]

F F's safely arrived. Glad you have such a voluminous market for back numbers. But the passing of the magazine is certainly a pity, for nothing close can take its place. F M[2] is, of course, too devoted to science fiction to take its place—but I'm glad it will handle some of the departments. Hope they can use the Rimel & [?Petaja articles] for which those clever linoleum blocks have been [?made]. No hurry about the return of anything. ¶ Hope to see you in August—I think you'll find considerable of interest around Providence—which, as I told you, is an ancient place like your own Elizabethtown. ¶ Had a call lately from a remarkably bright boy—Kenneth Sterling—who knows you & the science fiction circle. He showed me some excellent stories of his—which would go [?firmly] in any of the science-fiction magazines. I imagine he has quite a brilliant career ahead of him. ¶ Crawford of M T writes of some plans to take over the F F & continue it—but I'm afraid he could never swing it . . . judging from his schedule on his own paper. ¶ Expressions of regret for

the loss of the magazine come in from all quarters—Barlow, Rimel, &c. &c. I am keeping 2 complete files besides my personal one, & slowly letting any worthy recipients have the odd copies. ¶ All good wishes, & hoping to see you in August—[3]
HPL

Notes

1. *Front:* Arch Bridge, Roger Williams Park, Providence, R.I.
2. *Fantasy Magazine* (1934–37), edited by Julius Schwartz.
3. See letter 131. Hornig in fact visited HPL on 25 May (*Essential Solitude* 697).

[131] [ANS][1]

[Postmarked Providence, R.I.,
20 May 1935]

Delighted to see you Saturday, but sorry you can make it only a single day. Young Sterling will be on hand, too—making quite a fantasy convention of the occasion. Shall I meet you downtown anywhere, or do you know your way up the hill? Have you any hotel in mind? The best moderate-priced one I know is the Crown, where Sterling lives. (He, by the way, is returning to N.Y. next month.) In case you have occasion to telephone, my number is *Plantations 2044* (instrument in the name of my aunt, Mrs. Gamwell). To find #66, go to Market Square & take the steep street leading straight up the eastward hill—which is College. You'll note the immense brick court house—in Georgian architecture, with a tall belfry—on the right-hand corner. But if you'll drop me a line telling your hotel, I'll be glad to meet you there. Otherwise, I'll be waiting for you at #66. In any case I hope to see you at *10 a.m. Saturday, May 25.* Hope you'll get rested well after the nocturnal or semi-nocturnal trip. There'll be plenty of sights to keep you busy during the next 13½ hours! ¶ I may possibly be going down to De Land to visit Barlow again next month—after he returns home. All good wishes—& see you Saturday morning.
—HPL

Notes

1. *Front:* The Carrie Tower, Hope, Manning and University Halls at left, Brown University, Providence, R. I.

[132] [ANS][1]

[Postmarked Fredericksburg, Va.,
6 June 1935]

Greetings from the first stage of a trip which promises to be a winner! I thought of you as the stage-coach passed through ancient Elizabethtown around 11 o'clock last night (Wednesday the 5th). Left Providence at 10:55 a.m., & arrived 7:00 p.m. in New York. Had dinner & wrote some postcards. Then on the Washington coach. Ran into a thunderstorm, but it cleared by dawn—which came [word(s) crossed out] somewhere beyond [?Aberdeen], Md. Did not stop in Washington at all, but came right on to ancient Fredericksburg—where I have 7 hours for writing & sightseeing. ¶ This is a great old place—Genl. Washington's home town. A vast amount of 18th century material of the _____. Shall take a Richmond coach 3:15 p.m., & take a Charleston coach at Richmond at 5:00. In Charleston 5:25 a.m. Friday. Shall ___ & [stop] there—then Savannah Saturday & Jacksonville that night. De Land Sunday [morning]—meeting the Barlows around [noon]. [Expect] a ___ good __! ¶ Hope [you] __ a good [ride] home. May ___ for the Elizabethtown [train?]. And I trust I shall see you again when I re-pass through N.Y. ___ ¶ All good wishes
Yrs most cordially,
HPL

Notes

1. *Front:* "Mary Washington Home, Fredericksburg, Va."

[133] [ANS, JHL][1]

[Postmarked Charleston, S.C.]
June 7[, 1935]

Hit Charleston at 5:25 a.m. & rested at the Y. Now absorbing colonial antiquity & delectable heat, & getting a coat of sunburn on the Battery. What a place! I hate to leave so badly that I may cut out Savannah & spend the bulk of tomorrow here. You ought to see the churchyards—overhung with live-oak & Spanish moss. The climate peps me up immensely—I feel 50 years younger. Got some ice cream at the oldest apothecary shop in the U.S. founded 1784.
                    Regards—H P L

Notes

1. Old Powder Magazine, Charleston, S. C.

[134] [ANS, sold by Carl's Bookstore (Spring 1969)]

[location unknown
19 September 1935]

[135] [Christmas card, signed][1]

[Envelope postmarked Providence, R.I.,
19 December 1935.]

[May the joy that comes at CHRISTMASTIME linger with you all the Year.]
H.P.L.
—1935

Notes

1. *Front:* Mary Washington Home, Fredericksburg, Va.

[136] [ANS]

[Postmarked Providence, R.I.,
30 January 1936]

Greetings! I envy you the glimpse of New Orleans, which I haven't seen since 1932. I also envy Koenig his glimpse of Charleston—which he is seeing on his way back from an electrical convention at Boca Raton, Fla. ¶ Was in N.Y. over New Year's, & saw Long, the Wandreis, & [the rest?] of the old group. Since then have been [inundated?] with [work?] & largely under the weather—grippe or some damn thing. ¶ Sterling has been in Prov. both before & since my N.Y. trip, & we have had many interesting conversations. While in N.Y. I met Arthur J. Burks, Otto Binder,[1] & other fantasy authors for the first time—also saw the Hayden Planetarium. Was so crowded for time that I had to miss seeing several—including Koenig. Hope to see you next time. ¶ I trust your trip was uniformly pleasant. Which route did you take? Did you see old Natchez?

Best wishes
HPL

Notes

1. Weird writers Arthur J. Burks (1898–1974) and Otto Binder (1911–1974), the latter of whom published stories collaboratively with his brother Earl under the pseudonym "Eando Binder."

To John H. Birss

John Howard Birss (1907–1994) attended New York University, Harvard, and Columbia. Lovecraft wrote to his aunt Annie: "Stopped at Kirk's a while, & then over to Loveman's shop—where we met a very pleasant young fellow (a critic of some note) named John Birss, who knows of my tales & wants to read more of them. Next to Talman's office, where we had a pleasant chat" (*LFF* 959). Birss had written to Lovecraft at Loveman's suggestion, and, as he did with so many others, Lovecraft sent him a handwritten list of his stories to facilitate lending.

Birss was an instructor of English at Rutgers and later a professor of English and American Literature. He also was a noted Melville scholar. Birss published *Two Letters: Hart Crane* (for The Friends of Jack Birss, 1934; 50 copies), consisting of two letters by Crane to Samuel Loveman, and various other booklets. In later life, he assembled the greatest scholarly collection of Mary Baker Eddy material in private hands. In a letter to Dr. Irving A. Beck (1911–1998), transmitting the list of stories as presented here, Birss wrote: "Incidentally, my letters from Lovecraft—plus a short story he sent in typescript, signed—I gave to a student of mine at Rutgers in 1941, James Blish" (11 June, 1971; TLS, JHL). The whereabouts of the other letters and the story manuscript are unknown.

[137] [ALS]

66 College St.,
Providence, R.I.,
Jany. 19, 1934.

Dear Mr. Birss:—

In accordance with my promise of last month I am herewith sending a list of the thirty-odd tales of mine which exist in lendable form. If you'll check off those you have seen & return the list, I will begin at once to lend the desiderate residue—in small batches, or in any way you prefer, until ennui & disgust impel you to call a halt. I felt highly flattered at learning that you like the specimens you have seen, & hope you may not be too badly disappointed by the rest. I regret that our friend Loveman's favourite—"The Shunned House"—cannot be on the list, but a recent loss of my only copy (a set of wretched galley-proofs) in the mails has temporarily bereft me of the text. I hope, however, to get a set of the loose sheets of the al-ready-printed edition before long. It is scheduled to appear in the course of time as a separate brochure.[1]

　　With vast appreciation of the interest you have expressed,
　　　　　Believe me,
　　　　　　　Yrs most faithfully,
　　　　　　　　　H. P. Lovecraft

[On envelope:]
John H. Birss Esq.,
1401 University Ave.,
New York, N.Y.

[Enclosure]　　　[AMS, JHL]

　　　　　Tales by H P Lovecraft available for lending
　　　　　　　　[66 College St
　　　　　　　　Providence
　　　　　　　H. P. Lovecraft.][2]

The Tomb
Dagon
The Statement of Randolph Carter
The Terrible Old Man
The Cats of Ulthar
The Temple
Arthur Jermyn (pub. as "The White Ape")
The Picture in the House
The Nameless City
The Moon-Bog
The Outsider
The Other Gods
The Music of Erich Zann
The Lurking Fear
The Rats in the Walls
The Unnamable
The Festival　　　　　　　　　　　　　　　　[Written in
The Horror at Red Hook　　　　　　　　　　　Lovecraft's
He　　　　　　　　　　　　　　　　　　　　　hand.]
In the Vault
Cool Air
The Call of Cthulhu
Pickman's Model
The Silver Key

The Strange High House in the Mist
The Colour Out of Space
The Dunwich Horror
The Whisperer in Darkness
At the Mountains of Madness
The Shadow Over Innsmouth
The Dreams in the Witch House
The Thing on the Doorstep

Check off the ones you have seem & return list—I will then lend others, a few at a time or as desired.

Notes

1. *The Shunned House* was set in type and printed in 1928 by W. Paul Cook of the Recluse Press, but the sheets were not bound until R. H. Barlow bound a very small number in 1934–35 and again until Arkham House bound and distributed some sets in the 1960s.

2. The bracketed text comprises notations made by Birss.

To Anthony Pryor

[Two autograph picture postcards signed to Anthony Pryor in Ozone Park, N.Y. were sold by Sotheby's in 2006.]

To Lloyd Arthur Eshbach

Lloyd Arthur Eshbach (1910–2003) was a science fiction writer and publisher from Reading, Pa. Since 1931, Eshbach had published several stories in the science fiction pulps, and he was also associate editor of *Marvel Tales*. In early 1935 he began a general magazine called *The Galleon: A Journal of Literary Excellence* (November 1934–September/October 1935) and asked Lovecraft to contribute. Lovecraft sent "The Quest of Iranon" and two sonnets from *Fungi from Yuggoth*, but only "Background" (May–June 1935) and the story (July–August 1935) were published before the magazine changed focus and became a regional Pennsylvania magazine. Accordingly, Eshbach returned "Harbour Whistles," which he had also accepted. After World War II Eshbach successively founded two small presses in the fantasy field, Fantasy Press and Polaris Press. He also published a collection of his science fiction stories (*The Tyrant of Time*, 1955) and an anthology of essays on science fiction writing (*Of Worlds Beyond*, 1964).

[138] [AHT]

De Land, Fla.
May 13, 1934

Dear Mr. Eshbach:—

[. . .] Glad you have found enjoyment & interest in some of my yarns. Of my stuff, I like the "Colour Out of Space" best & "Erich Zann" next; but am dissatisfied with virtually all my yarns. I fail somehow to attain the level of Blackwood & Machen, & am constantly analysing & experimenting with a view to the possible amendment of my defects. No—all propositions for the issuance of my tales in book form have so far fallen through. . . . . With all good wishes for you, Yrs most cordially & sincerely, H. P. Lovecraft

[139] [ALS]

66 College St.,
Providence, R.I.,
March 19, 1935.

Dear Mr. Eshbach:—

Let me thank you most heartily for the issue of *The Galleon* which has just reached me! It is not flattery but simple fact when I say that I have never seen a magazine of more tasteful & appealing aspect. And the contributions are fully commensurate. The verse is of a high standard &

cleverly varied, while the prose has that authentic closeness to the soil so appropriate in brief compositions. Your "Nocturne" has a quiet beauty which grows on the reader, & "Above the Canal" has a curiously haunting potency. As a lifelong antiquarian I delighted in the exquisite etching of Old Trinity & its accompanying description. Mr. Luft is certainly a craftsman of enviable power.[1]

Regarding the whole enterprise—& the spirit & energy behind it—I can scarcely find words strong enough for the praise I would like to give! Such exercise & encouragement of literary expression for its own sake—free from the commercial considerations which clog & debase the ordinary channels—seems to me altogether admirable in the highest degree. I certainly hope it will succeed in establishing itself on a permanent basis—a not unreasonable hope in view of the survival of many kindred enterprises.

Your suggestion that I contribute something is indeed flattering, & I fervently wish I had something suited to the *Galleon's* requirements. If weird material of substantial length were acceptable, I would promptly inundate you—but alas! in all my existence I have never written a story which was *not* weird! As for verse—my earlier stuff *was* non-weird, but it is so poor that it would never make the *Galleon* standard. More recent specimens (of which there are not many) *are* weird—or at least, on the borderline of weirdness. Possibly you've seen some in *Weird Tales* or *Driftwind*. The only thing I can think of which would be acceptable to you is something already in *local* print. Would you object to a piece of verse which appeared in the *Providence Journal* 5 years ago? If not, I might shoot along a kind of pseudo-sonnet which (as my junk goes) is perhaps not as bad as it might be.

In future scribbling I shall certainly keep *The Galleon* in mind—sending in anything which may seem to fall within your requirements. Lately, however, I have written less than usual—both through a lack of time & energy, & through a growing distrust of the quality of my own products. There will, however, undoubtedly be future spurts of production & experimentation.

Derleth mentioned hearing from you, & I feel sure he can supply excellent & appropriate material. Other possible sources of good material are the following:

> Frank B. Long, Jr., 230 W. 97th St., New York, N.Y.
> Clark Ashton Smith, Box 385, Auburn, California.
> Donald Wandrei, 155 W. 10th St., New York, N.Y.
> Henry G. Weiss, 125c, Route 1, Tucson, Ariz.
> Robert E. Howard, L.B. 313, Cross Plains, Texas.
> Mrs. Natalie H. Wooley, 20 N. Early St., Rosedale, Kansas.
> Carl F. Strauch, 812 Washington St., Allentown, Pa.
> Richard E. Morse, 115 B St., S.E., Washington, D. C.
> Samuel Loveman, 17 Middagh St., Brooklyn, N.Y.
> Richard A. Thomas, Jr., 1094 N. Parkway, Memphis, Tenn.
> Maurice W. Moe, 1034 N. 23d St., Milwaukee, Wis.

———

At any rate, I think that you may never lack a plenitude of good material.

Again expressing my gratitude both for the copy of the magazine & for the compliment of your invitation, I remain

Yrs most cordially,

H. P. Lovecraft

Notes

1. *Galleon* 1, No. 3 (March 1935) contained the etching "Old Trinity" (facing p. ii) by "Mr. Luft"; "Above the Canal" (pp. 26–27) by Wm. J. Meter; and "Nocturne" (p. 46) by Eshbach.

[140] [ALS]

April 3, 1935

Dear Mr. Eshbach:—

I am very glad to hear more of *The Galleon's* requirements, & to learn that I am not as definitively barred out as I had thought. Most of the qualitatively ambitious magazines nowadays have a prejudice against the weird, & it is refreshing to encounter one exempt from that idiosyncrasy. Yes—I have written plenty of non-weird stuff, but it is not fiction & it is not short. Largely argumentative material in various aesthetic, scientific, historical, & philosophical fields, & narratives connected with antiquarian travel. Virtually none of this is designed for publication. Of non-weird verse I wrote floods in the old days—but began to see how generally lousy it was about a decade ago, & cut off short. No—I don't think it's modesty which makes me dissatisfied with my stuff nowadays. Rather is it an increased realism & a raising of my critical standard. I see defects in my attempts which I did not see ten or even five years ago.

Glad Derleth has supplied something good.[1] To that list of names I sent, another really ought to be added—*Miss Elizabeth Toldridge, The La Salle, Washington, D.C.* This is an old lady of great poetic accomplishment, some of whose wistful, delicate lyrics you may have encountered in the various poetry magazines. Another possible verse contributor whom I may have failed to list is *Mrs. E. G. Lee, 5 Linden Ave., Greenwood, Mass.*[2]

Now about my stuff—I can't conceive of the *Journal's* demanding credit for something printed in their literary page five years or so ago, hence don't see why you couldn't use my old lines "Background" just as if they were unpublished. I enclose them. Am also sending "Harbour Whistles"—which is, so far as I can recall, unpublished. If it has ever appeared, it can have been only in an *amateur* paper.[3] I don't keep much track of the publication of my junk, hence cannot always be sure of the past use of this or that item. However, I did note on one MS. of 35 different verses just where each (if printed) appeared. This is now with *Fantasy Magazine*, but when I get it back I can straighten things out & send one or two things which I *know* have never previously seen type.

As for prose—I run so to *length* nowadays that I fear I'm a hopeless case . . . unless, indeed, my present course of experimentation produces some diminutive specimens. In carefully going over my files, I find only *one* unpublished story (if you call it that) within the 3000-word limit—but here it is . . . . to be returned if it doesn't make the grade. This thing—"The Quest of Iranon"—was written 14 years ago, when I was almost slavishly under the Dunsany influence. Today it sounds mawkish to me—although those who saw the MS. back in '21 seemed to like it. It has very little kinship to my present attempts, & I can offer it as objectively (& regard its rejection as detachedly) as if it were the product of another person. It has, incidentally, never been published in any form.

I have showed the copy of *The Galleon* to several persons of discrimination, & each has echoed my own admiring opinion. Most sincerely do I wish it a long & successful existence. ¶ Hoping that the enclosed efforts may not seem too disappointing—I remain

Yrs most cordially,
H. P. Lovecraft

[Enclosure: "Harbour Whistles."]

Notes

1. "Mass at Eight" (May–June 1935).
2. Marion E. Lee (c. 1882–1969), author of *Flame and Songs and Other Poems* ([Greenwood, MA: Privately printed by Will Bates Grant, 1935]). HPL discusses the brochure in "Report of the Bureau of Critics" (March 1935; *CE* 1.389).
3. It had, in fact, been published twice previously, in amateur journals, although one was issued in New Zealand.

[141] [ALS]

66 College St.,
Providence, R. I.
April 16, 1935.

Dear Mr. Eshbach:—

I am surely gratified to hear that you found my fantasy & two verses worthy of acceptance for The Galleon, & shall be tempted to venture other items for your consideration later on. Let us hope that the readers may not curse your decision! Meanwhile I trust that some good material has come from some of the others I have mentioned. Clark Ashton Smith and Samuel Loveman are about at the top of the list. Smith can furnish any amount of original verse—both in English & in French—to say nothing of some splendid translations from Baudelaire. One of the other poets I listed—Mrs. E. G. Lee,

5 Linden Ave., Greenwood, Mass.—says she wishes she could have a sample copy of The Galleon in order to study your especial wishes & needs.

Regarding the subscription from Brown University—I regret to admit that I had nothing to do with securing it . . . . although, as coincidence would have it, I live in a house owned by the college, & situated next door to the marble John Hay Library of that institution! This library contains the famous Harris Collection of American Poetry—greatest of its kind in the world—& of that collection The Galleon is likely to form a part by virtue of its ample poetic contents. Virtually all of the small high-quality magazines are kept in complete files—things like Driftwind, Kaleidograph,[1] &c. This collection is visited from all over the world by scholars exploring arcane caverns of American poetic literature, & is rich in rare items like the work of Thomas Holley Chivers.[2] Its curator—Prof S. Foster Damon[3]—is the author of Chivers' only biography . . . & an important poet in his own right. Poetry, indeed is quite an activity at the college. Annual series of poetry readings by figures as important as Archibald MacLeish, T. S. Eliot, & Stephen Vincent Benét are regularly given, & a group of professors, alumni, & friends edit the magazine Smoke[4]—whose present editor is Mrs. Susanna Valentine Mitchell Gamwell[5]—granddaughter of Dr. S. Weir Mitchell[6] of Philadelphia. Another of the Smoke group is the poet & novelist David Cornel de Jong.[7] So—all told—I fancy The Galleon will be in appreciated hands as it climbs the steep hill to our loftily perched citadel of learning!

[*balance (closing) not seen*]

Notes

1. *Driftwind* (1926–48?), edited and published by Walter J. Coates (1926–41), W. Paul Cook (1941–48), and Arthur Murphy (1948–?). *The Kaleidograph: A National Magazine of Poetry* (1929–59 [as *The Kaleidoscope*, 1929–May 1932]), edited and published by Whitney Montgomery and Vaida Stewart Montgomery. See Vaida Stewart Montgomery, *A Century with Texas Poets and Poetry* (Dallas, TX: Kaleidograph, 1934).

2. Thomas Holley Chivers (1809–1858), poet and physician. Chivers wrote a memoir of Poe that was published posthumously in 1952.

3. S[amuel] Foster Damon (1893–1971), professor of English (1927–71) at Brown, curator of the Harris Collection at JHL, and author of *Thomas Holley Chivers, Friend of Poe* (New York, 1930). Damon later oversaw the setting up of JHL's Lovecraft Collection.

4. *Smoke* (1931–37), edited by Winfield Scott, R. Wade Vliet, and W. H. Gerry. It does not appear that Gamwell was involved in the editing of the magazine.

5. Susanna Valentine Mitchell Gamwell (1896–1979), American poet, playwright, and novelist.

6. S[ilas] Weir Mitchell (1829–1914), American physician and author.

7. David Cornel De Jong (1905–1967), American novelist and poet best known for the novel *Benefit Street* (1938), set in Providence.

To George W. Macauley

George W[illiam] Macauley (1885–1969) was an amateur journalist of Grand Rapids, Mich., editor of the *O-Wash-Ta-Nong*,
which published several items by Lovecraft posthumously. At
the sixty-first annual meeting of NAPA, held at Grand Rapids,
MI, 2–4 July 1936, Macauley, as host of the convention, dedicated the "Presidents' Field" at Pine Springs. Pine trees were
planted in honor of each president of the NAPA (including
Lovecraft) since 1876, spelling out the letters "NAPA."

[142] [ALS]

66 College St.,
Providence, R.I.,
August 12, 1934.

My dear Macauley:—

Yours of the 31st—which I would have acknowledged
sooner but for a devastating pressure of various tasks—was surely a welcome
breath from other days! It must surely be 16 or 17 years since the letters were
whizzing back & forth between Grand Rapids & Providence—though in many
ways, I can scarcely realise that any time has elapsed.[1] Those early days of my
amateur affiliation seem only a moment ago—yet what a gulf of aeons really
stretches between! A world changed—systems of values shifted—emperors fall-
en & kingdoms risen—the age of traditional economics tottering to its close—a
generation then unborn grown to maturity—old things forgotten & strange
things sprung into being . . . . . Indeed, the gap is not merely one of 20 years (a
vast enough space at best), but of whatever cycles or kalpas separate two worlds!
And, yet, as I said before, the events of two decades ago in amateurdom's small,
unconvulsed world still seem removed by only a moment. Going to an old cabi-
net which has never, despite many moves, been unpacked or rearranged since
the old days, I found at once (as if I had placed it there but yesterday) the manuscript of your medieval tale "When Swords Were Bold", which (you'll perhaps
recall) I touched up a bit & meant to publish or place sooner or later. Alas for
my negligence! It seemed very fresh to me, & only when I observed the yellowed
paper & the long-vanished twists of my 1915 handwriting could I fully appreciate the abyss of years separating its writing & its exhumation. Curious how my
script has changed—retaining only its basic characteristic of discouraging illegi-
bility! I think I'll enclose the story for your perusal (if you can peruse such writing!), since it cannot but give you a feeling of picturesque linkage with the past.
Really—we ought to get it published somehow!

I am indeed interested to hear of the rise of a new Macauley generation.[2] Robie's name attracted my attention on the membership lists some time ago, & I wondered whether he were your son or nephew. I had heard of your marriage,[3] but could scarcely realise that enough time had elapsed to bring a child of yours to the active amateur age. Fancy a second generation taking over the institution, when only a moment ago the previous generation was itself in the heyday of enthusiastic youth, with the newcomers not even existing! Only with an effort can I grasp the fact that the present leaders are persons who did not exist when I sent in my application blank & penned my first critical reports in those remote, misty & half-fabulous days of 1914. Well— I'm [. . .] Macauley is still [. . .] & hope that Charleston [. . .] of Robie. *The Pod*[_ . . .] clever, & it [?would . . .] is naturally [?gra_ . . .] time sort. The convention—which I'm sorry I could not attend—must have been a very pleasant event, both for you & for your heir; in your case, a reminder of old times, in his case a gateway to new & alluring vistas. It seems to have regenerated enthusiasm in more than one bosom [. . .] you doubtless [. . .] after a quiescence [. . .] for my part, have never actually dropped out; though my share in the work has subtly changed from that of a full-fledged participant to that of a quasi-advisory elder. When the old [. . .] the section to which I belonged— went into abeyance in 1927, my activity reached its nadir . . . . . being [kindled?] afresh in the National by the Boston convention of 1930, when the present renaissance was started by a happy alliance of old-timers & young blood. The youngsters are certainly doing splendidly nowadays—your fellow Michigander Bradley[4] being about the most promising of the lot now in the saddle. He has very wisely seen the need of a qualitative as well as quantitative renaissance & is working for literature of a radically better grade. A kid named Adams[5] in Oklahoma also seems to be strong on quality, if what he says of his coming paper be correct.

Your plan for a pine-grove memorial to the presidents of the National strikes me as unique & admirable, & I certainly hope that nothing may interfere with its successful maturing. The location, arrangement, & markers all seem ideally appropriate; & in time the place ought to become a leading shrine for devotees of amateurdom. Needless to say, I feel superlatively flattered by your suggestion that I write some verses for the spot. I really fear that my creaking couplets are not good enough for so important a purpose— since the knowledge & taste of later years have taught me how stilted & artificial those early effusions of mine actually were. My verse has always had more rhetoric than poetry in it, & nowadays I write practically nothing in metre. The more I know about poetry, the more strongly do I realise that I am not a poet myself. However, I suppose writers of verse to order are not easy to find—so if no better candidate presents himself, I'll be delighted to do what I can in the matter. Let me have all the suggestions you can think of— especially as to the desired length. Anything pertaining to the appearance, history, legends, Indian background, & general folklore of the spot would certainly be a help—so that all pictures, stories, &c. would be exceedingly welcome. Of course, it isn't likely that one would want to weave any long descriptions or tales into a brief memorial verse; but the more the writer knows of the aspect & background of the place, the more aptly & effectively he can shape whatever he does include in his lines. I assume there would be an especial hurry about the completion of the verse. Such a thing ought not to be forced or hurried, but ought to spring spontaneously out of a leisurely consideration of the occasion & the material. Again let me express my appreciation of your choice of a bard—an honour I wish I more thoroughly deserved. The whole memorial project ought to prove exceedingly popular in amateurdom—as you will doubtless discover when you publicly announce it. It will finely supplement the recent housing of the Fossil Library as a symbol of the permanent value & dignity of amateur journalism.[6]

It is easy to understand how the pressure of outside affairs must have hampered your amateur activity, but I hope that during the coming years you can find a way to return to the familiar field—at least to a slight degree. I'd surely hate to be without any remaining link with the good old institution—even though that link might be very slight.

As I general thing, I don't believe my tastes & methods have changed very much *in essence* since the old days, although wider reading & increased observation have altered many of the details. When I re-read some of my critical articles & editorials of the 1914–16 period I have to smile at their naivete, limited vision, & ill-founded dogmatism—yet the major motivating forces remain about the same. I am still a natural-born antiquarian, revelling in the scenes & symbols of the past, & still a devotee of the fantastic & macabre. Since 1917 I have been devoting more & more time to spectral fiction of the Poe, Machen, & Blackwood type—this forming my only main product today. I have had tales in several magazines—especially *Weird Tales*—& several of these have been reprinted in anthologies. I have also done a good deal of the hateful work of professional revision.

My health is infinitely better than it was in the 1914–16 period, so that I am able to be away from home more. This has caused me to indulge my antiquarianism through visits to ancient places all along the Atlantic & Gulf coasts—observing different kinds of colonial architecture & traditional scenery from Quebec & Montreal on the north to Key West & New Orleans in the south. Through a fortunate chance I now reside (with an aunt who is my only remaining near relative) in a Georgian house 130 years old—at the rear of a quaint, village-like court on the crest of Providence's steep hill in the university district. Most of my travelling is toward the South, on account of the need of my constitution for warm climates. I spent the past spring in De Land, Florida, as guest of R.H. Barlow (last year's N.A.P.A. story laureate), incidentally stopping in such ancient places as St. Augustine, Savannah,

Charleston, Richmond, Washington, & Philadelphia en route. I enclose a few views illuminating this expedition.

Just had an enjoyable visit from James F. Morton. We took in most of the local sights, & also went to old Newport—a place as quaint as Charleston in its way. On Aug. 23 I am going to Wollaston to visit Edward H. Cole for a few days—& W. Paul Cook (now in Vermont) will probably be present. That will make quite an amateur convention!

Well—again let me say how glad I was to hear from you, & how much I appreciate your present project.

With every good wish—yrs most cordially & sincerely—HPL

P.S. Those finely copied & framed verses to my late uncle Dr. Clark,[7] which you so generously prepared back in 1915, have always hung in a place of honour on my walls. They now hang in my study above the bookcase containing Dr. Clark's scrapbooks of original articles.

Notes

1. This sentiment is quite similar to that of the profound shift in time as expressed in "The Shadow out of Time," written later in the year; so is the comment about HPL viewing his own handwriting of years past.

2. HPL discusses Macauley's son Robie Mayhew Macauley (1919–1995), who became a well-known novelist, critic, and editor (*Kenyon Review, Playboy*, and Houghton Mifflin). In his earlier years Robie was involved in amateur journalism. Macauley had another son, C[harles] Cameron Macauley (1923–2007), who became a prize-winning photographer and filmmaker.

3. Macauley married Emma Anne Hobart (1886–1979) in 1918 in Grand Rapids, MI.

4. Chester P. Bradley (1917–1983) of South Lyon, MI, Official Editor of the NAPA (1934–35) and editor of the *Perspective Review*.

5. John D. Adams of Frederick, OK.

6. The Library of Amateur Journalism, also known as the Edwin Hadley Smith Collection, was first housed at the Benjamin Franklin Institute in Philadelphia on 6 April 1935. The collection moved several times since, and is now in the Special Collections of the University of Wisconsin–Madison. Macauley's project was to plant a memorial field honoring former NAPA presidents. See *National Amateur Press Association: The First Hundred Years* (ed. by Harold Segal): "Presidents' Field, a six-acre plot on the grounds of George W. Macauley, publisher of O-Wash-Ta-Nong near Grand Rapids, Michigan, was dedicated in 1936. The pine trees were arranged to form the letters NAPA and each was marked with the name of the president whom it honored. Willard O. Wylie, the oldest living ex-president at that time (elected in 1883), made the dedication speech, bringing tears to many by his tributes, uttered in the reverent stillness, broken only by an occasional rustle of a gentle summer wind." HPL had been asked to provide suitable verses for the occasion, but it appears he did not.

7. HPL is referring to his tribute "An Elegy on Franklin Chase Clark, M.D."

[143] "Extracts from H. P. Lovecraft's Letters to G. W. Macauley"

To that sterling, hard-working, old-time amateur journalist, Edward F. Daas, goes the honor of having introduced Howard Phillips Lovecraft to our hobby. In March, 1914, "Eddie" as he was affectionately known to friends discovered Lovecraft's name and that of John Russell appearing in a magazine controversy. Eddie wrote both writers obtaining Lovecraft as a member of the UAPA and over a year later Russell joined.

Lovecraft later joined the National Amateur Press Association as well and became President, first of the United and later of the National.

Much has been written by better pens than mine of the brightness of Lovecraft's star in our miniature world of letters but I will state here that he was the greatest amateur of the period of my connection with amateur journalism, i.e., from 1911 to the present. In some ways Lovecraft ranked as the greatest amateur of all time and has been appropriately called "The Sage of Providence" by Maurice Moe.[1]

Referring to my files of letters received from amateurs over a period of some years I find the first letter from Lovecraft dated October 23rd, 1914. A contrast my eyes quickly register is much better legibility of these letters than in the letters of later years.

An October letter states, "I am a rank outsider in amateur journalism, having joined the United only six months ago, so of course I do not know whether or not it is the custom for the recruit committee each year to perpetuate its fame in print. . . . Of all branches of the Association our committee affords the least opportunity for enjoyment . . . obliged to write scores of letters to persons of whom we never heard before and will never hear of again. Only about a tenth of those to whom we write have the ordinary manners to answer our letters, and only about a third of them join the association. . . . We leave no record of our toilsome activities and are not able in our regular work to be connected with literary work at all." Ah, but were it only possible that Lovecraft could have known that his letter, written back there 24 years ago, would lend much to the inspiration which worked out the National's Publicity Letter which is a reality today!

Lovecraft's ability had gained quick recognizance with Eddie Daas and he was put at work on "the thankless task of the 'recruiting sergeant'" at which he turned in a very creditable record. Having had some "recruiting sergeant" work myself I could sympathize with Lovecraft and I have always deplored the lack of suitable literature with which to put over the story of Amateur Journalism to prospects.

In this same letter Lovecraft enclosed a newspaper clipping of the monthly department he conducted as an amateur astronomer in the *Providence Evening News* which has the usual Lovecraft thoroughness and reader interest. This subject recalls a question I later put to Lovecraft. One clear, cool August evening I was called from the house by my father, who has always been interested in the sky, to witness the most unusual sight it has ever been my fortune to gaze at in the heavens.

Almost directly over head was an arch of light brighter and more regular than the Milky Way but not as clear cut as a bright rainbow. The band of light was slightly north of direct west, arching, it seemed, south of a direct east position. There was a slight resemblance of northern lights but yet seemingly so different when, if they were such, one found them in his own back yard. I had hopes our local paper would mention and explain the phenomenon but this not occurring I sent a more complete description of the occurrence to Lovecraft and upon his inability to give a proper explanation the belief I had seen a rare sight began also to blend into the belief I had seen the unknown. Then, some two or three years later, I happened to see a torn copy of *The Scientific American* lying in some rubbish. Having some time on my hands I picked up the few readable pages left and in a moment I had spotted a letter from a reader asking for an answer to almost the identical phenomenon question which was still unanswered in my mind. The answer given by *The Scientific American* was covered in the term "detached Aurora" although the answer was lengthy in detail.

The great war then raging was much a subject of our letters. Lovecraft's letters often touched on it and from this passage one can gain much of his attitude. "Since you are taking such an interest in the European War, the enclosed verses of mine may interest you. I am the grandson of a true-born Englishman and feel very English myself, so that I fear my treatment of this subject is not sufficiently impartial for publication in America . . . an acquaintance thinks he can get these verses published in an English magazine."

In homage to a fellow poet I read: "As to Loveman, I am amazed. I am not given to extravagant expression as a general thing, and as a critic, have been called rather cold, but that man's poetry is marvelous. . . . He is completely dissociated from the sordid influence of the modern school, and his work is a page torn out of the literature of Queen Elizabeth's reign. . . . While my verses are mere mechanical imitations of the Queen Anne poets, Loveman's are fairly alive with the whole glorious spirit of the Renaissance. There is nothing in his technique that would lead one to think his work of a later date than 1600 or 1615. I have only read a little of what you have sent me, and by the time I am through I shall doubtless be even more of an admirer.

"His 'Ianthe Brooke' story is an effective bit of psychology, all apart from its merit as a 'fake'. It seems as though the critics could have seen that this was far above the ability of a half-grown girl."[2]

This last passage calls to mind Loveman's clever literary ambush of one National Critic who had remarked that a writer, even talented, who was so immersed in an outmoded literary age as was Loveman, could not do modern writing.

Loveman, under the nom de plume of "Ianthe Brooke," wrote a story for *The Quaker* which quickly won appeal from the same critic and many a laugh at the critic's expense when the ruse became known.

From another letter comes this passage, "It is strange how few old friends an amateur can persuade to enter his association. There are many young men, now from 21 to 26 years of age, whom I have known intimately since early childhood, yet who for some reason or other lack interest in amateur journalism. One of them, the son of the Chief Justice of our Superior Court, named Tanner,[3] is a very thorough student, a graduate of Brown University, but will not acknowledge the merit of the associations, since *they are so easy to enter.* He argues that their tone cannot be very dignified nor conservative since anyone can join without difficulty. In fact, this is the principal thing to which most seem to object, the promiscuousness of membership and the freedom that is extended to all."

Lovecraft had not, at this period, yet grasped the precept that "Amateur Journalists are born not made" and he proceeded, at this period, to teach "an evening school club which has become affiliated with the United" of "Irish workmen from the other side of the city."[4] But he refers enthusiastically to his one friend-recruit Chester Munroe,[5] hoping he "will become sufficiently interested to write some other Providence friends and try to arouse some amateur activity."

At another point in this same letter interesting light is thrown on cost of amateur papers of that day as Lovecraft writes, "Irving Sinclair must have been an enthusiastic amateur indeed to issue a $40.00 edition. Daas, though, says that one issue of Campbell's *Scotchman* cost $80.00![6] I dare say that the latter closely approaches the limit of size and quality in amateur journalism."

To contrast these costs with Bradofsky's *Californian* which I understand runs in cost over $100.00 per issue. Robie's[7] *Pine Needles* Clan issue cost 80 cents per copy or, if it had the usual circulation, the cost would have been over $300.00, while the last *O-Wash-Ta-Nong* cost about $40.00 not including the press work. Aside from *The Monadnock*[8] the cost of present day amateur journals ranks higher as to costs than those of yesteryear.

An extract from a February letter of 1915 protests, at my urging of Lovecraft to turn his pen from poetry to story writing, with these words, "I am such a poor fiction writer that after all I may defer the story and use verse instead."

About this time I had occasion to send Lovecraft a long story I had written asking for his criticisms. On receipt of the lengthy and elaborated [*sic*] criticisms I knew at once that he, the critic, should have written my story. I persisted in my belief that Lovecraft would find himself in the field of story writing which he eventually did but not in the type of story to interest me. Yet I was pleased to believe I had encouraged Lovecraft to venture into story writing where many thousands have, and still are, enjoying the tales from his pen.

Referring to a letter in which I had written of my disgust with ambiguous and archaic English spelling believing reforms would aid my own wretched spelling of words, Lovecraft remarks "I note your remarks on spelling reform. You ask if the English language is perfect enough to warrant the suppression of all change. I answer that it is no more perfect than any other human institution, [yet] it gained such a polish and stability in the 18th century that we ought to beware of tampering with it. . . . The new reforms are not truly progressive; they are rather steps backward, for their radical nature would plunge English again into the same old chaos from which Dr. Johnson rescued it."

On the fifth page of this letter I quote "I wish that I could write fiction, but it seems almost an impossibility." Again I violently disagreed.

So rich in interest are these letters I regret now that I did not plan to print them in full for the mere mention of a topic brought forth a scholarly discourse of interesting views. The letter before me gives a view of the World War, then at half tide, in respect to Lovecraft's feeling towards Germany. "I see that you do not approve of my pan-Teutonic ideas and in view of the horrors of the present war I can hardly blame you for differing, yet I am convinced that any racial fusion which would affect the purity of the Teutonic stock would be a disastrous thing for the future of the world." And of the Russian he shows that truly English attitude towards the Slavs in these words, "The Slav is unfit to sustain a high type of culture. . . . As Napoleon truly said, 'grattez le Russe, vous trouverez le Cosaque.'[9] I, for one, have no wish to live under a Slavo-Oriental despotism. . . ."

I approached Lovecraft on the subject of publishing a paper with him, he answering, "I should be very pleased to issue a paper with you this spring, perhaps using the long short story 'The Alchemist'. . . . I am no artist in fiction, but will say that I have seen worse in the amateur press."

In answer to my view of amateur journalism fellowship he writes, "Your sentiments regarding the essential unity of amateur journalism are highly commendable" and in [*sic*] the same letter contained the declaration "I am the most ardent of all advocates of total abstinence." While Lovecraft's political views changed from the straight laced conservative to what he himself viewed as broad liberalism, I do not know if his view on alcohol abstinence also changed but I do like to believe it did not. For myself I agreed completely with his views on this subject then and have never seen reason to change those views.

In a later letter I quote this passage wherein Lovecraft views the hobby as purely a training school idea as he says, "I believe that the United is destined eventually to develop into more than a mere press association, and become a means of systematic literary instruction for ambitious aspirants." I could not agree with this view believing it would completely divorce itself from amateur journalism and some of the features would be missed.

Lovecraft practiced what he preached, however, and many an aspirant received a helping hand from him as it may be noted from this quotation "I should much like to see your poetical attempts. . . . Never mind how crude . . . send them along! I am always looking for the sense beneath the metre. The latter is very easily re-cast. For instance—one stanza I received some time ago went as follows, though supposedly in 7-syllable trochaic verse:

> "'Ah, now, Spirit, thou hast left me!
> Farewell, fair creature, it were better so;
> Thou are [*sic*] far too frail a being
> The chills of night to know.'"

I immediately made it metrical, as follows:

> "'Ah, sweet Spirit, thou hast left!
> Farewell, now, 'tis better so;
> Thou art far too frail a thing
> Chills of cruel night to know.'"

The same letter had a newspaper clipping of an eulogy on Dr. F. C. Clark, "whose [passing] has deprived the world of [a] sincere and valuable, even though not widely acclaimed, scholar and worker. Dr. Clark . . . earnest student of literature and science, graduate of Brown (A.M.), M.D. of College of Physicians and Surgeons . . . also took special courses at Harvard under Oliver Wendell Holmes.

"His influence on me from childhood upward was very strong and any precision which my English may possess is due largely to his training. His retiring nature kept him from wider fame. . . . He is one who will not easily be replaced."

As the eulogy here mentioned was never published in an amateur journal I take pleasure in reprinting it in this issue.[10] Some passages on amateur politics I must pass by because even now they might open wounds but I must say here that Lovecraft never stooped to malice and pretence he liked or disliked from honest opinion [*sic*]. As Shakespeare said, "Mine honor is my life; both grow in one."[11] So I like to remember Lovecraft.

The next letter dated August 1st and amusingly addressed to Geo. Washington Macauley, Esq. in imitation of General Washington's handwriting comes with news of illness and "enormous amount of criticism and correspondence has accumulated. I have had to prepare a stupendous report for the September *United* and have written a great deal of verse for various individuals who have requested it. For instance, I have just mailed Daas a 52-line poem on his 'Scribblers Club'.[12] . . . But do not think I have forgotten any individual critical duties. . . . [it is] 4 a.m. and I cannot use the machine for fear of waking my mother whose room is just across the hall . . . . At present I have too severe a headache to sleep."

Due to the rather confused state of my old letter files and pressure of other matter just at this time I find that I am unable to continue this delightful browsing through Lovecraft's letters. When my amateur collection is sorted and housed in new files I will run across material for later articles.[13]

From my recollections our correspondence dropped to cards on Christmas after the 1920, or so, period and it was not until Robie started his amateur publishing career in 1932, did the flow of epistles from Providence begin once more. Lovecraft's penmanship had taken on a cramped style, the writing was much smaller and the letters so much longer I knew changes had come with the years but little did I realize how great until I found the Conservative of 1913 to 1920 a Liberal of nearly complete New Deal thought.

I like to remember my correspondence with Howard Phillips Lovecraft with these words of La Fontaine's, "Friendship is the shadow of the evening, which strengthens with the setting sun of life." He was, I feel, one silent yet most understanding friend whom it was my lot to never meet.

Notes

1. See Maurice W. Moe, "Howard Phillips Lovecraft: The Sage of Providence," *O-Wash-Ta-Nong* [2, No. 2] [1937]: [3].
2. Samuel Loveman, "A Ruined Paradise," *Quaker* 3, No. 2 (January 1910): [13]–16. In *Out of the Immortal Night* (2021).
3. Willard Brooks Tanner (1858–1946), Associate Justice, Superior Court of Rhode Island. His son Kenneth Tanner (1890–1979), was HPL's boyhood friend. Kenneth graduated from Brown in 1912, received an LL.B. from Harvard (1918), and became assistant trust officer of the Rhode Island Hospital Trust Co. (1926f.).
4. The Providence Amateur Press Club, which produced two issues of the *Providence Amateur* (June 1915 and February 1916) before disbanding.
5. Chester Pierce Munroe (1889–1943), who was briefly a member of the UAPA. Chester and his brother, Harold Bateman Munroe (1891–1966), were among HPL's closest boyhood friends.
6. Irving MacDonald Sinclair edited an amateur journal, *Cartoons* (c. 1905–10). The *Scotchman* was edited by Paul J. Campbell, a correspondent of HPL.
7. Robie Macauley issued *Pine Needles* in at least 10 issues in 1938.
8. The *Monadnock Monthly* (1901f.) was edited by W. Paul Cook.
9. "Scratch a Russian and you will find a Cossack." Alternatively, "Grattez le Russe, et vous trouverez un Tartare" ("Scratch a Russian and you will find a Tartar").
10. The poem ("An Elegy on Franklin Chase Clark, M.D.") was not in fact reprinted in the *O-Wash-Ta-Nong*.
11. Shakespeare, *Richard II* 1.1.182.
12. "To 'The Scribblers,'" written in the summer of 1915 and unpublished in HPL's lifetime.
13. In all, Macauley published seven items by HPL, aside from these extracts.

To the Coryciani

The first of Lovecraft's letters in the "Coryciani" cycle dates to December 1934 and is addressed "To the Members of the Neo-Kleicomolo." It is not an inaugural letter, for much of it is given to what appears to have been a discussion already initiated on the subject of the poem "The Grapes of Eshcol" by Emily Huntington Miller. But it is, in any case, Lovecraft's first letter to the group. The name Coryciani refers to the Corycian Cave on Mount Parnassus in Greece, named after the nymph Corycia. The name therefore signifies that the correspondence will focus on poetry. (Mt. Parnassus was believed to be the home of the Muses.)

It appears that the impetus behind the new round-robin cycle, as with most of the earlier cycles, was Maurice W. Moe. At the inception of the new group, no name had been decided upon, hence Lovecraft's address to the Neo-Kleicomolo. He acknowledges that the name is really not suitable to the group because Kleicomolo consisted of four individuals, whose names contributed to the overall group name. In the case of the new group, there seem to have been many members, and only Moe and Lovecraft were part of the Kleicomolo. There were so many individuals in the proposed new group that concocting a name based on all their names would have been even more unwieldy than *Kleicomolo*, and the nature of the group was poetry criticism, whether of poems of the participants or of any poetry at all. Thus, Lovecraft suggested some possibilities derived from terms associated with poetry, but avoiding overworked titles.

Lovecraft addressed the group in his second letter as "The Corycian–Goliard–Neo-Kleicomolo–or Whathaveyou," recognizing his, Moe's, and yet another suggested name, but also indicating nothing had been settled on. In what appears to be the fourth letter (there was clearly one from late 1935 that is nonextant), Lovecraft opened his letter with the greeting "Ave, Coryciani" (i.e., "Hail, Corycians"). The actual name of the group is not known; Lovecraft had suggested the adjectival form, but there is no known reference to the group outside these letters.

Nor is the membership entirely known. There is Lovecraft, of course, and comments by him are directed to or mention Maurice Moe. Another person whose name is mentioned often is Natalie Hartley Wooley (1904–1973) of Rosedale, Kansas, a correspondent of Lovecraft whom he recruited into the NAPA, and a Mr. [John D.] Adams of Frederick, OK (1908–1986), another NAPA member and editor of the *Literati*. But there is a plethora of other names, none identified with a first name, of whom we know little or nothing: Miss Pegis, Mr. Hille, Miss Adams (Elsa Elizabeth Adams [1910–2004], sister of John Adams), Mr. [Richard Alexander] Thomas[, Jr., (1915–2011)], Mr. Baker [Aaron A. Baker, 1911–1981, co-editor of *Literati*], Mrs. Yanger, and Miss Spaulding. It is unknown if they were all amateur journalists, or if some were Moe's students, or something else.

The Coryciani letters seem to have been circulated infrequently. Lovecraft's own contributions are fairly long (despite his professed desire to be brief) and cover a wide range of topics, not only matters poetical but also social.

[144]   [first leaf in *SL*[1]; JHL last 3 leaves only]

66 College St.,
Providence, R.I.,
Dec. 1, 1934.

To the Members of the Neo-Kleicomolo:

It is a pleasure to see & read, at last, a poem which I have heard praised for many years by one whose judgment is to be depended upon. Confronted by "The Grapes of Eshcol",[2] I find, as usual, that the enthusiasm of my old friend Maurice Winter Moe is indeed well justified. In its delicately vivid imagery, uniformly musical rhythm, & pervasively haunting atmosphere of tempered pensiveness, this distinguished specimen fulfils the requirements of true poetry in every particular. The liquid softness of sound, & the union of sound & sense, so manifest in every part, proclaim the verse as an untainted product of the old tradition; even though its date brings it close to the dawn of the present era of experiment. It is very clearly steeped in the mellow lore of antique scholarship, with its basis of biblical allusion & its subtle reflection of the classical spirit. The mysterious Passer, with his vine-clustered Thyrsus, is a typical avatar of Dionysus & the ecstatic spirit of adventurous expectancy associated with him; & one may feel an almost Ovidian touch in such lines as:

"Onc pass'd, his staff with purple clusters bent;
The winy juices dripp'd along the sand,
And all the air throbb'd fragrance as he went."

Centuries—even millennia—of song & folklore & memory have given to passages like this a curious power to evoke tenuous, half-familiar vistas of wonder & beauty. We recall such imperishable pictures as that in the third book of the Metamorphoses:

"Inpediunt hederae remos, nexuque recurvo
Serpunt; et gravidis distinguunt vela corymbis.
Ipse racemiferis frontem circumdatus uvis,
Pampineis agitat velatam frondibus hastam.
Quem circa tigres, simulacraque inania lyncum,
Pictarumque iacent fera corpora pantherarum."[3]

Since the primary function of a poem is not to tell a story but to present a picture or mirror a mood, & since the given specimen fulfils this function so well, it will not be necessary to enquire too closely into the detailed meaning of the verses. It would appear that the message is one of philosophic & not unhopeful disillusionment; as of a person of middle years who, having tasted the buoyant & expectant light-heartedness of youth, finds the extravagant promise of those days unfulfilled, yet who continues to feel with the pathetic confidence of naivete that perhaps the promise may yet be realised—or at least that the state of expectancy may return in all its roseal colours. This purport is indicated not only by the specific imagery, but by the groundwork of allusion; for in the scriptural tale (Deuteronomy I, 24–5) the fruits of the valley of Eshcol, in the Promised Land which the Hebrews sought to conquer, were secured by spies & brought to their leader Moses as a sample of the teeming opulence of the region. Thus there is a suggestion that the figurative grapes—the joys of youth—are regarded as specimens or harbingers of kindred joys lying ahead, to be gained through patience or effort. The precise interpretation is rather difficult, since some degree of apparent contradiction exists. In the biblical account, the recipient [page 2 begins here] of the grapes dies before he can enter the Promised Land (though he beholds it from a mountain top); whereas in the poem there is mention of 'smiling meadows' & 'shining vineyards' through which (it is perhaps implied) the poet will walk in the company of Joy. Conceivably, the parallel of Moses & the Promised Land is intentionally departed from. A more careful reading, however, suggests that the pleasing prospect of meadows & vineyards may not after all be anything actually reached; but may, like the vista glimpsed by the prophet from Pisgah, be merely something *seen from afar*—the delight of seeing, with its concomitant restoration of expectancy & the hope of vague blessings ahead, being sufficient to bring back the old companioning presence of joy, so long absent. This idea of continued remoteness coupled with vision is borne out by the imagery* of some of the lines:

---

*The only contradictory note is the epithet *cool* as used in the picture of the prospect. This *tactile* image scarcely belongs in a depiction of a scene glimpsed at a distance . . . . although it might be associatively justified. On the other hand, the image of the vineyards is purely visual, without the olfactory element used in the image of the closely passing Dionysus.

"   . . . . . on some raptur'd morn,
Astir with wings & tremulous with light,
The grapes of Eshcol, thro' the desert borne,
May gleam again upon my eager sight."

Discarding all attempts at literalism, we may reasonably judge that the poem represents a rather emphatic case of that reaction from the joyous, mystical expectancy & light-heartedness of youth, which is the all-but-inevitable lot of dull maturity. With the pensiveness of this dull-grey disillusionment is mixed a wistful residue of hope that the bygone bliss may somehow return—a typical psychological process which has enriched our mythologies with every variety of Paradise, Valhalla, Elysium, & Aidenn, & every sort of legend of a returning Golden Age.

"Ultima Cumaei venit jam carminus aetas;
Magnus ab integro saeculorum nascitur ordo."[4]

Whether the intention is to reflect, in emphasised form, the ordinary undulations of mankind's sense of hopeful expectancy through the years, or whether there is a design to portray an especially disappointed life, it would be hard to decide in the absence of specific information. The present commentator would incline toward the more general interpretation; seeing in the thyrse-bearing Liber-figure a symbol of youth's blithely causeless ecstasy & Dionysiac abandon. It is worthy of note that this ivy-crowned god does not figure in the wistfully foreseen return of the vision beyond the shining, deep, silent river of reality—the groping hopes of old age being without the Maenadic fire of those youthful expectancies which they seek to parallel. The whole conception is extremely poignant, & soundly true to human nature—all the emotions depicted being basic & genuine ones operating in their natural & characteristic fashion. The hollowness, overstressing, & feigned emotion which go to form *sentimentality* are happily absent throughout.

It is, however, as a series of pictures & impressions—or as a reflection of a mood—that the poem is chiefly valuable. One might single out a dozen images & suggestions & associations of the utmost keenness & authenticity—such as the Dionysian description quoted on the preceding page, & the supremely lovely line in the quotation on this page—"Astir with wings & tremulous with light." Also, the exquisite pastoral vignette toward the close—

"Tranquil & cool, a little path will run
Thro' smiling meadows downward to the sea,
Thro' shining vineyards shining in the sun.["]

In the last-quoted line the repetition of the epithet *shining* leads to a query as to whether any error in transcription has occurred. Such close repetition, without any earmarks of intentional symmetrical use, seems distinctly unusual, though it does not really mar the grace of the passage. If it could be done without impairing the auditory value of the line, one might be tempted to assay some substitution—as, for instance—"Thro' *laden* vineyards shining in the sun."

Like all true lyrics, this poem really carries a separate message to every separate reader. For each it brings up a shimmering, misty pageant of remembered things & long-dormant moods; & some of the pictures it leaves behind are, of necessity, curiously unlike anything which the author either wrote or had in mind. With me, the final persistent impression is that of a richly verdant plateau traversed by a shrub-bordered winding road & dotted with groves of oaks & olive-trees, through which the rose-tinted marble of low, columned buildings can be seen. It is sunset, & on ascending ground to one side a shepherd's pipe stirs a half-seen fleecy flock. Afar off on the road is the young Dionysus with thyrsus & vine-leaves, two panthers following silently in his wake. In the air is the perfume of the Naxian grape, mixed with that of unknown & unseen blossoms. Ahead is a precipice, with a deep river below it, litten with the apocalyptic flame of the westering sun. And beyond the river, rising gently like one of the landscape backgrounds in an Italian primitive, is a distant plain of meads & groves, temples & vineyards, magical in the golden light, & full of vague hints of a wonder, beauty, & ecstasy about to be revealed.

—H. P. Lovecraft

Comment after reading other contributions

The epistle of Mr. Moe well defines the purpose & methods of the newly established circle, & one could scarcely wish for a better arrangement—save that I shudder at the thought of the permanent preservation of such careless comments as I shall doubtless continue to make! The ancient Kleicomolo drew some absurd specimens of callowness from this now-aged pen, & (notwithstanding their over-kindly appraisal by our honoured leader) I would give much if all copies of them were safely incinerated. Regarding a name for the neo-Kleicomolo—it is truly difficult to think of anything at once unforced & perfectly appropriate. Most of the common terms relating to poetry are hopelessly hackneyed, this list including Parnassus, Helicon, Pegasus, Hippocrene, Apollo, the Muses, &c. &c. Let us, then, see whether there are any other names connected with this cycle, which have suffered less from common repetition. Ideally, a name should be neither *over-familiar* nor *absolutely unfamiliar*. Here are some suggestions: Tithorea & Lycorea,[5] the twin peaks jointly constituting the chief eminence of Parnassus; Aganippé, the sister-fountain of Hippocrene on Mt. Helicon; the Corycian cave, home of the Muses on Parnassus; Castalia, the famous fountain of Apollo & the Muses on Parnassus. Whatever name is chosen, ought to assume an adjectival form if used alone as a title for the circulating letter. As to the relative triteness & obscurity of the names just suggested—*Castalia* is rather well-worn. Aganippé & the Corycian cave are distinctly familiar. Tithorea & Lycorea, on the other hand, seem to be popularly unknown. Of all the titles cited, I fancy I would prefer—both from its intrinsic euphony & from its degree of vague familiarity—*The Corycian.* Such is my vote—though I shall not unduly obtrude this choice against the selections of others. What has the sage Mocrates to say? And The Editor of *The Literati?* And all the rest?

Coming to the other appraisals of "The Grapes of Eshcol"—I find nothing to debate in the acute comment of Mr. Moe, even though he tends to emphasise the element of *specific frustration or disappointment* more than I do after repeated readings. Now that I peruse his comment, I am half inclin'd to sway in his direction—though in truth I believe the matter must remain for ever unsettled. In Our Sage's high opinion of the poem, I can concur without reservation.

The interpretation of Miss Pegis is clever in the extreme, though I do not agree in deducing so specific a story from the lines. All of this commentator's observations on the imagery & associations of the poem are admirably acute & just; shewing a quick & sensitive perception, & a sound aesthetic taste. The style of the criticism is exceptionally graceful, fluent, & mature—speaking much for its author's imagination & literary attainments

Mr. Hille, in his comments, gives evidence of a gratifying responsiveness to poetry's most basic appeals. Each image seems to stir in him a rich profusion of associative responses—visual, auditory, olfactory, & imaginative—so that one is tempted to believe him a poet in his own right. One can find no fault with any dictum of his—& he is perhaps wise in eschewing any detailed interpretation of the latent "story."

Mr. Adams—whose enterprise & initiative in establishing the present circle cannot too warmly be commended—devotes his energy to deducing a meaning rather than analysing the poetic appeal. While I do not coincide with him in identifying the lost & possibly regained joy with anything as specific as theistic belief, I think he is right in rejecting a still more concrete interpretation. He likewise reveals acuteness in emphasising the dependence of the meaning upon the personality & background of each reader.

In conclusion, let me extend the present venture my heartiest good wishes & hopes of permanent success. It seems to me that the members—aside from the present unforgivably ponderous scribbler—have been very wisely selected, since every one shows signs of serious interest, keen insight, & sound judgment, in approaching the chosen activities of the enterprise. I shall await with pleasant anticipations the future visits of the latter, & trust that its personnel may soon be satisfactorily completed.

—H. P. Lovecraft

Decr. 1, 1934.

Notes

1. *SL* 1, facing p. 194.

2. Emily Huntington Miller (1833–1913), "The Grapes of Eshcol" (with two decorations by Frank Vincent Du Mend), *Century Illustrated Monthly Magazine* 85 n.s. 63, No. 1 (November 1912): 94–95; *Art and Progress* 4, No. 1 (November 1912): [inset between pp. 772–73, reprinted from *Century*].

> I have not entered in; across my way,
>   Shining and deep, a silent river lies;
> But sometimes, in the dawning of the day,
>   I see the vision of its vineyards rise.
>
> And once, when Joy and I walked hand in hand,
>   One passed, his staff with purple clusters bent;
> The winey juices dripped along the sand,
>   And all the air throbbed fragrance as he went.
>
> He spake no word, but in his eyes there shone
>   The steady radiance of the evening star.
> And wooing breath of music, lightly blown
>   By fitful winds, came stealing from afar.
>
> And still I wait till, on some raptured morn,
>   Astir with wings, and tremulous with light,
> The grapes of Eshcol, through the desert borne,
>   May gleam again upon my eager sight.
>
> Tranquil and cool, a little path will run
>   Through smiling meadows downward to the sea.
> Through fruitful vineyards shining in the sun,
>   And Joy, that fled, will walk again with me.

Miller edited the *Little Corporal,* a children's magazine, and was associate editor of the *Ladies' Home Journal.* See Num. 13:23–25.

3. Ovid, *Metamorphoses* 3.664–69, tr. Brooke Moore: "But twisting ivy tangled in the oars, / and interlacing held them by its weight. / And Bacchus in the midst of all stood crowned / with chaplets of grape-leaves, and shook a lance / covered with twisted fronds of leafy vines. / Around him crouched the visionary forms / of tigers, lynxes, and the mottled shapes / of panthers."

4. "The final age of the Cumaean song has now arrived / The great series of ages begins anew." Virgil, *Eclogues* 4.4.

5. Now known as Liakoura, the highest peak of Parnassus.

[145] [ALS, JHL]
The Corycian–Goliard–Neo-Kleicomolo–or Whathaveyou
Providence, R.I.,
March 17, 1935

Round II

Brevity will be an aim this time [Added note:] Later: (missed by a mile!)—both on account of congestion at this end & out of regard for those machine-trained members of the younger generation who have lost the knack of deciphering handwriting outside the copy-books. Typing is a highly repulsive process with this ancient correspondent, & the obligation to employ it would take the zest & spontaneity out of the whole venture. It is bad enough to type the MSS.—professionally intended—which *have* to be typed!

Mr. Moe's leading contribution is welcome & illuminating, & ought to be of great assistance in driving home to everyone a clear idea of just what poetry is, & how its principles are actually applied. There is an unmistakable danger today that the practice of poetry may degenerate into a more & more overstrained application of sheer theory at the expense of genuine artistic value. The principle of symbolic expression has been so divorced from considerations of rhythm & background, & so tortured into eccentric & emotionally unrealisable figures through an excessive fear of triteness, that a sterile, wholly subjective school of verse has sprung up—with results admirably summarised in the phrase of Max Eastman—"poets talking to themselves".[1] Of course this has nothing to do with free verse or polyphonic prose. A writer can be just as much a poet in broken lines or solid paragraphs as in sonnets & rondeaux, provided these lines & paragraphs possess a true rhythm & mellifluousness of their own kind. What ought to be avoided is the affected, largely meaningless kind of thing which runs something like this:

> Moon spirals epistemologically,
> Following sharpened tetrahedra . . . . .
> Mephitis chinga[2] extrapolates inverse chypre
> Orbital, melancholy parallelopipedons.
> Thallophytes crucify tenebrous zithers—
> Neutrons reanimate
> Equine plumage.

Regarding the free verse specimens submitted for arrangement—both are certainly real poetry. Whether this correspondent has enough of a natural rhythmical ear to arrange them in lines more effective than solid paragraphs, remains to be seen. Probably it would take a better poet to turn the trick. But here is a casual & timorous attempt:

Childhood

Stardust.
Twinkling & serious all at once.
Fairies
Made of faith in god.
Dreams
Moving with clouds
Into eternity.

Wind Magic

When the wind ~~breathes~~
Breathes through a dreaming tree at night
~~of myriad stars~~
There is the sound ~~of myriad stars~~
Of myriad stars ~~loosely dangled~~
Loosely dangled from silver threads
~~From silver threads~~
And all jingled together

When the wind
Crisps the water
Into billowy pleats that will not stay
There is a sense
Of mystery & happened things
That can never be again.

When the wind
Passes over one's head
And tangles his fingers
Through one's hair
There is a feel of things
(Who has ever fully understood?)
That one can never tell
In words.

When the wind ~~moves~~
Moves among the grass <~~Like silenced footsteps~~>
Like silenced footsteps—oh, gently passing!—
It is like someone in the night
Forming words of deepest silence
~~Of deepest silence~~
To tell you that he knows.

This—i.e., the original words—is really splendid poetry!

N.B. To non-readers of hieroglyphics—cf. original text in Mocratic section. ¶ It is here assumed that no transpositions of words are expected—i.e., that the original sequence is to be maintained, with only the division into lines altered.

Later—I see by Capt. Mocrates's note that verbal changes *are* permissible. However—let this stand 'as is'. Pardon lack of margin below. Better memory hoped for next time!

And so it goes. If this be Boeotian tone-deafness, think the best of it!

Regarding the "Commemoration Ode"—there is no doubt of its excellence as verse, even poetry, in the best classical tradition. Whether it possesses, in addition to its correctness & rich allusive background, the genuine emotional fire & non-mechanical boldness of figure which constitute *great* poetry, this correspondent leaves to abler critics than himself. Certainly, it does not make any expressive demand on the reader's store of traditional images. To fancy that an effective body of poetry can be constructed to suit the half-baked illiterati of a slipshod 'proletarian' or machine culture without roots is to entertain a vain hope. Modernists may boast of their absence of tradition—but their products are the poorer thereby, & will survive only in rare examples. They have deliberately sacrificed most of the normal sources of power—the touching of sensitive & abundant strings of memory—to cater to a tenuous theory of very doubtful foundation.

Well—now to select something especially appealing to this correspondent as poetry. As a "credo", one might say that poetry requires first of all a strong & genuine emotion connected with the perception of beauty (= rhythm, harmony, & ideas associated with it). Second, it requires the presentation of that emotion in the form of symbols or sense-images based on association or analogy. Just these two elements *can* make poetry of a sort, but for maximum effectiveness a third element is tremendously desirable—i.e., euphony of form, based both on the vocal qualities & agreements of the various words, & on the rhythmical flow of the entire text. The desirability of formal metre depends greatly on the extent to which it is expected in the national culture-tradition to which the given specimen belongs. Probably there is more to be said for than against it as a dominant poetic device, since it seems to be connected with many natural factors of regular recurrence in human experience. Seasons, tides, day & night, pulse, cardiac action, symmetry in crystals—dozens of basic facts in nature seem to incline men spontaneously to patterns in highly emotional expression. Even free verse often falls into unconscious approximations to regularity.

As for personal choices—all of these are appallingly non-academic, based largely on the visual beauty of the images they conjure up. To attempt an explanation of them, & of the long trains of subjective association which give them their particular magic to one especial auditor, would be virtually impossible & probably futile if possible. Here is something by the late Percy B. Shelley which persistently clings within the consciousness—

> "The young moon has fed
> Her exhausted horn
> With the sunset's fire—"[3]

From Gray's Elegy—

> "The breezy call of incense-breathing morn"[4]

From Keats:

> "Drows'd with the fume of poppies, while thy hook
> Spares the next swath & all its twinèd flowers."[5]

From Clark Ashton Smith: [Memnon]

> "And music still'd to monumental stone"[6]

From Samuel Loveman:

> "A broken column under a Grecian sky."[7]

And—trite as it is—good old Bill's "Bare ruin'd choirs" &c.—also his famed Tempest thing—"Cloud-capt towers" &c.[8]

From Johannes Miltonus:

> "Russet lawns & fallows gray
> Where the nibbling flocks do stray;
> Mountains on whose barren breast
> The lab'ring clouds do often rest;
> Meadows trim with daisies pied,
> Shallow brooks & rivers wide;
> Towers & battlements it sees,
> Bosom'd high in tufted trees . . . ."[9]

Tennyson's "Horns of Elfland" would have to be included.

Later: it seems that others have chosen *recent* verse specimens, but since Mr. Moe laid down no rule of contemporaneousness, these absolute choices may well stand. Of these, 3 are by living poets.

And our old friend P. Maro:

> "Molli paulatim flavescet campus arista
> Incultisque rubens pendebit sentibus uva,
> Et durae quercus sudabunt roscida mella."[10]

and for delicate *pathos*, nobody has yet beaten Pub's well known standby:

> "Sternitur infelix alieno vulnere, caelumque
> Adspicit, et moriens dulces reminiscitur Argos."[11]

And Mr. Pope's Iliad:

> "As when the moon, refulgent lamp of night,
> O'er heav'n's pure azure spreads her sacred light,
> When not a breath disturbs the deep serene,
> And not a cloud o'ercasts the solemn scene,
> Around her throne the vivid planets roll,
> And stars unnumber'd gild the glowing pole,
> O'er the dark trees a yellower verdure shed,
> And tip with silver ev'ry mountain's head;
> Then shine the vales, the oaks in prospect rise,
> A flood of glory bursts from all the skies:
> The conscious swains, rejoicing in the sight,
> Eye the blue vault, & bless the useful light;"[12]

From Bryant:

> "There thro' the long, long summer hours
>   The golden light should lie,
> And thick young herbs & groups of flowers
>   Stand in their beauty by.
> The oriole should build & tell
> His love-tale close beside my cell;
>   The idle butterfly
> Should rest him there, & there be heard
> The housewife bee & humming-bird."[13]

And Algernon Charles contributes this sonorous roll:

> "Out of the golden remote wild west where the sea without shore is"[14]

And our own Eddie:

> "Bottomless vales & boundless floods,
> And chasms, & caves, & Titan woods,
> With forms that no man can discover
> For the dews that drip all over;
> Mountains toppling evermore
> Into seas without a shore;
> Seas that restlessly aspire
> Surging, unto skies of fire;
> Lakes that endlessly outspread
> Their lone waters, lone & dead . . ."

> "Up shadowy long-forgotten bowers
> Of sculptur'd ivy & stone flowers—
> Up many & many a marvellous shrine
> Whose wreathed friezes intertwine
> The viol, the violet, & the vine."[15]

And Verlaine—trans. by Samuel Loveman

> "The shadow of trees in the hazy river
> Dies like the mists that shiver . . ."

> "The moon of snow
> Shines in the wood;
> From every bough
> Thin voices brood
> That the green sprays cover . . ."[16]

And Baudelaire—trans. by C. A. Smith:[17]

> "Babel of stairs & of arcades,
>   There is a place infinite,
>   Where fountains fall in chrysolite
> On the dull gold of long estrades.

> Where from the ramparts far & high
>   Enormous cataracts have sprung,
>   Like heavy crystal curtains hung
> On the huge walls within the sky.

No bloom, nor bower, but pools enchanted
 Where lies the columns' mirrored frieze—
  By the titanic Naiades
 Of pale & amber marble haunted

Blue waters endlessly are whirled
 Between the quays of malachite
  And quays of sand, that run in light
A million leagues athwart the world."

And Ossian—or Macpherson . . . . .

"The murmur of thy streams, O Lora! brings back the memory of the past. The sound of thy woods, Garmallar, is lovely in mine ear. Dost thou not behold, Malvina, a rock with its head of heath? Three aged pines bend from its face; green is the narrow plain at its feet; there the flower of the mountain grows, & shakes its white head in the breeze. The thistle is there alone, shedding its aged beard. Two stones, half sunk in the ground, shew their heads of moss. The deer of the mountain avoids the place, for he beholds a dim ghost standing there. The mighty lie, O Malvina! in the narrow plain of the rock."[18]

And Theocritus, as Mr. Calverley translates him:

"And sweet is sleep by summer brooks upon the breezy lea;
 And acorns they grace well the oak, apples the apple-tree",[19]

And Edward John Moreton Drax Plunkett, 18th Baron Dunsany:

"Clad though that city was in one robe always, in twilight, yet was its beauty worthy of even so lovely a wonder: city & twilight both were peerless but for each other. Built of a stone unknown in the world we tread were its bastions, quarried we know not where, but called by the gnomes *abyx*, it so flashed back to the twilight its glories, colour for colour, that none can say of them where their boundary is, & which the eternal twilight, & which the City of Never; they are the twin-born children, the fairest daughters of Wonder."[20]

Well—one could keep this up indefinitely, but this present anthological hash ought to serve for a while. A representative group of selections based less on one person's accidental set of tastes, & more on absolute aesthetic value, would be infinitely different—including pieces of wide emotional & pictorial range, & drawing on bards not mentioned in this brief list.

           —H. P. Lovecraft

Comment after Reading Other Contributions

Virtually everyone seems to have produced better arrangements of the free verse specimens than this correspondent—proving, no doubt, that the latter's ear for intrinsic rhythm isn't any too hot . . . . & that old dogs aren't distinguished in the learning of new tricks. Mr. Hille's choice of a favourite poem is sound & excellent, & his own sonnet—though a little didactic & given to prose expression ("The writer"—"merits still remain"—"is in itself"—&c) instead of the symbolic language of poetry—exhibits much thoughtfulness. Mr. Moe's remark on the "—dy" false rhyme is eminently sound. One might also point out that the rhyming of two syllables, *both* of which bear a merely *secondary* accent (mel″-o-dy′; mon″-o-dy′), is not the most graceful possible thing—though it is found extensively even in standard poets. Mr. Moe considers this too finical a point to mention in his unpublished (& marvellously fine!) manual, "Doorways to Poetry",[21] but there is no harm getting it on record somewhere! As to whether certain metres are especially adapted to certain types of subject-matter—there can be little doubt but that they are, in the main. But there are exceptions, as one might readily cite. It is never well to be dogmatic in any field—even though a *general* condition may be dominantly true.

Mr. Adams's observations, arrangements, & selections are all extremely interesting. It is clear that he likes the sort of verse which overlaps into the psychological & philosophical fields rather than 'just plain poetry'. The poems he chooses as favourites are all delightful—especially his first choice, the elfin & delicate "Path to the Sky."

Miss Adams's arrangement of "Wind Magic" is especially fine, & her remarks on poetry & its source can scarcely be disputed. The selections which she makes are of unmistakable power—& involve a dramatic element which seems to differentiate her taste from that of her Oklahoma namesake.

Mrs. Wooley's contribution is rich in illuminating comment & examples. She is, it would seem, right in believing that both simple & involvedly mystical & allusive (within reasonable limits) verse have a definite & unchallengeable place in the aesthetic scheme. Like Mr. Adams's, her preferences run to the philosophical—albeit in a somewhat less concrete fashion. A certain wistful, elusive mysticism—involving touches of the whimsical, the fantastic, & the delicately spectral—often characterises Mrs. Wooley's own verse[22]—as the columns of amateur journalism amply attest. The favourites she chooses reveal a taste definitely but conservatively modern. "The Grasshopper", by Merrill Root",[23] has a curious charm. As the final form of the immortality-endowed Tithonus, the grasshopper is a far from inappropriate symbol of eternity! "The Falling Gold", by Louise McNeill, is a very sound choice.[24] Mrs. Wooley's suggestion that translations of ancient & of foreign poetry be brought up for consideration is excellent—though copies of such might be hard to obtain in some places. Old Hindoo stuff—Vedas, Ramayana, Mahabharata, Kalidasa, Jayadeva, Sakuntala, Pankatantra, &c.,—is full of the philosophic tone relished by some of the circle. The Persian Avesta has its devotees, & Egypt has bequeathed its hymns, proverbs of Ptah-hotep, Pentaour, Book of the Dead, & romances & fables . . . . from the last-named of which came the familiar story of the lion & the mouse. The Tigris–Euphrates civilisation also has its reliques—whilst the Judaean products are known to all survivors of the Sunday-school. Chinese literature is a world in itself—& one with many cultural values far sounder than our own. Books on & of the ancient Confucian & Taoist classics are generally possible to secure—& the exquisite poetry of Cathay is available through excellent translations—such as Arthur Waley's.[25] All of which reminds me—does anybody in this circle know of an English translation of the Shah-Namah of Firdausi, whose millennium has just been so extensively celebrated? A friend of this correspondent is anxious to get hold of one, & would appreciate a postcard of information from anyone less ignorant on the subject than said correspondent. Address: Richard F. Searight, 19946 Derby Ave., Detroit, Mich. Incidentally, it must be realised that no amount of exotic Eastern lore can take the place of the Graeco-Roman classics which are culturally ancestral to us. The Orientals speculate thinly & sententiously—but the pages of Homer, Æschylus, Sophocles, Aristophanes, Pindar, Theocritus, Lucretius, Virgil, Ovid, Horace, Juvenal, Tibullus, Catullus, Propertius, & Martial are part & parcel of our Aryan life itself. There is no western civilisation without them. Likewise of vital import are our blood-ancestral epics—the Eddas & Sagas of the North. Modern foreign literature is another world in itself—which, beginning with the French, stretches off in ever-widening circles. One ought to know something of Baudelaire, Mallarmé, Rimbaud, Verlaine, Leconte de l'Isle, & their fellows— probably the greatest poets of the later 19th century. Of most of these translations are generally available.

Miss Spaulding's arrangement of the vers libre is exceedingly graceful, & her principles of poetic judgment are manifestly sound . . . . as is indeed proved by her selections. "Night Flowers in the Tropics" is splendidly vivid. "Slow Tempo" has power—but why, alas, did the author deliberately (twice!) give the *monosyllable rhythm* a *dissyllabic* value, as if it were *rhyth'-um?* Miss Spaulding's handwriting needs no excuse (would that the same could be said of *this!*), & certainly gives no evidence of the inconvenient posture!

Turning to Mr. Thomas's breezy contribution—the name-suggestion, "The Goliards",[26] certainly combines appropriateness & unhackneyedness in the most delightful fashion. Wider voting would seem to be in order! Hope the present correspondent's cacography will not cause Mr. T. more trouble— if it were not for the five-day limit, time for typing might be found, but the very thought of it is formidable, discouraging, & silence-producing to at least one elderly gent! Regarding amateur poetry—one can of course expect only a small fraction of it to have actual merit. Amateurdom is a great sieve—& if it can manage to catch even one or two real poets in the course of a year it may be said to be doing well. The columns of one or two papers like *The Literati* would seem to indicate that general paucity does not mean complete extinction by any means. The idea of encouraging the better amateur bards in this circle is worth considering. Incidentally—Mr. Thomas would make an excellent N.A.P.A. poetry critic for next year. How does the idea sound to him? One fancies an incoming president[27] could be made to see things the same way. The poem "Pursuit" displays gratifying freshness, even though one might wish it made fewer concessions to the fashion of the moment in matters of imagery & vocabulary. But the important thing is that it *does* speak in imagery—the test of true poetry.

Mr. Baker, one sees, is very literal in his interpretations of poetry—revealing his predominant inclination toward prose. It is obvious that he misses the point altogether in considering the appeal of "The Grapes of Eshcol"—mistaking a really original allusiveness for unoriginality merely because the background of allusion involves stable racial traditions. Further study of verse—& of the poetic principle—will open Mr. Baker's eyes to many things which now necessarily escape him. Amateur journalism will provide the opportunity if taken seriously—though it is to be wished that the associations had at their disposal some more specific sort of helpfulness, such as Mr. Moe's "Doorways" will provide when published.

> [pardon the non-margin again!!]
> ——H. P. Lovecraft

Notes

1. Max Eastman. "Poets Talking to Themselves," *Harper's Magazine* 163, No. 5 (October 1931): 563–74. Eastman's article quotes the entirety of Hart Crane's short poem "At Melville's Tomb" and criticizes it for obscurity.

2. I.e., the common American skunk.

3. "Twilight and Desire," ll. 1–3.

4. Thomas Gray, *Elegy Written in a Country Churchyard*, l. 17.

5. John Keats, "Ode to Autumn," ll. 17–18.

6. "Memnon at Midnight" (l. 14), in *Ebony and Crystal* (1922).

7. "Terminus," l. 8 (where read "The column . . ."), in *The Hermaphrodite and Other Poems* (Caldwell, ID: Caxton Printers, [January] 1936), 130. In *Out of the Immortal Night: Selected Works of Samuel Loveman*, ed. S. T. Joshi and David E. Schultz (New York: Hippocampus Press, 2021), 84.

8. Shakespeare, Sonnet 73.3 and *The Tempest* 4.1.152.

9. "L'Allegro," 71–78.

10. Both "P. Maro" and "Pub" (below) refer to Virgil (Publius Vergilius Maro). This quotation from *Eclogues* 4.28–30.

11. *Aeneid* 10.781–82.

12. Alexander Pope, *The Iliad of Homer* 8.687–98.

13. William Cullen Bryant, "June," ll. 19–27.

14. Algernon Charles Swinburne, "Hesperia," l. 1.

15. Edgar Allan Poe, "Dreamland" (1844), ll. 9–18; "The City in the Sea" (1831), ll. 19–23.

16. Samuel Loveman, "Romances sans Paroles," ll. 1–2; "La Bonne Chanson," ll. 1–5. From "Translations from [Paul] Verlaine," *Saturnian* 1, No 3 (March 1922): 12–15 (seven poems); in *Out of the Immortal Night* 181, 182.

17. Clark Ashton Smith, "CXXVI. Parisian Dream" (translation of "CXXVI. Rêve parisien" by Charles Pierre Baudelaire), *Sandalwood* (Auburn, CA: Auburn Journal Press, 1925), 31–32. In *The Complete Poetry and Translations*, ed. S. T. Joshi and David E. Schultz (New York: Hippocampus Press, 2007–08), 3.219, 221.

18. James Macpherson (1736–1796), "Carthon: A Poem," in *The Poems of Ossian* (1765).

19. Charles Stuart Calverley (1831–1884), "The Triumph of Daphnis" (by Theocritus), *Idylls* 8. In *The Complete Works of C. S. Calverley* (London: George Bell, 1901), 346–47.

20. Lord Dunsany. "The City of Never," in *The Book of Wonder* (1912; rpt. New York: Boni & Liveright, 1918), 60–61.

21. Moe's *Doorways to Poetry*, a treatise on the appreciation of poetry revised by HPL in 1929, was never published.

22. HPL's *Letters to Robert Bloch and Others* reprints a selection of Wooley's poetry.

23. "The Grasshopper" by E[dward] Merrill Root (1895–1973) appeared in the *Marshall* [TX] *News Messenger* (11 September 1934): 4.

24. Louise McNeill, "The Falling Gold," *Kaleidograph* 5, No. 2 (June 1933): 44.

25. Arthur David Waley (born Arthur David Schloss, 1889–1966), British Orientalist and sinologist, achieved popular and scholarly acclaim for his translations of Chinese and Japanese poetry.

26. The goliards were mostly young clergy in Europe in the 12th and 13th centuries who wrote satirical Latin poetry. They were chiefly clerics who served at or had studied at universities in France, Germany, Spain, Italy, and England, who protested growing contradictions within the church through song, poetry and performance.

27. The president of NAPA for the 1934–35 term was Ralph W. Babcock, Jr., whose conduct gained disapproval from HPL. The president for 1935–36 (elected in July 1935) was Hyman Bradofsky, editor of the *Californian*.

[146] [ALS, JHL]

66 College St.,

Providence, R.I.,

July 14, 1936.

Ave, Coryciani:—

Floundering in the midst of an unprecedented vortex of duties, & only recently emerged from a half-year nightmare of poor health & nerve-strain (aggravated by the very severe illness & hospital absence of the aunt who heads this household[1]—& who is now, fortunately, back & nearly recovered), I shall not be able to offer much of value on this round of the epistle. My comments will be dull & hasty, & probably devoid of any fresh perspective or original thought. In the case of Basileus[2] Mocrates, however, I shall have a chance to offer an oral postscript, since I expect the pleasure of a personal glimpse of our eastward-faring leader (the first such glimpse in 13 years) less than a week hence.[3] Surveying the interesting array of material before me, I observe that my own contribution of last winter has not been returned. Can it be that some hapless Corycian, exasperated by the wretched hieroglyphs, tore it to pieces in a fit of ungovernable rage? In any case the loss is small. Incidentally, it was with great interest that I learned of the fresh link— that of atrocious script—which binds me to my fellow non-poet, the prolific & prosaic Mr. Guest![4] Years ago the discovery that Mr. Guest & I have a common birthday filled me with sorrow & humiliation. Today I accept such symbols of kinship more philosophically—for after all, I ain't such a riot myself, while Mr. Guest (according to his recent letter) at least has the perspicacity to realise that the result of his quantity-production is not poetry.

Proceeding with my listless-sounding & unimaginative footnotes on various topics as they occur—let me say that I shall be glad to do my feeble best in the second contest-balloting when the time comes. Let us hope that the new set of entries may include some as good as the best three or four in the preceding contest. ¶ Regarding snapshots—I was much pleased to see the various "Strange Faces" (as well as Il Duce Mauricio's far-from-strange features), & am adding a clock-stopper perpetrated in Charleston, S.C. on April 30, 1934. Its representativeness is fair—the subject's aging in the intervening 2¼ years being somewhat too subtle for so primitive a four-for-a-dimer to contradict. ¶ Let me endorse the Mocratic recommendation to obtain a free subscription to *Travel in Japan*. I have done so, & am thoroughly enthusiastic over the charm of the publication—its illustrations of Japanese scenery & architecture, its sidelights on Japanese art & design, & its glimpses of Japanese thought & feeling—musical, poetic bits like the extract cited. Mr. Moe has certainly not overrated the charm of this material—& I am led to wonder whether some English or American translator has prepared the visible text of the various articles & poems from originals in Japanese. In the Spring 1936 issue there is an article on the Japanese spring which well matches the earlier autumnal article. In it is quoted a very fine & typical hokku by the poet Saigyo Hoshi—

> "Oh, would that I could
> Split myself into many,
> 　　And, missing not a twig,
> See all the glory of the flowers
> In all the unnumbered hills."[5]

Incidentally—I abundantly share Mr. Moe's appreciation of the curious spell woven by exotic place names as illustrated by the poem "Like Silver Gongs".

The various analyses by recognised poets of the processes behind their work are extremely interesting to study—all the more so because they tend to be so meagre, vague, & essentially non-committal. They tend to confirm the idea that the truest poetry is largely unconscious, & that the more a bard knows about his own products, the less truly poetic the latter are likely to be. Mr. Prokosch's "Persian Idyll"[6] is a thing of extreme beauty—& if it has a meaning beyond the decorative & pictorial, I would guess that its chief symbolisation is that of the constant, close pursuit of everything living—in all seasons & under all conditions—by the inevitable black hand of death. The ensuing poem by Mr. Ficke[7] presents, more subjectively & elliptically, an emotional response to one phase of that selfsame truth. The parallel interpretations by a high-school pupil & by the author are highly illuminating. The third poem—"The House on the Dunes"[8]—is unusually vivid, & it would be interesting to obtain the author's account of it. Like Mr. Adams, I believe the pupil was wrong in attributing the second stanza's assertions to anyone other than the original sea-reviler. The whole set of invectives against the sea come from one person—the person who, though revolting outwardly against a marine environment, is actually too saturated with it through heritage & experience ever to break away. The rhyme-liberties, I feel certain, are intentional & calculated. Whether they contribute anything to the poem's effect would form an interesting subject of debate. I agree that nothing is really *lost* through the experiment. My own position in the matter of rhyme is perhaps not quite as rigid as Mr. Moe's remark would imply. I have indeed said that I am now convinced of the *general preferability* of perfect rhyme—yet this position was almost forced on me in middle life by fastidious technicians. My own original inclinations were all toward the degree of liberty exercised by the classic bards of the late 17th & 18th centuries—Dryden, Addison, Pope, Parnell, Tickell, Gay, & so on—whereby considerable latitude in the *vowel* sounds of rhymes (*above—grove—move*) was permitted. It took a long time to convert me from this position, & my conversion is not yet perfect enough to make me take violent issue with Mr. Moe's liberal position. I do *not* endorse Mr. Kleiner's objection to a rhyme of a monosyllable with the secondarily accented syllable of a longer word (*thee—liberty*), since I regard such a rhyme as *perfect*—not even merely "allowable". What I *do* object to, however, is the rhyming of *two or more* syllables whose accents are merely secondary. Thus although I fully accept a rhyme of *me* & *victory*, I would *not* accept one of *liberty* & *victory*. In this matter I have had an amiable fight with our leader. I want him to embody the precept in his "Doorways to Poetry", while he thinks it too trivial for such citation. I admit that many standard poets have violated this principle, but believe it is a freedom not to be imitated by the novice. The opinions of others of the circle would be interesting. The rough-rhymed poem by Clem-

ent Wood[9] is very vivid & attractive, & I agree quite fully with Mr. Moe's remarks upon it. Like him, I admire its richness & freshness, & also like him, I
find only the *glitter-flutter* assonance really irritating. At this particular period it
is perhaps better to err on the side of over-precision than on the side of slip-
shodness, since so many disintegrative tendencies are at work. Some of the
more radical poets are now trying to employ crude assonances which make
no pretence to "allowability" as rhymes, & which sharply grate upon the ear
whenever they occur. There is really no excuse for such extremes, since the
offending specimens nearly always occur in verses where real rhymes pre-
dominate. If the assonances were recognised as a conscious tradition (as in
Spanish poetry) & employed with some degree of consistency, they would not
be so unpleasantly obtrusive. It is their mixture with true rhymes which
makes them offensive.

The Markham verse-form cited by Mr. Moe is indeed clever & original.[10]
Regarding the Mocratic verses "One Hour to Live", based upon a student's
theme, my criticisms would be only of small points like the word *weepy* for
tearful, plaintive, mournful, grieving, wailing, &c. ("weepy" is slang, with humorous
or contemptuous overtones) in line 4, or the naively trite phrase "joys that
wait above" in the concluding line. The apparently redundant syllable in line
6, pointed out by Mrs. Adams-Moore, is probably a conscious result of an
attempt to view the line in terms of rhythmic *feet* rather than formal *syllables*.
The phrase *"to receive"*, I imagine, is designed for a virtually dissyllabic pronunciation, thus: *t're-ceive'*. Thus the line scans:

Their own / proud strength / to re ceive / the mor / tal stroke

It would not do to eliminate *proud,* for then a strong accent would fall on the
relatively unimportant words *own* & *to,* leaving the important word *strength* in an
unaccented position. Mr. Moe's notes on the composition of these lines shed a
valuable light on the careful & discriminating methods followed by fastidious
versifiers. The refusal to accept any but the one inevitable word or phrase or
image for each impression to be conveyed is something which marks the true
artist. Were everyone to exercise this degree of care & conscientiousness, less
bad verse would be loosed upon the world. As for the general idea of what one
would do if certain of death in an hour—I fancy most persons in normal health
tend to sentimentalise & romanticise a bit about it. For my part—as a realist
beyond the age of theatricalism & naive beliefs—I feel quite certain that my
own known last hour would be spent quite prosaically in writing instructions
for the disposition of certain books, manuscripts, heirlooms, & other posses-
sions.[11] Such a task would—in view of the mental stress—take at least an
hour—& it would be the most useful thing I could do before dropping off into
oblivion. If I *did* finish ahead of time, I'd probably spend the residual minutes

getting a last look at something closely associated with my earliest memories—a picture, a library table, an 1895 Farmer's Almanack, a small music-box I used to play with at 2½, or some kindred symbol—completing a psychological circle in a spirit half of humour & half of whimsical sentimentality. Then—nothingness, as before Aug. 20, 1890.

Turning to Mr. Hille's contribution—I have read the poem "Vraisemblance" with keen admiration, but wish the metre were less conspicuously irregular. How is one to scan lines like these:?

> Honeyed viands from heaven's hand above
> Of the silver poplars. And as she rests

I am aware that some moderns take strange liberties with prosody, but of the value of such liberties I am very sceptical. Another thing I'd criticise in the poem is the use of *immortal* for *immortally* in l. 3. The substitution of one part of speech for another was permitted in the artificial verse of the 18th century; but unless a poem be frankly archaic throughout, any such "poetic licence" as this tends to grate on the reader. The free verse "Love Knot" is clever, though the effectiveness of the rugged & colloquial medium seems open to question. Where a veteran like Sandburg succeeds in spite of a clumsy medium, a beginner is likely to be less successful. The lines of Logan Kean, "Under Ether", are surely ingenious & full of apt images. But why the overweighted second line?

Mrs. Moore is to be congratulated on the advent of a younger generation. The coming pageant would seem to offer great opportunities—to all of which I am sure the family will be equal. "To A Chinese Night", by Anne Atwood, is a phenomenally vivid poem which catches the Chinese spirit better than most Occidental attempts. "Papago Love Song" reminds one that all American Indian lore is full of poetry—which should be made more easily accessible & potentially popular than it is at present.

I am sorry to hear of Mr. Adams's enforced dropping-out—especially since he is the founder of the circle. Could he not adopt a less drastic course—remaining a recipient & reader even if he cannot for the nonce be an active participant? Sorry also to hear of the suspension of amateur activity. Mr. Adams's contribution to the quoted-poem galaxy is a very apt one—for "Planter's Charm", though simple, is admirably direct & graphic & redolent of the soil. The explanatory letter from Mrs. Yanger adds to its interest.

Mr. Baker's comment on the subtle & indefinite way in which real poetry takes form is very sensible & acute. The quoted poem by Paul Bowles[12] will be found a bit too modernistic to suit most tastes, though T. S. Eliot, e. e. cummings, & dozens of others have prepared us for such things. Some of the isolated images have a vigour which would be valuable if one were quite certain about what they express.

I can sympathise with Mr. Thomas in his temptation regarding book bargains—having been much the same myself until household congestion made the acquisition of any more volumes (present total perhaps 2500 in the house on shelves; 200 or 300 more in attic or stored in a neighbouring stable) absolutely impossible except through sacrifice of existing ones. The Bibliotheca Ricardana is obviously getting to be an ample & diverse one—& I surely hope it won't have to be transported too many times.

The circle will surely rejoice at Mrs. Spaulding's recent visit home—& will hope that improving health may soon make such visits more & more frequent, culminating in a permanent return. Mrs. Spaulding has surely earned our abundant gratitude by the ample letters of explanation elicited from poets—& from Mr. Guest—the material from Robin Lampson[13] being especially illuminating. As for the question of whether people like to be made to think, or only to be made to think they think, I would say that the answer depends on the type of individual concerned. What is more—it depends to some extent on the subject-matter concerned. Some types—complacent, conventional, tradition-bound bourgeois souls—simply *will not* think on any subject, & savagely resist any effort to bring them in contact with genuine facts or logical conclusions. Hence, to a great extent, all orthodoxies & forces of intellectual, social, political, & economic reaction. Other types are willing & eager to think on *some* subjects, but pompously or affrightedly close their minds to certain *others*—being content in these *verboten* fields to accept stupidly & supinely the fantastic & mythical concepts evolved in primitive ages of ignorant speculation & fastened on succeeding generations by the intellectually crippling process of childhood inoculation—irrational & arrogant indoctrination at an age when the plastic mind & emotions are ready to accept *anything,* true or false. A very small minority, however, really enjoy genuine thought in *all* fields, & welcome any influences which increase the radius of their rational comprehension. The smallness of this minority is tragic—but it cannot be helped under the existing system of unintelligent education & superstitious traditional indoctrination. The very basis of human philosophy & education will have to be revolutionised—with the training of the individual's logical capacity, & the liberation of his emotions from all dogmatic influences, as a paramount policy—before any appreciable multitude of people can be expected to think fearlessly & enjoy the art of thinking. At present the few who think do so in spite of hereditary cultural influences rather than because of them. And many current attempts to replace the rotten heritage with a sounder one involve misconceptions & extravagances scarcely less absurd than those of the blindly groping past. Indeed, the vicious crime of juvenile indoctrination & intellectual & emotional crippling is as typical of modern Marxism & Nazism as it ever was of blind royalism or clericalism. There will be no progress in the advancement of mankind to thinking stature until juvenile education ceases to impress on its objects the arbitrary notion (as often fallacious as not) that this or that debated imponderable *"positively is"* of this or that nature, & begins to impress upon them the one paramount duty of keeping their eyes & minds always open for valid evidence, of refusing to form any conclusion *except* on such valid evidence, & of dropping any formerly accepted belief the moment new evidence shows it to be false. There must be a revolution in education as profound as any effected by Lenin or Hitler—but in a direction equally remote from that followed by either of these examples. Some evolution in the right direction has indeed occurred during the past century—but the ground covered is so slight as compared with the ground lying ahead, that we may well look upon the problem as one still to be solved. Until that final solution is achieved, we must acknowledge the melancholy truth of Mr. Marquis's cynical epigram[14] so far as the majority are concerned. Today the man who forces the reluctant human herd to think will meet with the same savage & ignorant hostility which beset Socrates, Hypatia, Roger Bacon, Giordano Bruno, Galileo, Spinoza, Voltaire, Charles Darwin, Huxley, Freud, Bertrand Russell, & every other champion of truths which happen to run counter to the inherited & ingrained folk-delusions of an emotionally crippled race. He who wishes to be popular will be supine, gullible, acquiescent, carefully stupid, & conventional.

This topic leads quite naturally to Mrs. Wooley's section, with its reference to my criticism of her essay "Intimations—The Hand in the Dark". This essay, by the way, was a fine rhetorical achievement, & my criticism was entirely favourable. My "violent disagreement" was something wholly irrelevant to the quality of the work—a mere "aside" or postscript having nothing to do with the criticism but incidentally stating my opposition to the philosophic background or system of underlying concepts on which the essay was based. Mrs. Wooley now enquires whether a discussion of that background & its rivals would not form an interesting & appropriate topic for the circle as a whole. Well—I'd tend to reply that it all depends on moods & circumstances. Since the matter in question is so wholly philosophical & scientific as distinguished from poetical or aesthetic, one may doubt its adaptation to a purely poetic letter-series. On the other hand, one may enquire whether it is desirable to restrict the subject-matter so closely to a single art—which with many of the members is only a minor interest. The old Kleicomolo of 1915–20 was not thus restricted—philosophy indeed having a tremendous lead over aesthetics in most of the rounds. Of course the transformation of an avowedly poetical circle into a philosophical or semi-philosophical society might seem as amusing as the frequent transition of "Browning" Clubs into sewing or bridge-playing circles, or the imperceptible evolution of "Athletic" Clubs into nuclei of ward politics. However, an arbitrary limitation of the field in the face of a really popular demand for expansion would be even more ridiculous . . . . so I fancy it is most emphatically a matter to put to vote. I'll tentatively cast a ballot for expansion, since at the present time I probably have more to say on various problems of ideas than I have to say on poetry. But let nobody else vote likewise unless he really has a strong wish for the change. The introduction of a topic boring to even one member would be a mistake. There are likewise other disadvantages—one of which is the fact that Capt. Moe & I have vehemently discussed the selfsame problems from 1914 onward, & have long ago reached that deadlock which comes when each party knows in detail every idea which the other holds, & every argument which the other could possibly devise & advance. The crux of the debate is simply the age-old struggle of rational materialism—as represented by the long line of thinkers including Leucippus, Democritus, Epicurus, Lucretius, Hobbes, La Mettrie, Helvetius, Comte, Nietzsche, Huxley, Santayana, John Dewey, Sigmund Freud, Bertrand Russell, &c.—with the opposite & irreconcilable mystic doctrine of spirit or dualism as represented by Plato & the various supernatural religions of the world. I am a materialist without belief in "spirit", cosmic purpose & consciousness, or personal "immortality". I regard these beliefs as natural growths of primitive ages, unsupported by any real facts in the cosmos as we now understand it, & persisting into the present age solely through ignorance, mental inertia, & the emotional crippling resulting from juvenile indoctrination. That they could possibly occur to anyone *on the basis of today's knowledge* I regard as inconceivable—since modern psychology has revealed the emotions—themselves material phenomena of neural & glandular physiology & biochemistry—from which the "intuitions" & concepts of "spirit" & theistic cosmic governance spring. It is *the overpowering force of blind tradition,* I believe, which causes so large a percentage of "solid, respectable citizens" to retain a nominal or emotional belief in the old myths, & which causes a small residue of men of science (always exponents of the sciences of *dead* matter— seldom a sociologist, biologist, or psychologist) to share this vestigial clinging. Even many theists reject the unanalysed & absurd claim that the physics & mathematics of the 20th century overturn the scepticism of modernity in general. Prof. James Leuba of Bryn Mawr has shown in an article in *Harpers* (Aug. 1934) that in 1933 only 5% of the greatest sociologists (of the U.S.), 12% of the greatest biologists, & 2% of the greatest psychologists believed in an orthodox deity—believers in some sort of "immortality" among the corresponding groups being respectively 10%, 15%, & 2%.[15] So much for my own side. Mrs. Wooley, as I gather from her essay & from other scattered references, is a liberal deist with a belief in cosmic purpose (& possibly human immortality of some sort) though without belief in any organised orthodoxy. Mr. Moe is a hard-shelled though always courteous Presbyterian Christian, & I take it that Mr. Thomas is also of theological predilections. Moe–Lovecraft arguing reached a deadlock 20 years ago. The question is, would the circle enjoy separate arguments between the centre & each extreme—i.e. Moe– Wooley arguments with Mrs. Wooley on the iconoclastic side, & Wooley– Lovecraft arguments with Mrs. W. on the traditional side . . . or such other arguments as some of the rest of the personnel would care to sustain? Whether such debates would prove harmonious or acrimonious depends wholly on the personal temperaments of those concerned. I enjoy any sort of argument & never get angry, though some tell me that my emphatic formulations of my case occasionally offend very sensitive opponents—at least, until they get to know my perfect impersonality & underlying good will. So it's up to the members—I'll either debate or keep my mouth shut, according to the will of the majority. If anybody believes in the conventional maxim of "good breeding" which forbids the discussion of "religion or politics", let him vote a placid negative!

¶ I must read "Lost Horizon".[16] Much in the philosophy of the Far East claims my whole-hearted support. Though without the Oriental's *active & assertive* fatalism, I am a determinist & utterly without respect for financial prosperity or "success" as objectives. ¶ Good idea to purchase pivotal books on intellectual questions, as well as standard classics. I'd be lost if I had to depend on public libraries. ¶ Again I will close, with usual apologies as to boresomeness. In 4 days I hope to deliver this letter to our august leader in person instead of through the usual postal channels. ¶ My blessings on you all for your patience with this script!—H. P. Lovecraft

[At top of leaf III, recto:] I crave pardon for not turning this page the new trick up-&-down way!

Notes

1. HPL's aunt Annie E. P. Gamwell had been hospitalized for breast cancer, which resulted in a mastectomy.

2. An ancient Greek title meaning "king."

3. Moe visited HPL in Providence on 18–19 July 1936.

4. Edgar A. Guest (1881–1959), British-born American poet whose work—widely syndicated in newspapers—became a byword for triteness and conventionality. HPL learned of their shared birthday in 1931.

5. Saigyō Hōshi (1118–1190), quoted in Genjiro Yoshida, "Spring in Japan," *Travel in Japan* 2, No. 1 (Spring 1936): 6. See also letter 146.

6. Frederic Prokosch (1906–1989) was an American writer, born in Madison, WI, known for novels, poetry, memoirs, and criticism. "Persian Idyll" had appeared in *Harper's* 164, No. 4 (April 1932): 533.

7. Arthur Davison Ficke (1883–1945). HPL may be referring to his "Emblems of Spring," *Harper's* 162, No. 4 (March 1931): 418.

8. By Margaret Marks, *Harper's* 171, No. 1 (June 1935): 91.

9. Clement Richardson Wood (1888–1950), American writer, lawyer, and political activist (member of the Socialist Party). His work appeared frequently in pulp magazines.

10. Presumably a reference to American poet Edwin Markham (1852–1930).

11. HPL in fact did this in the not too distant future. In late 1936, some months before he died on 15 March 1937, he prepared a document he called "Instructions in Case of Decease," indicating how he wanted his library and papers distributed.

12. Paul Frederic Bowles (1910–1999), American expatriate composer, author, and translator. The poem to which HPL alludes is unidentified.

13. Robin Lampson (1900–1978), a neo-classicist poet preferring rhyming sonnet structures to free verse, who invented a sonnet type that borrowed rhyme schemes from Renaissance Italian terza rima. He is best remembered for his verse novels, *Laughter out of the Ground* (1936) and *Death Loses a Pair of Wings* (1939).

14. Don Marquis (1878–1937), humorist, novelist, poet, newspaper columnist, and playwright, best remembered for creating the characters Archy and Mehitabel, supposed authors of humorous verse. The epigram to which HPL refers is unknown, but may well be "An idea is not always to blame for the people who believe in it."

15. James H. Leuba, "Religious Beliefs of American Scientists," *Harper's* 169, No. 3 (August 1934): 291–300. HPL discussed this article at length in his letter to Moe of 15 February [?] 1935.

16. By James Hilton, regarding the origin of Shangri-La, a fictional utopian lamasery located high in the mountains of Tibet.

[147]   [TMS (by Maurice W. Moe), Wisconsin Historical Society][1]

[1936]

There is something very great in Far Eastern aesthetics which the Western World misses almost completely—a feeling born of a truly rational philosophy which recognises the insignificance of mankind. The genuine un-Westernised Chinese or Japanese poet—or artist—sees the supreme beauty in large rhythms of nature, & in momentary perceptions of natural objects, or arrangements of things, which symbolise those rhythms. In all this, making & its emotions are necessarily subordinated in just proportion to the whole scheme of cosmic entity—or visible cosmic entity. The Oriental does not slop over—hence his classic disapproval of effusive amatory lyrics.

Some of the most fascinating Japanese hokkus (17-syllable poems) are to be found in the essay "Butterflies," by Lafcadio Hearn, in his volume called *Kwaidan*. Speaking of the prominence of the butterfly in Japanese art & lore, Hearn assembles a number of hokkus on the subject—presenting both the Japanese sounds in Roman letters & a literal prose translation of the meaning. Of course to us the beauty comes mainly from the translation; but we can also catch from the original sounds something of the grace & music of the language & poetic form. I append some which appeal most strongly to me:

> Rakkwa éda ni
> Kaëru to miréba—
> Kochō kana!

(When I saw the fallen flower return to the branch—lo, it was only a butterfly!)

Chiru-hana ni—
Karusa arasoü
Kochō kana!
(How the butterfly strives to compete in lightness with the falling flowers!)
Tsurigané ni
Tomarité nemuru
Kochō kana!
(Perched upon the temple bell, the butterfly sleeps.)
Chō tondé
Kazé naki hi to mo
Miëzari ki!
(Even though it did not seem a windy day, the fluttering of the butterflies———!).[2]

Notes

1. Published as "Japanese Hokku." Moe's typescript states: "Extract from a Lovecraft letter, 1936," but does not identify the recipient. The content, and HPL's overall tone in the piece, suggests that the letter from which it was extracted may have been another Coryciani letter.

2. The text used for the haiku is that of the 1904 edition rather than Moe's typescript. The first and fourth are on p. 189, the second on p. 190, and the third on p. 188.

To W. G. Bautz

Walter George Bautz (1883–1964) of Milwaukee was for some years a bookkeeper for the Fred Miller Brewing Company. He later worked as a manufacturer's representative for a vacuum cleaner concern. As early as 1922 and as late as 1944 he published several pieces of popular music. He probably came into correspondence with Lovecraft through their mutual friend Maurice W. Moe.

[148] [AHT]

66 College St.
Providence, R.I.
May 16, 1935

Dear Mr. Bautz:—
[. . .]

Regarding American political parties—I think they are all obsolete today, in view of the new conditions brought about by the almost simultaneous development of two basic changes in human life—the application to industry of the mechanical technique of swift and easy duplication with a minimum of human labour, and the collapse of several philosophic illusions traditionally favouring certain false values and unconsciously barbaric methods. The Republican philosophy (which is, incidentally—with its Whig and Federalist antecedents—that of my own family) strikes me as being least adaptable to the needs of the future because of its bland trust in certain laissez-faire economic principles no longer operative and never more than approximate. The Democrats, through their willingness to experiment, are a shade less impossible—but the only sort of government with any effective future will have to savour largely of socialism and fascism. Most of the younger thinkers are going over to Marxian communism—but to me this represents a tragic waste of traditional values . . . a medicine which kills more than it cures. In these latter years I have an increasing regard for the social opinions of the La Follette group in your own state.

As for the war-time issues—I am so far from a Marxian that I line up with the conservatives on these . . . even today. I see no possibility of harmonious internationalism except through a general rationality backed by individual strength. Increased avenues of discussion, plus a clearer realisation of the ruinous effects of war, may help to avert many conflicts which might have taken place in the past; but a certain residue of quarrels are too basic to adjust peacefully. They involve hopelessly irreconcilable and mutually destructive ambitions among groups whose hereditary cultures are too different to make yielding conceivable except through physical force. That is, certain national groups cherish certain conditions so tenaciously, that they will never relinquish them so long as any possible mode of retention—rational or forcible, fair or foul—remains to be tried. To gain certain ends, a group will stop at nothing. There will always be a possibility of war as long as any group retains the hope of being able to defeat any possible force or combination of forces which can be brought to bear against it—and it is difficult to see how any future arrangement can ever destroy that hope. It is useless to point to the harmonious federal union of American states. These were all of the same basic tradition and culture-pattern to start with—and even so, the war of 1861–5 between them could not be averted. With nations as utterly different—in many cases completely antipodal—in race, ideas, standards, desires, and ambitions—as those of Europe and Asia, the very idea of an harmonious federation becomes comic. Each has its own ideas of what is desirable and important—and when two or more sets of ideas irreconcilably clash, there is only one possible result. Reason may decrease the number of hopelessly irreconcilable clashes, but it cannot guarantee their abolition. The duel was abolished in certain countries only because a superior and impartial physical force existed to check the actions of both sides. With the nations of the world, no such superior and impartial force exists. All each nation can do is to use its intelligence in minimising its points of friction with other nations—and to keep itself strong enough to avoid being the prey of a probable aggressor. The alternative to strength and courage is subjection—or the constant likelihood of subjection—and we can see in the cases of the Jews and the Chinese and the Greeks of the Roman period how high a price a group pays when it allows itself to be overridden. Obviously, each separate culture-group cannot be prepared to fight in order to keep itself inviolate and in a position of importance. It should not be needlessly aggressive, but should be ready to check any international development threatening either its direct subordination or series of steps leading to its final subordination.

In the case of the World War—previous events on both sides were undoubtedly foolish and short-sighted to the point of criminality. There were really no issues so basically irreconcilable that reason could not—if given a chance—have adjusted them. When war did occur, however, there was nothing for each group concerned to do except see that its subordination by any other group be averted if possible. Whichever side won, it would be a bad business not only for those directly on the other side, but for those whose culture is identical with that of any of the losing groups.

So far as the United States was concerned, this meant that a British defeat would be a disastrous and menacing event—for despite all the internal quarrels, typified by the American revolution, the great stream of massed Anglo-Saxon ideas, attitudes, modes of feeling and expression, ways of doing things, and instinctive standards of value, as transmitted with the language, laws, literature, art and basic institutions, is forever an indissoluble one. Anglo-

phobia in America and Americanophobia in England are mere surface phenomena based on externals. Whether the average individual of each national
division realises it or not, the two divisions really stand or fall together. Neither
can afford to see the other defeated or subordinated by the representatives of
any external culture. When either is involved in a war imperilling its position
of eminence and security, it is both a duty and a matter of advantage and necessity for the other to sustain it by auxiliary or parallel action.

Now in the World War there was a great deal of emotional talk on both
sides which was meaningless. Neither side was a band of savages trying to
wipe out a superior civilisation with inhuman methods. But just the same,
each side knew well that, if defeated, its own type of culture would be placed
at a disadvantage. This was true of the U.S., through Great Britain, and it was
therefore necessary for future American interests that Britain be not subordinated. My great objection to Wilson at this stage of things is that he did not
enter the war soon enough—although it is claimed that he entered it as soon
as popular psychology was ripe. There ought not to have been any war—but
that evil having been accomplished, the best thing from the Anglo-Saxon
standpoint would have been a speedy victory for the side on which Anglo-
Saxons were arrayed. No group can afford the risk of having its heritage of
speech, folkways, perspectives, and aesthetics subordinated or menaced.

Of course the same was true of the Central Powers. It was their duty, too, to
stand together and see that their own joint heritage of speech, emotions, attitudes, art, and methods be safeguarded as far as possible. That is the essential
tragedy of all wars—the rightness of each side from its own point of view.
Somebody was going to suffer—but each side could do no more than try to
prevent its own culture from being the sufferer. The really philosophic American in 1914–18 could realise at one and the same time that his own action, *for the
same reason,* would have to put forth corresponding exertions on the opposite side.

Subsequent events have tragically proved the truth of this general principle. The outcome which meant continued safety for Anglo-Saxon culture has
meant melancholy disaster for Germanic culture—disaster which no Anglo-
Saxon would wish to see inflicted on a virile opponent. The imposition of
barbarous and excessive terms upon Germany and Austria at Versailles has
led to the rise of strange elements in the defeated nations, and to the decline
of that vigorous freedom of art and scholarship which placed the old German
culture ahead of all others in many fields. This tragedy is both Germany's and
all the world's—but it shows what happens when a great civilisation is placed
at a disadvantage. Had England been defeated, all Anglo-Saxon culture would
have suffered. A triumphant Germanic penetration of all the colonisable corners of the globe would have ultimately placed the Anglo-Saxon speech and
heritage and way of life at a definite disadvantage, so that every part of the
English-speaking world would have declined more or less. While this might
have meant no loss to western civilisation as a whole, it is inconceivable that

an Anglo-Saxon could consider the prospect without all the resistance in his power. The French of course thought the same about their culture—which had already suffered in its previous conflicts with ours. There again was the old struggle for supremacy. From 1689 to 1760 the French could not do otherwise than fight for the dominance of their culture in Europe and America. They lost—and today our cultural influence in the world at large infinitely surpasses France's, while in America only Quebec, and such bits as Guiana, St. Pierre and Miquelon, and some of the West Indies, still harbour French speech and ideas. Even in Louisiana, proud second capital of New France, the speaking of French is virtually extinct. Fight or perish is, alas, the savage motto of every form of life. We cannot strike lest we be struck down ourselves. And so I cannot stand with those who censure America's participation in the war.

I may add that I am just as opposed to any *needless* attack on another culture as I am to a failure to defend one's own. Safety for one's own group, and *not* the excessive injury of any other, is the legitimate policy of a nation. Thus I hold no brief for Versailles and the really outrageous terms laid down there to the Central Powers. Such disproportionate burdens ought never to be laid upon any nation, defeated or otherwise, and it is only natural that Germany today should seek to remove them. Were it not for those burdens, Germany would never have suffered the vicissitudes which have placed her in such a peculiar and culturally maladjusted position since 1933. One only hopes that the reaction against the unjust load will not lead to some fresh shattering of international equilibrium.

As for Woodrow Wilson—he is a hard bird to analyse. I was for him in 1912 because I thought he represented a civilised form of government as distinguished from the frankly thieving plutocracy of the Taft die-hards and from the blindly rebellious well-meaningness of the Bull Moosers.[1] His vacillating policy toward Mexico, however, alienated me almost at once. I could see its basis in punctilious well-meaningness, but I could not consider it properly applicable to the given conditions. Then, as later, I considered Wilson as excessively given to ethical theories of a tenuous and occasionally even meaningless nature. I did not and do not consider him a conscious hypocrite or double-dealer, but I did think his lofty idealism considerably tinctured with subtle, unconscious egotism and involuntary affectations. His tendency to concentrate authority in himself I did not condemn *per se*, because I then believed and still believe that no effective government—especially in a complex industrial nation involving policies and decisions of a sort beyond any layman's reach—is possible except by concentrated authority. I believe that the people at large should exercise their collective power in determining *major goals* of importance to themselves—matters such as economic safeguards, territorial expansion, and the like—but that, once the goals are decided upon, the details of administration should be left to a small group of trained and competent men who really know what they are doing and who are free from the constant checks and confusions of parliamentary squabbling and electoral ignorance. If this group does not serve the people, it can be turned out at the next election—but while it's in, let it work effectively and without interference! Thus I didn't oppose "Wilson the autocrat" *as such,* but simply lamented certain things he did. I thought he affected too much war-time neutrality when no real neutrality was possible—and after the war, I thought his policy at Versailles excessively cloudy and high-flown. Had his aims been less airily lofty, they would have been less easily twisted and nulli-fied by wise old birds like Clemenceau.[2] I thought he ought to know better—and yet I admired his ability to think objectively and impartially in a time of savage stress and bias. I thought, and still think, that he meant well. I didn't like him—yet I felt that his egotism was unconscious, involuntary, and unal-terable . . . a defect rather than a fault. His League of Nations idea I could never take seriously. I was amused equally by those who frantically advocated America's entrance, and by those who frantically opposed it. To me it was simply a joke—an impossible and ineffective phantom, membership or non-membership in which meant nothing one way or the other. I was mildly anti-League—merely because I thought membership meant a bit of needless ex-pense and bother. Today I think my opinion is fairly well vindicated.

But pardon this extended harangue—verboseness is a weakness of mind, and of all provocations, nothing is so tempting as some reminiscence-making echo of the past. Your acrostic[3] stimulates so many bygone memories and bygone moods that I become subject to a sort of loquacious, quasi-rejuvenation, as if 1919 were with us once more!

Buckling down at last to the technique of the acrostic—it is certainly ex-tremely clever, getting its initial message across as smoothly and with as little verbal straining as does its geographic successor of a decade later. At the same time I fancy you can see that it is not quite as fluent as the later one. Your style has improved, without question, since 1924. The *metre* of the Kaltenborn[4] vers-es is all right—and so are all the rhymes except that of *autocrat* and *democrat,* where the rhyming syllables (-crat— -crat) are *identical* instead of with different initial consonants. As you probably realise now, a syllable cannot rhyme with itself. The main trouble with the verses, if there is any, is the somewhat forced and unnatural way in which the *accents* fall within the various lines. It is an axiom of prosody that accents ought to fall, in general, upon important or emphasised words—and in the same idiomatic relationship to each definite phrase that would occur in ordinary oral discourse. Now the accents in lines like

— ◡   ◡   — ◡   ◡   —   ◡   —
Lover of / liberty / and human / rights*

---

* — ◡   ◡ — ◡◡   —   ◡ ◡   —
Lover / of liberty / and human / rights

This would make a typical heroic line—iambic pentameter with a trochee substi-tuted for the first foot.

(Also—the *you* rhyme is repeated too soon.)

or—

Tell me how / this man who / all of thence / blights

certainly do not conform to true requirements. In one or two places there does seem—despite the general fluency—to be a little heaviness in the handling of the words to make rhyme and metre come out right. In other spots the substitution of a word or two might add just an infinitesimal touch of aptness. Enclosed is a version, embodying all these points, which I hope will meet with your approval. Most of the changes were made to improve the rhythm—the easy "swing". Read it aloud and the effect will perhaps be apparent. In other cases I have sought to give the expression a slightly more effective turn—always, of course, remaining faithful to the original spirit. I hope these liberties don't seem excessive. Remember, of course, that I am not criticising your *present* style, but your work of a decade ago. There was no occasion to make written changes in your clever geographic acrostic.

Trusting that any comments may prove helpful—if only in slight degree—and again thanking you for the compliment of sending your sprightly lines, I am

Yrs most cordially and sincerely,

H. P. Lovecraft.

Notes

1. In the presidential election of 1912, Wilson ran as a Democrat; Taft, the incumbent, ran as a Republican; Theodore Roosevelt, formerly a Republican, had broken with Taft and ran a third-party campaign on the Bull Moose ticket.

2. Georges Clemenceau (1841–1929), Prime Minister of France (1906–09, 1917–20) who influenced Wilson to agree to harsh punitive measures against Germany in the Treaty of Versailles (1919–20).

3. Bautz said (18 June 1935; TLS, JHL) that he had entered a "Douglas acrostic" in a contest and had written "a recent acrostic for the Palmolive contest," presumably for a radio contest.

4. Hans von Kaltenborn (1878–1965), otherwise known as H. V. Kaltenborn, American radio news commentator.

[149] [AHT]

Charleston, S.C.
June 8, 1935

Dear Mr. Bautz:—

[. . .]

Just now—as I sit in the sun on Charleston's Battery, I am being pestered by dozens of coal-black pickaninnies of the average age of eight, who want (a) to black my already-blacked boots, and (b) to dance a jig for my benefit in exchange for a penny. Dey jes nochally ca'n't un'erstan' wha de genmum ruther write letters than improve his personal appearance or advance his choreographic education! Damn hard little wasps to shoo off—but one doesn't want to be cross with them. I feel quite flattered and bewildered by the importance which you and Moe seem to attach to my recent casual ramblings on yesterday's war-time issues. Bless me, but I had no wish to pose as an oracle! I dare say dozens of persons think about the same and say it much better. Likewise with the remarks on Roman architecture and the lines on '04.[1] As for lines on 1911—(my own class would have been 1912 had health not kept me from college) I don't believe I could have done them as well as '04. Somehow my extreme youth—and the period in which it lay—have for me a greater glamour than the middle period of young manhood. The world was fresher—and seemed fuller of golden glamour and adventurous expectancy than it ever did again. Also, my health was slightly better—and my environment was more congenial. My grandfather's death, and removal to smaller quarters in 1904 took something of zest out of existence. 1902-3-4 will always be seen through a transfiguring haze which 1911 lacks. I was quite broken down nervously in 1911—the year I came of age.

Every good wish,
Yrs most cordially,
H. P. Lovecraft.

Notes

1. HPL refers to items he had provided to Maurice W. Moe: "A Living Heritage: Roman Architecture in Today's America" and "An Epistle to the Rt. Honble Maurice Winter Moe, Esq. of Zythopolis, in the Northwest Territory of HIS MAJESTY'S American Dominions" (i.e., the lines on 1904).

To Ernest A. Edkins

Ernest A[rthur] Edkins (1867–1946) was a longtime amateur journalist with whom Lovecraft began corresponding in 1932. Lovecraft, who regarded Edkins as one of the shining lights of the "halcyon" age of amateur journalism (1885–95), persuaded him to rejoin the movement, and Edkins subsequently edited several issues of the journal *Causerie.* In the 1940s he co-edited the *Aonian,* an amateur journal that contained material by and about Lovecraft, with Timothy Burr Thrift. Lovecraft thought so highly of him that he preserved all the letters he received from Edkins (a total of 141 letters, now at JHL). In his memoir of Lovecraft, Edkins wrote: "All but one or two of the considerable number of letters that I received from him [Lovecraft] have been either lost or passed on to others, but I have a keen recollection of their archaic urbanity and charm" ("Idiosyncrasies of Lovecraft" [1940]; in Joshi and Schultz, *Ave atque Vale* 360). Only the incomplete draft letter that follows survives.

[150] [AL][1]

% R. H. Barlow
Box 88,
De Land, Florida
June 22, 1935.

O Stylus Chrysostomick:—[2]
Yours of the 17th, with its cargo of Aonian wealth, arrived on Thursday & at once precipitated a dust of admiring appreciation. What a wealth of delightful verse! And I do not say so in any spirit of insincere flattery! These things certainly catch the essence of vivid moods & authentic beauty; & are definitely powerful & haunting, no matter how much they may fall short of your original purpose as an artist. No one can 'put across' *all* of what he feels as he approaches & treats a certain subject; but when anyone 'puts across' as rich a proportion of the total as these verses seem to contain, he certainly cannot say that he has not succeeded. I don't think these poems can be called obscure or esoteric, or that their prosody is in any way harsh or involved. In many cases you have chosen a metre intentionally rugged as judged by syllable-counting & sing-song recitation (cf. Phaëton),[3] but the beat & cadences never fail to fulfil the chosen plan & satisfy the ear. Regarding "Bizarres"[4]—I do not think there is any real inadequacy in expressing the given concept, even if some of the specific references (embat-

tled gnomes, &c) are not instantly recognisable by the casual reader. The essentials are plainly & concretely suggested, & the major images are unmistakable in their implications. Barlow is particularly fond of this poem, & craves permission to use it in that prospective paper for which the "Letter to a Young Poet"[5] is already scheduled . . . . a permission which I trust you will grant.

"King Arthur's Keep" is a splendid picture—a scene which lives glowingly & realistically in the reader's imagination. The change of cadence in the last three stanzas, where the descriptive gives place to the reflective, seems unmistakably suggested by the change in approach. Since a general type of metre so intimately bound up with mood was chosen for the first two stanzas, it is inevitable that the metre change when the mood changes. The two forms are not incongruous, & the transition from one to the other is very smooth & outwardly imperceptible. Certainly, there is no more unjustified abruptness about the shift than in any musical composition where the movement naturally changes. It would have been far less justified if no change had been made in order to preserve an artificial smoothness & uniformity. The strong emotion behind the poem is certainly well realised. Phaëton [don't run together the A & E in the name—they do not form a diphthong] is powerful even if elusive. The appeal is manifest throughout, & the images partake of the aërial, flamelike, wistful quality of the whole. "Heimwehfluh" appeals to me tremendously, & I don't consider its *simplicity* as a defect of any sort. Indeed, this directness—in view of the theme—contributes to its power.

Altogether, these four poems strike me as forming a highly remarkable group—or perhaps I should not say "remarkable", since expression of this kind seems to be something not by any means unprecedented with you. What I mean is that they are remarkable when viewed either as amateur journalism's products, or as the performances of one whose poetic utterance has been so relatively infrequent. They are full of that charm, grace, & mellowness which characterise genuine & well-grounded poetry; & fit delightfully into the picture of Golden Age Aonianism which has since 1916 or 1917 been symbolised in my mind by the composite & almost abstract type-figure of "Edkins 'n' Emery."[6] Great stuff—& I like them all prodigiously! Barlow won't be happy till he has captured one for his future paper—& I won't be contented till they have all helped—in print somewhere or other—to promote the aesthetic renaissance of amateurdom. You have every reason to be proud of these things—& it is only because of old times, & because of that traditional connexion betwixt yourself & the N.A.P.A.'s Golden Age, that I suggest *amateur* papers as a preferred medium of publication. I hate to follow out your command to return these fascinating items—& indeed, I may defy authority & keep a copy of the poem Barlow wants . . . (Bizarres) . . . . subject, of course[,] to your approval & veto. *All* of the poems, I trust, will eventually find a proper place in papers of the right sort.

Notes

1. Beneath the final paragraph, R. H. Barlow has written: "(discarded because it was not sufficiently tactful)."

2. A pen is one of many symbols associated with St. John Chrysostom (c. 347–407), an important and prolific Early Church Father who served as archbishop of Constantinople. The epithet *Chrysostom* means "golden-mouthed" and alludes to his eloquence.

3. *Californian* 6, No. 1 (Summer 1938): 49.

4. "Bizarres," *Dragon-Fly* No. 1 (15 October 1935): 32.

5. "Fragment of a Letter to a Young Poet," *Dragon-Fly* No. 1 (15 October 1935): [11]–26.

6. Brainerd Prescott Emery (1865–1917). HPL discusses Emery throughout the essay "Looking Backward" (1920), his survey of amateur papers from 1885 to 1895 (*CE* 1.239–53).

To Alvin Earl Perry

It appears Lovecraft wrote only one letter to Alvin Earl Perry (1918–1968). Perry was a fan of the science and weird fiction pulps and had numerous letters published in them. He also wrote "biographical sketches" of Robert E. Howard, E. Hoffmann Price, and A. W. Bernal for *Fantasy Magazine* in 1935 and 1936. Lovecraft's letter is largely cribbed from his essay "Notes on Writing Weird Fiction." If Perry wrote an article about Lovecraft, it was not published.

[151] [ALS][1]

66 College St.,
Providence, R.I.
Oct. 4, 1935.

Dear Mr. Perry:—

I found your card of Septr. 4 awaiting me upon my return from an absence of 3½ months—& such was the engulfing pressure of piled-up work that I have not until now been able to acknowledge it. Your wish to cite my methods of story-writing in the *Fantasy* article gives me a very flattered feeling, & I trust the ensuing remarks may not arrive too late to be of any use.

In a way, it is impossible for me to give a detailed account of how I write a story—from the moment of conception till it is sent out to gain one of Wright's rejection slips—since I've scarcely ever used the same method for any two stories. It all depends upon the individual circumstances.

The one thing I never do is to sit down & seize a pen with the deliberate intention of writing a story. Nothing but hack work ever comes of that. The only stories I write are those whose central ideas, pictures, or moods occur to me spontaneously—beforehand—& virtually demand formulation & expression.

These ideas, picture, & moods come from every possible source—dreams, reading, daily occurrences, odd visual glimpses, or origins so remote & fragmentary that I cannot place them. Naturally, they come in different stages of development—sometimes a bare incident, effect, concept, or shade of feeling which requires a whole fabric of deliberate story-construction to support it, & sometimes a sequence of incidents which forms a goodly part of the final story. In at least one case I dreamed a story in full—"The Statement of Randolph Carter" being a literal recording of what sleep brought me one night in December 1919.

If there is any one method which I follow, I suppose it is to be found by taking an average of my lines of procedure in all the cases where I have done a great deal of deliberate construction. For example—behind "The Whisperer in Darkness" lay only two initial impelling concepts: the idea of a man in a lonely farmhouse besieged by "outside" horrors, & the general impression of weirdness in the Vermont landscape, gained during a fortnight's visit near Brattleboro in 1928. Upon these notions I had to build a story—& in doing that I followed a course which may or may not be typical. Here, then, is a rough idea of what I did in that case—& what I do more or less in similar cases.

First, a coherent story—or a rough approximation of one—must be thought out. This is a mental process, before pen & paper are approached. It is not often necessary to fill in details, or even to carry the plot forward to a definite end. The point is to think up some sort of definite series of developments which shall give the initial concept or concepts a plausible reason for existing, & make it or them appear to be the logical, inevitable outgrowth of some vital & convincing background. This "plot" or series of steps need not be a permanent one. Perhaps it will lose all its salient points during later manipulation—other & better ways of accounting for the central idea being discovered. But it is a useful starting-point—something to work with & build upon. When it has attained some definite shape in one's head, the time has come to turn to writing materials.

Yet even the second—or first recorded—stage is not that of actual story-writing. Instead, one had better begin with a synopsis of the given plot—listing all developments *in the order of their supposed actual occurrence*, not the order in which they will finally reach the reader. This is to provide a logical working background for the writer, so that he can envisage his plot as something which has really happened, & decide at leisure on what narrative devices to adopt in preparing a dramatic, suspense-filled version for the reader. In writing such a synopsis I try to describe everything with enough fulness to cover all vital points & motivate all the incidents planned. Details, comments, & estimates of the *consequences* of certain points are often desirable. The result is rather like an official report of some chain of happenings—each event set down prosaically in precise order of occurrence. Often the previously-planned plot will suffer great changes in the course of this recording.

Then comes the next stage—deciding *how to tell* the story already thought out. This begins mentally—by thinking of various effective ways to arrange certain unfoldings & revelations. We speculate on what to tell first, & what to save for later presentation in order to preserve suspense or provoke interest. We analyse the dramatic value of putting this thing before that thing, or vice versa, & try to see what selection of details & order of narration best conduce to that rising tide of development & final burst of revealing completion which we call "climax." Having roughly made our decisions regarding a tentative arrangement, we proceed to write these down in the form of *a second synopsis*—a synopsis or "scenario" of events *in order of their narration to the reader*, with ample fulness & detail, & with notes on such things as changing perspective, modulated stresses, & ultimate climax. I never hesitate to change the original synopsis to fit some newly devised development if such a devising can increase the dramatic force or general effectiveness of the future story. Incidents should be interpolated or deleted at will—the writer never being bound by his original conception, even though the ultimate result be a tale wholly different from that first planned. The wise author lets additions & alterations be made whenever such are suggested by anything in the formulating process.

The time has now come to *write the story* in the approximate language which the reader is to see. This first draught should be written rapidly, fluently, & not too critically—following the second synopsis. I always change incidents & plot whenever the developing process seems to suggest such change—never being bound by any previous design. If the development suddenly reveals new opportunities for dramatic effect or vivid story-telling, I add whatever I think advantageous—going back & reconciling early points to the new plan. I insert or delete whole sections when I deem it necessary or desirable—trying different beginnings & endings till the best is found. But I always take infinite pains to make sure that all references throughout the story are thoroughly reconciled with the final design. Then—in completing the rough draught—I seek to remove all possible superfluities—words, sentences, paragraphs, or whole episodes or elements—, observing the usual precautions about the reconciliation of all references. So open-minded do I keep during this stage of writing, that several of my tales (such as "The Picture in the House", "The Dunwich Horror", & "The Shadow Over Innsmouth") end in a manner totally unforeseen when I began them.

Now comes the *revision*—a tedious, painstaking process. One must go over the entire text, paying attention to vocabulary, syntax, rhythm of prose, proportioning of parts, niceties of tone, grace & convincingness of *transitions* (scene to scene, slow & detailed action to rapid & sketchy time-covering actions & vice versa . . . &. &c. &c.), effectiveness of beginning, ending, climaxes, &c., dramatic suspense & interest, plausibility & atmosphere, & various other elements. That finishes the story—& the rest is merely the preparation of a neatly typed version . . . the most horrible part of all to me. I detest the typewriter, & could not possibly compose a story on one. The mechanical limitations of the machine are death to good style anyway—it being harder to transpose words & make the necessary complex interlineations when bound to keys & rollers, while delicate prose rhythms are defeated by the irrelevant regular rhythms of line-endings & roller-turnings. Nothing was ever composed on a typewriter which could not have been composed better with pen or pencil.

Well—as I have said, this list of composition-steps is merely an average or idealised one. In practice, one seldom follows every step literally. Often one or more of the things supposed to be done on paper can be better done in one's head—so that many tales (such as my "Music of Erich Zann" or "Dagon") never had any kind of a written synopsis.

Nor should the given method be followed even mentally in some cases. Sometimes I have found it useful to begin writing a story without either a synopsis or even a bare idea of how it shall be developed & ended. This is when I feel a need of recording & exploiting some especially powerful or suggestive mood or picture to the full—as in "The Strange High House in the Mist." In such a procedure the beginning thus produced may be regarded as a problem to be motivated & explained. Of course, in developing this motivation & explanation it may be well to alter—or even transform, transpose beyond recognition, or altogether eliminate—the beginning first produced. Once in a while, when a writer has a marked style with rhythms & cadences closely linked with imaginative associations, it is possible for him to begin *weaving a mood* with characteristic paragraphs & letting this mood dictate much of the tale. This is what I did in "The White Ship"—though it must be owned that the result was not very successful.

I try always to keep a supply of story-ideas on hand—recording all bizarre notions, moods, dreams, images, concepts, &c., (& keeping all press clippings involving such) for future use. I do not despair if they seem to have no logical development. Each one may be worked over gradually—surrounded with notes & synopses, & finally built into a coherent explanatory structure capable of fictional use. I never hurry, nor seek to emulate the commercial writers who boast of their wordage per day or week. The best stories sometimes grow very slowly—over long periods, & with intervals in their formulation. *Too long* intervals, though, are to be discouraged; insomuch as they often alienate the writer from the mood and tempo of his task.

Random notes: ¶ In a tale involving complex philosophical or scientific principles, I try to have all explanations *hinted* at the outset, when the thesis is first put forward (as in Machen's "White People"), thus leaving the narrative & climactic sections unencumbered.

¶ I am always willing to spend as much time & care on the formulation of a synopsis as on the writing of the actual tale—*for the synopsis is the real heart of the story.* The real creative work of fiction-writing is originating & shaping a story in synopsis form.

¶ In order to ensure an adequate climax it is in rare cases advisable to prepare one in considerable detail *first,* & then construct a main synopsis explaining it. I followed this plan in "The Tree", "The Hound", & other minor pieces. With one it works less satisfactorily than with others.

¶ I always endeavour to read & analyse the best weird writers—Poe, Machen, Blackwood, James, Dunsany, de la Mare, Wakefield, Benson, Ewers,[2] & the like—, seeking to understand their methods & recognise the specific laws of emotional modulation behind their potent effects. Such study gradually increases one's own grasp of his materials, & strengthens his powers of expression. By the same token, I strive to avoid all close attention to the prose & methods of pulp hack writers—things which insidiously corrupt & cheapen a serious style. I would advise all serious literary aspirants to cultivate a sort of defensive semi-blindness in skimming cheap magazine fiction—developing an ability to sift out incidents & follow a plot without closely paying attention to the language. And most plots of this sort had better be followed very lightly & emulated not at all. In a year's output of pulp magazines there are scarcely a dozen stories seriously conceived & artistically written to an extent justifying remembrance, preservation, or imitation. The genuine writer must forget editors & possible audiences, resign himself to very infrequent sales, & labour only to express himself & satisfy his inward standards of taste. Commercialism & decent literature have no meeting-point save by accident.

And so it goes. I don't know whether any of this meandering will be of use to you, but it's the best I can provide amidst my present rush of work. Use it as you like, & let me know if there are any other points which you'd like to have covered. Hope my rotten handwriting isn't giving you too much trouble—I ought to type this, but I simply haven't the energy to spare. If you wish to make any extended verbatim quotations, you might send the final MS. to me—leaving blank spaces for the words you cannot decipher. I'll then go over the text, supplying the absent words & straightening out all the difficulties as best I can. But perhaps this arrives so late that you won't be able to use it at all.

No—I have no accepted stories awaiting publication in W T or any other professional sheet. W T has gone detective, & for a long time Wright has been hostile toward my MSS. He says my newer stories are *too long*—& then proceeds to accept some interminable serial by one of his regular hacks! There's no use trying to land anything with an editor who frankly caters to illiterates. I haven't submitted any MS. to Wright in two years . . . . although stories which I have "ghost-written" for various clients have occasionally appeared. If you'd care to see any of my recent work, I'll lend you MSS. Most of it is probably destined to remain in manuscript form!

With best wishes for your coming series, & apologies for this late response to your card, I remain

Yrs most cordially & sincerely,
H. P. Lovecraft

Notes

1. At the very top of the letter, someone (perhaps Perry's mother) has written "I opened by mistake thinking it was mine. *Pardon.*"
2. The weird writers Walter de la Mare (English; 1873–1956), H. Russell Wakefield (English; 1888–1964), E. F. Benson (English; 1867–1940), and Hanns Heinz Ewers (German; 1871–1943).

To Julius Schwartz

Julius Schwartz (1915–2004) was a prominent science fiction fan and the editor of *Fantasy Magazine*. He acted as Lovecraft's agent in selling *At the Mountains of Madness* to *Astounding Stories*. In later years he was a comic book editor and an agent for science fiction writers. He is best known as a longtime editor at DC Comics, where for a period he was primary editor over the publishers' two great superheroes, Superman and Batman.

As editor of *Fantasy Magazine*, Schwartz commissioned Lovecraft (along with C. L. Moore, A. Merritt, Robert E. Howard, and Frank Belknap Long) to write the weird version of "The Challenge from Beyond" for the September 1935 issue (also a science fiction version with five other writers). At a party in New York, probably in the fall of 1935, Lovecraft agreed to let Schwartz market his material; Schwartz sold *At the Mountains of Madness* to *Astounding* for $350 (he took a 10% commission). In late 1936 he contemplated marketing Lovecraft's tales in England, but if he did so he was unsuccessful. Schwartz published his memoirs, *Man of Two Worlds* (2000).

[152]

December 20, 1935

I am certainly grieved by the news of Weinbaum's death.[1] His stories were first called to my attention last spring, and I saw with pleasure that some one had at last escaped the sickening hackneyedness in which 99.99% of all pulp interplanetary stuff is engulfed. Here, I rejoiced, was somebody who could think of another planet in terms of something besides anthropomorphic kings and beautiful princesses and battles of spaceships and ray guns and attacks from the hairy sub-men of the "dark side" or "polar cap" region, etc., etc. . . . Somehow he had the imagination to envisage wholly alien situations and psychologies and entities, to devise consistent events from wholly alien motives and to refrain from the cheap dramatics in which almost all adventure pulpists wallow. Now and then a touch of the *seemingly* trite would appear—but before long it would be obvious that the author had introduced it merely to satirise it. The light touch did not detract from the interest of the tales—and genuine suspense was secured without the catchpenny tricks of the majority. The tales of Mars, I think, were Weinbaum's best—those in which that curiously sympathetic being "Tweel" figure[s].

Notes

1. Stanley G[rauman] Weinbaum (1902–14 December 1935) died of throat cancer at the age of 35. His writing career lasted a scant 18 months, but he is considered one of the greatest of science fiction writers for his realistic portrayal of alien creatures. Tweel was the central figure in Weinbaum's first and groundbreaking story, "A Martian Odyssey" (*Wonder Stories*, July 1934). He also appeared in "Valley of Dreams" (*Wonder Stories*, November 1934). Weinbaum belonged to the Milwaukee Fictioneers along with Robert Bloch, Roger Sherman Hoar ("Ralph Milne Farley"), Raymond A. Palmer, Arthur Tofte, and others.

To Forrest J Ackerman

Forrest J Ackerman (1916–2008) was an American agent, author, and editor. He was a science fiction fan since the late 1920s; he corresponded sporadically with Lovecraft from around 1931 onward. He instigated a controversy in "The Boiling Point" column (*FF*, September 1933f.; see letters to Charles D. Hornig herein) when he criticized Clark Ashton Smith's "The Dweller in Martian Depths" (*Wonder Stories*, March 1933); Lovecraft and his colleagues wrote numerous responses sharply criticizing Ackerman. Lovecraft poked fun at Ackerman in "The Battle That Ended the Century" (1934; with R. H. Barlow), referring to him as "the Effjay of Akkamin," and in "In the Walls of Eryx" (1936; with Kenneth Sterling), where mention is made of "wriggling" and "slimy akmans" and "efjehweeds." He was later editor of *Famous Monsters of Filmland* magazine (1958–82), which was instrumental in maintaining fan interest in weird fiction (and specifically horror films) during an otherwise lean period for the horror genre.

The letter published herein appeared initially with the following note: "2 yrs ago *HPL* rcvd from *FJA* a composite Kodak of the 'Master Maniac & Damsel in Distress' from macabre movie 'Mad Love', accompanied by a card expressing weird wishes for a 'Cthulhui*christmas* & Necronomico*new* yr'. The day before Xmas, 1934, *HPL* acknowledged receipt of this still of the cinema's 'Lord Hi Minister of All That Is Sinister'. '*HPLovecraft* re *Peter Lorre*' We publish following exactly as rcvd by Forry—precisely as penned by . . . *Lovecraft!*" The few other letters Lovecraft wrote to Ackerman have not come to light.

[153]

66 College St.,
Providence, R.I.,
Dec. 24, 1935

My dear Ackerman:—
Let me thank you most sincerely for the malignly hypnotic photograph of the egg-domed gentleman which reached me yesterday. Surely this pleasant chap looks as if he had but recently wriggled forth from an accursed tomb, & were prepared to wreak upon mankind any & every sort of evil from mere vampirism to cosmos-blasting invocation of the ultimate

black powers of horror! It's a wonder that the accompanying lady doesn't look more frightened than she does . . . . & one may imagine the hideous bass dissonances which issue forth from that shadowy Chickering[1] as clammy corpse-fingers draw a danse macabre on its time-stained ivory keys!

This portrait is really very timely, since a great many correspondents have been urging me to see some film—in fact, any film—in which the sinister Mr. Lorre is featured. "Mad Love"[2] has been especially recommended, & I have been quite alertly on the lookout for it, but somehow or other it has escaped me so far. After this glimpse I shall double the alerttness [*sic*] of my vigil. Ordinarily I see very few films—& most of the allegedly weird ones which I have seen ("Frankenstein", "The Ghoul",[3] &c.) were so naive & conventional in their appeal that they did not encourage persistence in the quest for thrills. Lately, however, so many have assured me that Lorre is the real thing, that I am determined to make his projected acquaintance at the very first opportunity. Again let me thank you for the vivid view—which I shall add with appreciation to my files.

With the season's best wishes, & trusting that your New Year may be replete with startling messages from the trans-galactic ether, I am

> Yrs most cordially,
> H. P. Lovecraft

Notes

1. Chickering & Sons was an American piano manufacturer located in Boston.
2. *Mad Love* (MGM, 1935), directed by Karl Freund; starring Peter Lorre, Frances Drake, and Colin Clive. Based on the novel *The Hands of Orlac* by Maurice Renard.
3. *Frankenstein* (Universal, 1931), directed by James Whale; starring Colin Clive, Mae Clarke, John Boles, and Boris Karloff. *The Ghoul* (Gaumont British Picture Corp., 1933), directed by T. Hayes Hunter; starring Boris Karloff, Cedric Hardwicke, and Ernest Thesiger.

To Mrs. H. H. Hughes

Kathleen Compere Hughes (1904–2000), wife of Herald Hall
Hughes (1902–1993), lived in Lawton, Okla., at the time Lovecraft wrote what seems to be his only letter to her. A letter by
her to "Dear Friend" of 6 April 1937 survives at JHL addressing
some of the points in the following letter, but the recipient may
have been R. H. Barlow. Her letter mentions returning some
borrowed manuscripts and hoping to see more, and asks if recipient is still writing stories. It is unknown how Lovecraft came
to hear from her, although she may have written him care of
Weird Tales. A letter by her was published in "The Eyrie" for the
August–September 1936 issue (pp. 255–56). Equally mysterious
is the fact that her letter from him was received at Arkham
House for transcription, for it survives only in the transcripts.

[154] [AHT]

[c. October 1936]

About these books on Atlantis, Lemuria, and Mu—I regret to say that
they all belong in the domain of charlatanry, semi-charlatanry, and self-
delusion. There is absolutely no basis in fact for any of the assumptions they
purvey—while on the other hand there is overwhelming evidence that none
of the fabulous "vanished continents" ever existed since the appearance of
mankind on the earth. In very early geologic ages, before man existed, all the
continental outlines were indeed different—Asia and North America being
joined, land bridges spanning what is now the Atlantic, Australia stretching
from Indo-China to Antarctica, South America and Graham Land continuing
into Antarctic, etc. etc.—but all this preceded any age when man or civilisation was on the scene. In the world of early man there were some differences.
The British Isles were probably *parts* of the European continent, while the
Mediterranean may have consisted of two inland lakes. The East Indies, too,
may have been joined to Asia, whilst a great sea covered inner North America. But there was nothing corresponding to Atlantis, Lemuria, or Mu. We can
tell this because of the radically different *recent* fauna and flora in the lands
which would be one if such continents existed. The *very ancient* life forms of
these lands were indeed identical, showing that they were *once* connected—
millions of years ago. But by the time the mesozoic age is over we find differ-
entiations beginning to appear—so that the lands once joined have *increasingly
different* sorts of plants and animals. This proves that they had begun to be
separated by water as they are now. And all this was millions of years before

man had evolved. It is safe, then, to say that accounts of Atlantis, Lemuria, and Mu—so far as they relate to human habitation—are sheer myths based on false, mistaken, or deliberately manufactured evidence. A good deal of the talk of vanished lands and races comes from a loose interpretation of imaginative oriental mythology—especially as fostered by the modern cult of theosophy. But none of this has any scientific standing. As for pre-human or pre-mammal civilisations of the sort that I and other fictioneers spiel yarns about—all we can say is that the known facts of biology and zoology make any such thing *extremely improbable*. Our imaginations are at liberty to weave pictures—but the chances are all against their reality. Man probably took vague form some 3,000,000 or 2,000,000 years ago, and attained something like his present physical and mental development about 1,000,000 years ago—many parallel sub-human races perishing side by side with him. Settled life and civilisation were probably slow in appearing, so that they do not very far antedate the dawn of history. I doubt whether this planet ever knew any civilisation prior to the one founded by true human beings in the uplands of Central Asia between 15,000 and 25,000 year ago. Even this is hypothetical. We know only that mature, fully developed civilisations existed in the Tigris-Euphrates valley some 8,000 years ago, and that these and other cultures in India, China, and elsewhere suggest a spread outward from a certain focal point at a certain rate. In speculations of this sort, the works of Sir Arthur Keith, and the latest books of Prof. G. Elliot Smith, will be found most illuminating.[1] Clark Ashton Smith and E. Hoffmann Price are also highly erudite in this way—though Price has never made use of his knowledge. One may add that real history offers one *miniature* parallel to the Atlantis–Lemuria–Mu idea in the case of the small volcanic *islands* (especially in the Aegean Sea and Pacific Ocean) which are known to have sunk or risen during the existence of man and even of civilisation. Thus the sunken-land idea cannot be regarded as wholly fictitious. While it is absurd to call Easter Island a former mountain or a vanished continent, it is by no means improbable that it once had close insular neighbours, and that it formed the sacerdotal headquarters of a kind of archipelagic civilisation. (See J. MacMillan Brown: "The Riddle of the Pacific.") Col. Churchward, the author of the "Mu" books, was a curious old chap—who probably believed more or less implicitly in his own extravagant yarns and deductions.[2]

I surely hope that you can some time see Newburyport and the other ancient towns of the East. There is a whole string of such places from Quebec on the north to St. Augustine on the south—to say nothing of the southwestern extension formed by Natchez and New Orleans. A summer season in New England would form a far from costly vacation as such things go. In most of the picturesque districts there are homes where one could obtain a room as low as $5.00 per week, while food is not more expensive than elsewhere. Cape Cod is a bit overdone by tourists, and has always seemed to me somewhat overrated. Different vacationists, of course, seek different things; so that no all-inclusive recommendation is possible. But if what one seeks is quaint and ancient village atmosphere, *Marblehead* has no competition. If I had a whole summer to spend in New England vacationing, I would not stay in any one place but would spend a week each in many different places. I would (if coming in from outside) not enter in the usual way, but would go from Albany to Greenfield over the Mohawk Trail. From Greenfield as a base I would take side-trips to Vermont and to ancient Deerfield. Then I'd go on to Boston and do the metropolitan zone. After that, the North Shore—Salem, Marblehead, Gloucester and Cape Ann, Newburyport, Portsmouth, N.H.— perhaps achieving a side-trip to the White Mountains or to marvellous *Quebec.* Then down to the region south of Boston—Plymouth, Cape Cod, New Bedford—and above all a trip to quiet Nantucket Island. Then Providence and Newport, and after that a leisurely jaunt through Connecticut, seeing such fine old villages as Wethersfield, Farmington, and Guilford, and the splendid city of New Haven. But for a long-term stay, *Marblehead* is the place! I've never seen California, but would like to. My travels have never extended west of Cleveland in the North, nor west of the Mississippi in the South. I envy you your sight of Santa Fe—of which I've heard much, and which probably resembles St. Augustine more than any other town I know. Next to New England (and much *more* so far as climate is concerned, since I can't stand cold) I like the South best of all places. Virginia is exquisite (Fredericksburg especially), while Charleston, S.C., is really my favourite of all cities. I am also fond of Natchez, Miss., and of St. Augustine, Fla. I shall probably have to live in the South eventually, since the climate here is increasingly intolerable to me. I am at my best around 80° or 90°, and can't guide a pen under 75°. Under 20° alarming symptoms develop, so that I am virtually a prisoner all winter. Florida is the only place where I feel continuously well.

I also wish I could see the Old World—the sources of our civilisation, and the shards of dead civilisations. Mexico and Central America would also be a delight—and I envy Price his trip of a year ago to Mexico City and the prehistoric ruins at Teotihuacan. And in imagination rather than in person I rejoice in explorations of sunken lands and brooding polar wastes. The *Antarctic continent* and its unseen leagues of black mountains and icy death is a theme which has haunted me ever since I was ten years old. I have a small collection of ancient and exotic objects including an Egyptian statuette, an Aztec calendar-stone, some Mayan images, a Greek lamp, etc. etc.

Your family link with Newburyport will doubtless heighten your interest in the "Innsmouth" story. Newburyport is a strange old city—half-deserted by its former industries, and with that air of sleepy hush and partial desertion typical of a town which has lost about half its population since its heyday. The harbour is half-filled with drifting sand, the wharves and marine warehouses are moss-grown and ruinous, whole blocks of vacant shops can be found in water-front streets, and certain sections are almost completely uninhabited, with long rows of 200-year-old houses boarded up and condemned. The business blocks of the main section are quaint, slant-roofed affairs put up just after the great fire of 1811, and there are some fine old churches with white Georgian steeples—in one of which the famous evangelist George Whitefield is buried. Far back from the waterfront is stately High St., with the great mansions of the colonial gentry and early-republic ship-owners. Newburyport was a great maritime centre around 1800—the period in which it harboured the famous eccentric "Lord" Timothy Dexter, about whom you have doubtless heard or read.[3] Just now—for history repeats itself—Newburyport has another rated eccentric in the person of its present mayor—an ex-sailor named Andrew G. Gillis, whose uncouth "rough-house" methods command many columns of newspaper space and form an inexpressible shock to the staid citizenry.[4] There is no place quite like Newburyport—for its retarded business life has preserved its sleepy antique flavour to an astonishing extent. It would form a rival to Marblehead if it were less regular in topography and layout, and if its houses were quite as old and quaint as those of the smaller port. In some ways it conveys a better impression of early America than does Salem or Gloucester. I can lend you some postcard views of Newburyport and environs if you'd care to see them.

Providence, though a large city, is also very quaint—especially on the precipitous hill where I live. Federal Hill is not so ancient, but is fascinating as a transplanted bit of Southern Italy. That old church has no sinister history, but looks as if it might have.

As for the "hellish and forbidden volumes" mentioned by various Mu writers—the monstrous *Necronomicon* of the mad Arab Abdul Alhazred, the portentous *Book of Eibon,* the shocking *Unaussprechlichen Kulten* of von Junzt, the Comte d'Erlette's *Cultes des Goules,* Ludvig Prinn's *De Vermis Mysteriis,* the Pnakotic Manuscripts, the Eltdown Shards, the unmentionable *Ghorl Nigral,*[5] etc. etc. etc.—they are all purely imaginary, like some of the "terrible tomes" mentioned in Poe, Bierce, Machen, Blackwood, Hodgson, etc. I think I started the ball rolling myself with the good old *Necronomicon* and the Pnakotic Manuscripts, but others of our group were quick to take up the idea and invent hellish volumes of their own. Clark Ashton Smith evolved the *Book of Eibon;* the late Robert E. Howard invented von Junzt and his "Black Book"; Robert Bloch is responsible for Ludvig Prinn and his mysteries—and also for the *Cultes des Goules.* R. F. Searight conceived the Eltdown Shards—and so on and so on. We all make references to one another's blasphemous secret tomes in order to build up an atmosphere of convincing naturalness concerning them (as we also do with our artificial gods and devils—Azathoth, Nyarlathotep, Cthulhu, Yog-Sothoth, Shub-Niggurath, Tsathoggua, etc. etc.), though we never try to put them across as actual hoaxes. We would, indeed, feel sincerely sorry if we led anybody to waste time in searching for books which do not exist.

Have I ever been in Newburyport? I should say I have! It is one of my favourite towns—a sleepy little city full of ancient houses and looking much as it did a century ago. It is precisely the sort of place I write about so often in my tales—and indeed, in "The Shadow Over Innsmouth" I mention it by name and speak of many of its streets. It is very interesting to know that you have relatives there. About "Arkham"—yes, *Salem* is its general prototype, although "Miskatonic University" is an interpolation. There is no college in Salem. I may add that "Kingsport" is *Marblehead*—a very quaint seaport contiguous to Salem—while "Dunwich" roughly reflects the Wilbraham region near Springfield. The Providence geography and descriptions in "The Haunter of the Dark" are true to fact—the house on College Hill being this one. At this moment I am looking out the window at Federal Hill and the spectral church—which latter, however, has now lost its slender spire through a lightning-stroke. Old towns fascinate me more than anything else—indeed, my chief hobby is architectural antiquarianism. Whenever I have any cash I spend it on trips to ancient places—Quebec, Salem, Philadelphia, Annapolis, Fredericksburg, Charleston, St. Augustine, Natchez, New Orleans, etc.

There is a great fascination in curios of all kinds—and I especially relish those with extreme antiquity behind them. I have quite a few genuine Egyptian objects, a good lamp and funerary jar, a few Roman coins, and several other odds and ends of the remote past in addition to the Aztec-Maya material. Archaeology most surely forms a fascinating pursuit. The other day I was vastly interested by a lecture on the early coastal civilisations of Peru—by a museum curator newly returned from there. It seems that the pre-Inca lowland races built great cities and had highly developed arts and crafts as early as the second or third century A.D.—at the same time that other cultures were arising in the Andean highlands. Lantern slides and a large assortment of reliques (pottery, textiles, etc.) helped to make this address exceptionally vivid.

About the way I write my tales—certainly I do them all in longhand. I couldn't possibly compose anything of importance on a typewriter. Some *do* compose on a machine—but I couldn't. Incidentally I'm enclosing something about my writing methods which I prepared at the request of one of the young "fan magazine" editors.[6] Please return it some time—for I'm not sure when the printed version will appear. About those snaps of "the gang"—I'll lend them as soon as Finlay returns them.[7] I don't like to hurry him up, since he's been ill.

Notes

1. Sir Arthur Keith (1866–1955), Scottish anthropologist, and G[rafton] Elliot Smith

(1971–1937), Australian-British Egyptologist, both propounded the theory that Europe was the cradle of humanity, but Smith also asserted a significant influence of Egypt upon ancient European culture.

2. Col. James Churchward (1851–1936), British occultist, wrote many fanciful books on the purportedly lost continent of Mu (in the Pacific). HPL mentions him in "Through the Gates of the Silver Key" and "Out of the Aeons."

3. "Lord" Timothy Dexter (1747–1806), as he was known to his contemporaries, was an eccentric American businessman and author of *A Pickle for the Knowing Ones* (1805), who dubbed himself "first in the East, the first in the West, and the greatest philosopher in the known world." He was a source for the character Obed Marsh in "The Shadow over Innsmouth."

4. Andrew Jackson ("Bossy") Gillis (1896–1965) was inducted mayor of Newburyport in January 1928. A former sailor, Gillis had several minor troubles with the police, including parking in a restricted area. In general, Gillis conducted himself in a flamboyant and undignified manner. He served six two-year terms as mayor between 1927 and 1960.

5. Invented by Willis Conover. HPL first discusses it in a letter to Conover (14 August 1936); *Letters to Robert Bloch and Others* 385.

6. "Notes on Writing Weird Fiction." The essay was published after HPL's death.

7. Virgil Finlay (1914–1971), celebrated weird artist.

To James Blish and William Miller, Jr.

James Blish (1921–1975) was a pioneering American science fiction writer. Blish and William H. Miller, Jr. (1921–1995, name later changed to Christian William Miller), living in East Orange, N.J., edited a mimeographed magazine called the *Planeteer*. Several issues appeared in 1935–36. Although they printed some sheets that included Lovecraft's poem "The Wood" (2, No. 1 [September 1936]: 5–6), the issue was not completed nor published. Blish published a mimeographed parody of Lovecraft and Clark Ashton Smith: "The Eldritch Goo: Manuscript Found Under a Bed in the Ruins of the Bronx," as by "H. Ashton Bloke," *Grotesque* 1, No. 1 (Spring 1937).

[155]

May 13, 1936

I am very glad to hear that you liked *At the Mountains of Madness*—which I like as well as anything I've ever attempted. The idea of the great white antarctic—an alien world of death, and the last great *Terra Incognita* on this planet—has haunted me ever since I was ten years old; and in this yarn I tried to express, after a fashion, the feeling of mystery it inspires in me. . . .

You are fortunate in securing copies of the hellish and abhorred *Necronomicon*. Are they the Latin texts printed in Germany in the fifteenth century, or the Greek version printed in Italy in 1567, or the Spanish translation of 1623? Or do the copies represent different texts? I am forced to depend upon the copy kept under lock and key in the library of the Miskatonic University in Arkham. It surely is a pity that the Arabic original is lost!

[156]

May 19, 1936

About the *Necronomicon*—bless my soul, but I thought you knew that was a strictly imaginary institution! The paragraph about its being for sale at $1.49 was a joke—I don't know who wrote it, but suspect young Bloch.[1] All the terrible and mysterious books so darkly mentioned in weird magazine stories are imaginary. I invented the *Necronomicon*, Clark Ashton Smith thought of *The Book of Eibon*, Robert E. Howard is responsible for *Unaussprechlichen Kulten*, Searight "discovered" the *Eltdown Shards*, Bloch is the parent of Ludvig Prinn's *De Vermis Mysteriis*, and of the shocking *Cultes des Goules* and so on.

[157]

June 3, 1936

Yes—it's too bad those Hellish and Forbidden Volumes exist only in the library of Miskatonic University and kindred places, and I really wish somebody had the time and skill to write them. The nearest things to them in reality are certain fragments of mythology and magical lore which actually do exist scattered about here and there. Bits of Oriental tradition such as those cited in Sinnett's *Esoteric Buddhism* (the kind of stuff from which theosophists concoct their fake traditions), and odd scraps of European and Near-Eastern rituals—mostly mediaeval incantations for summoning various spirits—such as A. E. Waite and "Eliphas Levi" (Alphonse-Louis Constant) reproduce in treatises on magic really *do* constitute something vaguely like what the *Necronomicon* and its congeners are supposed to be—but of course they are merely fragments, and are far less darkly impressive than the pre-human volumes which one may imagine!

As for bringing the *Necronomicon* into objective existence—I wish indeed that I had the time and imagination to assist in such a project . . . but I'm afraid it's a rather large order—especially since the dreaded volume is supposed to run to something like a thousand pages! I have "quoted" from pages as high as 770 or thereabouts.[2] Moreover, one can never *produce* anything even a tenth as terrible and impressive as one can awesomely *hint* about. If anyone were to try to *write* the *Necronomicon*, it would disappoint all those who have shuddered at cryptic references to it. The most one could do—and I may try that some time—is to "translate" isolated chapters of the mad Arab's monstrous tome . . . the less terrible chapters, which ordinary humans may read without danger of laying themselves open to siege by the Shapes from the Abyss of Azathoth. . . . It would be delightful if illustrations could be supplied by the sorcerer Klarkash-Ton, High-Priest of Tsathoggua—Abbot of Averoigne, and Direct Descendant of the Wizard Eibon in the 100,789th generation. A collected series of such extracts might be offered as an "abridged and expurgated *Necronomicon*"—although I am opposed to *serious* hoaxes, since they really confuse and retard the sincere student of folklore. I feel quite guilty every time I hear of someone's having spent valuable time looking up the *Necronomicon* at public libraries.

Notes

1. "How I Get My Inspiration" by A Weird Tales Author (i.e., Robert Bloch), *Phantagraph* 4, No. 2 (November–December 1935): 11. Rpt. *Operation Phantasy*, ed. Donald A. Wollheim (Rego Park, NY: Phantagraph Press, 1967), 29–30. In *Letters to Robert Bloch and Others* 432.

2. HPL cites p. 751 of the *Necronomicon* in "The Dunwich Horror."

To Earl Peirce, Jr.

Earl Peirce, Jr. (1917–1983) was a weird fiction writer who published a few stories in *WT* and other pulps. He corresponded with Lovecraft in the 1930s at the instigation of Robert Bloch, briefly a fellow-Milwaukeean. (The July 1937 issue of *WT* indicates he was then living in Washington, DC, as suggested by Lovecraft's comment below about Georgetown, Annapolis, and Fredericksburg "down your way.") His first published story was "Doom of the House of Duryea" (*WT*, October 1936). Lovecraft read and thought highly of his story "The Last Archer" (*WT*, March 1937).

[158] [Transcript, WHS]

66 College St.,
Providence, R.I.,
Nov. 28, 1936.

Dear Mr. Peirce:—

        I was very glad to hear from you, and to learn that you liked my recent "Haunter of the Dark"—which describes quite literally this house and the view from the window at which I am now sitting. As you may know, it is a sort of reply to our friend Bloch's "Shambler from the Stars". In that tale he killed me off, so I decided to return the compliment![1] Bloch is certainly an admirably brilliant chap, and will go far in the writing world.

        Incidentally—let me congratulate you on your own recent story, "Doom of the House of Duryea", which I have been praising to many correspondents. You managed to create an admirable atmosphere of suspense and menace, and then led on a completely stupefying and unsuspected—yet perfectly logical and inevitable—climax by having the supposed victim-elect turn out to be the predestined killer. I trust you will keep on contributing to W.T., and shall keep my eyes open for your work.

        As for my own stuff—no, I've never had anything in the so-called "slick" magazines. These are for the most part just as insincere and formula-bound as the "pulps", except that their formula is a slightly different one, and they have no use for serious weird material. The really high-grade magazines which *do* accept sincere work seem to have a prejudice against the macabre and fantastic—and what is more, I doubt whether any of my work comes up to their standard. I have endeavoured to keep free of the cheapening influence of the "pulps", but the fault is an insidious one, and I can see that my stuff is the worse for my having written so much for W.T. Several times book publishers have asked to see my tales with a view to collected publication, but in each case they have turned down the idea at the last moment. About the relative merit of my tales—of course, the ones in anthologies (Cthulhu, Red Hook, Erich Zann, Rats) are not necessarily the best, chance playing a great part in selection. Of my various attempts, the only one which satisfies me to any extent is "The Colour Out of Space". Yes—our "five-foot shelf" of imaginary necromantic works is rather picturesque—and is made more convincing by the common use of one another's dark allusions.

I'm interested to know that you've visited the Boston North End section mentioned in "Pickman's Model". This region used to be a good deal more picturesque than it is now, and the sinister alley described in the story was more or less literally based on a real alley (Foster St., I think) which zigzagged peculiarly up from Commercial St. to Charter St. not so very far from Copp's Hill. I'll never forget my mystification when I tried to show this region to Donald Wandrei (whose work in the magazines you've doubtless read) in 1927, on his first visit to the East. I had been all over it only the year before, and had told Wandrei what curious sights to expect, when lo!—as we approached the district we found only a barren waste of exposed foundations with the line of the former alley traced amidst the wreckage under a blazing sun! The whole damn tangle of alleys had been torn down in the few months between Dec. '26 and June '27, and I had nothing tangible to back up the glowing accounts I had given! There is nothing of quaintness and suggested menace in the nondescript new buildings now covering the site, and I believe Foster St. is wholly obliterated. Alas—all our larger ancient towns are gradually losing their mellow picturesqueness. May Yuggoth preserve Georgetown, Annapolis, and Fredericksburg down your way! Around here, Salem ("Arkham"), Marblehead ("Kingsport"), Newburyport, and a few other old places still uphold the colonial atmosphere and tradition.

Your archaeologist friend sounds tremendously interesting, and I must try to get in touch with him when my programme is a bit less congested. "The City of the Worm" surely must be a sinister place—and one capable of effective weird exploitation by anyone familiar with the local colour and details. I'd like to see the Southwest. Somewhere in New Mexico—in the Navajo country—there is a hellish area of broken lava called "The Desert of the Black Blood", which is rifted by great chasms and which has probably never been penetrated beyond a few miles by any white man—or living Indian for that matter. Yet aëroplanes, flying over it, have spied what look like ruins at its very heart; and local legends tell of an ancient and mysterious city whose crumbling walls now harbour carnivorous dragons.

With all good wishes, and hoping to see more of your work as time passes, I am

     Yours most sincerely,
      H. P. Lovecraft

Notes

1. Robert Bloch, "The Shambler from the Stars" (*WT*, September 1935).

[159] [Transcript, WHS]

> 66 College St.,
> Providence, R.I.,
> February 17, 1937

Dear Mr. Peirce:—

I shall certainly welcome the reprinting of "Sup. Horror in Lit." in the new Conover–Stickney magazine, whose neatness and careful typography put it in a class apart.[1] Conover now has the idea of beginning the treatise at the beginning instead of where the late F.F. left off—arguing that comparatively few of his prospective audience will ever have seen the F.F. I suppose you know of the plans to merge Schwartz's *Fantasy Magazine* with the S.F.C.[2]

Yes—I'd very much like to meet Bloch, and hope he can get East within the next year. We shall have plenty to discuss, even if the meeting is less spectacular than the recent S.F.C. would indicate.

"Mirage" and "The Elder Pharos" were set to music by Harold Farnese in 1932, but I don't think the result was ever published. As a matter of fact, I've never heard the music. It's a sadly safe bet that no gramophone record exists. Any information about the fate of the music would have to come from Farnese himself—from whom I haven't heard in three years or more. He was planning to write a weird opera based on my Yuggoth-Cthulhu cycle of elder gods, but no word of the project's completion has reached me. His address is—or was—4001 S. Harvard Blvd., Los Angeles, California. He is Dean of the Institute of Musical Instruction there.

Glad you like "At the Mountains of Madness", although the text of the *Astonishing* version is nearly ruined—especially toward the end—by the inept mangling of Street & Smith's obtuse editors. I wish I could get the correct version printed as a book, but there is very little chance of such. I've had uniform bad luck with book propositions. Again and again publishers have approached me concerning a collection of tales, but negotiations have always fallen through in the end. The one approximation to a book which did get printed—"The Shadow over Innsmouth"—is such a typographical mess that I hate to think about it.

I must congratulate you on your "Last Archer"—by a wide margin the best story in the March W.T. You certainly weave a magnificent atmosphere of elusive strangeness and gathering menace, and the concept of the duplicate castles and archers—the confusion of unity and duality—is masterfully handled. It would have been easy to present such an idea extravagantly and unconvincingly, but you really give the proper emotional and atmospheric prep-aration (something about which the conventional commercial pulpist never bothers) and succeed in putting it over powerfully. Glad you're also repre-sented in the next issue.[3] Keep this up, and you'll certainly rate as the spec-tacular W.T. "find" of 1936–7!

All good wishes—
Yours most sincerely,
H. P. Lovecraft

P.S. Pardon delay in letter. After 2 months of half-illness—intestinal grippe and allied ailments—I'm down at last. Doc is dosing me with 3 different nos-trums—and s[ta]y up only a little while at a time. I shall have to curtail all my activities for the rest of the winter.

Notes

1. HPL's revised "Supernatural Horror in Literature" did not appear in *Science-Fantasy Correspondent* as planned, neither as a continuation of the serial form from where it left off in *FF* (middle of ch. 8) nor in its entirety. The synopsis was not published until 1973.
2. I.e., Willis Conover's *Science-Fantasy Correspondent*. Such a merger did not occur.
3. "The Death Mask" (April 1937).

To Robert A. W. Lowndes

Robert Augustine Ward "Doc" Lowndes (1916–1998) was sta-
tioned at a CCC camp in West Cornwall, Conn. He later became a science fiction author, editor, and fan. He was best
known as the editor of *Future Science Fiction, Science Fiction,* and
Science Fiction Quarterly, among many other crime fiction, western, sports fiction, and other pulp and digest-sized magazines
for Columbia Publications. In 1963, he initiated the *Magazine of
Horror* (1963–71), which mixed reprints with new stories.

[160] [ALS]

66 College St.,
Providence, R.I.,
Jany. 20, 1937.

Dear Mr. Lowndes:—
        Yours of the 16th reached me yesterday, & I learned
with great pleasure of your familiarity with my fictional attempts. There was
no need to have hesitated in writing, for I can assure you that I am one of the
mildest-mannered & most benevolently-disposed old geezers alive—with not
a trace of that pompous & formidable quality which comes from an exagger-
ated ego or (much less commonly) a consciousness of truly substantial accomplishment. I have no illusions about the importance of the junk I
perpetrate. It's the best I can do—but not so hot at that! And, as just another
dub pottering around the edge of aesthetic problems too large for him, I certainly can't afford to do any metaphorical wearing of the silk topper!
    Your literary diet as suggested in your letter would seem to be all in the
right direction for one as artistically sensitive, & destined for expression on his
own book, as you appear to be. I assume that you realise the abysmal inferiority
of the pulp-magazine writers (among them titans like Clark Ashton Smith & the
late Robert E. Howard stand out as notable exceptions) as compared with real
authors of fantasy like Poe, Algernon Blackwood, Arthur Machen, Dunsany,
Walter de la Mare, M. R. James, & so on—or with the few real authors (H. G.
Wells, S. Fowler Wright, W. Olaf Stapledon . . . I can think of no more!) who
have produced "science fiction" of adult calibre. The less one reads of the magazine junk, the better for his taste & style. If you are not already familiar with
the principal classics of fantastic literature, I'd be glad to let you have the names
of some books which I look upon as almost "required reading." Not that I'm
any especially notable authority, but that I've done a bit of browsing in the
weird field in my day. A decade ago I summarised the results of my reading in

an article called "Supernatural Horror in Literature"—which is about to be seri-
ally reprinted in one of the little "fan magazines"—that issued by Willis
Conover of Cambridge, Md. Which reminds me that you might find some interesting suggestions & discussions in many of these miniature sheets—which
have become so numerous in recent months. If you are not already familiar
with the "fan" press let me know, & I'll give you the addresses of half a dozen
of these semi-amateur publications. They form good havens for one's early or
rejected MSS. as well as furnishing timely information & debate material.

From your remarks on your temperament & interests, I'd judge that you
have a good deal of the stuff of authorship—or artistic creation of some
sort—in you. At least, I fancy you won't be sidetracked into popular hack
writing for ready cash, as has happened to a tragically great number of those
who started out with serious literary intentions! I'd be interested to know
whether you've written anything as yet. Writing is always the best of practice,
but there's no need of attempting anything like a quantity production at the
outset. At your age the important thing is to saturate yourself with the best
literature, & to analyse & harness your own imagination with a view to its
most effective use. Your tendency toward introversion will form a substantial
asset in the fantasy field (if that is what you ultimately choose)—& all the
more so if disciplined & infused with perspective through a parallel cultivation of detached objectivity. I am a strong advocate of the impersonal, cosmic, or scientific point of view—the perspective not merely of Voltaire but of
Helvetius, La Mettrie, Locke, Huxley, Haeckel, Bertrand Russell, & the mate-
rialists in general. It takes nothing away from the charm of fancy to realise
that the whole universe is simply a vortex of aimless though patterned physical & chemical reactions without importance or absolute values. Imagination
is too local, momentary, specialised, decorative, & bound up in the unreflec-
tive enjoyment of the immediate, to suffer from a knowledge of the larger
objective probabilities of the cosmos. On the other hand, a full & disillusioned perception of the mechanical meaninglessness of the universe is a
great aid to good psychological adjustment. We never get worried about ourselves or anything else when we realise that nothing in the whole blasted
sphere of creation has any particular significance or matters a god damn. *Relative* values still hold good & can form a basis for mild enjoyment—but our
knowledge that they are not cosmically *absolute* helps us to avoid taking them
too seriously. The world of dreams & moods is none the less interesting because it is merely a world of illusions & symbols with only a local meaning.
What the hell of it—when nothing within our power of conception is other
than local & relative as scaled against unknowable infinity? No need of worry-
ing about the cosmos—from whose point of view the momentary incident of
terrestrial organic life is completely negligible. It is sufficient if we try to organise human existence as harmoniously as possible—taking man's psychological inheritance as it is, discovering as much as we can of its typical needs

& optimum environment, & modelling our standards & folkways accordingly. There is no such thing as perfection, & we'll worry less if we cease to expect it. The modicum of obtainable smoothness & harmony which a rational & well-organised life-pattern tends to foster is its own reward. The fact that it has no cosmic meaning, & that it can never even approximate the dreams of individual visionaries, ought not to give us the least concern. Why the devil *should* a rationally smooth-working set of institutions & mental habits "mean" anything beyond the immediate comfort it produces—or correspond to the pipe-dreams of this or that theorist or mystic?

Now as to my attempts at story-writing—a kind of attempt I've been making ever since I was 7 years old (& I'll be 47 next August)—I recently said in an article for one of the "fan mags"[1] that I perpetrate these in order to get the satisfaction of visualising more clearly & detailedly & stably the vague, elusive, fragmentary impressions of wonder, beauty, & adventurous expectancy which are conveyed to me by certain sights (scenic, architectural, atmospheric, &c.), ideas, occurrences, & images encountered in art & literature. I choose weird stories because they suit my inclination best—one of my strongest & most persistent wishes being to achieve, momentarily, the illusion of some strange suspension or violation of the galling limitations of time, space, & natural law which for ever imprison us & frustrate our curiosity about the infinite cosmic spaces beyond the radius of our sight & analysis. These stories frequently emphasise the element of horror because fear is our deepest & strongest emotion, & the one which best lends itself to the creation of nature-defying illusions. Horror & the unknown or the strange are always closely connected, so that it is hard to create a convincing picture of shattered natural law or cosmic alienage & "outsideness" without laying stress on the emotion of fear. The reason why *time* plays a great part in so many of my tales is that this element looms up in my mind (as in Dunsany's) as the most profoundly dramatic & grimly terrible thing in the universe. *Conflict with time* seems to me the most potent & fruitful theme in all human expression.

This ought to furnish at least a partial answer to your query as to why I always have characters repulsed, horrified, maddened, frozen into merciful silence, or wholly or partly destroyed by the achievement of the supernal knowledge or contact with the unknown which they seek. Whatever is unknown or alien *is necessarily horrible or "evil"*—because our only standard of comfort or restful equilibrium or "good" is the prolongation of some harmonious adjustment pleasantly known in the past. We are always dissatisfied with our narrow world, yet would inevitably be horrified & overwhelmed if we really could suddenly transcend its rigid boundaries. Whatever is not favourably known to us by experience is a subject of fear. The child instinctively fears the dark. The primitive geographer fills with nameless monsters whatever lands he knows nothing about. This has nothing to do with scientific truth. Actually, the new and alien region might, when gradually introduced to us, be very favourable as an environment. But it is a strong & ineradicable human instinct . . . & no weird story ever can be more than a picture of some traditional instinct or mood or belief or attitude. Our minds & emotions are so constituted that they do not wish to be removed from the repetition of known experiences. What has no reference to previous impressions can have no meaning—& what has no meaning is potentially dangerous. We fear & shun strange fruits or berries because they may be poisonous. Thus there is a basis of primitive cautionary logic in man's fear of the unknown & the strange. Then, too, there is a subtler psychological aspect based on something like *homesickness*. After all, apart from the most basic animal satisfactions, nothing really pleases or comforts us except by arousing pleasant associations based on past ideas & experiences . . . . nothing, that is, outside the realm of abstract intellectual curiosity. Even our sense of agreeable novelty & adventure depends wholly upon the real relationship of the "new" thing or experience to things or experiences we have known before. Without *reference-points* derived from our personal or traditional past, nothing has any meaning or value. In an unfamiliar, backgroundless void the illusions of value, direction, significance, & purpose cannot exist—& without these illusions we are lost. Bewilderment, loneliness, & ultimate horror are our only possible reactions. So in spite of all our impatience with the limited & the normal—that impatience to which fantasy owes its existence—we are still more overwhelmed by sudden confrontation with the unlimited or the totally alien. In order to face & become adjusted to anything really new or strange, we must make its acquaintance *very gradually*—giving ourselves time to correlate it with the body of our previous impressions, & to assign it a definite place in the understood scheme of cause & effect. Don't forget that the very chain of strict causation which sometimes galls us is also our symbol of *protection* against incalculable & unimaginable evils. Without it, *anything* might happen—& our experience in life, where pain & injury so vastly outweigh pleasure, leads us to visualise that "anything" as more often horrible & destructive than welcome & beneficent. Thus the deep-rooted human association of the unknown & alien with the sinister—an association so strong & natural & omnipresent that it cannot be disregarded in the artistic process of mood-picturing which lies behind serious fantasy. The Greeks wove a lot of sound psychology into the tale of Zeus & Semele![2] Intrinsically or absolutely or cosmically, such elements as "good", "evil", "happiness", "horror", "pain", &c. have no existence. These words signify only certain subjective reactions of certain local & negligible organisms to various (& sometimes different at different times & under different circumstances) environmental conditions. But from the point of view of those local & negligible organisms—ourselves—such reactions do indeed have a quasi-existence & relative significance . . . & we may deduce from experimentation that it is better for the organisms not to face too abrupt departures from their usual track of experience. For them—

i.e., us—the unknown & the alien are indeed closely connected, empirically speaking, with the emotion of fear & the quality of the sinister.

No—my central figures or narrators are never literal transcriptions of myself. My own psychology doubtless enters into most of them to a greater or lesser extent, & I suppose I've seldom bothered to draw elaborately different personalities; but my intention is simply to present that kind of a figure best adapted to the exhibition of the chosen phenomena. For *phenomena & conditions*—not persons—are the true protagonists of my yarns. ¶ All good wishes, & trust I'll hear more of your impressions. ¶ Yrs most sincerely, H P Lovecraft

Pardon my lousy scrawl—but I have an utter detestation of the typing process—which fatigues & enervates me oppressively. I never use the machine except under compulsion.

Notes

1. "Notes on Writing Weird Fiction."
2. In Greek mythology, Semele was a daughter of the Phoenician hero Cadmus who was seduced by Zeus in the guise of an eagle, later giving birth to Dionysus. But she demanded to see Zeus in his actual form and, when she did so, was consumed by fire from his lightning bolts.

[161] [ALS]

66 College St.,
Providence, R.I.,
Feby. 20, 1937.

Dear Mr. Lowndes:—

Your letter of Jany. 27 proved highly interesting, & I wish I might have answered it sooner. As it is, however, a persistent siege of intestinal grippe*—or some damned thing of the sort—is keeping my energies at such a low ebb that my whole programme is in chaos. About the matter of script versus typing—my dislike of performing the latter process is not based on any lofty scorn of machinery or any sentimental reaction against impersonal expression, but arises from the plain & prosy fact that working a typewriter any length of time makes me as nervous as hell, & finally gives me a cursed backache or headache or both. I don't know whether it's the noise or the position or both—but I do know that for me it's a gruelling grind. I *have* to do it in preparing MSS. for professional consideration, & sometimes have to fall back on it for important letters when illness makes my script to-

---

*The doc has me taking 3 cursed nostrums simultaneously, & I can stay up only a little while each day.

tally illegible—as was the case a week or two ago. But only necessity ever chains me to a keyboard. As for incoming epistles—I don't give a damn whether they're typed or written, so long as I can read them. I am, incidentally, rather a fairish script-decipherer; since I take whole words instead of single letters as basic units & quickly judge their identity by a panoramic survey of the context. Your writing—which, by the way, is remarkably neat & graceful—gives me not the slightest difficulty. To anybody who dares impugn *your* legibility, I would recommend a page or two of my own chaotic rooster-scratching as a perspective-rectifier!

Your devotion to the Middle Ages is very interesting—& is surely not without its justifying aspect. As a time which produced the Gothic cathedral, & which brought into literature that element of mysterious cosmic outreaching which is the Teuton's especial contribution, the western world's dark period can surely be forgiven much in the way of ignorance, bigotry, & hysterical irrationality. I, however, am too devoted to the element of reason in life to be any sort of a mediaevalist. The streak of Gothic fancy in my literary attempts is really a sort of contradiction of my general temperament—or at least, of the intellectual side of my temperament. Classical—& especially Roman—antiquity has always been my chief animator, & I have a parallel sense of identification with the eighteenth century, which drew so many of its typical elements from the classic Roman world. I like the free play of intelligence & of a critical sense, & dislike to see people kidding themselves with myths & superstitions. Heaven knows I enjoy fantasy & supernaturalism enough as aesthetic subject-matter, but I want to see them kept in their place as art material instead of running riot through the serious philosophy of adults. As for vigorous Renaissance figures like Leonardo da Vinci, Chaucer, Titian, Raphael, Michelangelo, Rabelais, Montaigne, the Elizabethan dramatists, Copernicus, Tycho, Kepler, & others whose mental & artistic activity from the 1300's onward astonished the world—I ascribe them not to the dark period which they ushered out, but to the age of classical revival which dawned & flowered simultaneously with them. The world recovered very slowly from the intellectual, artistic, & physical squalor of the worst period (say about 600–1000 A.D.), but in & after the 14th century the cumulative results of the gradual upturn began to be manifest. The Arabs in Spain had passed on a lot of Greek learning in the 11th & 12th centuries, & when the fall of Constantinople drove the Greek scholars westward in the 15th century the movement was accelerated. Whatever advantages in imaginative stimulation the Middle Ages may have possessed, seem to me to have been purchased at too high a price. Precious though they may have been, I cannot think that they were worth the filthy, disease-ridden, & verminous daily life, the dense universal ignorance, the vicious priestly arrogance, the grovelling intellectual degradation, & the hideously barbarous social organisation which in general characterised the period. And yet, in retrospect, we must be grateful for what the period did contribute, & correspondingly lenient about its evils. The present age of transition is another one calling for lenient judgment, & for a keen perception of merits as opposed to evils. Granting the dull texture of life fostered by the rampant commercialism of the 19th century & the unassimilated phenomenon of mechanical quantity-production, & the destructive hates & unrest caused by the lag of social & political evolution behind material invention & technology, we have today many redeeming things to behold. False ideas & ancient injustices are questioned on a wholly unprecedented scale—this being part of a larger movement, launched by the expansion of human knowledge & the growth of scientific method, whereby mankind is coming to demand more consistency & more logical justification in his institutions. With the opium of religion swept out of the way, greater stress is laid on the decent organisation of the life which is really ours. Of course, the present generation will not reap the benefits of this trend. Things move too slowly for that. But it is none the less encouraging to see that civilisation—despite some incidental losses—is dominantly headed away from caprice & cruelty & ignorance & toward the logical utilisation of human knowledge & resources. One may only hope that the trend will not be interrupted or retarded by suicidal wars or universal reactionary movements. Granted normal evolution, there will ultimately be achieved a stage of greater social & economic equilibrium amidst which the arts will have a chance to flourish more healthily & more integratedly than at present.

About fantastic literature—I haven't read "Lost Horizon", though many have recommended it. Sooner or later I hope to get around to its perusal. And now for those recommendations I spoke of. If you haven't read Blackwood, you have a treat ahead of you—but be sure to choose his best rather than worst products, since he is a curiously & bewilderingly *uneven* author. Some of his tales are among the finest products of the fantastic imagination—uniquely acute & serious studies of the deep-seated human emotions & processes which produce the illusion of the unreal—yet other things of his almost touch the nadir of bathos, sentimentality, & namby-pamby. Read "Incredible Adventures" & "John Silence—Physician Extraordinary"—& get hold of some collection containing the short stories "The Willows" & "The Wendigo." But *don't* waste time on "The Wave," "Tongues of Fire," "The Extra Day," & "The Garden of Survival." If you like, I can lend you "John Silence", "Willows," & "Wendigo." Machen is another revelation. Get hold of the Knopf edition of "The House of Souls", which contains "The White People" & "The Great God Pan." Read also "The Hill of Dreams," though it is psychological rather than supernatural. Don't miss "The Three Impostors", & "The Terror" is also worth going through. Almost anything of Machen's is worth reading—for he hasn't Blackwood's unevenness. As a mediaevalist, you'd probably like his "Secret Glory" & "Great Return". His story of the "angels of Mons"—"The Bowmen"—is so lifelike that it became a piece of folklore a week after its publication in 1914. People tried to tell Machen that he didn't invent the idea, but that soldiers actually saw the supernatural archers he describes! I can lend you a good deal of Machen. Montague Rhodes James is today best obtainable in "omnibus" form—all his stories bound together—but in most libraries you'll probably run across the separate books of the older edition—

> "Ghost Stories of An Antiquary"
> "More G. S. of an Ant."
> "A Thin Ghost & Others"
> "A Warning to the Curious"

The first three volumes here named contain the best stuff. I can lend you these. Of Walter de la Mare read the novel "The Return", & the short stories "Seaton's Aunt" (in "The Riddle & Other Stories"), "Mr. Kempe," & "All Hallows" (these last in "The Connoisseur & Other Stories"). Dunsany— petering out these days—is worth a special study. Besides what you've read & acted (congratulations on your leading role!), don't miss

> The Gods of Pegana   (I can lend these)
> Time & the Gods
> The Sword of Welleran
> The Book of Wonder
> Chronicles of Rodriguez
> The King of Elfland's Daughter
> Five Plays (with "The Gods of the Mountain")

Glad you know Shiel's "Purple Cloud". Try if possible to get hold of the book ("The Pale Ape & Other Stories") containing "The House of Sounds"—Shiel's real masterpiece. I'd give a lot to own that item! Stapledon's great work is "The Last & First Men"—a stupendous cosmic survey. Get hold of it if it kills you—I wish I had a copy! Of S. Fowler Wright read "The World Below", which I can lend. Of Ambrose Bierce read both short story collections—"In the Midst of Life" & "Can Such Things Be?" Of Robert W. Chambers read "The King in Yellow". Of William Hope Hodgson read "The House on the Borderland", "The Boats of the Glen Carrig", & "The Night Land"—despite the miserable & inaccurate attempts to ape archaic diction in the two latter. Going back to the elder classics, you ought to read Beckford's "Vathek" & "Episodes of Vathek", as well as Mrs. Radcliffe's "Udolpho", Lewis's "The Monk", & Maturin's "Melmoth, the Wanderer". Also Mrs. Shelley's "Frankenstein". I assume, of course, that you know Poe 'from kiver to kiver'. It would hardly be possible to give a full list in brief compass, but I'll put down suggestions when I think of them. Try to get John Buchan's "Witch Wood", Herbert Gorman's "The Place Called Dagon", Henry James's

"The Turn of the Screw", R. E. Spencer's "The Lady Who Came to Stay". Also ask for suggestions from others. Another fine fantasy is "The Worm Ouroboros" by E. R. Eddison. Some of the popular weird collections & anthologies contain excellent short stories. Be on the lookout for the various "Omnibuses of Crime", the Asquith "Ghost Books", the melanges called "Beware After Dark" & "Creeps by Night", Benson's "Visible & Invisible", & Wakefield's "They Return at Evening". The fantasy field is really a quite extensive one, & I never expect to get more than half way through it myself.

Glad you've had a chance to meet Wollheim, who is really a tremendously brilliant youth, & that you've placed some of your material in his publications. Aside from *The Phantagraph* & *Fanciful Tales,* the best small "fan mag" is *The Science-Fantasy Correspondent,* published by Willis Conover, Jun., 27 High St., Cambridge, Maryland. This magazine is about to absorb Schwartz's F M, & would certainly welcome material from you. If you don't despise the lowly mimeograph, try something on the following editors:

Supramundane Stories—Nils H. Frome, Box 3, Fraser Mills, B.C., Canada.
Phantasmagoria—John J. Weir, 223 John St., South Amboy, N.J.
Tesseract—C. Hamilton Bloomer, Jun., 464 Guerrero St., San Francisco, Cal.

Also—some day I suppose William Crawford (122 Water St., Everett, Pa.) will be rescuing his printed *Marvel Tales.*

Weird Tales is of course the best of the fantasy pulp mags, but even so, it's nothing to brag about. It caters to certain definite popular tastes, & has rejected some of the most serious efforts of Clark Ashton Smith & myself.

I trust that in time your work will have a professional as well as amateur acceptance—& indeed, the encouragement of the Cheyneys would seem to point that way. So far as insincere hack work goes—it's as honest as any form of cheap showmanship, & the only trouble is that it ruins its perpetrator for serious literary expression. I don't try to discourage anybody from attempting this source of revenue unless the person happens to be one whose contentment & good adjustment depend upon freedom to develop sincere expression. In that case I urge the ponderer to go slow. Just a few persons *have* got away with hack writing & escaped artistic injury, but the number is all too few. Far more common is the fate of Abe Merritt & Arthur J. Burks & Edmond Hamilton. Hell knows the economic situation of most writers is desperate enough—as a near-unemployable I myself have a perniciously high rating!—but I still think that in the long run it is wiser for the sincere artist to accept humble material conditions & turn to almost any source of food–clothing–shelter money other than style-wrecking pulp slavery. In my own case, I'm saved the trouble of choosing—for I simply *can't* cook up the kind of nauseous drivel which brings wide acceptance & substantial returns. Long & Wandrei have been pretty well sucked into the vortex of hopeless hackdom. Bloch & Kuttner[1] & Rimel still have a fighting chance. Price has touched bottom & may (thanks to a phenomenal abstract intellect) fight his way back. Smith never really hit the toboggan despite some perilous concessions in the *Wonder Story* days of 5 or more years ago. Derleth is getting through unscathed—but he is an exceptional case. Scribners is even now bringing out his first serious novel.[2] In general, the few who can get away with hack tripe are the ones who can reel it off so easily & mechanically that it doesn't actually touch their imagination.

Your remarks on the dreamer & the materialist contain a great deal of truth, though I think you somewhat underestimate the degree of tolerable balance & contentment achievable by the dreamer who is materialist enough to see through his own dreams—or (to view him from the opposite angle) the materialist who is dreamer enough to have dreams & enjoy them as such without forming grandiose & disappointing ideas about himself, life, & the cosmos. I can't get as enthusiastic about the Dionysiac stuff—the ideal of a full & varied life of the senses—as some aesthetes do. As one with the scientific point of view, I can't avoid the perspective which recognises all sensory phenomena as mere electro-chemical reactions & glandular discharges in a type of organism by no means dissimilar to a goat's or dog's. To me, the sort of activity worthy of a human mind is that which involves those tenuous & peculiarly human qualities centreing in *cosmic perception & recognition*—the sort embracing the gratification of intellectual curiosity, the enjoyment of cosmic rhythms & symmetries, & the exercise of those processes of creation & expression whereby we record our response to what we experience, & vicariously achieve what lies just beyond our reach. So far as I can see, the pursuit of this form of activity provides a perfectly tolerable goal & set of rewards for living—making the process of consciousness distinctly worth supporting even in the face of obstacles & drawbacks. Others may differ, but that's the way it looks to me. Naturally, we are happier if worldly things come our way—wealth, travel, fortunate marriage, security, recognition, esteem, & all that—but even if they don't, I believe that (barring the acutest hardship of physical pain) the residue provided by intellectual & artistic activity forms ample ground for preferring existence to non-existence if one is properly appreciative.

Getting back to that point about the linkage of horror with the unknown—the trouble with depicting exceptions is that they wouldn't be like human beings. They wouldn't ring true, & the thoughtful reader would at once recognise them as mere mechanical plot devices. The depiction of a human being as *welcoming* something utterly alien would require special treatment in order to have any semblance of vitality. The psychology of such a person would have to be treated as the central wonder along with the actual violation of cosmic law. It would have to be explained, & thrown into prominence in advance as a marvel in itself, if a later letdown & feeling of unconvincedness on the intellectual reader's part are to be avoided. The possible effect you foresee—a feeling of horror on the reader's part at the welcoming of alien conditions by a character or characters—could be achieved only through such adroit special preparation. It would be a horror at the discovery that a character or characters previously thought human *cannot in truth be purely human*—& the convincingness of this discovery would depend upon how cleverly & realistically the non-human elements in this character or characters had been suggested & motivated. It would be easier to have *one* character possess this "outsider" infusion (which might be either physical or psychological) than to have several so affected; though a skilled writer might get away with a case of mass alienage by postulating a group or community subjected to some abnormal influence. I tried the latter in my "Shadow Over Innsmouth", but fear I didn't succeed very well. It would also be possible to picture a *madman*—as distinguished from a non-human-being—as welcoming utterly alien conditions; but I fear a story with such a basis wouldn't have much point. One can't carry the word of Baudelaire too far, since it is too much of a disease-phenomenon to have limitless resources. When one makes a clinical study in literature, the element of outright supernaturalism subtracts from it. There is no real supernaturalism in diseased decadents like Baudelaire & Huysmans, *& that is where their power lies.* When you make a serious study of dementia, the reader will resent your dragging in assorted ghosts & monsters & other worlds & other dimensions. The ghosts, monsters, & alien worlds & dimensions of the mad exist only within their own minds. Poe bridged the gap as well as anyone could—but there was only one Poe! To me, the study of abnormal human personality does not belong in the fantasy field at all. It is another genre, whose resemblance to true fantasy is purely superficial & accidental. The true fantaisiste is not interested in diseased persons, but in the illusion of abnormal cosmic phenomena—hence his method is to show strictly normal human beings against a background of violated cosmic law. The people are puppets—symbols of the dreamer's detachment & passivity in the face of the phantoms that troop past him. The *phenomena* are the true protagonists.

Your idea of a novel depicting a horror or cosmic abnormality solely through the psychological responses of those confronting it—without any first-hand or directly presented picture—is surely clever & potentially fruitful. This principle has been very successful in many short stories, & its use in ampler compass would seem to depend a good deal upon the skill of the author.

Well—at your stage of the game *free experimentation* would seem to be the logical watchword. Your business at the outset is to find your own natural metier, & the only way to do that is to try first one form & theme after another—letting your innate aptitudes & inclinations tell you which to linger over & exploit. I hope to see some of your work in the course of time. Meanwhile fill your mind & imagination with the best fantasy obtainable—letting me know if you'd like me to lend some of those books mentioned, 2 or 3 at a time. I assume that you have facilities for their preservation in reasonably good condition. How are you off for public library facilities? If my wholly theoretical map-&-gazetteer knowledge be correct, your nearest sizeable town is Torrington . . . whose 25,000-odd status ought to ensure at least some sort of bibliothecal competence.

I skimmed over the March *W T* recently, & was glad to see the progress made by young Peirce. That "Last Archer" of his certainly is quite a yarn.

All good wishes, & hopes for your eventual literary success, yrs most cordially,

H P Lovecraft

Notes

1. Henry Kuttner (1915–1958), author of weird, fantasy, and science fiction who corresponded with HPL in 1936–37. For HPL's letters to him, see *Letters to C. L. Moore and Others.*

2. *Still Is the Summer Night.*

To Ben Abramson

Ben Abramson (1898–1955) was the proprietor of the Argus Book Shop in Chicago, from which Lovecraft occasionally and August Derleth regularly ordered books. He published the magazine *Reading and Collecting,* Derleth's *H. P. L.: A Memoir* (1945), and Lovecraft's *Supernatural Horror in Literature* (1945). Derleth's review of *The Shadow over Innsmouth* (1936) mentioned in this letter ultimately was recast somewhat to become part of his eulogy on Lovecraft, "A Master of the Macabre." The postscript to Lovecraft's letter appeared in *Reading and Collecting* 1, No. 5 (April 1937): 21.

[162] [ALS]

> 66 College St.,
> Providence, R.I.,
> Feby. 15, 1937

Ben Abramson, Esq.,
    Argus Book Shop,
        Chicago, Ill.,

Dear Mr. Abramson:—
        My young friend August W. Derleth of Sauk City, Wis. has just asked me to send you a photograph of myself for use in an all-too-generous review which he says he is writing for your fascinating publication *Reading & Collecting.* I have not had a formal photograph in over 20 years, but in lieu of such am enclosing a rather close-up snap taken a couple of years ago—which shews my present general appearance rather well so far as the Rembrantesque lighting scheme shews anything at all.[1] If this is of any use, & if the sour & grotesque phiz which it depicts does not seem likely to scare potential readers away from the makeshift "book" [that's what the publisher euphemistically calls it] forming the subject of the review, I shall be glad to have it employed as you see fit. You might change its title & let it go as one of the monstrous entities in "The Shadow over Innsmouth"!
    Appreciating your share in giving notice to my obscure lucubration, believe me,
    Yrs most sincerely,
        H. P. Lovecraft

P.S. I can't resist adding a wholly irrelevant word concerning something in the Jany. issue of *Reading & Collecting* which took my notice—namely, the reference to Andrews' (Freund's) Latin-English Lexicon in Mr. Paul's article "Books of the Dead."[2] The author speaks of this work as though it were a quaint & useless rarity; whereas in all truth it is one of the leading Latin-English dictionaries in existence—a standard work which has been through edition after edition, & which is in every way thoroughly adequate to the needs of the student of any of the recognised Roman classics. I don't know how minutely its later editions have kept abreast of the latest delvings in philology, or even whether it has been in print for the last 20 years or so [though I don't know why it shouldn't be]; but I can certainly attest that it formed the principal American work of its kind throughout the second half of the 19th century. I still use as my principal Latin dictionary the 1854 copy which was my grandfather's—& up in the attic there is still another & more battered copy reaching me through another source. I have come across it repeatedly in homes & libraries, & can in general be pretty certain that its status is that of a famous & authoritative reference-work (comparable to Liddell & Scott's Greek-English Lexicon) rather than that of a somewhat comic curiosity whose publication required vast courage on the part of Messrs. Harper & Bro. Wilhelm Freund, born in 1806, was a German-Jewish classical scholar of the first rank; & his *Wörterbuch der lateinischen Sprache,* first published in 4 volumes between 1834 & 1845, forms the basis of most of the Latin lexicons published since then. Ethan Allen Andrews (1787–1858) of New Britain, Conn. was an American educator & lexicographer of high standing, in every way fitted to appreciate & to translate intelligently the monumental achievement of Dr. Freund.[3] Pardon this unsolicited excursus—but you can imagine the effect of seeing an old familiar *freund* treated patronisingly as a sort of literary cousin to the dodo & the dinosaur. Possibly it is Mr. Paul's expressed attitude toward Latin which makes him censure the lexicographer for not providing a Latin grammar as well as a dictionary—something no lexicographer has yet attempted in the long & eventful history of scholarship. Selah. Of Messrs. Freund & Andrews, one may do no better than to say, in a few words well chosen from their collaborative pages, *Indocti discant, et ament macuinisse periti.*[4]

Again yr most ob^t Servt H P L

Notes

1. The "Rembrantesque" portrait may have been the well-known photograph taken by R. H. Barlow (as opposed to another ill-lit photograph taken by Donald Wandrei). Instead one of the famous portraits taken by Lucius B. Truesdell c. May 1934 was used.

2. Louis Paul, "Books of the Dead," *Reading and Collecting* 1, No. 7 (January 1937): 24.

3. The Andrews/Freud lexicon did indeed serve as the basic of *A Latin Dictionary* (1879), compiled by Charlton T. Lewis and Charles Short, long the standard Latin dictionary until the publication of the *Oxford Latin Dictionary* (1982).

4. "Let the ignorant learn, and the learned take pleasure in refreshing their memories." A Latin translation by Charles-Jean-François Hénault of a couplet in Alexander Pope's *An Essay on Criticism*.

To Arthur Widner

Arthur Lambert Widner, Jr. (1917–2015), 114 Co. C.C.C., Waterbury, Vt., helped organize "The Stranger Club" in 1940, Boston's first science fiction club. He later edited the fanzine *Fanfare*. Lovecraft probably wrote him only the two following missives, and those late in life.

[163]   [ANS][1]

[Postmarked Providence, R.I.,
16 January 1937]
66 College St.,
Providence, R.I.,
Jany. 15, 1937.

Dear Mr. Widner:—

Very glad to hear from you, & to learn that you liked various tales of mine. "Mts. of Madness" was mangled very badly in the printing—the effect being nearly ruined toward the end. I'll be interested to see what your one objection to the "Haunter" is. Incidentally, I describe my own residence quite realistically in that tale. ¶ As a correspondent, I am getting worse & worse of late, since the slow, steady, inevitable increase in the *number* of correspondents has made it impossible for me to write very promptly or at length. It would take a secretary to straighten out my mail nowadays! However, I always like to hear from those interested in fantasy, & acknowledge communications when I can. So you do a bit of writing yourself? I shall look for your work in the fantasy sheets, & would be glad to give any remarks which might prove helpful. Do you know about the National Amateur Press Association? It ought to be right in your line. The Secy. is Walter Stevenson, 47 S. Washington St., Tarrytown, N.Y. He'd be glad to send you information. All good wishes
—Yrs sincerely,
H. P. Lovecraft

Notes

1. *Front:* Unknown.

[164] [*SL* 926]

66 College St.
Providence, R.I.
Feby. 20, 1937

Dear "Art":—

About your objection to the "Haunter"—the main idea of course is that the night-monster has secured a hold upon Blake's brain, partly penetrating it & almost effecting an exchange of personalities. Blake could not think for himself or protect himself—indeed, on one occasion the monster has hypnotically dragged him all the way across town to the dark church against his will. If the tension is relaxed at certain moments, it still leaves the victim in no shape to do anything. His only safeguard is the city lighting which keeps the Thing at a distance & takes the responsibility out of his hands. As for portable lighting facilities—if Blake had been in any condition to exercise judgment, one may suppose he would have taken vast precautions after that first failure of the lighting system. He would have provided powerful oil or acetylene lamps in his house, ready to light up in case any more failure of power occurred—for it is doubtful whether the one or two candles & single flashlight at hand could have stopped the Thing. Perhaps he meant to take such precautions—but neglected them just too long because of his weakened will. Even if he *had* taken them the Thing could have come quite close—above the house, & out of the glow of the lighted windows (assuming no searchlight was provided)—& at that short distance could have completed the mental exchange & forced Blake to turn off whatever lights he had provided. However—having neglected the advance precautions, Blake couldn't be expected to do much when the lights went out. With mind half numb & haunted by the Thing, he would scarcely be apt to think of rounding up many candles from mantelpieces all over the house & getting them all grouped & lighted in time. And if the power stayed off long they would be burned out—& if he went out to buy candles or lamps from neighbours, what might not get him in the unlighted streets? If he begged shelter within a candle-lit house (most people were asleep) would he be admitted or ejected as a drunk or madman? Could he keep a blaze of paper going in the fireplace or in some tin basin? With a clear head something might have been done—but the Thing had already seized his brain. The whole point of the climax is that Blake was no longer capable of helping himself. Mentally, the Thing had got him—& his only hope of preservation lay in the maintenance of lights *by other people* not under the hellish Entity's control. Note that people free from such control—like the Italians of Federal Hill—*did* provide emergency lights. It is hardly correct to attribute Blake's inability to act to "a Hamlet-like nature"; since the cause was a *specific hypnosis from outside.* Left to himself, Blake was not necessarily of an indecisive temperament. I may add that I am rather fond of depicting central figures as helpless in the face of oncoming horrors, because that is the way people largely *are* during real nightmares. I have found it effective to make a spectral horror-story resemble an actual nightmare as closely as possible—& nothing helps this resemblance better than a helpless & inactive "hero" with the monstrous shapes of doom closing in relentlessly around him. Indeed, the secret of all dream-literature is to have the central figure largely passive (symbolising the dreamer himself), with the events floating more or less detachedly & uncontrolled by him. Another tale of mine with a "hero" whose helplessness might puzzle some readers (though explained in the text) is "The Whisperer in Darkness"—laid in your own Vermont. By the way—is your "Doc" Lowndes one Robert W. Lowndes of West Cornwall, Conn.? If so, I have heard from him & found him an extremely intelligent & artistically sensitive person.

About the N.A.P.A.—here is an application blank. It is a nationwide society of persons who either publish small amateur papers or write for them, & in my opinion forms one of the most truly encouraging aids for the young writer in existence. One can get a good deal of material published which would be rejected by the professional press, & once it is published it is carefully read by the limited circle of members (200 or 300) & usually criticised & reviewed in a good many of the papers. The society has been in existence nearly 61 years, & has been a substantial developing influence in the career of many writers—among them the fantasy author Frank B. Long Jr. A number of the youthful publishers & readers of fantasy "fan" magazines are now joining—Donald Wollheim, Duane W. Rimel, R. H. Barlow, & Emil Petaja being among our new members. I've been in "amateur journalism" (as the field covered by the N.A.P.A. & one or two similar associations is called) for 23 years, & have always found it extremely helpful. If you're interested I'll send you sample amateur papers.

[. . .]

No—I don't care for science fiction of the sort published in cheap magazines. There's no vitality in it—merely dry theories tacked on to shallow, unreal, insincere juvenile adventure stories. But I do like the few real masterpieces in that field—certain of H. G. Wells's novels, S. Fowler Wright's *The World Below,* & that marvellous piece of imagination by W. Olaf Stapledon, *Last and First Men.*

My latest story? "The Haunter of the Dark"! Haven't had a single chance to write a story since November 1935. Other tasks press heavily upon me, my correspondence utterly swamps me, & my health has of late been very poor. I had hoped that I might arrange for some fiction-writing leisure this winter, but the prospects now seem very slim. If I can keep up with revision work I shall be doing well. However, whenever I *do* get at yarn-spinning again, I shall no doubt drag in the primal pre-human entities of Earth's youth as often as of yore.

[. . .]

All good wishes—
Yrs. most sincerely—
HPL

Published Letters

Long Distance Predictions:
Weather Guessers Willing to Take Any Sort of Chances and Trust to Providence

The following unsigned article tells of a contest sponsored by Frederick R. Fast, a lawyer in New York, in which Lovecraft participated. The article is taken from the *Amsterdam* [NY] *Evening Recorder and Daily Democrat* (6 September 1905), but, as stated in the first paragraph, it first appeared in the *New York Herald Tribune*, presumably a day or two earlier (this appearance has not been located). In his hectographed paper, the *Rhode Island Journal of Astronomy* (3 September 1905), Lovecraft states that he has entered the contest. Presumably he did not win. The article constitutes the first known mention of Lovecraft in print and the first time any writing of his (presumably a portion of a letter to Fast) was published.

[165]

Six hundred prophets are at work on the weather, which accounts for its infinite variety. They are sending bulletins to Frederick R. Fast of New York, who has offered $100 for the most successful forecast. The New York Herald tells the story thus:

The long distance seers are the only ones who have favored him with replies, and they have prepared prophecies for months in advance. The official forecaster for a patent medicine almanac, who furnishes accurate programs of the rain and shine for fourteen months ahead, has forwarded his views, with the explanation that he guessed at the conditions and that he stands pat on the whole program. He supplements his information with the phases of the moon in which to plant corn with success, saying also that the condition of any corn will presage a downpour of rain.

The seer who is guided by his rheumatism, the forecaster who travels up and down all day in an elevator in an office building and the man from Winnebago whose glimpses into futurity are guided by the thickness of the fur of [*sic*] animals have all threatened to send contributions later.

De Voe, the Lone Prophet of the Hackensack Meadows, notified Mr. Fast that he would call upon him, but he was unavoidably detained. The New Jersey wiseacre takes orders for weather from various patent medicine firms and agricultural interests and makes out a scheme for the entire year. He is one of the champion guessers of the country and for twenty years his observations have been very close to the actual conditions.

The goose bone expert, the keeper of the royal ground hog and the man who, like the augurs of old, watches the flight of birds have written to Mr. Fast for further details of the contest. Many would like to send their ideas by telegraph, so as to have the advantage of as many hours as possible, for the forecast must be made for the twenty-four hours after its receipt.

One who prefers to keep his name secret despatches from the Hotel Lafayette the information that from October 15 to November 15, inclusive, there will be all kinds of weather, the most of which he says will be "nice." On October 15 the morning will be rainy and in the afternoon the skies will clear. There will be some "nice" days after that and on October 24 there will be snow. The days of November up to the fifteenth will be "nice" and snowy in alternation.

H. P. Lovecraft, who says he forecasts for Rhode Island, writes to say that he thinks his predictions will reach over into New York and New England.

"It may interest you to know," he writes, "that I have one mercurial thermometer by Spooner, six maximum and minimum thermomemeters [*sic*] by Casella, [*sic*] one psychometrical apparatus, one rain, one hair hygrometer and a wind vane." He spells the name of the thermometer a syllable longer than usual to indicate a superior length of column.

"It will be well worth while," said Mr. Fast, "to see if the guesses of the prophets are not as good as, if not better than, the calculations of the United States weather bureau. The official predictions are right forty-three per cent. of the time, while the unofficial average is sixty-six per cent in correctness."

To the *Providence Sunday Journal*

The first item is a letter to the editor commenting on a letter in the issue of 27 May by Thomas Hines, Jr., of Central Falls, R.I., published under the title "Hard Times Coming" (Sec. 2, p. 5). Hines had remarked: "According to the transit of Mars and Saturn, I judge that Providence and Boston will suffer from great fires this summer." The second letter is a refutation of an unsigned article a day before the letter was written, pertaining to the hollow earth theory.

[166]

No Transit of Mars

To the Editor of The Sunday Journal:

In the Journal for May 27, I notice among the letters to the editor a set of astrological predictions for 1906. Passing over the fact that astrology is but a pseudo science, not entitled to intelligent consideration, I wish to call attention to a striking inaccuracy in the aforementioned article. Its writer mentions a transit of Mars over the sun in July. Of course, as Mars is a superior planet, or one outside the earth's orbit, it cannot transit over the sun. Perhaps the astrologer refers to the conjunction of Mars July 15, but on that occasion the planet would pass behind and not across the orb of day.

H. P. LOVECRAFT.

Providence, May 27 [1906].

[167]

The Earth Not Hollow

To the Editor of the Sunday Journal:

In the Sunday Journal for Aug. 5 appeared an article concerning a book which advances the doctrine that the earth is a hollow sphere, with openings at the poles.[1] A few convincing arguments were brought up in support of the theory, but it seems to me that in most points it is contradictory to fact.

Among his arguments the author of the book, which is called *The Phantom of the Poles,* suggests that the compression at the ends of the earth is due to the apertures leading to the centre, but astronomy proves that a planet's polar compression is the result of centrifugal force, i.e. the power that causes the particles of a rotating body to retreat from the centre. All the members of the solar system are thus compressed, yet we see that they possess no polar apertures, which fact alone would almost prove by analogy that the earth is solid.

Another hypothesis introduced is that the Auroras of both hemispheres are burning volcanoes or fires, the "proof" being that they do not affect the magnetic needle. This is positively untrue, for the compass is not only disturbed but often deflected several degrees from the meridian during displays of the Northern and Southern lights. In fact, the general character of Auroral phenomena precludes the supposition that they are fires of any kind.

The rocks, gravel, wood, etc., often found in icebergs is also one of the facts with which he strengthens his theory; but they are, in all probability, the result of ocean currents.

"The open Polar seas" which are referred to as existing around both poles are likewise nearly proved to be figments of imagination, as the latest results of Arctic and Antarctic exploration seem to indicate that the North Pole is in the midst of a closely frozen ocean, while the southland is occupied by a great ice-bound continent the northern limits of which are already known to us as Graham, Victoria, and Wilkes Lands.

In regard to the surface gravity of the earth, which the new doctrine holds to be greatest at the "turning points" between the outer and inner worlds, it must simply be said that theory and experiment prove the attraction to be at its maximum on the equator, where, of course, is situated the largest amount of the earth's mass, owing to the polar compression before mentioned.

Again, the "hollow earth" theory at once becomes untenable when one reflects on the volcanic and seismic disturbances which so often convulse the crust of our planet and which, together with the fact that the heat of the ground increases with depth, tends to prove that the earth's centre is a mass of molten rock and fire.

From this we can easily see that the comparative warmth of the poles, which is emphasised most strongly, probably arises from the tenuity of the earth's crust in these localities.

In short, novel and attractive as the strange hypothesis may seem, it is certainly not possible, so we can still regard the earth as a solid body.

H. P. LOVECRAFT.

Providence, Aug. 6 [1906].

Notes

1. [Unsigned], "Is the World a Hollow Mockery? Mr. William Reed Thinks It Is in a Material No Less Than in a Moral Sense.—The Facts to Back Up His Ingenious Argument Set Forth," *Providence Sunday Journal* (5 August 1906): Sec. 4, p. 7. The article discussed Reed's *The Phantom of the Poles* (New York: W. S. Rockey Co., 1906).

Letters between H. P. Lovecraft and Orville L. Leach

These letters comprise an exchange between Lovecraft and Orville Livingston Leach (1859–1921) of Auburn, a village in the township of Cranston, R.I. All appeared in the "Letters to the Editor" column of the *Providence Sunday Journal.* At the time of the exchange (1908), Leach was forty-eight and Lovecraft was seventeen.

Leach engaged in various trades throughout his life, including Providence city lamplighter in 1879, seller of quack medicines in the 1890s, patented inventor in the 1900s and 1910s, author of a number of pamphlets and of at least one book, and proprietor of a picnic ground from the late 1890s until his death.

[168]

About the Vacuum

To the Editor of the Sunday Journal:

I notice an inquiry in the Evening Bulletin, about the conduction of heat by a vacuum, and beg to say that what your reader has read about the non-conduction of heat by a vacuum is erroneous—all text books on chemistry state that light and heat are conducted by the most perfect vacuum ever made.

I think your reader must have received his idea from the editorial which the Boston American printed some months ago in relation to a "double bottle" with a vacuum or exhausted space about the inner bottle—this editorial, which showed the lack of knowledge of science, explained that a vacuum was a non-conductor of heat and therefore any hot or cold liquid placed in the bottle would remain at the same temperature indefinitely, the editorial explained that this bottle was in imitation of the "cosmic principle of our earth" which did not lose its heat as it was surrounded by a vacuum, this editorial was something like the same paper printed from Ella Wheeler Wilcox once, which stated that "all water contained microscopic animals, and that it would be lifeless and inefficient if it did not," every scientist knows that pure water contains no organic matter whatsoever—and that when it does it is dangerous.1

While heat or force will pass through a vacuum it may not be exactly heat while it is in the vacuum, it is again refracted into heat when it impinges on the other side—the sun emits warm rays, but they are reduced by the vacuum or the interstellar space—thus mountain tops are cold but when the rays are

refracted by our atmosphere they become warm again—the varying sensations of force or rays are from different wave lengths, caused by rarefaction
or refraction.

While a vacuum will transmit light and heat a galvanic current can not
pass through a vacuum and an electric spark from the positive terminal in
passing into a vacuum forms into rivulets of light while the negative terminal
send [*sic*] a luminous glow into a vacuum.

A vacuum is always cold as all heat is produced by a twisting of rays of
force in passing through or around the molecules of matter, and as no matter
exists in the ether or a vacuum, there is nothing to refract straight magnetic
rays into heat, but practically the result is just the same as if heat passed
through the vacuum unchanged as we can not produce a vacuum except by
having matter on all sides of it.

I have made a study of vacuo, in my radio-active investigations and it is
ap-apparent [*sic*] that much interest is manifested by the public in regard to
the subject.

ORVILLE L. LEACH.

Auburn, June 1.

Notes

1. Neither the "inquiry" in the *Providence Evening Bulletin* nor the editorial in the *Boston
American* has been located. Ella Wheeler Wilcox (1850–1919) was an American author
and poet interested in spiritualism and theosophy.

[169]

Heat and Radiant Energy

To the Editor of the Sunday Journal:

In the Journal for June 7 I notice a letter on heat and the vacuum, written
by an Auburn man named Leach, who has recently been identified with many
speculations of a more or less scientific nature. In the course of his letter he
makes two statements so incorrect that I take the liberty of rectifying them.
First, it is stated that the difference between the temperature of a mountain top
and of the earth's surface is due to the different wave lengths of the radiant heat
at the two places. This is manifestly untrue, as it is a well-known fact, taught in
any high school, that the wave length of any certain form of radiant energy is
constant and invariable.

Radiant energy consists, in general, of undulations or waves in the ether
of space. There are many different forms, depending on the wave lengths.
Thus radiant energy resulting from very slow vibrations in ether and consequently having very long waves, produces electrical effects (relating to the

conductivity of certain metals) upon striking an obstacle. These waves are the undulations upon whose existence wireless telegraphy depends. Another form of radiant energy gives out somewhat shorter waves, which generate heat when intercepted. It is, therefore, called radiant heat. The amount of heat depends upon the wave length, but when one wave motion is sent out into the ether, its length never changes, and cannot be made to do so. Heat waves of short length are identical with long light waves, i.e., they produce both light and heat. Waves of a somewhat shorter length are wholly luminous, affecting chemical substances such as photographic plates, hence being called "Actinic" waves of light.[1] The shortest waves are the Roentgen or X rays.[2] Now the sun transmits to space waves of various lengths, mainly as light and radiant heat. Some of these reach the earth, where the radiant heat is stopped, raising the temperature. At all parts of its course, however, the wave length of each kind of energy remains unchanged. When thermal rays strike a mountain top, its temperature is raised, but since there is not enough air present to receive any large amount of heat, a person there feels very little warmth. At the surface the comparatively dense air is itself heated, hence persons surrounded by it experience a sensation of heat. In both cases, each wave length is, of course, the same. In connection with this point, where the Auburn "scientist" asserts that the "different wave lengths are caused by the rarefaction or refraction" (of the air) it must be said that no amount of refraction can alter the wave length of any form of radiant energy. If this were so, no telescope could be constructed that will show objects in their natural colors, as color depends on the wave length of light.

The second error in Mr. Leach's letter is still more ridiculous. This is the statement that "all heat is produced by a twisting of rays of force in passing through and around the molecules of matter." As nearly everyone knows that ordinary heat consists of rapid motions on the part of the molecules themselves, it would be interesting to know just what this Auburn gentleman's apparently hazy idea of force and matter is.

Finally, it is amusing to see how absolutely Mr. Leach now contradicts a statement which he published through a local paper not quite a year ago, at the time when he so widely promulgated his now notorious "hollow earth" theory, which was recently described in the Journal.[3] He then asserted that the earth will never lose its thermal energy "because a vacuum cannot conduct heat." Since then, it is evident that the Auburnite's knowledge of radiation has increased, and it is to be hoped that it will continue to do so.

H. P. LOVECRAFT.

Providence, June 9.

Notes

1. The word "actinic" derives from the Greek word for ray or beam, and refers to solar rays that produce photochemical effects.
2. Wilhelm Röntgen (1845–1923), German physicist who in 1895 discovered X-rays (or Röntgen) rays.
3. "Inhabitable Land Inside the Earth," [Providence] *Evening Tribune* (12 August 1907): 7.

[170]

Scientists at War

To the Editor of the Sunday Journal:

I notice that my letter in the Sunday Journal of June 7 has brought forth a protest from a much-perturbed individual who signs his name as "Lovecraft." He refers to my "apparently hazy idea of force and matter," but there is nothing "hazy" about this gentleman's ideas; they are decidedly ancient.

He says: "Finally, it is amusing to see how absolutely Mr. Leach now contradicts a statement which he published through a local paper not quite a year ago, at the time when he so widely promulgated his now notorious 'hollow earth' theory which was recently described in the Journal. He then asserted that the earth will never lose its thermal energy, 'because a vacuum cannot conduct heat.' Since then it is evident that the Auburnite's knowledge of radiation has increased, and it is hoped that it will continue to do so."

This statement is untrue. I have never published any such statement in any local paper. Perhaps Mr. Lovecraft means to refer to a statement made in a Boston newspaper, but this was not a publication of my own, and in publishing a reprint from this paper I corrected this statement.

I learned from a textbook on chemistry, written by Edward Yeomans [*sic*], in my youth that heat and light would pass through the most perfect vacuum ever made, or that its equivalent would do this.[1]

Mr. Lovecraft is a disciple of Count Rumford, who claimed that heat was not a material, but simply a motion; but he has had many opponents to his theory, and Dr. Samuel Metcalfe wrote two large volumes on "Caloric," in which he disproved the Rumford theory and proved that heat was a material "fluid."[2]

Mr. Lovecraft says: "As nearly everyone knows that ordinary heat consists of rapid motions on the part of the molecules themselves." Again, he says: "Radiant energy consists in general of undulations or waves in the ether of space."

I would like to know who contradicts themselves if this erudite gentleman does not. Surely there are no molecules in the ether.

The most ridiculous statement made by this gentleman is this: "The wave length of any certain form of radiant energy is constant and invariable." All textbooks state that the forces are corelative, and heat, light and electricity can be transmuted into one another. Mr. Lovecraft impugns the knowledge of Sir Oliver Lodge.[3] There was recently published in a Boston Sunday paper a description of Sir Oliver's discovery of condensing the fogs of London by sending rays of force into the fog from an electrical device and a diagram was printed showing that the rays were nearly straight when they started, but were refracted into long, deep waves when they had passed through the fog.

My critic finds trouble with my statement that the sun's rays are cold or straight on mountain top [*sic*] and refracted into heat in the valleys. He hatches up a funny idea that on mountains "there is not enough air present to receive any large amount of heat," and anyone knows that there is but very little difference in the amount of air on a mountain from what is found lower down. People live and breathe on mountains; our air extends upward for 250 miles, and the mountain tops penetrate only a short distance into this—there is more dust and moisture near the surface, and consequently more refractive power.

Aeronauts who have ascended into high altitudes in balloons say that it grew dark and the sun appeared like a red ball—again the proof of the fact that magnetic rays from the sun or ether are refracted into light by our low atmosphere.

Because the telescope shows objects in their natural colors, my opponent thinks that no amount of refraction can alter the wave length of any form of radiant energy, but does he forget that the spectrum can be produced by glass prism?

This "judge and jury" of his own appointment says: "Radiant energy from very slow vibrations in ether, and consequently having very long waves, produces electrical effects," and then he says: "Another form of radiant energy gives out somewhat shorter waves, which generate heat when interrupted [*sic*]."

The most commonplace scientists know that this is incorrect; the red rays or hot rays of the spectrum are the longest and slowest, while the violet rays or electrical rays are the quickest and shortest.

He says: "When one wave motion is sent out into the ether, its wave length never changes." Again, this gentleman shows that he has not emerged from his incubus—a ray will always go in a straight line except from some obstruction, and as there is no obstructing power to the intangible ether, there is nothing to cause a heat ray or any other ray to go in any way but straight—the sun may send out warm rays, but when they strike the ether, they immediately become cold and straight.

ORVILLE L. LEACH.

Auburn, June 17.

Notes

1. Edward L. Youmans (1821–1887), American writer who founded the magazine *Popular Science*. The book to which Leach refers is probably *A Class-Book of Chemistry* (1852).
2. Sir Benjamin Thompson, Count Rumford (1753–1814), inventor and physicist best known for creating the more efficient Rumford fireplace. Samuel L. Metcalfe (1798–1856), an American physician and chemist who wrote the two-volume work, *Caloric: Its Mechanical, Chemical, and Vital Agencies in the Phenomena of Nature* (1843).
3. Sir Oliver Lodge (1851–1940), British physicist, pioneer in wireless telegraphy, and dabbler in spiritualism and occultism.

[171]

Vacuums, Wave Lengths, Etc.

To the Editor of the Sunday Journal:

In your issue of the 21st I observe that Orville L. Leach, the scientific gentleman from Auburn, has made a valiant endeavor to refute some facts which I expressed in my letter of June 14, hence I am again forced to correct some of his statements.

In regard to the Auburnite's assertion that my reference to his publication, through a local paper, of the statement that a vacuum will not conduct heat, is "untrue," and that he never published such a statement save through an error in a Boston paper, I must simply say that the article referred to appeared, with a portrait, in the form of a direct interview, in a local paper Aug. 12, 1907. I have the cutting in my possession at present, and if Mr. Leach desires to see it at any time he may do so.

The next statement in Mr. Leach's reply is that he learned, in his youth, from Youman's Chemistry, that heat and light would pass through the most perfect vacuum ever made, or that its equivalent would do so. This is correct, in fact, my letter of the 14th did not contradict it, although the Auburn gentleman seems to labor under that impression.

Following directly upon this, Mr. Leach asserts that Rumford's theory of heat "has had many opponents." He is wise in using the perfect tense, since the theory is now accepted without question, as can be seen by consulting any modern textbook of physics.

As to the assertion that I "contradict myself" in stating that heat is molecular motion and that radiant heat is ether vibration, the sage of Auburn evidently errs in his conception of the nature of ether. Ordinary heat, it is true, cannot exist without the presence of molecules, that is, ordinary matter, but it must not be forgotten that according to every modern authority, ether is itself a certain form of matter, not molecular, but continuous, and capable of sustaining wave motions or vibrations. Radiant heat is the name applied to vibration of a wave

length greater than that of red light, giving thermal phenomena when intercepted. In no part of my letter of the 14th do I confuse this form of energy with ordinary or molecular heat.

Mr. Leach observes that "his critic finds trouble with his statement that the
sun's rays are cold and straight on a mountain top, and refracted into heat in
the valley, and hatches up the funny idea that on mountains there is not enough
air to receive any large amount of heat." His critic does find trouble. The density of the air decreases with the altitude, owing to the lesser gravity, as can be
shown by the fall of mercury in a barometer taken up a mountain. Aeronauts,
and those first going to high altitudes, find difficulty in living and breathing,
so insufficient is the supply of air. At the tops of mountains the density of the
atmosphere is so small that not enough molecules of its component gases are
present to form an obstruction sufficient to transform the radiant heat, or obscure radiations, into ordinary heat. This is why the air is cooler than at low
altitudes. This is not a theory "hatched up" by myself, but a fact well known
to all who study physics. (See Brocklesby's Meteorology, p. 25 section 36.)[1]

Mr. Leach states that his "opponent" forgets that a spectrum can be produced by a glass prism. His "opponent" does not forget, but the spectrum
does not show that the wave length of light can be changed. White light (as
sunlight) is composite, being a mixture of many colored lights, that is, is
composed of different forms of radiant energy. The prism simply breaks up
the beam of white light into the different forms of radiant energy of which it
is composed, the wave length of each being the same as before the dispersal.
The only change is in the direction of the wave fronts.

Mr. Leach tries to dispute the fact that "when one wave motion is sent
into the ether its length never changes." In refutation (?) he informs us that
"a ray will always go in a straight line, except from some obstruction, and as
there is no obstructing power to the intangible ether, there is nothing to cause
a heat ray, or any other ray, to go in any way but straight." While all this is
true, I fail to see how such a statement has any bearing on the well-known
truth which Mr. Leach attempts to contradict.

H. P. LOVECRAFT.

Providence, June 30.

Notes

1. John Brocklesby, author of *Elements of Meteorology* (1848), a copy of which HPL
owned. "We thus perceive, what all observations have proved, that the upper regions
of the atmosphere must be colder than the lower. It is not, however, to be forgotten,
that the rarefaction of the superior strata contributes to this condition" (25).

[172]

Holes in the Ether

To the Editor of the Sunday Journal:

I again receive the very kind attention of Prof. Lovecraft in the Sunday Journal of July 5, and for fear that he might feel slighted if I did not respond I will ask you for space for this letter.

I understand that H. P. Lovecraft is a Professor of Astronomy and was formerly at Brown University. He is one of "the old schoolers," who still holds to the idea of the "persistence of wave lengths of force." He has also been an advocate of "the persistence of matter" and the "immutability of the elements," but the latest discoveries by Prof. Ramsey [*sic*] and others prove one element can be changed into another, and Sir Oliver Lodge says: "Atoms can be broken up into electric discharges."[1]

My "strange ideas" are not the result of ignorance of the tenets of the old textbooks. I have studied the same books as the professor, but I have discarded them as old and effete.

I notice that in the professor's letter in the Sunday Journal of July 5 he practically corroborates the statement in my first letter which was the "bone of contention" of his letter in the Sunday Journal of June 7. In my letter I claimed that the reason why the surface of the earth was warmer than mountains was because of the obstructing power of the denser materials in the atmosphere of the surface.

In his letter in the Sunday Journal of June 14 he says: "When thermal rays strike a mountain top, it (temperature) is raised, but since there is not air enough present to receive any large amount of heat, a person there feels very little warmth."

Now in his letter in the Sunday Journal of July 5 he says: "At the tops of mountains the density of the atmosphere is so small that not enough molecules of its component gases are present to form an obstruction sufficient to transform the radiant heat.['] This is exactly my idea, as I expressed in my first letter.

Prof. Lovecraft in his last letter says: "Mr. Leach tries to dispute the fact that when one wave motion is sent into the ether its length never changes."

["]In refutation (?) he informs us that "a ray will always go in a straight line except from some obstruction, and as there is no obstructing power to the intangible ether there is nothing to cause a heat ray or any other ray to go in any [way] but straight."

"While all this is true, I fail to see how such a statement has any bearing on the well-known truth which Mr. Leach attempts to contradict."

It is evident that the professor has a constriction on the word refract. Webster's Dictionary defines the word in this way: "To bend a ray out of its course." But the professor seems to think refraction means simply a bending from a straight trend, the same as a bow is bent; but is not a wave or a spiral a lateral bending out of its course?

An ostrich may go in a "bee line" from Providence to Boston, but he goes zig-zag, and this is not straight. His path is refracted just as much as if he went to Boston by way of Worcester or in a half circle.

The professor will not deny that the forces are correlative. I am sure, and if one force can change into another it positively must be from a changing of its wave lengths, for if heat retained its regular wave lengths it would still remain heat and the same with any force.

Prof. Lovecraft says I am wise in using the perfect tense in saying that the Rumford theory has had many opponents, but I will say now that it has many opponents, and the new stellar photography proves that the orbits of the planets are great paths of moving force or ether, like streams of water, and on these paths the planets are floated or borne along—not by any undulation or wave motion, but by great moving ribbons of force. Has the professor heard of this, and does he ridicule the idea?

He states one great fundamental principle of my scientific creed when he says: "Ether is itself a certain form of matter, not molecular, but continuous." This means, of course, unparticled matter or spirit, which I claim is the only matter in the universe. I was the first man to give out the theory that matter was simply space spots, outlined by a moving wall of spirit. I was in correspondence with Sir William Crookes several years ago and sent him my theories and received his acknowledgment of the data.[2] At the same time I sent the same data to Sir Oliver Lodge. The ideas were discussed before the British Association for the Advancement of Science, and Sir Oliver averred that the theories were correct.[3] The English papers published the reports and they came back to America and Prof. Serviss wrote an article for a Boston paper, explaining that Sir Oliver averred that the ether was the only real thing in the universe, and Prof. Serviss in the same article says: "One savant (this is myself) says matter is simply a hole in the ether—we are holes in the ether—a mountain is a hole in the ether," etc.[4]

I claim that the matter of our bodies is "a hole in the ether," but that our nerve cells contain vacuo or spaces filled with spirit, which has consciousness and a potential of motion.

It will be seen that I am a Pantheist, but if science proves that I am right, who can deny my claims?

The truths of God and nature are ever open to the Auburnite as well as to a Brown Universityite, and the professor may fight as he retreats, but he cannot release himself from the iron grip of truth and progress.

ORVILLE L. LEACH.

Auburn, July 7.

Notes

1. Sir William Ramsay (1852–1916), Scottish chemist who received the Nobel Prize in

Chemistry in 1904 for his discovery of inert gases in earth's atmosphere. The quotation from Lodge appears to be inaccurate or invented.

2. See letter 3n12.

3. The British Association for the Advancement of Science was founded in 1831 and is now known as the British Science Association.

4. Garrett P. Serviss (1851–1929), American astronomer. HPL owned Serviss's *Pleasures of the Telescope* (1901), *Astronomy with an Opera-Glass* (1906), *Astronomy with the Naked Eye* (1908), and a Barrett-Serviss Star and Planet Finder (planisphere). The quotation comes from a syndicated newspaper article by Serviss, "A Paradox of Science." The appearance in the Boston newspaper has not been found, but the article was published in the *Windsor* [Ontario] *Star* (2 November 1907): 5.

[173]

Waves in the Ether

To the Editor of the Sunday Journal:

Once more I observe that Mr. Orville L. Leach has favored the public with a contribution on ether physics, in which he again makes some statements that compel me to contradict them. In his letter he asserts that I am an "advocate of the persistence of wave length, persistence of matter and immutability of the elements." The first statement is true, for every student knows that the length of an ether wave cannot be changed save by absorption and re-emission by a fluorescent body. The second is not quite so correct, because, as with all modern readers, I recognize the fact that certain observations slightly tend to discredit the law of the conservation of mass. According to the electrical theory of matter, the mass of a body depends on the velocity of the electrons or corpuscles which compose its atoms, hence, should their energy diminish or increase, the mass of the body would correspondingly diminish or increase.

I am also conversant with the claim of Heydweiler that cupric sulphate and water have a different weight when taken separately from that of their solution; and with that of Walace [*sic*] that water changes weight with freezing, yet after all, are these meagre theories and claims sufficient to overthrow such a well-established idea as that which holds matter uncreatable and indestructible?[1] As to the transmutation of elements, neither I nor any other student, so far as I am aware, now contradicts the fact that elements may be degraded into others of lesser atomic weight. The change of copper into lithium, as made by Sir William Ramsay in his recent radium experiments, would be sufficient to establish such a belief.

Mr. Leach states that he has cast aside as "old and effete" the textbooks which I have studied. Does he refer to Mumper's Physics (1907), The New Knowledge (1907), or others of similar date?

He also says that in my letter of June 14 I "corroborate the statement in his first letter, which was the 'bone of contention.'" If I read correctly, Mr.

Leach stated in his first letter that "mountain tops are cold, but when the (sun's) cold rays are refracted by our atmosphere they become warm again, the varying sensations of force of [*sic*] rays being from different wave lengths, caused by rarefaction or refraction."

In no place do I concur to this peculiar statement. In my letter of June 14 I stated the recognized facts, and on July 5 gave the explanation, showing that the heat felt at any place is due not to the radiations directly, but to the molecular heat caused by their interception by the air, the amount of which, of course, determines the amount of heat formed. The radiations themselves can, of course, produce no sensations.

My objection to Mr. Lynch's [*sic*] statement lay in the fact that he assumed a change of wave length due to refraction, a manifestly impossible thing. In discussing wave motion Mr. Leach falls into the error of supposing that the bends of the wavy line which a transverse wave describes are the results of refraction. In physics, the direction of a wave is considered as the direction of the vibratory impulse, or line of propagation, which is, of course, a straight line. Refraction, in its scientific sense, is defined as "the bending of the line of propagation of a wave" (Avery's Physics).[2] Thus the Auburnite's interesting comparison to the ostrich on his weary journey from Providence to Boston falls flat. When luminous rays are ordinarily transformed into heat, the wave length is not changed, but lost, because heat is molecular, not wave motion. Light cannot be transformed into radiant heat except in the phenomenon of absorption and re-emission. In speaking of the Rumford theory of heat, it is almost unnecessary to state that it is now accepted without question as being the only possible explanation of the observed facts. Mr. Leach construes my statement that the ether is continuous and not molecular into an expression of one "great fundamental principle of his scientific creed.["] I must, however, remark that the continuity of the ether has been assumed almost ever since the existence of the medium itself was acknowledged. As to any theory that matter consists of "space spots, outlined by a moving wall of spirit," I must say that nothing of the kind has ever been accepted by the scientific world. Sir Oliver Lodge, J. J. Thomson,[3] and other eminent investigators have outlined the new electric theory of matter, assuming that all masses are aggregations of, and not holes in, the ether. According to this theory, all matter is electrical, the ether being "bound" by moving electrons or corpuscles which compose atoms. If the "holes in ether" theory be the "iron grip of truth and progress" from which Mr. Leach asserts that, although I may "fight as I retreat," I cannot release myself, I have great doubts as to the efficiency of the "iron grip."

H. P. LOVECRAFT.

Providence, July 13.

Notes

1. Adolf Heydweiler (1856–1925), adjunct professor at Breslau (1895–1901), professor at the Universität Münster (1901–08), and professor of experimental physics at the Universität Rostock (1908–21). "Cupric sulphate" is simply another term for "copper sulfate." "Heydweiler claims that copper sulphate and water do not have the same collective weight before and after solution. Wallace claims that a mass of water does not have the same weight before and after freezing. Altogether, both from theoretical and experimental considerations the absolute validity of the law of the conservation of mass is certainly challenged." Duncan R. Kennedy, *The New Knowledge* (New York: A. S. Barnes & Co., 1905), 250. "Walace" is probably Alfred Russel Wallace (1823–1913), British biologist and explorer, who carried out some experiments on water.

2. Elroy M. Avery (1844–1935), historian and author of *School Physics* (1895) and *Elementary Physics* (1897). However, this exact quotation appears in neither of these two books, though very similar quotations do.

3. J. J. Thomson (1856–1940), British physicist, discoverer of the electron, inventor of the mass spectrometer, and recipient of the 1906 Nobel Prize in physics.

[174]

Matter the Deficiency of Mass

To the Editor of the Sunday Journal:

In answer to a very courteous letter of inquiry from A. E. Williams, I would say that I claim the molecules of matter are caused to rotate by impinging lines of force, and taking to greater orbits cause matter to expand.[1]

It was not my intention to pay any more attention to H. P. Lovecraft, but he says: "As to any theory that matter consists of 'space spots outlined by a moving wall of spirit,' I must say that nothing of the kind has ever been accepted by science. Sir Oliver Lodge, J. J. Thomson and other eminent investigators have outlined the new electric theory of matter, assuming that all masses are aggregations of and not holes in the ether."

Prof. Serviss quotes from the report from the British Association for the Advancement of Science, saying that "matter instead of being, as we innocently believe on the evidence of our senses, the only real and solid thing in nature is, in fact the absence or deficiency of mass."[2]

And again: "Inside the solidest substances we should find emptiness."[3]

ORVILLE L. LEACH.

Emery Park, Auburn, July 20.

Notes

1. The letter from A. E. Williams was sent either directly to Leach or through the *Providence Sunday Journal*, as it does not appear in the "Letters to the Editor" column.
2. From Serviss's article in the *Windsor Star* (see letter 172.n4), where Serviss attributes it to Osborne Reynolds (1842–1912), British innovator in fluid mechanics.
3. From the same article by Serviss.

The two following letters are among the few surviving works from Lovecraft's period of hermitry (1908–14) following his withdrawal from high school. If nothing else, the second letter testifies that Lovecraft did venture out of doors on rare occasions.

[175]

Venus and the Public Eye

To the Editor of the Sunday Journal:

The general ignorance of the public as regards the science of astronomy has often been noted and deplored. Garrett P. Serviss, in his well-known work entitled "Astronomy With an Opera Glass,"[1] tells of an instance in which the planet Venus was mistaken for an electrically lighted balloon by the greater part of the population of New York city. This occurred in 1887, yet the following incident tends to illustrate the lamentable fact that the public knowledge of celestial science has advanced little, if any, since then.

While in the business section of this city on Christmas Eve, at about 6 p. m., the writer noticed excited groups of people on the street corners, and mystified individuals everywhere pointing to the western sky. Following the direction of the many upraised fingers he beheld the planet Venus, which was shining with great brilliancy, and appeared to be the centre of attention. This great apparent concern in astronomy seemed encouraging, to say the least, and the writer began to believe that the general apathy which the public usually exhibits was being thrown off, and that an awakening of scientific interest was taking place within the breasts of the population, when this belief was shattered by remarks overheard from a knot of cultivated and apparently well-educated men.

It seems that the general idea existed that the planet was nothing more or less than the searchlight from some airship, either that which was recently purchased by a local merchant, or that supposed to be owned by Wallace E. Tillinghast of Worcester, Mass. Upon further listening the writer heard many remarks as to the "perfect control to which the aëroplane must be subject, in order that the light shine so steadily," and many estimates of its "distance above the earth," varying from half a mile to two miles. When apprised of their error, the gentlemen of the aforementioned group exhibited only mild surprise.

Such a revelation of general ignorance is depressing in effect. In all probability the reports of strange lights lately seen in the sky have caused the multitude to turn their gaze heavenward, and to seize upon Venus, which is by far the brightest of all star-like objects, as the searchlight of the supposed "airship," for which they really look in vain.

Yet, actually, the appearance of Venus should not cause people of intelligence to indulge in such suppositions, as its brilliant presence in the heavens is by no means uncommon. Even now it is not as bright as it will be next month.

The moral of the preceding is that if the general public will not avail itself of the astronomical information afforded by the publication of Prof. Upton's excellent articles in the Journal on the first of each month,[2] suitable free lectures should be provided to impart such knowledge to it.

H. P. LOVECRAFT.

Providence, Dec. 24 [1909].

Notes

1. HPL's "Celestial Objects for All" (1907; *CE* 3.89–99) speaks of the use of an opera glass for astronomy. For Serviss see letter 172n4.

2. Winslow Upton (1853–1914), professor of astronomy at Brown University and a friend of the Lovecraft family, wrote a long-running monthly astronomy column in the *Providence Journal*. For this reason, HPL's own astronomy columns had to be written for other local papers. HPL owned Upton's *Star Atlas* (1896; *LL* 990).

[176]

Seats for Park Concerts

Room for 'Greek Theatre' on Bank Above Lake.

To the Editor of the Sunday Journal:

As a frequent auditor at the municipal concerts, held during the summer in Roger Williams Park,[1] I feel impelled to remark the utterly inadequate provisions there made for seating the great numbers who assemble three times a week by the bandstand on the lake.

The public owes, it is true, much gratitude to the city for furnishing this admirable series of musical entertainments, especially since the financial assistance of the local street railway has been withdrawn; yet withal it seems not unreasonable to desire that some sort of auditorium be erected to replace that which was recently condemned and demolished.

We are, according to the present state of things, listening to a band of the very first quality under conditions which forbid us properly to appreciate its excellence. For who can fully enjoy hearing even the most carefully selected and skilfully rendered music when he is at the same time pacing up and down a narrow concrete walk amidst a jostling crowd; standing awkwardly in one place until fatigue or the resistless crush of humanity compels him to move on; or else sitting, crouching, or reclining in an uncomfortable posture upon the bank which rises west of the lake? Only a few fortunate first-comers are enabled to secure space on the benches which line the walk, and many are deterred altogether from attending the concerts on account of this miserable lack of facilities.

Last Wednesday evening, while viewing the situation and considering various methods whereby it may be ameliorated, the writer and several others were very much impressed by the resemblance of the grassy bank with its numerous occupants to an ancient Greek theatre with its tiers of auditors, and by the possibility that this bank might be properly excavated in a semi-circular outline facing the bandstand, fitted from top to bottom with rows of seats, and made in truth a lineal descendant of the old Dionysiac Theatre at Athens.

Such an arrangement would surely provide for the comfortable seating of a very large proportion of the audiences, would be by no means unsightly, would be exempt from the charge of dampness brought against the old auditorium over the water, would be unexceptionable from an acoustic point of view, and lastly, would not interfere with the enjoyment of the music by the canoeists on the lake, and by the motorists on the opposite shore.

This suggestion has perhaps been offered by others before, but if so, deserves renewed attention now that the old seats have been removed, and the public is without suitable accommodations; wherefore it is here presented for the consideration of the Metropolitan Park Commission, or such other authorities as may possess jurisdiction over matters of this sort.

H. P. LOVECRAFT.

Providence, July 31 [1913].

Notes

1. At the time, HPL lived at 598 Angell Street, a little more than 4 miles from the park.

To the *Scientific American*

A prescient recommendation to search for planets within the solar system beyond Neptune by the use of celestial photography. The search for such planets gained momentum during the early 20th century, resulting in the discovery of Pluto (now deemed a dwarf planet) in 1930 by Clyde Tombaugh. At the time, Lovecraft was writing "The Whisperer in Darkness," in which he identifies his imaginary planet Yuggoth (first cited in *Fungi from Yuggoth* [1929–30]) with Pluto. Following the fly-by of Pluto in July 2015 by the *New Horizons* spacecraft, an elongated dark region on the surface was named Cthulhu Macula (formerly called Cthulhu Regio), named after Lovecraft's fictional entity.

[177]

Trans-Neptunian Planets

To the Editor of the SCIENTIFIC AMERICAN:

In these days of large telescopes and modern astronomical methods, it seems strange that no vigorous efforts are being made to discover planets beyond the orbit of Neptune, which is now considered the outermost limit of the solar system. It has been noticed that seven comets have their aphelia at a point that would correspond to the orbit of a planet revolving around the sun at a distance of about 100 astronomical units (9,300,000,000 miles).

Now several have suggested that such a planet exists, and has captured the comets by attraction. This is probable, as Jupiter and others also mark the aphelia of many celestial wanderers. The writer has noticed that a great many comets cluster around a point 50 units out, where a large body might revolve. If the great mathematicians of the day should try to compute orbits from these aphelia, it is doubtful if they could succeed; but if all the observatories that possess celestial cameras should band together and minutely photograph the ecliptic, as is done in asteroid hunting, the bodies might be revealed on their plates. Even if no discoveries were made, the accurate star photographs would almost be worth the time and trouble.

H. P. LOVECRAFT.

Providence, R. I., July 16, 1906.

To the *New-York Tribune*

[178]

The English Language

Writer Sees No Need to Replace It by an American Tongue.

To the Editor of The Tribune.

Sir: I was extremely surprised and inexpressibly pained at reading in the Tribune of Sunday, September 10, an open letter advocating the adoption by the people of this country of a so-called "American language."[1] That such a terrible blow to civilization can be seriously planned or even calmly contemplated by a broad minded or public spirited citizen I am loath to believe. It cannot but be plain to any sane thinker that even the present number of tongues in the world is by far too great and that the various enlightened nations of our globe can never attain that degree of intellectual sympathy and community which should be theirs till they have a common speech.

It is the good fortune of the American people to possess the noblest language spoken by man. Almost the youngest of tongues, it has grown up among the Anglo-Saxons, who by their racial superiority have been able to enrich its literature by more and greater names than may be found in the annals of the most favored of foreign speeches. Transplanted over all parts of the globe by the mighty race that has developed it, it is above all others fit and likely to become the future universal means of communication, and is, indeed, already spoken by more persons than is any other language.

Is it this symbol and instrument of advancement that it is purposed to reject? Do the short sighted pseudo-patriots who prate against it realize what a calamity its loss would mean to this nation? Let me not think so; rather say that they are blinded by that painful sort of "spread-eagleism" which so oft afflicts the superficial.

Undermined as we now are by a polyglot mass of sodden foreigners, we are certainly incapable of rivalling in intellect our English relatives, so is it not wisest for us to remain in closest touch with them and enjoy in their company the sunlight of literary and scientific excellence which pours forth from the Britannic pen and press? The English of our books, and especially of our periodical literature, is far below the proper standard, and in the improvement of this state of things will be found a far more proper employment for uneasy brains than in disturbing and debasing the speech of a great nation by such ruinous practices as "simplified spelling" or "American languages."[2]

H. P. LOVECRAFT.

Providence, Sept. 14, 1911.

Not all Anglo Saxons
Writer Finds English Speaking Celts Predominant in America.[3]

There are only two points in Mr. Lovecraft's rather hectic inviting notice—his references to the "racial superiority of the Anglo-Saxons" and to the "polyglot mass of sodden foreigners." It is curious that he and his type do not see that those incessant lapses from good taste spoil arguments that are the blatant outcome of overweening racial vanity. Mr. Lovecraft is certainly not as "Anglo-Saxon" as he imagines; but if he desires to prove his point let him stop crowing and produce the Anglo Saxon who will beat Sheridan as an all-around athlete, or MacDonald at hammer throwing, or Roosevelt as statesman, or Bryan as orator, or Johnson as boxer. His opponents will then be dumb.

We hear more about the "Anklo-Saxung" here than in England, where the local Hodge or Scrooge regards with awe the Harcourt or De Montmorency. Remember that the Anglo-Saxons did not really begin to shed their barbarism till after six centuries in England. Lanigan cites as an instance of their depravity; as late as the thirteen century, their practice of selling their own children, in spite of Pope and King, as slaves to Irish nobles. Mackintosh, as well as Havelock Ellis in his "Study of British Genius," admits that the unmixed Saxon is "marked by mental mediocrity."

Cambrensia, the Norman, who hated the Irish, but said the strength and majesty of their physique was unequalled in Europe, wrote in the twelfth century: "Who dares compare the English, the most degraded of all races under heaven, with the Welsh celts? In their own country they are serfs, the veriest slaves of the Normans. In our (Wales) who else have we for our herdsmen, shepherds, cobblers, skinners, cleaners of our dog kennels?"

I regard the Celt or Gael of Western Europe as the highest human type of the past. The American, who is an English speaking Celt predominantly, promises, with a little more discipline, to be the man of the future. I would therefore like to see him prefer fact to argument, and drop talking grotesque nonsense that excites the laugh and wink of Englishmen.—Herbert O'Hara Molineux in New York Tribune.

Notes

1. John L. M. Allen, "Wants an American Language," *New-York Tribune* (10 September 1911): 6.

2. Herbert O'Hara Molineux responded to this letter with "Not All Anglo-Saxons," *New-York Tribune* (25 September 1911): 6, which was carried in various newspapers.

3. *Pioneer Press,* Martinsburg, WV (7 October 1911):1

Letters to the Munsey Magazines

American publisher Frank A. Munsey (1854–1925) began a line of popular magazines with the *Golden Argosy* (1882; later retitled the *Argosy*), followed by *Munsey's Magazine* (1889f.), the *All-Story Weekly* (1905f.), and others. Lovecraft began reading some of these magazines as early as 1903; in the *Rhode Island Journal of Astronomy* (27 September 1903) he cites an article from *Munsey's*. In his letter to the *All-Story* (see letter 184 below), he notes that he had been reading that magazine since its inception. In 1913, Lovecraft's objections to the romance stories of Fred Jackson in the *Argosy* led to a furor that lasted well over a year and incited him to write the verse satire "Ad Criticos" (only two of the four "books" were published in the magazine). Other readers responded with both letters and verse attacking Lovecraft. (For the complete texts of the letters by and about Lovecraft, see Joshi, *H. P. Lovecraft in the Argosy*.) An editor at the *Argosy*, Matthew White, Jr., asked Lovecraft and John Russell (one of Lovecraft's leading antagonists) to conclude the debate; they did so by each writing a poem published in the October 1914 issue (Lovecraft's was "The End of the Jackson War" [*AT* 209]). Lovecraft's letters were noticed by Edward F. Daas of the UAPA, leading to his recruitment into amateur journalism.

[179]

[October 1911?]

And now comes H. P. L., of Providence, Rhode Island, who prefers war to humor, for he says: "According to my idea, Albert Payson Terhune[1] is the leading feature of the magazine. His stories are of surpassing merit, in selection of historical period, development of plot, and purity of English. For these alone I would willingly purchase *The Argosy* at its present price, or at a greater." He then goes on to say that the rest of the magazine is likewise of meritorious quality, but takes exception to the lack of descriptive matter in some of the stories, superabundance of slang in others, and the tendency of the writers to lay their scenes in the present age instead of the past. He also says: "Some of the tales are founded upon too commonplace and trivial incidents, events unworthy of the writers' efforts. This defect, however, seems less prominent in the more recent issues, perhaps owing to the policy of the magazine in providing stories with an outdoor setting." He signs himself a "Reader since 1905" and I can assure him that he is a much appreciated one.

Notes

1. Albert Payson Terhune (1872–1942), prolific American author, dog breeder, and journalist, perhaps best known for *Lad: A Dog* (1919).

[180]

[January 1913?]

[A Few Lines about "Fishhead"]

. . . It is the belief of the writer that very few short stories of equal merit[1] have been published anywhere during recent years. It is easy to imagine with what genuine regret the editors to whom it was submitted declined to print it. . . .

H. P. LOVECRAFT.

598 Angell Street,
Providence, R.I.

Notes

1. HPL writes about "Fishhead" by Irvin S. Cobb (1876–1944), which was published in *Cavalier* (11 January 1913).

[181]

Objects to Jackson

Editor, Argosy:

> Too long hath love engross'd Britannia's stage,
> And sunk to softness all our tragic rage:
> By that alone, did empires fall or rise,
> And fate depended on a fair one's eyes;
> The sweet infection mixt with dang'rous art,
> Debas'd our manhood, while it sooth'd the heart.
> *Tho. Tickell on Addison's Cato.*[1]

When Mr. Pope desired that his pastoral poetry should be preferred to that of his rival, Ambrose Philips, he published an anonymous criticism, wherein, by affecting to condemn his own work, he artfully managed very considerably to praise it.

That the "Josh Billings-gate"[2] classic, signed F. V. Bennett, R. 2, Hanover, Illinois, which appears in your July Log-Book, is in reality a sly attempt at augmenting the fame of your contributor, Fred Jackson,[3] is scarce to be doubted; yet despite its concealed intent, it seems to me that a literal reading of it expresses a far juster opinion of the modern Jacksonian novel.

In the words of the Hanoverian correspondent, the subscribers of *The Argosy* are undoubtedly receiving "to mutch" of Mr. Jackson's erotic fiction.

Whilst I am not wishful to be unduly censorious of any author, I must own that the Jacksonesque style of narrative inspires in me far less of interest than of distaste, and must express my wonderment at the extraordinary favour accorded its originator by the publishers of *The Argosy* and *Cavalier*.

To the eye of a disinterested observer it appears as though an effort were being made forcibly to obtrude Mr. Jackson upon the reading public by an unexampled campaign of advertising, and by the selection for publication in the Log-Book of those letters wherein he receives the greatest amount of adulation.

The opinion that Mr. Jackson's novels are wholly wanting in merit would be as unjust as is their present praise fulsome, for in certain quarters they might find a fitting place and furnish material for multitudes avidly to read.

There is a numerous set of people whose chief literary delight is obtained in the following of imaginary nymphs and swains through the labyrinthine paths of amorous adventure, and who deem an account of an affection won or lost quite as exciting and entertaining as that of a kingdom saved or destroyed.

To such as these are the fictions of Jackson well suited; but these, methinks, are not the average readers of *The Argosy*. The latter prefer, I am sure, a sprightlier sort of story, where acts of valour are more dwelt upon than affairs of Venus. For mine own part, I have ever preferred the Aeneid of Virgil to the Ars Amatoria of Ovid.

Apart from the mere choice of subject, let me venture to describe the Jacksonine type of tale as trivial, effeminate, and, in places, coarse.

The author remarks the costumes of his heroines with the minute attention of a mantua-maker and describes the furnishings and decorations of their apartments like a housewife or chambermaid.

Into the breasts of his characters, and appearing to dominate them to the exclusion of reason, he places the delicate passions and emotions proper to negroes or anthropoid apes.

His literary style is feeble, and often excessively familiar. He abounds in "split" infinitives, and occasionally falls into the use of outlandish words, as, for instance, "live-in-able", instead of "habitable".

From the general tenor of his works I am inclined to believe that the name "Fred Jackson" serves to veil an identity no more masculine than that of "George Eliot", "George Sand", or "John Strange Winter".[4]

In short, whilst he is indubitably clever in his way and well fitted to please that portion of the public which once read with joy the effusions of Laura Jean Libbey, Mrs. E. D. E. N. Southworth,[5] and others of the saccharine, gelatinous school of literature, Mr. Jackson is not in harmony with the policy of *The Argosy* and certainly should not be allowed to occupy so much space, crowding out the work of such really able authors as Albert Payson Terhune, Lawrence Perry, or William H. Greene.[6]

I have, in all, succeeded in enduring about three and a half of Fred Jackson's stories. The first, whose name I forgot, I began in ignorance of its nature, and continued in the hope that its quality might improve toward the end. I was disappointed.

The second, which was entitled "The House of Unrest", I perused in order to determine whether or not all of this author's productions were as bad as the first. I found little difference.

The third was "The First Law", which I read because I thought that since it appeared in *The Argosy* it must be superior to its predecessors. My expectation was not fulfilled. I lately cast my eye upon "The Third Act" in order to discover some reason why Mr. Jackson was so strongly recommended to the readers of *The Argosy*, but after reaching Page 540, or thereabouts, I found myself too weary to continue, and resolved to give over so profitless and dull an occupation.[7]

I had not intended bursting into defamatory rhetoric over this matter, but am now induced to do so by reason of the humorous letter of Mr. Bennett, who so ingeniously praises Jackson with faint damning.

Think not that I write in hostility, for such is the very opposite of my feeling for *The Argosy*, which is, I assure you, "the Best Story Magazine I Ever Read". I desire merely to call your attention to the fact that there is at least one amongst your readers who does not welcome "Jackson In about Ever nomber".

Because of its strictures on such a laurelled literary luminary, I may with safety predict that no part of this my lucubration will appear in print; however, this will cause me no pangs, for I have already been guilty of an inch or two in the Log-Book and am now seeking only to avert a flood of 2 mutch Jackson.[8]

Yours truly,

H. P. Lovecraft.

598 Angell Street,
Providence, Rhode Island.

Notes

1. Thomas Tickell (1685–1740), minor British poet, "To the Same [Joseph Addison], on His Tragedy of Cato" (ll. 1–6), included in most editions of Addison's play *Cato* (written 1712; performed 1713).

2. A portmanteau word of HPL's coinage. Josh Billings was the pen name of Henry Wheeler Shaw (1818–1885), famous humor writer and lecturer in the U.S.; billingsgate is coarse or foul language.

3. Fred Jackson (1886–1953) was a prolific American author, playwright, and screenwriter. He wrote for more than 50 films between 1912 and 1946.

4. John Strange Winter was the pseudonym of the British novelist Henrietta Eliza Vaughan Stannard (1856–1911).

5. Laura Jean Libbey (1862–1924), American writer. Emma Dorothy Eliza Nevitte Southworth (1819–1899), American writer of more than 60 novels in the latter part of the 19th century, and perhaps the most popular American novelist of her day.

6. Lawrence Perry (1875–1954), author of adventure fiction. William H. Greene, author of "The Savage Strain" (*Argosy*, November 1911) and other works.

7. "The House of Unrest" (*Cavalier*, 11 January 1913); "The First Law" (*Argosy*, April 1913); "The Third Act" (*Argosy*, June 1913).

8. HPL is imitating the illiterate letter by F. V. Bennett (July 1913) in which he stated: "It was Fred Jackson to mutch of him I should say."

Ad Criticos

[182]

Liber Primus

What vig'rous protests now assail my eyes?
See Jackson's satellites in anger rise!
His ardent readers, steep'd in tales of love,
Sincere devotion to their leader prove;
In brave defence of sickly gallantry,
They damn the critic, and beleaguer me.
Ingenious Russell, I forgive the slur,[1]
Since in such clever lines your sneers occur.
Your verse, with true Pierian heat inflam'd,
Should be at some more worthy object aim'd.
Think not, good rhymester, that I sought to shew
In my late letter merely what I know,
Nor that I labour'd, with my humble quill,
To bend the universe to suit my will.
My aim, forsooth, was but to do my best
To free these pages from an am'rous pest.
With no false hopes did I so strongly plead;
Small chance had I, unaided, to succeed.
Of Russell's rhymes, thus briefly I dispose,
And next consider Crean's perspicuous prose.[2]

Forbear, kind sir, to think my plaint was made,
That I my store of language might parade:
In truth, my words are not beyond the reach
Of him who understands the English speech;
But Crean, I fear, by reading Jackson long,
Hath lost the pow'r to read his mother tongue.
Yet hark! I face another diatribe;
My critic says, I am a luckless scribe.
Dismiss the charge! From that disgrace I'm free;
No line of fiction e'er was writ by me!
So much for Crean, but ere my song I end,
I porze, Fonetik Bennett too Kummend.³
His rugged wit hath such a solid worth,
'Tis not amiss to doubt his rustic birth,
And guess he toils, his protests to prepare,
Safe seated in an editorial chair,
From whence he hurls deceptive ridicule
'Gainst all who fight soft Jackson and his school.
Scrawl on, sweet Jackson, raise the lover's leer;
'Tis plain, you please the fallen public ear.
As once in Charles the Second's vulgar age,
Gross Wycherley and Dryden soil'd the stage;
So now again erotic themes prevail,
However loud the sterner souls bewail.
Pure fiction wanes, and baser writings rise—
But cease, my Muse! No more I'll criticise.

[183]

Liber Secundus

Still louder bawl the bold Boeotian band,
And seize their arms at sentiment's command:
The lovers' legion, martially array'd,
To tender Jackson bears its eager aid.
Their acid quills, fresh pluck'd from Cupid's wing,
At me the Myrmidons of Venus fling.
Intrepid Saunders heads the hostile horde,⁴
And hurls with deadly skill the poison'd word;
Help'd on by books, both sacred and profane,
He seeks to shine in the satiric strain.
Peace! Oklahoman, cease my words to rate:
"Jacksonian", "Jacksonine", "Josh Billings-gate"

Claim no existence but as satire's tools;
Owe no allegiance to linguistic rules,
Whilst as for "Hanoverian", take care
Lest as a faulty scholar you appear;
Too much upon your lexicon you lean,
For *proper names* in such arc seldom seen.
As studious Saunders, like the kangaroo,
Jumps in a hansom, and is lost to view,
Laconic Bonner takes the leader's place,[5]
And throws his modest "classic" in my face.
Now fairer forms from out the ranks emerge;
The Amazons in reckless fury charge.
Good Madam Loop,[6] like Crean of Syracuse,
Protests unkindly 'gainst the words I use:
Whoe'er this lady's firm esteem would seek,
In monosyllables must ever speak.
The North and West have now their rancour spent,
And Old Virginia joins the tournament.
Here once a nobler JACKSON wag'd his wars,
And died a hero in a glorious cause.
Lost is the cause, but deathless STONEWALL'S fame.
Alas, that lesser men should bear his name!
But down, my Muse, to present actions skip;
And meet th' attack of Mistress Blankenship.[7]
The maid of Richmond, with romantic mind,
Considers my opinions most unkind;
And finds in Jackson's tales of love intense
A charming sweetness; beauteous innocence.
What fascination! Ah! what loveliness—
Save us, ye Gods, from such a nauseous mess!
Exactitude the fair one hardly heeds,
Since she "erratic" for "erotic" reads,
But unimportant 'tis, for by my troth,
Jackson's erratic and erotic both!
How vain the task such champions to oppose;
Fred's fond battalion ev'ry moment grows.
Naught can I do, save here and now to close.

Notes

1. John Russell (1871–1929) was a Scotsman living in Tampa, FL; he joined the
UAPA sometime after HPL (see HPL's "Introducing Mr. John Russell" [*Conservative,*

July 1915; *CE* 1.55]). HPL remained in touch with him after the *Argosy* controversy and even met with him in New York in April 1925. In the *Argosy* controversy, Russell had begun the practice of writing letters in verse with "Verses for Jackson" (November 1913).

2. T. P. Crean of Syracuse, NY, wrote a letter attacking HPL (November 1913).

3. F. V. Bennett had written a letter defending HPL (November 1913).

4. F. W. Saunders of Coalgate, OK, in a letter titled "Bomb for Lovecraft" (December 1913), wrote a lengthy attack on HPL.

5. G. E. Bonner of Springfield, OH, wrote a letter attacking HPL (December 1913) entitled "Challenge to Lovecraft."

6. Elizabeth E. Loop of Elmira, NY, attacked HPL in a letter titled "Elmira vs. Providence" (December 1913).

7. Miss E. E. Blankenship of Richmond, VA, attacked HPL in a letter entitled "Virginia vs. Providence" (December 1913).

[184]

Correction for Lovecraft

Editor, Argosy:

In the verses which I sent last October, appeared the couplet:

> "Think not, good rimester, that I sought to *shew*
> In my late letter, merely what I *know*."

As printed in the January *Argosy*, with "modernised", "simplified" or "Americanised" spelling, I see that it reads:

> "Think not, good rimester, that I sought to *shew*
> In my late letter, merely what I *knew*."

I fear that this will create a wrong impression, and convey the idea that I pronounce the verb "to shew" like "shoe", or "shoo", instead of the proper manner, rhyming with "sew". It seems as though if an alteration of the spelling had to be made, your compositor might have changed "shew" to "show", thus preserving both rhyme and sense, and making the couplet conform to that style of spelling which is used in other parts of your magazine.

As it is, three faults remain: (1) The rhyme is destroyed. (2) The sense of "know" is changed from present to past, and (3) "shew" remains unaltered and inharmonious with the general spelling of the verse.

I now write only to free myself from the suspicion of pronouncing "shew" to rhyme with "blue"; I realise that the original fault is mine, and that in writing to a magazine wherein a changed or modern form of spelling is employed, I ought to lay aside my own orthographical system and make my manuscript correspond to the usage of the magazine in question.

Any writings which I may in future inflict upon *The Argosy* will, I assure you, *show* none of the personal idiosyncrasies which may have characterised my past performances. I shall labour sincerely to forget the good old Johnsonian way of spelling and shall endeavour to master the patois which the modern periodical seems inclined to favour.

> "With old orthography I now am thru
> Since printer's devils *rime* my "shew" with "knew";
> I'll watch the glorious modern method *rize*
> And rival Bennett when I crit*icize*."

Do not imagine that I fail to appreciate the space in the Log-Book which has been allotted to me, especially since you *show* by your editorial comment that you do not share my opinion in regard to Jackson.

H. P. LOVECRAFT.

598 Angell Street, Providence, R.I.

P.S. I have a design of writing a novel for the entertainment of those readers who complain that they cannot secure enough of Fred Jackson's work. It is to be entitled: "The Primal Passion, or The Heart of 'Rastus Washington."[1]

H. P. L.

Notes

1. HPL did not write this story; but at some point between 1919 and 1924, he wrote "Sweet Ermengarde," a parody of the Horatio Alger stories with perhaps a satirical nod to Jackson.

[185]

PROVIDENCE, Rhode Island.
[February 1914?]

EDITOR, THE ALL-STORY MAGAZINE.
SIR:

Having read every number of your magazine since its beginning in January, 1905, I feel in some measure privileged to write a few words of approbation and criticism concerning its contents.

In the present age of vulgar taste and sordid realism it is a relief to peruse a publication such as *The All-Story*, which has ever been and still remains under the influence of the imaginative school of Poe and Verne.

For such materialistic readers as your North-British correspondent, Mr. G. W. P., of Dundee, there are only too many periodicals containing "probable" stories; let *The All-Story* continue to hold its unique position as purveyor of literature to those whose minds cannot be confined within the narrow circle of probability, or dulled into a passive acceptance of the tedious round of things as they are.

If, in fact, man is unable to create living beings out of inorganic matter, to hypnotise the beasts of the forests to do his will, to swing from tree to tree with the apes of the African jungle, to restore to life the mummified corpses of the Pharaohs and the Incas, or to explore the atmosphere of Venus and the deserts of Mars, permit us, at least, in fancy, to witness these miracles, and to satisfy that craving for the unknown, the weird, and the impossible which exists in every active human brain.

Particular professors and sober Scotchmen may denounce as childish the desire for imaginative fiction; nay, I am not sure but that such a desire is childish, and rightly so, for are not many of man's noblest attributes but the remnants of his younger nature? He who can retain in his older years the untainted mind, the lively imagination, and the artless curiosity of his infancy, is rather blessed than cursed; such men as these are our authors, scientists, and inventors.

At or near the head of your list of writers Edgar Rice Burroughs undoubtedly stands. I have read very few recent novels by others wherein is displayed an equal ingenuity in plot, and verisimilitude in treatment. His only fault seems to be a tendency toward scientific inaccuracy and slight inconsistencies.

For example, in that admirable story, "Tarzan of the Apes", we meet Sabor, the tiger, far from his native India, and we behold the hero, before he has learned the relation between vocal sounds and written letters, writing out his name, Tarzan, *which he has known only from the lips of his hairy associates,* as well as the names of Kerchak, Tantor, Numa, and Terkoz, all of which he could not possibly have seen written.

Also, in "The Gods of Mars", Mr. Burroughs refers to the year of the red planet as having 687 *Martian* days. This is, of course, absurd, for while Mars revolves about the sun in 687 *terrestrial* days, its own day or period of rotation is almost forty minutes longer than ours, thus giving to Mars a year which contains but 668⅔ *Martian* solar days. I note with regret that this error is repeated in "Warlord of Mars".[1]

William Patterson White, in writing "Sands o' Life",[2] has shewn himself to be an author of the first order. The very spirit of the old Spanish Main pervades the pages of this remarkable novel. It is worthy of permanent publication as a book.

In the domain of the weird and bizarre, Lee Robinet has furnished us a masterpiece by writing "The Second Man".[3] The atmosphere created and sustained throughout the story can be the work only of a gifted and polished artist. Very effective is the author's careful neglect to tell the exact location of his second Eden.

I strongly hope that you have added Perley Moore Sheehan permanently to your staff, for in him may be recognised an extremely powerful writer. I have seen Mr. Sheehan's work elsewhere, and was especially captivated by a grim short story of his entitled "His Ancestor's Head".[4]

William Tillinghast Eldridge set such a standard for himself in "The Forest Reaper" that it seems almost a pity for him to be the author of "The Tormentor" and "Cowards All".[5]

William Loren Curtiss tells a homely yet exciting sort of tale which exerts upon the reader a curious fascination. "Shanty House" seems to me the best of the two he has contributed to *The All-Story*.[6]

Donald Francis McGrew is one of the "red-blooded" school of writers; he describes the Philippine Islands and the army there with an ease indicative of long residence or military service on the scene of his literary productions.[7]

I hardly need mention the author of "A Columbus of Space"[8] further than to say that I have read every published work of Garrett P. Serviss, own most of them, and await his future writings with eagerness. When a noted astronomer composes an astronomical novel, we need not fear such things as years of 687 Martian days upon the planet Mars.

As to your short stories, necessarily second in importance to the novels and serials, it may be said that some of them rise much above the middle level, while few of them fall beneath it. The merry crew of humorous writers, such as T. Bell, Jack Brant, Frank Condon, and Donald A. Kahn,[9] are, though light and sometimes a trifle silly, nevertheless distinctly amusing. Kahn is especially clever in drawing the characters of callow college youths.

I hesitate to criticise adversely such an excellent magazine as this, but since my censure falls upon so small a part of it, I think I may express myself openly without giving offence.

I fear that a faint shadow from the black cloud of vileness now darkening our literature and drama has lately fallen upon a few pages of *The All-Story*. "The Souls of Men", by Martha M. Stanley, was a distinctly disagreeable tale, but "Pilgrims in Love", by De Lysle Ferrée Cass,[10] is contemptibly disgusting, unspeakably nauseating. Mr. G. W. S., of Chicago, has written that Cass "diplomatically handles a very difficult subject—Oriental love".

We do not care for subjects so near allied to vulgarity, however "diplomatically" they may be "handled". Of such "Oriental love" we may speak in the words of the lazy but ingenious schoolboy, who when asked by his tutor to describe the reign of Caligula, replied, "that the less said about it the better". We prefer a more idealised Orient to read about; let us have "nature to advantage drest", as in the beautiful romance of "Prince Imbecile", by C. MacLean Savage, or "The Invisible Empire", by Stephen Chalmers.[11]

Speaking of the last novel, is not the title somewhat misleading? In the United States the name "Invisible Empire" is forever associated with that noble but much-maligned band of Southerners who protected their homes against the diabolical freed blacks and Northern adventurers in the years of misgovernment just after the Civil War—the dreaded Ku-Klux-Klan.

The broad editorial policy of *The All-Story* in making the magazine not merely a local American publication, but a bond of common interest between the United Kingdom, the United States, and the various British Colonies, cannot too heartily be commended.

Blood is thicker than water; we are all Englishmen, and need just such a leveler of political barriers as this to remind us of our common origin. Let the London reader reflect, that in Boston, Toronto, Cape Town, Calcutta, Melbourne, Auckland, and nearly everywhere else, his racial kindred are perusing the same stirring stories that delight him.

America may have withdrawn from the British Empire of government, but thanks to such magazines as *The All-Story*, it must ever remain an integral and important part of the great universal empire of British thought and literature.

I cannot praise *The All-Story Magazine* by comparing it with others, since it stands alone in its class, but I think I have made it clear that I hold this publication in the highest esteem, and derive much pleasure from its pages. What I have said in criticism of some parts of it I have said only with friendly intent, believing that the humble opinions of one more reader may prove not unacceptable to you.

But ere I grow more tedious still, let me close this already protracted epistle, and, with the best wishes for the future of *The All-Story*, subscribe myself as

Your obedient servant,

H. P. L.

Notes

1. The works by Burroughs (1875–1950) appeared in the *All-Story* as follows: *Tarzan of the Apes* (October 1912); *The Gods of Mars* (January–May 1913); *Warlord of Mars* (December 1913–March 1914). All were later published in book form.

2. William Patterson White (1884–?), "Sands o' Life" (*All-Story*, January 1913).

3. Lee Robinet (pseud. of Robert Ames Bennet, 1870–1954), "The Second Man" (*All-Story*, February 1913).

4. Perley Poore Sheehan (1875–1943), "His Ancestor's Head" (*Popular Magazine*, 1 August 1913).

5. William Tillinghast Eldridge (1881–1941), *The Forest Reaper* (*All-Story*, July–December 1911); "The Tormentor" (*All-Story*, November 1912); "Cowards All" (*All-Story*, April 1913).

6. William Loren Curtiss, *The Shanty House* (*All-Story*, December 1909–April 1910). Curtiss had three other stories in *All-Story* from 1909 to 1913.

7. Donald Francis McGrew (1886–1955) wrote prolifically for *Argosy*, *All-Story*, *Popular Magazine*, and many other such periodicals. HPL must have also read his work in *Railroad Man's Magazine*, as he reports reading the entire run of that magazine.

8. *All-Story* (February–June 1909).

9. T. Bell published several tales in *All-Story* between 1912 and 1914. Jack Brant published many stories in this and other magazines between 1911 and 1915. Frank Condon (1882–1940) published widely in popular magazines between the 1910s and the 1930s. Donald A. Kahn published in *All-Story*, *Black Cat*, and other magazines between 1911 and 1918.

10. Martha M. Stanley (1867–1950), "The Souls of Men" (*All-Story*, September 1912). De Lysle Ferrée Cass (1887–1973), "Pilgrims in Love" (*All-Story*, September and October 1913).

11. C[harles] MacLean Savage (1884–?), *Prince Imbecile* (*All-Story*, January–June 1912). Stephen Chalmers (1880–1935), "The Invisible Empire" (*All-Story*, October 1913).

[186]

For England and the All-Story

To the Editor:

While I have not lately been a reader of *The Cavalier*, I have read *The All-Story* continuously from its beginning to the current issue, and I take the liberty of assuming that the present periodical is still *The All-Story;* in fact, I cannot but believe that *The Cavalier* element will soon be lost in the more virile atmosphere of the older magazine.

Many writers, familiar and unfamiliar, good and bad, come from *The Cavalier* to the readers of *The All-Story*. Out of these I trust the best will be permanently retained, and the others gradually eliminated.

The greatest benefit derived from the amalgamation undoubtedly will be the return to *The All-Story* of George Allan England,[1] who, to my mind, ranks with Edgar Rice Burroughs and Albert Payson Terhune as one of the three supreme literary artists of the house of Munsey. Mr. England's "Darkness and Dawn" trilogy is on a par with the "Tarzan" stories, and fortunate indeed is that magazine which can secure as contributors the authors of both.

Other *Cavalier* authors of extreme merit are Zane Grey, whose novels of the West have such a fund of graphic local colour; and Edgar Franklin, whose stories, both serious and humorous, have so long entertained the readers of the Munsey magazines.[2]

I hope that the department of announcements and correspondence, this week called "Heart to Heart Talks", will later return to its more dignified title of "The Editor's Desk", which was not long ago accepted in preference to "Table-Talk". "The Editor's Desk" is a name extremely well suited to this department, and will bear comparison with the apt designation of "The Log-Book", used by *The Argosy* for a similar column.

I hope also that you will in time revert to the regular *All-Story* policy of choosing bits of verse to fill in at the bottoms of pages, and make your selections from the works of the older standard authors instead of publishing the efforts of modern bards. Some of these new rhymesters are quite clever, but most of your readers could probably rhyme just as well; besides, the custom of *The All-Story* in printing standard poetry helped to improve public taste.

I now approach a subject which fills me with trepidation.

Ever since last August I have been engaged in a wordy warfare with some of the readers of *The Argosy* concerning an alleged author whose erotic, effeminate stories fill me with the most profound disgust. This author was one of the principal contributors to *The Cavalier;* in fact, his tales formed the reason for my ceasing to read the later periodical. Now he is to be inflicted upon the readers of *The All-Story.* For my somewhat severe criticisms of this writer, I have received every imaginable sort of ridicule and opposition, both in prose and in verse, through *The Argosy* Log-Book.

In order to avoid another such affray in case this letter should be printed, I will here do no more than to quote and uphold the words of your anonymous correspondent, "One Who Reads Between Lines", whose letter appears in *The All-Story* for May 16. He says, and I say with him, "Tell Fred Jackson to can all of his heroines and then send the can to the government to be tested as an explosive."

This interlinear reader has in truth a very just opinion of modern love stories, although I cannot accept his low estimate of the work of George Allan England.

You have lately set a very high standard for your magazine, and I hope that it may ever be maintained. "The Castle on the Crag" is extremely well written, and reflects the highest credit on Mr. Chalmers.[3] "Wandering Men", by William Patterson White, is a masterpiece,[4] and I think that the criticism of M. A. H., in the issue of April 18, is most unjust. Assuming the scene of "Wandering Men" to be laid in England just after the Conquest, this critic says that Mr. White should have applied the title "Earl" instead of "Count" to his noblemen.

M. A. H. continues thus: "There are no English counts, *nor have there ever been; the title has never been known in the country.*" Now while it is true that at the present time the title of "Count" is not used in England, it is ridiculous to state that it was not employed by English noblemen in the Middle Ages.

M. A. H. should remember that in Norman England the language of the nobility and gentry was not English, but Norman-French, only the peasantry using the old Saxon speech, which was held in great contempt. It is hard for us to think of a French dialect as the language of England, but we all know the lines of Chaucer, where he says of the Prioress:

> "And Frenche she spake ful fayre and fetisly,
> After the scole of Stratford-atte-Bowe."[5]

All titles were derived without change from the Continent. The French word "Comte" or "Compt" was in universal use, and not until the revival of Teutonic forms of speech in the thirteenth or fourteenth century did the title "Earl", derived from the old Saxon "Ealderman", come into existence and displace the Norman-French word. Mr. White has made no error in this matter, and indeed, all his work is singularly free from blunders of any sort.

H. P. LOVECRAFT.

598 Angell Street,
Providence, Rhode Island.

Notes

1 . George Allan England (1877–1936), American writer and explorer, best known for speculative and science fiction. The "Darkness at Dawn" trilogy was first serialized in the Munsey magazines: 1) *Darkness and Dawn* (*Cavalier/Cavalier and Scrap Book,* January–20 January 1912); 2) *Beyond the Great Oblivion* (*Cavalier,* 4 January–8 February 1913); 3) *The Afterglow* (*Cavalier,* 14 June–5 July 1913).

2. Zane Grey (1872–1939), pioneering writer of westerns; Edgar Franklin (pseud. of Edgar Franklin Stearns, 1879–1958), prolific author of humorous stories, early science fiction, and other works.

3. Stephen Chalmers (1880–1935), *The Castle on the Crag* (*All-Story Weekly,* 7 March–4 April 1914).

4. William Patterson White, *Wandering Men* (*All-Story Weekly,* 14 March–18 April 1914).

5. "Prologue," *The Canterbury Tales.*

[187]

To the All-Story

Lovecraft to Clark Ashton Smith, 13 December 1933: "By the way—this business about special lunar radiations is highly interesting. If Prof. Stetson is right about the matter, then my chief objection to the original 'Moon Pool' (as an All-Story novelette, June 22, 1918) falls flat. I panned Merritt in the readers' column for having moonlight open the strange door in the primal

Ponapean masonry when sunlight (chemically identical) had no such effect."[1]

Notes

1. *Dawnward Spire* 504. HPL's letter on the subject has not been found. He refers to Harlan True Stetson (1885–1964), American astronomer and physicist, for whom a lunar crater is named. The following text was omitted from the book version: "'There is a powerful quality in moonlight, as both science and legends can attest. We know of its effect upon the mentality, the nervous system, even upon certain diseases. [¶] 'The moon slab is of some material that reacts to moonlight. . . .'"

Letters between H. P. Lovecraft and J. F. Hartmann

Lovecraft wrote six letters in late 1914 to the Providence *Evening News* to combat the astrological articles of J. F. Hartmann. Local astrologer Joachim Friedrich Hartmann (1848–1930) published an article in the *Evening News*, "Astrology and the European War" (9 September), in the exact location (the top of the last page) where Lovecraft's astronomy columns typically appeared. Lovecraft replied with two hostile and intemperate letters, to the first of which Hartmann replied with a letter of his own (published 7 October). Lovecraft then employed the satirical method of Jonathan Swift, who in his "Isaac Bickerstaffe" articles predicted the death of John Partridge (1644–1714?), English astrologer, author and publisher of a number of astrological almanacs and books. He then wrote a convincing account of Partridge's death, whereupon Partridge had a difficult time proving he was still alive. Lovecraft's pieces merely parody astrological technique by making vague and absurd predictions of the distant future. Hartmann feebly rejoined with two further pieces in which he ridiculed the Bickerstaffe pieces, unaware that Lovecraft had written them.

[188]

Astrology and the European War

The vulgar prejudice against the noble science of astrology by otherwise learned men is greatly to be deplored.

Almost every author on astronomy, mythology, anthropology and philosophy; school teachers, professors of universities and the clergy, while willfully ignorant of astrology, yet never tire loading it with slurs and abuse, ridicule and misrepresentation; ever insinuating that astrologers must either be fools or knaves.

Proctor, banking on his knowledge of astronomy, though ignorant of astrology, fills page after page with ridicule of what he disdained to properly investigate.[1]

Garrett P. Serviss, also banking on his astronomical knowledge, parades as an authority on what he don't [*sic*] know when he says, "Astronomy finds no indication of the existence of any such influences."

It is only those who have never studied this science who in their self-sufficient conceit dare assume authority to condemn it.

They argue that they "cannot understand how the planets can influence human events," as if their ignorance was the limit of truth.

With like reason might all the sciences be argued away by those ignorant of them.

Astrologers themselves are not agreed among themselves about planetary influence. Some say the planets influence our lives; others say they only indicate events, while yet others hold no opinion either way. A good astrologer need not have any opinion about it.

Another argument is that astrology teaches fatalism. But all science is fatalistic. The study of astronomy cannot cause the sun to rise a minute sooner or later than fate decrees it.

Study mathematics a lifetime and you cannot alter the relation of numbers.

Fatalism gives assurance that we can depend upon certain things, such as the multiplication table; without it there could be no dependence upon anything, and there could be no knowledge, no science, and all thinking would be of no use to us.

The other sciences would gain much if pursued in connection with astrology, such as evolution, eugenics, agriculture and statecraft.

Franz Cumont, the Belgian scholar, condemns astrology as a pagan superstition, establishing the divine right of kings to oppress the people.[2]

But a king's horoscope shows only his exaltations over his fellow men, that he will be kind or cruel, wise or foolish, strong or weak, etc. Cumont writes strongly against astrology, but shows how its introduction from Asia into Rome transformed the many religions of Italy into a unison preparatory to Christianity, which was constructed out of these "pagan" religions, thanks to astrology, without which there would have been no Christian religion.

The church has ever fought astrology, which teaches that the immutable laws of nature will not be suspended for a God to answer prayer.

Nor can the Christian doctrine of the freedom of the will stand before the astrological doctrine that we are creatures of conditions, and must ever will and act within the laws of our being; that our bodies and our surroundings force upon us motives which determine what our will shall be.

This conflict between the church and astrology, and the tremendous influence which the church still wields over popular thought, goes far to explain the antagonism of learned men to a science which prejudice prevents them from studying.

The church condemns the prediction of future human events, as if that was a crime, and holds that there is no authentic case of prophecy on record since "Bible times." That God has forbidden it. As if prognostication was astrology's only or most important claim, whereas it constitutes a great philosophy and connects with all the other sciences and philosophies. And the art of practical astrology is well worthy of the best minds.

The English astrologers publish annually ephemerises of the planet's daily places, which have tremendous sales throughout the English-speaking world.

Raphael's reaches nearly a half million copies at 40 cents each, but years ago was sold at a dollar.

A page of pictures, printed in color, depicts events to come. These are printed in the summons previous to the year in which the events are to happen.

The Messina earthquake was thus foretold, the latitude and longitude given. Had the people of that region believed in astrology they could have fled the city in time with their animals and goods.

In these picture predictions, for 1912 published in 1911, there is shown a huge steamship going down in front of a great iceberg and small boats with people in them nearby.

This was literally fulfilled by the Titanic disaster. While the danger was there it could nevertheless have been avoided by the owners of the ship consulting the ship's horoscope, and sailing only when in that way a safe voyage was indicated.

Another picture shows the assassination of a statesman, who is lying on the ground with the assassin nearby trying to sit up. Literally fulfilled by the assassination of Canalejas, where the assassin failed to commit suicide, but only disabling himself so he could not get away.[3]

Another picture shows Turkish soldiers fighting among rough mountains; fulfilled by the Balkan war.

The pictures for 1914 show besides the horrors of war, a royal funeral, and the coffin of the Pope,[4] covered with a purple cloth, and around the base a scarlet cloth, with a crown on top and four large candles at the corners.

While historians publish the pictures of events after they have happened, the astrologer publishes the pictures before the events come to pass.

But the opponents of astrology call such proofs "mere coincidences that prove nothing." However, everything is "coincidence," without it existence would be inconceivable.

Raphael's ephemeris, published a year ago, makes the following predictions concerning European conditions for 1914:

ENGLAND.

The influences operating in King George's horoscope are very unfavorable.[5] The sun has reached the parallel of Mars, which is evil for health, and denotes the continuation of warlike tendencies. As Mars is in transit over the progressed moon twice during the early months of the year, the danger of war predicted in last year's *Messenger* will continue. Saturn is also stationary on the radical sun, denoting much depression of trade and commerce and trouble among the people. The autumn is an evil time, for the moon meets the square of Saturn, indicative of bereavement.

A critical period is forming for the fortunes of this country, but as the sun meets the sextile of the radical moon after it leaves the evil direction of Mars, it will be but the darkest hour before the dawn, and a brighter future awaits the empire. Neptune's transit over the progressed sun is indicative of much socialistic aggression, which will cause anxiety and worry.

THE PRINCE OF WALES.[6]

The autumn is very unfavorable, for Saturn falls stationary on the sun's place at birth, which is evil for health and constitution. Some honors are shown in November.

GERMANY.

The kaiser[7] is under very adverse directions, and danger both to health and person is indicated. The year opens with Mars in square to the radical sun, and with Uranus transiting the sun's place at birth, and Mars passing over the ascendant, the indications for war and disaster are strongly marked. The moon is opposed to Uranus in January, a further indication of trouble. A crisis is apparent in the history of the German Empire; the terribly evil array of influences will leave their mark for many a long day to come.

AUSTRIA.

The sun is closer to an evil direction of Mars, and with that planet near the meridian in the early months of the year, war is threatened. As Saturn is in close parallel with the radical moon, the condition of the health of the emperor[8] will be very precarious, and the end may come at any moment. The stationary position of Saturn on the meridian of the horoscope in the autumn is evil for reputation.

FRANCE.

The president of France[9] was born on Aug. 20, 1860, with the sun conjoined with Saturn in the sign of Leo and the moon in square to Mars. These are not reassuring influences. The sun is now just leaving the square of Mars, and with that planet in transit over the opposition of Mars, and square of the sun, the indications of war are very powerfully shown; still, as the sun leaves the evil direction of Mars it meets the sextile of Jupiter, which should bring about a more favorable time.

RUSSIA.

Adverse influences are shown in the Tsar's horoscope,[10] for the sun meets the conjunction of Uranus at birth, which will cause much trouble in his empire, and great personal danger. Saturn is stationary in opposition to the progressed moon in the autumn and this denotes bereavement and indisposition.

ITALY.

Martial influences are still in operation in the king of Italy's horoscope.[11] The sun is still close to the parallel of Mars, and Mars in stationary opposition to the progressed sun in the early months of the year is ominous of war. Mars has also progressed to the opposition of Uranus, which points to some outrage, or an attempt on his life.

SPAIN.

The King still remains under adverse influences.[12] The sun is still near the square of Mars and both August and December are evil months, and his health and person will be in danger.

JAPAN.

The Mikado[13] is now coming under some severe afflictions which will bring a crisis in his empire. The sun is forming an opposition to Saturn, and is in semi-square to Mercury. The moon has only just left the conjunction of the radical Mars. With Mars stationary on his meridian war is probable, and serious trouble. Disputes with the other powers are shown, and there is grave danger of an Anglo-Japanese difference.

The above illustrates how astrologers publish prognostications year after year—"since Bible times," too.

There are good and evil times for beginning any new undertaking. The emperors of both Austria and Germany chose about the most evil time in the whole year. The sun was going to a close opposition of Uranus, a planet which when evilly aspected brings evil surprises and utterly unlooked for disappointments like lightning out of a clear sky. It breaks up families, partnerships, agreements between nations, etc.

But the wise men of this world don't know everything, and therefore suffer for their ignorance.

J. F. HARTMANN.

Notes

1. Richard Anthony Proctor (1837–1888), British scientist and author of such works as *Essays on Astronomy* (1872) and *The Moon* (1886).

2. Franz Cumont (1868–1947), French archaeologist and historian; author of *Astrologie et religion chez les grecs et les romains* (1912; translated as *Astrology and Religion among the Greeks and Romans*).

3. José Canalejas y Méndez (1854–1912), prime minister of Spain who was assassinated by an anarchist on 12 November 1912.

4. Pope Pius X (b. 1835) died on 20 August 1914.

5. George V (1865–1936), King of England (1910–36).

6. Edward, Prince of Wales (1894–1972), later King Edward VIII (1936–37).

7. Wilhelm II (1859–1941), Emperor of Germany (1888–1918).

8. Franz Joseph I (1830–1916), Emperor of Austria-Hungary (1848–1916).

9. Raymond Poincaré (1860–1934), president of France (1913–20); also prime minister (1912–13, 1922–24, 1926–29).

10. Nicholas II (1868–1918), Czar of Russia (1894–1917).

11. Victor Emmanuel III (1869–1947), King of Italy (1900–46).

12. Alfonso XIII (1886–1941), King of Spain (1886–1931).

13. Taishō (1879–1926), Emperor of Japan (1912–26).

[189]

Science versus Charlatanry

To the Editor of the Evening News:

It is an unfortunate fact that every man who seeks to disseminate knowledge must contend not only against ignorance itself, but against false instruction as well. No sooner do we deem ourselves free from a particularly gross superstition, than we are confronted by some enemy to learning who would set aside all the intellectual progress of years, and plunge us back into the darkness of mediaeval disbelief.

As a lover of Astronomy, and a writer on that subject, I was the other day very much pained and shocked to see in the Evening News an article on the pseudo-science of Astrology, which has ever been the bane of the seeker after truth. While I entertain no doubt as to the sincerity of the author, a Mr. Hartmann, [it is impossible] for me to comprehend how any person of judgment and education can now give credence to the doctrines of a false and ridiculous system completely exploded over 200 years ago. In this age of enlightenment it ought not to be necessary to shew the utter absurdity of the idea that our daily affairs can be governed by the mere apparent motions of infinitely distant bodies whose seeming arrangements and configurations, on which the calculations of judicial astrology are based, arise only from perspective as seen from our particular place in the universe. It seems very provoking that astronomers and other men of sense should be obliged to waste their time and energy in proving Astrology to be false, when there exists not the slightest reason to believe any part of it true; yet the perverse sophistry of certain misguided individuals still raises up such a body of specious evidence in favour of it, that we must needs attack again what we had thought finally conquered. The fallacies of Astrology are like the many heads of the Lernean Hydra; chop off one, and two grow in its place.

Mr. Hartmann, in his recent article, seems to defend Astrology by assertions that the astronomers and scientists who shew its falsity are unacquainted with its precepts. This statement loses force when we reflect that the whole mass of nonsense which constitutes this study is only a vague distortion and misuse of astronomical principles; indeed, the study of Astronomy absolutely proves the spurious nature of Astrology by elimination, or reductio ad absurdum. It is very amusing to read Mr. Hartmann's hostile allusions to Mr. Garrett P. Serviss and the late Richard A. Proctor. These two popular astronomical writers, similar in many ways, have by means of their double gifts of scientific and literary skill accomplished marvels in dissipating superstition and propagating truth; it is no wonder that they are hated and feared by the leaders of the hosts of ignorance.

Still more amusing is Mr. Hartmann's sober reference to the English astrological almanacks. These wretched pamphlets, though much perused by the vulgar and the ignorant, have been the laughing-stock of the intelligent British public since Queen Anne's time, when Dr. Swift destroyed with such exquisite humour the pretensions of the conceited astrologer and almanack-maker, John Partridge. In 1827 the Society for the Diffusion of Christian Knowledge severely attacked annuals of this sort and later caused most of them either to suspend publication or to discontinue their astrological predictions, so that today only two, Zadkiel's and Raphael's, are in existence. The prophecies of these almanacks are like the utterances of the Delphic Oracle; so vague and ambiguous that they can be made to suit any subsequent events. In many a time of peace have the mystics and seers given forth warnings fully as dire and dreadful as any that have preceded the present war.

The ravings of Raphael about lamentable losses to kings and emperors may be made to fit alike the loss of a handkerchief or of a throne. War in the Balkans, unrest in Russia, and revolutions in Central or South America are among the events most successfully predicted. Mr. Hartmann's mention of the predictions of Pope Pius' death reminds me that this same event was scheduled in 1906 by a learned astrologer of Central Falls, R.I.[1]

I should not take up your time nor seek to occupy your columns with this reply to Mr. Hartmann if I did not consider Astrology a dangerous as well as a silly subject. In the minds of the masses it tends to become confused with Astronomy, and thereby to injure the reputation of that science.

The News has ever been a friend to the improvement and instruction of the public, so that I am confident it will not begrudge me a little space besides that which I regularly occupy on the first of each month, in my humble efforts to diffuse truth and to expose fallacy regarding the heavens.

H. P. LOVECRAFT.

598 Angell Street, Providence, R.I.

Notes

1. HPL refers to Thomas Hines, Jr., whom he had criticized in his 1906 letter to the *Providence Sunday Journal*, "No Transit of Mars" (see letter 166).

[190]

[Letter to the Editor]

To the Editor of The Evening News:

It is unfortunate that the advocates of unpopular truth must contend against the prejudice, venom and false teachings of the influential and learned who misuse their reputation for knowledge in their warfare against truth.

My critic, Mr. Lovecraft, "was very much pained and shocked to see in The Evening News an article on the pseudo-science of astrology, which has ever been the bane of the seeker after truth."

If Mr. Lovecraft had studied the textbooks of astrology, and tested their rules he could not have called it a false science; assuming, of course, that he is a seeker of truth, possesses the scientific spirit and is honest with himself.

He queries: "How any person of judgment and education can give credence to the false and ridiculous system completely exploded over 200 years ago."

No one ever heard the explosion; where and when did it occur? We have only heard mere fizzles that have never exploded anything, and these fizzles are still being set off by learned men; weak-minded on this particular subject.

The ancient Greeks, enemies of Astrology, wrote the most plausible arguments against it, plausible to the ignorant. But to astrologers such writings have merely advertised the ignorance of their authors. And no modern critic has gone beyond the ancients.

The moderns, wilfully ignorant of its rules, and mentally too indolent to study and test them, content themselves with making themselves funny over it, indulging in pointless ridicule, cheap denunciation, misrepresentation and downright lying. A course quite unworthy of men parading as scientists.

Mr. Lovecraft complains: "It seems very provoking that astronomers and other men of sense should be obliged to waste their time and energy in proving astrology to be false—that we must needs attack again what we had thought finally conquered."

But no astronomer has ever disproven it, and there is no piece of literature in existence that disproves it.

If they really feel "obliged" to disprove astrology, why don't they try it, and in a manner becoming the scientific method.

Years ago W. H. Chaney contracted with a New York publisher to write a scientific refutation of astrology, seeing that no one had written such a book. After writing all he could think of, he consulted the astrologers for more points to refute, when to his amazement he found it a real science, broke his contract with the publisher, studied it and became a skilful astrologer.[1]

Under the religious persecution of astrologers Boss Tweed locked him up, quite curiously in the same cell which Tweed occupied later on.

He wrote improved books on the science and promulgated it in the West, becoming known as the "Father of Astrology" in the region from the Mississippi to the Pacific.

And so any one who will honestly attempt a sincere and scientific refutation of it will surely become converted to it.

Mr. Lovecraft continues, "Mr. H. seeks to defend astrology by asserting that the astronomers and scientists, who show its falsity, are unacquainted with its precepts."

They certainly are when at the People's Forum we once interrupted a clergyman's rantings against astrology by asking, "What astrological textbooks have you studied?" He replied, "None," and continued his ignorant ranting. And this man is but an example of the enemies of astrology everywhere.

My critic continues: "The whole mass of nonsense, which constitutes this study is only a vague distortion and misuse of astronomical principles; indeed the study of astronomy absolutely proves the spurious nature of astrology."

What astronomical principles, please tell us what you mean. It certainly is not a distortion and misuse of astronomy when we apply it for the promotion of truth and the good of mankind in a more beneficent way than the astronomers are willing for us to use.

The astronomers hurt their own science by narrowing it down to its lesser uses, valuable enough as these are. To set limits to the usefulness of astronomy, when there is already a greater field for it, comes very near being a "misuse of the principles."

There exists not the slightest reason to believe that "the study of astronomy proves the spurious nature of astrology."

There should be just as much sense in saying that the study of anatomy "absolutely proves the spurious nature of medical science." Or that the healing art "is only a vague distortion and misuse of anatomical principles."

Once a learned botanist, ignorant of medicine, meeting a physician, denounced herbal medication as an exploded superstition, and refused to listen to any facts in support of it, because his botanical studies had disproved all medical virtues in herbs. Which well illustrates the astronomer's attitude toward astrology.

Again he says: "The English astrological almanacs. These wretched pamphlets, though much perused by the vulgar and the ignorant, have been the laughing-stock of the intelligent British public since Queen Anne's time." Yes, the laughing-stock of conceited bigots.

And again: "In 1827 the society for the diffusion of Christian Knowledge severely attacked" (severely, that's right) "annuals of this sort and later caused most of them either to suspend publication or to discontinue their astrological predictions, so that today only two, *Zadkiel's* and *Raphael's,* are in existence."

There is no such thing as Christian knowledge or Christian science. But there is Christian faith, Christian bigotry and Christian persecution.

The British astrologers were "severely attacked" by Christian policemen, sheriffs, courts and jailors, ruined by Christian persecution, ever the last resort of bigots in the warfare against truth.

In the early Christian centuries astronomy was idolatry, blasphemy, and all that was vile. The astronomers faced the maledictions of the church, its dungeons, hot pinches, the faggot and the ox. If force is a good argument against astrology why was it not against astronomy?

Again he says: "The prophecies of these almanacs are like the utterances of the Delphic Oracles; so vague and ambiguous that they can be made to suit any subsequent events."

How do you know that the Delphic Oracles were "vague and ambiguous"?

I published in *The Evening News* a long list of European predictions from Raphael's Ephemeris published in August, 1913, to come to pass in 1914. There is nothing vague about them, and the daily papers report their fulfillment.

It is hard to comprehend how any person of common sense can stigmatize such proof of correct predictions as "vague and ambiguous."

When the prediction of the Titanic disaster was accompanied by a picture of the great steamer going down in front of an iceberg, how can that be called "vague," "made to fit subsequent events"?

It is hard to argue with men who stubbornly refuse to be shown any facts in support of truth.

Mr. Lovecraft refers to prophets whose predictions went wrong as disproving astrology. But just think of all the astronomers who have made mistakes. Then astronomy must be a superstition. There is no science but its votaries have made mistakes. Then all the sciences must be false.

Think of all the mistakes in calculation made by bookkeepers and bank clerks. Then what a wretched pseudo-science must be arithmetic.

What a poor rule that won't work both ways!

Mr. Lovecraft might make himself interesting if he would demand of us the kind of evidence he would consider proof of the truth of astrology. He might think of something and then challenge us to produce it.

Our enemies never do that for they are determined to listen to no facts.

Mr. Lovecraft considers astrology a dangerous subject which "in the minds of the masses tends to injure the reputation of astronomy." How can that be when astrology gives astronomy a far more respectful and broader meaning. A respect akin to reverence additional to our ordinary conception of it. Mr. Lovecraft has given not a single fact against astrology. Calling names proves nothing.

At another time I hope to illustrate the benefits of astrology, and how that, if universally applied, it would be a most far-reaching means for the progress and uplift of the human race.

J. F. HARTMANN.

77 Aborn Street, Oct. 5, 1914.

Notes

1. W. H. Chaney (1821–?) wrote several books on astrology. The work in question is either *Chaney's Primer of Astrology and American Urania* (1890) or *The Astrologer's Vade Mecum* (1902).

[191]

The Falsity of Astrology

To the Editor of the Evening News:

Since the ordinary modern astrologer is merely a mountebank who seeks to defraud the ignorant by means of crude gibberish which he knows to be untrue, his tribe may very easily be silenced by the proper legal authorities. During the past few years hundreds of these impudent quacks have been disposed of by the United States government through the diligent efforts of the postal inspectors.

Far more difficult, however, is the task of dealing with that honest minority of star-gazing prophets who actually believe in their own ridiculous teachings, and who can therefore invest their fallacious arguments with the convincing force of genuine though misplaced enthusiasm.

To the latter class belongs our distinguished local author and astrologer, Mr. J. F. Hartmann, whose long and laboured letter in defence of his belief appears in The Evening News for Oct. 7. Mr. Hartmann is nothing if not sincere. He is very obviously a blindly fanatical devotee of the false science of the heavens; being on that account the more dangerous foe to knowledge, since he appears to deem it his duty to spread the pernicious superstition which he himself so innocently holds.

In his recent letter Mr. Hartmann says little that he has not said before, and but for the superficial plausibility of some of his attempts at reasoning, I should have taken no notice of it. As it is, I feel impelled to comment a little further on the one oft-repeated foundation of his arguments: the alleged ignorance of astrology on the part of astronomers.

Mr. Hartmann errs very gravely when he denies that astronomy proves the falsity of astrology. Astronomy investigates every force and influence exerted by the various bodies of space upon one another, measuring with the utmost care and exactitude each slightest manifestation of energy. No considerable influence could possibly escape the attention of the astronomer, for he attacks the subject at every angle, and follows up with the keenest activity every principle for which he can discover any real data whatsoever. The true student, comparing the motions of the heavenly bodies with the varied affairs of mankind, has never found a trace of evidence that there is any connexion between the two, nor has he discovered any reason why there should be. Indeed, astrology is based wholly upon apparent celestial motions, which, as I pointed out in my previous letter, are merely the result of perspective as viewed from this one puny planet which we call Earth. No rational and unprejudiced scholar could for a moment tolerate a "science" thus unsupported. He needs no such "astrological textbooks", as Mr. Hartmann recommends, in order to perceive its absolute unsoundness. Mr. Hartmann himself appears to possess just those intellectual characteristics which he deplores in others. He is certainly bigoted in his astrological belief, and he has evidently studied astronomy no more than the astronomers whom he censures have studied astrology. A simple course in astronomy might do much toward destroying his mediaeval ideas.

Very ridiculous is the statement that any fair-minded astronomer would become a convert to Astrology if he should study the latter subject. It were more correct to say that any astrologer, if unprejudiced and properly instructed, would quickly abandon his superstitious notions. Has Mr. Hartmann forgotten that the great Danish astronomer Tycho Brahe was at first a sincere and enthusiastic believer in Astrology, becoming convinced of its falsity only after he had profoundly studied it for years; or that the eminent French philosopher Gassendi had delved deeply into astrological lore before he cast it aside in disgust?

We need comment but little on the prophecies which Mr. Hartmann in his first article quoted from Raphael's almanack. Though the coincidence concerning the Titanic is very interesting, the general ambiguity of the prediction is self-evident. Prof. George Lyman Kittredge[1] of Harvard University gives similar examples, extracted from Zadkiel's annual, in his interesting book entitled "The Old Farmer and His Almanack".

In replying to one of my arguments, Mr. Hartmann asks: "How do you know that the Delphic Oracles were vague and ambiguous?" My inquisitor would do well to engage in some elementary classical research.

As a supreme test of his pseudo-science, Mr. Hartmann invites me to demand the sort of evidence of its truth which I would deem convincing. I might ask him on what principle the various and complex destinies of men can be connected with the apparent positions of immensely distant bodies, all moving in accordance with regular mechanical laws, and exerting no perceptible influence upon the earth save that of gravitation. I might ask him to state the nature of the powerful, mysterious celestial force which, he declares, moulds our acts and fortunes, and to explain why a few erratic sophists claim the ability to detect and study in detail without instruments a species of energy which no other scientist has yet noticed even with the most elaborate and delicate appliances. But I should pay too much respect to a contemptible system of charlatanry were I to consider these matters seriously.

The baleful effect of Astrology upon the reputation of Astronomy is far too patent for Mr. Hartmann to argue away. I was not long ago asked by a man who had seen my astronomical articles, 'if I did not cast horoscopes or calculate nativities'! It is not pleasant for a serious student of the heavens to be taken for a petty fortune-teller.

I shall not seek to persecute Mr. Hartmann and his false art. Astrology thrives on persecution, as Juvenal knew well when he wrote in his Sixth Satire: "Nemo mathematicus genium indemnatus habebit."[2] My only wish is to warn the reading public against these dead, ancient fallacies which now and then rise like unwelcome spectres from their graves.

Astrology is the legacy of prehistoric ignorance. Since our primitive ancestors saw that the motion of the sun through the Zodiac influenced their affairs by the change of season which it causes, or that the movements and phases of the moon affected their nocturnal pursuits by the alternative presence and absence of moonlight, they must have believed themselves under the direct control of these bodies. Since certain stars appear at certain seasons, apparently announcing such periodic events as the rising of the Nile or the autumn rains, the untutored man of remote antiquity must quite easily have acquired the false belief that events of any sort are predicted by the lanterns of the sky. In time, the ancients came to seek explanations for all the phenomena of earth in the phenomena of the heavens, and arbitrarily to assign a celestial cause for every terrestrial occurrence. Naturally, their religious system became merged into their astrological scheme, and each governing god became identified with some particular "governing" planet; whence comes our present planetary nomenclature.

With such a beginning, it is not difficult to account for the prevalence of astrological beliefs in ancient and mediaeval times, or, on the other hand, to see why such notions cannot hope to survive in this scientific age.

H. P. LOVECRAFT

598 Angell St., Providence, R.I.

Oct. 8, 1914

Notes

1. George Lyman Kittredge (1860–1941), *The Old Farmer and His Almanack* (1904; *LL* 539). See HPL's discussion of the book (*SL* 2.174).

2. "No astrologer who has not been imprisoned will have any reputation." Juvenal, *Satires* 6.562.

[192]

Astrology and the Future

Editor, Evening News:

Very regrettable is the reluctance lately shewn by the professors of the sublime science of astrology in publishing their predictions. Persecuted as they are by arrogant, intolerant, and materialistic students of less lofty subjects, they seem to confine their glorious art to relatively unimportant matters, as though too proud to exhibit to a cynical, unenlightened, and undeserving world the full majesty of their power.

The most authoritative astrological information now to be obtained is that published each year in Raphael's Ephemeris, as recently quoted by your gifted contributor, Mr. Hartmann; yet this scholarly annual forecasts events only for each following year, neglecting to prepare us for occurrences in the more remote future.

Now since all astrological prophecies are founded on the exact, eternal, and undeviating motions of the heavenly bodies; their houses, exaltations, progressions, aspects, and transits; their oppositions, trines, quartiles, sextiles, and conjunctions; and since by mathematics we can calculate these motions for an infinite distance into the future; why do the astrologers of today content themselves with predictions a mere year in advance, instead of extending their researches through the coming centuries, even to the end of the world itself? It is true that the universal deluge predicted by Stöffler[1] for the year 1524 failed to appear, but we have at the present time far more exact methods of calculation, and are undoubtedly able to determine future events with a much greater degree of accuracy and certainty.

The writer, who was born under the planet Mercury, has spent many years in astrological study, following in general the methods of William Lilly,[2] and giving special attention to remote future. As early as 1897 I predicted the present European conflict, as well as the annexation of Mexico by the United States, which will take place next year, after the anarchy resulting from the displacement of Carranza by Gen. Villa.[3]

In my unpublished book, "The History of the Future", I have recorded many startling things which would not be believed were I to reveal them now. I foresee within the next 2000 years events of the most stupendous nature in the Western hemisphere.

A fortunate ascendant of Mars shews that a man will arise whose fame will outrank Caesar's.

I see changes of a most revolutionary nature about to occur in the very State of Rhode Island. A conjunctional eclipse of Mercury by Saturn indicates that the English language will cease to be spoken in America after the year

2344, at about which time Emperor Theodore IX of the United States will retake California from the Japanese through the remarkable strategy of Field-Marshal Patricio Coeno. The crossed transit of Jupiter and Uranus over the alternately radical sun and moon on March 9, 2448, is certain evidence that the American monarch will be overthrown in that year as a result of a popular uprising led by Gen. Jos. Francisco Artmano and a new republic established; the capital being moved from Mexico City back to Washington.

In Europe every familiar condition will vanish. An opposition of Neptune with the asteroid Ceres tells us that in 1916 the present war will end with a complete victory for the allies, this being followed by the dismemberment of the German and Austrian Empires.

The Tsar will take German and Austrian Poland, as well as the whole of Hungary. France will regain Alsace and Lorraine. England will take over all German colonies, and establish a naval base on the Baltic in Schleswig-Holstein. Holland will enter the war on the side of Germany, and after the defeat will be annexed to Belgium. Italy, having fought bravely with the Allies, will receive a large share of Austrian territory, and will annex all Albanian territory as well. Japan will take but little part in the war, and indeed will engage in no tremendous hostilities until the great Mongolian invasion of 2142. Prussia will retain but little territory outside its own boundaries. Austria, deprived of Hungary, will join with Bavaria, forming a powerful and prosperous Teutonic empire which will conquer Spain in 2010 during the Hapsburg succession to the Spanish throne.

Kaiser Wilhelm and his family will be exiled in Napoleon's old quarters at Longwood on St. Helena, but a supreme ascendant of Mars in Scorpio shews that the crown prince's eldest son will escape in June, 1937, and later reign as king of Prussia. A progressed double quartile of Pallas and Mercury in Taurus and Venus and Juno in Libra indicates the conquest of all Europe by Russia in 1998, and a general invasion of Mongolians in Europe and America in 2142. This invasion will give rise to a frightful struggle between the white and yellow races lasting two and a half centuries, and resulting in the complete defeat of China and Japan, together with the conquest of their lands. A descendant of the circumpolar constellation Ursa Major, accompanied by a corresponding progressive exaltation of the radical Zodiacal sign Leo in 2517, indicates the overthrow of the Russian power in Europe by the English and the subsequent joint rule of earth by America and England.

With Uranus stationary in conjunction with the seventh house of the sextile opposition of Vulcan in Gemini on Aug. 18, 2814, I foresee a terrible plague which will annihilate a quarter of the world's population.

Last and most terrible of all, the collusive quaternary trine of Mars, Mercury, Vulcan, and Saturn, in the 13th progressed house of the sign Cancer on Feb. 26, 4954, stands out as plainly as the handwriting on the wall to shew us the awful day on which this earth will finally and infallibly perish through a sudden and unexpected explosion of volcanic gases in the interior.

Scoffers and unbelievers may smile at my predictions, but these astrological computations are founded on a science as old as the human race; a science that has for centuries resisted every attempt of the sceptical and the ignorant to overthrow it.

Were it not a wiser and nobler course for our upstart teachers and scientists to cease their vain cavillings at astrology, to mould their lives and actions in accord with the infinite and the inevitable, and to bow with proper humility before the time-tried precepts of this sacred and venerable species of truth?

ISAAC BICKERSTAFFE, JR.

South Main Street, Providence, R.I.

Notes

1. Johann Stöffler (1452–1531), German astrologer and student of the astrolabe. HPL's information on him comes from the article "Astrology" (by Jules Andrieu) in the 9th edition of the *Encyclopaedia Britannica* (*LL* 318).
2. William Lilly (1602–1681), British astrologer and author of almanacs such as *Merlini Ephemeris* (1644–81).
3. During the Mexican Civil War, revolutionary leader Francisco ("Pancho") Villa (1878–1923) struggled against forces led by Venustiano Carranza (1859–1920). Carranza defeated Villa at the Battle of Celaya in 1915, thereafter ruling Mexico as constitutional president until shortly before his death.

[193]

The Science of Astrology

Astrology, built up through observation, reflection, and experience, long ages ago became a science, a philosophy and an art; continually verifiable by whosoever may come to test its rules and aphorisms on himself, his friends or strangers.

It rests upon the relation that is proven to exist between what we are in body and mind, the events of our lives, the evolution of life, and geological disturbance on the one hand and the ever changing mutual aspect between the celestial bodies of our solar system and their places in the zodiac as seen from earth.

We don't know the final explanation more than we know the final secret of gravitation which affects every little particle of matter, or why invisible Neptune billions of miles away affects our earth by perturbation.

The zodiac, from the Greek circle of beasts, is the circle of 12 star groups, or constellations, in the apparent path of the sun, pictured as animals on our star maps from Aries the ram to Pisces the fishes, and as shown in almanacs.

Astrology, however, does not use the constellations, but the 12 signs of the celestial circle measured from the vernal equinox, the sun's place in spring when the days and nights are of equal length.

The signs, or twelfths of a circle, are named like the constellations, but do not coincide with them, for the equinoctial points recede through them 52½ seconds per year.

The "malefics" are those planets which denote evil more often than good.

The "benefics" are those which denote good more than evil.

The evil aspects, as seen from the earth, as square and opposition, denote evil; the trine and sextile denote good.

The hour of the day is also important, the daily horoscope being divided into 12 parts, or "houses," each "house" having its special meaning, as the house of money, of friends, home, health, etc. It makes a difference in reading a horoscope whether a given planet be rising or setting, whether on the midheaven or at the nadir, whether the planets, sun or moon, above or below the earth in the horoscope.

A horoscope is a star map for some particular time at some particular place. Many persons born at the same time but in different parts of the world would not have the same horoscopes, each one's horoscope would be different from that of all the others, but they would be alike only in some particulars.

A "chart" is a written delineation or "reading" of a horoscope.

In mind and body persons are classified by signs and planets, for these denote various characters.

The sign rising at birth, those containing the sun, moon or most planets describe the person. The sign that is stronger than the rest is the chief ruler of the person.

A Taurus person is short and stout with broad shoulders.

A Gemini person is tall and straight, with straight arms.

An Aries person has much mental energy, is a natural leader, organizer and pioneer, headstrong and impulsive.

An Aquarius person is patient, quiet, unobtrusive, fond of art, science, music and literature.

Where one planet is decidedly stronger than the rest the person is known by such a planet. As when a planet is above the earth and the rest under the earth.

A representative Mercury person is tall and thin, with a narrow face, long nose, thin lips and chin, and little beard. A subtle imagination and good memory; philosophical and mathematical; writer, poet, orator, etc.

A Saturn person is of middle stature; small, black, leering eyes, thick nose and lips, large ears, dark hair and of melancholy expression. Tends to engage as a farmer, miner, brick maker, butcher, etc.

Every person, however, is a combination of the 12 signs of the 9 sun, moon and planets.

The planets being in constant motion, each with a different velocity, never twice form the same combination throughout eternity. Hence no two persons can be exactly alike nor have precisely the same fate.

Inasmuch as astrology reveals to each person his strong and weak points, and to what line of efforts he is best adapted it follows that his education and training should accord with it. A child so brought up would learn faster with greater pleasure, and with greater profit to itself and to society than under our present ignorantly conducted school systems.

Hence applied astrology would revolutionize our educational methods.

In our ex-Governor Dr. Garvin's horoscope the medical sign Scorpio is decidedly strong, showing that he would naturally incline to the medical profession.[1]

The planet Uranus is in trine to the sun, denoting that he rises to a high position in government. Which could have been foreseen from his horoscope when he was yet an infant.

In Edison's horoscope is rising a "fixed" sign denoting great persistency of purpose and bodily endurance, and skill in chemistry.

The Sun and Mercury in the scientific and humanitarian signs Aquarius, with the planet Uranus in Aries, denotes great inventive ability.

The symbol for Aquarius is the lightning. It denotes electricity, light, sound, the voice, music, art, etc., and great ability for mental application. Edison's inventions have been well along these lines.

Jupiter alone above the earth is a scientific sign, of itself denotes him a high-minded and noble man of science; and all the other planets below the earth denote that his greatest success and his most brilliant achievements will come in the closing years of his life.

But most persons with such similar horoscopes have no means for engaging in their natural mission. Hence it would pay society to seek them out, particularly the thousands of children with such horoscopes, and put them back to work at the public expense. Financially and for the progress of civilization society could make no investment more profitable.

Natural affinity between two persons is determined by comparing their horoscopes; a matter of supreme importance in sex relations.

Permanent affection is shown where the planets in one horoscope make good aspects to those in the other.

More temporary affection followed by aversion is shown where the mutual aspects are some of them good and some evil, with the evil ones stronger than the good.

When all persons shall know how to compose horoscopes, each will carry his horoscope as he does his watch, and will ally himself only with those whose horoscopes agree with his own.

We live for happiness, in sex relations as in all else. And a happy sex union is a most important factor in begetting improved offspring.

Astrology also shows how so to conduct the marital indulgence by the aspect between Venus and the moon as to regulate the number of offspring within the bounds of reason, for large families are a curse to themselves and to society as the Malthusians have well made clear.

And again, as there are good and evil times to be born, the parents can so time conception that the birth nine months later shall fall under fortunate planetary configurations, thus producing children far superior to those conceived like brutes in man's present ignorance.

Such a course universally practiced would in a few generations create an ideal race having a state of enjoyment not possible to the kind of people that now inhabit the earth.

In the great pyramid of Cheops is an inclined shaft to the south, not for making astronomical discoveries, but for astrological purposes.

On one side of its floor are steps for the astrologers to ascend, and benches to sit upon, while observing the shadows of the sun or moon on the floor of the tube, or the planets' places in the zodiac.

The flattened apex of the pyramid shows a horoscope blank whereon to chalk the planets' places when calculating horoscopes.

It must have well paid the kings to maintain numerous astrologers to decide for them the fortunate times and seasons for engaging in their projects, to learn what dangers threaten, the intentions of their enemies, what friends to trust, the disposition of their subjects, and a thousand other things.

This pyramid, not built as a tomb for kings, like other pyramids, but for occult purposes, is the largest telescope ever built, a most mighty monument to astrology.

We may well infer that astrology must have been very old and widely known even before this pyramid was built.

Much of the astrological literature has no doubt perished in the wreck that overtook the great writings of ancient times. But some of it has come down to us in most of the 60-odd pamphlets which constitute the Bible, written by astrologers. A book which, without a knowledge of astrology, cannot be properly understood.

In Genesis the zodiac is called "the tree of the fruit of knowledge of good and evil," which by "eating," or appropriating thereof, is calculated to make one wise concerning the good and evil in ourselves and our fate, and of the best "times and seasons" for engaging in the important matters of life.

This "fruit," or knowledge, was forbidden the tillers of the soil and tree keepers of rich men's gardens, lest they become wise "even as one of us" and make an end of their oppressors.

Jacob and his twelve sons is the story of the sun and the twelve signs of the zodiac, each sun, or sign, denoting an astrological character.

The "twelve tribes of Israel" are the twelve classes of persons whose characteristics answer to the twelve signs respectively. Each of us answers to one or more of these "tribes," the tribes of Aries, Taurus, etc.

The astrologers who were to interpret Belshazzar's dream feigned inability, for it was no doubt dangerous to tell the king of impending misfortunes, as dangerous as it would be to tell the kaiser to his face that he would lose the war.

The Apocalypse calls the zodiac "the tree of life which is the midst of paradise." Paradise, from the Persian, means among the stars, and of course that is where we find the zodiac to be.

It is also called "the book of life," which is to be "eaten" or studied, wherein everyone's life is written, and which only the astrologer knows how to read.

The ancients knew only the seven visible bodies of our solar system, but understood certain influences in their horoscopes which we know to be those of Uranus and Neptune, to be seen through our telescopes.

The ancient Hindu astrologer, however, charted nine bodies, having discovered the two invisible ones from their effects on the horoscopes.

John writes: "The seven stars are the angels of the seven churches; and the seven candlesticks are the seven churches."

Here we are classified by the seven planets instead of by the 12 signs of the zodiac. Each planet is called an angel, as when Jacob, lying on his back at night, watched the "angel" stars rising and settling in their celestial paths, or "ladder."

The "seven candlesticks" are seven star clusters in which the seven "angel" stars exert their most beneficent influence.

The "seven churches" are the seven classes of people that answer to the astrological influence of these celestial candlesticks. The 12 candlesticks being the 12 constellations of the zodiac.

"In the midst of the street of it, (path of the Sun and planets) and on either side of the river, (equinoctial circle) was there the tree of life, (zodiac) which bore 12 manner of fruits, (12 manner of people) and yielded her fruit (births) every month, and the leaves (teachings) of the tree were for the healing of the nations."

When "the nations of them which are saved shall walk in the light of it; and the kinds of the earth do bring their glory and honor into it," "there shall be no more curse."

Disease, poverty, vice and war will disappear and in its place will appear the Christian "millennium."

Then the tears of the world shall be wiped away "from their eyes; and there shall be no more death, (fear of death) neither sorrow, nor crying, neither shall there be any more pain; for the former things are passed away." Rev. xxxi, 4.

J. F. HARTMANN.

77 Aborn Street.

Notes

1. Lucius F. C. Garvin (1841–1922), governor of Rhode Island (1903–05). He was trained as a physician at Harvard Medical School and had a practice in Pawtucket, R.I.

[194]

Delavan's Comet and Astrology

The influence of cometary bodies on the horoscope of mankind is one which most astrologers of the present time have sadly underrated. The uninstructed majority seem to have lost faith in the benefic and malefic potency of these tenuously constructed celestial wanderers, and to condemn as superstitions what they should investigate as scientific phenomena.

Shakespeare knew well the significance of a comet's visitation when he wrote in his immortal tragedy of "Julius Caesar": "When beggars die, there are no comets seen; the heavens themselves blaze forth the death of princes."[1]

Little did I dream when I published my astrological predictions in The Evening News for Oct. 12, what marvellous revelations of interplanetary communications should be made to man through the recent aspect of Delavan's comet, coupled with the retrograde motion of Saturn, the greater in fortune. Prof. Hartmann, the recognised leader of astrological thought in New England, seems even now to have missed these startling disclosures from the sky, though he utters a multitude of profound truths in his masterly essay of Oct. 22.

In brief, I have now been enabled to solve the momentous problem of the future of the human race after the destruction of the earth by the great volcano explosion of February 26, 4954!

It was ever difficult for me to believe that our noble species of mortals could be completely annihilated in an instant; that all the flower of uncounted centuries of evolution could thus be cruelly blasted in the twinkling of an eye; yet what could a true astrologer do but believe it when all the stars, suns, worlds, planets, moons, constellations, and zodiacs in their courses pointed with a grim unrelenting finger to the world's inevitable end?

But the computed alternating back eccentric transit of the future projection of Delavan's comet around the progressed quartile square of the prolonged inclination of the retrograde orbit of Saturn clears up the perplexing situation in a moment, renders the whole matter most simple and obvious, and restores to man that hope without which the heart would sicken and break.

As every schoolboy may perceive, the inequalities in the gravitational direction of the 23d house of Saturn cause a pronounced deflection in the course of the seventh inner circle of that mysterious comet known to astrologers as XY4. Now before the discovery of Delavan's comet it was thought that comet XY4 would not approach that part of space until 4975, or 21 years after the destruction of the world, but the occult separative influence of the new-found body introduces a new factor into our calculations, and our conclusions. From this same cause, most important and hitherto obscure data concerning the ascendant of the 16th benefic of Jupiter over the 11th malefic of Mars in the year 4824 are explained.

From all of which we may easily deduce that on June 29, 4898, or nearly 56 years before the great catastrophe, the comet XY4 will harmlessly encounter our terraqueous globe, safely taking away on its tail the entire human race! The anaesthetic gases of which the comet is composed will preserve in a state of suspended animation the mortals thus whisked off into space, allowing them to be carried toward perihelion and deposited unhurt on the planet Venus, which much resembles the Earth in size, and on which mankind will forevermore dwell in peace and plenty. The processional quadratic equation of Ariel and Callisto in Sagittarius shews that the present inhabitants of Venus are much superior in intellect to our earthly race, being especially skilled in astrology.

When our remote descendants are set down amidst this enlightened people, they will doubtless lose that stubborn, sceptical devotion to so-called "reason" or "common sense", which now sadly hinders their progress in the higher and more mystical branches of spiritual learning.

It is obvious that all astrological computations beyond the year 4898 must be made not for the Earth but for Venus, where mankind will then reside. I have commenced my labours in this direction, and have succeeded in making certain predictions as far as the year 5025. I find to my extreme regret that several fragments from the terrestrial explosion of 4954 will strike the planet Venus, there creating much damage, and causing grave injuries to Señor Nostradomo Artmano, a lineal descendant of our talented Prof. Hartmann. Señor Artmano, a wise astrologer, will be hit in the cranial region by a large volume of astronomy, blown from the Providence Public Library, and his mind will be so affected by the concussion that he will no longer be able to appreciate the divine precepts of Astrology.

In 5012 an unfortunate event will occur, for the double crossed note of the trine of Neptune and Umbriel on Jan. 3 of that year shews that an evil-minded individual named Serviss will introduce amongst the people a false and pernicious art called "Logic", which will work great havoc with the noble doctrines of astrological truth.

As I delve deeper into the mysteries of the remote future, I shall endeavour to keep the public informed from time to time of my progress; but until then, I must leave the field clear for Prof. Hartmann's expert and brilliant work.

ISAAC BICKERSTAFFE, JR.

Providence, Oct. 24, 1914.

Notes

1. Shakespeare, *Julius Caesar* 2.2.30–31.

[195]

A Defense of Astrology

To the Editor of The Evening News:

Dear Sir—Mr. Lovecraft's abusive treatment of astrology and the astrologers, of Oct. 8, exemplifies the unreasoning attitude of the influential intellectuals, the clergy, college professors, authors and scientists, especially the astronomers, toward a science as thoroughly established in fact and reason as is any science, but whose claims these proud, self-sufficient men will not investigate. Keeping themselves wilfully ignorant of this noble science, they yet imagine themselves fair judges of what they don't understand, and belabor with vilest abuse and slander those learned therein.

Ridicule and bitter denunciation should only be employed when accompanied by facts that justify it, a rule of fairness that is never observed by the enemies of astrology.

Mr. Lovecraft begins this his second tirade:

"Since the ordinary modern astrologer is merely a mountebank" (what about the ancient, or not ordinary one?) "who seeks to defraud the ignorant by means of crude gibberish which he knows to be untrue, his tribe may very easily be silenced by the proper legal authorities."

Here he justifies the revival of the brute force, prison and torture of medieval practices as the proper argument for a scientist to use as a substitute for facts and reason when debating with astrologers. Ever the first and last word of bigotry.

The pulpit, which never defiles itself with science lectures, while it cannot now crush all the sciences as once it had the power to do, allies itself with the scientific bigots in including legislatures to enact laws for the suppression of all such other sciences as remain as yet unpopular in their superstitious, knowledge-fearing circles. Superstitious, because their frightful terror of astrology seems unaccountable to right-thinking people.

Many astrologers, good, honest, useful men, have thus been persecuted, cast into prison, their lives ruined through the machinations of these learned bigots; and the people are by law denied their rightful liberty to consult astrologers, men and women more useful than lawyers. People should have the same right to choose their science that they have to choose their religion, the same right to visit their astrologer that they have to visit their pastor and their prayer meetings.

If everything is to be suppressed whereby the ignorant are defrauded nearly all the religious institutions would be the first to go, and all those astronomers who by misrepresentations defraud the ignorant of the knowledge of astrology.

Honest opponents never attack a thing without first testing it. Before denouncing astrology they would test hundreds or thousands of horoscopes, reading them by the rules in the textbooks, on friends and strangers.

It is a rule of science that to be a science it must be predictive, that like phenomena will recur under like conditions; a rule to which astrology conforms remarkably, placing it among the sciences.

Knowing that under certain celestial phenomena certain mundane phenomena do occur we can predict with assurance that under a recurrence of the celestial the mundane will also recur and to this the astrologer's daily experience continually testifies.

Until our defamers will make and test horoscopes they have no argument that appeals to reason.

Of the many books on astronomy none show how to make a horoscope, one of the first lessons an astronomy student ought to learn, namely a map of the heavens for a given time and place. Innocent as it seems to calculate such a celestial map the professors think it something disgraceful for an astronomer to perform.

As Mr. Lovecraft complains: "The baleful effect of astrology upon the reputation of astronomy is far too patent for Mr. Hartmann to explain away. I was not long ago asked by a man who had seen my astronomical articles, if I did not cast horoscopes or calculate nativities! It is not pleasant for a serious student of the heavens to be taken for a petty fortune-teller."

Rather should astronomers feel shame for not knowing how to calculate such a map. A nativity being a horoscope at birth.

How any astronomer can feel annoyed at being thought capable of making a star map seems beyond comprehension.

That astrologers don't talk "gibberish" any one can see by consulting them, but which our enemies never do, and cannot therefore know how the astrologers talk. But no doubt they call "gibberish" everything that comes from the mouth or pen of an astrologer, however serious.

Two recent articles in these columns, by an enemy falsely posing as an astrologer, are real "gibberish," the kind which our critic does not criticise.

Real astrologers never write such ridiculous parodies upon their own sacred science, which Mr. Lovecraft calls a "base superstition."

But what is superstition? Edward B. Tylor in "Primitive Culture", defines it as derived from two Greek words meaning that which has "stood over" from past times.[1] The implication being that the past can teach us nothing. As if we who now live in the world were the only people who ever knew anything worth knowing.

Under Tylor's definition all literature, history, sciences, and art of past times is superstition.

Andrew D. White, in "Conflict Between Science and Religion", defines it as derived from the Greek "super," the supernatural, and "stitio," to fear—"the fear of God."[2]

But astrology is not "the fear of God." Fear and the supernatural are no more a part of it than of astronomy or any science. Hence astrology is not a superstition, save in the diseased imagination of those learned ignoramuses, who, trembling in mortal fear, beseech governments to help them, and cry "Police! Police!" at the mere sight of an astrologer.

As for astrologers defrauding the ignorant, they enlighten and help them, and frequently serve poor persons with troubled minds free of charge, which they would not do were they "mountebanks." Not only are they studious persons, which their science requires them to be, but they are sympathetic, feeling pity for suffering, which is the foundation of the moral sense.

Astrology goes deep into human nature and deals with the good and evil of existence, which is more evil than good, with the joys and sorrows, hopes and fears of struggling mortals, with whom sorrow and fear outweigh the passing joys of life; and where the astrologer's knowledge becomes of far greater value, a hundred fold, than the person's beliefs and prayers.

Mr. Lovecraft's charge [is] that astrologers are the enemies of knowledge, when their very mission is, in the nature of things, one of enlightenment. Wherever you meet a good astrologer, you almost invariably meet a person of broad views and a well-informed mind: one who wants to see the world wiser and happier, and who never thinks of calling the police to help him settle a question in science.

How any self-respecting astronomer can make such a false charge against astrologers one is at a loss to explain.

It is the astronomer who, by means of base falsehoods, causes disrespect for astrology, and to that extent prevents the spread of knowledge.

Mr. Lovecraft objects to my article: "The one oft repeated foundation of his arguments: the alleged ignorance of astrology on the part of astronomers. He errs very gravely when he denies that astronomy proves the falsity of astrology. Astronomy investigates every force and influence exerted by the various bodies of space upon one another, measuring with the utmost care and exactitude each slightest manifestation of energy."

As if the astronomer's brass and glass tools had now reached their final perfection, further improvements being for all time impossible.

But astrology has means not made of metal incomparably more sensitive than anything the astronomer has yet known, the human brain itself.

When physicians say the moon's phases influence their patients the astronomers call it truth, but when the astrologers say it they call it superstition, and run to the telescope to prove it so.

The astronomer refuses to test astrology by its own methods, which of course would prove it a true science. But if it was a "false science," as Mr. Lovecraft charges, then its own methods would be just the course by which to prove it false.

The astronomer's method is like that of the anatomist who disproved the existence of mental faculties in the head by sawing up skulls and finding none.

My critic continues: "The astronomer attacks the subject at every angle, and follows up with the keenest activity every principle for which he can discover any real data whatsoever. "

Just what the astronomer does not do. He rejects the very data and principle that alone will give him results. He stubbornly insists that his ignorant ways which he knows and admits give no results are the only means to be employed.

He never really tests astrology at all, if he thinks so he is deluded, misled by his ignorant professors.

Again he says: "The true student, comparing the motions of the heavenly bodies with the varied affairs of mankind, has never found a trace of evidence that there is any connexion between the two."

He means the false student who doesn't want to find out, for he denounces astrological literature as "miserable pamphlets," unfit for serious study.

The true student of these despised books does find what the untrue-to-truth student can never find. Hence it seems ridiculous to have him conclude: "No rational and unprejudiced scholar could for a moment tolerate a science thus unsupported"—namely, unsupported by himself and all those who keep wilfully ignorant of the facts that do support it, as found in those "miserable pamphlets," in study which he thinks a waste of time and a lowering of his dignity.

The Australian bushman who can't count over three thinks the multiplication table "unsupported." So is the astronomy "unsupported" with those who don't believe in it. And the infallible Bible has often proven astronomy to be of the devil, while early Christian governments made short shrift of the "mountebank" astronomers.

Our critics err when they imagine that the disproving of planetary influence disproves astrology. They don't seem to know that our science does not rest on planetary influence but on the fact that mundane affairs coincide with celestial phenomena and can be read by them.

If your watch keeps good time, what matters it whether you think it makes the time or only indicates it. To prove that it doesn't create time doesn't hurt the watch; just so with astrology.

"Planetary influence" becomes a convenient technical term, because from reading horoscopes they come to seem or appear as if they influenced mundane affairs.

The astronomer also speaks of appearances as if they were real. He speaks of sunrise and sunset, knowing that the sun doesn't rise and set; of retrograde planetary motion, when he knows that planets don't retrograde, and of circular orbits that are only apparent.

About all the books on astronomy in our public library leave the reader with the impression of circular orbits. One author merely adds as a sort of afterthought, "but these are not the real motions."

There is probably but a single explanation of the true planetary motions in all this literature, and that is in the Popular Astronomy magazine. Hence a carping critic could have a better case against astronomy as a "false science" than has the astronomer against astrology.

Mr. Lovecraft having been challenged, in a former reply to his strictures, to test the rules and aphorisms of our textbook, replies: "No rational and unprejudiced scholar needs astrological textbooks in order to perceive its absolute unsoundness." An admission of wilful ignorance of the contents and teachings of astrological books.

What would he think of a "rational and unprejudiced' judge who refused to hear his side, on the ground that he didn't "need" to, and then sentence him with abusive language, insults and billingsgate?

Mr. Lovecraft continues: "Mr. Hartmann himself appears to possess just those very intellectual characteristics which he deplores in others. He is certainly bigoted in his astrological belief, and he has evidently studied astronomy no more than the astronomers whom he censures have studied astrology. A simple course in astronomy might do much toward destroying his mediaeval ideas."

Mediaeval ideas used to imprison astronomers as now the astronomers imprison the astrologers. We are by no means ignorant of astronomy, which we must study in order to become astrologers. It is in astronomy that we find our astrology.

A bigot is one who will not reason, one who persistently condemns a science whose textbooks he will not study, and whose results he will not test. He is a bigot who seeks to refute another's ideas by mere bald denials, abusive language and vulgar personalities, and a bigot is he who in a scientific debate gloats over the tyrannical arrest and imprisonment of those whose views he cannot meet with fact and reasons; one who sets up false reasons and misstatements which he thinks to drive home with a policeman's club and prison bars.

Having been invited to tell what sort of evidence he would consider as proving astrology to be true, my critic evasively refuses the challenge by asking: "on what principle the various and complex destinies of men can be connected with the apparent positions of immensely distant bodies?"

Easily answered by comparing men's lives with their horoscopes.

But as our critic is wilfully ignorant of how to read a horoscope, and has resented it as an annoyance when a man asked him if he could do it, he has no way to test the matter, and can be no judge of it.

Inability to explain all about why observed facts are facts is no argument against their being facts.

Some astronomers don't seem to know that.

What lovely logic: That a thing is not a thing unless we can explain it is a thing.

He asks: "explain why a few erratic sophists claim the ability to detect and study in detail without instruments a species of energy which no other scientist has yet noticed even with the most elaborate and delicate appliances. But I should pay too much respect to a contemptible system of charlatanry were I to consider these matters seriously."

Mr. Lovecraft is mistaken in thinking that astrologers study certain species of planetary energy, which they don't need to study, being no part of astrology, which is a complete science without that sort of study.

He might make himself interesting by telling us what sort of instruments astronomers have used, and how and in what way they have gone about it to decide that there is no astrological relation between earth and sky, and have they gone to any considerable expense of time, money, study and patience in the matter.

Evidently they have done nothing whatever, for in the language of our critic they do not "consider these matters seriously."

Until they tell their story we will doubt their having anything to tell.

So far only false statements, angry contempt, abusive language, and vulgar personalities have come from their lips and pens. Methods so very unbecoming the dignity of scientific gentlemen, the professor's gown, or the sacred cloth.

As for "Tycho Brahe and Gassendi" abandoning astrology for other studies being any argument against it, if it were legitimate, would prove every one of the sciences false. What about the thousands of astrologers who did not abandon their art? And what about their opponents who upon investigation became converted to it? And have not astrologers the same rights as have all men to abandon one profession for another?

While the astronomers have not disproven planetary influence, but only the failure of their instruments to detect any, they have persistently rejected the only instrument suitable for the purpose of proving the astrological relationship between the heavenly bodies—the horoscope. If their failure to discover astrological energy refutes astrology, then, to be consistent, their failure to discover energy in the stars that make them rise and set every night ought to be a sure refutation of astronomy.

J. F. HARTMANN.

77 Aborn Street.

Notes

1. Edward Burnett Tylor (1832–1917), pioneering British anthropologist and author of *Primitive Culture* (1871). In ch. 3 he writes: "The very word 'superstition,' in what is perhaps its original sense of a 'standing over' from old times, itself expresses the notion of survival."

2. Andrew Dickson White (1832–1918), *A History of the Warfare of Science with Theology in Christendom* (1896). See ch. 15: "It is significant . . . that the Greek word for superstition means, literally, fear of gods or demons." White is referring to the word *theiasmos;* he is not claiming that the word superstition is itself a Greek derivative.

[196]

The Fall of Astrology

To the Editor of The Evening News:

In perusing Mr. Hartmann's somewhat belated reply to my letter in The Evening News of October 10, I am impressed with the resentment the astrologer seems to harbour against me for what he deems my abusive treatment of him. It may be that contempt for the puerile fallacies of astrological lore has led me into a rather too caustic procedure with my opponent, yet I would assure him that I respect the sincerity of his opinions, and admire the spirit with which he defends his pseudo-science. In the present letter I shall strive to avoid the use of that denunciation and ridicule against which Mr. Hartmann so strongly protests; but shall instead try the novel experiment of suspending my attack, and of assuming a defensive attitude, endeavouring merely to justify the present universal rejection of astrology by the intelligent public.

Astrology was coeval with astronomy. It was indeed, as I pointed out in a previous article, the natural result of the contemplation of the celestial vault by a young and undeveloped race. In very ancient times it was of real value to science on account of the incentive which it offered to the precise observation and careful study of the heavenly bodies. The astronomical knowledge of the Chaldaeans was in fact wholly due to the zeal of their astrologers. Thus before the advent of modern scientific exactitude, the true and the false studies of the sky were pursued side by side and in perfect harmony. If either one might be said to have precedence over the other, astrology was the one so favoured. Throughout the Middle Ages and the early Modern Period astrology enjoyed the condition of a respected branch of learning. Each monarch had his astrologer or astrologers, to whom he referred all projected affairs of state, both in war and in peace. Though at the time of the Renaissance some keener minds penetrated the specious exterior and discovered the fundamental unsoundness of the art, it was none the less very generally cultivated by all classes, foremost among them being the astronomers. Kepler, while discarding many of its more patently absurd notions, stoutly defended the underlying truth of astrology, and made known his views in a pamphlet entitled "De Fundamentis Astrologiae Certioribus" (1602). Lord Bacon and Sir Thomas Browne were likewise believers in the influence of the heavens. As late as Charles the Second's reign the public had scarce begun to doubt the genuineness of astrology, and the notorious William Lilly, though probably a conscious charlatan himself, was credited to a marvellous degree, even being summoned at one time by a committee of the House of Commons to predict the result of a certain piece of legislation.

Thus it may be perceived, that before the discovery of conclusive contrary evidence, astrology encountered no opposition either from the astronomers or from the people in general. So long as any man of science could find any reason to believe it true, it was accepted on a plane of equality with other serious studies. The only bigotry and blind prejudice which astrology ever aroused emanated from the early church; but this hostility did not extend to every department of the subject, and has no connexion with the later overthrow of the art on rational grounds.

The downfall of astrology was the inevitable result of intellectual progress; of new discoveries in science, improved methods of reasoning, more intelligent examination of history, and more discriminating investigation of the prophecies of astrologers. It became apparent that very few definite astrological predictions had ever been fulfilled even approximately, that almost all forecasts were couched in a vague style which might be interpreted in practically any way, that the most successful astrologers were obviously impostors who arrived at their conclusions only through shrewd guesses or profound knowledge of human nature, and that those who most honestly practiced astrology were the most conspicuous in their failures. At the same time, earnest students perfectly familiar with astrology and astrological methods commenced to realise the utter absurdity of the study. They saw that the very fundamental principle of casting horoscopes rests on mere allegory; the analogy of a man's birth to a star's rising. They saw that the various qualities attributed to the several planets and their positions in the Zodiac we derived wholly from the mythical gods and monsters after which the planets and stars were named. Not only was it shewn that astrological predictions were untrue, but also that every method employed to make them is false. Besides, no reason was found why the heavens should in any manner whatsoever influence or indicate the lives and destinies of mankind. What excuse, then, could any man have for adhering to a belief unsupported by the least particle of evidence, and possessing not the slightest shadow of probability? Even had there been no direct evidence against astrology, the complete absence of evidence for it would have been sufficient to justify its abandonment. Astrology died a natural and honourable death; and had the world been content to let it rest in peace, it would never have become an object of contempt and ridicule. But the greed of the charlatan and the vagaries of the eccentric kept it before the eyes of a public who had outgrown belief, and who could not but be intolerant of an art which they knew to be obsolete. The first opponents of astrology were perfectly conversant with its principles, and derived from their knowledge only the more material for use against it. But the study of the pseudo-science naturally disappeared amongst the intelligent as soon as its falsity was well demonstrated. It would of course be ridiculous for men to waste their lives in amassing information which is well known to be false, and which would seriously interfere with their acquisition of real learning. We cannot spend our precious years in repeating all the errors of our remote forefathers; we must rather profit by old blunders, and seek to avoid the false in favour of the true. Wherefore reputable authors, publishers, and institutions of learning have ceased to disseminate the fallacies of astrology, and the present generation have no hesitation in declaring their absolute unfamiliarity with that subject. It has been disproved so many times by those versed in its mysteries, that even were astronomy not enough to brand it false, we should not need to repeat such a redundant performance. Why does not Mr. Hartmann demand that we disprove the old, abandoned Ptolemaic theory of the universe once more?

Let me now consider some of my opponent's statements in greater detail. He declares quite gravely, that "when physicians say the moon's phases influence their patients, the astronomers call it truth". I hardly need answer that no astronomer of the present time would credit such an absurd assertion, nor would any rational physician make it.

Another paragraph of Mr. Hartmann's is truly amazing. He tells us that with but one exception the astronomical books in our public library leave the reader with the impression that planetary orbits are circular. I have read nearly all the volumes in question, and can say with certainty that none of them could possibly convey such an idea to any intelligent person. The elliptical nature of orbits is too well known to be concealed even by the vaguest of books.

Mr. Hartmann inquires of me, in connexion with my denunciation of the "ordinary modern astrologer" as a mountebank, what I would consider an ancient or an extraordinary astrologer. Since the ancient astrologers believed to a greater or less extent their own predictions, I should call them somewhat misguided scientists; while as for the extraordinary modern prophets like Mr. Hartmann himself, I think I gave them sufficient credit for their fanatical sincerity in my previous letter.

Before concluding, I should like to comment on Mr. Hartmann's curious attempt at etymological derivation of the word "superstition". Surely he could not have obtained such a mass of nonsense from the authorities he quotes, for any man of education knows that the word comes directly from the Latin and not from the Greek. "Superstition" is from the Latin "superstare", and in turn derived from "super", over, and "stare", to stand still; the implied meaning being a standing still over anything in dread amazement or reverence. All of this information is obtained from Webster's Unabridged Dictionary, which should invariably be consulted on points of this sort. However, I fail to see how the origin of the word can interest Mr. Hartmann so much more than its present use, which is sufficiently well-known to all.

I have here endeavoured to treat seriously a subject which can scarce be contemplated without a smile. This rather inappropriate method must find its justification in the sober and extremely zealous tone of my opponent's arguments.

H. P. LOVECRAFT

Dec. 15, 1914.

[197]

[Isaac Bickerstaffe's Reply]

Editor News:

Seasoned though I am to the heartless attacks of the vulgar scientific public, I was cut to the quick by the recent insinuations concerning me, made by my fellow-astrologer, Prof. J. F. Hartmann. I cannot but infer that it is to my work that he alludes, when he says that "Two recent articles in these columns, by an enemy falsely posing as an astrologer, are real gibberish. Real astrologers never write such ridiculous parodies upon their own sacred science." How can Prof. Hartmann hope to secure belief for his own writings, when he thus basely attacks the humble efforts of a brother? Heretofore only stupid outsiders have cast aspersion and ridicule on our labours. Is the professor about to desert our sublime study, and join the ranks of the mocking unbelievers? In denouncing my work as "gibberish", Prof. Hartmann shews as little genuine spiritual comprehension of the inner truths of astrology as do the pompous pedants who attack us both.

Astrology is indeed like a delicate flower; in its entirety a thing of rare grace and beauty, but utterly ruined when picked to pieces by gross, ungentle hands. Why seek for cold logic in the inspired utterances of a prophet? Obtuse indeed is that intellect which can mistake for parodies the predictions in whose preparation a grave scholar has spent the better part of a long life. Could Prof. Hartmann himself duplicate my achievements in the art of judicial astrology? Does he extend his own timid forecasts to the end of the world and beyond? When he can thus compete with me in my own wider sphere then let him taunt me with his charge of levity and insincerity!

But when the professor pronounces my writings mere "gibberish", he pays me a far greater compliment than he dreams. I perceive by his profound etymological analysis of the word "superstition", wherein he traces it back to

the Greek, that he is a thorough master of classical languages; yet his ignorance of the Arabic tongue leads him astray in the use of what he thinks to be
an epithet of opprobrium. In employing the word "gibberish", Prof. Hartmann doubtless falls into the error commonly found in the cheap dictionaries, assuming the noun is derived from the Icelandic verb root "gifra", to
jabber; but as a student of Arabic, I am able absolutely to controvert this fallacy, and to ascribe the word to its proper root. "Gibberish", or to use the
more primitive noun, "al geber isch", arose from the name of Geber, an eminent Arabian astronomer and alchemist, who flourished in the eighth century
A.D.[1] The purest signification of "gibberish" is "words of Geber", which later gave rise to the secondary meaning, "astrological wisdom", referring to the
Wisdom of Geber's conversation on that subject. Thus do I stand trium-
phantly vindicated! Prof. Hartmann has indirectly and unwittingly admitted
that I am a wise astrologer!

But let me now leave this distasteful controversy and proceed at once to
the work which I was preparing before the professor so rudely attacked me. I
have the honour herewith to submit my carefully calculated prophecies for
the first half of the coming year 1915. I may with all due modesty affirm their
complete accuracy, and challenge any of my emulous rivals to produce equal
or superior results.

JANUARY.

Conjunction of Mercury and Mars on first indicates prosperous and disastrous year. Earth in perihelion on second, conjoined with greatest brilliancy
of Venus, and lunar conjunction of Neptune, predicts cold weather in January
and February. Moon on Equator Jan. 19 shews that European war will still be
raging. Opposition of Neptune on 20th signifies English or German success
about this time.

FEBRUARY.

Greatest elongations of both Venus and Mercury on 6th indicate the following February will have 29 days, that being one extra. Eclipse of Sun on
13th is malefic [so that] several men will die either in Belgium, France, or
Prussia.

MARCH.

Entrance of Sun into sign Aries shews that spring will begin on the 21st.
Conjunction of Mars and Jupiter on 23d shews disturbances in the Eastern
hemisphere.

APRIL.

Moon's double Perigee on 1st and 30th tells one that Kaiser Wilhelm will
not yet put into practice his principle of universal peace.

MAY.

Superior conjunction of Mercury in 1st shews that weather will be much warmer than January. Lunar conjunction of Saturn on 17th foretells ill feelings between Austrians and Serbians.

JUNE.

Summer will probably commence this month. Quadrature of Jupiter on the 19th indicates much anxiety felt by Kings and Princes. Conjunction of Saturn on 28th renders it likely that July will arrive no sooner than usual.

The arduous labour necessary for the computation of these prophecies has left me with but little time in which to enlarge my vaster researches into the more remote future, hence I can be sure of very few facts after 5020 A.D.

In concluding, I must again lament the apostasy of my talented colleague, Prof. Hartmann. How can we astrologers hope successfully to promulgate our glorious science, if we have such bitter dissensions amongst ourselves? In exhibiting scepticism of a brother's work and thereby seeking to destroy our faith with the worldly weapons of reason and scorn, the Professor has perpetrated a serious infraction of astrological ethics.

ISAAC BICKERSTAFFE, JR.

Notes

1. "Geber" is the westernized form of Jabir ibn Hayyan, an Arabic alchemist of the 8th century who wrote several immensely influential astrological works. Geber is cited in *The Case of Charles Dexter Ward* (1927).

To Gavin T. McColl

Gavin T. McColl, a "crippled Scotsman" of Dundee, produced 96 numbers of his amateur journal, *The Scot*. He published Lovecraft's "The Doom That Came to Sarnath."

[198]

Appreciations

[early 1916]

Permit me to thank you very sincer[e]ly for The Scot, and upon whose excellence I desire to congratulate you. It is indeed a welcome new-comer to the Amateur world, and I believe will within a short time be one of the very foremost amateur journals. The articles are all attractive and well written, whilst the typographical work is equally commendable. It is difficult to believe, from the quality of your journal, that you are a new-comer in the literary field.

To Charles W. Smith

Lovecraft rebuts Graeme Davis (Official Editor of the NAPA for 1917–18), who in an unlocated issue of his amateur journal, the *Lingerer*, attacked the UAPA, in which Lovecraft himself was apparently mentioned. Lovecraft's correspondence with Smith is lost. A single letter, unseen, is known to exist.

[199]

A Reply to the Lingerer

[May 1917]

Editor Tryout:—

It was with no little interest that I perused the recent attack on the United Amateur Press Association made by the Rev. Graeme Davis in his excellent publication *The Lingerer*. Since the culture and intellectual quality of Mr. Davis forbid one to charge him with the trivial and illiberal prejudices of association politics, it is an inevitable deduction that his anti-United attitude arises from lack of recent information concerning the two major societies and their places in the amateur world today.

It is entirely true that much puerility and much immaturity does exist within the United. The discovery of this condition requires no considerable acumen, nor does its mention in an United paper constitute either a treasonable revelation or a naive admission. The *Conservative* editorial[1] from which Mr. Davis derives such unholy glee was a frank criticism of a remediable fault; and was directed against a small clique, also active in the National, whose maleficent energy seems now quite spent. For evidence of a puerility that is permanent and an immaturity that is immutable, our critic should look elsewhere; nor should he close his eyes to his own association whilst sifting out the flaws of another.

To speak brutally and impartially, all amateurdom is more or less homogeneously tinctured with a certain delicious callowness. To confound this callowness with downright density would be most unjust, for it is merely a healthy adolescence which results from the continual infusion of young blood. But why exclude the United from this charitable interpretation? Is the ancient and honourable lineage of the National a fetish so potent that what passes for budding genius within its own fold, must in the United be branded with alliterative ingenuity as "permanent puerility and immutable immaturity"? I would admonish Mr. Davis that it ill becomes the pot to call the kettle black.

When Mr. Davis essays a direct comparison between the United and National, he exhibits most clearly the effects of his long absence from amateurdom. Proud of the justly famous personages in the old association, he is entirely ignorant of the new and commanding figures in the literary life of the United; men and women of ideals and scholarship who have appeared above the horizon during his seven years of retirement.

Perhaps it is the dormant state of the amateur press which has kept many of these gifted recruits from his notice, but he at least owes it to the United to withhold invidious comparisons before acquainting himself with our present personnel.

To refute Mr. Davis' none too generous suggestion that my own loyalty to the United is caused by a conceited desire to stand out against a background even more mediocre than myself, I need only mention the names of a score of fellow members, to each of whom I can justly and gladly concede the palm of vastly superior genius, scholarship, and expression. Were I desirous of shining at the expense of youth and crudity, I am sure that my search for suitable "foils" would lead me through pastures much closer to Mr. Davis than the United.

If in the preceding paragraphs I have seemed to bear criticism with less than Christian meekness and acquiescence, it is because of the peculiarly unprovoked and uncalled-for nature of Mr. Davis' attack on the United. It would perhaps have been more seemly and logical to explain to *The Lingerer* some of the ceaseless and laborious enterprises undertaken by the United in the ill-rewarded cause of serious educational service; enterprises whose very spirit and essence are unknown to the basically dilettante mind of the typical Nationalite; but I feel that he should have known of these before seizing upon an exceptional case of criticism as grounds for a polite sneer. The standards of a decade ago are no longer to be applied to amateurdom, for the United has left the beaten path and is pioneering in fields to which the National does not aspire. Each association has now its separate niche, and the need for mutual rivalry, jealousy, and hostility is past.

Rev. Graeme Davis is deservedly classed as one of the elect in our miniature world. His *Lingerer* is one of the few papers of which no recipient will ever throw away a copy. Must he not, considering the intellectual height from which he views the panorama of amateurdom, soon grasp the scene as a whole, without the prejudices common to less disciplined mentalities?

Notes

1. Evidently a reference to "Amateur Standards" (*Conservative*, January 1917; *CF* 1.138).

[200] [ALS]

[13 March 1928]

Two-page letter, part of the Grill/Binkin collection (#509), the only known surviving (but unseen) letter to Tryout Smith.

To the Bureau of Critics

Lovecraft satirically takes the side of two amateur writers offended at the severity of the criticism directed against them in the NAPA's Bureau of Critics. (He was often critical of the poets himself.) Lovecraft tended to regard the NAPA's department as being far more lenient on mediocrity than the analogous department in the UAPA, the Department of Public Criticism, of which he was chairman for much of the period between 1914 and 1919.

[201]

To the Honourable Bureau of Critics,
   National Amateur Press Ass'n.,
      Athol, Mass., U.S.A.

Gentlemen:

Having lately observed the just and manly protests of Messrs. F. C. Reighter and J. Osman Baldwin[1] against the biased and inhuman tone of your published reviews; we, the undersigned, desire to add our voices to this chorus of wronged and aggrieved merit.

Are you not aware, gentlemen, that you have no right to pronounce judgment upon the effusions of genius greater than your own? What if we poets do occasionally overlook the inconsequential minutiae of such trivial things as rhyme, metre, and good taste? We would have you know, that these things are but trifles to great souls, and that if you fail to forget them in admiration of our larger impressionistic efforts, you forthwith convict yourselves of deficient super-aestheticism.

Mr. Reighter has very acutely observed, that there is only *one* (the italics are his own) truthful side of every question. We are impelled to add, that of course a poet always *knows* (these italics are ours) when he has hit upon the truth; and that consequently when we bards say a thing, it is invariably above criticism. Why waste your ink, gentlemen of the bureau, in these days of conservation?

Now, gentlemen, we rise to protest against some of the *de*-structive criticism we have received at your hands. One of us some years ago wrote a poem containing the eminently correct rhyme of *brown* and *ground*,[2] and one of your brutal department had the effrontery to say it was erroneous, *despite the fact that he offered no substitute*. Members of the National, I appeal to you against this tyrannic oligarchy of littlewit reviewers! Think of this case; a critic protesting against a rhyme, *when he is incapable of making any rhyme whatsoever himself!* We declare this to be an outrage against the citizens of a free country, and a violation of the constitution and the Magna Charta! Let the critic seek, as our fellow-sufferer Mr. Reighter suggests, the sanctified privacy of his chamber; and in solemn accents utter repeatedly the words *brown* and *ground*, passing over the final consonant of *ground* as a non-essential, and giving the whole a most sonorous and resounding roll. We say to you, that if you do this you will find our—that is, Mr. Softly's—rhyme absolutely "A-1 Perfect".

Now while of course we care naught for the cruel things you have said of our work—we are above such petty censure, since we belong to the "so-few"—we must intervene in Mr. Reighter's behalf concerning the "widow's cruse of oil" allusion.[3] Evidently your ancestors are not Roman, else you would have recognised the simile as referring to the inexhaustible bowl of Baucis and Philemon, in Ovid—you all know the passage.

> "——haustum cratera repleri
> Sponte sua, per seque vident succrescere vina."[4]

The "widow" reference was a trivial *lapsus calami*, or figure of speech.

[N.B. My friend Mr. Softly is in error; I am of opinion that Mr. Reighter alluded to the very pretty incident in the history of Elisha, the Semitic Prophet, as related in the fourth chapter of Second Kings.[5] However, deem me not an Hebrew because I am familiar with the legend. Neither is Mr. Softly, who quoted Ovid, a Roman!—

Ward Phillips.]

My—or rather *our*—sympathy goes out abundantly to Mr. Baldwin. As he says, the fiendish malignancy of the critics of amateurdom has deterred all of our beginners from exhibiting their embryonic but inspired products to the world. In fact, we *never* see any crude products in amateur papers nowadays. Gentlemen, you are discouraging incipient genius by attempting to assist writers.

Infant poesy must never be vexed by the precepts of a guide or *de*-structive critic. Like a delicate flower it must blossom of itself, assisted only by gentle showers from the benevolent watering-pot of polite panegyric.

Far be it from us to take umbrage at what is said of our own work; we are, as we said before, steeled against the darts of envy, and appreciative of any genuine attempts at *con*-structive criticism; but we cannot bear your unjust and heinously harsh estimates of recent poetry in *The Tryout*. Mr. Softly is most contemptuous of your ill-timed censure against his serious artistic attempt entitled "Damon and Delia", and vows you shew vast ignorance in declaring it 'not always successful, too long, and sometimes awkward and unmusical'. He spent several years in the composition of this masterpiece, and has been told by his landlady's cousin (a graduate of grammar-school) that it surpasses even the best of the "Love-Epistles of Aristaenetus", as translated in 1771 by Halhed and Sheridan.[6]

As for Mr. Phillips's "Eidolon"—he maintains an haughty silence at your ungenerous strictures, but wants information as to why you dare call the piece lacking in those contrasts necessary to produce full horror, *when you do not offer an improved version yourself.* I am not—that is, Mr. Phillips is not—egotistical in the least; but we consider "The Eidolon" one of the most graphic and impelling Poe-ems to appear in the amateur press since the dawn of our hobby; one whose beauties are desecrated by the earthly appraisal of a mere critic.

As we terminate this friendly communication, we entreat of you not to deem us in the least incensed or even mildly perturbed. Our remarks, we assure you, are but philosophical observations—altogether impersonal—designed to assist you in conquering the grave faults of criticism which have made your bureau an object of detestation amongst all sensitive members of the so-few, and all disciples of the obscurely beautiful in poesy.

Permit us to subscribe ourselves as your devoted and obedient servants,

Ned Softly,
Ward Phillips.

P.S. Mr. Softly desires that you will look up what Mr. Addison, a *real* critick, said about his lines "To Mira"; in No. 163 of the *Tatler*.[7]

Notes

1. Frank C. Reighter (1865–?), whom HPL characterized as a "didactic" poet, and John Osman Baldwin (1871–1942), an amateur poet from Ohio. The latter is presumably the subject of HPL's poem "To Mr. Baldwin, upon Receiving a Picture of Him in a Rural Bower" (1923; *AT* 169).

2. No such verse has been found among HPL's known poems.

3. An inexhaustible supply. From 1 Kings 17:8–16. In particular, "And the barrel of meal wasted not, neither did the cruse of oil fail, according to the word of the LORD, which he spake by Elijah." Elijah instructed a widow to prepare him some bread, in the middle of a famine. She demurred because she had only a little left for herself and her son. She did as instructed, and found that her supply of flour and oil was never diminished.

4. From Ovid, *Metamorphoses* 8.679–80: "They saw that the mixing bowl, as often as it was drained, kept filling of its own accord, and that the wine welled up of itself" (tr. Frank Justus Miller).

5. 2 Kings 4:1–7 tells the story of a widow who appeals to the prophet Elisha because her sons are to be taken as slaves by a creditor. Elisha arranges for the widow to gather as many jars of oil as she can find, and she finds that the supply of oil she had (which she believed would fill only one jar) filled all the jars.

6. *The Love Epistles of Aristaenetus* (1771), tr. from the Greek by Richard Brinsley Sheridan and Nathaniel Brassey Halhed. Aristaenetus (d. 358 C.E.) was a Greek grammarian; the letters are probably attributed to him falsely.

7. In *The Tatler* No. 163 (25 April 1710), Addison (under the pseudonym "Isaac Bickerstaffe") pretends to praise a poem, "To Mira on Her Incomparable Poems," by "Ned Softly," calling it "a little nosegay of conceits, a very lump of salt: every verse has something in it that piques."

To the Omaha *World-Herald/Daily Bee*

The letters below are both extracted from Lovecraft's essay "Literary Composition," *United Amateur* 19, No. 3 (January 1920): 56–60. It is almost certain that someone else submitted these extracts to the newspaper; but the only member of the UAPA in Nebraska at the time was Kate L. Humphrey of Omaha, with whom Lovecraft is not known to have been acquainted. Possibly she submitted the items without Lovecraft's knowledge or permission.

[202]

The Bible as Literature

Omaha, Feb. 18—To the Editor of the World-Herald: All attempts at gaining literary polish must begin with judicious reading, and the learner must never cease to hold this phase uppermost. In many cases the usage of good authors will be found a more effective guide than any amount of precept. A page of Addison or of Irving will teach more of style than a whole manual of rules, whilst a story of Poe's will impress upon the mind a more vivid notion of powerful and correct description and narration than will ten dry chapters of a bulky text book. Let every student read unceasingly the best writers.

It is also important that cheaper types of reading, if hitherto followed, be dropped. Popular magazines inculcate a careless and deplorable style which is hard to unlearn, and which impedes the acquisition of a purer style. If such things must be read, let them be skimmed over as lightly as possible. An excellent habit to cultivate is the analytical study of the King James Bible. For simple yet rich and forceful English this masterly production is hard to equal, and even though its Saxon vocabulary and poetic rhythm be unsuited to general composition, it is invaluable for writers. Lord Dunsany, perhaps the greatest living prose artist, derived nearly all of his stylistic tendencies from the scriptures.   II. P. LOVECRAFT

Style in English

Omaha, Feb. 20.—To the Editor of The Bee: All attempts at gaining literary polish must begin with judicious reading, and the learner must never cease to hold this phase uppermost. In many cases, the usage of good authors will be found a more effective guide than any amount of precept. A page of Addison or of Irving will teach more of style than a whole manual of rules, while a story of Poe's will impress upon the mind a more vivid notion of powerful and correct description and narration than will 10 dry chapters of a bulky text book. Let every student read unceasingly the best writers.

It is also important that cheaper types of reading, if hitherto followed, be dropped. Popular magazines inculcate a careless and deplorable style which is hard to unlearn, and which impedes the acquisition of a purer style. If such things must be read, let them be skimmed over as lightly as possible.

An excellent habit to cultivate is the analytical study of the King James Bible. For simple yet rich and forceful English, this masterly production is hard to equal; and even though its Saxon vocabulary and poetic rhythm be unsuited to general composition, it is invaluable for writers. Lord Dunsany, perhaps the greatest living prose artist, derived nearly all of his stylistic tendencies from the scriptures; and the contemporary critic, Boyd,[1] points out very acutely the loss sustained by most Catholic Irish writers through their unfamiliarity with the historic volume and its traditions.

> H. P. LOVECRAFT

Notes

1. Ernest A. Boyd (1887–1946), Irish critic and editor and author of *Ireland's Literary Renaissance* (1916).

To John Milton Heins

John Milton Heins was the editor of the *American Amateur*. Letter 202 is Lovecraft's only known publication in that periodical, aside from the essay "Life for Humanity's Sake" (September 1920).

[203]

[c. March 1921]

I shall vote for E. Dorothy McLaughlin[1] for President of the National because of her individual fitness for the post, as well as her representation of the elements devoted to honest literary endeavour. The encroachment of factions dealing only in personal malice and debased and scurrilous journalism should be resisted at the polls for the good of the whole amateur cause.

Notes

1. McLaughlin (later the wife of George Julian Houtain) in fact was elected president of the NAPA (1921–22).

[204]

598 Angell St., Providence,
November 4, 1921.

My dear Mr. Heins:—

Permit me to thank you most sincerely for the attractive silver medal which your Association has been so kind to award me.[1] The honourable mention is as gratifying as any ordinary laureateship, since my superior is no less a person than James F. Morton, Jr. The idea of the medals, for which I believe your Association is indebted to you alone, is certainly a most desirable one; since it stimulates in the contests a keen interest otherwise lacking. I regret that my prime allegiance to the United Association forbade me to contribute to your medal fund in these lean times, but am sure you can appreciate the principle involved. If you ever join the United and start such a fund, you may depend upon my fullest coöperation!

It was not without a qualm of conscience that I accepted the medal when informed of it by Mr. Houtain—it seemed to some degree unethical to step into another Association, grab a valuable prize, and then step out again with only a brief word of thanks. My qualms were overruled, however, and I now tender the thanks with as much contrition as the occasion demands.

Thanking you again—both you and your association, in fact—and assuring [*sic*] you to have any part of this letter published if you so choose,
Believe me,
Most sincerely yours,
H. P. Lovecraft

Notes

1. HPL acknowledges an award as runner-up in the essay laureateship in the NAPA for 1921; the laureateship was won by James F. Morton. HPL received the award for "The Street."

To the Board of Executive Judges, NAPA

When William J. Dowdell resigned as president of the NAPA late in 1922, the NAPA's Executive Judges appointed Lovecraft interim president for the balance of the 1922–23 term.

[205]

November 30, 1922

Board of Executive Judges,
National Amateur Press Association,
Mrs. E. D. Houtain, Chairman,

Dear Mrs. Houtain:—
I am in receipt of your communication of the 27th inst., notifying me of the Board's appointment of myself as President of the National Amateur Press Association.

In reply I take pleasure in giving my acceptance, with the assurance that no matter how inadequate my efforts may seem, I shall at all times endeavour to discharge my duties to the satisfaction of the membership and the best interests of amateur journalism.

Appreciating the Board's confidence in my qualifications, and its offer of administrative support, I am

Most cordially and fraternally yours,
H. P. Lovecraft

To the Members of the N.A.P.A.

"I have this day written a long report for Martin's *National Amateur*, & design immediately to publish an appeal for official organ funds, in the form of an epistle to be mimeographed by Lynch. In my message, I am requesting volunteer critics & reviewers to communicate with Loveman;[1] in the hope that the National may gradually acquire that helpfulness to the novice which marked the United before its recent destruction" (*Letters to Rheinhart Kleiner and Others* 198–99).

In "President's Message," *National Amateur* 45, Nos. 2–3 (November–January 1923): 2, Lovecraft discusses the status of the *National Amateur* and lists one donation and ten pledges in addition to the two donations mentioned in the mimeographed letter (*CE* 1.318–19). In "President's Message," *National Amateur* 45, No. 4 (March 1923): 4, he writes: "Responses to the mimeographed appeal [i.e., the item below] have been gradual, but sufficient to relieve the acutest phases of the situation" (*CE* 1.323–24).

[206] [Printed broadside][2]

[before 11 January 1923]

NATIONAL AMATEUR PRESS ASSOCIATION

To the Members:

The dawn of 1923 reveals amateur journalism in the midst of a depression almost unparallelled in its history. The National, totally inactive during the first half of the official year, is only just started in the task of administration; with an official board to assemble and a literary renaissance to launch, so that some imperative call to action is necessary if we are to recover from stagnation and ensure the unbroken continuity of the amateur tradition. To put it mildly, we have a year's worth to do in exactly half that time.

Now the one essential to any kind of progress, or for that matter to the bare prevention of retrogression, is an official organ of proper size and regularity. At great personal sacrifice Mr. Harry E. Martin has consented to remain as Official Editor, and is now preparing a NATIONAL AMATEUR to be dated November–January; but if the work is to be carried on adequately, it must receive special financial support from the membership at large.

SUPPORT THE OFFICIAL ORGAN! A fund has been started under the custodianship of the undersigned, to be devoted exclusively to the maintenance of the NATIONAL AMATEUR; and it is to be hoped that contributions from all members will be received. While each is urged to give as much as he conveniently can, donations of any size are received with gratitude. Donors will be given credit in the columns of the NATIONAL AMATEUR. To open the list the following contributions are announced:

> H. P. Lovecraft........................$10.00
> Leonard A. Merritt $2.00

Donations are payable to H. P. Lovecraft, 598 Angell St., Providence, R. I., and will be transmitted to Editor Martin as demanded by publishing conditions. Members who have pledged sums to the fund are especially urged to materialize these pledges, since the year's plans have been somewhat modelled on the expectation of such payments. THE NATIONAL AMATEUR is the nucleus of all our associational life—SUPPORT IT!

But a mere official organ is not enough to vitalize the whole fabric of amateur journalism. Where is the interest and individual publishing activity of other days? Are our aesthetic and intellectual impulses either atrophied or diverted to non-amateur channels? Surely the basic impulse of amateurdom—the desire to utter thoughts and images before a sympathetic audience, or to exchange impressions with congenial minds, cannot have vanished in six months' time!

But whatever we may say of impulses, the amateur press *has* largely vanished; and without it we are helpless and inarticulate. Never before have we so gravely needed an application of the honoured motto, "PUBLISH AN INDIVIDUAL PAPER—NOW!" Everything depends upon the appearance of more papers, and we should deem no sacrifice too great to make in issuing them. The undersigned hopes to set a good example with THE CONSERVATIVE, and is glad to announce many heartening pledges of kindred action by others. Later in the term we hope to establish some co-operative publishing activity for the benefit of those for whom the individual burden is too great.

An effective official board is now forming. Miss Juliette H. Haas (formerly Historian) is now Secty. A new Historian, Second Vice-President and Publicity Secty. will be announced later. The machinery is starting—now for the whole membership to play its part!

Sincerely and fraternally yours,

H. P. LOVECRAFT
President.

Notes

1. Loveman was head of the Bureau of Critics of the NAPA for 1922–23.
2. Apparently printed by Howard Jeffreys; see *Letters to James F. Morton* 48.

To the *Gothamite*

The Gotham Press Club was a group of amateur journalists in New York City, led by George Julian Houtain. The official organ of the club, the *Gothamite*, began publication in the early 1900s. When Houtain resigned his position as NAPA President, Lovecraft was appointed to replace him in early 1923, hence Lovecraft's "greeting" below. In various President's Messages and other writings from that time, Lovecraft describes the Gotham Club at the time as "new," suggesting that the group reformed in Houtain's absence.

Greetings from N. A. P. A.
President Lovecraft

[207]

"Continue as brilliantly as you have begun and you will gain an instantaneous fame which nothing can challenge or tarnish" was Howard P. Lovecraft's written greeting read at the Gotham Dinner.

To the Ohio Amateur Journalists' Club

[208]

Lovecraft's Greeting

As President of the National Amateur Press Association to the members of the Ohio Amateur Journalists' Club in convention at Warren, Ohio, Decoration Day, 1923.

It will give me pleasure if this greeting can reach you in time for reading at your annual banquet; for, as I can honestly say without the speaker's usual insincerity, I have a particularly high regard for the amateur journalists of Ohio.

Your state has developed the greatest aesthete ever known to our hobby—Samuel Loveman, of Cleveland—and in William Dowdell of the same place has produced a publicity worker without a peer. For organised activity no other, to my knowledge, has so much to shew; since you can point to local clubs in Cleveland, Akron, Columbus, Warren, and Lorrain—the latter only just established. Ohio contains the president and official editor of the United Association—Messrs Conover and Fritter[1]—and the gifted Official Editor of the National—Mr. Harry E. Martin. Both the *United Amateur* and *National Amateur* are published within its borders by Mr. Howard Jeffreys of Columbiana.

But I cannot attempt to catalogue all the amateur glories of Ohio—they are too numerous. I can only commend in a general way the genuine and healthy literary spirit of the state as I have found it, as attested by the contents of *The Clevelander* and the rise of such new figures as Dudley Carroll[2] and Carroll E. Lawrence.

The past is altogether too broad a field to cover, one to which an amateur recruit of 1914—as I am—cannot do thorough justice. But here also I seem to find evidences of Ohioan eminence, for the names of Thrift, Brodie, Sinclair,[3] and the Cincinnati circle of some 35 years ago are things to conjure with.

With such long-standing and well-diffused activity, it is only natural that Ohio should today have the only sectional association in existence. To this association the National extends its sincerest congratulations and good wishes, together with a hope that it may by increasing its usefulness and in a period of reconstruction serve as a model and inspiration for the foundation or revival of others of like nature in various parts of the country.

As an individual and as a representative of the National I salute you. Would that I were present that the cordiality of my words might be more manifest.

H. P. LOVECRAFT
May 29, 1923

Notes

1. Howard R. Conover (1900–1980), UAPA Historian, of Cozzadale, later of Cincinnati, and Leo Fritter (1878–1948), lawyer and member of the Woodbee Press Club. HPL supported Fritter's campaign to be president of the UAPA (1915), which Fritter won. (HPL was first vice-president.)

2. HPL referred to Dudley Carroll as a "psychological fictionist *par excellence*" (*CE* 1.348).

3. Timothy Burr Thrift (1883–1947), owner of a printing and advertising business in Cleveland, editor of *Lucky Dog, Tim Talks,* the *Aonian,* the *Mailbag,* and *Tim Thoughts,* and president of the NAPA (1905–06). Warren J. Brodie, independent printer and secretary of an amateur club in Cleveland. Irving MacDonald Sinclair (1885–1969), who affected the spelling "SinClair," was publisher of *Cartoons,* an amateur journal.

To the *Haldeman-Julius Weekly*

The *Haldeman-Julius Weekly* (1922–29) was founded by Emanuel Haldeman-Julius (1889–1951), publisher of an extensive array of inexpensive books, such as the Little Blue Books, designed to sell to the masses at 5¢. Lovecraft owned dozens, perhaps hundreds, of them. He was apparently reading the *Weekly* during 1922–23, as evidenced by the two letters printed below. The first one inspired a response by a reader, to which Lovecraft's second letter is a reply.

[209]

[December 1922?]

Of all the letters I have received regarding great men (and many of them were of real interest) the very best, by far, comes from *H. P. Lovecraft*, 598 Angell Street, Providence, R.I., whose letter it was a pleasure to read and a privilege to pass on. He lists the following candidates for immortality: *Homer,* who first mirrored with natural fidelity the world and the men-vermin who crawl over it; *Epicurus,* who first made plain and coherent the rational mode and object of existence; *Alexander,* who gave to Hellenic civilization a permanence and extent which preserved it as a dominant force; *Caesar,* who opened the western world to civilization, and supplemented *Alexander* in fixing classical culture as an universal endowment; *Shakespeare,* who most completely expressed the mind and moods of man; *Balzac,* who most intelligently dissected modern society, and closely seconded *Shakespeare* in representing human thought; *Poe,* who gave reality to the unreal, and first made articulate and beautiful the faint clawings of the daemons of outer voids on the farthest unseen rim of space; *Schopenhauer,* who first appraised life as it is, founded the art of modern conduct, and taught the only rational *vie cerebrale; Nietzsche,* who destroyed the rubbish of the ages, and explained the pseudo-values which generations of babbling cattle have worshipped without understanding; *Remy de Gourmont,* who has added that final touch of disillusion needed by the alert intellect, and has crystallized that cosmic irony which all penetration must ultimately reach.[1] Such are *Mr. Lovecraft's* heroes. He tells me his pet aversions are too numerous to catalogue, though an infinitesimal part of his "hates" might thus be represented: *Plato,* whose good sense masked enough infernal nonsense to tinge half the world's philosophies with absurdity, and who is responsible for that execrable bore, *Ralph Waldo Emerson; Jesus,* who, if he existed, formed the excuse for the world's most blighting system of rabble ethics and emotional dissipation; *all the Church Fathers,* a snivelling crew whose imbecilities and distorted values did more than the barbarians to wreck the world's greatest civilization; *Heliogabalus,* who is responsible for the ethical conceptions of the ultra-moderns, especially the *Dial* group; *Dante,* who would be an atrocious nuisance if anybody tried to read him through; *Rousseau,* an especially obnoxious conjunction of silliness, swinishness and sentimentality; *Kant, Hegel* and other founders of Nineteenth Century metaphysical mystification; *Walt Whitman,* Pan turned poseur—arch affectationist amidst whose awkward artificialities and clamorous cacophonies we see a small lump of real genius spread out over an infinite area of sentimentalism and false social theory; *Karl Marx,* glib theorist who has lent a pseudo-scientific rationalization to the herd's lunacy, stupidity and enviousness; *Harold Bell Wright,* who typifies the reigning American boobery;[2] *Lenin,* intellectually agile ass who has made Russia even more impossible than it was before; *T. S. Eliot,* author of *The Waste Land,* who has done to American "poetry" what *Lenin* has done to Russia. Such are his devils, and a mighty good devil-swatter he is. I can promise *Mr. Lovecraft* that he is going to be the target for a bushel basket of letters, for I can see what disastrous effect his lists are going to have. The air is going to ring with cries, shouts and tumults. All I, as pastor of this flock, ask is that the letters of castigation be as exciting reading as *Mr. Lovecraft's.* This man is the sort of a person I'd like to have in my library for a long night. I wager you, we could talk ourselves to exhaustion. If you ever get out this way, *Mr. Lovecraft,* please remember to stop off in southeastern Kansas. I like you immensely. I am also mighty glad that you are a vast admirer of the pocket series. Don't worry— this enterprise won't go the way of the *Cassell's National Library.* The promoters of that enterprise made the mistake of trying to obtain distribution through the bookstores, and anyone who knows anything at all knows that the book dealers are the most stupid and impossible people in the world. I sell my books direct to the public, via the mail order route, and every now and then I turn to the dealers and give them the merry ha-ha. The dealers are able to destroy any good thing that comes along, but I'm not going to give them a chance to kill the pocket series. I tell them frankly, again and again, that I don't want their cooperation, because they make me tired. But to return to *Mr. Lovecraft's* list. I agree with him that to select the world's ten greatest men is, in view of the subjectivity and evanescence of human standards, a task of obvious absurdity. That is why it is interesting. "The prime equipment for such a labor," says *Mr. Lovecraft,* "is clearly an absence of thought, since a comprehending approach to the problem would but exaggerate its complexity and demonstrate its insolvableness."

Notes

1. Remy de Gourmont (1858–1915), French poet and critic. HPL appreciated his *Une Nuit au Luxembourg* (1906; translated as *A Night in the Luxembourg*). See *SL* 1.250.
2. Harold Bell Wright (1872–1944), prolific and bestselling American novelist.

[210]

John Mason, Caney, Okla., is a reader I like to hear from now and then. He has a viewpoint that I respect, even though I do not agree with him most of the time. He writes me that he is pleased with this line of mine: "Every belly full of stew and every broad bottom settled on the seat of a Ford can make a very dull nation." I rather liked it myself. *Mr. Mason* feels very strongly about *Mr. H. P. Lovecraft,* whose letter I commented upon very freely a few weeks ago. *Mr. Mason* writes:

> "Of Mr. H. P. Lovecraft (whose letter you praised so highly) my opinion is that he is an intellectual snob. His 'hates,' and his reasons therefor, prove it. He seems to have it 'in for' every one who has helped or tried to help the 'herd,' 'rabble,' 'boobs,' as he terms us common mortals. Does he regard himself as one of Nietzsche's super-men, already arrived? He should re-member that, whatever heights he may have himself attained, he is related by blood, closely or remotely, to that same race of despised boobs."

Mr. Mason suggests another question for discussion: *What is the paramount end, aim and object of life?* He gives his answer as: Self-development and self-expression. Without self-development and self-expression there is no genuine happiness in life. This is a most interesting question and I am ready to open these columns to interesting comments. Get busy, readers, and write me what you think is the paramount aim and object of life. Make it short and to the point.

[211]

[February 1923?]

H. P. Lovecraft, 598 Angell Street, Providence, R.I., treads on firmer ground. He writes:

"I am interested in the communication of Mr. John Mason of Oklahoma, who calls me an 'intellectual snob' and wants to know what life is for. Wheth-er or not Mr. Mason is right about me is an interestingly debatable point, probably depending on the exact interpretation of his phrase. If he thinks that I possess any especial sense of personal distinction or importance, he is indu-bitably wrong; but [if] he simply means to point out that I cannot accept the ideas of a public uninstructed in the weighing of evidence and values, he is indubitably right. I might put the matter rather simply by saying that I am an extremely insignificant individual; who, looking at the universe as a cat may look at a king, arrives at certain conclusions through a very humble self-effacement and a most unassuming and impartial objectivity.

"When I object to the misdirection of energy involved in coddling the herd, it is not because I wish to disclaim relationship with the latter; but merely because I refuse to accept the traditional delusion about the sanctity and importance of mankind. I refuse to accept the unfounded and unphilo-sophical notion that the condition of humanity at large is of any particular significance, and do not care to blind myself to the obvious truth that mobocracy as a goal kills the finest development of all those things which cause men to struggle out of a purely animal state.

"Now this brings us around to Mr. Mason's interesting query about the paramount end, aim and object of life. If I understand him correctly, I think I agree with him; for he names self-development and self-expression, and esteems them because they produce happiness. One could ask for nothing more logical, and the only possible criticism would be a request for more explanation and definition.

"For my part, I think that in view of the now acknowledged purposeless-ness of the cosmos as a whole, it is most sensible to concur with the Epicurean in calling painlessness or tranquil contentment the only sensible end and object of life. So much is easy, but we begin to debate when we consider how we shall get our small and imperfect share of it. A certain school of thinkers, guided mostly by sentiment and by traditional conceptions of justice which are pure illusions, seeks to experiment with the uplift of the masses as masses, and to defy with fine words and attitudes the basic and far-reaching biological laws by which humanity naturally tends to stratification. They think it ought to be done even if it can't; though if you should ask them why they could only talk about 'justice,' without telling what justice is or why it is of such extreme importance. This is what I should call the 'ethical complex' if I belonged to the younger generation. One can sympathize with these people a great deal, for their state of mind is one that makes for delightful amiability. But they have to go down on the list of nuisances when we see how greatly their misplaced activities retard the growth of the real bits of color and contrast, dramatic conflict and individuality, glamour and glitter, splendor and refinement, wonder and beauty, which alone can furnish pleasure enough to make life worth living.

"Our platitudinarians call these things the 'shams' and their own illusions the 'realities,' 'things that count,' 'higher values,' 'worth-while things,' or 'big things of life'; but with a little impersonal analysis we can see that matters are just the other way around. The popular 'big things' are mere tenuous ideas based on visionary theories, whereas the pomps and pageants of vanity are solid realities—defining reality as the ability to produce truly poignant and pleasurable sensations in the mind of fancy. Of course this question of sensation can be used in a metaphysical way by Epicurean ascetics who contend that equal impressions may be derived from purely imaginary ideas. They are partly right, in that every man does not have to live in palaces and gardens in order to gain certain pleasurable pictures from these ideas. But it remains a fact that the idea would never have existed but for the reality in some shape or other—the only true Platonism is an inverted one.

"It seems to me a clear fact, that amidst the hopeless muddle of conflicting emotion and futile ambition which we call life, the only sensible course is to leave the way open for the free development and encouragement of sensation and beauty. Nothing really matters except that we have wondrous domes and spires and roofs to make our horizons beautiful; that we have flowers in majestic gardens to delight our esthetic senses; that we have poignant books and paintings and statuary to thrill us, and dreams of wonder and glamour, and a few human beings bred to comeliness, sensitiveness and delicacy. These alone are real, because they do not profess to be more than the stimuli of agreeable sensations. They are real because they make no claim to mythical 'deeper meanings' in a blind, bland cosmos devoid of deeper meanings.

"To appreciate them, however, one must have the intellectual independence to reject the unfounded ethical tradition and accept the inevitable aesthetic remainder. I try to have it, and am consequently able to delight in seeing the classically imposing or venerably beautiful college buildings, and the finely bred Nordic types of college boys, whereby the patience of your admirable contributor, Mr. Upton Sinclair, is so sorely tried. I don't care how these things came into being or how they are maintained; for the forces behind them, whatever they are, are amply justified by the beauty they have produced. Nasty kerosene makes lovely light—and I can forgive anything which has enabled me to see Harvard Yard or Morningside Heights[1] in the sunset.

"Energy spent in inciting social rebellion is destructive to the last degree. It will never benefit those whom it seeks to benefit, but may conceivably bring about a catastrophe by which every real incentive toward life and progress will perish as such things have perished before at the collapse of great civilizations. Personally I think our civilization is on the decline, and that it will peter out like that of Rome in the fifth century A.D., oppressed by its own old age and harassed by attacks of the proletarian class as Rome was harassed by attacks of external barbarians. It would be folly to hope that any civilization can be immortal.

"Thus it seems to me that we can, during the life of our civilization, gain more by worshipping refinement and beauty than by ignoring these things in attempts to thwart human nature. This does not mean that caste lines should be enforced; indeed, there is nothing more stupid than an effort to suppress natural merit; but it does mean that the standards of patrician art and intellect should not be lowered under any circumstances. It means that the rising newcomer ought, in deference to the forces creating beauty, to respect the field he is entering, and to exercise patience in dealing with that coolness at the gate which is after all merely the pettily disagreeable by-product of instincts which perform valuable preservative functions. We must all come to acknowledge that certain sacrifices are absolutely necessary to the maintenance of the supreme values of our futile and directionless existence. Am I a snob? It matters little. One should avoid prejudices against words. The only important thing is to say candidly what one thinks. That is self-expression, and possibly self-development; both excellent Masonian wishes.

"As a final word, I would remind Mr. Mason that my list of 'hates' was by no means prompted by any emotion so narrow and one-sided as sheer anti-democracy. Indeed, I recall some emphatic exceptions which ought not to have been overlooked. Heliogabalus was surely as arrogant a prince as any good democrat could desire for hating purposes. The German metaphysicians have never been claimed as voices of the people, while Mr. Harold Bell Wright is so overwhelmingly bourgeois that I fancy few genuine bolsheviks love him. And it would not take much wading in the turbid puddle of Mr. Eliot's effusions to discover that this gentleman is not only no ochlocrat, but an aristocratically ironic modern whose aesthetic personality really merits the designation of 'intellectual snob.'

"P.S. Aim and object of life 'short and to the point'? It can't be did! But if you want to print anything you might say:

"The paramount end, aim and object of life is contentment or tranquil pleasure; such as can be gained only by the worship and creation of beauty, and by the adoption of an imaginative and detached life which may enable us to appreciate the world as a beautiful object (as Schopenhauer tells us it is) without feeling too keenly the pain which inevitably results from reflecting on its relation to ourselves."

Mr. Lovecraft may be an "intellectual snob," but he is entirely right in observing that his view cannot be dismissed by this simple anathema. He is definite as an express train—though perhaps this is too roaring a simile for the quiet detachment of his letter. I am sure *Mr. Lovecraft* is mistaken, however, in thinking that the social rebels who quarrel with his view will have nothing but phrases with which to answer him. He is in for heavy fire, or my knowledge of rebels is a poor guide.[2]

Notes

1. The area in the Upper West Side of Manhattan where Columbia University is located.

2. A hostile response to this letter, written by D. H. Ashley of Wabash, IN, was published in the *Haldeman-Julius Weekly* No. 1431 (5 May 1923): 1.

To Edna Hyde

Edna von der Heide McDonald (1893–1962), known by amateur journalists around the world as "Vondy," was perhaps the most highly regarded poet in the field. She published her own journal, the *Inspiration,* and a book of verse as Edna Hyde titled *From under a Bushel* (1925). The subject of Lovecraft's letter was Albert A. Sandusky, an amateur journalist given to colorful slang.

[212]

[c. 1924]

And now there is Albert Sandusky's friendship with Howard Lovecraft, and who is there who will put on a par with Albert our erstwhile recluse? What common ground it is on which they meet, only they and the good lord know. But those of us who heard Albert speak at the Cleveland Convention banquet last summer can have no doubt of the earnestness and sincerity of that friendship. Albert has taken the trouble to dig out Lovecraft. And he has made me jealous of his findings. And to have Howard Lovecraft write me himself and say 'Bless the child. He wields a curious influence over me, for who else could have taught me to chant with jocose abandon, the contemporary shortage of the noble banana',[1] is to have an admission of the feat that Albert has achieved with natural-selfness, what the rest of us have never taken the trouble to attempt.

Notes

1. HPL refers to a popular novelty song of his day, "Yes! We Have No Bananas," by Frank Silver and Irving Cohn, from the Broadway revue *Make It Snappy* (1922).

To the Editor of the *Providence Sunday Journal*

After he returned to Providence on 17 April 1926, after two years in Brooklyn, Lovecraft found a renewed interest in the antiquities of his native city. His first letter is a general discussion of the significance of these antiquities to the cultural heritage of the city. In 1929 he was determined to urge the preservation of a series of warehouses built in the early 19th century, called Brick Row, that were scheduled for demolition to make way for a Hall of Records. Lovecraft wrote a letter in March 1929 (it was published in abridged form in the newspaper, but Lovecraft's T.Ms. survives). In December he wrote a letter and persuaded his friend James F. Morton to sign it: "But the big thing is to have the important Mortonian letter sent! I can't imagine that yᵉ ed won't print it—if he doesn't, he's a cursed traitor to the traditional beauty of his home burg!" (*Letters to James F. Morton* 203). But by this time the fate of Brick Row was already decided, and the buildings were torn down in 1930. Lovecraft wrote a poem, "The East India Brick Row" (7 December 1929), that was also published in the newspaper.

[213]

Asks Preservation of Old Buildings

Providence, Oct. 5[, 1926]

To the Editor of the Sunday Journal:

The interesting responses in the Evening Bulletin's "Why I like Providence" column, the recent publication of such popular or juvenile volumes as Miss Gleeson's "Colonial Rhode Island,"[1] the increasing array of historical pamphlets prepared by Dr. Carroll for the State department of education,[2] the illustrated series on "Odd Phases of Rhode Island History" by Mr. Chapin in the Sunday Journal,[3] the attention given by the Journal and Bulletin to neglected historic sites, and the widespread following of Colonial models in contemporary building operation, would all seem to indicate a wholesome and spontaneous awakening of this city to the unique wealth of antiquarian background.

It is refreshing to watch the emergence of the community at large from an almost un–New Englandish absorption in material gain and quantitative expansion to a mature appreciation of the more thoroughly grounded ancestral values in which other old towns like Philadelphia, Annapolis, Salem and Portsmouth have long taken so just and keen a pride.

In virtually no American city of equal size may one find such vivid and dramatic linkages with sources and developments as here; where the ancient hill still bears its graceful Georgian steeples and pilastered doorways, while bits of walled garden and steep green lane even now keep alive the memory of old home lots stretching back from the Towne Street.[4]

With the 1773 Market House, the 1761 Colony House, the 1770 College Edifice, the intact home of the old Providence Gazette, the 1783 Golden Ball Inn, the 1760 schoolhouse in Meeting street, four Georgian churches, the incomparably colourful row of 1816 warehouses in South Water street, and the notable variety of Colonial mansions and unchanged streets to be found for nearly a dozen squares east of the Great Bridge, Providence has a heritage of cumulative life-deposits and a fountain of deeply genuine beauty, interest, fascination and picturesqueness which most metropolitan districts must envy in vain, and which can be parallelled only by the mellower corners of such lovely old world towns as travellers haunt.

These things, the very vital spark and soul of a place from any aesthetic or really enlightened standpoint, are gifts not freely granted in our age and nation, and form so rare and so absolutely irreplaceable an endowment that we ought to live up to them by the exercise of a constant and diligent alertness lest they be impaired or swept away through coarser-grained conceptions of progress and urban splendour.

These remarks are impelled by the tidal wave of building replacement in which our city is just now immersed, and which though in the main undoubtedly a healthy process, might easily reach the proportions of vandalism if encouraged without a due regard for traditional landmarks. No one, it is true, can be sorry to witness or anticipate the end of such Victorian pests as Butler Exchange, Infantry Hall and the unspeakable Superior Court House; but when a well-balanced Georgian structure like the old Butler mansion next the Arcade[5] is removed, it would seem to be time to inquire whether the change be a real civic necessity or a mere expression of crude, restless commercial adventuring.

The Butler mansion is, of course, relatively a minor case; but its passing tends to renew one's apprehensions regarding the future of such really important scenic, historic, artistic, or atmospheric relics as the Arcade, the exquisite Joseph Brown mansion[6] recently vacated by the Providence National Bank, the quaint warehouses in South Water Street, and the characteristic Colonial homes—austere wooden affairs with their carved doorways—on the glamourous lanes that climb the hill.

Treasures like these are too precious to lose without a struggle, and deserve all the effort and finance which can be brought to [their] aid against the encroachments of boom-town "Babbitry." Any mushroom oil centre can have bright lights, skyscrapers and apartment blocks, but only a well-loved seat of centuries of pure taste and gracious living can have the urn-topped, ivied walls, the gabled and steepled vistas, the unexpected vista of cobbled court and alley, and all the manifold touches of elder landscape which mean Providence to those real natives who have grown up in it and cherish its every mood and aspect, summer and winter, sun and rain.

Organized protest saved the Old South Church in Boston and timely organization might do much toward preserving those buildings and landscape effects which contribute most to the matchless charm of our city. We shall be fortunate if the rising interest in local history and tradition can reach this stage of effectiveness before modern progress shall have wrought any further damage.

One might speculate pleasantly on the later evolution of such a movement if once successfully established—an evolution broadening it from antiquarian to general artistic aims and supplementing a purely defensive programme with one involving the rehabilitation (as successfully practiced in Boston and New York) of venerable neighbourhoods like northern Benefit street, whose appealing old houses and romantic topography merit a better fate than the slumdom now overtaking them.

This critical vigilance might ultimately be extended to the buildings and skyline of the city as a whole, old and new, with a view to the promotion of one harmonious architectural plan, and the discouragement of incongruous or excessively tall structures, which violate the traditional atmosphere of an old Georgian town. Boston has long enjoyed such intelligent zoning laws.

Whether all suggestions of this sort belong to the realm of impracticable visions, only time can tell. But if anyone need an incentive for active efforts in behalf of Old Providence, let him stand in Market Square some late afternoon when the slanting sunlight touches the Market House and the ancient hill roofs and belfries with gold, and throws magic around the dreaming wharves where Providence Indiamen used to ride at anchor. Then let him scale the slope in the dusk past the old white church and up the precipitous ways where yellow gleams begin to appear in small-paned windows and through fanlights set high over double flights of steps with curious wrought-iron railings. That is Old Providence—and any civilised spirit must agree that it is amply worth saving!

H. P. L.

Notes

1. Gleeson was the author of radio plays (1935–37) about early Rhode Island history, written for elementary and junior high schools in Rhode Island.

2. Charles Carroll (1876–1936), author of "Rhode Island Historical Calendar" (1922), "Outline of the Constitution of Rhode Island" (1925), "Outline of the Constitution of the United States" (1925), "Outline of the History of Rhode Island" (1925), and others.

3. Howard M. Chapin (1887–1940), Librarian of the Rhode Island Historical Society.

4. Cf. W. Paul Cook, *In Memoriam: Howard Phillips Lovecraft* (1941), who noted that "and where" was "one of Howard's favorite phrases when showing visitors around the city. He would stop at a spot where the view would be comparable to that of a country village. 'Where, except in Providence,' he would ask, 'in the midst of a large city, will you find a view like that?' The next view would be a sylvan scene. 'Where save in Providence, in the midst of a large city . . .' he would say. The next step it would be, 'Where, save in Providence. . . .' And after that the single word 'Where . . . ,' with an expressive gesture embracing the scene before him" (Joshi and Schultz, *Ave atque Vale,* 67).

5. The Westminster Arcade (1828) (called "Butler's Folly" when it was constructed) is a historic shopping center at 130 Westminster Street and 65 Weybosset Street in downtown Providence. The Arcade was built for Cyrus Butler (1767–1849). Butler, known locally as a miser, was persuaded to contribute generously to the construction of the Butler Hospital for the Insane, where HPL's father remained for the last five years of his life. Butler conducted business at 38 Weybosset and lived at 30 Westminster.

6. Built 1774, at 50 South Main Street.

[214]

The Old Brick Row

To the Editor of the Sunday Journal:

Discussion in these columns of the area between South Main and South Water Streets near Market Square, proposed either as a site for a Hall of Records or as a cleared plaza to enhance the effect of the new Court House, brings into very pertinent debate the future of the quaint, graceful old buildings now standing there. Behind it looms the far broader clash of city-planning ideals which it typifies; the eternal warfare, based on temperament and degree of sensitiveness to deep local currents of feeling, between those who cherish a landscape truly expressive of a town's individuality, and those who demand the uniformly modern, commercially efficient, and showily sumptuous at any cost.

Beyond doubt, the plans hitherto mentioned take a very superficial view in considering a permanent landscape for this focal, historic meeting-place of bay and hill. The side of tradition, which finds the soundest beauty in a retention of forms and proportions evolved from the continuous history of a proud old seaport, is well-nigh unrepresented; all the commentators apparently accepting for granted the cruder, flashier ideal of a stridently modernised city of pompous vistas and spruce, mid-Western architectural luxury—not a haven to charm the connoisseur of richly mellow old-world lanes, but a tungsten-drenched Midway to lure the hard-boiled buyer from Detroit, or a scenic flourish in deference to Seattle and Los Angeles aesthetes attuned to a futuristic Chicago or the maltreated Paris of Haussmann and Viollet-le-Duc.[1]

Amid such complacent "progressiveness" one feels almost timid in suggesting that the history and topography of Providence's older sections call for a decorative standard far removed from the expansive, the lavish, and the monumental. Suggest it one must, however, since the whole matter of a basic standard is evidently overlooked by those who glibly urge majestic spaces and imposing facades as fixed, absolute boons regardless of environment or atmosphere. To a chorus clamouring indiscriminately for lavishness and modernity in any and every place, the fact ought surely to be pointed out that what is appropriate in one type of locality is not necessarily so in another, and that the neighbourhood of our picturesque old "Market Parade" and head of navigation is distinctly unsuited to a formal, radical transformation upsetting its traditional character.

If Providence must have a sumptuous region of modern vistas like Boston's Back Bay, let it further emulate the latter by choosing an empty or unhistoric zone for the experiment. We have many sections topographically suited to this purpose; Exchange Place, Cathedral Square, and "Newmarket" (the confluence of Broad, Weybosset, Chestnut and Empire Streets) being typical examples. These sections, ugly or Victorian in their dominant motif except for the Exchange Place park and mall, would have little to lose through a change; and their renovation would form a net addition to the city's beauty. How much more sensible to make monumental developments where they are fitting and where nothing of importance need be sacrificed, than to purchase a new and doubtfully appropriate splendour at the expense of an historic elder beauty which is absolutely irreplaceable and perhaps of greater worth!

Specifically, there can be little question but that the proper treatment of the Market Square region is a modest one preserving its colonial and maritime lines and maintaining an atmospheric harmony with the ancient Market House and the two exquisite Georgian steeples visible close by. There is space in abundance at present, with a promise of still more when the complete covering of the river is accomplished. The line of slant-roofed brick warehouses in South Water Street, built in the decade following the "Great Gale" of 1815, rounds out a satisfying picture and symbol of the old Yankee seaport spirit which ought to be precious to every native Providentian, and which surely would be if a greater sense of its historic significance were aroused. We are singularly lucky in possessing this quaint, characteristic waterfront at our advanced stage of civic growth, for very few ports of this size have been able to keep such links with the romantic days of brigs, privateers, and East-Indiamen. As it is, with a splendidly intact row instead of merely a few scattered examples, we can rival the choicest of New England's coast towns in colour; presenting the unusual synthesis of a busy and populous life against a bit of visible background comparable to anything in Portsmouth,

Newburyport, or Newport. To lose such a generous, vivid fragment of the poetry of history at this late date, and for no valid reason, would be a tragedy peculiarly ironic.

But it is not merely as historic colour that this ancient brick row is worth cherishing. That indeed might be reason enough, for local fixity breeds a beauty of its own—a beauty of memories with very valid claims against the outward beauty of the eye. In this case, however, we have an actual visual beauty as well; for only a barbarian warped by garish standards could be blind to the intrinsic charm of these humbly harmonious structures. To call objects of such graceful simplicity and artlessly fine proportions "shabby, ramshackle old rookeries" is merely to display a stunted artistic feeling or ignorance of good design. They have been conspicuously praised by nearly every discriminating visitor who has seen them, especially Europeans of taste who know the magic of old-world towns and famous waterfronts. Offhand one recalls among these admirers the names of James Stephens, John Drinkwater, and Padraic Colum.[2] Nor are the best-qualified local judges any different in their verdicts. Only a year ago the supreme architectural authority of all, Mr. Norman M. Isham,[3] was quoted in the Journal as admiring the old brick row and wishing that it might be saved.

Just now the readers of that much-discussed novel "A Dead Man Dies" cannot fail to notice how the caustic author, blind though he is to nine-tenths of the city's good buildings and landscapes, is forced momentarily into a grudging appreciation by the sight of ancient Market Square. "There," he sourly concedes in somewhat laboured prose, "the old brick buildings facing the Providence river have a mellow redness that brings with it a glamour that neither the Italians vending garden truck nor the stench of the river can kill. Only a hundred yards away there is the harbour, and so long as there is salt water with a mast rising above it, there is romance."[4]

The arguments for removing the old buildings are of two kinds, aesthetic and practical. Those who stress the first set are perhaps the more misled in their premises; for their one major plea, whether they wish a new Hall of Records or a wholly cleared plaza, is that the present brick row forms an inadequate environment for the massive new Court House now rising on the hillside behind it. To one who has studied the design of the Court House as it will ultimately look, or even to one who has carefully noted the part already reared, it ought to be obvious that such a plea is almost the sheerest nonsense.

The builders of this edifice, like the builders of many other recent local structures, have a truer instinct for Providence atmosphere than have the present destruction-advocates; and are creating something which not only does not clash with the old waterside warehouses, but which actually carries on their tradition and derives an additional grace and mellowness from their presence. Naturally, a neo-classic or Renaissance temple of gleaming white marble would be at variance with the quaint Yankee market-place which history has given us, and would demand a stilted new landscape to match it; but as it happens, the designers had too much sense and taste to rear such a thing. Instead, they have provided a marvellously adroit group of wings or units in the familiar red brick of the local tradition; so that in effect the spacious new pile will be not one continuous mass of incongruous and overawing vastness, but a graceful cluster of separate roof-lines and gables, many of them reproducing Providence colonial types, whose total impression will be that of the artistically irregular skyline of a terraced hillside town—just such a town as Old Providence.

The harmony with the old brick row facing the water will be complete, since these genuine survivors of the Georgian era will set the keynote for the soaring tiers of neo-Georgian gables above them; forming an ideal starting-point for the eye and the imagination, and bridging the years between the early maritime Providence and the modern metropolis. No other building or buildings, and no open landscape development, could compare with this old row as a frame for the tall, white-belfried newcomer. The glamourous loveliness of clustered roofs rising over roofs in an ancient town is something which artists have always appreciated abroad, and which they are beginning to appreciate here, as attested by Mr. Henry J. Peck's recent exhibition of captivating local drawings and etchings.[5]

The practical arguments for removing the old buildings involve both the wish to widen South Main Street and the need for a Hall of Records. Regarding the first: this could of course be accomplished without disturbing the best group of structures concerned—the old brick row—since the latter fronts on South Water; yet it seems doubtful if even this programme of partial destruction is necessary in view of the continuous highway afforded by Canal and South Water Streets. The narrowness of South Main at this point is a quaint and not unbeautiful reminder of the old "Towne Street", as we may appreciate in the fine Duphinney[6] [*sic*] painting reproduced on a calendar two years ago; and it would surely be a pity to destroy such a picturesque survival without adequate reason. Moreover, one of the buildings in South Main (Nos. 27–31) is the old Nicholas Brown house, erected about 1760 and used during the sojourn of Rochambeau's troops as the abode of three of his officers—de Vauban, de Damas, and that appealing Swedish adventurer Count Axel de Fersen.[7] It is one of only three surviving Providence houses in which French officers lodged during the Revolution.

Much better than street-widening would be a judicious reconstruction of the old-time atmosphere on the west side of South Main Street, involving the removal of the hopelessly decrepit and already mutilated houses, and the restoration of the remainder. The one desirable alteration of street lines may perhaps be the razing of the two buildings north of Leonard's Lane, which would open a larger area around the foot of College Street and give a broader spaciousness to Market Square. Of these buildings one is nondescript and Victorian, while its colonial companion is too much altered and defaced to be of architectural value. This removal, of course, gives the South Water Street brick row an improved scenic position.

As for the need of a Hall of Records—it may reasonably be asked why no one has yet thought of using the old brick row itself for this purpose. By closing one or more of the alleys between South Main and South Water Streets—Wyeth, Hutchinson, and Mark Lane—as large a continuous structure as desired can be made of the venerable warehouses, linked where the gaps occur. The interiors, of course, would be totally removed and replaced by floors, partitions, and stacks of modern fireproof construction; but the grace of the ancient walls and roof-line would remain, and the ends of practicality prosper without loss to quaintness and tradition. There would, besides, be actual economy in such an arrangement; for the brickwork of Georgian times is as toughly solid as the Pyramids, and would form an admirable nucleus for the fresh interior. Successful experience [*sic*] with modern fireproof construction inside old brick walls, as in the Municipal Museum Building of Paterson, N.J.,[8] proves that the notion is by no means extravagant or chimerical. The long, narrow dimensions of the composite building thus formed could hardly constitute a major objection.

Urban mellowness, picturesqueness, and historic colour are rare enough in America, and it is not unreasonable to hope that as much as possible will be spared in the few towns lucky enough to retain them. This could be made certain if appreciative persons would reflect maturely on the relative values of things; balancing the aesthetic against the baldly commercial, and recognising the need of discrimination and local feeling in landscape standards.

—H. P. L.

Providence, March 20, 1929.

Notes

1. Georges-Eugène Haussmann (1809–1891), prefect of Seine (1853–70) who carried out an extensive renovation of Parisian boulevards, parks, etc. Eugène Emmanuel Viollet-le-Duc (1814–1879), French architect who restored many buildings in Paris and elsewhere in France destroyed or damaged during the French Revolution.

2. HPL refers to the writers James Stephens (Irish; 1880–1950), John Drinkwater (English; 1882–1937), and Padraic Colum (Irish; 1881–1972).

3. Norman Morrison Isham (1864–1943), prominent architectural historian, author, professor at Brown University and Rhode Island School of Design, ardent preservationist, and pioneer in the study of early American architecture.

4. Percy Marks (1891–1956). *A Dead Man Dies* (New York: Century Co., 1929), 222.

5. Henry J. Peck (1880–1964) had an exhibition of his work at the Providence Art Club, 7 to 18 November 1928. See HPL to Maurice W. Moe, 13 December 1928 (*MWM* 193–94): "I had the honour of meeting him in person, & told him, I wou'd not be satisfy'd till he had publisht a book of his collected urban sketches." *Glimpses of*

Providence: from Crayon Drawings, with Notes ([Warren, RI: Henry J. Peck, n.d.]) probably contains work from the exhibition.

6. Wilfred Israel Duphiney (1884–1960), portrait artist born in Central Falls, RI. He taught courses at Rhode Island School of Design for nearly 40 years. He made a living from commissioned portraits of (mostly) Rhode Islanders, and also illustration work. He was a member of the Providence Art Club and had a studio at the Fleur-de-Lys building at 7 Thomas Street on College Hill in Providence, RI.

7. Jacques Anne Joseph Le Prestre de Vauban (1754–1816), French general of the Ancien Régime who took part in the American War of Independence. Joseph François Louis Charles, duc de Damas (1758–1829), Rochambeau's aide de camp in 1780–81. Axel von Fersen the Younger (1755–1810), a Swedish count, Marshal of the Realm of Sweden from 1801, and aide-de-camp to Rochambeau in the American Revolutionary War. He was the mastermind behind a failed attempt to spirit the French royal family out of France during the Revolution.

8. Where James F. Morton (see following letter) was a curator.

[215] [TMS, JHL]

Save the Old Brick Row

To the Editor of the Sunday Journal:

For the past few months I have been astonished and grieved to hear from correspondents in Providence, where I am an appreciative annual visitor, that plans have been prepared for the destruction of that incomparably fine row of old brick warehouses in South Water Street, whose simple lines and perfect adaptation to the waterfront scene make them such a notable architectural asset to your lovely Georgian seaport. It increases my amazement to be told that this destruction is not planned for the usual commercial reasons, but in the interest of a "more beautiful" approach to the new court house in South Main Street; as if any sort of artificial landscape or monumental beauty could match the unstudied and spontaneous exquisiteness of the present arrangement; whereby the artistically grouped neo-colonial gables of the court house are seen rising gracefully out of the splendid line of really old slant roofs which the threatened warehouses form.

Cannot something be done to open the eyes of the "powers that be" to the real aesthetic merits of the situation? That the architecture of a city ought to sum up its spirit and history is a truth evidently well known in Providence; since a number of splendid new Georgian buildings—including the great court house itself—attest the local determination to preserve the Georgian tradition. Should it not then be obvious that this ancient and graceful row forms exactly the setting demanded by an old New England waterfront where history revolves around brave, glamorous memories of ships and cargoes and the Indies? Rows of warehouses like this are the most vivid of all symbols of the glorious maritime days which laid the foundations of New England's prosperity. They stretched along the wharves of all the great seaports—Portland, Portsmouth, Newburyport, Salem, Boston, New Bedford, and so on—and are still to be found in many of these cities. Providence, in view of its size and activity, is unusually lucky to have so magnificently intact a row of them; and it would be an act of peculiarly myopic vandalism to sacrifice this rare and harmonious heritage for the sake of a raw, "synthetic" beauty of more formal and coldly statuesque character. As one of New England ancestry, birth, and education, I may be pardoned for feeling very strongly in this matter.

That I am not alone in my opinion has been amply demonstrated to me by the fondness of artists for the old brick row as a subject, by various statements, and by several letters clipped from the Journal. I am told that many persons of the highest taste in Providence, including the eminent architectural authority Norman M. Isham and the late Henry A. Barker,[1] have strongly regretted the threatened doom of these artistic buildings; and that several European visitors of aesthetic distinction—John Drinkwater, James Stephens, and Padraic Colum among others—have given warm praise to their seasoned exquisiteness, and to the quiet way in which they carry on the picturesque seaport traditions of the old world. Not long ago, too, I saw them praised in a current novel—where it was said that their "mellow redness . . . . brings with it a glamour."

But what has impressed me most of all in the printed pleas for the row's retention is the suggestion that the buildings be carefully restored and given a new fireproof interior in order to serve as the city's much-needed Hall of Records. This has a very personal interest for me, insomuch as I happen to be writing these lines in just such a restored brick building—the Municipal Museum of Paterson, New Jersey, of which I have the honor to be Curator. Indeed, I noticed with pleasure that one of the letters in the Journal expressly cited the Paterson Museum as a case of successful restoration. This museum, established only five years ago, was allotted one of the city's older brick buildings as its initial unit; and at once proceeded to use the splendidly solid and graceful walls as the shell of a new interior. The result, as I think every visitor must agree, has been eminently satisfactory; for the retention of the massive old walls has in no way interfered with the modern arrangement and effectiveness of the hundred-per-cent-fireproof stories installed within. The economy of such a course is naturally very great—in fact, it is seldom that the most disinterested demands of art so exactly coincide with the most practical interests of municipal finance.

Pictures of the old brick row in the latest Netopian—receipt of which has called forth this eleventh-hour plea—increase the sense of sadness that one cannot help entertaining at the thought of Providence's losing this fine and eurythmic legacy of its adventurous past. It will seem strange to visit the city next spring and find a barren waste where I have been used to seeing this delicious bit of New England congruity, and I fervently hope that some determined and vigorous move on the part of local citizens and art-lovers may spare me such a painful experience.

JAMES F. MORTON.

Paterson Museum,
Paterson, N. J.,
Dec. 17, 1929.

Notes

1. Henry Ames Barker (1868–1929), city planner and corporation manager who died on 27 February.

To *Dragnet*

At the behest of August Derleth, Lovecraft dutifully composed a letter praising Derleth's story "The Adventure of the Black Narcissus," the first in a long series of detective stories featuring Derleth's sleuth Solar Pons, an imitation of Arthur Conan Doyle's Sherlock Holmes.

[216]

One for "The Black Bag"

[January 1929]

My dear sir:

Having lately come across a copy of the *Dragnet* for the first time, and noting your desire for opinions from readers, I am compelled to express my pleasure at the excellent quality of the publication.

In the February issue, to my mind, two stories stand out as of especially distinctive merit. One of these—"The Black Bag"[1]—handles the elements of suspense and surprise with a skill and assurance not often met with in popular magazine fiction; and somehow achieves a naturalness which causes the rather free use of coincidence to pass unnoticed.

The other—and perhaps the better technically—is "The Adventure of the Black Narcissus"[2] by August W. Derleth. The extremely fine craftsmanship of this tale creates a sense of constantly impending revelation and never-flagging interest; whilst the denouement comes with such a mingled inevitability and shock of surprise that we feel not only dramatically satisfied, but moved with a conviction of reality which no mere theatrical claptrap could supply. There is an element of unusual proportion and sanely consistent verisimilitude which does not clash at all with the rapid and brilliant movement and the expert knitting of plot-developments. I sincerely hope that Mr. Derleth is a permanent member of your writing staff, for his "Solar Pons" seems eminently qualified to take rank with the standard detectives of fiction.

With best wishes for your group of publications, I am

Yours very truly,

H. P. LOVECRAFT,
10 Barnes Street,
Providence, R. I.

Notes

1. By Mignon Eberhart. *Dragnet Magazine* 2, No. 1 (February 1929): 7–61.
2. *Dragnet Magazine* 2, No. 1 (February 1929): 69–75.

To "The Sideshow"

B[ertrand] K[elton] Hart (1892–1941) was the literary editor of the *Providence Journal,* who wrote a column, "The Sideshow," six days a week (i.e., in every daily issue except the *Sunday Journal*). In mid-November 1929, Hart had conducted a discussion of the weirdest story in literature. Lovecraft wrote to August Derleth that "his choices were so commonplace that I couldn't resist writing him myself & enclosing transcripts (with my own tales omitted) of your & Belknap's lists of best horror tales" (*ES* 230). Lovecraft refers to the fact that, since late September, Love-craft, Derleth, Long, and Donald Wandrei had been discussing this very subject in correspondence, in part as a result of Der-leth's work on his honor's thesis, "The Weird Tale in English Since 1890." Accordingly, Lovecraft sent lists by himself, Long, and Derleth to Hart, who published them in two separate col-umns. (Lovecraft alludes to a list by Wandrei [*ES* 218]; no such list was published.)

This discussion led to Hart's reading "The Call of Cthulhu" in T. Everett Harré's anthology *Beware After Dark!* (1929) and his observation that the home of Henry Anthony Wilcox (the Fleur-de-Lys Building at 7 Thomas Street) was one that Hart had once occupied. In response to Hart's jocular threat to send a ghost to haunt Lovecraft at 3 A.M., Lovecraft wrote "The Messenger" at 3:07 A.M. on 20 November and sent it to Hart; its appearance in "The Sideshow" for 3 December 1929 consti-tutes its first appearance in print. Hart apparently expressed a wish to meet Lovecraft, but Lovecraft felt awkward doing so and declined the opportunity.

Extracts from some of these columns were printed in Phil-omela Hart's compilation *The Sideshow of B. K. Hart* (Providence: Roger Williams Press, 1941).

[217]

[23 November 1929]

We told the story here, not long ago, of a lost railroad train which appeared in the dead of night on a main division and then drifted away as mysteriously into the nowhere. From one source and another it now appears the weird leg-end is known the world around, wherever the iron horse upon his twin steel strands penetrates lonely and barren regions.

But I like best a version which comes from France, and in particular from the low, unpeopled stretches of the Department Gironde, which lie by the Bassin d'Arachon. Here a great train bound in the night from the south for St. Vivien and le Verdon simply did not arrive. Nor has it ever arrived, and no stick nor bolt nor axle of it has ever been found. The likeliest theory is that it leaped a bridge into a small stream and was swallowed in the quicksands which abound there. . . . But 400 years ago, in the same countryside, there was a story of a prince's coach, journeying by night, and neither did that arrive; and so also did the quicksands swallow it.

It was while talking of the lost railroad train that we discussed also the question of the most eery story ever written. You may possibly remember that we spoke of Kipling's "Morrowbie Jukes," of "Halpin Frayser," of "The Rue Morgue" and many more.[1] I have since had an extremely interesting correspondence with Mr. H. P. Lovecraft of Providence, who has made a lifelong study of the macabre in literature, and who has written with high authority on the subject; and I have likewise many other letters, chiefly recommending single stories for consideration, for which I am grateful.

Mr. Lovecraft, and I think rightly, suggests that our casual list leaned toward the mechanically clever in eery stories, whereas the best examples of the mood are to be found (often in less well known authors) among those whose work "is actually profound and disturbing in its intimations of morbid violations of the order of the universe." A good definition of the field we are hunting! He cites Poe's delicately artistic "House of Usher" as against his "Rue Morgue" and some other merely ingenious works. "The difference is one between the workings of the deepest subconscious emotions and the conscious but superficial processes of a brilliant objective intellect. 'Usher' represents art; 'The Rue Morgue,' scientific image-carpentry."

The intimations of an exhaustive research embodied in Mr. Lovecraft's letters sent me on a somewhat gruesome but vastly stimulating lark through the libraries. He provided me with several tables of selections of "the best" in the field from which I endeavored to reach an independent opinion; and I am convinced that his own list is a little masterpiece of comparative criticism.

Here it is—and by no means must you consider reading these stories by midnight lamplight in a lonely house:

THE WILLOWS, by Algernon Blackwood.
THE WHITE POWDER, by Arthur Machen.
THE WHITE PEOPLE, by Arthur Machen.
THE BLACK SEAL, by Arthur Machen.
THE FALL OF THE HOUSE OF USHER, by Poe.
THE HOUSE OF SOUNDS, by M. P. Shiel.
THE YELLOW SIGN, by Robert W. Chambers.

The superiority of Machen in his metier is undoubted. It is not at all out of proportion to allot him three places in a list of seven, and I am glad Mr. Lovecraft offers an opportunity to print Machen's important but steadily forgotten name here. Welsh by origin—perhaps that explains something of his mood. Welsh from the hills which adduced the "Garthowen" of Allen Raine, and the wild scenes in Owen Rhoscomyl and Ernest Rhys,[2] and even in London, as a youth, he read (so he admits somewhere) Poe and DeQuincey above all others, and became a devotee of Burton's "Anatomy."[3]

"As a group of second choices," writes Mr. Lovecraft, "I would suggest these":

COUNT MAGNUS, by M. R. James.
HALPIN FRAYSER, by Ambrose Bierce.
THE SUITABLE SURROUNDINGS, by Ambrose Bierce.
SEATON'S AUNT, by Walter de la Mare.[4]

Surely De la Mare is a lone master in his kind. Where is there a more astonishing book than "The Return"? The second Bierce story, "The Suitable Surroundings," incidentally embodies the whole problem of whether to believe or to doubt. It hinges neatly on what Mr. Powys was saying the other night about ghosts, and his unquestioning acceptance of them. The story (if you happen not to know it) concerns a man who (like myself) has no room for ghosts in a busy week, and who defies a professional writer of eery yarns (say like Mr. Machen, or Mr. de la Mare) to provide him with a spook. The author hands the doubter an ancient manuscript, charged with ghoulish and unearthly details, and bids him read it by candlelight in a lonely haunted house, far from the town. As the doubter reads, and sharpens his sceptical resolution against the depressing surroundings, a boy who is out late looking for strayed cattle, sees the light in the window of the evil house and creeps up in fear and trembling to see what is taking place. Spellbound, with consummate courage, he presses his face against the glass, in terror-stricken awe, to watch this queer candlelight business; and at that precise moment the reader, feeling a presence, glances up swiftly. He sees a stark white face, leering at him through the glass, and falls dead of shock in a huddle beside his chair.

"I fight shy of tales dependent on a trick ending," notes Mr. Lovecraft. "Real horror dwells in atmosphere—even in language itself—and not in obviously stage-managed denouements and literary cap-pistol cracks." . . . I am sorry I can't reprint here an article Mr. Lovecraft published in a magazine some years ago,[5] for it gives a quick and useful grasp of the whole shivering subject. . . . He appends two other lists, from different hands, which I shall certainly use directly.

Mr. Powys suggested a test for ghost-doubters the other night which has the ring of practicality. . . . "You doubt them, of course," he said, "because we are here, six in a brightly lighted room, in a well inhabited city. But if you were alone at midnight in a notoriously haunted house, and something tapped on the back of your shoulder—what then?"[6]

For my part I should go home, rather swiftly.

Notes

1. Rudyard Kipling, "The Strange Ride of Morrowbie Jukes"; Ambrose Bierce, "The Death of Halpin Frayser"; Edgar Allan Poe, "The Murders in the Rue Morgue."

2. Allen Raine (1836–1908), *Garthowen: A Story of a Welsh Homestead* (1900). Owen Rhoscomyl was a Welsh novelist and author of *Flame-Bearers of Welsh History* (1905). Ernest Rhys (1859–1946) was an Anglo-Welsh novelist, essayist, and poet, and also longtime editor of Everyman's Library.

3. See Machen's autobiography *Far Off Things* (1922), in which he admits to a fondness for the authors in question (the last being Robert Burton, author of *An Anatomy of Melancholy*, 1621).

4. Of the above eleven stories, all but the last two appear on "The Favorite Weird Stories of H. P. Lovecraft" (*FF*, October 1934). That list also adds A. Merritt's "The Moon Pool."

5. "Supernatural Horror in Literature."

6. Hart refers to the British writer John Cowper Powys (1872–1963), some of whose work borders on the weird. The source of the quotation has not been located.

[218]

[25 November 1929]

A knocking in the chimney? There's a ghost in your grave.— Surrey Proverb.

The oftener ghosts are mentioned here, the more am I convinced that there is a great popular reluctance to surrender these foggy and insubstantial people to the enlightenments of progress. Because I spoke entirely about macabre tales, the shivering yarns of masters, the unseen beyond the certain, in this column the other day, I have been engulfed with useful information which will keep me pondering and sorting for many an hour. Mrs. Edgewood assures me (and doesn't care whether I laugh or not) that a ghost once took the pillows off her bed and hid them in the pantry; and I am quite ready to believe G. O. M., who met a queer man on a New Hampshire road looking for the way to Dublin. I don't in the least see why ghosts may not get out of their own country. And if you read the wonderful incident in Padraic Colum's "Boy in Erin," [*sic*] where the Little People tried to help Daniel O'Connell 40 years too late, you will agree with me that the time factor and the geographic dimension may very well become confused when you are no longer a physical and taxable fact.

The proper way to approach ghosts, of course, is with an open mind and one jib bent to the leeward. So long as it is pleasant to explore the infinite possibilities of the theme it seems too bad to take a didactic position. You can, if assailed by a logical minded materialist, always slip back into the orthodox attitude; and meanwhile the diversions of spook-chasing will keep you from remembering the desolate certainties of the impending winter.

The lists of eery stories, with which Mr. Lovecraft supplied us on Saturday, offer a sensible avenue of inquiry. In books you need accept nothing, for you may always enjoy a tale without framing a judgment, provided you are of the sort content to accept hospitality without abusing your host. . . . I have just been re-reading "Ghost Stories of an Antiquary,"[1] and I recommend it, in its entirety, to advanced explorers of the unearthly. And I also suggest that you get hold of the stories of Mr. M. P. Shiel, whether the ghostly ones or that good yarn, "How the Old Woman Got Home."

I mentioned some other lists of eery stories which Mr. Lovecraft sent me. The two which follow are clearly indicative of differences in the manner of approach. There is a temperament and an inclination in everything.

The first was drawn up by Mr. Frank Belknap Long, Jr., of New York; and I find myself bound to like it enormously because it contains so much that has already appealed very strongly to me. The John Buchan thing is especially pleasant to meet here. (He calls himself "Buckon" by the way.) And Andreyev's "Lazarus" is unforgettable. Andreyev could adduce terror, and stark tragedy, beyond the hope of any in his heyday—as much outside the macabre tale as in it. I mind that horrible and heart-breaking closing scene in "The Waltz of the Dogs," where Henry Tile plays his silly little piece over and over again at the piano, half undressed, and then saunters out to shoot himself.

Here is Mr. Belknap Long's list of "the twenty-eight best tales of supernatural horror":

LAZARUS, by Leonid Andreyev.
NEGOTIUM PERAMBULANS, by E. F. Benson.
THE WILLOWS, by Algernon Blackwood.
THE WENDIGO, by Algernon Blackwood.
SKULE SKERRY, by John Buchan.
HALPIN FRAYSER, by Ambrose Bierce.
THE YELLOW SIGN, by Robert W. Chambers.
THE UPPER BERTH, by F. Marion Crawford.
BETHMOORA, by Lord Dunsany.
THE MONKEY'S PAW, by W. W. Jacobs.
COUNT MAGNUS, by M. R. James.
THE TREASURE OF ABBOT THOMAS, by M. R. James.
AN EPISODE OF CATHEDRAL HISTORY, by M. R. James.
(With a certain neat efficiency Mr. James pitched his Cathedral tales in the memorable non-existent Barsetshire cathedral close of Trollope.)
THE WHITE PEOPLE, by Arthur Machen.

THE WHITE POWDER, by Arthur Machen.
THE GREAT GOD PAN, by Arthur Machen.
THE BLACK SEAL, by Arthur Machen.
(It may be remembered that two of these were in Mr. Lovecraft's first list.)
THE HORLA, by Guy de Maupassant.
THE BAD LANDS, by John Metcalfe.
METZENGERSTEIN, by Edgar Allan Poe.
LIGEIA, by Poe.
THE FALL OF THE HOUSE OF USHER, by Poe.
THE MASQUE OF THE RED DEATH, by Poe.
MANUSCRIPT FOUND IN A BOTTLE, by Poe.
THE HOUSE OF SOUNDS, by M. P. Shiel.
HE COMETH AND HE PASSETH BY, by H. R. Wakefield.
THE 17TH HOLE AT DUNCASTER, by H. R. Wakefield.

Apparently Poe's "Usher" will get into any and every list we may compile on this theme. But I have always suspected that there is a good deal of deliberate leg-pulling in the heavy rhetorical style of it.

Mr. August W. Derleth, of Madison, Wisconsin, began the second list, like Mr. Lovecraft, with The Willows, of Blackwood. He introduces a less well known one from Bierce—The Inhabitant of Carcosa—and follows with The Yellow Sign, by Robert W. Chambers; The Upper Berth, by F. Marion Crawford; The Monkey's Paw, by W. W. Jacobs; A View from a Hill, by M. R. James (one of his best); Seaton's Aunt, by De la Mare; The House of Sounds, by Shiel; A Dream of Armageddon, by H. G. Wells (I can't go with him there!), and Mary E. Wilkins Freeman's Shadows on the Wall.

If it's a creeping spine you need most of all, then here you have it. If you read all these you'll be a bit surprised to find how homely and comfortable it is to get out in the public traffic again!

Notes

1. The 1904 collection by M. R. James.

[219]

[29 November 1929]

We have been talking a good deal lately about ghosts, and revenants, and the weird things which do or do not happen over the borderline of fact, and consequently I have been paying more than usual attention to books that touch on the theme. And when I stumbled on a new one called "Beware After Dark" (which is a collection of strange tales selected by Mr. T. Everett Harré) I was greatly pleased. It is a good book in its kind. The Arthur Machen story of the white powder is here, and Benson's "Negotium Perambulans," and Andreyev's "Lazarus," and many more lately recommended in this column. But what startled me wide awake and brought back the two-headed dog and the white morning rain over the broken back of Waterman Street Hill, was a passage that leaped to my eye the moment I opened the book.

> "The manuscript was divided into two sections, the first of which was headed: 1925—Dream and Dream Work of H. A. Wilcox, 7 Thomas Street, Providence, R. I."

We always tend to shy a little at a familiar label, caught in the bat-wing flight of print, but this was so precisely the house in which I had lived, and so much the place for a ghost to happen in a book called "Beware After Dark!" that I fancy I gasped. We do not look for our everyday neighbors in works of fiction, in any case, and least of all do we expect to find them haunted.

Now mark how well the author achieved verisimilitude in this tale. Henry Arthur Wilcox is a name with an accurate Providence timbre to it. He had been (and what more plausible) a student at the Rhode Island School of Design, and lived alone at 7 Thomas Street, rather a dark and puzzling fellow, who was looked upon as eccentric. "Even the Providence Art Club, anxious to preserve its conservatism, had found him quite hopeless." Presently we see him conferring with "George Gammell Angell, professor emeritus of Semitic languages at Brown University;" and before long Professor Angell is (as the tabloids might phrase it) strangely dead in city street. Skillful, that! And disconcerting. I do not mind discovering my mystery-story victims strewn ten thick upon the London Embankment or down the mean streets of Liverpool; and you have only to murmur Hammersmith to adduce for me the linked vision of a corpse and a Scotland Yard inspector. But when you drop your snarled skein of horror and death into my own dooryard I begin to grow a little nervous about the business. . . . The tale (as strange a thing as ever I set eyes upon!) is entitled "The Call of Cthulhu" and it implies, entirely without my consent, that the whilom tenant of my old chambers used to toss in his dreams and hear vast abysmal voices summoning him from a terrific void in the world's heart. Linked to those once-pleasant rooms, where birch-wood generally flamed on a cheerful hearth, I must now believe there stretches a ghastly, eldritch chain ending in a voodoo-like pool of carking horror far down in the antipodes. . . . I won't have it. My own little ghost shadows, slinking home to the sun in the healthy dawn, are quite enough for Thomas Street, and I reject these sinister brutes from the other side of the beyond, cluttering up the traffic with their gargantuan bulk.

Yet they have a power over me, as the old people used to say, because there is something more than a chance connection between the Thomas Street devils and The Sideshow. I had only to turn to the title-line to find it out. And there, to be sure, sailed the name of one of our most engaging contributors—indeed the one who set us all off on this ghost hunt—Mr. H. P. Lovecraft. . . . He is, by the bye, widely recognized as a skillful writer of weird tales. Mr. E. J. O'Brien, in "The Best Short Stories of 1929" gives the laudatory three-star ranking to his yarn, "The Dunwich Horror," and other large distinctions have befallen him. . . . Personally I congratulate him upon the dark spirits he has evoked in Thomas Street, but I shall not be happy until, joining league with wraiths and ghouls, I have plumped down at least one large and abiding ghost by way of reprisal upon his own doorstep in Barnes Street. . . . I think I shall teach it to moan in a minor dissonance every morning at 3 o'clock sharp, with a clinking of chains.

Or would it be better to have it prowl through the cellar, murmuring "Hushhushshsh" the livelong night?

[220]

[30 November 1929]

Mr. August W. Derleth, of Madison, Wisconsin, whose list of "best" weird stories was cited here the other day, writes me he is preparing a thesis on the twelve best written in English between 1890 and 1930;[1] and here they are—to be taken as all of equal merit:

> A View from a Hill, by Montague R. James.
> The Monkey's Paw, by W. W. Jacobs.
> The White People, by Arthur Machen.
> A Dream of Armageddon, by H. G. Wells.
> The Willows, by Algernon Blackwood.
> The House of Sounds, by M. P. Shiel.
> The Shadows on the Wall, by Mary E. Wilkins Freeman.
> Seaton's Aunt, by Walter de la Mare.
> The Upper Berth, by F. Marion Crawford.
> The Yellow Sign, by Robert W. Chambers.
> The Death of Halpin Frayser, by Ambrose Bierce.
> The Outsider, by H. P. Lovecraft.

Pray notice the last item, which I have purposely shifted to the foot for emphasis. This is the gentleman (but not the story) involved in the ha'nting of Thomas Street.

One of the most charming ghosts I have ever heard of is described in a letter from A. L. H., of Pawtucket, who met it (more than once) on an old farm near Woonsocket; but I am not at liberty to put black print upon its head as yet. The same writer commends Kipling's "They"; and so do I. . . . There used to be a ghost in Kingston (writes D. L. D.); who pumped at the well at night on an abandoned farm and rattled the pails prodigiously. Evidence indisputable: the well finally went dry.

Notes

1. The thesis, "The Weird Tale in English Since 1890" (Univ. of Wisconsin, 1930; *Ghost* No. 3 (1945): 5–32), was actually a wide-ranging study of weird fiction during this period; it borrowed heavily from "Supernatural Horror in Literature."

[221]

[3 December 1929]

Really, I hardly meant it when I announced the other day that I would send a ghost up to Barnes Street to ha'nt Mr. H. P. Lovecraft, the ingenious doctor of mysteries, as a reprisal for the vast creatures he had sent stalking down Thomas Street in "The Call of Cthulhu." You know how it was: he happened to pitch his lumbering great devils into the very room I used to occupy, and I thought the least I could do, in a spirit of mischief, was to ask my favorite wraith the favor of rattling his doorlatch at three in the morning. . . . With (I think I said), a clanking of chains. . . . But all I can do now is to advise amateurs not to tinker around with the slippery half-people of the night, because you never know when one of them is loaded. I merely spoke sketchily about it to my ghost (a good fellow, though given to playing chess in the chimney) and away he went. And next morning I found this in my mail, dated from Mr. Lovecraft's study, at 3:07 a.m., and dedicated to me—pensively:

> The Thing, he said, would come that night at three
> From the old churchyard on the hill below;
> But crouching by an oak fire's wholesome glow
> I tried to tell myself it could not be.
> Surely, I mused, it was a pleasantry
> Devised by one who did not truly know
> The Elder Sign bequeathed from long ago,
> That sets the fumbling forms of darkness free.
>
> He had not meant it—no—but still I lit
> Another lamp as starry Leo climbed
> Out of the Seekonk, and a steeple chimed
> THREE—and the firelight faded, bit by bit.
> Then at the door that cautious rattling came—
> And the mad truth devoured me like a flame!

You see what happens when you toy with immeasurable properties. I no more intended—. But there! it's done. And the best I can do now is to try to get my hired ghost to come home and leave off his reckless latch rattling. . . .

He ought to be a proud ghost. That is a very adroit poem he inspired. No connoisseur of sound verse will fail to notice that it is a skillful exercise in one of the best forms of the Petrarchan sonnet. . . . That point matters. The half-people prefer to be discussed either in sonnets or in iambic pentameter—never in rondels or galloping couplets. And least of all in limericks.

[222]

[18 March 1930]

I hoped that a reference to "The Turn of the Screw" as one of the greatest mystery yarns would draw fire from Barnes Street, where Mr. H. P. Lovecraft sits (as I picture him) sorting out the ha[']nts and were-wolves of the world with the fingers of a prestidigitator. I tried to trace this great Jamesian story to the effect of the Newport pavements. . . . Barnes Street has obliged:

Dear Showman:
　　I'd hesitate to dispute any dictum assigning a high place to "The Turn of the Screw" in American macabre literature. Really, it impresses me even more in retrospect—when I can evoke its shadowy intimations in terms of vague impulse and imagery—than it did during actual perusal, when I could not be unconscious of the prolix, palaeoparthenoid finicality of the language which Mr. James felt impelled to employ in order to secure his precise shadings of mood and meaning. It is news to me that the "Turn" has achieved Modern Library reprinting! This means one more Spanish milled dollar drawn forth from the stocking in the chimney-niche, even as did the late reprinting of Lafcadio Hearn's "Kwaidan" in the Riverside Library!
　　And it would take more than a liqueous prop to alienate ME from old Newport! As the last surviving Georgian (I–IV, not V!) I could not exist without an occasional sight of its elder charm. If they tear down any more ancient buildings in Providence I vow I shall transfer my loyalty altogether to the earlier seat of Rhode Island civilization. . . . At present I don't even bother to invent other reasons for visiting Newport and saluting the gold crown on Trinity's spire!
　　　　Yours, etc.
　　　　　　BARNES STREET.

　　What was the famous mot about James's changing style and his three stages of progress? . . . "James the First, James the Second, and the Old Pretender".[1] . . . A. B. M. recalls it. . . . James's "prolix, palaeoparthenoid finicality" of style affected more than James! When you find dark passages in Conrad—passages harried about with the attenuate qualification and the anticipatory negation—you will know they are there because the two great men

held communion over the riddle of style. The American who became an Englishman was stronger here than the Pole who followed him. . . . The simplicity begotten of long nights under the Southern Cross, with high winds
sweeping the stars, was all muddled up the moment that Lord Jim's creator
came under the syntactical psychotherapy of the man from Newport. . . . The
interpolated parentheses stunned the old sailor like a marlin spike, and without so much as a protest he began to call a spade a utilitarian implement of
husbandry.

Notes

1. The anecdote is found in Philip Guedalla, *Supers and Supermen: Studies in Politics, History and Letters* (New York: Knopf, 1924), 45. Guedalla refers to two kings of England
and the Stuart "pretender" James [III] (1688–1766). The Young Pretender, Charles
[III] (1720–1788), "Bonnie Prince Charlie," was the son of the Old Pretender.

[223]

[13 November 1931]

It was late twilight when the Rev. Mr. Jennings departed from London for his
distant rectory at Kenlis, in the Warwickshire reaches, and the lonely old omnibus that rumbled along the road with no other passenger aboard was unlighted and doubly dark for the increasing blackness without. It might,
almost, have been driven by a blind force, rather than a busman, for there
was no touch of human kinship between the solitary passenger and the opera-
tor, remote on the seat outside. . . . Overtired with late nights in his library
and long days in his parish, the Rev. Mr. Jennings was low in spirit. . . . Let
me quote his own words to Dr. Hesselius:

> "The interior of the omnibus was nearly dark. I had observed in the cor-
> ner opposite to me at the other side two small circular reflections, as it
> seemed to me of a reddish light. They were about two inches apart, and about
> the size of buttons. I began to speculate, as listless men will, upon this trifle.
> From what centre did that faint but deep red light come, and from what—
> glass beads, buttons, toy decorations—was it reflected? We were lumbering
> along gently, having nearly a mile still to go. I had not solved the puzzle, and
> it became in another minute more odd, for these two luminous points, with
> a sudden jerk, descended nearer the floor, and then as suddenly rose to the
> level of the seat on which I was sitting and then I saw them no more."

Yes, this is taken from a ghost-story—from "Green Tea", by Mr. J. Sheridan
Le Fanu; and I am printing it to anticipate unfairly a letter that presently follows. . . . Dr. Jennings, by riveting his eyes closely upon the phenomenon, at
length discerned that it was a little black monkey, sitting on the seat and grin-

ning at him. . . . He poked at it with his umbrella—and the umbrella went
right through the monkey, who didn't at all mind!

"I can't in the least convey to you the kind of horror I felt. As I looked
again it made a little skip back, quite into the corner. . . . I stopped the bus
and got out."

So did the monkey. It followed him home. It came into the house. It remained there always! . . . Sitting on a shelf, crouching under a chair, brooding
evily [*sic*] across the table with venom and malice in its eyes, the strange, insubstantial creature remained until——.

Never mind the rest of it now. If you care to know, look up the story. I
merely want to get a head-start by demonstrating (at least to my own satisfaction) that Mr. Le Fanu has written here a very ghoulish and completely successful ghost-yarn. . . . Because my ancient and immensely-informed mentor
in these matters, Mr. H. P. Lovecraft of Providence (himself the author of
many such tales, and one among the best ever I have seen), thinks otherwise. . . . You may remember that I called upon him the other day to express
a view on the Colin de la Mare collection of tales of witchery and wanderers by
night. His answer came to me, appropriately enough upon a card from Salem,
carrying a view of a house where hanged witches still congregate at night:

Dear Showman:

Barnes Street would be delighted to effuse opinions regarding "They
Walk Again" had this desiderate volume yet become visible on that thor-
oughfare. The lack is surely one which the near future must supply! But I
will say, without having seen the book, that if J. Sheridan Le Fanu has ev-
er written anything with a REAL (as distinguished from a conventional)
shudder, I still have a treat in store for me.[1] And if one wants a genuine
Dunsanian shiver, what's the excuse for not choosing "Bethmoora" or
"Poor Old Bill"?[2] And who can, on second thought, place anything of
M. R. James's above "Count Magnus" or "The Treasure of Abbot Thom-
as"? De gustibus, etc. I'd like to concoct an anthology some day!
Yours, etc.,
H. P. L.

I wish he'd do that! You may recall that a year or so ago, while engaged
in an examination of the same territory, he adduced for us a number of remarkable lists of possibilities. I have amused myself since with hunting out all
the stories he listed that were new to me and I am now convinced that he is
either a master of black magic or possesses an extraordinary sense of the weird.

It is a fault of the majority of current anthologies of spooky tales that little distinction is made between the purely fantastic and the psychologically
plausible. The perfect story of apprehension and terror, it seems to me, will

be in the order of Henry James's "Turn of the Screw," and not at all in the order of, let us say, Kipling's "Morrowbie Jukes." . . . There is a third order of ghost stories which I like very much indeed but which certainly has no standing with such experts as Mr. Lovecraft and Mr. Blackwood and Mr. James and the rest—the comic spook yarn. Possibly the best available example of what I mean is Richard Middleton's "Ghost Ship," in which, during a night of terrific rain and wind, the little village of Fairfield beyond Portsmouth Road was visited by a pirate galleon and its captain, who came to anchor miles and miles from the sea in a turnip field. . . . "I seem to have brought her rather far up the harbor," murmured the captain. . . . Fairfield had always prided itself on its ghosts, and didn't very much mind the intrusion—at first. It was regular practice there for the lads and lassies who had left this world to foregather on the village green and talk away the night; and most everybody in town was on hobnobbing terms with his great grandfather or his aunt's uncle's grandmother. Some of them, indeed, boarded around in the different houses, and came and went very much like ordinary people. . . . But suddenly they all started to get drunk—especially the younger ones. Citizens began to complain that their great-uncles had come home at two in the morning and fallen downstairs, or that veterans of the Battle of Hastings were holding reunions in the attic and making too much noise about it. . . . The upshot of it was that the captain of the galleon had been giving away free rum, in an effort to recruit a new ghost crew for his voyage to sea. The minister went down to remonstrate and the captain was very polite. He pointed out that a storm was coming up and that he would sail away with it. . . . He did. And all the young ghosts with him, singing in the night: high against the moon, with all lights blazing. And Fairfield was never the same old place again. . . . Such a yarn leaves no shiver behind it, but only laughter.

Notes

1. HPL wrote to August Derleth (14 November 1931): "I hardly fancied that B K H would print a postcard which merely disclaimed knowledge in the desired field—but anything makes copy" (*ES* 411). It is unclear whether HPL ever saw or read *They Walk Again.*
2. "Bethmoora" and "Poor Old Bill," in Lord Dunsany's *A Dreamer's Tales* (1910).

To the *Exeter* [NH] *News-Letter*

[224]

[November 1930]

Again we hear something more about Captain Huse's elephant. H. P. Lovecraft, of Providence, Rhode Island, writes: "I am an interested follower of 'Rockingham's Rambles.' Not long ago I noticed an item concerning an elephant exhibited at a New Hampshire tavern at some time around or subsequent to 1800 and tentatively mentioned as the first of its kind in the United States. This leads me to volunteer an account of a considerably earlier exhibition of the sort in Providence—the central figures of which, according to dimensions, is not likely to have been the pachyderm involved in the later display.

["]The Providence Gazette for July 1, 1797, and the U. S. Chronicle for June 29 of that year, carry advertisements of an elephant exhibited in the rear of The Exchange Coffee House (now demolished) on Market Square. It was to remain only a single week, before moving on for an exhibition at Cambridge, Mass. The animal was advertised as of '3000 weight,' and of less than full growth; present measurements being 15 feet 6 inches from tip of trunk to tip of tail, 10 feet 6 inches around the body, 7 feet 2 inches around the head, 3 feet 2 inches around the leg above the knee, and 2 feet 2 inches around the ankle. The advertisement adds: 'He eats 130 weight a day and drinks all kinds of spirituous liquors; sometimes he has drunk 30 bottles of porter, drawing the corks with his trunk. The price of admission to view this stupendous monster is for adults a quarter of a dollar; for children an eighth of a dollar, or a bit.'

["]The second elephant in Providence was advertised in the Gazette for August 22, 1818, and was exhibited in the rear of Daniel Hemmenway's Inn. Some historians, overlooking the beast of 1797, have spoken of this as the first.

["]Let me say in conclusion that, as a person of retrospective cast and very fond of New England antiquities, I always peruse 'Rockingham's Rambles' with the greatest pleasure. It is interesting to have these sidelights on the daily life of a northern community, to compare with the annals of a somewhat differently founded and developed region on New England's southern coast.["]

Mr. Lovecraft adds this: "P.S. It is barely possible that the Providence elephant of 1797 might be the later Greenland one—growth accounting for the greater dimensions of the latter. This assumes, of course, that the 'he' of the Providence advertisement was merely rhetorical in its implications of gender."

Notes

1. HPL's letter is in response to "Rockingham's Rambles" of 10 October 1930. Exeter, NH, is in Rockingham County.

To Vincent B. Haggerty

Vincent B[artholemew] Haggerty (1888–1943) was an amateur journalist and publisher of *Amateur Affairs*. He was associated with the NAPA in the 1920s and 1930s. With Lovecraft and Jennie K. Plaisier, he was a co-author of "Report of the Executive Judges," *National Amateur* (June 1936).

[225]

[mid-1935]

[. . .] Tarrytown is the sort of place that fascinates me more than any other kind. I love the steep streets that climb dizzily from the river front, the old traditions, and the picturesque hinterland. It is hard to beat the old Dutch church with its adjacent cemetery and the impressive ravine behind it.[1]

Notes

1. HPL first visited Tarrytown, NY (where Washington Irving had set "The Legend of Sleepy Hollow"), in May 1928. At that time he saw the Old Dutch Church of Sleepy Hollow (1685). He describes it in the essay "Observations on Several Parts of America" (1928; *CE* 4.18–19).

Report of the Executive Judges

Lovecraft, as one of the three executive judges for the 1935–36 term, gives his opinion on the debates between Hyman Bradofsky and others (as related in "Some Current Motives and Practices" [1936; CE 1.399–403]).

[226]

Chicago, Illinois,
April 25, 1936.

To the Members of
The National Amateur Press Association:

Although no report has hitherto appeared from the office of the Executive Judges, the year has been a very busy one for the members of the Board. Much of the work placed upon their shoulders has remained unfinished for reasons beyond their control, but of sufficient importance to warrant the delays involved. Reports on these unfinished problems would have been very misleading to the members as well as unfair and unjust to those concerned.

In August, 1935, the Board received the request of Mr. O. W. Hinrichs[1] for permission to increase the number of pages in the September *National Amateur*. Mr. Lovecraft being absent on a vacation, the desired permission was granted on August 23, 1935, by Judges Plaisier and Haggerty.[2]

On October 31, 1935, Edwin Hadley Smith protested the 1934–35 History and Story Laureate awards to Ralph W. Babcock, Jr., and Richard Foster, respectively, for contributions appearing in *The Red Rooster* for May 1935; offering evidence to prove that this number of *The Red Rooster* was actually not completed or published until September 1935. An investigation of the case showed that the disputed entries were printed each in a separate 8-page 6 × 9 advance section of the issue in question, both seen by a limited number of members on or around the first of May. The requirements of the constitution are:

"Article XI, Section 2: Laureate Title. In order to compete for the title 'Laureate' in any department except that of editorials, an active member must publish his entry in an amateur paper by May 1 and send two marked copies of the paper to the Vice President."

Notice of this protest was at once sent to Mr. Babcock and Mr. Foster, and Mr. Babcock agreed to furnish information on the disputed points upon his return from college at Thanksgiving time. The holiday season being too short to permit Mr. Babcock to make a thorough search through his files for evidence concerning the completion and distribution of the May *Red Rooster*, time was extended until the Christmas vacation. Meanwhile Mr. Babcock relinquished his right to the History Laureateship awarded his article, "The Decline and Rebirth of the N.A.P.A.," which appeared in the History Section of the disputed issue, but requested an extension of time until his spring vacation to furnish proof regarding the date and distribution of the Feature Section containing the story by Richard Foster: "As Fate Wills It," which received the Laureate award.

Mr. Babcock having ultimately furnished sufficient proof of the completion and distribution of the Feature Section in compliance with the requirements of the Constitution, Executive Judges Lovecraft and Plaisier find that the Story Laureate award to Richard Foster for "As Fate Wills It", appearing in Section II (Feature Section) of the May *Red Rooster*, was properly made. Mr. Haggerty declined to rule on this question, having been the Judge of Histories at the time.

In view of Mr. Babcock's withdrawal, and of the doubtful circulation of the History Section, the Board finds that the History Laureateship for 1934–35 devolves upon the winner of the Honourable Mention title, Chester P. Bradley, for his "History of the N.A.P.A. 1933–34" in *The Perspective Review* for Autumn, 1934.

Resolutions adopted by the Oakland Amateur Press Club on December 15, 1935, regarding omissions from President Bradofsky's reports of appointments, changes in official personnel and reappointments, were forwarded to the Judges in January. After careful consideration of the evidence submitted, the Judges unanimously agreed that the omissions in President Bradofsky's messages were without censurable intent. The matter having been called to the President's attention, the explanation was accepted by the Oakland Amateur Press Club without further comment.

On January 8, 1936, President Bradofsky requested a ruling regarding his functions as a member of the Constitution Committee in reconciling apparently conflicting or overlapping amendments submitted by Edwin Hadley Smith and Harold Segal,[3] and an interpretation of the ruling of the previous year's judges (*Nat. Am.* June 1935, p. 14) regarding the general functions of the Committee in relation to the formulation of defectively framed amendments. He was given the necessary information and advised that the Committee is not required to formulate amendments which are submitted merely in outline and without the final text intended.

On January 14, President Bradofsky requested a specific ruling on a case involving the same principle; that of a set of unformulated suggestions for amendments submitted to the Constitution Committee by Victor A. Moitoret and Marion C. Morcom.[4] He was advised that the re-writing of these suggestions as true proposed amendments formed no part of the Committee's duty and that they should be returned to their authors for preparation and re-submission in proper form. The Judges also ruled that the authors, in view of their good faith in submitting the suggestions before the expiration of the time allowed for amendments, should be granted a reasonable period after the official time-limit for the necessary preparation and re-submission.

Also on January 14, Pres. Bradofsky requested a ruling on a complete new Constitution submitted by Ex-Pres. Babcock, and a general ruling on the right of members of the Constitution Committee to propose amendments themselves. He was advised that Mr. Babcock's submission of the new Constitution was legal, and that there is no barrier against the proposal of amendments by members of the Committee. He was, however, further advised to suggest to Mr. Babcock that the proposed new constitution be voluntarily withdrawn and re-submitted in the more logical form of separate amendments. In all three of these constitutional matters President Bradofsky acted promptly in accordance with the Board's rulings.

On March 18, 1936, Edwin Hadley Smith preferred charges to the Board regarding the delay of Ralph W. Babcock, Jr., in printing a set of Laureateship Certificates which had been ordered from him and for which he had received the sum of $15.00 in advance. He showed that in Sept. 1934, $25.00 had been given to the Association by Hyman Bradofsky for the printing of such certificates, and that up to the time of the complaint none of the nine winners of the 1935 awards had been supplied as per agreement notwithstanding the placement of the order with Mr. Babcock and the advance payment to him of $15.00 in October 1934. Exhibits were furnished and the complainant appeared to proceed on the assumption that the order was for a large stock of blank certificates for future use, only a fraction of which were to be used for the nine 1935 winners. Mr. Babcock was notified and sent a preliminary reply scarcely in keeping with the seriousness of the complaint. It later developed that his understanding of the order differed from Mr. Smith's, his impression being that only a single set of nine certificates for the 1935 winners had been ordered; these to have the individual names printed in and to be of a de luxe quality warranting the seemingly high price of $25.00 for a single set. Upon receipt of the flippant preliminary reply, the following resolution was adopted by Judges Haggerty and Plaisier, Mr. Lovecraft not voting:

"The Board of Executive Judges have received a complaint from Mr. Edwin Hadley Smith that Ex-President Ralph W. Babcock, Jr., received $15.00 in October 1934, for the printing of laureate certificates, and that up to the present time these certificates have not been printed. The Board communicated with Mr. Babcock and received his reply, which was flippant and very discourteous, and which seemed to show no recognition of the gravity of the charges.

"We recognize that Mr. Babcock's absence from home will probably prevent him from printing the certificates, which are so long overdue, until his return from college, and we feel that a reasonable opportunity should be given him. We therefore refer this matter to the incoming Board of Executive Judges, to be elected at the Grand Rapids convention, for such action as the circumstances will warrant at that time."

Since this resolution additional testimony has been received; Mr. Babcock stating his conception of the order, citing other witnesses with a similar understanding and indicating that work on a single set of elaborate certificates had begun long previously; being later halted by the Smith complaint concerning the History and Story awards, which threw into uncertainty the identity of the winners in these classes and rendered the printing of their names impossible. On the other hand, testimony from Mr. Bradofsky indicates that in making his gift of $25.00 he had in mind a large stock of blanks instead of a single set of certificates with printed names; thus sustaining the assumption in Mr. Smith's charges. Obviously there has been a grave and definite misunderstanding in the terms of the printing order, which will have the strongest bearing on the final judgment of the case. If the present Board is unable to arrive at a ruling within its term of office, its successor is urged to apply the most painstaking and liberal consideration to this delicate problem.

On April 10, 1936, the Judges were requested by the President to prepare the form and text of the proxy ballots to be used at the coming election. Since this duty is one not ordinarily required of the Board and not specifically mentioned in the Constitution, the Board referred the matter back to the Secretary, through the President.

All papers covering matters brought before the Executive Judges for the 1935–36 term will be turned over to their successors at the Grand Rapids convention.

Respectfully submitted:
VINCENT B. HAGGERTY
H. P. LOVECRAFT
JENNIE K. PLAISIER
Executive Judges

Notes

1. O. W. Hinrichs (1887–1982), Official Editor of the NAPA (1934–35) and Official Printer for the 1935–36 term.

2. Jennie K. Plaisier (1882–1962), Executive Judge of the NAPA (with Vincent B. Haggerty and HPL) for 1935–36. Vincent B[artholemew] Haggerty (1888–1943), amateur journalist associated with the NAPA in the 1920s and 1930s.

3. Harold Segal (1915–2009), editor/publisher of *Good Timers' Club News*, the *Sea Gull*, and *Campane*. Official Editor of the NAPA (1932–33) and President (1933–34), taking over the post from Edwin Hadley Smith.

4. Victor A[ntoine] Moitoret (1919–2005), son of the amateur writer Anthony F. Moitoret (who was a known antagonist of HPL) and editor of *Moitoret's Midget* (1935f.). Marion Cummings Morcom (1919?–?), president of a local amateur journalist group in Oakland in the mid-1930s; editor of *Marionette* and associate editor of *Scarlet Cockerel*.

To the Convention of the
National Amateur Press Association, 22 June 1936

The letter was presumably solicited by Hyman Bradofsky, as it appeared in a booklet containing praise of his work, and therefore constituted a rebuttal to other amateurs (including Ralph W. Babcock) who had attacked Bradofsky during his term as NAPA president (1935–36).

[227]

I keenly regret the circumstances which prevent me from being present on this occasion, and wish to extend my greetings to those who are more fortunate. From what I have heard of local plans, I feel sure that the gathering will prove to be one of the Association's most active and enjoyable conversations.

I shall await very eagerly the results of the election, and hope that they may ensure a continuance of those upbuilding efforts which the retiring administration has so valiantly and on the whole successfully conducted despite the most serious handicaps. The past year has seen a perceptible rise in the Association's standards, as shewn in such new journals as *Causerie* and *The Dragon-Fly*,[1] and in the increasingly helpful quality of the official criticism under Messrs. Spencer[2] and Kleiner. During the year to come there will be great opportunities to build upon these foundations, and to carry out such plans as were blocked by the special obstacles of the past.

Our thanks are due to President Bradofsky, and to the colleagues who have loyally stood by him, for an uphill fight in behalf of progress and quality. I am sure we all appreciate the sacrifices which have made possible the issuance of *The Californian* with its unprecedented chances for our prose writers, and which have kept *The National Amateur* up to its present standard. A high example has been set—and we can ask no more of the new administration than that it preserve the same aim and zeal, and make the most of its more favourable conditions.

It is a matter of much regret to me that my own contributions to the year's activities have been few—an unavoidable result of obstacles outside the Association. But that the N. A. P. A. has been no real loser thereby, will be obvious to all who have studied Mr. Kleiner's critical articles.[3]

It is my most earnest hope that the new board will see fit to reappoint Mr. Kleiner to the post of verse critic, which he has filled with distinguished ability and raised to a new level of importance.

The dedication of the Presidents' Field, a memorial which places the Association for ever in Mr. Macauley's debt, will help to make the present convention an historic one. Let us trust that it may prove no less historic in its dedication of the officers and members to a task of continued constructiveness and renewed harmony.

Again, my most cordial greetings and sincere regrets.

Fraternally yours,

H. P. Lovecraft.

Notes

1. Published by Ernest A. Edkins and R. H. Barlow, respectively.

2. Truman J[oseph] Spencer (1864–1944) of Hamden, CT, historian of the amateur journalist movement, author of *A Cyclopedia of the Literature of Amateur Journalism* (1891) and *The History of Amateur Journalism* (1957; completed in 1940, but revised continually by Spencer until his death), and editor of *The Fossil*.

3. HPL was to have been a member of the Bureau of Critics for 1935–36, but illness and other work prevented him from writing any articles after the one that appeared in the December 1935 *National Amateur*. Kleiner took over HPL's responsibilities as verse critic.

Addenda

Leaf from letter to Elizabeth Toldridge

In *SL* 2.336–37, the following passages appear as the concluding paragraphs to a letter to Elizabeth Toldridge dated 4 May 1929. The manuscript of the Toldridge letter at JHL indicates that these paragraphs are not part of that letter. A T.Ms. of the fragment exists at WHS. (Toldridge's letters were not part of AHT.) The letter must date to c. 1929–30, since it mentions Franklin C. Clark as having died "nearly 15 years ago." Lovecraft refers to the recipient's "fellow-Marylander H. L. Mencken." Toldridge was born in Maryland and lived there in the 1870s and 1880s but was in Washington, DC, by 1890; a correspondent living in Maryland has not been identified.

[228]

[n.d. c. March 1929]

[. . .] a curb upon the fancy, so that the poetry of the period tends to be rhetoric rather than inspiration. For the soul & substance of poetry, there is no richer source than *Keats*. Join his spirit & fire to the simple language of straightforward conversation, & you have the utter apex of poetic possibility! As for modern writers—the reading of whom would form a good introduction to contemporary modes of thought—I don't recall that I mentioned any to you; all my own favourites being fantaisistes who are of course wholly outside the modern tradition. The best way to bridge the gap between the Victorian age & the present is to begin with the earlier works which represented the first revolt against artificial convention & falsity—works written by vigorous individual minds in the midst of the prevailing delusion. Meredith & Hardy are the best to start off with, & Pater & Wilde ought not to be overlooked. Then one simply must grit one's teeth & plough through Samuel Butler's "Way of All Flesh", despite the violence it does to many of one's possibly cherished sentimentalities. Another important thing is to know the foreign streams which have coloured our own increasingly since 1900. Of course everyone must read Balzac—& to this I'd add a good bit of Gautier, Flaubert, de Maupassant, & Zola. Baudelaire, Mallarmé, & Verlaine are poets which one absolutely must know in translation. I don't think it would pay to study other languages unless one had the most elaborate possible ambitions. Even Latin literature can be known pretty well though good English renderings of Caesar, Cicero, Lucretius, Catullus, Propertius, Tibullus, Virgil, Horace, Ovid, Seneca, Livy, Martial, Juvenal, Tacitus, the Plinies, &c.—not all of them complete, of course, but in balanced rations as recommended by university extension courses. The same is true of Greek—which ought to begin with Homer in the magnificent prose version prepared by the late Andrew Lang & his colleagues. Another great modern thought source is

535

Russian literature, of which Dostoievsky's "Crime & Punishment" & "Brothers Karamazov" will give the most representative glimpse. And finally come the approaches to modernity itself. John Galsworthy, H. G. Wells, Edith Wharton, Joseph Conrad, &c. are eminent old-schoolers getting close to the brink. Theodore Dreiser is of the new order, as is Sherwood Anderson. Don't miss James Branch Cabell, either. And a very good critical perspective can be obtained by reading the various "Prejudices" (with due allowance for certain violent habits of expression) of your brilliant & mordant fellow-Marylander H. L. Mencken, of 1524 Hollins St., Baltimore. This background is a desirable thing for anyone living today to know, & an *essential* thing for any prose-writer dealing directly with life. It is not, however, so rigidly indispensable for a poet or for a fantaisiste. My own interest in it is purely intellectual, not aesthetic-emotional. For imaginative enjoyment I turn to that narrow group of special writers (all of them representatives of an ancient rather than modern tradition) of which I have often spoken—Machen, Dunsany, de la Mare, Blackwood, &c. I shall very shortly send along the two Machen books I spoke of. By the way, though—don't fancy that I even dream of competing with these titans myself. My work has very grave limitations visible both to myself & to others, whilst my scholarship is the merest drop in the bucket as compared with that of a real scholar. I have reason to know this from direct & disillusioning comparison—for an uncle of mine who died nearly 15 years ago was the real thing![1]

I note all the enclosures with keen interest, & think you amply deserve the graceful sonnet addressed to you. "Shallow Water" is good of its kind, but too conventional & too bound up in a turn of thought to satisfy my notion of poetry. "White Frost" is thoroughly delightful—the poignantly visual decorative material which means real poetry. It seems to have had good luck with the press, & I don't wonder! The other cuttings are also entertaining—I must send that one about gloomy poetry on the rounds of the gang! Wilder lectured here recently, but I did not attend—for lectures bore me unless I am absolutely unable to get the material in printed form. "The Bridge of San Luis Rey"[2] is a fine & brilliantly written novel, though I have a feeling that it has been somewhat overpraised. Its dramatic vividness & mechanical facility seem almost *too* clever for realistic vitality, whilst I think the author strains unduly after elemental universality & cosmic significance. But for all that it's a great novel which no one ought to miss. I was woefully late in reading it. The Roman item is interesting, & I wish I had the cleverness & initiative to concoct & market things like that. Heaven knows I need the cash desperately enough! The best Roman antiquarian I know of is Edward Lucas White, whose "Andivius Hedulio" I shall soon lend you. The cat article impels me to enclose an old MS. of my own, which you can peruse & return at leisure. It was written to be read by my friend James F. Morton as part of a "Cat & Dog" controversy programme at the Blue Pencil Club of N.Y., to which I had formerly belonged. You may find it absurd & extravagant, disconcertingly pagan,

& full of references to personal matters & friends which may make it obscure, but it will at least express something of my lifelong & sincere idolatry of the felidae. You don't have to finish it if it gets more & more tedious as you advance!

Well, anyway, I'm glad the envelope of MSS. wasn't lost. I hope the enclosed comments on your poems may not prove wholly without value, & that the rambling discontinuity of the present epistle may be pardoned. ¶ With best wishes—

Yr most obt Servt   H P Lovecraft

Notes

1. Franklin C. Clark.
2. By Thornton Wilder.

To Clark Ashton Smith

[229] [ANS, privately held]

Jany. 17[, 1927]

Dear C A S:—

The Wandrei MSS safely arrived today, & I am really quite enthusiastic about them. The author has a genuine grasp of the strange, & a verbal facility & richness which needs only practice to evolve into a powerful & compelling style. The cosmic pieces are perhaps the most distinctive, but all the others have qualities which it is impossible to praise too highly. "The Chuckler" certainly is a hair-raiser deluxe! I hope Wandrei will keep up his writing, & am anxious to see more of his material.

Am adding slowly to my novel, but am very dissatisfied with the result. Still, I must get it out of the way in order to tackle something else! Hope you're evolving some poetical & pictorial material—did I say I've discovered a new artist fond of the weird?[1] Best wishes, & thanks for the Wandrei mss.

H P L

Notes

1. I.e., Bernard Austin Dwyer, poet and artist.

[230] [ANS, privately held][1]

[Postmarked Boston, Mass.,
5 January 1929]

Greetings from a section of the gang! Loveman is making a business trip to New England, & I am showing him the sights & antiquities of Providence,

Boston, & other historic sights. Tomorrow we go to Salem & Marblehead—the old town of the witchcraft, & the best preserved Colonial village in America.
Best wishes—
Yr obt Servt H P L

Dear Clark
I am here on business and having a marvellous time. Marblehead and Salem tomorrow! Much affection to you—Sam

Notes

1. *Front:* Old South Church.

[231] [ANS, privately held][1]

[Postmarked Providence, R.I.,
9 May 1932]

Thanks enormously for the impressive view of California's scenery. I must get around your way some day—for here we have nothing as bold & rugged as this. Congratulations on Ubbo-Sathla! Now if Wright will only take The Double Shadow, I'll feel that I have some influence in his sanctions![2] We have good outdoor weather here. Still in doubt about travel potentialities, but will be getting started on whatever trip I do take in about a week.
Yrs in the Nighted Brotherhood of the Andean Monolith—
E'ch-Pi-El

Notes

1. *Front:* University Hall and Manning Hall, Brown University.
2. "Ubbo-Sathla" (*WT,* July 1933). Wright rejected "The Double Shadow."

[232] [Enclosure, privately held][1]

[9 June 1934]

Later—June 9. Young Ar-E'ch-Bei has held this epistle up several days, wishing to get in an enclosure. Meanwhile the envelope of your drawings has come, & he is in ecstasies over them. He keeps them always within reach, & takes them out to gaze at every few minutes—& has made *copies* of many of them as best he can. ¶ Hope you can fix him up regarding the mythological matters. He wants all the available data on Tsathoggua—have you still the bits from "The Mound" that I sent you when cooking up that tale in 1930?

¶ Went yesterday to Silver Springs, where the bottom of a lake is riddled with picturesque [caves?] seen from a glass-bottomed boat. Also sailed 10 miles down a tropical river[2] which looked every inch like the Amazon or Congo. The

scenes for the cinema of "Tarzan" were made here. I must send you a folder of the place—one of the most distinctive & fascinating spots I have ever seen. ¶ Yrs for the Eternal Infra-Red Flame
—E'ch-Pi-El.

Notes

1. *Front:* A fine bunch of bananas, Florida.
2. HPL misspeaks. Silver Springs is 60 miles from DeLand. The boat excursion was about 10 miles.

[233] [ANS][1]

[Postmarked Providence, R.I.,
28 July 1934]

Congratulations on the remittance from Hugo the Rat! Wish I could have been in on Sultan Malik's second visit. Glad that Xeethra is to adorn the pages of W.T. No hurry about the Hodgson books—I came home into a devastating accumulation of tasks, & don't know when I'll ever get a chance for extra reading! Thanks for the view of High St.—a very attractive scene! ¶ Two-Gun Bob visited the Carlsbad Caverns last month, & gives a tremendously powerful description of them. They must be one of the world's most stupendous wonders. ¶ Little Bloch has placed a story in W.T. at last—"The Secret in the Tomb." ¶ My trip home was very enjoyable. St. Augustine was fascinating, & I stopped off 2 days in Charleston. In Richmond I stopped at a cheap hotel only 2 doors from the site of the old Allan home where Poe grew up. An afternoon in Fredericksburg, & then 2 days in Washington. Then Philadelphia—where I saw the newly opened Poe home (1842–44) in N. 7ᵗʰ St. A very neat brick cottage, furnished just as in Poe's time. In N Y I found the Longs about to leave for a week end in Asbury Park, & went along with them. Too broke to stop much in N Y, hence couldn't look up anybody except Loveman. Reached home July 10, & was surely glad to see New England's rolling hills, great elms, stone walls, & white village steeples again! Aunt in good health—goes everywhere without a cane now. And there is an exquisite black kitten at the boarding house across the back garden. ¶ Have you heard of the new magazine *Terror Tales?* ¶ Just got new F F & *Marvel Tales*—latter greatly improved. Glad to see "Epiphany of Death" in print. I've written an article on interplanetary fiction for Crawford. ¶ Expect a visit from James F. Morton Aug. 2–3–4. ¶ Yrs for the green crescent of Zarth—
E'ch-Pi-El

Notes

1. *Front:* First Baptist Church, Providence, R. I.

[234] [ANS][1]

[Postmarked De Land, Fla.,
1 July 1935]
Yoh-Vombis—
Hour of the Red Moon

Dear Klarkash-Ton:

Thanks effusively & overwhelmingly for the two nameless eikons which arrived this afternoon. Iä! Shub-Niggurath! The Goat with the Thousand Young! Didst find them amidst the shunn'd ruins of Uzuldaroum, or didst carve them in dreams induced by sleeping in the crumbling citadel of Commorium? They haunt & fascinate me. I hope they're both mine—but if one is for Ar-Ech-Bei I'll pass it along with a sigh. ¶ Still having a great time & feeling like a prize fighter. A fortnight ago we explored a strange tropical river—Black Water Creek—where corpselike cypresses rise amidst festooning moss, & palms with twisted, writhing roots lean over the edge of the glassy stream. It is a scene like the Congo or Amazon—with pallid flowers & fungi in the black earth of the twilight forest aisles, & lush creepers interlacing with ghoulish fallen logs. It is like that river at Silver Springs which I described last year . . . but I enjoyed it more because we had a slow rowboat instead of a speeding launch. ¶ All hands went to Daytona Beach last Friday. ¶ Hope all flourishes in brooding Averoigne. Thanks again for the cryptic eidola from the Caves of Ngranek. ¶ Yrs for the Faceless Image of Thok—

Ech-Pi-El

Notes

1. *Front:* Where you love to linger, on the coast of beautiful Florida.

To Unknown

[235] [AN]

The following is a note to an unknown person, written on the verso of his bookplate.

[c. September 1929]

What do you think of my new bookplate? Designed by young Wilfred B. Talman of the amateur crowd. I am enthusiastically pleased with it. The colonial doorway typifies both the spirit of Old Providence & my especial antiquarian tastes.

¶Incidentally—Windsor, Vt. looks as if it might have some good specimens of this sort.[1] Thanks for the card—which goes at once into my collection.

The following fragments were sold in an eBay auction in 2012 along with Lovecraft's letters to Robert Nelson. The earliest known letter by Lovecraft to Nelson dates to 19 October 1934, and it is not clear that Lovecraft was in touch with him so early as 1932.

[236]

[26 November 1932]

[Written on a prospectus for *For the Glory of France,* by Everett McNeil.] The author of these books is a member of our gang in N.Y. Keep him in mind if you ever want to buy a present for a youngster.

[237]

[Written on an envelope piece:] Just got $21.61 for reprinting of Erich Zann in *London Evening Standard.* In a note from Whitehead I get the idea that *Astounding* is to follow S.T. into oblivion. Is this correct? Speaking (as inside) of deaths—did Hugh Walpole die recently? I just saw his name bordered in black on the *New Am. Spectator* but haven't noticed a word of his decease anywhere else.[2] People drop off faster that an old man can keep track of!

[238]

[Written on an envelope piece:] Sudden bad news. Whitehead died last Wednesday.[3] I knew he was in rotten health, but had no idea it was as bad as all this. He wrote breezily & optimistically less than a fortnight ago with no reference to health. Really, this gives one a damnable jolt. He was such a splendid chap in all ways—brilliant, courageous, generous, attractive, learned, & everything else admirable. This will be a frightful blow to his father now 84.

Notes

1. HPL refers to the fanlighted doorway depicted on the recto side of his bookplate.
2. The novelist Hugh Walpole died in 1941. Perhaps the notice HPL saw was regarding publication of *The Fortress.*
3. Henry S. Whitehead died 23 November 1932, age 50.

To Wilfred B. Talman

In *Letters to Wilfred B. Talman and Helen V. and Genevieve Sully,* letters 238 and 239 below were printed only in part because only a photograph of the rectos of each page were visible in Owings and Binkin.

[239] [ALS]

Colonial Shades of #66
July 22, 1933

Jonckheer:—

Well, well, well, Son—Grandpa sure is glad to hear that the Dutch-Yankee article suited your requirements so aptly! Hope your Secretary-Censor will have an equally kind opinion. As I said before—change as much or as little as you like. Never mind my spelling—I believe all magazines & papers have their "style sheet" of individual usage, to which all contributions are made to conform. "Connexion" is a very old & common usage, & remains the dominant form throughout the Mother Land & a good part of the Dominions .... God Save the King! But as for Adriaen Block's Dutch—if I were you, I'd let it alone. Remember what you told me about diverse dialects. Of course, Adriaen wasn't a Nieuw Nederlander—but presumably there must have been some flexibility of usage back home. The form *een rodtlich Eylandken* (get this straight—EEN RODTLICH EYLANDKEN) is quoted precisely as given (spelling, capitalisation, & all) in at least two Rhode-Island histories—Field's & Richman's, & I never heard any other version. It may have been bum Dutch—Jersey Dutch, or what the hell—but the chances are that it's what honest Adriaen, bluff old sea-dog that he was, put down on paper, take it or leave it. It is my impression that modern historians quote verbatim et literatim from some account of Block's, printed contemporaneously with himself. There has long been a *popular folklore impression* 'that Block named the island of Aquidneck Roodt Eylandt'—a thing perpetuated in a work as semi-authoritative as Munro's "Picturesque Rhode-Island"—but modern serious works ignore this, since it errs in two points. Actually, the island Block called *rodtlich* (or what have you) was *not Aquidneck* but (by Block's own account) one to the west of Aquidneck—the name being transferred later through confusion; & also, the name given came not through a direct proper-noun christening, but merely through a common adjectival description ... "a reddish islet". If I were you, I'd quote as given unless some definite contrary evidence comes up. If you can dig up any explanatory data, so much the better—nothing boosts an article like a learned editorial footnote. If the given phrase is *too* bad, according to *any* valid dialectic standard, you can justify it & yourself by means of a bracketed [sic] after the quotation. But this is really a minor & pedantic point. The important thing is that, almost undoubtedly, one of the foremost of the New-England colonies received a permanent name of Dutch origin.

Do as you like about the derived words & culinary products—I know that many are subject to dispute. But I think you're wrong in attributing *boss* to African Boer influence. In the first place, Bartlett's "Dictionary of Americanisms" (ed. of 1877, p. 59) says of *boss*, "The word probably originated in New York, & is now used in many parts of the U.S." In the second place, *boss* was undoubtedly known in New England during the first half of the 19th century—a date apparently precluding any substantial South African influence. What contact had Americans with the Boers in 1840 or before? Even if England had picked up the word from its settlers in South Africa, it would not have been very likely to spread here unless of great popularity on British soil—& the fact is, that America seems to have had the word long before England. Bartlett records *boss* as an Americanism, & even today it has not the wide usage in England that it has here. How could America get a South-Africanism *ahead* of England? It is true that the Dutch settled Cape Colony as early as 1652, but what trade had Americans with these Afrikanders? I may be wrong, but I believe that the bulk of the American sea-trade had to do with the gold, ivory, & slave coasts of West Africa, far north of any region which could know Boer influence. When we reflect on the *very slight* connexion [sic] of Americans with the African Dutch prior to 1840, & on their *very close* connexion [sic] with the New-Netherland Dutch, we cannot but draw conclusions favourable to Bartlett's opinion. If, however, any *new evidence* pointing to the African derivation of *boss* has been unearthed since Bartlett's day, I will cheerfully accept correction—for I admit that my statement was a very lay-manlike one, unverified by the fruits of recent scholarship. All I know is that, a generation ago, *boss* was usually considered by New Englanders as a Nieuw-Nederland importation.

I shall be glad to look over a typed copy of the revised article prior to publication. Glad that your society has Wendells & Updikes in prominent posts, so that my wholly disinterested reference to these notable families will count in my article's favour! The Jacob Wendell house (1760) in Portsmouth, N.H. is one of the most distinctive & best-preserved Middle-Georgian houses in New-England.

My aunt appreciates your message & sends you her best regards. She ought to be up & on crutches within a week if the doctor's latest assurances mean anything. The nurse is very accomodating about staying in on after-noons when I want especially to be free, & will make it possible for me to spend next Monday & Tuesday with Sonny Belknap & his papa & mamma at Onset (near Cape Cod), where they are sojourning for a week. The Long party flashed through Providence very briefly last Wednesday—bringing with them & leaving a friend of Clark Ashton Smith's (a very gifted young gentle-woman named Helen V. Sully) who is touring the East & looking up all of Smith's friends. She left for Gloucester Friday morning, after being shewn the leading antiquities of Providence & Newport. Belknap, in his momentary glimpse, thought that Grandpa's new colonial quarters were not half bad—an opinion which I am sure you will share when you see them. Don't you recall the little yellow Georgian house behind the John Hay Library? Next Wednes-day, when the Longs return eastward, Sonny, papa, & mamma will probably spend the afternoon here. And Mortonius is due here around Aug. 1—quite a social season after all!

I trust that all the household at Knollwood towers are flourishing—including Carbie & her posterity. At the boarding-house whose rear abuts on our rear garden there are two tiger kittens with their eyes just open—& I will leave it to your imagination how often I borrow them .... & how often I shall borrow them when they grow more vigorous & playful!

Well—so it goes. I'm glad the article suited, & hope you can smuggle me an extra Haelve Maen or so next October when (or if) it appears. Come along & see Grandpa's Georgian dump when you can! ¶ Yr obt hᵇˡᵉ Servt   Petrus O'Casey

P.S. Hope this reaches you sooner than its predecessor seems to have done. The post-horses must have been spavin'd & jaded beasts!

[240] [ALS]

Thor's Dæg
[3? August 1933]

Jonkheer:—

Yrs. duly arrived—just after my adieu to my distinguish'd & mountainous guest ... whose joint postcard with me doubtless reached you. We had a great time—Jake's, Maxfield's, rural exploration, & a boat trip to Newport.

As for Mynheer van Twiller's[1] dimensions—I never met the genial soul, but merely repeat hearsay. This is what C. B. Todd says in his "Brief History of N.Y. City" (Am. Book Co. 1899), p. 23.

> "But, burlesque aside [he had been quoting Knickerbocker] Van Twiller was a grotesque figure, a mountain of flesh, slow & narrow of mind, with a petty spirit, & a burgomaster's fondness for good dinners & sound wine."

Is Mr. Todd too much of an Anglo-Saxon outsider to be an authority? All I know is what I *read* in the papers &c! Glad John Clarke is good material.

For Dutch tenure in Maine, my *immediate* source is one of the really important historical works issued by the State St. Trust Co. of Boston—"France & New England" Vol. III—by Allan Forbes & Paul F. Cadman (1929). See pp. 70–80. The site of Fort Pentagoët, Castine, Maine, is covered with tablets which refer to the Dutch such as the following:

FROM THIS BASE OF ATTACK
Extending to the West
FORT PENTAGOËT
Defended by Captain de Chambly, Baron de Saint-Castin his Lieutenant & 38 soldiers & fur traders was carried by assault August 10, 1674 by Captain JURRIAN AERNOUTS & 110 Seamen from the Dutch frigate *Flying Horse* after one of the most desperately contested of the many engagements fought upon this peninsula.

Aernouts (Drake: Nooks & Corners of the New England Coast [1876], p. 78) is considered by some as a buccaneer, but Charlevoix shows that he had a commission from the Prince of Orange; so that, although the *older* histories do not consider the incident as a formal break in the French occupation, *modern* historians seem to agree in maintaining that Pentagoët was really under the Dutch flag.

Thanks abundantly for the Georgia brochure, which I have just perused with avidity & appreciation. I long to see Savannah again! Material herewith returned as per request.

Had a letter from Knopf Co. (inspired by our friend Samuelus) asking to see some of my MSS. with a view to possible book publication—but at this late date I know how little comes of such inquiries. By the way—note the enclosed, which refers to an amateurish new magazine.[2] CAS & I are going to let it print our old rejected MSS. for the sake of lending copies.

And so it goes.

      Pax Vobiscum

        ——Grandpa O'Casey

Notes

1. Wouter van Twiller (1606–1654), who succeeded Peter Minuit as director of New Netherland (1633–38).
2. I.e., *Fantasy Fan.*

[241] [ALS]

                                 Sept. 25, 1933

Jonckheer:—

    Ædepol! You people had better have a staff research bureau, & not contaminate yourselves with unknown articles from the ignorant outside laity!

As to the latest point, I don't like to seem unduly critical, but that change as suggested is so completely *redundant* that I would recommend something else if possible. What needs doing, of course, is simply to remove the perplexity of those who can't believe the Dutch had any hold on North America after the Treaty of Westminster (Oct. 31, 1674). Therefore, the logical thing is not to repeat the just-asserted fact that the French took the fort, but simply to rub in the fact that the Dutch were on hand over time.

Accordingly, what I'd advise—& what I am writing into the carbon—is the following new version of the whole passage in question: (beginning immediately after the words ". . . . submitted to the invaders.")

In November, 1676, two years after the second and peaceable transfer of New Netherland to the English by the Treaty of Westminster (Oct. 31,

1674), a French force under Baron de St. Castin recaptured the stronghold, expelling the settlers because of their readily granted allegiance to the Dutch. Thus for over 24 months after the treaty with England by which the Netherlands nominally resigned all claim to North American soil in exchange for a recognition of their rights in the West Indies and in Surinam, an actual Dutch hold on this continent existed.

You can't get round that. *Any* damn fool can see what that means. Hope it's all right, but let me know when you or somebody else wants more changes. Quite a game! Use your own judgment about *Het Vliegende Parde.*[1] I wish some of your wise guys would take the time to nose the whole episode out of the obscure records in which its details seem to be buried. I wouldn't mind the reading the real close-up dope on the affair! Incidentally—by the time this article is really done, it ought to be quite a good-sized affair. Better leave it unpublished for a year, open to the suggestions of their High Mightinessess of the States-General, & it will have grown to a book!

Glad the gang has had a meeting, & that Editor Hall is getting worked into it. And so the anthologist Harré, too! Wish I would have been on hand. The old circle really does need new blood.

I envy you your trip to Texas—or rather, I *would* if I thought it would last till the hellish northern winter is over. do you suppose you'll get a chance to make a land journey to Cross Plains & confabulate with Two-Gun Bob, the Terror of the Range? Drop me a card from any quaint & ancient parts you may take in!

Glad the camera is doing well, & that you have a business neighbor & fellow-enthusiast in young Melmoth the Wandrei. No doubt you'll snap quite a few marine & Texan views during your coming voyage.

Thanks abundantly for that generously scaled map of the ancient Accomac peninsula, which I surely hope I can see & describe some day. According to all accounts, it's a region far above the average in picturesqueness.

I had a glorious time in ancient Quebec—4 days of fine hot weather. Absorbed all the familiar sights & stumbled on quite a few new ones, besides taking a walk to Sillery & inspecting the Georgian mansion of the Duke of Kent (Queen Victoria's father) at Montmorency Falls. The French up there look quite happy after their expulsion of you Dutchmen from Pentagoët (by force, not treaty) in 1676 (not 1674). Saw a marvelous sunset effect on Labour Day—golden glamour everywhere, yet a thunder-cloud sending down streaks of lightning over the opposite shore of the St. Lawrence, & a fragment of rainbow above the Isle d 'Orleans. On the return trip I called again on Cook, & made a digression to Salem & Marblehead. Marvellous reproduction of the pioneer settlement of 1626 at Salem.

My aunt is now all around the house on cane or crutch—nurse gone. We have a new electrical device so she can open the front door from upstairs. I'm not as badly tied down as I was, & have been taking several rural walks despite the approach of autumnal chill. ¶ Price is back in New Orleans. ¶

Thanks for the map, & let me know when you want some more changes in the article. Yrs. for accuracy & clearness.

—Grandpa

P.S. I learn from Klarkash-Ton that a new low-paying weird (scientifiction) magazine is about to appear—UNUSUAL STORIES.[2]

Notes

1. The frigate *The Flying Horse.* It is not mentioned in "Some Dutch Footprints in New England."
2. *Unusual Stories* was one of several semi-professional magazines edited and published by William L. Crawford (1911–1984). It ran for 3 issues (March 1934, May/June 1935, Winter 1935). It contained no work by HPL or WBT.

To Emil Petaja

[242] [TLS][1]

> 66 College St.,
> Providence, R.I.
> [late February 1937]

Dear Petaja:—

Reduced to the hated machine by a spell of bad health (more or less allied to grippe, and involving swollen feet, intestinal disorders, and general weakness) which has rendered my script illegibly shaky in any substantial quantity.

That N.A.P.A material wasn't a mere loan—I didn't need it back at all. Such shipments can always be passed on to possible recruits or others if you haven't any use for it yourself. Glad various bundles of papers have begun to reach you. Did you get the splendid Winter CALIFORNIAN and the December official organ? Before long the MS. bureau will begin to show results regarding the placement of your material.

Congratulations on your congenial Seattle visit, which must surely have been a rare treat. Even in winter the scenery en route was doubtless tremendously impressive. That's the advantage of mountain regions—their charm and grandeur do not depend upon anything seasonal. Seattle alone, w[i]th bookshops and other facilities, was doubtless a delight in itself.

Sorry to hear of your influenza—about which, as you may see, I can sympathise very eloquently. Hope all traces are now worn off, and that you are rapidly repairing the scholastic damage. Glad you are increasing your Murphy courses. The results will undoubtedly be manifest in your literary products—and in the public's reception of them.

Glad you liked the "Haunter" and "Doorstep". Finlay belied the narrative a bit in illustrating the first, but his "Doorstep" drawing is a classic. Wright has given me the originals of these two sketches, and they far excel the reproductions in effect. Much is lost in even the best cuts. As for Utpatel's "Innsmouth" illustrations—I enclose (please return) the set. They really are excellent, even though the white-bearded nonagenarian does appear as smooth-faced. The book is out now, and is rather a damned mess in format, typography, and binding. Crawford's printed list of errata leaves many uncorrected, so that I am asking purchasers of the book to let me know and receive a supplementary list. Sorry your "World of Sensation" didn't quite land—but the next attempt may bring better luck. I was glad to see Rimel's "Disinterment" in print, and found it as powerful on a second reading as when I first saw it in MS. I've just seen another good story of Rimel's—"From the Sea"—which Wright ought to accept eventually.[2]

Glad you liked "The Purple Cloud". Yes—I've seen "Shapes in the Fire".[3] Isn't this the book which contains a powerful but florid and over-ornate tale (I can't recall the title here used) about a tower of brass amidst the swirling waters of the Norwegian coast? If so, you've read the crude prototype of one of the finest weird stories ever written—for about 1907 Shiel resurrected and revised this opus and presented it (in "The Pale Ape and Other Stories") [*sic*] as that unforgettable classic, "The House of Sounds". I'm rather sorry that you won't have the chance good luck (as I had) to read the superior version first, and thus get the effect of the better craftsmanship combined with absolute freshness and unexpectedness. The resemblance to Poe's "House of Usher" is obvious, but not offensive. Shiel has not plagiarised, but re-created. "This Above All" sounds like quite a delicate and tragic character-study.

Hope you receive most of the small weird magazines—whose numerousness is now quite bewildering. Did you know that the SFC is about to absorb FANTASY MAGAZINE?

Commiserations on the cold winter! Ours has proved very warm—seldom below 40—so that I've been able to get occasional bits of air and exercise. A really cold winter would have finished me!

All good wishes—yrs most sincerely,
HPL

Later—This damn grippe has got me down at last! Doc has me taking 3 nostrums at once, & I can't stay up very long at a time.

Notes

1. On the verso, Petaja wrote: "Lovecraft's last letter to me. He died two weeks later."
2. The story was not published.
3. "The House of Sounds" initially appeared as "Vaila" in *Shapes in the Fire*.

To Howard Wandrei

[243] [ALS, held privately]

66 College St.,
Providence, R.I.,
Dec. 27, 1934

Dear H E:—

Very glad to hear from you again! No—I have had no bulletins from the House of Wandrei between a card from Montreal & a message from Auburn, Cal. I fancy that Young Melmoth's sojourn in the Hesperian groves of Averoigne must have been extremely pleasant, as it certainly was for his hosts. Does he intend to settle again in New York? There is a vague possibility that I may visit that region briefly within the next fortnight—& if I do, I hope I can somehow get in touch with him.

I'm certainly sorry to hear that Comte d'Erlette has been seriously ill. He has been having indigestion off & on during the autumn, but *smallpox*—even as tempered by vaccination—is something else again! It could scarcely have been a long or severe attack, since I heard from A W as recently as the 10th, with no mention of such. I must drop him a line & ask how he is!

I surely hope you'll be able to get to N Y again if that's where you want to be[1] (it's about the last place in the U.S. I'd ever wish to inhabit permanently!)—& I can abundantly sympathise with your attitude toward the Minnesota winter! You can probably appreciate the sentiment behind one of the stanzas of a juvenile "poetic" effusion of mine:

> It was in the cold season
>   It* dawn'd on my gaze;
> The mad time of unreason,
>   The brain-numbing days
> When Winter, white-sheeted & ghastly, stalks onward to torture & craze.[2]

As you may see, the hyemal period was never exactly popular with me, even in my youth! And the long decades have done nothing toward reconciling me to it. Providence has just about as bad a climate as I can endure at all. Even here I have to hibernate closely all winter—& one shade more of cold would form the final straw. I may yet have to light out for the South—but sheer attachment to my native landscape & architecture has so far held me here. Key West is the town I would choose for climate—though antiquarian interests would probably cause me to compromise on St. Augustine or Charleston. But if I ever broke loose from Rhode Island, I would certainly live no farther north than Charleston.

Congratulations on the Munsey sales! You are fortunate in your ability to

---

*A sinister, unknown city of dream

suit remunerative markets—an accomplishment utterly beyond me. Long is just now doing very well in that line, & I hope his winning streak will keep up!

Meanwhile I hope your pictorial pen has not been idle. I have lent the set of small photographic reproductions to many correspondents old & new—the result in each case being spontaneous & unqualified admiration. Not long ago Barlow sent me a fine 4½ × 6 photograph of your Sabbat masterpiece—the nameless shapes disporting against a monstrous, trans-galactic orb. Its superiority over the small photographs is enormous—there being multitudes of details utterly lost in the smaller print of the same subject. It has more of the feel & atmosphere of the original, as I remember it, than I would have thought possible in a photograph so relatively small.

I trust you have been enjoying a pleasant Yule, & that the New Year may be one of great happiness & prosperity for you. Christmas hereabouts was exceptionally pleasant—we had a *tree* for the first time in over a quarter of a century! December as a whole was rather congenially crowded with events—largely a series of art lectures & exhibits at the local museum. This institution has recently acquired a set of 717 Japanese prints of the choicest sort, which give it a quite eminent distinction in the far eastern field. The autumn was not especially genial, so that I had fewer trips than last year; but I managed to see something of the changing leaves, & visited the Boston region twice. I dropped you a card, I fancy, from my memorable Nantucket trip of late August.

All good wishes—& hopes for a mild winter.

Yrs most sincerely—
H P L

P.S. Enclosed is an issue of the Fantasy Fan—dedicated to me—which may be of some mild interest. The editor generously flooded me with duplicates. The Nov. issue was dedicated to Clark Ashton Smith, & the Dec. to the late Edgar Allan Poe!

[P.P.S., on envelope:] Just learned (a) that Donald has hit N.Y., & (b) that Belknap expects me to be on hand Monday. Barlow is also in N.Y. Some gathering!

Notes

1. HPL addressed the letter to the Wandrei home in St. Paul, but it was forwarded by DAW to New York, postmarked 3 January 1935.

2. "The City" (1919), ll. 6–10 (the first line should read "I remember the season" [*AT* 65]).

Appendix

Elegy

Harold S. Farnese

Style No. 10 — 12 Staves (9 x 12)
Printed in the U. S. A.

G. Schirmer, Inc., New York

Style No. 10 — 12 Staves (9 x 12)
Printed in the U. S. A.

G. Schirmer, Inc., New York

Sources for Lovecraft's Letters

Abramson, Ben. ALS, WHS. Extracts published in *Reading and Collecting* 1, No. 5 (April 1937): 21.

Ackerman, Forrest J. *Imagination!* 1, No. 4 (January 1938): 9–10 (includes facsimile of greeting and signature from ALS).

Bacon, Victor E. ALS, [private collection].

Bautz, W. G. AHT. Name misspelled as "Bantz."

Birss, John H. ALS, Harvard. The list of tales that accompanied it is held at JHL.

Blish, James, and William Miller, Jr. *Phantastique/The Science Fiction Critic* No. 13 (March 1938): 3–4.

Braithwaite, William Stanley. ALS, JHL.

Bryant, William. 25 April 1927 and 18 May 1927: ALS, Natural History Museum at Roger Williams Park. ALS, JHL. 27 April 1927: TLS, JHL (on verso of A.Ms. of "History of the 'Necronomicon'").

Bullen, John Ravenor. ALS, Manuscripts and Archives Division, New York Public Library. Letter fragments are on versos of the A.Ms. of "The Horror at Red Hook."

Coryciani. ALS, JHL (save for leaf 1 of the first letter, which is reproduced in *SL* 1, facing p. 194). "Japanese Hokku." From a typescript prepared by Maurice W. Moe; published in *O-Wash-Ta-Nong* 3, No. 1 (January 1938): 13.

Davis, Edgar J. AHT.

Eddy, C. M., Jr. Mixed: one ALS exists at JHL, another held privately; another at Place of Hawks, Sauk City, WI. Image of one obtained from the Internet.

Edkins, Ernest A. A.Df., JHL.

Eshbach, Lloyd Arthur. AHT; ALS, [private collection].

Farnese, Harold S. TLS, JHL; also AHT.

Gallomo. AHT. Letter #10 is held at JHL.

Greene, Sonia H. TLS, JHL. "Niet[z]scheism and Realism." *Rainbow* No. 1 (October 1921): 9–11. "The Psychic Phenomenon of Love." T.Ms., JHL. ANS, [private collection].

Hoag, Jonathan E. ANS, JHL. "Postcards to Jonathan E. Hoag." *Lovecraft Annual* No. 10 (2016): 121–57, with postcards printed in facsimile.

Homeland Company. T.Df., JHL.

Hornig, Charles D. 26 January 1935 and 7 June 1935: ANS, JHL. Other ALSs and ANS in private collections. Several extracts of letters published in the "Our Readers Say" column of *FF:* 1, No. 2 (October 1933): 14 (no. 108); 1, No. 3 (November 1933): 33 (no. 110); 1, No. 4 (December 1933): 50 (no. 111); 1, No. 7 (March 1934): 97 (no. 116); 1, No. 8 (April 1934): 113 (no. 117); 1, No. 9 (May 1934): 129 (no. 119); 1, No. 11 (July 1934): 162 (no. 120); 2, No. 2 (October 1934): 17 (no. 124); 2, No. 4 (December

1934): 49 (no. 125). Other items published in "The Boiling Point" column in *FF:* 1, No. 2 (October 1933): 27–28 (no. 108); 1, No. 5 (January 1934): 68 (no. 112). Part of no. 116 published in the "Your Views" column of *FF:* 1, No. 7 (March 1934): 105.

Houdini, Harry. ANS, lovecraftzine.com/2015/05/05/letter-from-lovecraft-to-houdini-about-edgar-allan-poes-desk/. Accessed 12 November 2021.

Hughes, Kathleen Compere (i.e., Mrs. H. H. Hughes) AHT.

Hyde, Edna. "My Memoirs of Amateur Journalism" *Oracle* 4, No. 3 (May 1924): 3–14; HPL quote on p. 14 and rpt in George T. Wetzel, *Collected Essays on H.P. Lovecraft and Others* Wildside Press, 2015, p. 38.

Jacobi, Carl. *SL* 4.24–25.

Kelley, Earl C. ANS, private hands.

Kirk, George W. [2 August 1926]: ANS, [private collection]. [25 September 1926]: ANS, [private collection].

Kleicomolo. AHT.

[Letter Seeking Employment.] A.Df., JHL.

Little, Myrta Alice. ALS, JHL.

Lowndes, Robert A. W. ALS, [private collection].

Macauley, George W. 12 August 1934: ALS, [private collection]. "Extracts from H. P. Lovecraft's Letters to G. W. Macauley." *O-Wash-Ta-Nong* 3, No. 2 (Spring 1938): 1–4.

Michael, Robert Hartley. *E'ch-Pi-El Speaks; The Occult Lovecraft; The Fantastic Worlds of H. P. Lovecraft.* Some ALSs offered by L. W. Currey.

Munn, H. Warner. 19 September 1930: [private collection]. 29 December 1935: ALS, JHL.

Peirce, Jr., Earl. Transcript, WHS.

Perry, Alvin Earl. ALS, JHL.

Petaja, Emil. ALS, JHL.

Quinn, Seabury. *SL* 3.410–11.

Schwartz, Julius. *Stardust* 2, No. 1 (1940): 8.

Smith, Clark Ashton. Assorted ANS and ALS, [private collections].

Smith, Edwin Hadley. "Lovecraft on Poetry Writing." *Boys' Herald* 71, No. 1 (October 1941): 7–8.

———. "View and Review" (containing an extract, unsigned, of a letter by HPL). *Boy's Herald* 65, No. 1 (March 1936): 2.

Stone, Lee Alexander. In HPL's letter to James F. Morton. *Letters to James F. Morton* 233–34.

Swanson, Carl. ALS, JHL.

Talman, Wilfred B. ALSs [private collections].

Tilden, Leonard E. ANS [private collection].

Ullman, Allan G. ALS, JHL.

Weiss, Henry George. AHT.

Wandrei, Howard. ALS [private collection].

Widner, Arthur. 15 January 1937: ANS, [private collection]. 20 February 1937: *SL* 5.413–16.
Worthington, William Chesley. ALS, Providence Athenaeum.
Ziegfeld, Henriette. TLS, [private collection].

Lovecraft's Published Letters

"Asks Preservation of Old Buildings." *Providence Sunday Journal* 42, No. 15 (10 October 1926): Sec. A, p. 5.
"The Bible as Literature." *Omaha World Herald* (21 February 1920): 6 (under "The Public Pulse").
"The Earth Not Hollow." *Providence Sunday Journal* (12 August 1906): Sec. 2, p. 5.
"The English Language." *New-York Tribune* (21 September 1911): 6.
[Letters between H. P. Lovecraft and J. F. Hartmann.] All letters in the Providence *Evening News*.
 J. F. Hartmann. "Astrology and the European War." (4 September 1914): 8.
 H. P. Lovecraft. "Science versus Charlatanry." (9 September 1914): 8.
 J. F. Hartmann. [Letter to the Editor.] (7 October 1914): 12.
 H. P. Lovecraft. "The Falsity of Astrology." (10 October 1914): 8.
 H. P. Lovecraft. "Astrology and the Future." (13 October 1914): 8
  (as "Astrlogh and the Future"; as by "Isaac Bickerstaffe, Jr.").
 J. F. Hartmann. "The Science of Astrology." (22 October 1914): 8.
 H. P. Lovecraft. "Delavan's Comet and Astrology." (26 October 1914): 8
  (as by "Isaac Bickerstaffe, Jr.).
 J. F. Hartmann. "A Defense of Astrology." (14 December 1914): 8.
 H. P. Lovecraft. "The Fall of Astrology." (17 December 1914): 8.
 H. P. Lovecraft. "[Isaac Bickerstaffe's Reply]." (21 December 1914): 3
  (as by "Isaac Bickerstaffe, Jr.").
[Letters between H. P. Lovecraft and Orville L. Leach.] All letters in the *Providence Sunday Journal.*
 Orville L. Leach. "About the Vacuum." (7 June 1908): Sec. 2, p. 5.
 H. P. Lovecraft. "Heat and Radiant Energy." (14 June 1908): Sec. 2, p. 5.
 Orville L. Leach. "Scientists at War." (21 June 1908): Sec. 2, p. 5.
 H. P. Lovecraft. "Vacuums, Wave Lengths, Etc." (5 July 1908): Sec. 2, p. 5.
 Orville L. Leach. "Holes in the Ether." (12 July 1908): Sec. 2, p. 5.
 H. P. Lovecraft. "Waves in the Ether." (19 June 1908): Sec. 2, p. 5.
 Orville L. Leach. "Matter the Deficiency of Mass." (26 July 1908): Sec. 2, p. 5.
 All articles included in "Letters between H. P. Lovecraft and Orville L. Leach," ed. Donovan K. Loucks. *Lovecraft Annual* No. 7 (2013): 36–59.
Letters to the Munsey Magazines.
 [October? 1911]. *Argosy* 67, No. 4 (November 1911): 768 (as by "H. P. L.").

[January 1913?]. *All-Story Weekly* 31, No. 26 (8 February 1913): 361 (as "A Few Lines about 'Fishhead'").

[August 1913?]. *Argosy* 73, No. 2 (September 1913): 478–79 (as "Objects to Jackson").

"Ad Criticos." AMS (JHL); *Argosy* 74, No. 2 (January 1914): 479–80 (Liber Primus; as "Lovecraft Comes Back: Ad Criticos"); 74, No. 3 (February 1914): 715–16 (Liber Secundus; as "Ad Criticos: Liber Secundus").

[January 1914?]. *Argosy* [74], No. 4 (March 1914): 956 (as "Correction for Lovecraft").

[February 1914?]. *All-Story Weekly* 34, No. 5 (7 March 1914): 223–24.

[July 1914?]. *All-Story Weekly* 35, No. 2 (15 August 1914): 344–45 (as "For England and the All-Story").

"Long Distance Predictions: Weather Guessers Willing to Take Any Sort of Chances and Trust to Providence." *Amsterdam* [NY] *Evening Recorder and Daily Democrat* (6 September 1905): 3.

"No Transit of Mars." *Providence Sunday Journal* (3 June 1906): Sec. 2, p. 5.

"The Old Brick Row." T.Ms., JHL. *Providence Sunday Journal* (24 March 1929): A5 (abridged; as "Retain Historic 'Old Brick Row'").

"A Reply to *The Lingerer.*" *Tryout* 3, No. 7 (June 1917): [9–12].

"Report of the Executive Judges." *National Amateur* 58, No. 4 (June 1936): 2–3. In *CE* 1.

"Save the Old Brick Row." T.Ms., JHL. *Providence Sunday Journal* (22 December 1929): Section A, p. 5 (as "Praises Beauty of 'Old Brick Row'"; as by James F. Morton).

"Seats for Park Concerts." *Providence Sunday Journal* (3 August 1913).

"Style in English." *Omaha Daily Bee* (24 February 1920): 4.

"Trans-Neptunian Planets." *Scientific American* 95, No. 8 (25 August 1906): 135.

To *Dragnet. Dragnet* 2, No. 3 (April 1929): 372 (as "One for the Black Bag"). *Phantagraph* 12, No. 3 (November 1944): 3–4.

To Elizabeth Toldridge. T.Ms. (fragment), Wisconsin Historical Society. In *SL* 2.336–37

To Gavin T. McColl. "Appreciations." *Scot* No. 7 (March 1916): 36.

To John Milton Heins. [c. March 1921]: *American Amateur* 2, No. 5 (April 1921); 153. 4 November 1921: *National Amateur* 44, No. 3 (January 1922): 27.

To the Board of Executive Judges, National Amateur Press Association, Mrs. E. D. Houtain, Chairman. *National Amateur* 45, Nos. 2/3 (November [1922]–January 1923): 6.

To the Bureau of Critics. *National Amateur* 41, No. 3 (January 1919): 93 (as by "Ned Softly" and "Ward Phillips"; in section titled "The Members' Forum").

To the Convention of the National Amateur Press Association. *Lest We Forget* (October 1936): 28.

To the *Exeter* (NH) *News-Letter* (21 November 1930).

To the Gallomo. In *Dreams and Fancies* (Sauk City, WI: Arkham House, 1962): 4–9; 43–50.

To the *Haldeman-Julius Weekly*. *Haldeman-Julius Weekly* No. 1416 (20 January 1923): 1; No. 1424 (17 March 1923): 1. [Letter by John Mason: *Haldeman-Julius Weekly* No. 1421 (24 February 1923): 1.]

To the Gotham Press Club. *Gothamite* No. 1 (new series) (April 1923): 6.

To the Members of the NAPA. Printed broadside, in a scrapbook owned by Edwin Hadley Smith, Library of Amateur Journalism, University of Wisconsin–Madison.

To the Ohio Amateur Journalists' Club, 29 May 1923. *Buckeye* 3, No. 1 (June 1923): 3 (as "Lovecraft's Greeting").

To "The Sideshow." In B. K. Hart's "The Sideshow." *Providence Journal* (23 November 1929): 2; (25 November 1929): 2; (29 November 1929): 10; (30 November 1929): 10; (3 December 1929): 14; (18 March 1930): 12; (13 November 1931): 14.

To Vincent B. Haggerty, mid-1935. *Amateur Affairs* 1, No. 9 (October 1935): [4] (in section titled "Fragments").

"Trans-Neptunian Planets." *Scientific American* 95, No. 8 (25 August 1906): 135; rpt. *Liverpool* [NSW, Australia] *Herald* (24 November 1906).

"Venus and the Public Eye." *Providence Sunday Journal* (26 December 1909): Sec. 2, p. 5.

Glossary of Frequently Mentioned Names

Babcock, Ralph W., Jr. (1914–2003), a lifelong writer and printer (since the age of seven). He was active in amateur journalism (President of the NAPA 1934–35 and Official Editor 1939–40), and publisher of the *Scarlet Cockerel* and other papers.

Baird, Edwin (1886–1954), first editor of *Weird Tales* (1923–24), who accepted HPL's first submissions to the magazine. Also editor of *Real Detective Tales and Mystery Stories.*

Barlow, R[obert] H[ayward] (1918–1951), author and collector. As a teenager he corresponded with HPL and acted as his host during two long visits in the summers of 1934 and 1935. In the 1930s he wrote several works of weird and fantasy fiction, some in collaboration with HPL. HPL appointed him his literary executor. He assisted August Derleth and Donald Wandrei in preparing the early HPL volumes for Arkham House. In the 1940s he went to Mexico and became a distinguished anthropologist. HPL's letters to him are published in *O Fortunate Floridian* (2007).

Bishop, Zealia Brown (Reed) (1897–1968), HPL's revision client. HPL ghostwrote "The Curse of Yig" (1928), "The Mound" (1929–30), and "Medusa's Coil" (1930) for her based on her slim plot synopses.

Blackwood, Algernon (1869–1951), prolific British author of weird and fantasy tales whose work HPL greatly admired when he read it in 1924.

Bloch, Robert (1917–1994), author of weird and suspense fiction who came into correspondence with HPL in 1933. HPL tutored him in the craft of writing during their four-year association. HPL's letters to him are published in *Letters to Robert Bloch and Others* (2015).

Bradofsky, Hyman (1906–2002), a prolific amateur journalist and president of the NAPA (1935–36). He edited the *Californian* (1933f.), one of the most distinguished—and voluminous—amateur journals of the period.

Bush, David Van (1882–1959), prolific author of inspirational verse and popular psychology manuals, many of them revised by HPL.

Campbell, Paul J. (1884–1945), amateur journalist, editor of the *Liberal* and numerous other journals, and president of the United Amateur Press Association (1916). HPL's letters to him are contained in *Letters to Rheinhart Kleiner and Others* (2020).

Clark, Franklin Chase (1847–1915), husband of HPL's aunt Lillian, a physician and writer on medicine and local and natural history. He translated Homer, Virgil, Lucretius, and Statius into English verse. HPL possessed

Clark's translations of the Georgics and Aeneid of Virgil and mentioned on several occasions his desire to see the work published.

Clark, Lillian D[elora] (1856–1932), HPL's maternal aunt. She married Dr. Franklin Chase Clark in 1902. From 1926 to her death she shared quarters with HPL at 10 Barnes Street. HPL's letters to her are published in *Letters to Family and Family Friends* (2020).

Coates, Walter J[ohn] (1880–1941) was a poet, printer, bibliographer, Universalist minister, and storekeeper in Vermont. He published *Driftwind*, a poetry magazine, for fifteen years starting in 1925. His Driftwind Press specialized in Vermont literature and small edition vanity books of poetry. He published ten sonnets from HPL's *Fungi from Yuggoth*.

Cole, Edward H[arold] (1892–1966), a longtime amateur associate of HPL, living in the Boston area, and editor of the *Olympian*. HPL's letters to him are contained in *Letters to Alfred Galpin and Others* (2020).

Cole, Ira A. (1883–1973) of Bazine, KS. Historian of the UAPA and member of the Kleicomolo. He edited the *Plainsman*, which published HPL's poem "On the Cowboys of the West" (December 1915).

Conover, Willis (1920–1996), weird fiction fan who edited *Science-Fantasy Correspondent* (1936–37) and was a late correspondent of HPL. HPL's letters to him are contained in *Letters to Robert Bloch and Others* (2015).

Cook, W. Paul (1880–1948), publisher of the *Monadnock Monthly*, the *Vagrant*, and other amateur journals; a longtime amateur journalist, printer, and lifelong friend of HPL. He first visited HPL in 1917, and it was he who urged HPL to resume writing fiction after a hiatus of nine years. In 1927 Cook published the *Recluse*, containing HPL's "Supernatural Horror in Literature."

Crawford, William L[evy] (1911–1984), editor of *Marvel Tales* and *Unusual Stories* and publisher of the Visionary Publishing Co., which issued HPL's *The Shadow over Innsmouth* (1936).

Daas, Edward F. (1879–1962) of Milwaukee, WI, joined the UAPA within one year of its founding in 1895. He was elected its President in 1907. He also served as Official Editor in 1913–14 and 1915–16.

Derleth, August W[illiam] (1909–1971), author of weird tales and also a long series of regional and historical works set in his native Wisconsin. HPL's letters with him are contained in *Essential Solitude* (2008). After HPL's death, he and Donald Wandrei founded the publishing firm of Arkham House to preserve HPL's work in book form.

Dowdell, William J. (1898–1953) of Cleveland, amateur journalist and editor of *Dowdell's Bearcat*, who abruptly resigned as president of the NAPA in late 1922, leading the executive judges to appoint HPL as interim president.

Dunsany, Lord (Edward John Moreton Drax Plunkett, 18th Baron Dunsany) (1878–1957), Anglo-Irish writer of fantasy tales whose work notably influenced HPL after HPL read it in 1919.

Dwyer, Bernard Austin (1897–1943), weird fiction fan and would-be writer and artist, living in West Shokan, NY; correspondent of HPL. HPL's letters to him are contained in *Letters to Maurice W. Moe and Others* (2018).

Ericson, E[ric] E[dward] (1879–1935) of Elroy, WI, for many years the official printer of the UAPA.

Gamwell, Annie E[meline] P[hillips] (1866–1941), HPL's younger aunt, living with him at 66 College Street (1933–37). HPL's letters to her are published in *Letters to Family and Family Friends* (2020).

Gernsback, Hugo (1884–1967), editor of *Amazing Stories, Wonder Stories,* and other pioneering science fiction pulps.

Goodenough, Arthur H[enry] (1871–1936), amateur poet who resided in Brattleboro, VT. HPL visited him there on several occasions.

Hamlet, Alice M. (1888–1967), an amateur living in Dorchester, MA, who introduced HPL to the work of Lord Dunsany.

Henneberger, J[acob] C[lark] (1890–1969), founder of *College Humor* (1922f.) and the original publisher of *Weird Tales.*

Houdini, Harry (stage name of Ehrich Weiss, 1874–1926), celebrated escape artist and opponent of spiritualism for whom HPL ghostwrote the story "Under the Pyramids" (1924; published as "Imprisoned with the Pharaohs") and for whom he did other revisory work in 1926, just prior to Houdini's death.

Houtain, George Julian (1884–1945), lawyer, amateur journalist, editor of the *Zenith,* and president of the NAPA (1915–17) who with his wife, E. Dorothy (McLaughlin) Houtain (1889–1980), established the semiprofessional humor magazine *Home Brew,* for which he commissioned HPL to write "Herbert West—Reanimator" (1921–22) and "The Lurking Fear" (1922).

Howard, Robert E[rvin] (1906–1936), prolific Texas author of weird and adventure tales for *WT* and other pulp magazines; creator of the adventure hero Conan the Cimmerian. He and HPL corresponded voluminously from 1930 to 1936. Their letters are published in *A Means to Freedom* (2009).

Jackson, Winifred Virginia (1876–1959), amateur poet in the Boston area and close colleague of HPL for the period 1918–21. For a time she was married to Horace Jordan and was known as Winifred Virginia Jordan. Some have speculated that at the time she and HPL were romantically involved. HPL's letters to her are contained in *Letters to Rheinhart Kleiner and Others* (2020).

James, M[ontague] R[hodes] (1862–1936), pioneering British writer of ghost stories whose work HPL much admired.

Koenig, H[erman] C[harles] (1893–1959), late associate of HPL who spearheaded the rediscovery of the work of William Hope Hodgson. He published HPL's "Charleston" as a booklet.

Leeds, Arthur (1882–1952?), movie script writer, associate of HPL in New York, and member of the Kalem Club. HPL's letters to him are contained in *Letters to Rheinhart Kleiner and Others* (2020).

Long, Frank Belknap, Jr. (1901–1994), fiction writer, poet, Kalem Club member, and one of HPL's closest friends and colleagues. He was recruited into UAPA by Paul J. Campbell.

Loveman, Samuel (1887–1976), poet, book seller, member of the Kalem Club, and longtime friend of HPL, Hart Crane, Clark Ashton Smith, and George Sterling. Author of *The Hermaphrodite* (1926) and other works. HPL's letters to him are contained in *Letters to Maurice W. Moe and Others* (2018).

McNeil, Everett (1862–1929), author of historical and adventure novels for boys; member of the Kalem Club.

Martin, Harry Edwin, a prominent amateur from Ohio, was the fifty-first NAPA President, and also Vice President of the UAPA (1905–06). He had served as NAPA's Official Editor in the Dowdell/Lovecraft administration, and continued to serve under that of Hazel Pratt Adams. Author of *The Tents of Grace: A Tragedy, and Four Short Stories* (1910).

Miniter, Edith (1867–1934), amateur author who also professionally published a novel, *Our Natupski Neighbors* (1916) and many short stories. HPL was guest at her home in Wilbraham, MA, in the summer of 1928.

Moe, Maurice W[inter] (1882–1940), amateur journalist, English teacher, and longtime friend and correspondent of HPL, living in Appleton and Milwaukee, WI. HPL's letters to him are published in *Letters to Maurice W. Moe and Others* (2018).

Moore, C[atherine] L[ucile] (1911–1987), late associate of HPL who later married Henry Kuttner and became a leading figure in science fiction and fantasy. Their joint correspondence has been published in *Letters to C. L. Moore and Others* (2017).

Morton, James Ferdinand (1870–1941), amateur journalist, author of many tracts on race prejudice, free thought, and taxation; longtime friend of HPL and Kalem Club member. In 1925 he became the curator of the Paterson (NJ) Museum. HPL's letters to him are published in *Letters to James F. Morton* (2011).

Petaja, Emil (1915–2000), science fiction fan and late associate of HPL; later a prolific author and editor. HPL's letters to him are published in *Letters with Donald and Howard Wandrei and to Emil Petaja* (2019).

Price, E[dgar] Hoffmann (1898–1988), prolific pulp writer of weird and adventure tales. HPL met him in New Orleans in 1932 and corresponded extensively with him thereafter. HPL's letters to him are published in *Letters to E. Hoffmann Price and Richard F. Searight* (2021).

Renshaw, Anne Vyne Tillery (1890?–1947?), prolific amateur journalist and professor. She met HPL during the latter's visit to Washington, DC, in April 1925. In 1936 she commissioned HPL to revise a textbook of English usage, *Well-Bred Speech* (1936), although much of the work HPL did for it was excised. HPL's letters to her are published in *Letters to Elizabeth Toldridge and Anne Tillery Renshaw* (2014).

Rimel, Duane W[eldon] (1915–1996), weird fiction fan and late associate of HPL, who revised some of his early tales. HPL's letters to him are published in *Letters to F. Lee Baldwin, Duane W. Rimel, and Nils Frome* (2016).

Russell, John (b. 1871–), an Englishman residing in Tampa, FL, who engaged with HPL in a controversy in verse, conducted in the letter column of the *Argosy* in 1913–14.

Samples, John Milton (1887–1944) of Macon, GA (later Atlanta), editor of the *Silver Clarion*, to which HPL contributed a few items around 1918.

Sandusky, Albert A[ugust] (1896–1934), amateur journalist whose use of slang amused HPL. HPL met him frequently during trips to the Boston area.

Searight, Richard F[ranklyn] (1902–1975), sporadic contributor of weird and science fiction tales to the pulp magazines. He corresponded with HPL from 1933 to 1937. HPL's letters to him are published in *Letters to E. Hoffmann Price and Richard F. Searight* (2021).

Smith, Charles W. (1852–1948) of Haverhill, MA, editor and publisher of the *Tryout*.

Smith, Clark Ashton (1893–1961), prolific California poet and writer of fantasy tales. He received a "fan" letter from HPL in 1922 and corresponded with him until HPL's death. Their joint correspondence is published in *Dawnward Spire, Lonely Hill* (2017).

Smith, Edwin Hadley (1869–1944), a leading amateur journalist of the period, chiefly associated with the NAPA. The Library of Amateur Journalism (also known as The Edwin Hadley Smith Collection and The Fossil Collection), initially housed at the Franklin Institute in Philadelphia, is now at the University of Wisconsin–Madison. HPL directed that, upon his death, his amateur journals be turned over to Smith.

Spink, Helm C. (1909–1970), printer and Official Editor of the NAPA in 1930 and again in 1935 (with O. W. Hinrichs). He printed and published HPL's *Further Criticism of Poetry* (1932) as a booklet because the report HPL had submitted for publication in the *National Amateur,* the organization's official organ, was too long for inclusion. Others of HPL's reports did appear in the organ.

Starrett, [Charles] Vincent (1886–1974), American poet, fiction writer, journalist, and critic, was known to HPL before the two corresponded. HPL recognized Starrett as the man "who introduced the work of Machen to America." HPL's letters to him are contained in *Letters to Maurice W. Moe and Others* (2018).

Sterling, Kenneth (1920–1995), young science fiction fan who came into contact with HPL in 1934. They collaborated on the science fiction story "In the Walls of Eryx" (1935). Sterling later became a distinguished physician. HPL's letters to him are contained in *Letters Robert Bloch and Others* (2015).

Stickney, Corwin F. (1921–1998), copublisher with Willis Conover, Jr., of *Science-Fantasy Correspondent* (1936–37), later titled *Amateur Correspondent* (1937f.), edited by Stickney alone.

Strauch, Carl Ferdinand (1908–1989), correspondent of HPL. He later became a distinguished professor and critic. For HPL's letters to him, see *Letters to J. Vernon Shea, Carl F. Strauch, and Lee McBride White* (2016).

Talman, Wilfred Blanch (1904–1986), correspondent of HPL and late member of the Kalem Club. HPL assisted Talman on his story "Two Black Bottles" (1926) and wrote "Some Dutch Footprints in New England" for Talman to publish in *De Halve Maen,* the journal of the Holland Society of New York. Late in life he wrote the memoir *The Normal Lovecraft* (1973). HPL's letters to him are published in *Letters to Wilfred B. Talman and Helen V. and Genevieve Sully* (2019).

Toldridge, Elizabeth (1861–1940), invalid poet living in Washington, DC, who corresponded with HPL from 1928 to 1937. His coaching of her on her poetry was very influential in his own significant change in his poesy in 1929. HPL's letters to her are published in *Letters to Elizabeth Toldridge and Anne Tillery Renshaw* (2014).

Wandrei, Donald (1908–1987), poet and author of weird fiction, science fiction, and detective tales, and co-founder of Arkham House, to publish HPL's work. HPL's letters to him are published in *Letters with Donald and Howard Wandrei and to Emil Petaja* (2019).

Wandrei, Howard (1909–1956), younger brother of Donald Wandrei, premier weird artist and prolific author of weird fiction, science fiction, and detective stories. HPL's letters to him are published in *Letters with Donald and Howard Wandrei and to Emil Petaja* (2019).

Whitehead, Henry S[t. Clair] (1882–1932), author of weird and adventure tales, many of them set in the Virgin Islands. HPL once described him as "Musician, artist, athlete, traveller, cleric, liturgiologist, author, boys' camp leader, psychologist, civic leader, anthropologist" as well as an alienist and psychiatrist." HPL corresponded with him and visited him in Florida in 1931. HPL wrote a brief eulogy of Whitehead for *WT*.

Wollheim, Donald A[llen] (1914–1990), editor of the *Phantagraph* and *Fanciful Tales* and later a prolific author and editor in the science fiction field. HPL's letters to him are contained in *Letters to Robert Bloch and Others* (2015).

Wright, Farnsworth (1888–1940), editor of *Weird Tales* (1924–40).

Bibliography

Works by Lovecraft

Books

The Ancient Track: Complete Poetical Works. 2nd ed. Edited by S. T. Joshi. New York: Hippocampus Press, 2013.

The Annotated Supernatural Horror in Literature. 2nd ed. Edited by S. T. Joshi. New York: Hippocampus Press, 2012.

Collected Essays. Edited by S. T. Joshi. New York: Hippocampus Press, 2004–06. 5 vols. [CE]

Collected Fiction: A Variorum Edition. Edited by S. T. Joshi. New York: Hippocampus Press, 2015–22. 4 vols. [CF]

The Dark Brotherhood and Other Pieces by H. P. Lovecraft et al. Edited by August Derleth. Sauk City, WI: Arkham House, 1966.

Dawnward Spire, Lonely Hill: The Letters of H. P. Lovecraft and Clark Ashton Smith, Edited by David E. Schultz and S. T. Joshi. New York: Hippocampus Press, 2017.

E'ch-Pi-El Speaks: An Autobiographical Sketch. Saddle River, NJ: Gerry de la Ree, 1972.

Essential Solitude: The Letters of H. P. Lovecraft and August Derleth. Edited by David E. Schultz and S. T. Joshi. New York: Hippocampus Press, 2008. 2 vols.

Further Criticism of Poetry. Louisville, KY: George G. Fetter, 1932. [Titled by HPL "Notes on Verse Technique."]

H. P. Lovecraft in the Argosy: *Collected Correspondence from the Munsey Magazines.* Edited by S. T. Joshi. West Warwick, RI: Necronomicon Press, 1994.

H. P. Lovecraft in "The Eyrie." Edited by S. T. Joshi and Marc Michaud. West Warwick, RI: Necronomicon Press, 1979.

Letters to Alfred Galpin and Others. Ed. S. T. Joshi and David E. Schultz. New York: Hippocampus Press, 2020.

Letters to C. L. Moore and Others. Edited by David E. Schultz and S. T. Joshi. New York: Hippocampus Press, 2017.

Letters to Family and Family Friends. Edited by S. T. Joshi and David E. Schultz. New York: Hippocampus Press, 2020.

Letters to James F. Morton. Edited by David E. Schultz and S. T. Joshi. New York: Hippocampus Press, 2011.

Letters to Maurice W. Moe and Others. Edited by David E. Schultz and S. T. Joshi. New York: Hippocampus Press, 2018.

Letters to Rheinhart Kleiner and Others. Edited by S. T. Joshi and David E. Schultz. New York: Hippocampus Press, 2020.

Letters to Robert Bloch and Others. Edited by David E. Schultz and S. T. Joshi. New York: Hippocampus Press, 2015.

Letters with Donald and Howard Wandrei and to Emil Petaja. Edited by S. T. Joshi and David E. Schultz. New York: Hippocampus Press, 2019.

O Fortunate Floridian: H. P. Lovecraft's Letters to R. H. Barlow. Edited by S. T. Joshi and David E. Schultz. Tampa, FL: University of Tampa Press, 2007.

The Occult Lovecraft. Edited by Anthony Raven. Saddle River, NJ: Gerry de la Ree, 1975.

Selected Letters. Edited by August Derleth, Donald Wandrei, and James Turner. Sauk City, WI: Arkham House, 1965–76. 5 vols.

The Shadow over Innsmouth. Everett, PA: Visionary Press, 1936. (*LL* 591)

The Shunned House. Athol, MA: Recluse Press, 1928 (printed but not bound or distributed until 1959–61).

Fiction

"The Alchemist." *United Amateur* 16, No. 4 (November 1916): 53–57. In *CF* 1.

"Arthur Jermyn." See "Facts concerning the Late Arthur Jermyn and His Family."

At the Mountains of Madness. Astounding Stories 16, No. 6 (February 1936): 8–32; 17, No. 1 (March 1936): 125–55; 17, No. 2 (April 1936): 132–50. In *CF* 3.

"The Beast in the Cave." *Vagrant* No. 7 (June 1918): 113–20. In *CF* 1.

"Beyond the Wall of Sleep." *Pine Cones* 1, No. 6 (October 1919): 2–10. *FF*, 2, No. 2 (October 1934): 25–32. In *CF* 1.

"The Call of Cthulhu." *WT* 11, No. 2 (February 1928): 159–78, 287. In *Beware After Dark! The World's Most Stupendous Tales of Mystery, Horror, Thrills and Terror*, ed. T. Everett Harré. New York: Macaulay, 1929. 223–59. In *CF* 2.

The Case of Charles Dexter Ward. In *CF* 2.

"The Cats of Ulthar." *Tryout* 6, No. 11 (November 1920): [3–9]. *WT* 7, No. 2 (February 1926): 252–54. *WT* 21, No. 2 (February 1933): 259–61. In *CF* 1.

"The Colour out of Space." *Amazing Stories* 2, No. 6 (September 1927): 557–67. In *CF* 2.

"Cool Air." *Tales of Magic and Mystery* 1, No. 4 (March 1928): 29–34. In *CF* 2.

"Dagon." *Vagrant* No. 11 (November 1919): 23–29. *WT* 2, No. 3 (October 1923): 23–25. In *CF* 1.

"The Doom That Came to Sarnath." *Scot* No. 44 (June 1920): 90–98. *Marvel Tales of Science and Fantasy* 1, No. 4 (March–April 1935): 157–63. In *CF* 1.

The Dream-Quest of Unknown Kadath. In *CF* 2.

"The Dreams in the Witch House." *WT* 22, No. 1 (July 1933): 86–111. In *CF* 3.

"The Dunwich Horror." *WT* 13, No. 4 (April 1929): 481–508. In *CF* 2.

"Facts concerning the Late Arthur Jermyn and His Family." *Wolverine* No. 9 (March 1921): 3–11; No. 10 (June 1921): 6–11. *WT* 3, No. 4 (April 1924): 15–18 (as "The White Ape"). *WT* 25, No. 5 (May 1935): 642–48 (as "Arthur Jermyn"). In *CF* 1.

"The Festival." *WT* 5, No. 1 (January 1925): 169–74. *WT* 22, No. 4 (October 1933): 519–20, 522–28. In *CF* 1.

"From Beyond." *FF* 1, No. 10 (June 1934): 147–51, 160. In *CF* 1.

"The Haunter of the Dark." *WT* 28, No. 5 (December 1936): 538–53. In *CF* 3.

"He." *WT* 8, No. 3 (September 1926): 373–80. In *CF* 1.

"Herbert West—Reanimator" (as "Grewsome Tales"). *Home Brew* 1, No. 1 (February 1922): 84–88 ("From the Dark"); 1, No. 2 (March 1922): 45–50 ("The Plague Demon"); 1, No. 3 (April 1922): 21–26 ("Six Shots by Moonlight"); 1, No. 4 (May 1922): 53–58 ("The Scream of the Dead"); 1, No. 5 (June 1922): 45–50 ("The Horror from the Shadows,"); 1, No. 6 (July 1922): 57–62 ("The Tomb-Legions"). In *CF* 1.

"History of the 'Necronomicon.'" Oakman, AL: Wilson H. Shepherd/The Rebel Press, [1937] (as *A History of the Necronomicon*). In *CF* 2.

"The Horror at Red Hook." *WT* 9, No. 1 (January 1927): 59–73. In *You'll Need a Night Light*, ed. Christine Campbell Thomson. London: Selwyn & Blount, 1927. 228–54. In *Not at Night!*, ed. Herbert Asbury. New York: Macy-Masius (The Vanguard Press), November 1928. 27–52. In *CF* 1.

"The Hound." *WT* 3, No. 2 (February 1924): 50–52, 78. *WT* 14, No. 3 (September 1929): 421–25, 432. In *CF* 1.

"Hypnos." *National Amateur* 45, No. 5 (May 1923): 1–3. *WT* 4, No. 2 (May–June–July 1924): 33–35. In *CF* 1.

"In the Vault." *Tryout* 10, No. 6 (November 1925): [3–17]. *WT* 19, No. 4 (April 1932): 459–65. In *CF* 1.

"The Lurking Fear." *Home Brew* 2, No. 6 (January 1923): 4–10; 3, No. 1 (February 1923): 18–23; 3, No. 2 (March 1923): 31–37, 44, 48; 3, No. 3 (April 1923): 35–42. *WT* 11, No. 6 (June 1928): 791–804. In *CF* 1.

"Memory." *United Co-operative* 1, No. 2 (June 1919): 8. In *CF* 1.

"The Moon-Bog." *WT* 7, No. 6 (June 1926): 805–10. In *CF* 1.

"The Music of Erich Zann." *National Amateur* 44, No. 4 (March 1922): 38–40. *WT* 5, No. 5 (May 1925): 219–34. In *Creeps by Night: Chills and Thrills*, ed. Dashiell Hammett. New York: John Day Co., 1931. 347–63. In *Modern Tales of Horror*, ed. Dashiell Hammett. London: Victor Gollancz, 1932. 301–17. *Evening Standard* (London) (24 October 1932): 20–21. *WT* 24, No. 5 (November 1934): 644–48, 655–56. In *CF* 1.

"The Nameless City." *Wolverine* No. 11 (November 1921): 3–15. *Fanciful Tales* 1, No. 1 (Fall 1936): 5–18. In *CF* 1.

"Nyarlathotep." *United Amateur* 20, No. 2 (November 1920): 19–21. *National Amateur* 48, No. 6 (July 1926): 53–54. In *CF* 1.

"The Other Gods." *Fantasy Fan* 1, No. 3 (November 1933): 35–38. *WT* 32, No. 4 (October 1938): 489–92. In *CF* 1.

"The Outsider." *WT* 7, No. 4 (April 1926): 449–53. *WT* 17, No. 4 (June–July 1931): 566–71. In *CF* 1.

"Pickman's Model." *WT* 10, No. 4 (October 1927): 505–14. In *By Daylight Only*, ed. Christine Campbell Thomson. London: Selwyn & Blount, 1929. 37–52. *WT* 28, No. 4 (November 1936): 495–505. In *The "Not at Night" Omnibus*, ed. Christine Campbell Thomson. London: Selwyn & Blount, [1937]. 279–307. In *CF* 2.

"The Picture in the House." *National Amateur* 41, No. 6 (July 1919 [*sic*]): 246–49. *WT* 3, No. 1 (January 1924): 40–42. *WT* 29, No. 3 (March 1937): 370–73. In *CF* 1.

"Polaris." *Philosopher* 1, No. 1 (December 1920): 3–5. *National Amateur* 48, No. 5 (May 1926): 48–49. *FF* 1, No. 6 (February 1934): 83–85. In *CF* 1.

"The Quest of Iranon." *Galleon* 1, No. 5 (July–August 1935): 12–20. In *CF* 1.

"The Rats in the Walls." *WT* 3, No. 3 (March 1924): 25–31. *WT* 15, No. 6 (June 1930): 841–53. In *Switch On the Light*, ed. Christine Campbell Thomson. London: Selwyn & Blount, 1931. 141–65. In *CF* 1.

"The Shadow out of Time." *Astounding Stories* 17, No. 4 (June 1936): 110–54. In *CF* 3.

"The Shadow over Innsmouth." In *CF* 3.

"The Shunned House." In *CF* 1.

"The Silver Key." *WT* 13, No. 1 (January 1929): 41–49, 144. In *CF* 2.

"The Statement of Randolph Carter." *Vagrant* No. 13 (May 1920): 41–48. *WT* 5, No. 2 (February 1925): 149–53. In *CF* 1.

"The Strange High House in the Mist." *WT* 18, No. 3 (October 1931): 394–400. In *CF* 2.

"The Street." *Wolverine* no. 8 (December 1920): 2–12. *National Amateur* 44, no. 3 (January 1922): 25–27. In *CF* 1.

"The Temple." *WT* 6, No. 3 (September 1925): 329–36, 429, 431. *WT* 27, No. 2 (February 1936): 239–44, 246–49. In *CF* 1.

"The Terrible Old Man." *Tryout* 7, No. 4 (July 1921): [10–14]. *WT* 8, No. 2 (August 1926): 191–92. In *CF* 1.

"The Thing on the Doorstep." *WT* 29, No. 1 (January 1937): 52–70. In *CF* 3.

"The Tomb." *Vagrant* No. 14 (March 1922): 50–64. *WT* 7, No. 1 (January 1926): 117–23. In *CF* 1.

"The Transition of Juan Romero." In *Marginalia*. Sauk City, WI: Arkham House, 1944. Pp. 276–84. In *CF* 1.

"The Tree." *Tryout* 7, No. 7 (October 1921): [3–10]. In *CF* 1.

"The Unnamable." *WT* 6, No. 1 (July 1925): 78–82. In *CF* 1.

"The Whisperer in Darkness." *WT* 18, No. 1 (August 1931): 32–73. In *CF* 3.

"The White Ship." *United Amateur* 19, No. 2 (November 1919): 30–33. *WT* 9, No. 3 (March 1927): 386–89. In *CF* 1.

Poetry [all in *AT*]

"Ad Balneum." Not published in HPL's lifetime.

"The Ancient Track." *WT* 15, No. 3 (March 1930): 300.

"Bells." *Tryout* 5, No. 11 (December 1919): [9–10] (as by "Ward Phillips").
"Damon and Delia, a Pastoral." *Tryout* 4, No. 8 (August 1918): [23–26] (as by "Edward Softly").
"The East India Brick Row." *Providence Journal* (8 January 1930): 13.
"The Eidolon." *Tryout* 4, No. 10 (October 1918): [3–6] (as by "Ward Phillips").
"An Elegy on Franklin Chase Clark, M.D.: (Died April 26, 1915)." [Providence] *Evening News* 46, No. 137 (29 April 1915): 6.
"An Epistle to the Rt. Honble Maurice Winter Moe, Esq. of Zythopolis, in the Northwest Territory of HIS MAJESTY'S American Dominions." Not published in HPL's lifetime.
"Epitaph on the Letter Rrr........" Not published in HPL's lifetime.
"[Fragment on Whitman.]" In "In a Major Key." *Conservative* 1, No. 2 (July 1915): 9–11.
Fungi from Yuggoth
    I. "The Book." *FF* 2, No. 2 (October 1934): 24. *Driftwind* 11, No. 9 (April 1937): 342.
    II. "Pursuit." *FF* 2, No. 2 (October 1934): 24.
    III. "The Key." *FF* 2, No. 5 (January 1935): 72.
    IV. "Recognition." *Driftwind* 11, No. 5 (December 1936): 180.
    V. "Homecoming." *FF* 2, No. 5 (January 1935): 72. *Science-Fantasy Correspondent* 1, No. 1 (November–December 1936): 24. [Cambridge, MD] *Democrat & News* (8 July 1937). *WT* 37, No. 5 (May 1944): 52–53. *WT* (Canadian) 38, No. 3 (January 1946): 56.
    VI. "The Lamp." *Driftwind* 5, No. 5 (March 1931): 16. *WT* 33, No. 2 (February 1939): 151.
    VII. "Zaman's Hill." *Driftwind* 9, No. 4 (October 1934): 125. *WT* 33, No. 2 (February 1939): 151.
    VIII. "The Port." *Driftwind* 5, No. 3 (November 1930): 36. *WT* 39, No. 7 (September 1946): 65. *WT* (Canadian) 38, No. 4 (November 1946): 40.
    X. "The Pigeon-Flyers." *Ripples from Lake Champlain* 2, No. 4 (Spring 1932): 31. [Cambridge, MD] *Democrat & News* (8 July 1937). *WT* 39, No. 9 (January 1947): 96. *WT* (Canadian) 38, No. 4 [*sic*] (March 1947): 110.
    XI. "The Well." *Providence Journal* 102, No. 116 (14 May 1930): 15. *Phantagraph* 6, No. 3 (July 1937): [1]. *WT* 37, No. 5 (May 1944): 53. *Crypt of Cthulhu* No. 20 (Eastertide 1984): 8 (as "Two Discarded Drafts of 'The Well'").
    XII. "The Howler." *Driftwind* 7, No. 3 (November 1932): 100. *WT* 34, No. 1 (June–July 1939): 66.
    XVI. "The Window." *Driftwind* 5 (April 1931 [special issue]): 15. *WT* 37, No. 5 (May 1944): 53. *WT* (Canadian) 38, No. 3 (September 1945):

75. *Hi-Lite* [Mannheim Township High School, Nettsville, PA] (30 October 1946).

XVIII. "The Gardens of Yin." *Driftwind* 6, No. 5 (March 1932): 34. *WT* 34, No. 2 (August 1939): 151.

XX. "Night-Gaunts." *Providence Journal* 102, No. 73 (26 March 1930): 15. *Interesting Items* No. 605 (November 1934): [6] (as "Night Gaunts"). *Phantagraph* 4, No. 3 ([June] 1936): [8]. *Science Fiction Bard* 1, No. 1 (May 1937): 2–3. [Cambridge, MD] *Democrat & News* (8 July 1937). *WT* 34, No. 6 (December 1939): 59.

XXIII. "Mirage." *WT* 17, No. 2 (February–March 1931): 175 (as No. 8).

XXIV. "The Canal." *Driftwind* 6, No. 5 (March 1932): 34. *WT* 31, No. 1 (January 1938): 20.

XXVI. "The Familiars." *Driftwind* 5, No. 1 (July 1930): 35. *WT* 39, No. 9 (January 1947): 96. *WT* (Canadian) 38, No. 4 [*sic*] (March 1947): 59.

XXVII. "The Elder Pharos." *WT* 17, No. 2 (February–March 1931): 175 (as No. 9).

XXIX. "Nostalgia." *Providence Journal* 102, No. 61 (12 March 1930): 15. *Phantagraph* 4, No. 4 (July 1936): [1]. *Stars* (December [1940]–January 1941): 2.

XXX. "Background." *Providence Journal* 102, No. 91 (16 April 1930): 13. *Interesting Items* No. 592 (September 1932): [1]. *Galleon* 1, No. 4 (May–June 1935): 8. *Lovecrafter* 47, No. 1 (20 August 1936): [1] (as "A Sonnet"; in fact, the only appearance of the publication, intended as a birthday present for HPL [actually his forty-sixth]).

XXXI. "The Dweller." *Providence Journal* 102, No. 110 (7 May 1930): 15. *Phantagraph* 4, No. 2 (November–December 1935): [3]. *WT* 35, No. 2 (March 1940): 20.

XXXIV. "Recapture." *WT* 15, No. 5 (May 1930): 693. *WT* 39, No. 3 (January 1946): 37. *WT* (Canadian) 38, No. 4 (March 1946): 78.

"A Garden." *Vagrant* [Spring 1927]: 60. The issue of the *Vagrant* was long delayed and should have emerged as early as 1923.

"The House." *National Enquirer* 9, No. 11 (11 December 1919): 3. *Philosopher* 1, No. 1 (December 1920): 6 (as by "Ward Phillips").

"In a Major Key." *Conservative* 1, No. 2 (July 1915): 9–11). In *CE* 1.

"The Isaacsonio-Mortoniad." Not published in HPL's lifetime.

"John Oldham: A Defence." *United Co-operative* 1, No. 2 (June 1919): 7.

"Medusa: A Portrait." *Tryout* 7, No. 9 (December 1921): [32–34] (as by "Jeremy Bishop").

"The Messenger." In B. K. Hart, "The Sideshow." *Providence Journal* 101, No. 288 (3 December 1929): 14. *WT* 32, No. 1 (July 1938): 52.

"Nemesis." *Vagrant* No. 7 (June 1918): 41–43. *WT* 3, No. 4 (April 1924): 78.

"Ode for July Fourth, 1917." *United Amateur* 16, No. 9 (July 1917): 121. *National Magazine* 46, No. 10 (July 1917): 616 (as "Ode to July 4th, 1917"). [Providence] *Evening News* 51, No. 26 (3 July 1917): 3.

"On a Grecian Colonnade in a Park." *Tryout* 6, No. 9 (September 1920): [11–12] (as by "Henry Paget-Lowe").

"On Reading Lord Dunsany's Book of Wonder." *Silver Clarion* 3, No. 12 (March 1920): 4.

"The Peace Advocate." *Tryout* 3, No. 6 (May 1917): [12–14] (as by "Elizabeth Berkeley").

"The Poe-et's Nightmare." *Vagrant* No. 8 (July 1918): [13–23].

"The Poem of Ulysses." Not published in HPL's lifetime.

"The Power of Wine: A Satire." [Providence] *Evening News* 46, No. 46 (13 January 1915): 5. *Tryout* 2, No. 5 (April 1916): [5–7]. *National Enquirer* 5, No. 26 (28 March 1918): 3.

"Psychopompos: A Tale in Rhyme." *Vagrant* No. 10 (October 1919). *WT* 30, No. 3 (September 1937): 341–48 (without subtitle).

"Sir Thomas Tryout: Died November 15, 1921." *Tryout* 7, No. 9 (December 1921): [31–32] (as by "Ward Phillips"). *Tryout* 21, No. 1 (March 1941): [3–4].

"Sonnet on Myself." *Tryout* 4, No. 7 (July 1918): [2] (as by "Lewis Theobald, Jun.").

"Spring: Paraphrased from the Prose of Clifford Raymond, Esq., in the Chicago Tribune." *Tryout* 5, No. 4 (April 1919): [15–16].

"To a Dreamer." *Coyote* No. 16 (January 1921): 4. *WT* 4, No. 3 (November 1924): 54.

"To a Young Poet in Dunedin." Not published in HPL's lifetime.

"To Alan Seeger." *Tryout* 4, No. 7 (July 1918): [1–2]. *National Enquirer* 6, No. 20 (15 August 1918): 10. *United Amateur* 18, No. 2 (November 1918): 24.

"To Charlie of the Comics." *Providence Amateur* 1, No. 2 (February 1916): 13–14 (unsigned).

"The Unknown." *Conservative* 2, No. 3 (October 1916): [12] (as by "Elizabeth Berkeley").

Nonfiction

"Commonplace Book." In *CE* 5.

"A Confession of Unfaith." *Liberal* 1, No. 2 (February 1922): 17–23. In *CE* 5.

"For Official Editor—Anne Tillery Renshaw." *Conservative* 5, No. 1 (July 1919): 11–12 (unsigned). In *CE* 1.

"Idealism and Materialism—A Reflection." *National Amateur* 41, No. 6 (July 1919 [actually spring/summer 1921]): 278–81. In *CE* 5.

"In a Major Key." *Conservative* 1, No. 2 (July 1915): 9–11 (unsigned). In *CE* 1.

"Life for Humanity's Sake." *American Amateur* 2, No. 1 (September 1920): 93–94. In *CE* 5.

"A Living Heritage: Roman Architecture in Today's America." *Californian* 3, No. 1 (Summer 1935): 23–28 (abridged; as "Heritage or Modernism: Common Sense in Art Forms"). In *CE* 5.

"Lucubrations Lovecraftian." *United Co-operative* 1, No. 3 (April 1921): 8–15. In *CE* 1.

"Nietzscheism and Realism." *Rainbow* No. 1 (October 1921): 9–11 (as "Nietscheism and Realism"). In *CE* 5.

"Notes on Writing Weird Fiction." *Amateur Correspondent* 2, No. 1 (May–June 1937): 7–10. In *CE* 2.

"Old England and the 'Hyphen.'" *Conservative* 2, No. 3 (October 1916): [1–2]. In *CE* 5.

"Preface." In John Ravenor Bullen. *White Fire*. Athol, MA: The Recluse Press, 1927 [actually January 1928]. 7–13. In *CE* 2. Earlier version as "The Poetry of John Ravenor Bullen." *United Amateur* 25, No. 1 (September 1925): 1–3, 6.

"A Reply to *The Lingerer*." *Tryout* 3, No. 7 (June 1917): [9–12]. In *CE* 1.

"The Simple Spelling Mania." *United Co-operative* 1, No. 1 (December 1918): 1–3. In *CE* 2.

"Some Self-Criticism." In James Van Hise, ed. *The Fantastic Worlds of H. P. Lovecraft*. Yucca Valley, CA: James Van Hise, 1999. 37.

"Supernatural Horror in Literature." *Recluse* No. 1 (1927): 23–59. Rev. ed. *FF* (October 1933–February 1935; incomplete). In *CE* 2.

"Supernatural Horror in Literature" (abridgment of 1936). *WT* 47, No. 2 (Fall 1973): 53–56. Rpt. *Supernatural Horror in Literature as Revised in 1936*. Arlington, VA: Carrollton-Clark, 1974.

"The Symphonic Ideal." *Conservative* 2, No. 3 (October 1916): [10–11]. In *CE* 5.

"The Vers Libre Epidemic." *Conservative* 2, N. 4 (January 1917): 2–3 (unsigned; part of the column "In the Editor's Study"). In *CE* 2.

"Verse Criticism." *National Amateur* 55, No. 3 (March 1933): 3. In *CE* 1.

"The Weird Work of William Hope Hodgson." *Phantagraph* 5, No. 5 (February 1937): 5–7.

Revisions and Collaborations [all in *CF* 4]

"The Challenge from Beyond" (with A. Merritt, C. L. Moore, Robert E. Howard, and Frank Belknap Long). *Fantasy Magazine* 5, no. 4 (September 1935): 221–29.

"The Crawling Chaos" (with Winifred V. Jackson). (*United Co-operative*, April 1921; as by "Elizabeth Berkeley and Lewis Theobald, Jun.")

"Deaf, Dumb, and Blind" (with C. M. Eddy, Jr.). *WT* 5, No. 4 (April 1925): 25–30, 177–79.

"The Electric Executioner" (with Adolphe de Castro). *WT* 16, No. 2 (August 1930): 223–36.

"The Ghost-Eater" (with C. M. Eddy, Jr.). *WT* 3, No. 4 (April 1924): 72–75.

"The Green Meadow" (with Winifred V. Jackson). *Vagrant* (Spring 1927): 188–95 (as by "Elizabeth Berkeley and Lewis Theobald, Jr.").
"In the Walls of Eryx" (with Kenneth Sterling). *WT* 34, No. 4 (October 1939): 60–58.
"The Loved Dead" (with C. M. Eddy). *WT* 4, No. 2 (May–June–July 1924): 54–57.
"The Mound" (with Zealia Bishop). *WT* 35, No. 6 (November 1940): 98–120 (abridged).

Works by Others

Alden, Abner (1758?–1820). *The Reader: Containing the Art of Delivery, Articulation, Accent, Pronunciation,* [etc.]. <1802> 3rd ed. Boston: Printed by J. T. Buckingham for Thomas & Andrews, 1808. (*LL* 25)
Andrews, Ethan Allan (1787–1858). *A Copious and Critical Latin-English Lexicon. Founded on the Larger Latin-German Lexicon of Dr. W. Freund.* New York: Harper & Brothers, 1854. (*LL* 39)
Andreyev, Leonid (1871–1919). *The Waltz of the Dogs: A Play in Four Acts.* Tr. Herman Bernstein. New York: Macmillan, 1922.
The Arabian Nights Entertainments. Selected and Edited by Andrew Lang. New York: Longmans, Green, 1898. (*LL* 49)
Asquith, Cynthia (1887–1960), ed. *The Black Cap: New Stories of Murder & Mystery.* London: Hutchinson, 1928.
———, ed. *The Ghost Book.* London: Hutchinson, 1927. New York: Charles Scribner's Sons, 1927.
Bartlett, John Russell (1805–1886). *Dictionary of Americanisms: A Glossary of Words and Phrases Usually Regarded as Peculiar to the United States.* 4th ed. Boston: Little, Brown, 1877. (*LL* 77)
Beckford, William (1759–1844). *The Episodes of Vathek* <1912> Tr. Sir Frank T. Marzials. Boston: Small, Maynard & Co., [1922?] or [1924?]. (*LL* 83)
———. *Vathek.* <1786> Introduction by Ben Ray Redman. Illustrated by Mahlon Blaine. New York: John Day Co., 1928. (*LL* 85)
Benson, E. F. (1867–1940). *Visible and Invisible.* New York: George H. Doran, 1923 or 1924. (*LL* 90)
Bierce, Ambrose (1842–1914?). *Can Such Things Be?* <1893> New York: Boni & Liveright (Modern Library), 1918. (*LL* 98)
———. *In the Midst of Life: Tales of Soldiers and Civilians.* <1891> Introduction by George Sterling. New York: Modern Library, [1927]. (*LL* 99)
Bierstadt, Edward Hale (1891–1970). *Dunsany the Dramatist.* New and rev. ed. Boston: Little, Brown, 1919. (*LL* 102)
Blackwood, Algernon (1869–1951). *The Centaur.* London: Macmillan, 1911.
———. *The Empty House and Other Ghost Stories.* London: Eveleigh Nash, 1906. New York: Donald C. Vaughan, 1915. New York: Alfred A.

Knopf, 1917. [Includes "The Haunted Island" and "Smith: Episode in a Lodging House."]

———. *The Extra Day*. London: Macmillan, 1915.

———. *Incredible Adventures*. London: Macmillan, 1914. New York: Macmillan, 1914.

———. *John Silence: Physician Extraordinary*. London: Eveleigh Nash, 1908. Boston: John W. Luce, 1909. London: Macmillan, 1912. New York: Vaughan & Gomme, 1914. New York: Alfred A. Knopf, 1917. New York, E. P. Dutton, [1920]. (*LL* 107, 108) [Includes "Ancient Sorceries."]

———. *The Listener and Other Stories*. London: Eveleigh Nash, 1907. New York: Vaughan & Gomme, 1914. New York: Alfred A. Knopf, 1917. [Includes "The Listener" and "The Willows."]

———. *The Lost Valley and Other Stories*. London: Eveleigh Nash, 1910. (*LL* 110) [Includes "The Wendigo."]

———. *Tongues of Fire and Other Sketches*. London: Herbert Jenkins, 1924. New York: E. P. Dutton, 1925.

———. *The Wave: An Egyptian Aftermath*. London: Cassell, 1916. New York: E. P. Dutton, 1916.

Blasco Ibáñez, Vicente (1867–1928). *The Four Horsemen of the Apocalypse*. Tr. Charlotte Brewster Jordan. New York: E. P. Dutton & Co., 1918. [Translation of *Los cuatro jinetes del Apocalipsis* (1916).]

Bleiler, Richard. "H. P. Lovecraft's First Appearance in Print." *Lovecraft Annual* No. 14 (2020): 26–36.

Braithwaite, William Stanley (1878–1962). *Anthology of Magazine Verse for 1926 and Year Book of American Poetry*. Boston: B. J. Brimmer Co., 1926.

Brocklesby, John (1811–1889). *Elements of Meteorology*. <1848> 3d rev. ed. New York: Pratt, Woodford & Co., 1849. (*LL* 133)

Brown, J. Macmillan (1845–1935). *The Riddle of the Pacific*. London: T. Fisher Unwin, 1924.

Buchan, John (1875–1940). *The Runagates Club*. Boston: Houghton Mifflin, 1928. (*LL* 141)

———. *Witch Wood*. Boston: Houghton Mifflin, 1927.

Bulfinch, Thomas (1796–1867). *The Age of Fable; or, Beauties of Mythology*. <1855> Edited by J. Loughran Scott. Rev. ed. Philadelphia: David McKay, [1898]. (*LL* 142)

Bullen, John Ravenor (1886–1927). *White Fire*. Athol, MA: The Recluse Press, 1927 [actually January 1928]. (*LL* 143)

Butler, Samuel. *The Way of All Flesh*. London: Grant Richards, 1903.

Cline, Leonard (1893–1929). *The Dark Chamber*. New York: Viking Press, 1927. (*LL* 198)

Cannon, Peter, ed. *Lovecraft Remembered*. Sauk City, WI: Arkham House, 1998.

Colum, Padraic (1881–1972). *A Boy in Eirinn*. New York: E. P. Dutton, 1913.

de la Mare, Colin, ed. *They Walk Again: An Anthology of Ghost Stories*. London: Faber & Faber, 1931; New York: E. P. Dutton, 1931.

de la Mare, Walter (1873–1956). *The Riddle and Other Stories*. <1923> New York: Alfred A. Knopf, 1930.

Derleth, August (1909–1971). *Evening in Spring*. New York: Charles Scribner's Sons, 1941.

———. "A Master of the Macabre." *Reading and Collecting: A Monthly Review of Rare And Recent Books* 1, No. 9 (August 1937): 9–10.

———. *Still Is the Summer Night*. New York: Charles Scribner's Sons, 1937.

Drake, H. B. (1894–1963). *The Rescue*. London: John Long, 1925. Rpt. as *The Shadowy Thing*. New York: Macy-Masius, 1928. Rpt. New York: Hippocampus Press, 2010.

Drake, Samuel Adams (1833–1905). *Nooks and Corners of the New England Coast*. New York: Harper and Brothers, 1876.

Dunsany, Lord (Edward John Moreton Drax Plunkett, 18th Baron, 1878–1957). *The Book of Wonder* <1912> [and *Time and the Gods* <1906>]. New York: Boni & Liveright (Modern Library), [1918]. (*LL* 288)

———. *Don Rodriguez: Chronicles of Shadow Valley*. New York: G. P. Putnam's Sons, 1922. (*LL* 289)

———. *A Dreamer's Tales and Other Stories* [*A Dreamer's Tales* <1910> and *The Sword of Welleran* <1908>]. New York: Boni & Liveright (Modern Library), [1917], [1919], or [1921]. (*LL* 290)

———. *Five Plays*. <1914> Boston: Little, Brown, 1923. (*LL* 292) [Includes *The Gods of the Mountain*.]

———. *The Gods of Pegāna*. <1905> (*LL* 277)

———. *The King of Elfland's Daughter*. London: G. P. Putnam's Sons, 1924. (*LL* 294)

———. *The Last Book of Wonder*. Boston: John W. Luce, 1916. (*LL* 295)

Eddison, E. R. (1882–1945). *The Worm Ouroboros: A Romance*. Illustrated by Keith Henderson. New York: A. & C. Boni, 1926. (*LL* 309)

England, George Allan (1877–1936). *Darkness and Dawn*. *Cavalier* (January–April 1912). Boston: Small, Maynard, 1914 (incorporates *Beyond the Great Oblivion* and *The Afterglow*).

Forbes, Allan (1874–1955), and Paul F. Cadman (1889–1946). *France and New England*. Boston: State Street Trust Co., 1925–29. 3 vols.

Gleeson, Alice Collins. *Colonial Rhode Island*. Pawtucket, RI: Automobile Journal Pub. Co., 1926.

Gorman, Herbert (1893–1954). *The Place Called Dagon*. New York: George H. Doran, 1927. New York: Hippocampus Press, 2003.

Goudsward, David. *H. P. Lovecraft in the Merrimack Valley*. New York: Hippocampus Press, 2013.

Grimm, Jakob Ludwig Karl (1785–1863), and Wilhelm Grimm (1786–1859). *Fairy Tales*. <1812–15> (*LL* 405)

Hammett, Dashiell (1894–1961), ed. *Creeps by Night: Chills and Thrills.* New York: John Day Co., 1931. (*LL* 421) [Contains HPL's "The Music of Erich Zann."]

Harper, Charles G. (1863–1943). *Haunted Houses: Tales of the Supernatural.* Philadelphia: J. B. Lippincott Co., 1907.

Harré, T. Everett (1884–1948), ed. *Beware After Dark! The World's Most Stupendous Tales of Mystery, Horror, Thrills and Terror.* New York: Macaulay, 1929. (*LL* 425)

Hawthorne, Nathaniel (1804–1864). *Tanglewood Tales for Girls and Boys: Being a Second Wonder-Book.* <1853> New York: A. L. Burt, [189-?] or [1907]. (*LL* 435)

———. *A Wonder Book for Boys and Girls, Comprising Stories of Classical Fables.* <1852> New York: A. L. Burt, n.d. (*LL* 437)

Hearn, Lafcadio (1850–1904). *Kwaidan: Stories and Studies of Strange Things.* <1904> Boston: Houghton Mifflin (Riverside Library), 1930. (*LL* 440)

Hecht, Ben. *Erik Dorn.* New York: G. P. Putnam's Sons, 1921.

Hilton, James (1900–1954). *Lost Horizon.* London: Macmillan; New York: William Morrow & Co., 1933.

Hoag, Jonathan E. (1831–1927). *The Poetical Works of Jonathan E. Hoag.* [New York: Privately printed], 1923. (*LL* 453)

Hodgson, William Hope (1877–1918). *The Boats of the "Glen Carrig."* London: Chapman & Hall, 1907.

———. *Carnacki the Ghost-Finder.* London: Eveleigh Nash, 1913.

———. *The House on the Borderland.* London: Chapman & Hall, 1908.

———. *The Night Land.* London: Eveleigh Nash, 1912.

Homer (fl. 750 B.C.E.?). *Tales from the Odyssey: For Boys and Girls.* Half-Hour Series. New York: Harper & Bros., 1890.

James, Henry (1843–1916). *The Two Magics: The Turn of the Screw; Covering End.* <1898> New York: Macmillan, 1911. (*LL* 498)

James, M. R. (1862–1936). *The Collected Ghost Stories of M. R. James.* London: Edward Arnold, 1931.

———. *Ghost-Stories of an Antiquary.* London: Edward Arnold, 1904. (*LL* 499)

———. *More Ghost Stories of an Antiquary.* <1911> (*LL* 500)

———. *A Thin Ghost and Others.* <1919> London: Edward Arnold, 1925. (*LL* 501)

———. *A Warning to the Curious.* London: Edward Arnold, 1925. (*LL* 502)

Joshi, S. T., ed. *H. P. Lovecraft in the Argosy: Collected Correspondence from the Munsey Magazines.* West Warwick, RI: Necronomicon Press, 1994.

———, and David E. Schultz. *Lovecraft's Library: A Catalogue.* 4th rev. ed. New York: Hippocampus Press, 2017.

———, ed. *Ave atque Vale: Reminiscences of H. P. Lovecraft.* West Warwick, RI: Necronomicon Press, 2018.

Kennedy, Duncan R. (1868–1914). *The New Knowledge: A Popular Account of the New Physics and the New Chemistry in Their Relation to the New Theory of Matter.* New York: A. S. Barnes & Co., 1905.

Krutch, Joseph Wood (1893–1970). *Edgar Allan Poe: A Study in Genius.* New York: Alfred A. Knopf, 1926.

———. *The Modern Temper: A Study and a Confession.* New York: Harcourt, Brace, 1929.

La Motte Fouqué, Friedrich Heinrich Karl, baron de (1777–1843). *Undine and Sintram.* <1811; 1815> Boston: Estes & Lauriat, [18—]. (*LL* 549)

Level, Maurice (1875–1926). *Tales of Mystery and Horror.* Translated from the French by Alys Eyre Macklin, with an Introduction by Henry B. Irving. New York: Robert M. McBride & Co., 1920. (*LL* 565)

Lewis, Matthew Gregory (1775–1818). *The Monk: A Romance.* <1796> London: Brentano's, [1924]. (*LL* 567)

Liddell, Henry George (1811–1898), and Robert Scott (1811–1887). *A Greek-English Lexicon.* <1843> (*LL* 569)

Lodge, Sir Oliver (1851–1940). *Raymond, or Life and Death: With Examples of the Evidence for Survival of Memory and Affection After Death.* London: Methuen, 1916.

Long, Frank Belknap (1901–1994). *The Goblin Tower.* Cassia, FL: Dragon-Fly Press, 1935.

Lucretius (T. Lucretius Carus) (98?–50? B.C.E.). *De Rerum Natura Libri Sex.* Recognovit Iacobus Bernaysius [i.e., Jakob Bernays]. Lipsiae [i.e., Leipzig]: Sumptibus et Typis B. G. Teubneri, 1879. (*LL* 600)

———. *Lucretius on the Nature of Things.* Tr. Cyril Bailey (1871–1957). <1910> Oxford: Oxford University Press, 1921.

Machen, Arthur (1863–1947). *The Hill of Dreams.* London: E. Grant Richards, 1907. New York: Alfred A. Knopf, 1923. (*LL* 617)

———. *The House of Souls.* <1906> New York: Alfred A. Knopf, 1923. (*LL* 618) [Contains "The White People" and "The Great God Pan."]

———. *The Terror.* New York: Robert M. McBride, 1917. London: Duckworth, 1917.

———. *The Three Impostors.* <1895> New York: Alfred A. Knopf, 1930. (*LL* 623)

Maturin, Charles Robert (1782–1824). *Melmoth the Wanderer.* <1820> London: Richard Bentley & Son, 1892. 3 vols. (*LL* 646)

Mencken, H. L. (1880–1956). *Prejudices.* New York: Alfred A. Knopf, 1919–27. 6 vols.

Merritt, A. (1882–1943). "The Conquest of the Moon Pool." *All-Story Weekly* (15 February–22 March 1919). Incorporated into *The Moon Pool.* New York: G. P. Putnam's Sons, 1919.

———. "The Moon Pool." *All-Story Weekly* (22 June 1918). (*LL* 26) Incorporated into *The Moon Pool.* New York: G. P. Putnam's Sons, 1919.

————. *The Ship of Ishtar*. *Argosy All-Story Weekly* (8 November–13 December 1924). New York: G. P. Putnam's Sons, 1926.

Middleton, Richard (1882–1911). *The Ghost-Ship and Other Stories*. London: T. Fisher Unwin, 1912.

Mills, Weymer Jay (1880–1938). *Historic Houses of New Jersey*. Philadelphia: J. B. Lippincott, 1902.

Moskowitz, Sam. "On Nils Frome and Blish, Lovecraft, et al." *Science-Fiction Studies* 12, No. 2 (July 1985): 229–36. In Sam Moskowitz, ed. *Howard Phillips Lovecraft and Nils Helmer Frome*. Glenview, IL: Moshassuck Press, 1989. 7–14.

Mumper, William N. (1858–1931). *A Text-Book in Physics for Secondary Schools*. New York: American Book Co., 1907.

Munro, Wilfred Harold (1849–1934). *Picturesque Rhode Island*. Providence, RI: J. A. & R. A. Reid, 1881. (*LL* 694)

Munroe, Kirk (1850–1930). *Snow-Shoes and Sledges*. New York: Harper & Brothers, 1895.

O'Neill, Eugene. *The Emperor Jones*. New York: Stewart Kidd, 1921.

Owings, Mark (1945–2009), and Irving Binkin (1906–1989). *A Catalog of Lovecraftiana: The Grill-Binkin Collection*. Baltimore: Mirage Press, 1975.

Priestley, J. B. (1894–1984). *Benighted*. London: Heinemann, 1927. Rpt. as *The Old Dark House*. New York: Harper & Brothers, 1928.

Radcliffe, Ann (1764–1823). *The Mysteries of Udolpho*. <1794> London: George Routledge & Sons, [1882]–[192-]. (*LL* 787)

Rohmer, Sax (pseud. of Arthur Sarsfield Ward, 1883–1959). *The Romance of Sorcery*. New York: E. P. Dutton, 1914.

Santayana, George (1863–1952). *The Life of Reason; or, The Phases of Human Progress*. New York: Scribner's, 1905–22. 5 vols.

————. *Scepticism and Animal Faith*. New York: Scribner's, 1923.

Sayers, Dorothy L. (1893–1957), ed. *The Omnibus of Crime*. <1928> Garden City, NY: Garden City Publishing Co., 1931. (*LL* 830)

————. *The Second Omnibus of Crime: The World's Great Crime Stories*. <1931> New York: Blue Ribbon Books, 1932.

Schopenhauer, Arthur (1788–1860). *Studies in Pessimism*. Tr. T. Bailey Saunders. London: Swan Sonnenschein, 1890.

Schultz, David E. "The Origin of Lovecraft's 'Black Magic' Quote." *Crypt of Cthulhu* No. 48 (St. John's Eve 1987): 9–13. Revised version in *The Horror of It All*, ed. Robert M. Price. Mercer Island, WA: Starmont House, 1990. pp. 32–38.

Serviss, Garrett P. (1851–1929). *Astronomy with an Opera-Glass*. <1888> 8th ed. New York: D. Appleton & Co., 1906. (*LL* 849)

Shaw, George Bernard (1856–1950). *Back to Methuselah: A Metabiological Pentateuch*. New York: Brentano's, 1921. (*LL* 861)

Shelley, Mary (1797–1851). *Frankenstein; or, The Modern Prometheus.* <1818> New-York: H. G. Daggers, 1845. (*LL* 864)

Shiel, M. P. (1865–1947). *How the Old Woman Got Home.* London: Richards Press, 1927.

———. *The Pale Ape and Other Pulses.* London: T. Werner Laurie, 1911. [Contains "The House of Sounds."]

———. *Prince Zaleski.* Boston: Roberts Brothers, 1895. (*LL* 870)

———. *The Purple Cloud.* London: Chatto & Windus, 1901. New York: Vanguard Press, 1930. (*LL* 871) Rpt. in Shiel's *The House of Sounds and Others.* Ed. S. T. Joshi. New York: Hippocampus Press, 2005.

———. *Shapes in the Fire* (London: John Lane; Boston: Roberts Brothers, 1896).

Sinnett, A. P. (1840–1921). *Esoteric Buddhism.* London: Trübner, 1883.

Smith, Clark Ashton (1893–1961). *Complete Poetry and Translations.* Ed. S. T. Joshi and David E. Schultz. New York: Hippocampus Press. 3 vols.

———. *Ebony and Crystal: Poems in Verse and Prose.* Auburn, CA: [Auburn Journal,] 1922. (*LL* 881)

———. *Odes and Sonnets.* San Francisco: Book Club of California, 1918. (*LL* 882)

———. *Sandalwood.* Auburn, CA: Auburn Journal, 1925. (*LL* 883)

———. *The Star-Treader and Other Poems.* San Francisco: A. M. Robertson, 1912. (*LL* 884)

Smith, Sir William (1813–1893). *Smith's Bible Dictionary.* Philadelphia: A. J. Holman Co., [1893].

Spencer, R. E. (1896–1956). *The Lady Who Came to Stay.* New York: Book League of America, 1931. New York: Hippocampus Press, 2009.

Stapledon, Olaf (1886–1950). *Last and First Men.* London: Methuen, 1930.

Todd, Charles Burr (1849–1928). *A Brief History of the City of New York.* New York: American Book Co., 1899.

Waite, Arthur Edward (1857–1942). *The Book of Black Magic and of Pacts: Including the Rites and Mysteries of Goëtic Theurgy, Sorcery, and Infernal Necromancy.* London: George Redway, 1898.

Wakefield, H. Russell (1890–1964). *They Return at Evening.* New York: D. Appleton & Co., 1928.

Wales, Hubert (1870–1943). *The Brocklebank Riddle.* New York: Century Co., 1914.

White, Edward Lucas (1866–1934). *The Song of the Sirens and Other Stories.* New York: E. P. Dutton, 1919. (*LL* 1037)

Wilde, Oscar (1854–1900). *The Picture of Dorian Gray.* <1890> New York: Boni & Liveright (Modern Library), 1918. (*LL* 1051)

Wilder, Thornton (1897–1975). *The Bridge of San Luis Rey.* New York: Albert & Charles Boni, 1927.

Wright, S. Fowler (1874–1965). *The World Below.* New York: Longmans, Green, 1930. (*LL* 1070)

Index

www.ingramcontent.com/pod-product-compliance
Lightning Source LLC
Chambersburg PA
CBHW070343030726
47504CB00001B/48